T5-CCW-771

1991-92

# Table of Contents

## National Single Adult Ministries Resource Directory, 1991-92

### Where To Find It:

# Welcome to the Second National Resource Directory

## The Only National "Yellow Pages" For Single Adult Ministry

hen you need information about ministry with single adults, this is the place to come. We have spent literally months collecting (and verifying) all the information found in these pages so that you might have helpful ministry guides and tools at your finger tips. And to help save you even more time, we've added two handy indexes (see page 257) in this second edition. (If you have an idea on how we might improve future editions of this Directory, we'd love to hear from you.)

Even though putting this resource together can sometimes seem like a never-ending project, we believe it's well worth it. Listen to what some leaders have said about the *Resource Directory*:

• "I wish a resource like this had been available twenty years ago when I began working with single adults. Within these pages is, without a doubt, the most comprehensive and complete listing of single adult ministries, resources, and leaders published anywhere. Anyone in singles ministry, particularly those who are just beginning, shouldn't be without it." **- Bill Flanagan, Minister with Single Adults, St. Andrew's Presbyterian Church, Newport Beach, CA**

• "This directory is the 'Yellow Pages' for anyone working with single adults today. No singles ministry leader should be without it." **- Jim Smoke, Founder, The Center for Divorce Recovery, Tempe, AZ**

• "I have appreciated the *National Resource Directory* because it provides concise, at a glance information about singles leaders and ministries across the U.S. . . . plus many helpful resources pertaining to single adult ministry. I highly recommend this directory to anyone involved in single adult ministry." **- Dennis Franck, Minister with Single Adults, Bethel Assembly of God, San Jose, CA**

• "If your filing system is anything like mine, this national directory is for you! It's a friendly guide to single adult ministry. Speakers, resources, ideas, how-to's and why-to's. In short, the help you need is here. When reading through this *Resource Directory*, I find myself saying, 'I didn't know that.' Keep it handy." **- Harold Ivan Smith, author and speaker**

Thanks to each of you who took the time to send us information for this directory. We could not have done it without you.

And for those of you who want to be included in the next edition, see page 249.

Until next time . . .

Jerry Jones, Editor

**NATIONAL SINGLE ADULT MINISTRIES RESOURCE DIRECTORY, 1991/92**

Published by Singles Ministry Resources/NavPress

**Editor**
Jerry D. Jones

**Editorial Staff**
JoAnne Hill, Marie Kohlwaies

**Production Staff**
Don Burmania, Linda Lawson, Ruth Lillie, Cyndi Sykes, Leslie Yeaton

**Graphic Design and Production**
Kim Brill

**Advertising Sales**
Ron Weide, (719) 548-9373

NATIONAL SINGLE ADULT MINISTRIES RESOURCE DIRECTORY, 1991/92
© 1991 by Singles Ministry Resources/ NavPress. All rights reserved. No part of this publication may be reproduced in any form without written permission from NavPress, P. O. Box 6000, Colorado Springs, CO 80934.
Library of Congress Catalog Card Number: 91-61547
ISBN 08910-93826

Scripture in this publication is from the Holy Bible: New International Version (NIV), Copyright © 1973, 1978, 1984, International Bible Society, used by permission of Zondervan Bible Publishers; the New American Standard Bible (NASB), © The Lockman Foundation 1960, 1962, 1963, 1968, 1971, 1972, 1973, 1975, 1977; the Revised Standard Version Bible (RSV), copyright © 1946, 1952, 1971, by the Division of Christian Education of the National Council of the Churches of Christ in the USA, used by permission, all rights reserved; The New Testament in Modern English (PH), J. B. Phillips Translator, © J. B. Phillips 1958, 1960, 1972, used by permission of Macmillan Publishing Company; the New King James Version (NKJV), copyright © 1979, 1980, 1982, Thomas Nelson Inc., Publishers; and the King James Version (KJV).

**FOR MORE INFORMATION, SEE PAGES 247-253.** **OR CONTACT:**
NavPress 1-800-366-7788 (USA)
or 1-416-499-4615 (CANADA)

Or Singles Ministry Resources
1-800-487-4-SAM (USA)
or 1-719-488-2610 (CANADA)

# Do You Have All The Answers They Need?

## Here's Help...

# RESOURCES FOR CHRISTIAN COUNSELING

**Dr. Gary R. Collins, Editor**

**. . . for shepherds who care—professionally**

## NOW AVAILABLE AT 20% OFF!

RESOURCES FOR CHRISTIAN COUNSELING is an ongoing series with an emphasis on resources that you can apply today in your counseling ministry. Each volume is written by a practicing Christian professional who writes of recent research, treatment techniques, and Christian applications of sound psychology.

**HOW YOUR SUBSCRIPTION WORKS:**

- Every four to six weeks we mail the latest volume in the series.
- You have a *10-day free review period*—if you are not totally satisfied, just return the book and there is no charge.
- You receive a 20% discount on each book you choose to add to your permanent, professional library—*a $12.99 value for only $10.39.*

**TOPICS TREATED IN THIS PROFESSIONAL SERIES:**

- Premarital counseling
- Drugs and alcohol abuse
- Homosexuality, AIDS, & unplanned pregnancies
- Anger and self-control
- Infertility
- Women's issues
- Family violence
- Marriage and family
- Meaninglessness
- Children's problems
- Crisis counseling
- Innovative ways to minister through counseling
- Counseling the depressed

Mail the attached order form today, and receive your first book, **Counseling the Depressed,** for a 10-day review period.

FREE NEWSLETTER

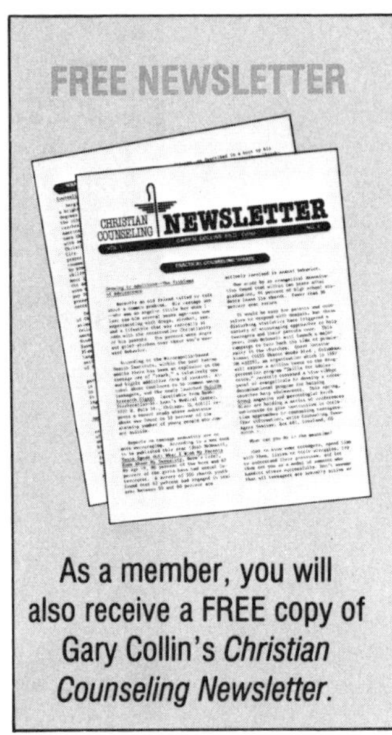


As a member, you will also receive a FREE copy of Gary Collin's *Christian Counseling Newsletter.*

**ENROLLMENT CERTIFICATE**

**YES** I wish to enroll in **Resources for Christian Counseling.** Send me my copy of *Counseling the Depressed* by Dr. Gary R. Collins and my FREE copy of the *Christian Counseling Newsletter.* I understand I may examine my book for 10 days. If not satisfied, I may return it to you and owe nothing. If I keep the books, you may then bill me $10.39, plus shipping and handling and I will begin receiving one new volume every 4-6 weeks until my set is complete. This price represents a 20% discount off the regular retail price of $12.99...and a 20% savings to me.

Name ______________________________
(please print)

Address ______________________________

City/State/Zip ______________________________

Signature ______________________________

CLIP AND MAIL TO: **Word Inc.** P.O. Box 10829
Des Moines, IA 50336-0829

SAMRD—91752

"I FIND PRACTICAL IDEAS AND INSIGHTS IN EVERY ISSUE OF SINGLE ADULT MINISTRIES JOURNAL. IT IS THE BEST RESOURCE AVAILABLE FOR PASTORS AND LEADERS WORKING WITH SINGLE ADULTS . . . . NOTHING ELSE EVEN COMES CLOSE."

- PAUL PETERSEN

HIGHLAND PARK PRESBYTERIAN CHURCH

DALLAS, TEXAS

Call toll FREE today to get your subscription started.
**800-487-4-SAM or 719-488-2610**
Or write: *SAM Journal*, P. O. Box 62056,
Colorado Springs, Colorado 80962-2056.

A one-year subscription is $24 (10 issues); $29 in Canada; $33 for all other countries.
*U. S. funds only*. Payment by Visa, MasterCard, or "bill me" also available.

# Part 1

# How Many Single Adults Are There? . . . And Other Facts

## Current Facts and Figures on Single Adults and Single Adult Ministry

### Where To Find It:

# U. S. Single Adult Population Nears 70 Million

*BY J. DAVID JONES*

## The Year 1989 Had the Largest One-Year Increase in the Number of Single Adults Since 1984

If there are those who may believe the need for a ministry with single adults is on the decline, this close look at some of the facts will be a valuable use of time.

According to the most recent report from the U.S. Census Bureau, the total number of single adults in America in 1989 (18 years or older) was 68,310,000, not including the separated. This is an increase of nearly two million over 1988 (compared to "only" 1.3 million in increase from 1988 to 1989).

Of those 68.3 million single adults, 39.9 million (58%) have always been single; 14.5 million (21%) are divorced; 13.7 million (20%) are widowed.

But more significant than the actual increase in numbers are the trends that show America continues to move towards a singles-oriented society (and away from what we have known as the more "traditional family" structure).

### Postponement of First Marriages

This trend continues upward, with no reversal in sight. The estimated median age at first marriage in 1989 was 26.2 years for men and 23.8 years for women. The comparable figures in 1970 were 23.2 years and 20.8 years, respectively.

*Since 1970, the proportion of persons ages 25 to 29 who have never married has tripled for women and more than doubled for men.*

### Single Parent Families

For the past 20 years, there has been rapid growth in the number of one-parent families. This trend is likely to continue in the 1990s. According to *American Demographics* magazine, "These 'other' families (they include all families not headed by a married couple) *are expected to increase by 16 percent between 1990 and 2000.*"

The proportion of children under 18 living with two parents declined from 85 percent in 1970 to 73 percent in 1989, while the proportion living with one parent doubled from 12 to 24 percent.

Although the number of "other" families headed by men is expected to grow faster than the number headed by women, by the

### Single-Parent Father Households on the Increase

Families not headed by a married couple that are expected to increase the fastest between 1990 and 2000 will be headed by the following:

| | Percent Change 1990-2000 |
|---|---|
| Men ages 45-64 | 53.1 |
| Women ages 45-64 | 34.4 |
| Men under 25 | 26.8 |
| Men ages 25-44 | 21.8 |
| Men 65 and older | 21.2 |

year 2000 there will still be three times as many "other" families headed by women.

## Unmarried-Couple Households

The growth in this category is staggering. These households totaled 2.8 million in 1989, compared to 523,000 in 1970. The Census Bureau defines an unmarried-couple household as one comprising two unrelated adults of the opposite sex, with or without children under 15 years old living in the household. About 7 out of 10 such households had no children present in 1989.

Here is a breakdown of those living in an unmarried-couple household:

**Marital Status**

- 59% have always been single
- 32% are divorced
- 4% are widowed
- 5% are separated

**Age**

- 42% are ages 25-34
- 27% are under age 25
- 17% are ages 35-44
- (60% are under 35)

## People Living Alone

*American Demographics* magazine projects a 17.7 percent increase from 1990 to 2000 in the number of householders who live alone.

The most dramatic growth in people living alone will be among those aged 45 to 64, as baby boomers become middle-aged.

Those living alone who are expected to show the largest increase over the next decade are:

**Percent Change 1990-2000**

| | |
|---|---|
| Men ages 45-64 | 50.5 |
| Women ages 45-64 | 35.2 |
| Men 65 and older | 19.4 |
| Women 65 and older | 13.0 |
| Women ages 25-44 | 9.8 |
| Men ages 25-44 | 6.1 |

There are 23.6 million people living alone in 1990. This is expected to increase to 27.7 million by the year 2000.

SOURCES: *American Demographics* magazine, March 1990, page 63; April 1990, page 55; U.S. Bureau of the Census, "Marital Status and Living Arrangements: March 1989" report and the March 1989 Current Population Survey.

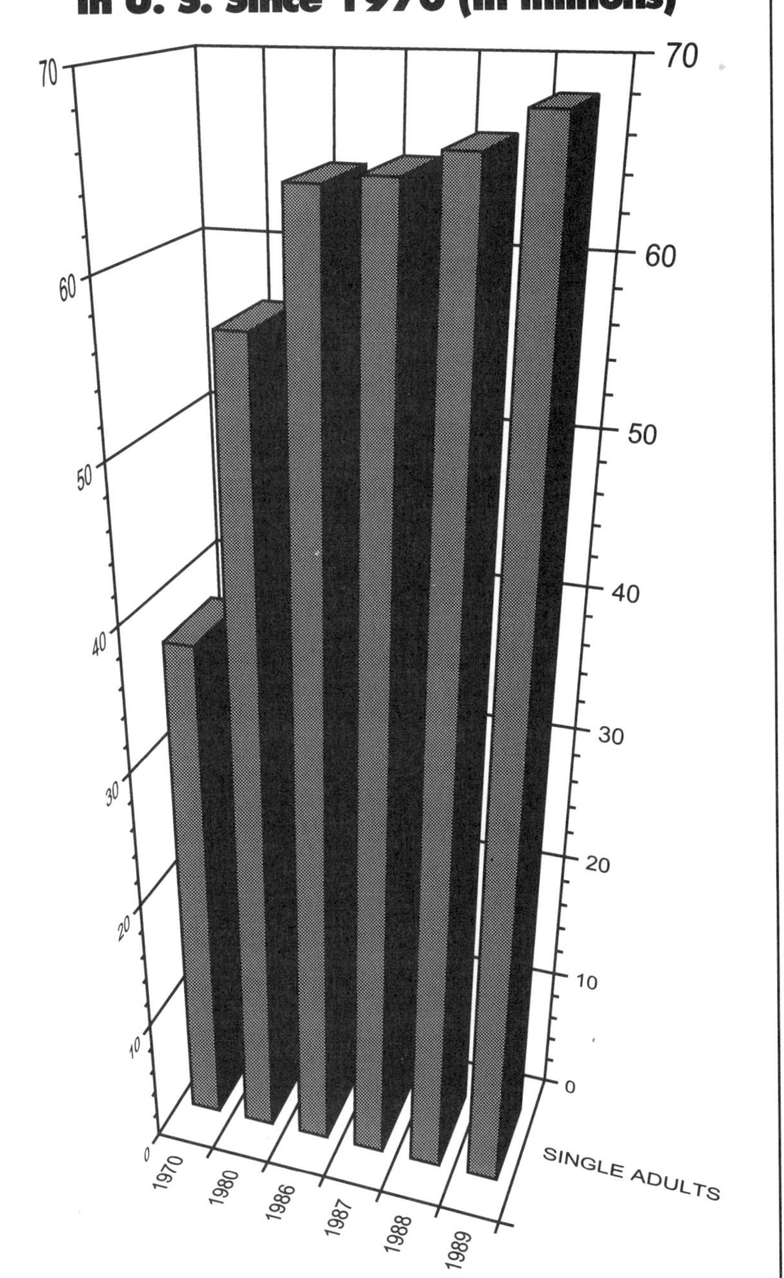

# Marital Status of U. S. Adult Population (18 and over)

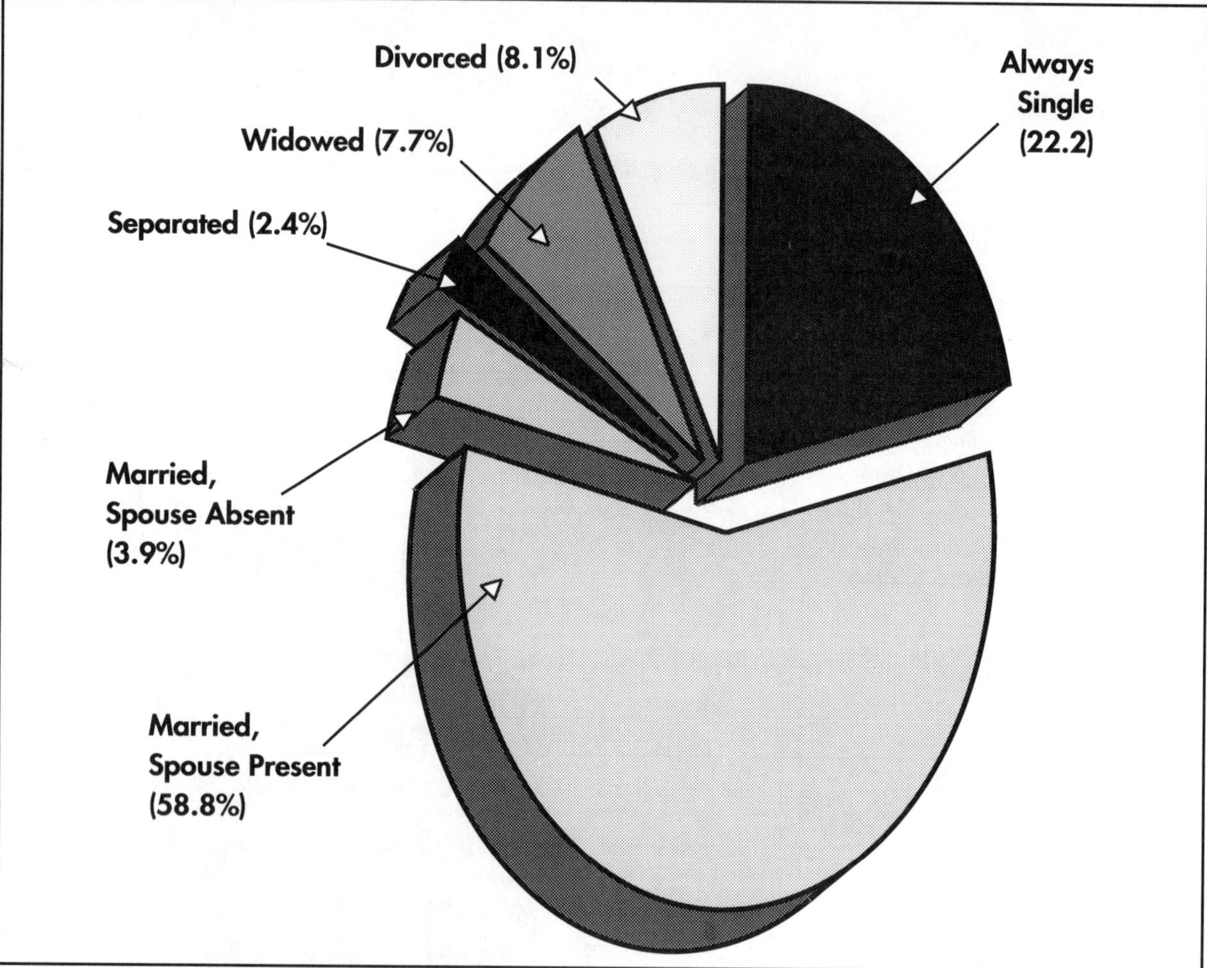


## How Many Single Adults Are There? (18 and older)

**Total numbers are as follows:**
In 1970 there were 37.5 million single adults
In 1980, 56.8 million
In 1986, 64.5 million
In 1987, 65 million
**In 1989, 68.3 million** *(most recent data available)*

**Of those who were single in 1989,**
58% had always been single
21% were divorced
20% were widowed

## Percent of Americans Who Are Single

According to the U. S. Census Bureau's most recent statistics (1989), here is the breakdown of single adults in America by percent:

| | |
|---|---|
| ages 15 and up | 41% |
| ages 18 and up | 38% |
| ages 20 and up | 36% |

**NOTE:** U. S. Census Bureau definitions for the graph at top are as follows: **"Married, Spouse Present"**-both husband and wife are reported as a member of the household; **"Separated"**-Legal and/or other separations due to marital discord; **"Married, Spouse Absent"**-Married persons living apart for reasons other than separation as defined above (work, miliary service, etc.)
**SOURCE FOR THE ABOVE:** U.S. Bureau of the Census, "Marital Status and Living Arrangements: March 1989" report and the March 1989 Current Population Survey.

# Development of America's Single Adult Population During the Twentieth Century

*FROM THE BOOK,* SINGLE ADULT PASSAGES: UNCHARTED TERRITORIES

## The Single Lifestyle is an Accepted Experience in America Today

Never before has there been such a major change in the family as there is now. The U.S. Census Bureau confirms it: Singleness is the highest its been since the early part of the century. According to Steve Rawlings, a Census Bureau family demographer, about 41 percent of all adults of marriageable age (15 and older) are now single. Our culture is changing. Our world has come a long way in its acceptance of the singles lifestyle as a valid exception from the norm of society. The American culture has always been founded on the concept of the nuclear family but that concept is changing. "The numbers are so high that we've begun to accept the idea of non-traditional households as being normal" says Susan Hayward of the Yankelovich Clancy Shulman market-research company.

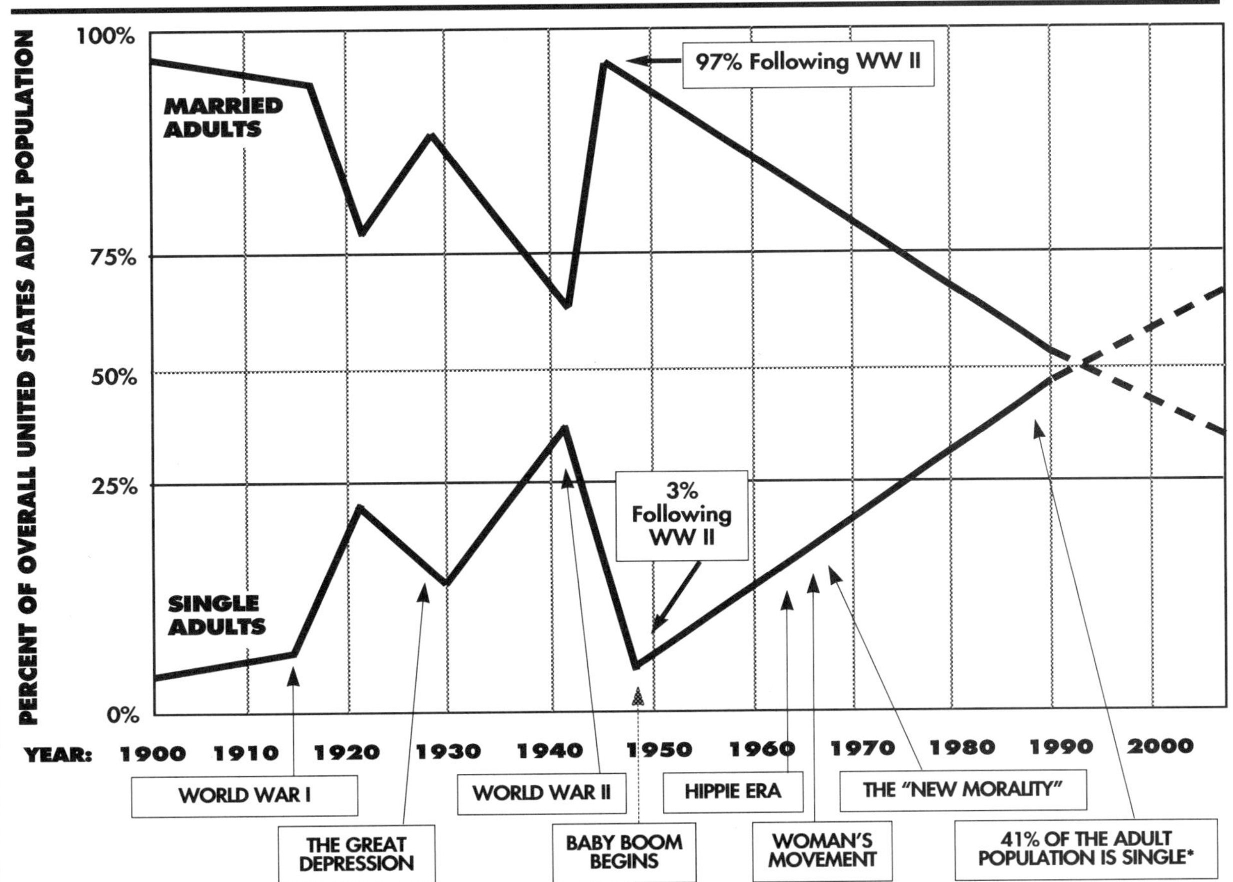


(*Of official marriageable age, 15 and older.)
The above material was reprinted with permission from the book, *Single Adult Passages: Uncharted Territories*, by Carolyn Koons and Michael J. Anthony (Baker Books, 1991). The above chart was also adapted from this book.

SINGLES IN AMERICA

# Attitudes About Sex and Being Single

*BY CAROLYN KOONS AND MICHAEL J. ANTHONY*

## Based on a National Survey of Nearly 1500 Christian Singles, Here is a Snapshot Look at Some of Their Attitudes, Experiences, and Opinions

his survey is one of the largest ever conducted among Christian single adults. Those who responded to this survey are—for the most part—actively involved in a church. They ranged in age from 18 to 65.

• *Of the men*, 85 percent attend church weekly (or more often); 40 percent read the Bible on a daily basis; 75 percent pray daily.

• *Of the women*, 90 percent attend church weekly (or more often); 36 percent read the Bible daily; 84 percent pray daily.

Here is how they responded to the following:

### Who Is Most Likely To Own a Home?

According to this survey, it is single women. 38% of the women own their own house or condominium, compared to 33% of the men. 61% of the single women lived alone compared to almost 50% of the men. (Only 14% still lived with their parents and only 2% are currently living with someone of the opposite sex.)

### What Are The Greatest DISADVANTAGES of Being Single?

MEN

1. Loneliness
2. Restricted sexual and social life
3. It makes me self-centered
4. I hate the dating grind

WOMEN

1. Loneliness
2. Financial insecurities
3. It makes me self-centered
4. Restrictions on sex life

### What Are The Greatest ADVANTAGES of Being Single?

MEN

1. Mobility and freedom
2. Time for personal interests
3. Privacy
4. Social life in general

WOMEN

1. Mobility and freedom
2. Time for personal interests
3. Social life in general
4. Privacy

### Sexual History and Current Involvement of Christian Singles

MEN

- 33% are virgins
- 35% have had as many as 4 or more previous sexual partners
- 22% have lived with a woman in a cohabitation arrangement
- 10% have had as many as 20 or more sexual partners
- 23% have been involved in sexual relations within the past 6 months

WOMEN

- 39% are virgins
- 27% have had as many as 4 or more previous sexual partners
- 22% have lived with a man in a cohabitation arrangement
- 5% have had as many as 20 or more sexual partners
- 14% have been involved in sexual relations within the past 6 months

Adapted from the book, *Single Adult Passages: Uncharted Territories*, by Carolyn Koons and Michael Anthony (Baker Books). Get a copy of this book for complete results of this national study.

SINGLES IN AMERICA

# BECOMING A Friend & Lover

## A conference for your single adults to strenghten their relationships and their commitment to Jesus Christ

Your single adults will enjoy this exciting weekend event as they hear Dick Purnell, nationally-known speaker and award-winning author, talk on friendship, intimacy and biblical principles for building lasting relationships.

Designed to meet the needs of single adults, the *Becoming a Friend and Lover* Conference attracts Christians and non-Christians alike. Here's what single adult ministers have to say about this conference:

*"Dick's presentation of a Christian view of friendships with the opposite sex is a breath of fresh air in a world where our single adults are barraged with secular relational and sexual values. Singles of all ages mention growth and benefit from this conference. I highly recommend Dick and his ministry to churches and organizations both as a man of God and as a captivating speaker."*

**Paul Petersen, Chairman of the Board**
**National Association of Single Adult Leaders**

*"Thanks for a job well done. We will have to do this again in the near future. Our single adults all had positive things to say about your seminars. They really listen to someone who has been 'where they are' and survived successfully."*

**Steve Cretin, Associate Pastor**
**Prestonwood Baptist Church, Dallas, Texas**

*"I was delighted to see that a number of people received Christ and many more were encouraged as they considered what a godly relationship is all about. You definitely had a positive impact here."*

**Scott Season, Ministries Coordinator**
**Perimeter Presbyterian Church, Atlanta, Georgia**

### Becoming a Friend and Lover Conference Topics

- Understanding the Opposite Sex
- Why Relationships Fail
- Friendship — The Basis for Love
- Building a Relationship That Lasts
- Intimacy Without Guilt

**Dick Purnell** is an international speaker and award-winning author, who has spoken to hundreds of thousands of people in eight countries. He holds a master's degree in counseling from Indiana University and a Masters of Divinity Degree, Magna Cum Laude, from Trinity Evangelical Divinity School. Dick is presently the national director of **Single Life Resources**, a ministry of Campus Crusade for Christ, designed to equip singles to live dynamic, godly lives.

***YOU CAN SCHEDULE THE BECOMING A FRIEND AND LOVER CONFERENCE TODAY!***

Contact Dick Purnell at P.O. Box 4410, Cary, NC 27519, (919) 460-8000

A MINISTRY OF CAMPUS CRUSADE FOR CHRIST.

NATIONAL SURVEY RESULTS

# SURVEY RESULTS: Single Adult Ministry in North America

## A Descriptive Look at the Leaders, the Single Adults Who Attend—and Some of the Ministry Trends

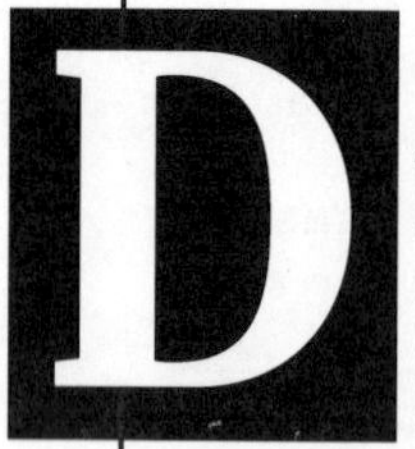

During 1990 *Single Adult Ministries Journal* conducted a nationwide survey of pastors and leaders involved in ministry with single adults. With over 600 people responding, this was the largest survey ever conducted to learn about the state of single adult ministry in North America.

This survey was mailed to readers of *SAM Journal* which represents a wide cross section of denominations and regions in both the U.S. and Canada.

*Single Adult Ministries Journal* is the largest publication specifically for those involved in ministry with single adults.

On the following few pages you will find many of the results of this survey, along with some comparisons to a previous and similar survey conducted by *SAM Journal* in 1988.

### Who Are the Pastors and Leaders Involved in Ministry With Single Adults?

Compared to the survey taken two years earlier:

- More singles ministry pastors/leaders are married.
- There has been an increase in the number of *paid* singles ministry leaders (versus those serving as volunteers).

| | 1988 % | 1990 % | Change % |
|---|---|---|---|
| **SEX** | | | |
| Women | 25 | **24** | ↓1 |
| Men | 75 | **76** | ↑1 |
| **MARITAL STATUS** | | | |
| Married | 57 | **61** | ↑4 |
| Always-Single | 18 | **17** | ↓1 |
| Divorced | 12 | **10** | ↓2 |
| Remarried | 10 | **9** | ↓1 |
| Widowed | 3 | **3** | — |
| **LEADERSHIP POSITION/RESPONSIBILITIES** | | | |
| Full-time associate minister *(with several areas of responsibility in the church, including singles ministry)* | 31 | **36** | ↑5 |
| Volunteer leader/director | 25 | **21** | ↓4 |
| Full-time paid singles pastor/director | 27 | **30** | ↑3 |
| *Ordained* | 21 | **22** | ↑1 |
| *Non-ordained* | 6 | **8** | ↑2 |
| Part-time paid singles pastor/director | 6 | **6** | — |
| Other | 11 | **6** | ↓5 |

## What Are the Most Frustrating Aspects of Being a Leader in Singles Ministry?

(Here are the top ten answers.)

1. Lack of commitment among the singles.
2. The constant need and challenge to recruit and develop leadership in the ministry.
3. High turnover rate of the single adults.
4. Too little time for personal renewal.
5. Lack of interest in spiritual growth among the singles.
6. Finding good curriculum and study discussion materials.
7. Lack of personal support system.
8. So many depression problems/ needs among the singles.
9. (*Two-way tie*) Heavy counseling load; An inadequate singles ministry budget.
10. (*Two-way tie*) The extent of inappropriate sexual activity of some of the singles; Inadequate personal income and benefits.

## How Many Leaders Have Taken Any Seminary or Graduate Course Work *Specifically in the Field of Single Adult Ministry?*

Sixteen percent say they have done so. (See page 94 for a list of the "most popular" seminaries.)

## How are Single Adult Ministries Doing Compared to Two Years Ago?

Here are the survey results to the following three questions:

**A. How effective is your church's ministry with single adults compared to two years ago?**

- More effective - 75%
- About the same - 20%
- Less effective - 5%

**B. Compared to two years ago, how supportive of the singles ministry is your senior pastor?**

- More supportive - 60%
- About the same - 36%
- Less supportive - 4%

**C. Compared to two years ago, the total budget (including staff salaries) for the singles ministry department in your church is:**

- Larger - 51%
- About the same - 44%
- Smaller - 5%

## Most Leaders Have Made a Long-term Commitment to Singles Ministry

In spite of the frustrations associated with being involved in singles ministry (see column at left), the vast majority of them apparently have no intentions of quitting their ministry. Here is how leaders answered when we asked the question: **"Do you plan to continue indefinitely as a singles pastor or do you see it as an interim ministry?"**

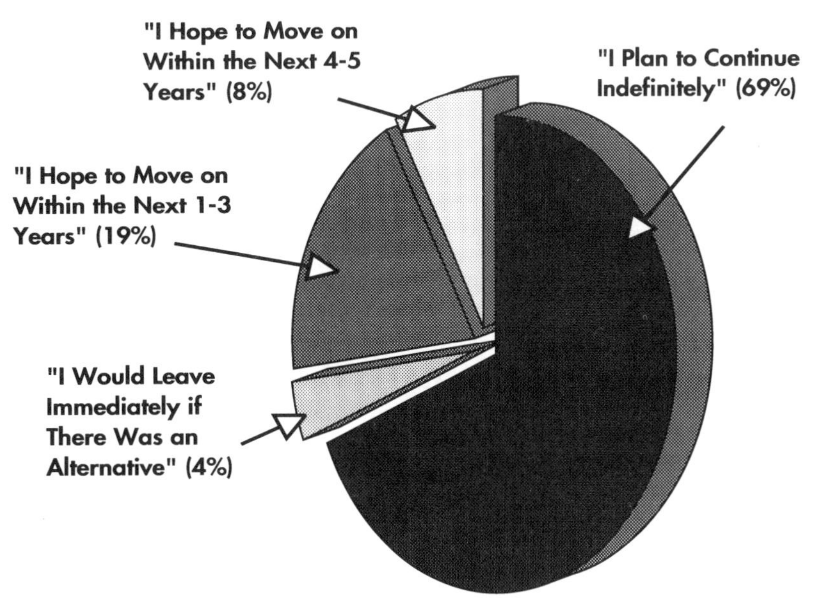

## What Are the Issues and Topics That Your Single Adults Most Need Addressed?

Here is how 600-plus leaders answered this question:

1. Spiritual growth and relationship with God.
2. Skills for developing close personal relationships.
3. How to develop and nurture a sense of community/belonging.
4. Developing a personal ministry (giving of self to others).
5. Living with inadequate finances.
6. (*Two-way tie*)
   Adult dating;
   Lack of self-esteem.
7. (*Two-way tie*)
   Growing through divorce;
   How to be a more effective single parent.
8. (*Three-way tie*)
   Life goals/planning;
   Discouragement/depression about not being married;
   Sex/physical intimacy.
9. Materialistic influences.
10. Relationship with ones ex-spouse.

## Volunteer Leaders Involved

According to the survey, the average number of people involved in leadership is 19 per group.

## Singles Ministry Newsletters Show Slight Increase

In the 1988 survey, 62 percent of all singles groups published a newsletter. In 1990, that number had increased to 64 percent.

## Demographic Picture Of Single Adult Groups

Compared to the survey taken two years earlier:

- Small singles groups are declining; larger groups are increasing.
- Percent of divorced persons in groups is increasing while percent of always-single adults is declining.
- Attendance by single adults under age 30 is declining while the over-30 group is increasing.
- Weekend nights are becoming less popular for regularly scheduled group meeting times.

| | 1988 % | 1990 % | Change % |
|---|---|---|---|
| **AVERAGE NUMBER OF SINGLE ADULTS ATTENDING LARGEST REGULARLY SCHEDULED EVENT** | | | |
| Less than 30 | 44 | **32** | ↓ 12 |
| 30-50 | 16 | **19** | ↑ 3 |
| 50-100 | 17 | **21** | ↑ 4 |
| 100-150 | 11 | **12** | ↑ 1 |
| 150-200 | 4 | **7** | ↑ 3 |
| 200+ | 8 | **9** | ↑ 1 |
| **Overall Attendance Average Per Group in 1990:** 87 | | | |
| **Average Sunday A.M. Total Church Worship Attendance:** 1,152 | | | |
| **MARITAL STATUS OF SINGLES IN GROUP** | | | |
| Always-Single | 50 | **48** | ↓ 2 |
| Divorced | 38 | **41** | ↑ 3 |
| Single Parent | 8 | **8** | — |
| Widowed | 4 | **3** | ↓ 1 |
| **AGES OF THOSE INVOLVED** | | | |
| 18-25 | 13 | **10** | ↓ 3 |
| 26-30 | 26 | **22** | ↓ 4 |
| 31-35 | 22 | **23** | ↑ 1 |
| 36-40 | 17 | **18** | ↑ 1 |
| 41-45 | 12 | **14** | ↑ 2 |
| 46-50 | 6 | **8** | ↑ 2 |
| 50+ | 4 | **5** | ↑ 1 |
| **MOST POPULAR REGULAR GROUP MEETING TIME** | | | |
| A. M. Sunday school class | 44 | **48** | ↑ 4 |
| Sunday night | 8 | **5** | ↓ 3 |
| Week night | 23 | **26** | ↑ 3 |
| Friday night | 12 | **10** | ↓ 2 |
| Saturday night | 7 | **4** | ↓ 3 |

# Most Effective Ways To Get New Singles Involved in Your Ministry

When we asked leaders what they considered to be their most effective methods of reaching new singles adults, here is how they answered (ranked in order of effectiveness):

1. Workshops and seminars (including divorce recovery workshops, financial planning, single parenting skills, relationship building, etc.)
2. Personal invitation from our singles.
3. Good reputation/visibility of our church in the community.
4. Personal follow-up of visitors.
5. Small study groups/support groups.
6. (*Two-way tie*) Strong, effective teacher/topic at our singles group meeting; Good Sunday school class.
7. Special interests/events (such as rafting, biking, tennis, theater, etc.)
8. Singles retreats.
9. Giving new people a position of leadership/responsibility in the group.
10. Personal evangelism.

# How Long Has the Average Singles Ministry Been in Existence?

According to the 1990 *SAM* survey results, 6.2 years. As would stand to reason, there were more long-term ministries in 1990 than in 1988. For example, 32 percent of ministries had been in existence for less than two years in 1988, compared to 16 percent in 1990.

# What Leaders Consider to Be Their Most Effective Area of Ministry

Compared to the survey taken two years earlier, here is how leaders rated their effectiveness, ranked in order (with 1 being most effective).

| | 1988 # | 1990 # | Change # |
|---|---|---|---|
| 1. Small group Bible studies | 2 | 1 | ↑1 |
| 2. Retreats/special events | 3 | 2 | ↑1 |
| 3. Divorce recovery and (tie) | 4 | 3 | ↑1 |
| Ministry with never-marrieds (25+) | 1 | 3 | ↓2 |
| 4. Single parent ministry, and (tie) | 5 | 4 | ↑1 |
| Evangelism/Outreach | 14 | 4 | ↑10 |
| 5. Remarriage ministry, and (tie) | 13 | 5 | ↑8 |
| College-career ministry (under 25) | 6 | 5 | ↑1 |
| 6. Conferences/seminars | 7 | 6 | ↑1 |
| 7. Short-term missions and, (tie) | 11 | 7 | ↑4 |
| Pre-marriage counseling | 9 | 7 | ↑2 |
| 8. Ministry with the widowed | 8 | 8 | — |
| 9. Ministry with children of divorce | 12 | 9 | ↑3 |
| 10. Reaching single men | 10 | 10 | — |

# Ages of Single Adults Involved in Singles Ministries: 1988-1990

As the baby boomer generation ages, so do those involved in our singles ministries. This increase in average age will continue.

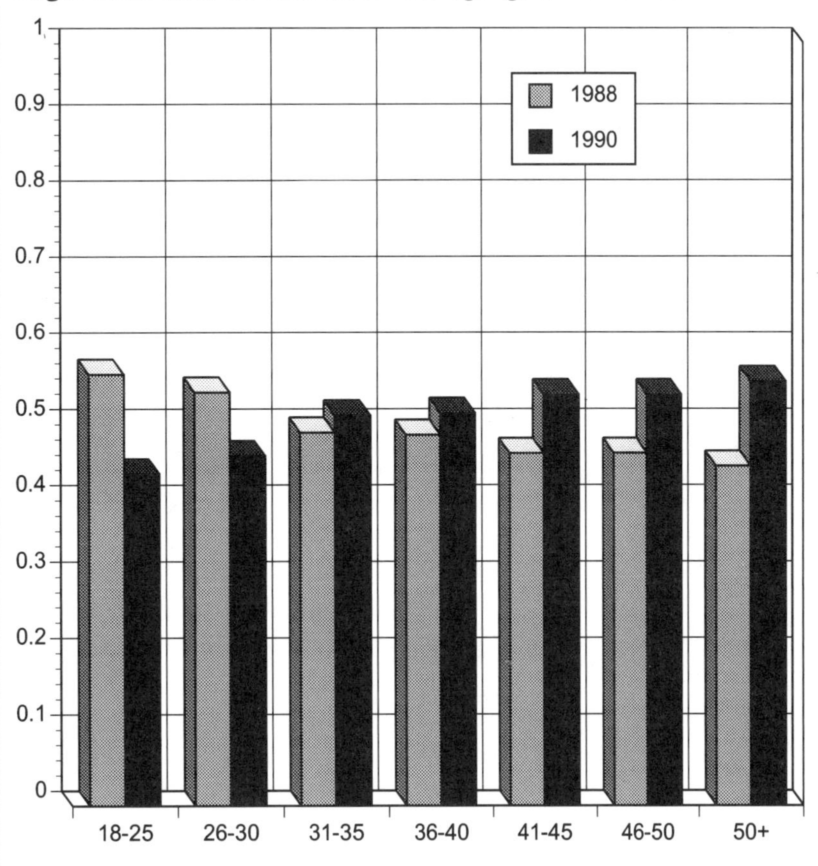

"I HIGHLY RECOMMEND

SINGLE ADULT MINISTRIES JOURNAL

TO OTHER PASTORS AND LEADERS

BECAUSE NO OTHER PUBLICATION

IS SO COMPLETE IN ITS COVERAGE

OF SINGLE ADULT MINISTRY."

- DENNIS FRANCK

BETHEL CHURCH, SAN JOSE, CALIFORNIA

Call toll FREE today to get your subscription started.
**800-487-4-SAM or 719-488-2610**
Or write: *SAM Journal*, P. O. Box 62056,
Colorado Springs, Colorado 80962-2056.

A one-year subscription is $24 (10 issues); $29 in Canada; $33 for all other countries.
*U. S. funds only*. Payment by Visa, MasterCard, or "bill me" also available.

# *Part 2*

# Guidelines for Singles Ministry

## Eighteen Helpful Articles from Experienced Leaders in Single Adult Ministry

### Where To Find It:

GROWING YOUR MINISTRY

# Twelve Realities About a Singles Ministry in the Local Church

*BY DR. MICHAEL ANTHONY AND CAROLYN KOONS*

## Here is a Brief Overview of How Singles Ministry Is Unique Compared to Other Forms of Ministry

There are a number of commonly accepted realities associated with starting and maintaining a single adult ministry. Leaders must face each reality or frustration will result. There are ways to handle some of these realities so they will not undermine your ministry.

**1. Transient singles.** The number one reason why single adults remain single, according to national polls, is the freedom and mobility that single living provides. Most church singles programs will have no shortage of visitors but the challenge is keeping the regulars from leaving before the newcomers become members. Turnover among single adults in most large churches is a critical issue of concern.

**2. Lack of church ownership.** Because of increased mobility among Christian single adults there is a lack of ownership to a particular church. They will stay long enough to observe the full spectrum of singles in the group, determine whether or not this group will meet their needs, and if not, then move on to new horizons. Single adult leaders must not get trapped into directing their ministry to this cross-section of the singles population. Each church must realize that it will not be able to provide something for everyone. It becomes imperative to know your limits and focus your ministry toward specific needs.

**3. No perfect singles ministry.** Not all groups are right for all people. Some groups may be able to specialize on recovery, either divorce or grief. Some may be able to provide their members with a haven for embattled single parents. Some may find that they attract the never-married college and career-aged single adults. The training of the single adult leaders will have a lot to do with the kinds of singles the church attracts.

It is a simple reality that no church can provide a balanced program for every type of single adult ministry available today. Some may be limited by financial or physical resources. Some may not have any trained staff for the singles ministry. At any rate, no ministry will be perfect. Most are doing the best they can with the resources that are available.

**4. A healing ministry.** Most ministry with single adults is marked by healing of emotional, spiritual and social hurts. A number of singles come into the church with scars and damaged emotions. It takes a great deal of time and energy to provide the kind of healing that these adults need.

A successful ministry to single adults must realize that there is a difference between holiness and wholeness. Although holiness is the standard that we as Christians pursue, such a goal will never be accomplished in our lifetimes.

Many single adults are living with the guilt and pain of compromised standards of living. They need to learn to see themselves as God sees them, forgiven and cleansed. A single adult ministry must foster the development of wholeness. Singles need to experience this state of wholeness in their lives in order to gain new hope and vision for what their lives can become.

**5. Total member involvement.** New Testament ministry was never designed to be done by just one person. God dispersed the spiritual gifts to all the members of the body of Christ in order to require total member involvement in a healthy church.

Single adults are capable of assuming leadership roles in our churches. They handle significant responsibilities during the week in their employment, yet are often treated as dependent children on the weekend by single adult leaders who take full responsibility for the details of the singles ministry.

**6. Advance planning.** Any successful program requires advance organization. The structure selected should be based on natural groupings. There should be opportunities to gather as a large group as well as a small group. When determining how best to break the group into smaller units, it is best to categorize them by age, not status (i.e. never-married, divorced, etc.). It is also a good idea to have written job descriptions for those serving on the leadership team, and to meet with the leaders on a regular basis.

**7. Ministry promotion.** Those churches able to provide for a singles ministry need to advertise it regularly in community newspapers, mailers and flyers, etc. Be certain that materials are printed in a quality manner. The single adult ministry that uses poorly-prepared materials communicates a half-hearted concern for quality.

**8. The dating game.** Because of the social and relational needs of single adults, there will always be a percentage of single adults who come through your church each week in pursuit of a mate. Their motives may be faulty but their resolve is focused and determined.

**9. Sex and the single Christian.** One of the most common realities often overlooked today is that Christian singles are sexually active. With this realization, a singles ministry must deal with the issues that such sexual activity will create. These singles may be experiencing guilt and emotional pain. They may have feelings of failure and rejection. Plan programs that will guide them in the Christian perspective of their sexuality. They need to see that sexuality is a God-given dimension of their humanness, but that it requires a degree of responsibility and control.

**Turnover among single adults in most large churches is a critical issue of concern.**

**10. Your Christian identity.** When some church single adult ministries begin to attract large groups of single adults, they are faced with the temptation to compromise their message so that they do not "turn off" those who come. They may be fearful of losing their momentum by presenting the gospel and integrating Bible studies into their programming.

There is no need to apologize for being Christian in focus. If single adults complain about the religious dimension of your programming, simply explain that a solid biblical foundation is the only answer to the needs that single adults face today. To undermine that foundation by omitting an emphasis on it would be to deny your mission as a church.

**11. Standards of conduct.** Each church has different teachings as to the degree of freedom that God's Spirit allows believers to exercise. For example, some churches allow their single adults to consume alcohol at social functions; others do not. There are diverse issues that need clarification in advance so conflicts do not arise. Have these standards written down and let the singles know what they are in advance. The church leadership should contribute to the setting of basic policies that will influence the church's reputation in the community.

A common issue is what to do with singles living together. Do you condemn them and require them to separate (and risk losing an influence on their lives) or condone their activities and say it is not the church's business (and in so doing ignore the scriptural teaching on marital fidelity)? Singles who are living openly together and do not wish to separate should be encouraged to attend a couples class. Attending singles functions would not have a positive influence on the sexual standards you are trying to maintain.

**12. Misunderstandings.** Any leader in ministry must realize there will be times when misunderstandings will occur. Some times they will come from the church body that does not fully understand the complexity of needs that singles face. Other times it may come from the singles themselves who may not understand that their singles ministry is a smaller part of the entire church's Christian education ministry.

These twelve realities of singles ministry in the local church are provided to assist single adult leaders in gaining an understanding about the uniqueness of a singles ministry compared to other forms of ministry in the church. Single adults are not to be treated like an extended youth group. They are adults and must be treated as such.

Single adult ministries help the church keep a balanced perspective in life. They help the church realize it is a body of diverse people; whether they are young or old, rich or poor, black or white, married or single, they are still members of God's eternal body of believers. Church ministry that is comprehensive will include a focused effort at meeting the needs of all its members.

**Michael Anthony, Ed.D., is chairman of the Department of Christian Education at Talbot School of Theology, Biola University. He also serves as associate pastor of Christian education at Woodbridge Community Church in Irvine, Calif. He has held various pastoral and teaching positions in the past ten years.**

**Carolyn Koons is dean of church relations and executive director of the Institute for Outreach Ministries at Azusa Pacific University. She is a graduate of the Christian Education Department at Talbot School of Theology and a popular author and conference speaker.**

*Excerpted with permission from* Single Adult Passages: Uncharted Territories, *Chapter 15, "Setting Your Compass: Designing a Single Adult Ministry," by Carolyn Koons and Michael Anthony, Baker Books, 1990.*

# Who Are the Single Adults in Your Community?

*BY KAREN GREENWALDT*

**Use this form to determine who the single adults are in your community and in your church. If you know these measurements, you can begin to assess priorities and project the various costs of your programs based on estimating the numbers who will participate.**

**Knowing My Community**

(Much of this information can be obtained by contacting your public library or Chamber of Commerce. Ask for demographic data on single adults in your town, city, or county.)

The number of all adults who live in my town, city, or county:__________

The number of single adults in my town, city, or county:_______________

The number of single adults between the ages of 19 and 30:___________
31 and 55:___________
over 55:___________
(You may want to find out numbers of persons in the older adult age range. If so, determine your age brackets and search for the information.)

The number of single parents in your town, city, or county:___________

What opportunities are available for single adults in your area? Supply names of organizations and number of persons served on an annual basis:

Other churches:

Dating services:

Single adult clubs or other area singles groups:

Restaurants or night spots which cater to single adults:

Sports teams for single adults:

Other options for single adults:

Where do concentrated numbers of single adults live in your town, city, or county? Apartment or condominium complexes: (List the complexes closest to your church. Then list those farther away.):

Particular neighborhoods:

Other information which you may want to collect:

**Knowing My Church**
(Your church records may have this in formation. If not, you may have to develop a survey or ask for approximate numbers.)

Your church's adult membership:____________

The number of single adults who are members:___________

The number of single adults between the ages of 19 and 30:_________
31 and 55:_________
over 55:_________
(You may want to break the numbers of persons over 55 into categories.)

The number of single parents who have children under 18 living at home:

The number of single parents who have children under 18 who are living with another person:

List single adults in leadership positions in your church (for example, Sunday school teachers, members of boards, committees, councils, task forces, etc., members of the choir, etc.):

List existing programs for single adults (for example, classes, study groups, weekday programs, visitation programs, activities for single parents, etc.):

What does your pastor think about single adult ministry? How supportive is he or she? How important does your pastor believe singles ministry to be? How will your pastor support your efforts in ministry with singles?

What do single adults in your church say? What are their needs, hopes, concerns? How would they like the church to help them with these issues?

What suggestions would they make for the kind of single adult program they would support? Who are potential leaders among these persons?

**Now What?**
What did we learn from the information we gathered?

What can we offer that is not already offered in the church or in the community?

**What is our next step?**

**Karen Greenwaldt is Director of Single Adult Ministries for the United Methodist Church. She travels the country extensively to train leaders and encourage programs for the millions of single adults in our communities and congregations.**
*Excerpted with permission from* Singles Care One for Another, *Karen Greenwaldt, pp. 79-84, Discipleship Resources, 1989. (P. O. Box 840, Nashville, TN 37202. Order #DRO72B. Price: $6.95)*

GROWING YOUR MINISTRY

# Starting a Single Adult Ministry

*BY SHERON C. PATTERSON*

## One Successful Singles Ministry Leader Shares a Gameplan . . . Plus Some Do's and Don'ts.

The decision to start a singles ministry in your church is a major decision, and a worthwhile one. A lot of effort will be required to get the program off the ground. Even more work will be needed to keep things going. Be prepared for anything. You will need a good bit of stamina. Most of all, rely on God to enable you in this most vital ministry.

Several years ago I decided that I wanted to see a singles ministry in my church because I saw a large portion of the congregation's membership in need. The needs were diverse, yet they were the same. A large group of unconnected individuals were in need of connection. So, with a wing and a prayer, I approached the senior pastor of my congregation, Rev. Zan W. Holmes, with the idea that we should have our own singles ministry. "Sounds good," he said. "What is it?"

Luckily, Dr. Holmes was (and is) a man with a futuristic vision. He was also able to see what was before his eyes each Sunday morning in the congregation, a congregation that was 50 to 60 percent single adult. With Dr. Holmes' blessing, and with a handful of other interested singles, we went to work and began carving out the kind of program that I had felt in my heart was needed. Today, the single adult ministry at St. Luke "Community" United Methodist Church, with over one hundred participants, continues to thrive and to serve as a model of ministry with singles.

### Starting from Scratch

Watching a flourishing ministry among single adults is a great joy. Helping such a ministry to happen is a lot of work. I want to share with you the five steps I have used, and now recommend, in order to build a singles ministry from scratch.

**1.** Discuss the idea with the senior pastor. Ensure that he or she is in favor of such a ministry. You cannot and should not try to begin such a group without pastoral consent and support.

**2.** Begin to meet with a small group of singles. These should be people who are interested in the idea of having a singles ministry at the church, and who are willing to work to make the group a reality.

This core group needs to be informed on the topic of single adults in general. Members of the group should research the topics of single adults, and of ministry to single adults, through magazine articles and books. The group should also examine church records, in order to determine the number of singles within the potential ministry of this congregation. Note also that this should include the number of those who live within the ministry area of the congregation. Singles ministries can be beautiful tools for evangelism.

**3.** The core group should produce a survey of the singles who are already part of the congregation. Such a survey can be distributed by mail or by hand during a worship service. The survey should poll singles as to their interest level in a singles ministry, and their willingness to attend meetings.

This survey should also be designed to find out what the church means to singles, and how they would like to serve if given the opportunity. In many instances the status of singlehood is a stigma. Single people are often excluded from church leadership. (Whether the exclusion is intentional or unintentional makes little difference.) A singles ministry can and should be a means of overcoming such indifference and building the participation of singles into the full life of the congregation.

**4.** Compile all of the information (i.e., the numbers of single persons, their status and interests, etc.) and use this to create a formal presentation to the appropriate boards, agencies, and pastoral staff of your congregation. This information will enable you to document the need for a singles ministry in your church should there be opposition.

In my experience, it is probably wise to anticipate some opposition. Some opposition may come, for example, from married persons who aren't quite sure what the role and purpose of a singles ministry will be. The term singles conjures up in some minds a swinging, irresponsible lifestyle. In this case it will be incumbent upon you to convince such doubters that a ministry to single adults will be just the opposite.

**5.** Once the plan to develop the ministry is approved, allow the core group to plan an opening event. Announce this event from the pulpit, and have it endorsed by the senior pastor. The first event might be a meeting in the fellowship hall after services, or a brunch at a nearby restaurant, or a Bible study at someone's home.

Let's say, for example, that the first event will be a combined Bible study and potluck dinner at one of the single's homes. Schedule the event about four to six weeks in advance, to ensure that it is included on all church organizational calendars. This advance planning also gives time for the printing of flyers or even invitations for the singles of the church. On the two Sundays prior to the event, ask the senior pastor to endorse the plan for the singles group and for the upcoming event from the pulpit. In the week before the event, ask the core group to launch a calling campaign to personally contact all of the singles of the church and to invite them to come.

**A good idea is to involve men on the planning team. As a rule, singles ministries are dominated by women. You will do well to break this rule in every way you can.**

At the initial event, allow all those present to express their ideas, dreams, and visions for the singles ministry. This will give them their proper sense of ownership in the group right from the start. From these initial comments and conversations, you should have the raw material for moving forward with your own plans in your own context. In any event, whatever the long-range vision, don't wait long to plan another group event. A great deal of ministry with singles happens just by being together.

## Do's and Don'ts

Along with these five steps for starting a ministry, I would also like to share some insights concerning how to keep the ministry healthy and growing.

***Do*** pray. Keep the power of prayer alive in the group and in the planning and upkeep of the group. Ask the entire congregation to pray for the success of the ministry.

***Do*** try to get men involved in the group. Men can and do benefit from the nurturing and care that stems from singles ministries. Many men, however, are not joiners by nature. A good idea is to involve men on the planning team. As a rule, singles ministries are dominated by women. You will do well to break this rule in every way you can.

***Do*** maintain a Christian purpose as your backbone and mainstay. The singles at St. Luke intended to keep the ministry of Christ at the center of their gathering, so they chose a special name to reflect this commitment. They decided to call themselves "S.O.L.E."—Singles of Life Everlasting. A vital element of any singles ministry is that it is a ministry. There are loads of social outlets for singles. The ministry of the church offers them the best in the world—Jesus Christ.

***Do*** recruit aggressively. Don't be afraid to gently approach a single person in the congregation and offer an invitation to an event.

GROWING YOUR MINISTRY

***Don't*** be upset by a low turnout or by apathy. It takes some people a while to warm up to the idea of a program designed to meet their specific needs, especially if they are rarely catered to in this way. It's a real treat to have a customized ministry offered just for your group. But some people may not be quite ready for this.

***Don't*** expect everyone to join. The idea of a singles ministry strikes some people as a group for losers. Also, many people today are overextended. They hold memberships in lots of groups and do not have the time for one more. Encourage such busy people to attend occasional events.

***Don't*** judge the group's members on the basis of their careers. A person who works as a waiter may have the same, if not more, skills than a corporate manager. Remember that in our community we have not all had the same chance to make it. Much to my amazement, the stalwart of the group I started was a custodian. He was talented, creative, and a good leader.

## Favorite Activities

In addition to the steps for getting started, and the "do's and don'ts" for growing as a group, every ministry with single adults will want to discover a list of favorite activities. Some activities are, however, time-honored and tested. Therefore, you might want to consider some of these in the short- and long-range planning for your group.

*Bible study.* An exciting opportunity for ministry and sharing is possible whenever two or more are gathered around the Word of God. Singles ministries should be biblically based.

*Happy hours.* Singles are looking for a place where they can truly "meet" one another. The idea of a Christian happy hour, therefore, is something about which to be creative and to rejoice. Why not pick a special meeting place, one that is conducive to listening and to sharing? Or provide a place in the fellowship hall of your congregation's building. This should be a place where singles can come to listen to music—gospel jazz, light jazz, or gospel rap. Create an inviting atmosphere and serve punch as the beverage of choice. In doing so you can provide a place for singles to meet one another and to form faithful friendships.

*Rap sessions.* Another activity that generates interest and involvement is a rap session. Rap sessions are opportunities to discuss topics such as sex, dating, marriage, etc. Christian singles need opportunities to discuss such topics openly and honestly. Since the opportunity for such discussions is often scarce, you may find that rap sessions attract singles from other congregations, as well as from your own. Rap sessions may also attract singles in your own congregation who have been reluctant to get involved in other kinds of activities. This can be a good opportunity to spark their interest in the group.

*Retreats/Outings.* Everyone loves to get away from the normal routine for a while. For singles, however, getting away can be a lonely experience. To remedy this, some singles groups plan occasional outings—for example, weekend retreats at local campgrounds, retreat centers, or hotels. A retreat with singles can be centered around a variety of relevant themes, and led by a person trained in that field. Outings are also popular because many singles dislike attending public functions alone. Singles outings to movies, plays, and restaurants are crowd pleasers.

**Sheron Patterson founded and began to direct a church-based singles ministry in 1983. Since then, she has lectured, preached, and written on the topic of singleness and Christianity. Currently she is an ordained deacon in the North Texas Annual Conference and an associate pastor at First United Methodist Church in Dallas, Texas.**

*Excerpted with permission from* Ministry With Black Single Adults, *by Sheron C. Patterson, pp. 47-52, Discipleship Resources, 1990. (P. O. Box 840, Nashville, TN 37202. Order #DRO87B. Price: $4.95.)*

**Use the Handy Order Form on Page 253 . . .**

*to receive some of the most helpful resources for your single adult ministry.*

# Sample Goals and Objectives for a Singles Ministry

*BY MIKE PLATTER*

## If You Don't Know Where You're Going, You'll Probably End Up Somewhere Else.

These words provide a great place to start talking about developing single adult ministries. They serve to remind us that without goals, our journey toward effective ministry may become mere back-to-back activity.

**Purpose:**
To train single adults to discover their spiritual gifts and effectively use these gifts in reaching other adults for Christ.

**Objectives:**
1. To recognize singleness as an acceptable lifestyle.

2. To equip single adults with necessary skills to live productive lives.

3. To minister to single adults during times of crisis.

4. To help single adults become integrated into the local church progra and family.

5. To help members of the church family see single adults as family members.

6. To provide single adults a place of service to minister in the church family.

7. To develop support structures within the church to meet the unique needs of the single adult and single parent family.

**Mike Platter, a single adult, is an active participant and leader in single adult ministries. He is director of Single Adult Ministries for the Iowa District Church of the Nazarene. He is associate pastor of First Church of the Nazarene, Oskaloosa, Iowa.**

*Excerpted with permission from* The Faces of Single Adult Ministries, *Linda G. Hardin, editor, Chapter 5, "How to Begin Single Adult Ministries in the Local Church," by Mike Platter, pp. 59-60, Beacon Hill Press, 1990. (Available through Nazarene Publishing House: 800-877-0700. Price: $4.95.)*

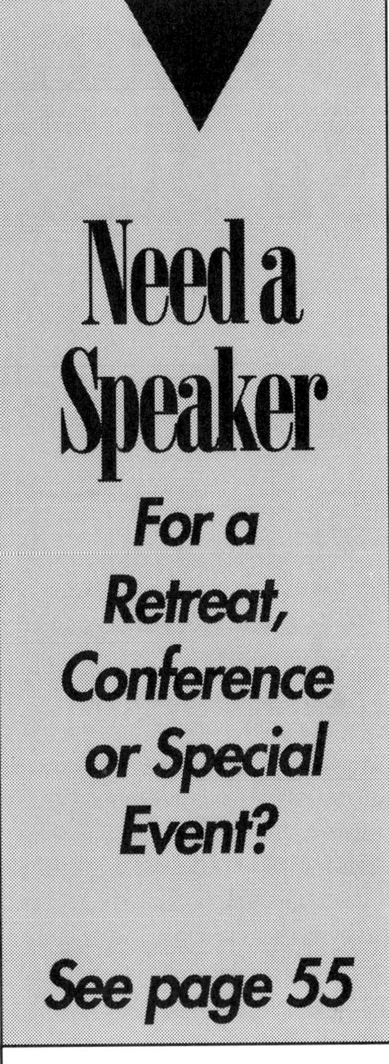

GROWING YOUR MINISTRY

# Building a Well-Balanced Singles Ministry

BY CHRIS EATON

## Are You Addressing Both the Spiritual and Social Needs?

Balance is as important to a ministry as it is to a high-wire walker. Even just a slight shift to one side or the other may create a disastrous imbalance. Therefore, the leadership of a singles ministry should think balance every step of the way. Unfortunately, too many ministries do not start thinking about balance until a fall has occurred and, at that point, the damage may be irreparable.

### Balance Defined

One reason balance sometimes escapes the planners of a ministry is that it seems an element too vague to incorporate into the planning. Therefore, it is wise to begin with a rather simple working definition:

*Balance in a ministry is attained when both the social and the spiritual needs of the participants are met in such a way that the two are viewed as inseparable.*

The ideal ministry situation is when both the social and the spiritual needs are treated as interdependent. This philosophy is especially important in a single adult ministry, where the social need is so much more apparent. The mistake often made is to view these needs as separate entities in the planning of the ministry. For example, a spiritual time is planned once a week and a social time is planned once a month. Yet in the Scriptures the two go hand in hand.

*A well-balanced ministry is reached when spiritual growth and relational development (community building) are both happening in some way at every function of the group.*

Now of course there will be times when there is more social than spiritual, and vice versa, but it needs to be balanced out in the end. Just as it would be ridiculous for the high-wire walker to continually lean in one direction, so also is it foolish for a leader to allow a ministry to continually lean in one direction.

### Importance of Balance

The importance of balance to a ministry can be understood by looking at the results of both proper balance and improper balance.

**Individual growth.** Participants will be growing in their spirituality. They will not just be learning material, rather they will be developing a "cutting edge" relationship with Jesus Christ. Learning is always more effective in the context of a community. In a community people are challenged not only to learn, but are stimulated to put that learning into practice.

**Group growth.** When there's proper balance in a group, there will be more of an interest in visitors. Obviously when there's an interest in the visitors, a larger percentage of them will return to the group. Some single adult ministries stagnate simply because there is nothing worth coming back to. Healthy growth will usually be a good indicator of proper balance.

The results of improper balance can be seen in one of two extremes. Group "too" spiritual. Primary focus is inward. The emphasis is only on the spiritual dimension. Motto: Study! The characteristics of this group (signs to look for) are:

(1) Social sought elsewhere. The need is still there and has to be met. A program may be great on Sunday morning, but chances are the single adults are not staying home Saturday night studying their Sunday School curriculum!

(2) Boredom within the group.

(3) Poor evangelistic/outreach attitude. Christians are commissioned to carry the Good News to the world they live in. However, when the concern of a group is only on their own spiritual growth, their concern for the needs of those around them can drop off.

(4) Low visitor return.

Group "too" social. Primary focus is outward. The emphasis is only on the social. Motto: Party! The characteristics of this group are:

(1) Little spiritual growth in individuals.

(2) Lack of a solid foundation in the group.

(3) Complaining in the ranks when personal needs are not met.

(4) Low visitor return. There's no community being developed when the spiritual is ignored. It is purely superficial.

In summary, both situations fail to insure longevity for the group. Chances are either type of group will die a slow, stagnating death.

## Hindrances to Balance

Imbalance is not something a leader decides one day to have. Instead it is usually a gradual slide to one side or the other—a slide that may at times go unnoticed until too late!

Ways a single adult ministry may slide out of balance:

**Demands of people.** It is quite obvious that what people demand may not be all they need. Therefore, it is important for the leadership to keep the demands in the proper perspective.

**Expectations of people.** Meeting everyone's expectations can be as unhealthy as meeting everyone's demands.

**Preoccupation with numbers.** This causes a leader to go for the "big" number events in programming. The problem is that often less glamorous needs go without being met.

**What has been done in the past.** Especially if the past includes a ministry way out of balance. The mentality will need to be gradually changed.

**Staff pressures/board pressures.**

**Lack of creativity.** The "rut" mentality of ministry results in doing the same thing year after year. Leaders fail to come up with innovative ideas.

When the leadership allows these to control or influence the direction of the group they run a high risk of imbalance.

## Maintaining a Balanced Ministry

**Leader.** Balance begins with a balanced leader. The leader should be an example of balance in his personal life. Participants should see both the spiritual and social needs of the leader being met in an integrated manner. A leader must not be so quick to lay the blame for the imbalance of the group on the people involved, the church board, or certain circumstances. Often the imbalance may simply be a reflection of the leader's own imbalance!

**Group.** As with anything else, attitude is of key importance to a group desiring balance. Maintaining these attitudes will play a major role in maintaining a balanced ministry.

**Understanding.** Leaders should understand that people are not exclusively spiritual or social.

**Sensitivity.** A leader must be sensitive to the changing needs within the group and in the world around the group. Without sensitivity a leader may try to do the same things over and over again even when the program or idea has outlived its usefulness.

**Adaptability.** Be willing to adapt a program or method to a certain situation or need.

**Flexibility.** The leader must avoid rigidity in the approach to people and ministry.

**Risk-taking.** Be willing to try new ideas, new methods, new strategies. A leader who desires a balanced ministry will be a leader who is willing to take some risks in that ministry!

A balanced ministry is a necessity for effective, long-term ministry in the single adult community. Therefore, the leadership needs to pause from time to time and get a feel for whether or not the ministry is balanced.

**Chris Eaton is Executive Director of Single Purpose Ministries in St. Petersburg, Florida and the founder of Bridge Builders, Inc. He is also a co-author of *Vacations With a Purpose*, an excellent resource for short-term missions teams. As a singles ministry leader, Chris has learned well the importance of achieving balance in ministry.**

*Excerpted with permission from* Singles Ministry Handbook, *Douglas Fagerstrom, editor, Chapter 45, "A Balanced Ministry," by Chris Eaton, pp. 219-222, Victor Books, 1989, Wheaton, IL.*

GROWING YOUR MINISTRY

# How to Attract Single Adults to Your Church

*BY KAREN GREENWALDT*

Any church that intends to build a healthy ministry with single adults will want to find ways to reach new people in the community. Here are several suggestions to consider that can help keep your doors open wide to the single adults in your community.

Single adults are invited by someone else. Most people respond positively to an invitation. "Come with me to ______."

By far, single adult groups grow best when members take responsibility to invite others, their friends, co-workers, and neighbors to attend. More persons respond positively when someone says, "I'll pick you up so that we can go to ________."

Some churches have developed visitation programs in which members of the single adult group visit in pairs those persons who are prospective members for the group. These teams often choose one night a week for visitation. Visitors meet at the church for their assignments. They spend two hours visiting with single adults in their homes, apartments, condominiums, or restaurants. (Many of these visitation teams have made appointments before they ring doorbells.) Following the visitation time, the teams meet for coffee and snacks and discuss their learnings, feelings, and stories.

Single adults respond to publicity. Some people respond to advertisements in the newspaper. Others respond to visual invitations on bulletin boards, in brochures, etc.

When publicity is used, single adult groups follow various procedures. Most do monthly newsletters. Others develop special brochures which advertise various programs for single adults. These brochures are distributed in many ways—through lawyers', doctors', and judges' offices; through the mail to selected persons; through visitation teams; and through bulletin inserts during worship. Some churches pay for advertising in the area newspaper. Others buy space in local single adult community papers or use free time allotted to public service announcements on the radio or TV.

**Some single adults will be referred to your program by others. Lawyers, mental health professionals, doctors, financial planners, and other community leaders often refer single adults to churches. Anticipate such referrals by getting acquainted with these community leaders.**

Whenever publicity methods are used, the materials need to contain these items:

• Clear messages—giving purpose of the program, time, place, dress required, baby-sitting available, cost, etc.

• Visual appeal—using color if possible and containing brief descriptions of the program.

• Descriptions of benefits to participants—suggesting ways the program will provide help with problems or concerns, information, ideas for living, contacts within the single adult population, etc.

Single adults sometimes initiate a call to the church when looking for a singles group. When they receive information, they decide whether or not to attend. Every church office needs to contain specific information so that callers can be given complete and up-to-date news about your single adult program.

In addition, names, addresses, and phone numbers of persons who call the church can be given to single adults. These singles can call or visit persons who have expressed an interest in the program.

Some single adults will be referred to your program by others. Lawyers, mental health professionals, doctors, financial planners, and other community leaders often refer single adults to churches. Anticipate such referrals by getting acquainted with these community leaders. Help them understand the ministry in which you are involved. Encourage them to refer persons to your program.

In addition, family, friends, and associates often refer single adults to churches where there are high-quality programs. Provide information to all church members about your program and encourage them to refer their friends and associates. Spread the word about your ministry to every person in your congregation.

Some single adults will come to your church looking for a singles program. These persons often attend worship first, or they may arrive at the Sunday school hour. Be alert and be looking for visitors who are single. Provide single adult greeters to the Christian education program who know how and when to direct visitors to your group.

Whenever your group meets, designate persons to watch for visitors. These designated people need to:

- Be friendly!
- Invite the visitor to sit with him or her.
- Introduce the visitor to other persons in the group.
- Learn something about who the visitor is so that caring can begin immediately.
- Make certain that the visitor fills out a card, giving name, address, and phone number.
- Be sure that this card is given to the persons who are committed to call or visit the visitor within a few days.
- If worship or other activities follow your group meeting, invite the visitor to go with you to that function.

**Karen Greenwaldt is Director of Single Adult Ministries for the United Methodist Church. She travels the country extensively to train leaders and encourage programs for the millions of single adults in communities and congregations.**

*Excerpted with permission from* Singles Care One for Another, *by Karen Greenwaldt, Chapter 16, "What You Wanted to Know," pp. 95-97, Discipleship Resources, 1989. (P. O. Box 840, Nashville, TN 37202. Order #DRO72B. Price: $6.95.)*

**"Call it intuition, a sixth sense, or discernment . . . . Whatever it was, there was something that disturbed singles director Paula Pingly about the new guy at their last meeting."**

GROWING YOUR MINISTRY

# Are Your Singles Part of the Mainstream?

*BY MARY GRAVES*

## Integrating Singles into the Life of the Church

**Single Adults Want to Be the Church Too**

"One of the most important concepts to catch in the single adult ministry is the idea that the church is composed of both two-adult family units and one-adult family units. Too often, by default, it is assumed that the church is the married adults and that when the singles get married and have homes, then they too can be the church. We need to stretch our vision of the church to include the single adult."

Such is the perceptive counsel of Britton Wood in his book Single Adults Want to Be the Church Too (Broadman). The proof that a church has this kind of vision is not in the number of programs offered for singles, but in the number of singles involved in all the programs of the church. A successful singles ministry helps the church realize that single adults are not just one part of the church to be ministered to (like the youth). They make up an important part of the ministry team, and the church must recognize their part in the body (Rom. 12:4-5).

One single adult leader claimed that if you took all the singles out of his church it would be paralyzed. That is what it looks like

# How to Select Leaders for Your Singles Ministry

*BY BOBBIE REED*

## Practical Steps for Interviewing and Recruiting Your Leadership Team

**In the Beginning**

Church leaders who are contemplating starting a singles ministry frequently ask "Where do we find leaders?" Obviously if you have only four singles in church, you won't be over burdened with would-be leaders. Your first step will be to decide who will be in charge of the new group. If one of your single adults has the right qualifications for a leader, you may wish to ask him to serve as director for an initial period of six months. After six months your group will have grown, and you may wish to increase the number of leadership positions.

**How Many Leaders?**

To determine the leadership positions you will want, analyze your group. The one most significant determinant is group size. How many regular members do you have? Do you have 5 to 15 singles? You may want only one or two leaders at first. Do you have 50 or more singles? You will want several leaders right away.

The basic leadership positions, or officers, are president (who may be called a Director of Singles), vice president, secretary, treasurer, and fellowship chairperson. This team directs and coordinates the group functions in all areas, including: membership, outreach, fellowship, family life, publicity, music, and spiritual life.

As your group grows, you may form committees for each of these major functions, and involve more of your members in the planning and conduct-

when singles ministry comes to full maturity. It isn't just providing a place where singles can learn and grow with other singles; it is connecting them to the larger body of Christ.

## The Attitude of Your Church toward Single Adults

When Highland Park Presbyterian Church in Dallas hired a singles pastor, it was spelled out in the job description that this person was to bridge the gap between singles and marrieds and, by a consciousness-raising on both sides, to bring singles into the center of the church's life. But when a large community church in southern California hired a singles pastor, he was to take care of single people and their needs and keep them "out there" as a separate department, apart from the whole life of the church—what you might call a "leper colony" mentality. Whether articulated or not, every church has an attitude toward singles and singles ministry, and that attitude is lodged in the leaders of the church. The task of integrating singles into the life of the church begins and ends with their vision.

## Two Prevailing Views

There seem to be two basic images of singles ministry: singles as a separate colony or as a necessary part of the whole. The first task is to determine the premise that prevails in your church and in the singles leader. If the "separate colony" image prevails, then consciousness-raising will have to happen in the leadership first before integration is even a possibility.

## Single Adults as a Problem or an Asset

In conversations about people it is hard to find the word "single" without also hearing words like lonely, divorced, depressed, swinging, sleeping around, etc. Most single adults don't like the title of "single" because of negative connotations. So with that kind of press, it is not surprising that many churches hold singles at arm's length, unable to ignore them and unwilling to draw them in.

But more and more churches are discovering that single adults are not a problem to be solved but a gifted work force to be employed for the work of Christ's church. Singles often ask the honest questions and come up with new solutions; they break out of the conventional and/or make the conventional more practical. Singles are an asset to the church not because they have more time and money (a mythical stereotype which is simply untrue) but because they bring a new and fresh perspective that allows God to do the "new thing" that needs doing.

CONTINUED ON PAGE 32

---

ing of your activities. Committees, of course, do not function autonomously, but rather take guidance from your group leaders. Committees have the advantage of getting several people involved in planning and carrying out the mission of your organization. The more people you have involved, the greater is your potential for creativity. Also, people who are actively involved tend to maintain enthusiasm for and interest in your singles ministry.

### Recruiting Leaders

Once your group has grown, you will have a broader base from which to select leaders. Then you can follow a more formal recruitment process.

1. Ask God to guide you in recruiting leaders. He knows which of your people are gifted and ready to lead.

2. Write clearly-defined job descriptions for each position of leadership in your group. These duty statements provide a basis for discussing the possibilities for service with potential leaders.

3. Look for singles who have demonstrated a gift for leadership and administration in any area of their lives—at home, on the job, in previous church experience. Get to know your members on a personal level and discover which ones put God first, are in a good personal and spiritual space, and are caring individuals.

4. Approach people with a positive attitude. You are offering people an opportunity to use their God-given talents, and to grow. Don't try to make people feel it is their duty to be a leader. Don't make them feel guilty if they say no. Remember that God is guiding you to the right person and when you find him, you will also discover that God has prepared his heart to listen to your offer and respond with a yes!

### Selecting Leaders

Every organization and church will have its own procedure for selecting and appointing leaders. The most common include recruiting candidates (which sometimes includes using a nominating committee), verifying that applicants meet an established qualification standard, interviewing all candidates, and final selection by member voting or executive appointment.

Interviewing potential leaders is one method of assessing candidate qualifications and appropriateness of appointments. Interviews may be conducted by a nominating committee, the Director of Singles, your Director of Christian Education, or pastor. Whoever conducts the interviews should plan questions which will give each person an opportunity to present his qualifications as a leader. Questions you might ask include the following:

CONTINUED ON PAGE 32

## The Attitude of Single Adults Toward Your Church

You must have a church that singles want to go to. The worship service must be enthusiastic, not lifeless. The preaching must be inclusive of the experiences single adults are facing. The church must express an openness to the wounded—especially to the divorced. Sunday Schools must address the needs of single parent homes with a sensitivity to custody arrangements.

## Singles Get the Message

There are many subtle ways that the church can say to singles, "You do not belong here." The leadership, program, and language of a church can say very loudly, "This is a family church," and singles will be left out. Singles will go where they aren't put on hold until they are married. They will go where they are recognized and counted.

## Cultivate in Your Singles a Desire to Serve

Single adults must first have a desire and willingness to serve before they will move into areas of ministry in the church. This grows out of discipleship; it results from people being nurtured and trained to think of themselves as belonging to Jesus Christ, His family, being His servants.

This happens at an academic and experiential level in Bible studies, in leadership training, and in one-on-one discipling. Talk about serving the needy and then follow that with a volunteer assignment to work at the local soup kitchen. With this training and exposure singles will already be thinking ministry and looking for ways to do more.

## Orient Your Singles to the Church

Singles need to know where they can serve in the church. It is important to note that different commitment levels are required for the various volunteer opportunities. Low-level commitments might include ushering, greeting, or serving coffee, whereas high-level would include teaching Sunday School or singing in the choir. Look for the commitment level suited for the different singles in your church.

## Identify Opportunities for Service

Singles seem to respond well to commitment responsibilities where high demands of energy and attention are required for a short period of time (the task force model). Planning a one-day conference on "Intimacy" or a New Year's Eve party for the whole church family. Other opportunities in this category might include teaching Sunday School just for the summer or organizing a mission trip.

High-level commitments require training and equipping and much encouragement. Perhaps the first high-level commitment for your singles is church membership. Every church has its own requirements, some more rigorous than others. But whatever the requirements, the commitment involves consciously making one particular church their church home. All other major commitments to the church spring from that.

## Orient Your Church to the Singles

Often church members are totally uninformed about their singles. It is not necessarily

---

CONTINUED FROM PAGE 31

—Why does this position interest you?

—What kinds of other leadership experience have you had?

—List your leadership skills.

—What responsibilities will you find most difficult in this position?

—Describe your relationship with God.

—Share a recent experience which helped you grow spiritually.

—How much time are you prepared to devote each week to this position?

—In what way would you hope to grow as a person if you were appointed to this position?

—What would you like to tell us about yourself?

Develop additional, or substitute, questions to fit your needs.

After you have interviewed every applicant, discuss and compare the qualifications of each. Then, following the leading of the Lord, choose the leaders for your single adult ministry.

**Bobbie Reed is Director of Staff Development for a California state agency, serves as managing editor of SOLO, a Christian magazine for single adults, and has coauthored several previous books on singles ministries.**

*Excerpted with permission from* Single on Sunday, *by Bobbie Reed, Chapter 4, "Develop Successful Leaders", pp. 24-31, Concordia Publishing House, 1979. Available through Concordia Publishing House, 3558 S. Jefferson Ave., St. Louis, MO 63118. Item #12-2735. 800-325-3040.*

because they don't care; they don't know!

Single adults and your singles ministry can be made more visible to the whole church in a variety of ways. Starting with the obvious means of publicity, use your church newsletter, featuring articles on the activities of your single adults (e.g., specific acts of service by an individual or reporting on group events).

## Be Creative

The singles at Calvary Community Church in Thousand Oaks, Calif., have an annual Single's Day at their church which features a big jamboree with a pastor's dunk booth, a chili cook-off, live music, and all kinds of fun for the whole church family. It is effective for the singles to sponsor events for the whole church, even simply a reception after church with good food and catchy displays of the things that your single adults are doing.

The singles leader should keep the staff and church leaders aware of the gifted people available and encourage them to invest these leaders in their own ministries. This means that you must be willing to let go of these leaders to let them serve elsewhere.

In the body of Christ we are one family with one Father and "He made known to us the mystery of His will . . . to bring all things in heaven and on earth together." It is in that union that we will attain "to the whole measure of the fullness of Christ," when we are "joined and held together" (Eph. 1:9-10; 4:13, 16). That is the vision. That is what it looks like when singles ministry comes to full maturity.

**Mary Graves is Associate Pastor and Minister with Singles at Solana Beach Presbyterian Church, Solana Beach, Calif. She has experienced the ministry of integrating singles into her church over the last four years.**

*Excerpted with permission from* Singles Ministry Handbook, *Douglas Fagerstrom, editor, Chapter 49, "Integrating Singles into the Life of the Church," by Mary Graves, pp. 243-247, Victor Books, 1989, Wheaton, IL.*

# Single Adult Survey

## Learn More About the Singles in Your Church and Community

*BY SHERON PATTERSON*

The following survey can be adapted in a variety of ways to serve the particular needs of your congregation. If you want to conduct a confidential survey, for example, you can simply remove the line related to "name." In any case you will want to encourage your singles to fill out the survey as candidly as possible.

1. Name:

________________________________________

2. Gender: Male _____ Female_____

3. Age range: 20's ( ) 30's ( ) 40's ( ) 50's ( ) 60's ( ) 70's ( ) 80's ( )

4. Single status:
Divorced _____ Widowed_____
Always-single_____

5. Children: No_____ Yes_____ How many?_____
Ages ____________

6. What is the greatest joy of being single?

7. What is the greatest problem with being single?

8. Does your church's singles ministry meet your needs? Explain.

9. What is more important in a potential mate: Christian beliefs, occupation, appearance, or personality? Why?

10. Is celibacy a realistic option for you? Why?

11. Please check or list activities below that interest you.

Bible Related ____ Sports ____
Enrichment Services ____ Bible Study____
Bowling____ Seminars____
Sunday School____ Bicycling____
Retreats ____ Special Worship____
Horseback Riding____ Workshops____
Other______ Other_______ Other_______

12. Please check or list activities below that interest you:

Eating ___ Arts & Crafts____Civic Activities____
Potlucks____ Plays____
Neighborhood Repair___ Barbecues____

Art Galleries____ Visit Sick____ Picnics ____

Model Building____ Volunteer Work____

Use your imagination to create a survey that is suited to the situation of your congregation and to the needs of your singles. Another excellent resource for helping people identify their areas of interest in congregational life and ministry is the Time and Talent Inventory, available from Discipleship Resources.

**Sheron Patterson founded and began to direct a church-based singles ministry in 1983. Since then, she has lectured, preached, and written on the topic of singleness and Christianity. Currently she is an ordained deacon in the North Texas Annual Conference and an associate pastor at First United Methodist Church in Dallas, Texas.**

SINGLES SURVEY*Excerpted with permission from* Ministry With Black Single Adults, *by Sheron C. Patterson, pp. 56-57, Discipleship Resources, 1990. (P. O. Box 840, Nashville, TN 37202. Order #DRO87B. Price: $4.95.)*

# Types of Single Adults to Develop A Ministry With

*BY KAREN GREENWALDT*

Here is a list of the various single adults who may be in your community or congregation. Can you think of others? How might you and your congregation be in ministry with some of these groups or individuals?

**YOUNG—19-30**
students
graduate students
professional/workers
single parents
divorced singles
widowed/widowers
financially troubled
those living as singles (spouses overseas/traveling)
runaways
homeless
separated
prisoners
unemployed/underemployed
emotional problems/mental or physical issues

**MIDDLE—31-55**
divorced
widowed/widowers
separated
single since birth
single parents (custody noncustody)
unemployed/underemployed
professionals/workers
absent spouse
remarriage issues
prisoners
homeless
emotional problems/mental or physical issues
more women who are single
dealing with children leaving home
financially troubled
grandparents
students/graduate students

**OLDER SINGLES—over 55**
young olders
middle olders
older olders
frail olders
widows/widowers
divorced people
singles always
grandparents
professional/workers
retired
those in complex living situations
financially troubled
emotional problems/mental or physical issues
unemployed/underemployed

(Persons have unique needs and gifts. Always take care not to use these sociological categories as labels which define or limit a person's worth or wholeness in God's world.)

**Karen Greenwaldt is Director of Single Adult Ministries for the United Methodist Church. She travels the country extensively to train leaders and encourage programs for the millions of single adults in communities and congregations.**

*Excerpted with permission from* Singles Care One for Another, *by Karen Greenwaldt, pp. 79-84, Discipleship Resources, 1989. (P. O. Box 840, Nashville, TN 37202. Order #DRO72B. Price: $6.95.)*

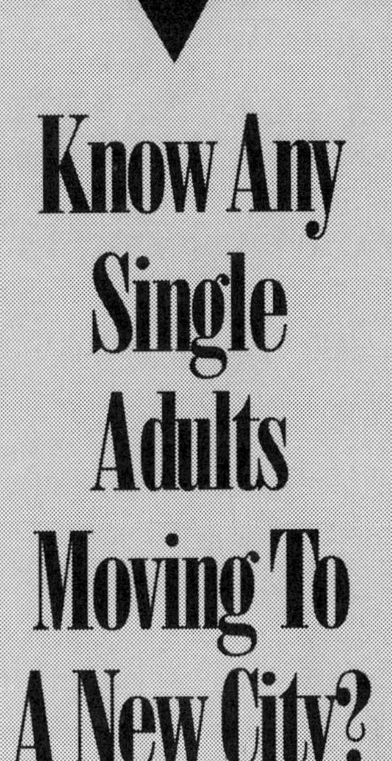


*When one of your singles—or a friend—is seeking to build a support system in a new city, refer to the Network on page 199.*

*Check to see what ministries are in the area. If you choose, you can even call one of the pastors or leaders listed to notify them of the new person moving into their area.*

*This can be one excellent way to help warm up a new home.*

# Understanding the Single Parent Family

## and Ministering to Their Needs

*BY CAROL J. MILLENSON*

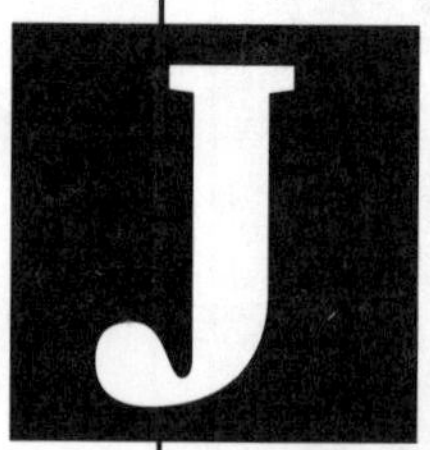

James 1:27 focuses our attention on the needs of the single parent family. "Genuine religion of the untainted variety is to visit and care for the fatherless, homeless, and parents without partners, and to keep yourself from adopting the attitude of the world toward those God calls precious" (paraphrase mine). James directs his words to ministers, church ministry leaders, and practicing Christians. We must face the impact of this warning on our attitudes and actions.

### Beyond Statistical Apathy

We cannot ignore statistics that highlight the increase in the numbers of single parent households. For instance, since 1970, married-couple families decreased to 56% of the United States population. Single parent homes represent 20%. Other single adult households grew to 29%. We cannot ignore this shift in family structure.

A hurting world often sees exemplary lives with little room for imperfection through the open doors of our churches. Sadly, growth statistics dominate our attention and dictate our success. Our ministries often neglect these untouched families.

What shall we say then? We are gifted and blessed by God. As Christians, it is time to move into the hurting world as ambassadors of Jesus.

### Beyond Obvious Needs

If we are to minister to the single parent family, our attitude of apathy is the first hurdle to overcome. We must minister with wisdom based on knowledge. We must learn the needs of those to whom we minister.

The obvious concerns of single parent families include financial stresses, parenting conflicts, and time and energy constraints. We see these difficulties impacting the adult in the home. We must also recognize the resulting strain on the children in the family. While the single parent struggles to meet basic survival needs, the child tries to appear normal and doesn't understand the financial strain. The custodial parent impresses upon the children the need for responsible handling of limited family funds.

Single parents face misunderstanding when the other parent or grandparents indulge the child's request. Also, the single parent often maintains a full-time job and a household while functioning in dual parenting roles. The children often develop adult perspectives and roles in the single parent family. Often, these guilt-ridden, exhausted parents only see their failures and shortcomings. The children's feelings of loss, guilt, and confusion overwhelm the parent.

The parent fears further loss and rejection by failing to provide adequately for the family. Another dimension is the loss of companionship and sharing in the parenting process. The single parent also fears rejection by potential spouses who are hesitant to date a ready-made family.

Another item of concern to single parent families is adequate and consistent role modeling for the children. When one parent is absent from the children's lives, a developmental deficit often occurs. It is not enough that boys have a male adult or girls a female. The opposite sex parent also has a marked impact on normal development.

While concentrating on the custodial home, we must include the needs of the other parent in our ministry. People often view the parent without custody of the children as unfit or suspect. Traditional pressure to place children with their mother does not require labeling male parents as bad. Mom, however, must bear the scrutiny of society when the father wins custody. The church must consider the loss and deep needs of the parent whose lifestyle no longer includes going home to family. It is this parent who may become lost to the church family.

In the eyes of the community and the church, the single parent family sometimes receives little respect as a family. Genuine ministry to single parent families requires us to examine our attitudes about the importance of the individual to God's heart.

## Beyond Problem Orientation

Our goal is to identify ministry opportunities as they parallel the needs of single parent families; to guide single parents to sources of aid while showing love and commitment to them.

## Financial Assistance

Finances are a critical need in single parent homes. The single parent often experiences added pressure to keep the family together. Consider the single mother who delayed career development during the child-rearing years. Now jobs for which she qualifies are low in both income and self-esteem. How can the church respond to the financial pressure faced by the single parent home? Consider the following suggestions.

A. Establish an emergency fund to help with needs not met through other resources. The Church (Hebrew tradition) provided for widows and the children. The Word of God specifies that such needs demand our attention.

B. Set up scholarship funds to help single parents attend unaffordable church activities and training.

**Since 1970, married-couple families decreased to 56% of the United States population. Single parent homes represent 20%. Other single adult households grew to 29%. We cannot ignore this shift in family structure.**

C. Provide affordable church, single adult, children, and teen activities. Be aware of the limited finances of single parent and low-income families.

D. Provide an occasional time-out for single parents by planning a day, half-day, or evening for their children.

E. Consider creating a co-op among your single parents to share their overload on a regular basis. Involve some of the single adults without children in this program.

F. Provide a systematic network of community resources designed to meet the needs of single parents. This may be a current list of resources.

The church need not rescue single parents. Address their needs while increasing their self-respect and personal worth. The financial difficulties they face need a helping hand—not a handout.

## Providing Support

How can we possibly respond to the needs of single parent homes and the parenting conflicts they experience? Perhaps the question here is, What role does the church play in the parenting process of our families? We truly minister to our families by providing support groups, special classes for single parents, and counseling facilities or referrals. Parenting is a task requiring insight, support, and direction. Unique factors complicate the single parenting process. The church guides and supports by bringing families together to share their needs and strengths.

## Stresses Added by the Church

The single parent home must meet the demands of the employer, the household, the family, and court-ordered visitations. Our churches add to the stress by expecting consistent church attendance and ministry involvement. Often I hear church leaders suggest the way to minister to single adults is to keep them busy and involved. This reflects a lack of understanding about the strain unique to single parent homes. The single parent family needs the church to diminish the time demands, often communicated

SINGLE PARENT FAMILIES

through guilt, without reducing the sense of belonging.

The church can choose to make a significant impact in the lives of the children of single parent homes. We need to train our Sunday School teachers and workers to increase their sensitivity to the unique circumstances of these families. Most children from single parent homes become frustrated with Sunday School contests. Attendance requirements often eliminate them, since they regularly miss due to court-ordered visitations. Another area is special days activities. Single parent youngsters may have difficulty with Father's Day or Mother's Day. Christmas and other family holidays often create stress and require careful handling. The children of single parent families need extra affirmation and genuine caring from the church family.

Often the strain on single parents is due to the expectations they try to meet. A single parent does not have the emotional resources to experience grief, help the children in their loss, and meet other demands. Loss recovery groups for parents and children help reduce the emotional pain and introduce the healing process. If your church cannot offer such ministries, you can help your families locate these necessary programs elsewhere.

Often our congregations experience their own grief at the loss of another traditional home. The distance between the divorced family and church friends becomes intolerable and confusing to the grieving. Friends are afraid to get too close. They don't know what to say and they fear that others think they condone divorce by their association. My question, the one repeated many times in Sheldon's book *In His Steps*, is "What would Jesus do?" Jesus responded most lovingly to needs and lifestyles embarrassing to the traditional church. He responded to the hurts and hearts of people. He provided an object lesson so that we might know how to minister. If you follow the example of our Lord, extend your outreach beyond your comfort zone, and move into lives otherwise lost to the church.

**Carol J. Millenson is on staff at the Orlando Central Church of the Nazarene, where she serves as pastor to single adults. She is forming an interdenominational network of ministries to single adults called Greater Orlando Network of Christian Singles Ministries. She is doing graduate work in marriage and family therapy. She and her husband, Bob, have a six-year-old son, Clay.**

*Excerpted with permission from* The Faces of Single Adult Ministries, *Linda G. Hardin, editor, Chapter 4, "The Ministry Challenge of the Single Parent Family," by Carol J. Millenson, pp. 50-58, Beacon Hill Press, 1990. (Available through Nazarene Publishing House. 800-877-0700. Price: $4.95.)*

**"Why not look at this difficult time in your life as a chance to grow some more?"**

# An Open Letter to All Professional Church Leaders

**FROM DR. EMIL AUTHELET**

**Dr. Authelet directs Conflict Management and the Young Adults Ministry for American Baptist Churches of the West. He has served for 25 years in pastoral ministry and family therapy. As a popular conference and workshop leader, he specializes in single family ministry.**

*Excerpted with permission from* Parenting Solo, *by Dr. Emil Authelet, pp. 225-6, Here's Life Publishers, 1989.*

## Dear Colleague in Ministry:

Greetings to you in the name of the One who came preaching, teaching and healing.

There is a special segment of people in your congregation who need Jesus' full ministry in their lives. These are the singles, particularly the single parents among your members. I point this group out because they need your sympathetic help and compassionate care.

Being a single parent in our culture is no small task. To be able to fulfill their role as Christian parents effectively, they require your help, support and encouragement.

One way your church can show this is by providing selected reading resources through your library for these single parents' study and help. Most of these people are on limited budgets and your making this material available would be of great encouragement to them.

Another way your church can show concern is through a single parent support group. A group like this can run itself if you will assist in getting it organized and going. Assigning a staff person the responsibility of liaison between the group and the church is the best procedure because it would show the church's commitment to this ministry.

Still another way to help is to seek ways of integrating single parent families into the full life of the church. They feel different enough already, so don't add to that feeling. Help to dispel it.

In the case of the death of a spouse bringing about a single parent family, a grief support group could be a real ministry. With divorce, a divorce recovery group can be the way to go. Sit down with those involved and explore their needs, and then respond to what you hear.

Single parent families do have specialized needs, but at the same time they can become whole just as any other family can. Being a church that takes its ministry to families—all families—seriously means more than just providing worship and fellowship experiences. These singles silently cry for support groups, information-sharing times, workshops and ongoing programs designed to meet their real needs. When these things are provided, your church indeed becomes a family church.

The need of your singles and single parents for specialized ministry was yesterday. Today is already late for many of them. Further delays will serve only to deepen their pain. Many have no one to turn to but their church. Be there for them. Act on their behalf. Minister to them and to their little ones. Do it "as unto Him."

Joy and peace,

Emil

SINGLE PARENT FAMILIES

# Helping Children Survive Divorce

*BY LAURENE JOHNSON AND GEORGLYN ROSENFELD*

## What Pastors and Leaders Need to Understand to Help Kids and Their Parents

irtually every American's life is touched by divorce . . . from the upper echelons of society to the homeless on the streets. In divorce, unfortunately, the real losers are the children. Divorce legally severs a marriage, but it also frequently severs the parental relationship, making the children feel that their parents not only divorced each other, but also divorced them.

Although adults experience a significant amount of trauma while going through a divorce, children not only suffer during the process but continue to suffer long after the final papers have been signed. Children of divorce battle fear and humiliation for many years, their perception of themselves drastically altered by the loss of their family. Struggling to find their own way to cope with the trauma, some children strike out with behavior problems while others succumb to crippling low self-esteem. In their weakened emotional condition, divorced kids often blame themselves for the divorce.

Unfortunately, kids are often the forgotten element in a divorce. Parents are truly in the driver's seat, with access to friends, divorce recovery groups, support groups, church groups, lawyers, and counselors. Children are all too often left to fend for themselves. To children, the family unit is all they have ever known. It is their world, containing their earliest and most profound memories. The split in the marriage cracks the deepest foundations of their life, and suddenly everything is unstable. What can they depend on? Can anything be trusted?

### Variety Of Responses To Divorce

There seem to be as many different reactions to divorce as there are different kinds of children. Nevertheless, most fall into several well-defined categories. And not surprisingly, the feelings children have are similar to the grieving process that adults experience during a tragedy. In addition, they suffer from a devastating loss of self-esteem, a feeling of responsibility for the divorce, and other emotions that are frightening in their intensity.

Let's consider a sampling of the most common responses children have to divorce.

### Sadness

One twelve-year-old boy wrote, "I wouldn't miss my dad so much if I didn't hear my mom crying so hard every night. It's not fair my dad isn't here to do his job."

Even children who welcomed their parents' divorce as an end to bitter fighting and distress still felt upset. "I felt glad," wrote one child, "but it was like losing a good friend, too."

No matter what other reactions children may demonstrate toward their parents' breakup, a deep, pervasive sorrow is always present.

And sometimes children cling to this sadness because letting go of it feels like a betrayal. Children may feel that if they are sad for "long enough," what they had will come back; by giving up the sadness, they are giving up the chance of a happy ending, as well as betraying the object of their loss.

What children need to know is that their sadness is not a "contract" that will bring back their lost parent, home, or family structure. At the same time they need to understand that it's OK to feel sad, and they will ultimately feel happy again.

One of the best things you can do for your children is allow them to express their grief. Prolonged crying and preoccupation with the lost relationship are normal responses. They can actually help the child move through the adjustment period after the divorce. Parents who are trying to deal with their own trauma, however, may find it difficult to deal with a grief-stricken, despairing child who is acting out feelings the parents may be trying to avoid. But children need to be assured that they will not drive their parents away if they act sad or angry. Parents frequently try to hide their own grief from their children, but by expressing it in front of them, they can validate their children's pain.

### Feelings of Abandonment and Isolation

"Daddy left. Will Mommy leave me too? What will happen to me?" an eight-year-old girl wondered.

"I thought it was my fault at first and I thought they hated me. Then they fought about custody and I thought nobody wanted me. The second and third times I was relieved about the divorce and had no negative feelings," wrote one tragic child.

The fear of abandonment often manifests itself as loneliness. Some of the pictures children drew for us describing divorce depict empty rooms with closed doors and windows, empty boxes and squares with nothing in the middle. One student caught the wrenching pain in a picture of a mangled dog lying in the street with tire treads over it and a car speeding away.

### Confusion and Disorientation

Far and away the most common problem for children of divorce is an inability to understand what in the world has just happened to them. In their resourcefulness and intelligence, they arrive at a number of conclusions—many, unfortunately, that are wrong—in an effort to simply find answers and just try to cope.

"I really didn't understand at first," said one teen, looking back on his parents' divorce when he was five, "but as the years went by, I thought it was my fault. It was a very confusing time for me."

Children's lives revolve around their family—it is all they have ever known. To hear from Mom and Dad that they will no longer be living together is more than a child can comprehend.

### Feeling Torn between Parents

This is perhaps the most wrenching feeling kids have to struggle with, and many times parents do nothing but add fuel to the fire.

Pictures describing these feelings included many houses that were being cut in two . . .

# Tips for Counseling Single Parents About Visitation

*BY LAURENE JOHNSON AND GEORGLYN ROSENFELD*

Visitation can be an awkward, painful experience that is as hard for the non-custodial parent as it is for the child. Sometimes it is so emotionally draining that a parent finds it easier to gradually withdraw from the children rather than experience the reopening of wounds every time they visit. Often the children arrive at a parent's home laden with animosity and bile pummeled into them by a spiteful custodial parent, and it may take hours or days to reestablish some kind of civil relationship with them—usually just about the time they are supposed to go back home.

Let's look at a few of the common mistakes parents make.

**1. Cramming a flurry of "fun" activities into the visit with little or no time for discussion or closeness.**

Devastated by his divorce and loaded with guilt, Jack determined to make his kids' visit a nonstop whirlwind of activity. From Saturday morning to Sunday night, his kids roller skated, went to the movies, and generally whooped it up. Although his kids reported what a great time they were having—they even saw more of him now than before the divorce—they were not exposed to each other in a realistic way.

Such behavior by the non-custodial parent leads children to the false conclusion that if they were to live with a father like Jack, life would be just like the weekend every day of the week. The parent providing all the thrills becomes the "good guy," and the other parent—the one who dispenses discipline—becomes the "meanie."

**2. No enforced responsibilities or discipline.**

This point is a natural consequence of the first, but even if children are not

CONTINUED ON PAGE 42

some even split by lightning. One picture showed four children trying to push the house back together while it was splitting down the middle.

"My mom cries when I tell her about Dad's girlfriend," one twelve-year-old said. "I can't help it if I like her just a little. She's nice to me."

Frequently, innocent remarks by the child become a battlefield for the parents. Kids soon learn that they can no longer share things with Mom or Dad. They just get bounced back and forth between vengeful parents, and everyone ends up in trouble.

A group of children, parents, lawyers, and psychologists were asked to name events they believed had a significant negative imp t on children in broken familie. Some of the events included:

• When one parent tells the child that he or she doesn't like that child spending time with the other parent.

• When one parent asks the child questions about the other parent's private life.

• When one parent says bad things about the other.

• When relatives say bad things to the child about his or her parents.

• When one parent tells the child not to tell some things to the other parent.

• When parents talk to children about which parent they want to live with.

• When parents make children feel like they have to choose between Dad and Mom.

## Forced Adulthood

A surprising number of the high school students who put their feelings into artwork drew pictures of nuclear holocausts or cataclysmic storms—the end of life as they knew it. No matter how old or young the child, divorce usually means experiencing grief and emotional trauma much sooner than most children would have.

Divorce shatters the safe, secure fantasy world of childhood, and children are suddenly forced to replace a parent's missing marriage partner and provide companionship for someone much older than themselves.

Divorce also imposes worries and responsibilities on children that are far beyond their age.

Arnold Lopez, a therapist in Phoenix who specializes in codependency, says he sees major lifelong issues develop when a child is placed in a parental role after a divorce. He works with adolescents who have been placed in the surrogate parent or spouse role and later find themselves in need of therapy.

Some children of divorce, after reaching adulthood, say that they feel like they've missed out on childhood by being forced to become their parents' missing partners, which is frequently regarded as a form of codependency. The most common form is when a child becomes a "surrogate spouse."

## Codependency

According to Lopez, when the other spouse is missing, the single

CONTINUED FROM PAGE 41

provided with nonstop entertainment, it can still occur.

When Joe's ten-year-old and fifteen-year-old daughters visited, he refused to make them do anything they didn't want to do. When Joe's wife asked the children to pick up after themselves, they threatened, "If we have to help, we're not ever coming here again." Joe insisted she not pester them anymore. When they realized their ploy had worked, the children carried their liberties to extremes. Again, this is an artificial atmosphere and can make the custodial parent appear wicked and tyrannical when he or she is forced to reinstate a code of conduct that was cast aside during the visit . . . to say nothing about how unfair it is to the stepmother.

This action not only engenders negative feelings toward the custodial parent, but it also plants seeds of rebellion in the children. When Mom tries to make them clean their room, they now have a weapon to use against her, "Well, Dad doesn't make us do that." Whereas before they probably would have obeyed, now they have a reason to issue an outright challenge to the authority of the custodial parent.

**3. Doing what the visiting parent wants without consideration for what the children enjoy or want.**

Without meaning to be inconsiderate, many parents assume that their kids will enjoy the same things they do. If a father's favorite Sunday activity is a football game on TV, he may inadvertently force a child whose greatest love is ballet into three grueling hours of boredom.

Remember that your visit is a special, limited time and should not be frittered away on activities you could do another day.

**4. Doing what the kids want without consideration for what the parent wants and enjoys.**

This is the flip side of the last problem.

John catered to the children's every whim during each visitation period. When one activity ended he always asked them what they wanted to do next, then did it. It wasn't long before his patience was overtaxed. He began to resent spending his entire weekend doing things he didn't want to do. Even though he never complained to the kids, his resentment surfaced as grouchiness, yelling, and flying off the handle over tiny violations of his perception of good behavior. The children didn't understand why he never seemed to be in a good mood.

parent's needs for love, belonging, and support are going unmet. This is why single parents tend to become emotionally enmeshed with their children. They discuss the details of financial burdens, daily exhaustion, loneliness, and depression with one of their kids. And the children begin to see themselves in the role of a spouse.

One boy said, "Dad left so suddenly that if I don't take care of Mom, she might leave me too." In later years children resent this role, and sometimes the resentment turns into anger in adolescence.

All too frequently single parents have limited financial resources and a weak support system of family and friends who are willing, able, and close enough to help. When this situation exists, the parent may end up not only being a poor parent, but may set up a situation in which the child ends up parenting the parent.

## How Long Does The Emotional Trauma Last?

In our workshops, when we asked children the question, "How long did it take you to get over the divorce?" some of the responses were:

"You never get over it" (fifteen years after the divorce).

"It's been four years but I'm still not over it."

"It took me about seven years to really get over it."

"I wasn't upset at the time. About a year later it hit and it lasted for a year."

"A few years of therapy."

The only "positive" response was: "Not long. My dad was pretty mean."

Clearly, the injuries sustained in a divorce heal slowly, if ever. One of the great tragedies of divorce is that children come to assume that the whole world operates like their own. They don't feel that "living happily ever after" is possible. Many feel destined to repeat their parents' mistakes.

Divorce may be the most catastrophic event the average American family is forced to overcome. For children, it violently interrupts the already tempestuous process of growing up. The adults involved in a pitched battle with each other have the advantage of a certain amount of control, even if it's minuscule, but children have none. This leaves the child in a wait-and-see posture, forever trying to adapt to changing conditions, torn between two parents, resiliency tested to the utmost.

Children are survivors by nature. With proper guidance their survival skills can be greatly improved.

**Laurene Johnson and Georglyn Rosenfeld are both divorced mothers of happy, well-adjusted children. Johnson, a therapist who works specifically in the area of divorce recovery, and Rosenfeld say, "Children are survivors by nature."**

*Excerpted with permission from Divorced Kids, Laurene Johnson and Georglyn Rosenfeld, Chapter 1, "How Divorce Affects Children," pp. 15-26, Thomas Nelson Publishers, 1990.*

---

The quality of the time John spent with his children was undermined, and soon he drifted away from them by scheduling business appointments on the weekend and finding excuses to leave the house on one errand or another. Eventually, the visits were less frequent and shorter.

**5. Everybody does his or her own thing.**

The story repeats itself here with a twist. When either the parent or the children have their way, someone suffers. But when everyone goes off in different directions, the visit is reduced to a mere ritualistic act by both parties. One can envision both parent and child, if asked how the visit was, to simply mumble, "Fine."

**6. Infrequent, inconsistent visiting habits.**

Even though decreed by the courts, visitation can break down in reality.

How often a child comes into contact with his or her parents following a divorce is a key factor in the time required to recover from all the trauma. Several studies reveal that the percentage of children living with their natural mothers who never see their fathers is as high as 46 percent. One child who was asked how often he sees his father replied, "He comes once every three years to make himself known again."

The confusion for kids who don't see their non-custodial parent regularly is evidenced in the following quotes:

"I don't know where he is or even if he is alive."

"When my dad left I never saw him again." This from a fourteen-year-old girl whose parents divorced ten years earlier.

When asked what might make this relationship better, the children's answers resembled one another:

"To see him more often."

"Longer visits."

Obviously, there are a multitude of reasons why a parent might not visit regularly—hostile ex-spouses, distance, and scheduling problems to name a few. But as far as the responsibility lies with the non-custodial parent, every attempt should be made to let children know they are cared for.

*Excerpted with permission from Divorced Kids, Laurene Johnson and Georglyn Rosenfeld, Chapter 6, "Common Visitation Mistakes," pp. 63-68, Thomas Nelson Publishers, 1990.*

DIVORCE RECOVERY

# The Spiritual Battle For Those Who Are Divorced

*BY H. S. VIGEVENO AND ANNE CLAIRE*

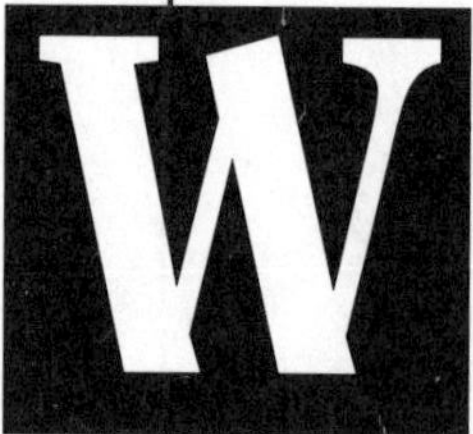

When Christians get divorced, often there is a spiritual battle going on. It is not unusual for many Christians to divorce the Church at the same time. Instead of looking to the Church for guidance, comfort and help when they end a marriage, they lose their spiritual moorings. This is not always the fault of the divorced individuals.

## The Family as Presented by the Church

Oftentimes the Church is to blame for presenting a cozy Christian family as the norm for Christian living. They show a husband (who is working), a wife (who remains at home) and 2.4 children. Whenever the Church pictures this stereotypical ideal and promotes programs for the family only, those passing through the gates of divorce may feel uncomfortable in that tidy family-oriented church.

Furthermore, there are churches that heap burdens of guilt upon the divorced. They preach the Law instead of grace, ideals instead of reality. Some Christians can't bring themselves to return to that kind of church and, in many cases, no longer attend at all.

Some Bible-taught believers reason: If God does not accept divorce, how can God smile on the divorced?

## Is There Room for Sinners?

Is it any wonder divorced Christians ask: Is there any place in the Church for the Christian sinner?

There is indeed. Jesus not only died for our sins, but He accepts sinners. In that case then, what can the Church do to minister to the people of divorce?

## When Christians Divorce

When a Christian husband and wife divorce, the tendency is for one of them to leave the church. The church now has the opportunity to minister to the remaining partner. The one who leaves may attend another church, but generally drops altogether.

Amy was divorced after 23 years of marriage. Her children were in their late teens, ready to leave home; the oldest was off to college.

"We were both active in our church when we were married, and when we separated he stayed. But where could I go? You can't both attend the same small church when you're divorcing. Everybody knows everybody else. It's awkward and embarrassing, but where can you worship when you've been in the same church for many years? With all the other trauma I was experiencing from the divorce, I had to find a new church.

"The church ought to be a place to meet friends and to get support, but my church's door was closed because my former husband was there.

"If I want male companionship now, where do I find it? I'm looking for someone who has similar goals, hopes, attitudes and faith in Christ."

## Divorce Recovery

**Workshops.** Some larger churches offer divorce recovery workshops, a unique experience for those who are hurting and facing the possible break-up of their family. In these workshops they meet other people who are also suffering, and that in itself can become the first step to healing.

**Counseling.** The Church's obligation and privilege is to counsel and care for the wounded and to bring all of its resources together in an attempt to promote a possible reconciliation. The Church needs to do more than it is presently doing in the area of counseling for the troubled, and to become more aware and sensitive to the needs of the people. When people come to the Church for counsel, often it is too late.

## Love Draws Singles to Groups

There are numerous single Christians who shy away from groups. They are embarrassed to be part of the singles scene, but few churches offer opportunities for mixing couples with singles. Once part of a couple, now single, some Christians feel it's a step down to attend a church's singles group.

"My secretary felt so strange the first time she walked into a singles group," commented one pastor. "This was a tremendous transition for her. A comedown in her mind from traveling first-class (being married) to having to be a single again, and a divorced one at that. And if Christian adults can't face this easily, how do you suppose the kids feel?"

All hurting people, including parents and children, need the support of the Christian community. They need to experience the Body of Christ at work, healing, forgiving, redeeming, for that is the task of the Church of Christ. Love is the heart of the good news. If people don't find grace and love (in the church), something is wrong! The fact is that the Church has much to offer single-parent families that they will never find anywhere else. It is comfort—"Comfort ye, comfort ye my people, saith your God" (Isa. 40:1, KJV).

## Ministry to Single Parent Families

There is no shame in being single. Statistics indicate that almost 50 percent of the U.S. population over 18 is single.

Some pastors working with single parents see in them more courage, more growth than anywhere else in the Church. It's sink or swim for them. Crucial issues are at stake and in their need divorced singles find God, as they minister to one another. The ones who swim become strong swimmers indeed!

Many churches are including children in their ministries to single families. They plan films, barbecues, picnics and retreats for single parents and their children.

Another church provides a unique program on Saturdays. Conceived and run by a group of single men, this program is known as Good Shepherds. Children of single moms are taken by these men to the mountains or the beach for a day. Recently mothers who have benefited from Good Shepherds hosted a thank you. They took the men to a major league baseball game, with the children of course.

Another congregation is considering a recovery program expressly for children. When they plan a divorce recovery workshop, they expect to offer a simultaneous program for children of divorce.

Some churches are exploring the possibility of a special class for remarried couples with children. "These couples need help to face the unique problems of blended families and step-parenting," a pastor stated.

## The Small Church

What if the church has limited resources? What if the church's membership is 200 to 300 and there aren't enough people for a singles group? What can the small church do?

Support and connect with a singles ministry of a larger church, said many pastors and singles we interviewed. The singles ministry requires a large number to attract others. Singles go where singles are. Instead of conducting a small group in a small church, it is best to provide an opportunity where ministry and counsel are available.

A pastor of a small church may be afraid to lose the few members he has to a larger church. He may even oppose someone attending a singles group at another church. But people who feel loyal to their own congregation return for worship and the responsibilities in their churches.

Include divorced people in leadership to integrate them into the life of the church. It is important to make single parents feel valuable.

Smaller churches can band together to form an association for singles across denominational lines. Any church that has no more than five or six singles together will not succeed with a singles program unless it's to enjoy a small after-church brunch. Even that will surely help the lonely.

What is your church currently doing for singles? Can you see a need for a change in attitude? What can you as an individual do to help and care for those who are recovering from divorce?

**H. S. Vigeveno has authored numerous books. He is a pastor specializing in personal counseling, small groups, and family retreats.**

**Anne Claire is a free-lance writer and a paraprofessional psychotherapist with the Family Stress Clinic in Los Angeles. She has had extensive experience working with women and children who have been abused.**

*Excerpted with permission from* No One Gets Divorced Alone, *by H. S. Vigeveno and Anne Claire, Chapter 17, "The Church Can Help the Divorced," pp. 206-217, 1987, Regal Books, Ventura, CA 93003.*

## Don't Be a Lone Ranger!

***Use the Network** (see page 199) **to make a lunch appointment.***

***Find some other singles ministry leader in your area and get together for lunch. Learn from one another. Share.***

***Or just play golf!***

**"Unraveling previous marital histories was sometimes a difficult job for singles pastor Marty Feltnik."**

# The "Am I Ready for Remarriage?" Test

*BY JIM SMOKE*

When counseling someone who is considering remarriage, here is a quick test to help them evaluate and think through some of the key issues. (See test results at the end of the test.)

1. Have I forgiven my former spouse as well as myself?
2. Have I experienced a healing of hurts caused by my divorce?
3. Am I still playing "get even" games with my former spouse?
4. When someone asks me about my divorce, do I have a hard time recalling events and situations?
5. Do I think of myself as a divorced person?
6. Has my self-esteem grown measurably over the past three years?
7. Do I enjoy my work?
8. Do people tell me they can't believe how well I'm doing?
9. Am I always looking for a potential mate?
10. Would I rather go out with others than by myself?
11. Am I haunted by loneliness?
12. Do I enjoy making decisions?
13. Am I glad there is no one there when I come home at the end of the day?
14. Do I enjoy going to singles groups?
15. Do I resent the word "single"?
16. Am I envious when I see happily married people?
17. Can I measure my growth in the three years since I became single again?
18. Am I looking for someone to take care of me?
19. Am I looking for someone to take care of?
20. Do I feel that the person I remarry has to be accepted and liked by my children and family?

21. Do I enjoy hearing other people's divorce war stories?
22. Do I believe I will make a good wife or husband for someone?
23. Do I still largely fear remarriage?
24. Do I feel comfortable with my singleness?
25. Am I excited about possible career advancements or changes?
26. Do I usually wait for someone to tell me what to do?
27. Am I angry that I am single at this point in my journey through life?
28. Am I still bitter about my divorce?
29. Do I feel good about my personal growth and accomplishments?
30. Do I make plans and work toward goals in my life?
31. Do I think all men (women) have a hidden agenda in remarriage?
32. Do I believe I am lovable?
33. Do I believe I can be a contributor to the happiness of someone else?
34. Am I a happy person?
35. Do I believe that God really loves me and has forgiven me for my divorce regardless of what other people might think?
36. Is my lifestyle mergeable?
37. Do I have a "who needs you" feeling toward the opposite sex?
38. Is the thought of remarriage an exciting challenge?
39. Am I willing to invest a year or two in building a relationship that could lead to marriage?
40. Would I feel safe with a prenuptial agreement?
41. Have I worked through my biblical concerns about the issue of remarriage?
42. Can I live happily ever after if I do not choose remarriage?
43. Do I believe there is only one person out there for me, and if I miss him (her), that's it?
44. Do I believe I am a loser if a long-term relationship does not end in marriage?
45. Have I traded in my "Happiness Is Being Single" shirt for one that says, "Happiness Is Being Human"?
46. Have I grown in my relationship with God? Is He real and vital in my life?

Every test demands some sort of grade. We are always eager to know whether we passed or failed. If you answered the above questions according to what I have observed, you are well on the way to growing and being prepared for remarriage.

**YES** on 1, 2, 4, 6, 7, 8, 12, 14, 17, 20, 22, 24, 25, 29, 30, 32, 33, 34, 35, 36, 38, 39, 40, 41, 42, 45, 46.

**NO** on 3, 5, 9, 10, 11, 13, 15, 16, 18, 19, 21, 23, 26, 27, 28, 31, 37, 43, 44.

**Jim Smoke is the author of numerous books and articles on singleness. He is an adjunct professor at Fuller Seminary in Pasadena, Calif., and Director of the Center for Divorce Recovery in Tempe, Arizona.**

*Excerpted with permission from* Living Beyond Divorce, *by Jim Smoke. pp. 154-157. Copyright 1984 by Harvest House Publishers, Eugene, OR 97402.*

**Do You Feel Left Out?**

If you were left out of this National Directory, we have good news. There will be another Directory... and we want to make sure you are not left out again. Help us make this Directory complete. Let us know about your group.

*See Page 247*

DIVORCE RECOVERY

# Guidelines for Becoming a More Effective Christian Divorce Counselor

*BY DR. GARY R. COLLINS*

## Helpful Advice for Counseling Couples When Reconciliation Seems to Be Out of the Question

Christian marriage counseling attempts to keep marriages together by helping couples develop smoother, more fulfilling, Christ-centered marital relationships. This type of counseling can be difficult, but it also can be challenging especially when the counselor is successful and the marriage improves.

It is more difficult to work with couples who have decided to separate and who have no mutual desire for reconciliation. These people nevertheless need counseling and this is the purpose of Christian divorce counseling. It attempts to help an individual or couple separate from a marriage (a) in a way that is consistent with biblical teachings, (b) with a minimum of pain or destruction to themselves or to others including their children, and (c) with a maximum of growth and new learning.

**I. Clarifying the Counselor's Attitudes.** Divorce counseling is rarely easy. If you feel frustrated, saddened, angry, or resistant to the concept of divorce, then it is unlikely that you will be able to listen carefully, understand, avoid condemning or be able to withstand the pressures or your own inclination to take sides.

The effective helper must take time for personal reflection on his or her attitudes toward divorce, divorced persons, and people who are going through divorce. As a follower of Jesus Christ, what is your responsibility to people who are frustrated, confused, angry, and despondent because of marital breakdown? No one can answer these questions for you. Before God, each counselor must consider some difficult questions.

**2. Determining Goals.** In divorce counseling, goal setting is not easy. Reconciliation and the development of a fulfilling, Christ-honoring marriage certainly are to be preferred, but often a couple has no such desire. When this is true, you can strive for a logical, respectful, mutually agreeable resolution of problems, but sometimes counselees have no desire to be logical.

Not all divorce counseling is like this, however, and it is possible to reach a number of goals, including the following:

- Helping counselees evaluate their marital situation realistically, including consideration of the prospects for avoiding divorce.
- Discussing biblical teachings on divorce and remarriage, and helping counselees make application of these teachings to their own marital situation.
- Discovering and discussing the counselees' expectations and desires for counseling, and evaluating whether these are (a) feasible, (b) consistent with the counselor's own moral and ethical standards, and (c) goals that you can, without hesitation, help the counselees achieve.
- Helping couples admit, confess (to God and to each other), and change attitudes and actions that are sinful.
- Helping counselees reach mutually acceptable agreements

concerning such practical issues as the division of property, alimony, or child custody and support.

- Encouraging couples to calm down from vindictive or self-centered hostile ways of relating.

- Helping counselees formulate ways of explaining the situation to children (sometimes this may mean including the children in some counseling sessions).

- Encouraging the couple to avoid belittling, blaming, and criticizing each other, especially in the presence of children.

- Helping the spouses understand the effects of divorce on children (including grown children) and encouraging counselees not to use children in manipulative ways, either to force children into taking sides or to get messages to the former spouse.

- Helping the couple (together, but more often separately) to cope with the emotions of divorce, including feelings of rejection.

- Guiding in the adjustment to post-divorce, single life.

- Encouraging counselees in their spiritual growth and in their involvement with other people, including church people and Christian divorce recovery groups, where there is support, encouragement, friendship, and spiritual nourishment.

**3. Work on Practical Issues.** Since divorce is a crisis, counselors should seek to give the support, guidance, and practical help that people in crises need. In addition you may want to discuss some of the following practical issues.

**(a) Handling Emotions.** It is difficult to make an emotional separation, even from a relationship that no longer is intimate. As we have noted, anger, anxiety, frustration, depression, and a host of other feelings flood the counselee, sometimes when they are least expected. Often there is a vacillation of feelings.

Most counselees will find it helpful to admit and express their emotions, but try to encourage growth beyond this emotional expression stage. Several guidelines may help counselees with this growth. Encourage them to:

- Admit and express emotions honestly as they arise.

- Ask God to help them resist hatred, resentment and bitterness. No matter how much one has been hurt, nothing is gained by revenge.

- Forgive, with God's help, and pray for those who have created pain and disappointment.

**Encourage counselees to select attorneys carefully, to hire someone who specializes in divorces, to refrain from signing anything until one's attorney is consulted, and to avoid do-it-yourself divorce.**

- Deliberately avoid the emotional traps of the past. These include developing self-fulfilling prophecies (like deciding, for example, that life will now be miserable—an attitude that, in turn, may make life miserable); wallowing in one's problems; blaming others perpetually (especially one's mate); and assuming that life can only be meaningful again when there is another marriage.

Feelings often follow thinking; if you change your thinking, this often leads to changed feelings. Encourage counselees to logically accept what may not be changeable (in this case, divorce), and then learn to resist dwelling on thoughts that can arouse painful feelings.

**(b) Guiding Mediation.** Until recently, divorcing couples almost always turned to lawyers for help in resolving such practical issues as child custody, division of property, alimony, or tax preparation. Within the past fifteen years, however, divorce mediation has become a fast growing profession among counselors and others who understand legal issues but may not be lawyers.

Mediation seeks to avoid the combative, adversarial approach. Instead it is a more cooperative approach to conflict resolution. People use it to get on with the business of living and to let go of the past. Any divorce counselor is likely to be involved in some mediation, but if you lack special training in this area, you may want to help couples find some competent and impartial person who can mediate successfully.

Encourage counselees to select attorneys carefully, to hire someone who specializes in divorces, to refrain from signing anything until one's attorney is consulted, and to avoid do-it-yourself divorce. Competent Christian lawyers, if available, are more likely to have an appreciation for the sanctity of marriage and be less inclined to stimulate hostility between the separating spouses.

**(c) Finding a New Identity.** Divorce plunges the formerly married person into singleness again. It is easy to think about better times in the past and to worry about life in the future.

Encourage counselees to

discuss these insecurities and to talk about life again as a single person. Many may need help with self-esteem, learning to accept themselves as God accepts them. Remind your counselees that it isn't easy to change our identities and it takes time to shift in the ways we think about ourselves.

**(d) Building New Relationships.** It can be difficult to form new relationships following a divorce. The person may look for new friends, but he or she also must redefine relationships with the former spouse, the children, old friends and relatives, or people in the church.

**(e) Facing the Future.** The divorced person cannot live in the past or bemoan the future. Bills must be paid, work must be completed, life must go on. The counselee can be helped to identify and learn from past mistakes, make immediate decisions about such practical issues as housing and finances, reestablish life priorities, set goals for the future, and move ahead to accomplish God's purpose for one's life.

**(f) Building Another Marriage.** The Christian must determine whether or not remarriage is permitted biblically. Christian counselors will differ in their views on this issue, but at some time the possibility of remarriage should be discussed with counselees.

Divorced persons often resent the need to start dating "like teenagers." Some fear that they will never find a spouse and others wonder if they will repeat earlier mistakes. At times there are fears about how the children would react to another marriage, especially if the new mate also has children that would be part of a blended family.

The counselor can help with these fears. Discourage people from marrying too quickly and help them choose another mate cautiously and wisely. Before marrying again, divorced persons could be encouraged to ponder what they learned from their past failed marriage. Premarital counseling should be considered essential.

If children are involved, it may be helpful to discuss some of the problems found in blended families: intrusions from previous spouses, fears that the new marriage will fall apart; wrangling over finances; children moving in and out; problems arising from the husband and wife having different authority over different children; the possibility of unequal financial realities for children in the same household; children's efforts to break up the marriage; and parental jealousy of children's allegiances.

In all of this, remind yourself and your counselees that God wants the best for his children. He forgives those who confess and guides those who want his leading. Divorced persons and their counselors are not left alone to fend for themselves. The Holy Spirit is the constant guide and companion of committed divorced believers and their Christian counselors.

**Dr. Gary R. Collins is a licensed psychologist with a Ph.D. in clinical psychology from Purdue University. In addition to his writing and speaking engagements, he teaches part-time at Trinity Evangelical Divinity School.**

*Excerpted with permission from* Christian Counseling: A Comprehensive Guide, *by Gary R. Collins, Ph.D., Chapter 30, "Divorce and Remarriage," pp. 458-464, Word Publishing, 1988, Dallas, TX.*

"No Church Leader Should Be Without It!"

*"Single Adult Ministries Journal* is the only professional publication geared to helping the clergy and laity stay in touch with the latest resources and ideas in the emerging field of single adult ministry. I recommend it everywhere I speak . . . No church leader should be without it."

-JIM SMOKE
nationally known speaker, singles ministry leader, and author of several books, including the best-seller, *Growing Through Divorce.*

**Begin your subscription today. Call toll FREE 800-487-4-SAM or 719-488-2610**

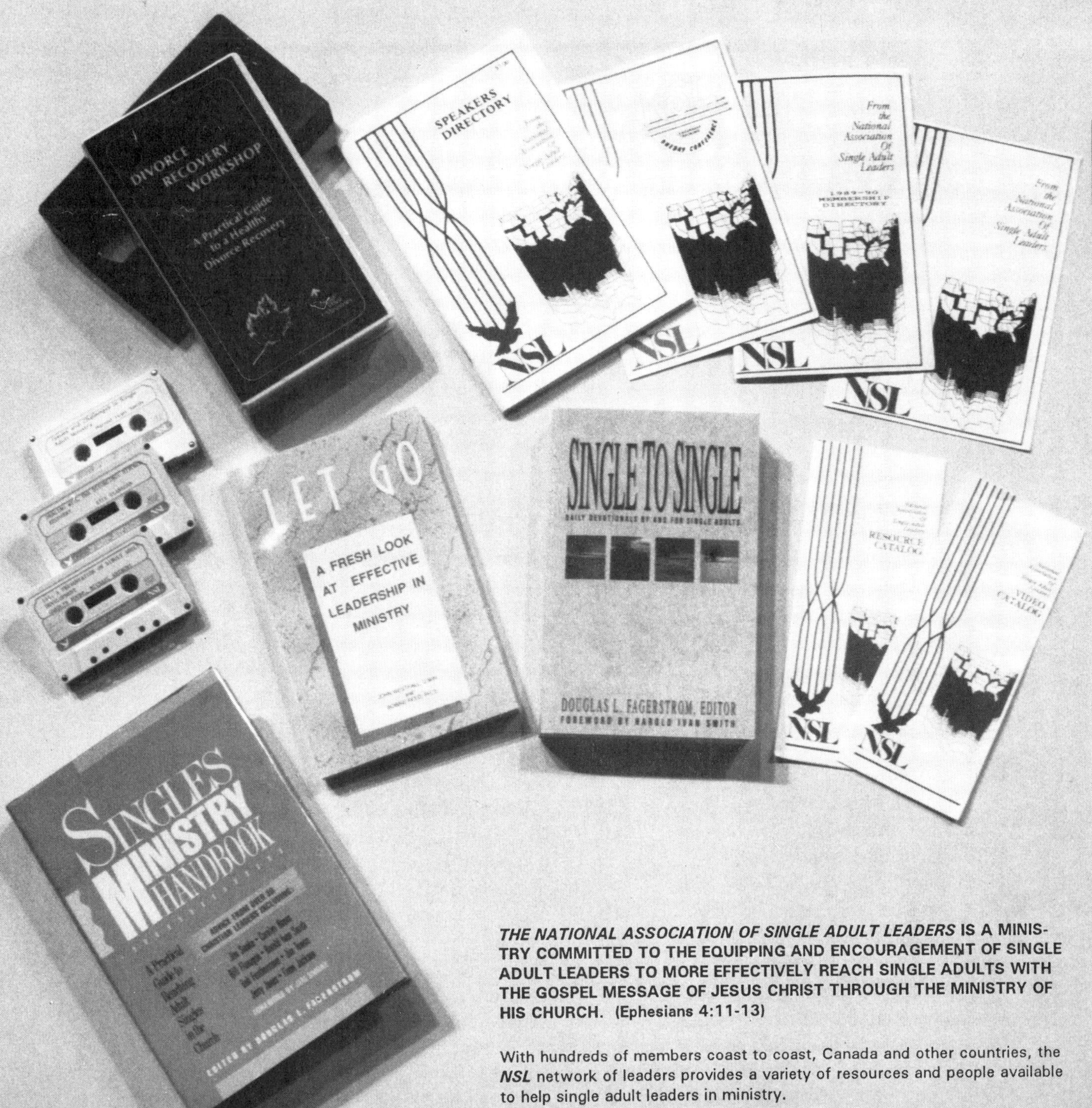

***THE NATIONAL ASSOCIATION OF SINGLE ADULT LEADERS* IS A MINISTRY COMMITTED TO THE EQUIPPING AND ENCOURAGEMENT OF SINGLE ADULT LEADERS TO MORE EFFECTIVELY REACH SINGLE ADULTS WITH THE GOSPEL MESSAGE OF JESUS CHRIST THROUGH THE MINISTRY OF HIS CHURCH. (Ephesians 4:11-13)**

With hundreds of members coast to coast, Canada and other countries, the *NSL* network of leaders provides a variety of resources and people available to help single adult leaders in ministry.

*NSL* provides:

- Teaching Cassette Tapes
- Video Tapes at Discount Prices
- Ministry Handbook
- Devotional Book
- Cirriculum Tools
- Speakers & Musicians Bureau
- Ministry Placement Opportunities
- Over 30 One-Day Training Conferences in major cities
- Annual Consortium for all members...
- And More!!

Membership in *NSL* will place you on the "cutting edge" of single adult ministry. Be a part of a fast growing network of single adult ministry leaders. *NSL* is making a difference and providing the tools and encouragement that you need. Contact us today.

To receive free information and the brochures pictured above, contact Executive Director Doug Fagerstrom, 616-956-9377, or P.O. Box 1600, Grand Rapids, MI, 49501.

National Association Of Single Adult Leaders

***THE NATIONAL ASSOCIATION OF SINGLE ADULT LEADERS***
**P.O. Box 1600, Grand Rapids, MI 49501**
**Telephone 616-956-9377**

ADVICE FOR LEADERS

# Avoiding Codependent Relationships in Your Ministry

*BY JAN SILVIOUS*

## Here Are Six Steps to Help Pastors and Leaders Avoid Illegitimate Emotional Entanglements

Be aware that Christian ministry is not exempt from emotional dependency. In fact, the opposite is true. Christian ministries often are led by appealing, charismatic people whose very temperament and personality attracts dependent people. Ministry, then, often becomes the perfect setup for codependencies to surface.

Great wisdom needs to be exercised in hiring personnel or taking on volunteers. Often leaders are so thrilled to have help that they are blinded to the potential danger of an emotionally dependent person attaching themselves to the ministry in order to meet their great need for acceptance and approval. Since Christian principles are based on tenderheartedness, kindness, forgiveness, and patience, dependent people often take advantage of these characteristics. They grab hard and hang on tight to the leaders, hoping to feel good about themselves—perhaps for the first time in their lives. And warm-hearted leaders can find themselves codependent before they realize what has happened.

### How It Starts

Wherever there is a strong, charismatic personality who seems self-assured and competent, there will be people who want to identify with that person to bolster their own lack of esteem and personal value. There are two common ways to get such a leader's attention. Offer to help in any way you can or ask for help with your needs. Either way, you can catch the unsuspecting with the hook of either "You need me and I can do a lot for you because you're so busy" or "I need you and you can do a lot for me because I'm so needy."

The workplace, whether secular or Christian, is a fertile field for codependent relationships to grow into infidelity. The cycle is rather commonplace. Unfortunately, it reads like a soap opera:

"I need someone to understand." *"I understand you."*

"I need more time to talk." *"I'll give you time."*

"I feel so alone." *"I'll hold you. I'm here."*

"I need you to hold me again." *"Of course I will."*

"I've never known anyone like you. *"Really?"*

"I need to talk. I know it's late. *"I'll be right there."*

"I never meant for it to go this far." *"I didn't either."*

"I think we shouldn't see each other." *"I can't leave you."*

"What if your wife (or husband) finds out?" *"We haven't been getting along lately anyway."*

It all begins with a genuine desire to meet a legitimate longing. And when it's all going on, it seems so right because feelings are being soothed, value is being restored, and longings are being fulfilled in both lives.

To have the need to be loved and accepted is not sin. To have a genuine desire to feel acceptable and approved is not sin. James 1:14-15 warns, "But each one is tempted when by his own evil desire, he is dragged away and enticed. Then, after desire has conceived, it gives birth to sin; and sin, when it is full-grown, gives birth to death."

No one wins when needs are met in an ungodly way. Adultery has never ended in anything but death to relationship, death to a good conscience, death to trust, death to dreams and hopes, and for the Christian, death to effective ministry.

## Steps to Avoid Illegitimate Emotional Entanglements

1. Turn from evil. Determine to live by the biblical injunction to "abstain from every form of evil" (1 Thess. 5:22 NASB). There is nothing good about "abstaining from evil" on the inside but playing with the appearance of it on the outside. The two are incompatible wherever they are found. Look at your own situation and answer the following questions. Let your answers put boundaries on your activities.

a. Will it appear evil if I work late with a co-worker of the opposite sex as the only other person in the office?

b. Will it appear evil if I go to lunch alone with a co-worker of the opposite sex?

c. Will it appear evil if I hug my secretary/boss?

d. Will it appear evil if I rub my boss's shoulders?

e. Will it appear evil if I ________________?

You fill in the blank. Self-examination that is candid and objective is a healthy step to wholeness. If you have doubts about any activity, then avoid it. What may seem perfectly harmless to you could give the wrong signals to a friend or co-worker.

2. Be ruthless with yourself. If you realize you are in a dependent relationship with another person, whether of the opposite or same sex, start to back off. Codependency is the first step toward personal and professional disaster. If you are a trusting, loving person, you may be naive about the background and experience of a co-worker. One woman nearly fell into a physically intimate relationship with another woman in her office. She felt uncomfortable with the hand holding and long, drawn-out hugs, but her friend and co-worker convinced her nothing was wrong.

**The workplace, whether secular or Christian, is a fertile field for codependent relationships to grow into infidelity.**

"Our conduct is perfectly harmless," she insisted. At that point the uncomfortable person followed her instinct and backed off. Don't go against your convictions. They will protect you when your emotions are not dependable.

3. Don't create a problem in the mind of the other person. If the relationship has just been fantasy for you, then deal with it by yourself and with the Lord. Don't put your notions into the other person's head, or you may get into deeper waters than you planned. Consider the following comments:

From a Christian counselor after a conversation with a woman in his congregation: "A woman came to speak to me to tell me that she had a strong attraction for me that she knew she should not have. My first response was, 'What have I done to make her feel like that?' My second response was an 'ego' response, which made me more interested in why she felt as she did. This could have set up the wrong set of dynamics for an ongoing relationship. Her expressing of her feelings to me created a difficulty for me to work through. In looking back, it created more of a problem for both of us than if she had not ever expressed it."

4. Ask the Lord to purify your heart and mind. As you go to the workplace each day, ask the Lord to put a hedge of protection around your mind (Job 1:10) to deflect Satan's fiery darts, which come in the form of sensual or suggestive thoughts (Eph. 6:16).

5. Study God's Word. Keep God's Word as a first priority in your life. "For the word of God is living and active. Sharper than any double-edged sword, it penetrates even to dividing soul and spirit, joints and marrow; it judges the thoughts and attitudes of the heart" (Heb. 4:12).

6. Change your behavior. The proof of your recognition of a real problem will be changed behavior. The degree of dependency you have on the other person will determine the degree of change needed. You may be able to detach yourself emotionally if you stop seeing each other altogether. It may even be necessary to leave your job. If your relationship is too entangled (physically and emotionally), the only way to get out is to cut the strings and separate.

Don't excuse yourself if you are only emotionally involved. Remember that emotional involvement is the first step in the process that leads to immorality.

**ADVICE FOR LEADERS**

If the other person knows about your feelings for him or her, tell the person that you realize the relationship is wrong and that you are going to change your part of it. Tell the person firmly but gently that you can no longer have personal conversations, that you will relate to him or her only on business. It is important to resist trying to convert the person to your point of view. Just say how things have to be—and go.

If the person questions your change in behavior, answer as briefly as possible in a matter-of-fact way. Be kind but avoid lengthy conversations. Discussing the problem will only keep the relationship going longer than is desirable.

If the relationship has been sexual, stop seeing the person immediately. To continue seeing a person with whom you have been physically intimate is keeping temptation too close at hand.

After you have broken off a relationship, you will be very vulnerable. Guard your emotions carefully. Develop new activities and relationships to help you resist the temptation to return to the unhealthy relationship.

I pray that if you see yourself in this chapter, you will run to the arms of Jehovah-Jireh, the all-sufficient one who can give you the strength, wisdom, and fortitude that you will need to pull yourself away from a relationship that can only bring tragedy to you.

**Jan Silvious served for 14 years as a counselor, administrator, writer, and teacher for Precept Ministries in Chattanooga, Tenn. She has authored Understanding Women and has her own radio program in Chattanooga, where she resides with her husband, Charles, and their three children.**

*Excerpted with permission from* Please Don't Say You Need Me, *by Jan Silvious, Chapter 7, "Codependency in the Workplace," pp. 110-119, Pyranee Books, 1989.*

**Make Sure YOU Are Included in the Next National Resource Directory!**

**See page 249**

**"The single's ministry candy sale poster had caused quite a stir among some of the members at First Church."**

# *Part 3*

# Speakers and Singers

## Resource People to Consider For Your Ministry

### Where To Find Them:


*Here is information on many of the best singles ministry consultants, retreat leaders and seminar speakers available in the country.*

# SPEAKERS AND SINGERS

**When you're looking for a speaker, singer or ministry consultant, this is the place to come. Here you will find information on the most experienced singles ministry leaders and resource people in the country.**

## ANDERSON, GILBERT W.

522 Belvedere Drive
Kokomo, IN. 46901
(317) 457-5544

**Occupation:** Psychologist and Consultant
**Full-Time Speaker:** Yes
**Years Involved In Singles Ministry:** 20
**Educational Background:** Ed.D. in counseling psychology and education; M. in Divinity
**Advanced Scheduling Required:** 1-2 months
**Workshops/Seminars:** "Development of Positive Self-Esteem"; "Values and Decision-Making"; "Intimacy and Sexuality"; "Mate Selection"
**Publications:** Emotional Aspects of Dealing with Serious Illness; Effect of Critical Parents on Children; Effect of Criticism on Persons at Any Age.
**Description of Ministry:** Gilbert's full time ministry is devoted to Christian counseling, speaking, workshop and seminar presentation. It is his goal to assist singles, families, and children in becoming more effective individuals and to make a difference with their lives, enabling them to be more effective Christians.

## ANTHONY, MICHAEL J. DR.

13800 Biola Avenue
La Mirada, CA 90639
(213) 903-4818

**Occupation:** Chairman, Department of Christian Education, Associate Professor of Christian Education, Biola University/Talbot School of Theology
**Full-Time Speaker:** No
**Years Involved In Singles Ministry:** 8
**Educational Background:** B.A., Christian Education, Biola College; M.A., Christian Education, Talbot Theological Seminary; M., Religious Education, Golden Gate Baptist Theological Seminary; Ed.D., Education Administration, S.W. Baptist Theological Seminary; Ph.D., Life Span Development, Claremont Graduate School
**Advanced Scheduling Required:** 2-3 months
**Publications:** "Single Adult Passages: Uncharted Territories"; "Help.. I'm A Camp Counselor"
**Workshops/Seminars:** "Living With Loneliness'"; "Christian Singles In The 90's"; "Involving Singles in Service Projects/ Missions" ; "Knowing God's Will"; "The Issues In Intimacy"
**Description of Ministry:** Dr. Anthony is a humorous Bible teacher who seeks to integrate Biblical truths with contemporary issues facing todays' singles across America. He has both academic and practical ministry experience. He offers solid advice to singles looking to grow in their faith. His travels around the world as a teacher/ speaker provide him with a wealth of practical illustrations on how to live the Christian life.

## BAKER, DAVID

15857 Deer Trail Drive
Chino Hills, CA. 91709
(714) 597-4266

**Educational Background:** B.A. Theology, M.A. Christian Formation
**Occupation:** Consultant, Executive Director for Personal Renewal Associates, Inc.
**Full-Time Speaker:** Yes
**Workshops/Seminars:** "Running To Stand Still: An Invitation to Personal Renewal"; "Who Cares?: Practicing a Compassionate Lifestyle"; Single and Young Adult Leadership Training
**Advanced Scheduling Required:** 6 months
**Description of Ministry:** David is Founder and Executive Director of Personal Renewal Associates, Inc., an interdenominational agency that exists to encourage work in spirituality, psychology and the arts, which promotes personal and professional enrichment and spiritual renewal through seminars, consortium, invitational conferences, research and consultation.
**SEE CHRISTIAN FOCUS AD ON PAGE 59**

## BARBER, BOB

11 West Avenue
Pitman, N.J. 08071
(609) 582-0222

**Occupation:** Assistant Pastor of Cloucester County Community Church; Director of "The Alternative for Single Adults"; Host of "The Single Alternative" - weekly Radio Broadcast on WZZD 990 AM, Philadelphia, PA.
**Full-Time Speaker:** No
**Years Involved In Singles Ministry:** 6
**Educational Background:** B.S. Rutgers University; M. Divinity, Eastern Baptist Theological Seminary
**Advanced Scheduling Required:** 30-60 days
**Publications:** Several tapes - audio, "You are Betrothed"; "Enjoying Our Children"; "Overcoming Temptation"; "The Foundation for Positive Single Adult Relationships"
**Workshops/Seminars:** "Understanding and Healing damaged Emotions"; "Raising and Enjoying Children in Single Parent Homes"; "The Foundation for Positive Single Adult Relationships".
**Description of Ministry:** Bob has a strong desire to see single adults mobilized and equipped to take their proper place in the Church and to help them to effectively lead the large number of unsaved singles in our country to Jesus Christ.

## BARTON, DAVE

Box 71, Dana Point, CA 92629
(714) 495-2761 FAX (714) 363-1458

**Occupation:** Christian Radio Talk Show Host and Senior Marketing Consultant at KKLA-FM, Los Angeles, CA
**Full-Time Speaker:** No
**Years Involved In Singles Ministry:** 7
**Educational Background:** M.A., Speech Communication
**Advanced Scheduling Required:** 2-12 months
**Workshops/Seminars:** "Communication: God's Gift For Relationship" - 4-session teaching series which reveals the keys to building stronger relationships through enhanced interpersonal communication. Brochure and tape available.
**Description of Ministry:** Dave Barton has a mission: To help others enjoy more rewarding relationships through increased communication skills. In a style that is both heartwarming and humorous, Dave Barton blends insightful communication principles and biblical truths with supportive illustrations from real life. Excellent for singles! Available for retreats, conferences and one-day seminars.

## BASHAM, ALAN

% Christian Focus
P. O. Box 2658
Woodinville, WA 98072
(206) 881-7270

SEE CHRISTIAN FOCUS AD ON PAGE 59

## BLACK, WILLARD

P.O. Box 7494
San Jose, CA. 95150
(408) 255-6885

**Occupation:** Director, Institute for Christian Resources, Inc. of San Jose, CA.
**Full-Time Speaker:** Yes
**Years Involved In Singles Ministry: 10**
**Educational Background:** B.A. University of Denver; M.A. San Francisco State University; B.A., M.A. Ozark Christian College.
**Advanced Scheduling Required:** 3-15 months
**Workshops/Seminars:** "Homesteading Your Single Parent Wilderness"
**Publications:** Video series, 1990
**Description of Ministry:** A teaching ministry of lay people... helping lay people. Our institute endeavors to help individuals with specific family issues (such as single parenting, step parenting, spouse abuse, grief and divorce); social issues (ecology and Christianity, Earth stewardship, Christian response to AIDS) and other areas such as conflict management, how churches and individuals can meet needs in conflict.

## BLACKMON, TOM

% Christian Focus
P. O. Box 2658
Woodinville, WA 98072
(206) 881-7270

SEE CHRISTIAN FOCUS AD ON PAGE 59

## BRILEY, PAT

50 Music Square West,
Suite 800
Nashville, TN 37203
(615) 327-3607

**Occupation:** Commercial Real Estate; Director of Leasing, Landmark Management Corp., Nashville, TN
**Full-Time Speaker:** No
**Years Involved In Singles Ministry:** 18
**Advanced Scheduling Required:** 2 months
**Workshops/Seminars:** "The Single Life and Christ"; "Obedience"; "Facing Life-Threatening Illness Alone"
**Description of Ministry:** Someone once said to me, "Pat, you have had so much tragedy in your life. How do you keep going?" I remember being stunned. I had never thought of my life as full of tragedy. But, I tell you, through each experience I have discovered a deeper grace and strength sufficient to carry me through...just as my Heavenly Father promised.

## BURKE, DAVID

1895 Wrightstown Rd.
Washington Crossing, PA 18977
(215) 493-5080

**Occupation:** speaker, director of Enthusiastic Ministries
**Full-time Speaker:** No
**Years Involved In Singles Ministry:** 10
**Educational Background:** B.A. in church history
**Advanced Scheduling Required:** 3 to 6 months
**Workshops/Seminars:** "Dating and Sexuality", "Our Identity in Christ", "How to Start and Grow A Singles Ministry", "Exciting Programs for Singles"
**Description of Ministry:** David is a humorous, challenging speaker with over 10 years of ministry experience in 35 states. In addition to serving as a pastor to singles, he speaks at retreats, conferences, training events, festivals and churches, challenging singles and leaders to be excited about Christ in their local church. Experienced, effective, evangelical, ministry-oriented, and a unique ability to be able to relate the scriptures to any audience.

## CARLSON, PETE

314 Cotton Lane
Franklin, TN 37064
(615) 371-1812 or (615) 790-2217

**Occupation:** Musician, song writer, PC Ministries, Franklin, Tenn.
**Educational Background:** B.S., Psychology, Duke University; B.A., Religion, (Christian Education) Taylor University; M.A., Student Personnel Administration/College, Ball State University.
**Years Involved In Singles Ministry:** 16
**Advanced Scheduling Required:** 4-6 months
**Style of Music/Type of Program:** Music is centered around acoustic guitar, piano, trax/adult contemporary; appealing to a wide range of ages centering in on Christian walk; practical and livable Christianity.
**Description of Ministry:** Pete Carlson's music is a seasoned but fresh voice to his varied audiences. His original tunes offer insight into the Christian life, the various positive struggles that we inwardly and outwardly find ourselves in, and the hope that is available through faith in Jesus Christ. His comments are honest, true to life, and transparent; never "formula bound", but committed to the process.

## CLINE, STACY

7245 College St.
Lima, NY. 14485
(716) 582-2790 or
(716) 582-1200

**Occupation:** Teacher/Minister, Dean of Students, Elim Bible Institute of Lima, NY.
**Full-Time Speaker:** No
**Years Involved In Singles Ministry:** 14
**Advanced Scheduling Required:** 4 months
**Workshops:/Seminars:** "Getting Serious (Dating Beyond the Friendship Stage)"; Friends First: God's Plan for Relationships"; "Sexuality and the Christian Single."
**Books/Tapes Published:** Tapes- on same topics as workshops listed above.
**Description of Ministry:** Stacy wants to see single adults mobilized and equipped to live a productive, fruitful life in Christ and be released for service in the body of Christ.

# Can you benefit from relationship resources that affirm, nurture and challenge?

## *"The Relationship Resource People"*

**Curriculum** Offering a variety of book and tape resources including, *Young Adult Ministry, Beginning Again: Life After a Relationship Ends, Giving the Ministry Away,* and Terry Hershey's newest book, *Go Away, Come Closer,* which Bookstore Journal calls "one of the most unsettling books you'll ever read, yet it's also one of the best gifts you can give to yourself and your 'identity'."

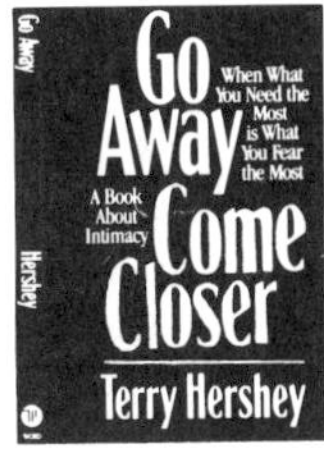

**Seminars:** Associates are professional and skilled. They speak from personal experience – presentations mixed with warmth, humor, conviction, and a healthy dose of reality. Their seminars are not crowded with cliches or band-aid platitudes – but offer grace and encourage personal responsibility. Subjects include: Intimacy / How to Be Me When the World Wants Someone Else/ The Few Things that Matter / Co-Dependency / A New Definition of Success / Truce: Ending the War Between the Sexes.

Terry Hershey, author and lecturer, Seattle, WA

Rich Hurst, Co-founder Leadership Training Group, Seattle, WA

Alan Basham, Graduate Faculty, Seattle Pacific Univ., Seattle, WA

Jerry Jones, editor, SAM Journal, Colorado Springs, CO

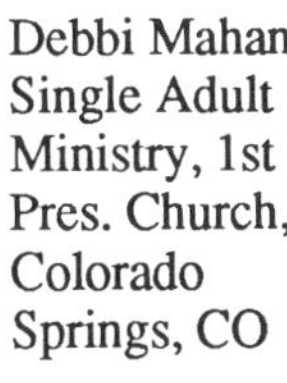

Debbi Mahan, Single Adult Ministry, 1st Pres. Church, Colorado Springs, CO

David Baker, Founder, Personal Renewal Assoc., Chino Hills, CA

Karen Fledderman, Christian Education, University Presbyterian Church, Seattle, WA

Kent Kilbourne, Assoc. Pastor, St. Lukes U.M., Houston, TX

Chris Eaton, Founder, Single Purpose Ministries, Tampa, FL

Tom Blackmon, Assoc. Pastor, St. Michael and All Angels, Dallas, TX

*Call or write for free tape and catalog:* **(206)881-7270**

Christian Focus • P.O. Box 2658 • Woodinville, WA 98072

## DUNN, DICK

814 Mimosa Blvd.
Roswell, GA 30075
(404) 594-0520

**Occupation:** Minister of singles and step-families, Roswell United Methodist Church, Roswell, GA.
**Years Involved In Singles Ministry:** 10
**Educational Background:** B.A., Baldwin-Wallace College, Berea, Ohio; Masters of Divinity, Boston University School of Theology; 1 year of Journalism, Ohio State University.
**Advanced Scheduling Required:** 3 months
**Workshops /Seminars:** "The Wholeness of Single Adults"; "Preparing To Marry Again"; "Recovering From Divorce or Grief"
**Books Published:** "Launching and Sustaining Successful Singles Ministry" and "Preparing To Marry Again"
**Description of Ministry:** Dick Dunn is a lecturer, author, publisher and minister of singles and step-families. He has been both divorced and married again, and comes to singles and step-family ministries with first hand experience. His workbook, "Launching and Sustaining Successful Singles Ministry" has been used in over 5,000 churches. The singles ministry at his church in Roswell, GA., serves over 3,000 single adults each year. His workbook "Preparing To Marry Again" comes out of his work with step-families and his own experience of remarriage.

**Do You Like to Read?**

If you'd like to serve on SAM's National Resource Review, let us know.

See Page 112 & 249

## DYKE, JAMES R.

Grace Church of Edina
5300 France Avenue S.
Edina, MN 55410
(612) 926-1884

**Occupation:** Minister with single adults
**Full-Time Speaker:** No
**Years Involved In Singles Ministry:** 12
**Educational Background:** B.A., University of California; M.Div., Western Evangelical Seminary; Doctoral Candidate at Fuller Theological Seminary.
**Workshops/Seminars:** "How To Be A Winner in the Dating Game"; "Reality Love"; "Building a Growing Single Adult Ministry"; "Money, Sex, and Power"; "Making Small Groups Work for You"; "A Single Adult Survival Kit"; "Leadership Training"
**Description of Ministry:** Jim Dyke is a seasoned speaker, published composer, musician, and writer whose articles have appeared in *Christianity Today*, *Youthworkers' Journal*, and *Single Adult Ministries Journal*. He has served in over a half dozen different denominational settings. His blend of personal insight and challenge have earned him a following among singles who are seeking a theological viewpoint on issues related to single adult life. His musical talents have added a special dimension to his ministry of teaching and public speaking.

## EATON, CHRIS

9925 7th Way North #102
St. Petersburg, FL 33702
(813) 576-4152

**Occupation:** Singles Director/Missions Coordinator and President of Bridge Builders, St. Petersburg, FL
**Full-Time Speaker:** No
**Years Involved In Singles Ministry:** 10
**Educational Background:** B.A.
**Publications:** "Vacation With A Purpose: A Manual for Developing Short-Term Mission Teams in Your Church"
**Workshops/Seminars:** Consulting on "Developing Short-Term Program In Your Church"; "Benefits of Short-Term Mission Teams"; "Challenge To Involve-ment In World"; "Friendships: The Neglected Relationship"; "Visionary Leadership."
SEE CHRISTIAN FOCUS AD ON PAGE 59

## FISCHER, JOHN

P.O. Box 1483
Bloomington, IL 61702
(800) 451-3784

**Occupation:** Author/Speaker/Musician
**Full-Time Speaker:** Yes
**Years Involved In Singles Ministry:** 20
**Advanced Scheduling Required:** 3 months to 2 years
**Publications/Tapes:** Books- "Real Christians Don't Dance"; "True Believers Don't Ask Why"; "Dark Horse"; "Single Person's Identity". Tapes—"Casual Crimes"; "Between The Answers"; "Dark Horse"; plus seven others
**Workshops/Seminars:** "Real Christians In A Real World"; "A Single Person's Identity"; "Asking Why"; "Real Christians Don't Dance"
**Description of Ministry:** John Fischer makes you think about your faith, about your world, and how those two co-exist. He speaks, and challenges the comfortable places in us all, then he sings, and strums the chords of our hope. It's a ministry that touches both the mind and the heart with equal passion.

## FLANAGAN, DR. BILL

St. Andrew's Presbyterian Church
600 St. Andrews Road
Newport Beach, CA 92660
(714) 631-2885

**Years Involved In Singles Ministry:** 20
**Educational Background:** B.A., U. of Redlands; M.Div., Princeton Theological Seminary; D.Min., Fuller Theological Seminary
**Advanced Scheduling Required:** 3 months
**Publications/Videos:** Video- "Rebuilding The Castle That Has Come Down - Divorce Recovery"; Books- "Developing a Divorce Recovery Ministry: A How-To Manual"; "Singles Ministry Handbook"; articles in: Leadership Journal, Decision, Single Adult Ministries Journal.
**Workshops/Seminars:** "Divorce Recovery"; "Single Adult Ministry Leadership Development"; "Growing Up Single - Considering The Issues (Love, Marriage, Relationships, Loneliness, Sex, etc.)"

## FLEDDERMAN, KAREN

% Christian Focus
P. O. Box 2658
Woodinville, WA 98072
(206) 881-7270

**SEE CHRISTIAN FOCUS AD ON PAGE 59**

## FULFER, KEITH

807 W. Glenwood
Tyler, TX 75701
(903) 592-3858

**Occupation:** Associate Minister
**Full-Time Speaker:** No
**Years Involved In Singles Ministry:** 2
**Educational Background:** M.S., Religious Education
**Workshops/Seminars:** Single Parenting; Single Lifestyle
**Description of Ministry:** As an associate minister my primary role is to see that the whole church ministers and is ministered to. There is a large gap regarding single adults in our church. Our goal is to: 1) reach lost singles; 2) provide ministry/ service to singles; and 3) provide opportunities for service by single adults.

## GNEGY, ROBERT C.

P.O. Box 164
Gig Harbor, WA. 98335
(206) 851-9991

**Occupation:** Grief and Memorial Counselor of Haven of Rest Funeral Home and Memorial Park.
**Full-Time Speaker:** No
**Years Involved In Singles Ministry:** 10
**Educational Background:** B.A. Howard University, STM Boston U. School of Theology.
**Workshops/Seminars:** "Grief Recovery: A function of the local church"; "Creative Adult Relationships"; "Intimacy"; "Singlehood: An opportunity for Spiritual Formation"
**Advanced Scheduling Required:** 60 days
**Books/Tapes Published:** "Launching and Sustaining a Successful Singles Ministry"
**Description of Ministry:** As a single person, my urge to belong to someone is basically an urge to belong to God. Once I have established an intimate relationship with God, then creative relationships with others are possible. Those relationships begin by my recognition of each human being as a child of God, made in His image. Each person has something unique in the way of a gift from God. It is up to me to discover or recognize the God-given gifts in others and then stimulate an awareness of that gift in each person I meet. My primary goal is to affirm others in their spiritual journey.

## GONZALES, GARY AND GEORGIA

1417 Blossom Circle,
Suite A
Upland, CA. 91786
(714) 985-7054

**Occupation:** *Gary*: Pastor, speaker, writer, adjunct professor; *Georgia*: Speaker, writer, consultant, Founder of Christian Singles United.
**Full-Time Speakers:** No
**Years Involved In Singles Ministry:** Gary, 5; Georgia, 20
**Educational Background:** *Gary*: B.A. Northeastern Illinois University; M.Div., Bethel Theological Seminary; D. Min. candidate, Talbot School of Theology; additional graduate work, Fuller Theological Seminary. *Georgia*: Fifteen years on staff with Campus Crusade for Christ, nine years in western Europe; self-taught singles ministry development; fashion model and image consultant.
**Advanced Scheduling Required:** 3-6 months
**Workshops/Seminars:** Week-end "Divorce Recovery" workshops; "How to Keep Your Single Adult Ministry Going and Growing"; "Reaching the Unchurched"; "Ministry Trends in the 90's and Beyond'; "Richer Relationships'; "Leadership"; "Life-style Evangelism"; etc.
**Description of Ministry:** Together, Gary and Georgia share a heartbeat for singles and in reaching the unchurched. They are available to speak as a couple or individually.
*Gary*- Speaking in a style seasoned with warmth, wit and unusual insight into everyday life, Gary skillfully applies biblical truth in ways that touch singles where they live.
*Georgia*- Having lived and worked for nearly 20 years as a single adult Georgia is in touch with the real issues of single life. Her fun style of speaking is both practical and inspirational.

## HASSELL, DAVID

P.O. Box 290-502
Nashville, TN 37229
(615) 885-9670

**Occupation:** Christian Music Artist
**Full-Time Speaker:** Yes
**Educational Background:** B.A., Music, Belmont College
**Advanced Scheduling Required:** 2-6 months (seasonal)
**Description of Ministry:** Specializing in conference music offering both praise and worship leading, and energetic concerts. Music is interspersed with relevant testimony and sharing on self-esteem in Christ, Daily Commitment, Relational evangelism, and Challenge to be real before God and others. Recent guest of Texas Baptist Singles Conference, Baptist Sunday School Board National Singles Events at Ridgecrest, Glorietta, St. Louis, in addition to single church events and youth activities.

## HEDGES, CHARLIE

% Christian Focus
P. O. Box 2658
Woodinville, WA 98072
(206) 881-7270

**SEE CHRISTIAN FOCUS AD ON PAGE 59**

## HERSHEY, TERRY

% Christian Focus
P. O. Box 2658
Woodinville, WA 98072
(206) 881-7270

**SEE CHRISTIAN FOCUS AD ON PAGE 59**

## HURST, RICH

% Christian Focus
P. O. Box 2658
Woodinville, WA 98072
(206) 881-7270

**SEE CHRISTIAN FOCUS AD ON PAGE 59**

## JACKSON, TIMM C.

8523 Bazemore Road
Cordova, TN. 38018
(901) 454-0034

**Occupation:** Associate Minister for single adults, Second Presbyterian Church
**Full-Time Speaker:** No
**Years Involved In Singles Ministry:** 15
**Educational Background:** Degree in pastoral theology and music.
**Advanced Scheduling Required:** 30 to 60 days

**Workshops/Seminars:** "Heart Attacks, What Keeps Us From Having Bigger Hearts"; A Divorce Recovery Series; "Leadership Renewal"; A weekend for fully devoted followers.
**Description of Ministry:** Having been involved with single adults for 15 years, Timm Jackson's ministry has allowed him the opportunity to learn in theory and first hand how to relate to single adults and build a ministry with them that truly meets needs. His ability to develop and execute creative programs has been one of his strongest assets. His involvement in divorce recoveryministry, where more than 4,000 singles have participated, has also been a significant focus. In addition to speaking at retreats and seminars on a variety of subjects, he has also developed a leadershop regeneration seminar to assist churches and groups in beginning a SAM or in renewing the focus and design of existing ministries with singles.

## JANSEN, REV. JOSEPH

7245 College St.
Lima, NY. 14485
(716) 582-2790

**Occupation:** Director of Ministry to Single Adults, Elim Fellowship of Lima, NY.
**Full-Time Speaker:** Yes
**Advanced Scheduling Required:** 4 months
**Workshops/Seminars:** "God's Call to Single Adults"; "Charting Your Course"; "Redeeming Rejection."
**Tapes:** On same topics as listed in workshops above.
**Description of Ministry:** Mobilizing and equipping singles for service in the Kingdom of God.

## JONES, JERRY

P. O. Box 60430
Colorado Springs, CO 80960-0430
(719) 579-6471

**Occupation:** Editor/Writer
**Full-Time Speaker:** No
**Years Involved In Singles Ministry:** 12
**Educational Background:** B.S., University of Tulsa (Communications)
**Advanced Scheduling Required:** 4-6 months
**Workshops/Seminars:** "Fresh Ideas for Your Singles Ministry," "Baby Boomers and the Future of World Missions," "Developing a Healthy Leadership Team," "Trends That are Shaping the Church and its Ministry

*we have it - together:* **T. K. & Company**
the Word and the music to serve your ministry

**Tony and Kimberly Bolton**
**T. K. & Company**

A highly talented Duo: Musicians/writers/ministers-in-music and anointed communicators of the Word, that will lift you to new heights. Versatile, fun, very effective. Affordable, and willing to serve. A ministry sold out to the Lord. Performance tailored to your function. A must for your next event!

Tony and Kimberly are also available individually to address your group with a program designed for your event.

**1-800-827-1332** T. K. & Company
servant heart ministries P.O. Box 5012 Fort Walton Beach, Florida 32548 (904) 244-1892

1-800-827-1332 T. K. & Company

With Single Adults."
**Description of Ministry:** Jones is the editor of Single Adult Ministries Journal, the most widely read publication specifically designed for those involved in ministry with single adults. He is also involved in developing a book line of resources for pastors and lay leaders in singles ministry. He previously served as editor of Solo and Spirit magazines.
**SEE CHRISTIAN FOCUS AD ON PAGE 59**

## KILBOURNE, KENT

% Christian Focus
P. O. Box 2658
Woodinville, WA 98072
(206) 881-7270

**SEE CHRISTIAN FOCUS AD ON PAGE 59**

## KOONS, CAROLYN

P.O. Box 1966
Glendora, CA 91740
(818) 812-3027

**Full-Time Speaker:** No
**Years Involved In Singles Ministry:** 15
**Educational Background:** M.A., Religion and Theology; M.A., Christian Education; M.A., Education; Ph.D. candidate - Human Development
**Advanced Scheduling Required:** 3 months to a year
**Publications:** "Beyond Betrayal: Healing My Broken Past"; "Tony: Our Journey Together" (single parenting); "Single Adult Passages - Uncharted Territory"; tapes on all the above topics plus: "Change - Key to the Future"
**Workshops/Seminars:** "Single Adult Passages: Uncharted Territories"; "Personal Change: Moving Up and Moving On"; "Memories: Healing the Past and Moving On"; "Single Parenting"
**Description of Ministry:** Carolyn Koons, a victim of parental rejection, emotional abuse and physical peril, shares how she experienced both the healing of memories and the renewing of her life beyond the pains of her past. Grasping hold of ongoing changes in her life, Carolyn has learned how to accept these changes and turn them into tremendous opportunities for growth and development. Whether single, married, young or young at heart, she offers listeners all over the world the opportunity to experience the joy of inner healing, the freedom of personal change and victory of the life in Christ. She opens doors which allow people to gain valuable insights into their identity and self-esteem. Carolyn does not live in the shadow of yesterday's sorrow. Her message is one of renewal and hope.

## LANDGRAF, JOHN R.

Central Baptist Theological Seminary
Seminary Heights
741 North 31st Street
Kansas City, KS 66102-3964
(913) 371-5313 or (800) 677-CBTS

**Fact:**
In 1990, for the first year ever, at least half of all marriages will be remarriages (for at least one partner).
*Special Report, Whittle Communications, Feb. - April 1990*

**Occupation:** Educator, author, administrator, pastoral counselor
**Full-Time Speaker:** No
**Years Involved In Singles Ministry:** 15
**Educational Background:** Diploma, Moody Bible Institute; B., Music, Wheaton College; M.Div., American Baptist Seminary of the West; Ph.D., School of Theology at Claremont
**Advanced Scheduling Required:** One year
**Publications:** "Singling: A New Way To Live The Single Life; "Creative Singlehood and Pastoral Care"; also numerous articles such as: "Singlehood by Divorce"; "Love and Friendship"; "Sexual and Single"
**Workshops/Seminars:** "Singling: A New Way To Live The Single Life"; "Counseling Issues of Single Adults"; "Understanding and Ministering to Singles"
**Description of Ministry:** My ministry goal is to raise a flag for singles liberation. I am called to help free single adults from the nefarious traps in their imaginations, teaching them how to be well-married to oneself, how to be whole without a "better half". The good news is that the single life can be an exciting concert instead of just a prelude, interlude or postlude. The bad news is that none of us is born single. Each of us is born profoundly non-single, and our natural bent is to stay that way. Like the skills of a concert artist, singling skills must be acquired. I want to teach people what these singling skills are and how to orchestrate and conduct a victorious single life through a healthy attitude and intelligent practice. As stated in my book, "Singling: A New Way To Live the Single Life", singling is a dynamic process one must intentionally enter and which one ought never to exit—never, even if one marries. Biblical models include Jesus, Ruth, Jeremiah, Esther, Lazarus, Rahab, Mary Magdalene, and the widow whose might Jesus extolled.

## MAHAN, DEBORAH

% Christian Focus
P. O. Box 2658
Woodinville, WA 98072
(206) 881-7270

**SEE CHRISTIAN FOCUS AD ON PAGE 59**

## MARSHALL, NORWIDA

3172 Oxbridge Way
Lithonia, GA. 30038
(404) 299-1832

**Occupation:** Administrator/Educator, Associate Director of Education at the Southern Union Conference of Decatur, GA.
**Full-Time Speaker:** No
**Years Involved In Singles Ministry:** 15
**Educational Background:** B.S. Elementary Education, M.Ed. Special Education and Ed. D. Curriculum and Instruction.
**Advanced Scheduling Required:** 2 months
**Publications:** "A Star Gives Light"; "Home and School Journal"
**Workshops/Seminars:** "Single and Satisfied"; "Burn Out-Spot it and Stop It"; "Managing Your Time and Your Life"
**Description of Ministry:** Norwida's goal is to share with others, especially the singles, how God can and will enhance our lifestyles once we have chosen to dedicate and commit our lives to Him. Also, that the basis for living a satisfied and contented single life is to develop that personal and meaningful relationship with Jesus Christ.

## MARTORANA, REV. TONY

7245 College Street
Lima, NY 14485
(716) 582-2790

**Occupation:** Minister
**Full-Time Speaker:** No
**Years Involved In Singles Ministry:** 9
**Educational Background:** Iona College
**Advanced Scheduling Required:** 6 months
**Workshops/Seminars:** "Single Parent Ministry In The Local Church," "Single Parent and Child Seminars," "Living in Excellence as a Single Adult."
**Books/Video:** "Developing A Single Parent Family Ministry Manual"; "Single Parent Day" (video series).
**Description of Ministry:** Tony presents a tender-hearted ministry to single parents and children with a special heart toward youth. He has appeared on 700 Club's 'Straight Talk' and the 'New PTL Show'. He is a motivator for Christian excellense, sought out for conferences and churches for both adult and youth."

## MENGER, JAMES ANDREW

3521 Nassau Drive
Augusta, GA 30909
(404) 733-2236

**Occupation:** Minister to Single Adults
**Full-Time Speaker:** No
**Years Involved In Singles Ministry:** 5
**Educational Background:** M.A., Clemson University; M.Ed., University of South Carolina, Religious Studies Certificate - Cambridge University; Doctor of Ministry, Pastoral Counseling-Graduate Foundation; National Board Certified Counselor
**Advanced Scheduling Required:** 6 months
**Workshops/Seminars:** "Life After Divorce"; "Remarriage and Blended Families"; "Single Parenting"; "Christ' Single Call: A Journey of Personal Faith Development".
**Description of Ministry:** To create a ministry to meet the unique needs of those who, for whatever reason, are single. To bring singles into the Body of Christ and to fully integrate them into Christian education and service. To provide nurture, and where needed, restoration. This is accomplished through a steadily evolving program of spiritual, social, recreational, and educational offerings. Grace is our watchword.

## MORGAN, ANDY

36685 Angeline Circle
Livonia, MI 48150
(313) 422-1854

**Occupation:** Associate Minister with Single Adults
**Years Involved In Singles Ministry:** 15
**Educational Background:** Graduate of Oral Roberts; Did graduate work at McCormack, Northern Baptist and Trinity Evangelical Divinity School
**Advanced Scheduling Required:** 3-6 months
**Publications/Tapes:** Divorce Recovery videos and tapes
**Workshops/Seminars:** "Relationships"; "Divorce Recovery"; "Developing A Single Adult Ministry".
**Description of Ministry:** Andy Morgan has been with Single Point Ministries of Ward Presbyterian Church for five years. He also hosts Solo Flight, a nightly call-in radio talk show for singles, which he would like to see syndicated.

## PETERSEN, PAUL M.

3821 University
Dallas, TX 75205
(214) 526-7457

**Occupation:** Minister to Singles
**Years Involved In Singles Ministry:** 8
**Educational Background:** B.S. Wheaton College; M.Div. Gordon-Conwell; D. Min. candidate Pittsburgh Theological Seminary.
**Advanced Scheduling Required:** 3-6 months
**Publications:** SAM Journal Articles: "Turn Your Meat Market Into a Meet Market"; "Counseling Single Adults."
**Workshops/Seminars:** "Why Does God Make Me Wait?"; "Single Adult Intimacy";

"Living Single in a Double World"; "Leadership Development"
**Description of Ministry:** Paul is the minister to singles of Highland Park Presbyterian Church, where he ministers to over 2,400 singles. He also serves on the board of directors of the National Association of Single Adult Leaders. At Highland Park, he focuses on a ministry of speaking, teaching, counseling, and facilitating. He speaks at conferences and churches around the country from a variety of denominational and independent backgrounds.

## PRATT, REVEREND AND MRS. GARY L.

3340 S. 16th Street
Chickasha, OK 73108
(405) 224-1599

**Occupation:** Single's Pastor, First Assembly of God
**Full-Time Speaker:** No
**Years Involved In Singles Ministry:** 5
**Educational Background:** Gary - B.S. Education
**Advanced Scheduling Required:** 2-4 months
**Workshops/Seminars:** "Triumph of Grace" (Life After Divorce); "The A.M.O.G. Looking for the A.W.O.G. (The Awesome Man of God Looking for the Awesome Woman of God)"; "Relationships" (Singles, Remarriage); "The Ready-Made Family" (Blending of Families); "Expect To Win" (motivational speaking for singles).
**Description of Ministry:** Gary has worked with single adults for several years. His experience as a layman in the church while employed as a High School Math Teacher, and then having worked as a full time staff minister of a large church, give him a unique perspective of ministry to, and leadership with singles. Gary has been a single adult and understands the issues and concerns facing the single in this decade. His wife, Debbie, shares in the ministry with singles and teaches classes among the singles as well. Debbie also directs the ministry to the S.A.M.'s Kids, a ministry for the children of single homes. The combination of Gary and Debbie's teaching offer a wide variety and a unique team for singles. Gary speaks at Single's Retreats, Advances, Conferences, as well as local churches pioneering Single's Ministries. (References available upon request.)

## PURNELL, DICK

Single Life Resources
1152 Executive Circle, Suite 300
Cary, NC 27511
(919) 460-8000

**Occupation:** Speaker, Author, Counsel and National Director of Single Life Resources, a ministry of Campus Crusade for Christ.
**Full-Time Speaker:** Yes
**Years Involved In Singles Ministry:** 15
**Educational Background:** B.S. - Wheaton College; M.Div. - Trinity Evangelical Divinity School, M.S. (Counseling) - Indiana University
**Advanced Scheduling Required:** 8 months
**Books/Tapes Published:** "Becoming A Friend and Lover"; "Building A Relationship That Lasts"; "Free To Love Again"; "Building A Positive Self-Image"; "Knowing God By His Names"; "Standing Strong In A Godless Culture"; "31-Day Experiment"
**Workshops/Seminars:** "Becoming A Friend and Lover Conference"; "Free To Love Again"; "Understanding the Opposite Sex"; "Developing a More Powerful Faith".
**Description of Ministry:** As an international speaker Dick has addressed hundreds of thousands of people on the subjects of successful relationships, intimacy, self-image and God's character. As an entertaining communicator and counselor, Dick pinpoints the unique problems that single adults face and offers practical, biblical solutions. With humor and sensitivity, Dick shares many of his personal experiences from 42 years of being single, prior to his marriage to Paula in 1982. His transparency challenges singles to grow in their relationships with God and each other, and maximize their lives as individuals.

## RABEY, LOIS MOWDAY

355 Doral Way
Colorado Springs, CO 80921
719-481-3442

**Occupation:** Speaker/Writer
**Full-Time Speaker:** No
**Years Involved In Singles Ministry:** 11
**Educational Background:** University of Maryland, Denver Seminary
**Advanced Scheduling Required:** 2-6 months
**Workshops/Seminars:** Dating Relationships; Male/Female Relationships (non-dating); Single Parenting
**Books Published:** "The Snare: Avoiding Emotional and Sexual Entanglements"; "Daughters Without Dads."
**Description of Ministry:** Living in a non-Christian culture requires an increasing amount of skill in order to maintain a Godly walk with Christ. Her ministry is focused on current issues concerning healthy relationships and encouraging people how to make wise choices in the midst of those relationships.

## RANDALL, BEN

207 Laurelwood Way
Vacaville, CA. 95687
(707) 448-3124

**Occupation:** Pastor of the Assembly of God of Vacaville, CA.
**Years Involved In Singles Ministry:** 4
**Educational Background:** U.California at Long Beach and University of San Francisco work toward Masters in education, B.A. in Administration, University of San Francisco, A.A. Business
**Advanced Scheduling Required:** 2-4 months

# About Jim Smoke

Jim Smoke is the author of seven books. His best seller, *Growing Through Divorce*, has sold over 300,000 copies with an estimated readership of over two million people. It is widely used in Divorce Recovery Seminars and Counseling Centers around the world.

Jim is a pioneer and veteran of over fifteen years experience in the Divorce Recovery field where he has counseled, taught, researched and written about the many facets of divorce. He has conducted over 500 seminars nationally in the past twelve years.

Jim is a former staff Minister to Single Adults at two Southern California churches: The Crystal Cathedral and Hollywood Presbyterian Church. He serves as an adjunct professor at Fuller Theological Seminary in Pasadena, California and is one of the founders of the National Association of Single Adult Leaders.

Jim is currently Executive Director of the Center for Divorce Recovery in Phoenix, Arizona.

This seminar is based on his new book, *Growing In Remarriage* published by Fleming Revell.

# Growing in Remarriage

*A Seminar for anyone who is single again, in a relationship that may lead to remarriage or those already in a remarriage!*

**Presented by Jim Smoke**

**Friday Night: 7:30 - 9:30 pm**
**Saturday: 9:00 am - 4:00 pm**

## *Some Topics the Seminar Will Cover...*

1. Why do as many as 70% of all second marriages fail?
2. Why are many second marriages merely emotional collisions?
3. Why do people often marry the same kind of person in a second marriage that they married in the first marriage?
4. How do you successfully blend two families with very different histories?
5. What kind of homework needs to be done prior to entering a second marriage?
6. How do you know if you are ready for remarriage?
7. How do you make expectations become a reality?

***These and many other questions will be explored in this eight hour seminar through the process of lecture, small group discussion and question and answer time.***

The *Growing In Remarriage* seminar will guide you in preparing for and living in a second marriage.

*For Further Information...*

Contact Jim Smoke at (602) 345-6266
or write to: P.O. Box 24450, Tempe, Arizona 85282

**Publications:** "Is There Life After Divorce"; "Vessels of Gold and Vessels of Clay"; "Recognizing the Need"; "Biblical Principles for Singles Leaders"; "So Much Wealth, So Little Worth"; "Hearing God Through the Static"
**Workshops/Seminars:** "Biblical Principles for Singles Leaders"; "What Singles Look for in a Leader"; "So much Wealth, So Little Worth"; "Hearing God Through the Static"
**Description of Ministry:** Ben founded the Single Purpose Ministries of California, a multifaceted outreach designed to offer the single adult a Christian alternative to the world's philosophy of single life. Ben does not see the single adult as being uniquely different in their desires from the rest of God's children. Rather he recognizes that the single has the same need for love, identity, and meaning with one exception; the freedom to choose how they will fulfill their needs and desires without parental influence or spousal guidance. Ben's vision and heart beat is that a "sanctuary" be established where the single adult can go to receive spiritual guidance, emotional comfort, and social interaction. The goal of this ministry is that the single adult will come to realize their potential in the Lord and thus go forward in His power with a "Single Purpose" of living a complete and committed life of service unto Christ.

## SAVAGE, DAVID W.

5409 91st.
Lubbock, TX. 79424
(806) 792-3363

**Occupation:** Singles Pastor of Trinity Church, Lubbock, TX.
**Years Involved In Singles Ministry:** 20
**Educational Background:** B.A. Southwestern College, Undergraduate-Presbyterian
**Workshops:/Seminars:** "Divorce Recovery"; "Guilt vs. Shame"; "Relationships-Junk Food Singles"; "Fig Leaf Religion"; "Misunderstood", "What to Do When You Don't Know What to Do".

## SCHILLER, BARBARA

7700 Davis Drive
Clayton, MO 63105
(314) 727-2777

**Occupation:** Assistant/Single Life Ministries
**Full-Time Speaker:** No
**Years Involved In Singles Ministry:** 5
**Educational Background:** Pursuing degree in Educational Psychology at Washington University
**Advanced Scheduling Required:** 3-6 months
**Publications:** "Building Effective Ministry for Children of Divorce"; "Ministry in the Local Church"
**Workshops/Seminars:** "Developmental Stress Within Children of Divorce"; "Loss, Separation, Anger and Guilt"; "Understanding Dilemmas of Single Parents While Offering Support"
**Description of Ministry:** The ministry in which Barbara Schiller is involved branched into three main areas: 1) Speaking directly to single parents, providing hope, encouragement and 'hands-on' practical guidelines in learning how to cope; 2) working with a leadership within various churches who desire to learn how to start a ministry to children of divorce; and 3) consulting with pastors and laity in understanding the dilemmas of single parenting, while learning to provide creative support.

## SHEMETH, REVEREND SCOTT

P.O. Box 9101
Springfield, MO 65801-9101
(417) 863-9160

**Occupation:** Evangelist
**Full-Time Speaker:** Yes
**Years Involved In Singles Ministry:** 8
**Educational Background:** B.S. Chemical Engineering, M.A. Biblical Literature, M.Div. Pastoral Counseling
**Advanced Scheduling Required:** Varies
**Publications:** Zondervan's "Dictionary of Pentecostal Charismatic Movements" - contributing author of several articles
**Workshops/Seminars:** "Unity/Community"; "God's Treasure (esteem, value, purpose)"; "Stress, Depression, Forgiveness"; "The Holy Spirit".
**Description of Ministry:** 1) Continue overseas crusades; 2) Continue U.S. crusades/seminars/retreats; 3) Continue to develop and publish a nationwide single's magazine

# More Than Fifty Years* of Singles Ministry Leadership Experience

**CHRIS EATON,** founder of Single Purpose Ministries, St. Petersburg, Florida; author of *Vacations With a Purpose*; involved as a singles ministry leader for more than ten years.

**TERRY HERSHEY,** Woodinville, Washington, is author of *Young Adult Ministry*; has served as a pastor and national singles ministry leader for more than ten years.

**ANDY MORGAN,** singles pastor for more than twelve years, has served on staff at Ward Presbyterian (Livonia, Michigan), and Arlington Heights Evangelical Free Church (Illinois); host of "Solo Flight," a radio program for singles in Detroit; voted National Singles Ministry Leader of the Year in 1990 by his peers.

**RICH HURST,** minister with Singles at Crystal Cathedral, Garden Grove, California; author of an upcoming book on building your singles ministry leadership team; singles ministry leader and consultant for more than ten years.

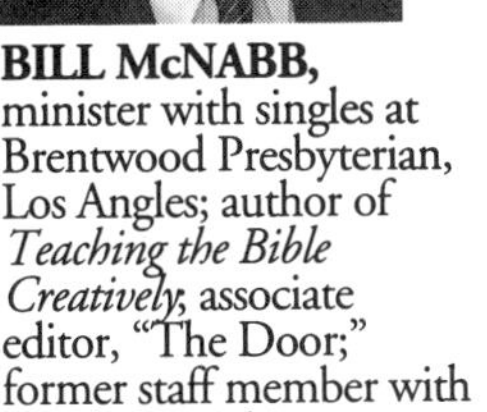

**BILL McNABB,** minister with singles at Brentwood Presbyterian, Los Angles; author of *Teaching the Bible Creatively*; associate editor, "The Door;" former staff member with Youth Specialties.

**JERRY JONES,** editor of *Single Adult Ministries Journal*; director of Singles Ministry Resources/NavPress product line, Colorado Springs, Colorado; involved in singles ministry leadership for more than 12 years.

## **The Singles Ministry Resources** Leadership Training Group

Call us for your Leadership Training Seminars,
Divorce Recovery Training, and Singles Ministry Consulting.

(And ask us for more details about our nationwide seminars and
National Singles Ministry Leadership Conference coming soon!)

LTG, P.O. Box 2658, Woodinville, Washington 98072 • (206) 881-7270 or (719) 579-6471

*(*Combined years in singles ministry leadership positions is 56+ years!)*

## SMITH, HAROLD IVAN

% McKinney Associates
P. O. Box 5162
Louisville, KY 40205
(502) 583-8222

**Occupation:** Writer, lecturer; President of Harold Ivan Smith and Associates
**Full-Time Speaker:** Yes
**Years Involved In Singles Ministry:** 9
**Educational Background:** Doctor of Ministry, Rice Seminary; Ed.S., Vanderbilt University; M.A., Scarritt College.
**Advanced Scheduling Required:** 6 months
**Workshops/Seminars:** "Dream Making in a Dream Breaking World", "Coming To Terms With Your Parents", "Coming To Terms With Friends", "You and Your Hormones", "Coming To Terms With Your Me", "Tear Catching: Developing The Gift of Compassion", "Forgiving is For Giving", "Is There Room In The Pew For Me?"
**Description of Ministry:** The ministry of Harold Ivan Smith is directed toward impacting single adults to make a difference in this season of life called singleness. The question is: singleness as a problem or as an opportunity. He also spends his time looking at issues which impact single adults and those who minister with single adults.

## SMITH-GREER, BECKY

Heart to Heart Ministries
900 Sussex Court
Spartanburg, SC 29301
(803) 439-8949

**Occupation:** Director of Single Adult Ministry
**Years Involved In Singles Ministry:** 8
**Educational Background:** B.S., M.A. degrees in Education
**Advanced Scheduling Required:** Varies
**Publications:** "Keepsakes for the Heart," (Focus on the Family Publishing). Keepsakes is a spiritual journey, a grief book, an inspirational message and challenge. It's a book about God's wondrous power to heal and rebuild broken lives.
**Workshops/Seminars:** Relational, Grief, Spiritual Growth. Especially for Women: Waiting on God's Best, Personal Development, Finding the Right Man
**Description of Ministry:** To challenge, motivate, instruct, inform and inspire single adults. To share God's love with those who are broken. To challenge new growth emotionally and spiritually. To inspire by example how God can re-construct broken lives. Heart to Heart Ministries also features Max and Becky Greer as a husband/ wife team who can minister separately or together.

## SMITHEE, CORY

404 Lena Lane
Burleson, TX 76208
(817) 295-7671

**Occupation:** Associate Pastor, Steppingstone Church
**Years Involved In Singles Ministry:** 6
**Educational Background:** CFNI - WOF Bible School
**Advanced Scheduling Required:** 2 months
**Workshops/Seminars:** College and Career; Inreach to Outreach; Leadership Training
**Description of Ministry:** My goal is simple - I'm an Associate Pastor and God has given me clear instruction that I'm to serve Pastors, helping them in any way that I can. I want to be a blessing to them, not a user of them.

## SMOKE, JIM

P.O. Box 24450
Tempe, AZ 85282
(602) 345-6266

**Occupation:** Executive Director, The Center for Divorce Recovery
**Full-Time Speaker:** No
**Years Involved In Singles Ministry:** 15
**Educational Background:** B.A., Kings College
**Advanced Scheduling Required:** 6-9 months
**Publications:** "Growing Through Divorce"; "Suddenly Single"; "Every Single Day"; "Living Beyond Divorce"; "Turning Points"; "What Ever Happened To Ordinary Christians"; "Growing in Remarriage."
**Workshops/Seminars:** Singleness and The Challenge of Change; Growing Through Divorce; The Way of the Spirit-Spiritual Renewal; Growing Strong At The Broken Places; Growing in Remarriage.
**Description of Ministry:** Traveling thousands of miles each year conducting

**Fact:**

About 60 percent of the children born in the U.S. today will spend part of their lives in single-parent households and in one or more step relationships.

*Special Report, Whittle Communications, Feb. - April 1990*

retreats, conferences, leadership seminars and workshops has earned Jim Smoke the title of 'America's Ambassador to Singles.' Jim has authored seven books and conducted over 500 speaking engagements in all denominations over the past 11 years which have helped him heal the hurts in the lives of many single, single again and married people across America.

## STOCKFORD, JEFF

1508 Fairview Rd.
Raleigh, NC. 27608
(919) 833-3000
(919) 266-7000 or
(919) 834-4729

**Occupation:** Wholesale manager at Carolina Window Display and part of praise and worship team at the Assemblies of God in Raleigh, NC.
**Advanced Scheduling Required:** 1 month
**Album Released:** "Late Night Buffets"
**Description of Ministry:** Jeff's ministry goal is to draw people into an intense pursuit of God, to extend the Kingdom of God, Exalt the Name of Jesus and to change the world.

## TALLEY, JIM

P.O. Box 4309
Modesto, CA. 95352
(209) 521-0181

**Occupation:** Minister of Single Adults at First Baptist Church.
**Full-Time Speaker:** No
**Years Involved In Singles Ministry:** 11
**Educational Background:** Masters Degree in Christian Education and Counseling
**Advanced Scheduling Required:** 6-10 months
**Publications:** "Too Close Too Soon" and Workbook; "Reconcilable Differences" and Workbook
**Workshops/Seminars:** "Too Close Too Soon," "Controlling Singles Ministries," "Divorce Recovery," "Single Parenting," "Reconcilable Differences."
**Description of Ministry:** Jim has been pastoring single adults on a full-time basis since 1970. He believes that ministry is the highest calling upon a man's life and has committed his life to serving Jesus Christ. He appeared on Dr. James Dobson's "Focus on the Family" and also was a special guest on CNN Nightline . In 1987 he had a weekly radio program called "Single Minded" on KAMB, a Christian station in Merced, California. Jim presents a large collection of seminars and is a national leader in the field of innovative singles programs.

## WEBSTER, BILL, DR.

3243 Grassfire Crescent
Mississauga, Ontario LHY3C5
(416) 762-3061
(416) 624-8080

**Full-Time Speaker:** No
**Years Involved In Singles Ministry:** 5
**Educational Background:** B.A. Psychology, B.D. D. Min.
**Advanced Scheduling Required:** 6-12 months
**Books/Tapes:** "Is One A Whole Number"
**Workshops/Seminars:** "Journey into Wholeness," "Identity, Intimacy and Integrity," "Reinterpretation of Lost Hopes," "Understanding the Grid Process," "Roots and Wings," "Single Parenting."
**Description of Ministry:** Widowed in 1983, Bill has turned his life situation as a single parent/widower into an effective ministry to other travelers on the road. He has pioneered and developed a ministry for singles in his own Church and denomination, including retreats, camps, etc. An effective speaker, Bill uses humor and insight to seek and minister to people and help them along the road to personal wholeness and healing, and to renewed hope.

## WESTFALL, DR. JOHN F.

4540 15th. Ave. N.E.
Seattle, WA. 98105
(206) 524-7300

**Occupation:** Pastor of Adult Ministries, University Presbyterian Church
**Full-Time Speaker:** No
**Years Involved In Singles Ministry:** 10
**Educational Background:** B.A. San Diego State University, M.Div. Fuller Theological Seminary, D. Min. Fuller Theological Seminary.
**Workshops/Seminars:** "Taking Risks in a Guarded World", "The Next Step - Personal Growth and Development, Sex and Intimacy", "Confessions of a Lousy Lover", "Growing Effective Leaders Into the World" "Short Term Mission Adventures, Discipleship for the Undisciplined", "The Shape of A Heart", "Nurturing Relationship"
**Description of Ministry:** As a pastor of adult ministries, Dr. John Westfall directs a single adult ministry involving nearly 1,800 singles. Our goal is not to build a strong singles ministry, but rather to build strong singles who are ministers. He is an enabler of people, encouraging singles to use all of life's experiences as opportunities for growth and ministry. Combining humor and clear Biblical insight, John is a popular speaker at retreats and conferences across the country. He also hosts "Everyday People", a weekly radio program on CBS radio in the Pacific Northwest.

## WHITE, WILLIAM A.

2935 E. 6th Street
Anderson, IN 46012
(317) 644-7721

**Occupation:** Children's Editor, Warner Press, Anderson, IN. 46012
**Full-Time Speaker:** No
**Years Involved In Singles Ministry:** 20
**Educational Background:** B.A., Anderson University; Master's of Divinity, School of Theology, Anderson University. Post graduate work.
**Advanced Scheduling Required:** 3 to 6 months
**Books Published:** "Single: Understanding and Accepting the Reality Of It All." book and leaders guide.
**Workshops/Seminars:** "Divorce Recovery Workshop"; "Creative Single Workshop"; "Single Parent Workshop".
**Description of Ministry:** Because of his own personal divorce (1975), because he has not remarried and because he's been involved over the years leading many workshops around the country, William White feels he brings to any singles event some unique experiences and information that speaks directly to the needs and concerns of single adults today. He sees his contribution in this area as ministry and is grateful for the opportunity to serve.

## WHITESEL, REVEREND SUE

3248 West 60th Street
Indianapolis, IN 46208
(317) 786-0426

**Occupation:** Minister of Youth and Singles, Garfield Park Church of God
**Years Involved In Singles Ministry:** 7
**Advanced Scheduling Required:** 2 months
**Workshops/Seminars:** "Building Healthy Relationships"; "Christian Romance"; "Dating and Relating"; "Leadership Training for Pastors and Lay persons".
**Description of Ministry:** Sue's eleven years of experience in single adult ministries have led her all over the state of Indiana. She provide in-depth training to pastors, lay leaders and singles who want to start a group, gain new insights, resolve conflicts or share available resources. Her leadership training and equipping have earned her recognition as a strong non-denominational resource person. Through conferences designed specifically for singles and leaders, opportunities have been provided for sharing, growth, fellowship and fun.

## WYRTZEN, MRS. CHRISTINE

Loveland Communications
P.O. Box 8
Loveland, OH 45140
(513) 677-1999

**Occupation:** Recording Artist, Public Speaker
**Full-Time Speaker:** Yes
**Years Involved In Singles Ministry:** 14
**Advanced Scheduling Required:** 3-12 months
**Publications/Recordings:** book - "Carry Me" (Autobiographical/Encouragement); 13 musical cassettes
**Workshops/Seminars:** "Encouragement For Those Who Hurt"; "Training Individuals To Minister To Those Who Hurt"; "Teaching Children Scripture Through Music/Critter Country".
**Description of Ministry:** Two messages Christine frequently gives at Women's Conferences, luncheons, church gatherings or retreats are: 1) Encouragement for Those Who Hurt, and 2) How To Minister To Hurting People. Often these speaking opportunities are combined with a special "Christine Wyrtzen Concert" held in the evening; a musical package created to encourage the entire family with Critter Country fun for the kids and a deeper ministry to adults. But, whether she is at the piano or behind the podium, Christine's purpose remains the same—encourage those who hurt, and to give HOPE based upon God's word. Paula Bussard, Christine's partner in the ministry, is also available for seminar speaking. The subjects she addresses complement Christine's and together they provide a full day of ministering, encouragement and hope.

*Part 4*

# Retreat Centers

## Camp and Conference Facilities For Your Group

### Where To Find It:

# RETREAT CENTERS

**Here is a list of Camps and Conference Centers across the country. Consider them as possible places to take your single adults for a retreat . . . or a place for those in your group to go for personal quiet time, reflection, and refreshment.**

## ALABAMA

### Camp Victory

Route 3, Box 212
Samson, AL 36477
205-898-7948
**SPECIAL ACTIVITIES:** February 1-3, 1991 - Retreat for College & Career. This retreat will emphasize Summer and short-term Mission opportunities.
**OTHER:** Year-round facilities for up to 175. Excellent family style food service. Seven acre lake, ideal for boating and fishing. Activities include: horseback riding, go-carts, nature trail and large recreation field, volleyball and basketball court. Available to Christian groups most weekends.

## ARIZONA

### United Christian Youth Camp

1400 Paradise Valley Road
Prescott, AZ 86303-4926
602-445-0391
**SPECIAL ACTIVITIES:** Tri-State Christian Singles Retreat: April 19-21, 1991, October 11-13, 1991, April 10-12, 1992.

## CALIFORNIA

### Alpine Covenant Conference Center

P.O. Box 155
Blue Jay, CA 92317
714-337-6287
**SPECIAL ACTIVITIES:** October 16-18, 1991 Singles Conference with Dr. Archibald Hart, Dean of Fuller Theological Seminary, School of Psychology.

### City Team Camp May-Mac

P.O. Box 357
Felton, CA 95018
408-335-3019

### Discovery Expeditions/ Christian Encounter Ministries

P.O. Box 1022
Grass Valley, CA 95945
916-268-0877
**OTHER:** Programs include wilderness adventures, rock climbing, camps, retreats, cross-county skiing. We use the mountains as classroom and teacher for the purpose of evangelizing, maturing, and training participants. Groups learn to work together in God's love and strength during a time of mind, spirit, and body challenge.

### Forest Home Christian Conference Center

40000 Valley of the Falls Boulevard
Forest Falls, CA 92339
714-794-1127 Ext. 316 (contact Greg Fields)
**SPECIAL ACTIVITIES:** March 22-24, 1991. Young Singles conference (up to 35 years old, approx.) includes a speaker, music, exceptional food and accommodations and recreation (relaxation, too!).

### Hartland Christian Camp

P.O. Box 25
Badger, CA 93603
209-337-2349
**SPECIAL ACTIVITIES:** November 29-December 1, 1991, Singles Conference with speaker, special music, fellowship, snow?; May 10-12, 1991, Single Parent Families - special speak and music, children's activities, counselors (psychologists) available, boating. Childcare available.

### Idyllwild Pines Camp

26375 Hwy. 243, Box 425
Idyllwild, CA 92349
714-659-2605
**OTHER:** A year-round camping opportunity in the midst of towering pines and cedars, with a view of the majestic Tahquitz Peak.

### Mount Hermon Christian Conference Center

P.O. Box 413
Mount Hermon, CA. 95041
408-335-4466
**SPECIAL ACTIVITIES:** February 15-18, 1991; May 24-27, 1991 and August 30-September 2, 1991. Summer Camps (June thru August) have single parent tracts at our family camps. Singles Conferences held at Ponderosa Lodge. The February and August Conference is for all ages of singles. The May Conference is for singles in their 20's and 30's. Biblical speaker, seminars, use of pools, etc., provided. Also offered: February 15-18, 1991 is an All-Comers Conference for single and married people - a biblical conference at the Conference Center.

### Victory Ranch

18080 Gilman Springs Road
Moreno Valley, CA 92360
714-654-7766 - Gordon Nicholson, Administrator
**SPECIAL ACTIVITIES:** February 22-24, 1991; August 23-25, 1991; February 21-23, 1992; all Single Young Adult Retreats. Friday night through Sunday am. Retreat at Church Camp (Victory Ranch). Bring your own bedding - dorm style accommodations with special speakers, recreation, horseback riding, hayride, campfire, good food, etc.

## COLORADO

### Hamilton's Glory Cabin at Breckenridge

2350 Flora Place
Denver, CO 80210
303-758-7632
**OTHER:** Attractive, large log cabin on 6 acres in a spectacular mountain valley above beautiful Blue River. Includes large living room or group meeting area with ample kitchen and eating space. Sleeping quarters includes 4 bedrooms - accommodates a total of 25 people.

**Do You Feel Left Out?**

If you were left out of this National Directory, we have good news. There will be another Directory... and we want to make sure you are not left out again. Help us make this Directory complete. Let us know about your group.
*See page 249*

### Living Rock Christian Retreat

P.O. Box 209
South Fork, CO 81154
719-873-5215
**OTHER:** We tailor our retreats for each individual group.

### Teocalli Outfitters

Box 1425
Crested Butte, CO 81224
303-641-6733
**OTHER:** First-come on any dates, June-September. Activities include: horseback trips into the beautiful wilderness. Perfect base camp setting for retreats of any length. Christian wranglers and owners.

## FLORIDA

### Camp Horizon

7369 Sunnyside Drive
Leesburg, FL 34748
904-728-5822
**SPECIAL ACTIVITIES:** October 26-17, 1990 Singles Retreat
**OTHER:** Camp Horizon is a favorite retreat year round: quiet, beautiful, convenient to all of Central Florida. We serve Christ by serving others.

## GEORGIA

### Lifeline Ministries, Inc.

Camp: Route 1, Box 2325
Lakemont, GA 30552
Home: P.O. Box 627
Louisville, MS 39339
1-800-726-8915
**OTHER:** Weekends/-week & 2-week expeditions in summer - whenever a group wants to go. Activities include backpacking, rock climbing, repelling, whitewater canoeing. Will custom-tailor expeditions in wilderness, small group living (12 maximum). Six years experience, emphasizing Biblical principles for successful Christian living.

### Thousand Pines American Baptist Outdoor Center

Box 3288
359 Thousand Pines Road
Crestline, GA 92325
714-338-2705
**SPECIAL ACTIVITIES:** May 24, 25 & 26, 1991 and August 31 - September 2, 1991. Both are single retreats designed to provide relaxation, spiritual challenge and social interaction. The May weekend runs a separate camp in another part of the facility for children of singles.

## INDIANA

### Brethren Retreat Center

Route 3, Box 162
Shipshewana, IN 46565
219-768-4519
**OTHER:** We are a retreat facility (located in the heart of Amish country) that is available for rental. We plan to hold College/Career Retreats and Divorced Singles Retreats in the near future.

### Indiana Regular Baptist Camp

205 North 700 W.
Warsaw, IN 46580
219-858-2451
**OTHER:** We have purchased a new facility in mid-Indiana and plan to open a Complete Camp Conference Center with Single Adult Programs in the Fall of 1992.

### North Indiana Conference of the United Methodist Church

P.O. Box 869
Marion, IN 46952
317-664-5138
**SPECIAL ACTIVITIES:** January 19-20, 1991, Single Parent Retreat; May 25-27, 1991, Single Parent Family Camp; July 19-21, 1991, Single Parent Retreat

### Solo Epworth Forest Conference Center

Box 16
North Webster, IN 46555-0016
219-834-2212
**SPECIAL ACTIVITIES:** Always the last Friday evening and Saturday of April and the first Friday evening and Saturday of October each year (6 pm Friday to 6 pm Saturday). April 1991 - "Creatively Single" a workshop/seminar led by a psychologist dealing with issues faced by single persons. Fall theme not chosen as yet. Contact Reverend Joe Smith, Box 5, Larwill, IN 46764 for information.

## ILLINOIS

### Manitoqua Ministries

c/o Reverend H. Curtis Bush
8122 West Sauk Trail
Frankfort, IL 60423
815-469-2319
**OTHER:** We want to be able to host/lead weekends for young singles. We can accommodate 30-34 people. Our interest would be in the area of providing facilities/resources for groups and/or facilitators.

## IOWA

### Heartland Bicycle Tours

1 Orchard Circle
Washington, IA 52353
319-653-2277
**SPECIAL ACTIVITIES:** Weekend bicycle tours summer-fall 1991. Dates not set at this time.
**OTHER:** We can provide special custom tours for groups of 10 and over. We can provide all rental equipment in addition to accommodations and meals. We have access to Christian Camp facilities.

### United Methodist Campground

Lake Okoboji
Spirit Lake, IA 51360
**SPECIAL ACTIVITIES:** July 5-7, 1991, Retreat "Life 101"

# MARYLAND

**Sandy Cove Bible Conference**
Box B
North East, MD 21901
301-287-5433
**SPECIAL ACTIVITIES:** April 19-21, 1991 - Singles Conference weekend, Speaker: Harold Ivan Smith; Guest Artist: John Fischer and Mike Faircloth
April 20, 1991 - Concert with First Call.
**OTHER:** Sandy Cove's an ideal vacation, retreat or conference center for single adults as individuals, conference events, groups, getaways.

# MICHIGAN

**Camp Amigo**
26455 Banker Road
Sturgis, MI 49091-9355
616-651-2811
**SPECIAL ACTIVITIES:** February 22-24, 1990 - Young Adult Weekend Retreat

**Camp Friedenswald**
15406 Watercress Drive
Cassopolis, MI 49031
616-476-2426
**SPECIAL ACTIVITIES:** February 8-10, 1991 and February 7-9, 1992, Winter Young Adult weekends, Inspirational speakers, winter sports and activities, dinner concert, volleyball tournaments.

**Cedar Campus**
P. O. Box 425
Cedarville, MI 49719
906-484-2294
**SPECIAL ACTIVITIES:** June 29-July 6, 1991: 4th of July vacation week. A program for singles, couples and families with small group studies, evening speaker and recreational opportunities. Cedar Campus is a 500 acre college and adult facility on Lake Huron in Michigan's Upper Peninsula.

**Geneva Camp and Conference Center**
3990 Lakeshore Drive
Holland, MI 49424
616-399-3150
**SPECIAL ACTIVITIES:** Single Parent and Child Retreat (dates to be set soon)

**Gull Lake Bible Conference**
1988 Midlake Drive
Hickory Corners, MI 49060
616-671-5155
**SPECIAL ACTIVITIES:** September 27-29, 1991 Fourth Annual Single Adult Conference. A weekend conference for single adults that includes general sessions, workshops, discussion groups, recreation, social times, meals, overnight accommodations, etc.

**Michigan Bicycle Touring**
3512 Red School Road
Kingsley, MI 49649
616-263-5885
**SPECIAL ACTIVITIES:** May-October 1991, the singles events are week-end bicycling vacations, in Northern Michigan, for beginner to advanced cyclists.

# MINNESOTA

**Big Sandy Camp**
HCR 3 Box 567
McGregor, MN 55760
218-426-3389
**SPECIAL ACTIVITIES:** April 26-28, 1990, A Singles Retreat, gathering people from a widespread area including Minneapolis-St. Paul. Enthusiastic and encouraging speakers along with exciting recreation top off a great weekend at a quality facility.

**Camp Lebanon**
Box 370
Upsala, MN 56384
612-573-2125
**SPECIAL ACTIVITIES:** February 1-3, 1991, Singles Retreat - "Mid -Winter Thaw".

**Covenant Pines Bible Camp**
HCR 4 , Box 440
McGregor, MN 55760
218-768-2610
**SPECIAL ACTIVITIES:** December 7-9, 1990, College/Career Retreat; December 6-8, 1991, College/Career Retreat. Retreats include winter fun: ice skating, broomball, gymnasium, relaxing, fellowship and worship.

**Wilderness Outreach**
P.O. Box 727
Grand Marais, MN 55604
218-387-1620
**SPECIAL ACTIVITIES:** Singles Canoe Trips July 1-6, 1991; July 8-13, 1991; August 31-September 2, 1991; or August 31-September 7, 1991 (or any week in September). Singles' canoe trips in the BWCA for 1991.

# NEW HAMPSHIRE

**Monadnock Bible Conference**
78 Dublin Road
Jaffrey Center, NH 03454
603-532-8321 or 603-532-6267
**SPECIAL ACTIVITIES:** October 5-8, 1990; May 5-7, 1990 and May of 1991. Messages, ropes course, off grounds trips, indoor pool swimming, hiking, new games.

**Singing Hills Christian Fellowship**
HCR #75 ,Box 206
Plainfield, NH 03781
603-469-3236
**OTHER:** Singing Hills is a non-denominational conference and retreat center with a maximum capacity for 250 overnight guests. We do not have a minimum group size requirement. Our ministry is to provide the lodging, meals, meeting areas and recreational areas to groups that come in an run their own programs. We are open year round to all age groups.

# NEW JERSEY

**America's Keswick**
Keswick Grove
Whiting, NJ 08759
201-350-1187
**SPECIAL ACTIVITIES:** Singles Conferences: November 23-25, 1990, January 4-6, 1991, August 3-10, 1991, November 29-December 1, 1991.

**Harvey Cedars Bible Conference**
P.O. Box 1000, Cedars and Atlantic Avenues
Harvey Cedars, NJ 08008
609-494-5689
**OTHER:** We are located on an island, six miles at sea. Summer conferences for teens and adults. Balance of year we host groups of 50-500. Motel, Victorian hotel, dormitories, chapel, gym, indoor pool, ocean beach. 60 miles to Philadelphia; 90 miles to New York City.

# NEW YORK

**Christian Camping Services**
54698A Nipher Road
Bath, NY 14810
607-776-6705
**OTHER:** Our organization is not a resident camp, but serves to help local churches or groups organize and direct camping activities and retreats. Our services range from as little as just speaking or helping plan, or as much as planning and arranging the whole thing including location, activities, menu, equipment and messages.

**Travel Companion Exchange, Inc.**
P.O. Box 833
Amityville, NY 11701
516-454-0880
**OTHER:** Our members constantly seek travel partners - all times of the year - but we only publish their travel plans in our newsletters. We do not sell or operate the trips they take, we find suitable travelling companions.

# NORTH CAROLINA

**Templeton Tours**
P.O. Box 2630
Boone, NC 28607
1-800-334-2630
**OTHER:** We sponsor Christian cruises, where the ship is filled with Christians, and the bars, casinos and slot machines are

closed. January 7-11, 1991; January 14-18, 1991; February 4-8, 1991; February 11-15, 1991; March 4-8, 1991; June 16-20, 1991; June 30-July 7, 1991 (Alaska); 1992 dates: January 6-10, 1992; February 3-7, 1992; March 2-6, 1992; June 21-25, 1992.

# OHIO

### Camp Burton
14282 Butternut Road
Burton, OH 44021
216-834-8984 FAX 216-834-0525
**SPECIAL ACTIVITIES:** February 15-17, 1991 Quality speaker, excellent food, winter sports, group worship, plenty of local attractions to visit.
**OTHER:** Camp Burton is 120 acres of woodland in scenic N.E. Ohio Amish country. We are a year-round facility with housing available for up to 200. We have hiking trails, hayrides, team sports, multiple meeting rooms and a beautiful A-frame chapel. We are very close to skiing, a beautiful state park, Seaworld, historic Century Village and numerous antique and gift shops.

### Marmon Valley Farm Group
5807 County Road 153
Zanesfield, OH 43360
513-593-8000
**OTHER:** We are a unique camp with a farm atmosphere and public riding stables Also will do barn dances and hayrides for groups.

# OKLAHOMA

### Church of God Camp Ground Association Camp Bristow
Route 3, Box 175
Bristow, OK 74010
918-367-6590

# OREGON

### Canon Beach Conference Center
P. O. Box 398
Cannon Beach, OR 97110
503-436-1501

Special Activities : May 31- June 2, 1991, Bible conference for Singles and Single Parents. Childcare provided; held in resort area.

### Twin Rock Friends Camp and Conference Center
18705 Highway 101 N.
P.O. Box 6
Rockaway Beach, OR 97136
503-355-2284
**OTHER:** Our camp and conference center is open to guest groups (churches, parachurch organizations, etc.) year round. We would welcome singles ministry retreats. Our capacity is 330 with full food service. We are 90 miles west of Portland on the Oregon coast.

# PENNSYLVANIA

### Black Rock Retreat
1345 Kirkwood Pike
Quarryville, PA 17566-9506
717-786-1266
**OTHER:** We are a facility that rents out our facilities to Christian groups (up to 250 persons) both weekends and during the week, year round, for their own retreats planned by them. We also have a challenge ropes course.

### CBM Ministries
3741 Joy-El Drive
Greencastle, PA 17225
717-369-4539
**SPECIAL ACTIVITIES:** KOINONIA KLUB: Regularly scheduled activities for 3 or 4 different groups of singles. 1) Singles who have never been married meet weekly for Bible study, also have extra social times each month. 2) SERENDIPITY (for divorced or separated) meet twice a month for Bible study, also have extra socials each month. 3) SINGLE PARENTS - meet monthly for programs, encouragement, helpful spiritual guidance, etc. 4) REBUILDERS -those who have lost their mates through death. Meet twice a month for spiritual encouragement, fellowship, etc.

### High Places Ranch Camp
P.O. Box 97
Mt. Morris, PA 15349
412-324-2770 or 324-2023
**SPECIAL ACTIVITIES:** October 27-28, 1991, haunted hayride - horseback riding.
**OTHER:** Ranch Camp is open year round for any group interested in hayrides, horseback riding, and winter bobsledding. Individuals are also welcome.

### Pocono Plateau Program Center
RR. #2, Box 1002
Cresco, PA 18326
717-676-3665
**OTHER:** We anticipate programming future events (retreats) for single adults. Our retreat center is available for use by single adult groups/ministries for weekend retreats or mid-week conferences. We have a beautiful center on 750 acres in the Pocono Mountains of Pennsylvania.

### Spruce Lake Retreat
Route 1 , Box 605
Canadensis, PA 18325
717-595-7505
**SPECIAL ACTIVITIES:** January 3-5, 1992, Cross County Ski Weekend, Tent Camping or Lodging.

### Twin Pine Camp, Conference and Retreat Center
3000 Twin Pine Rd.
Stroudsburg, PA 18360
717-629-2411
**SPECIAL ACTIVITIES:** May 24-27, 1991 and September 13-15, 1991, Retreats for Single Adults. Includes special speakers, hiking, music, campfires, volleyball and lots of fellowship and fun!
**OTHER:** We hold two retreats each year - Memorial Day Weekend (Friday evening through Monday noon) and one weekend in September (usually the first weekend after Labor Day).

# SOUTH CAROLINA

### Look-Up Lodge
100 Old Highway 11
Travelers Rest, SC 29690
803-836-6392
**OTHER:** We can schedule retreats for almost any size group at almost any time.

# SOUTH DAKOTA

### South Dakota United Methodist Camps
P.O. Box 460
Mitchell, SD 57301
605-996-6552
**SPECIAL ACTIVITIES:** August 30-September 2, 1991, Singles Weekend Camp

# TENNESSEE

### Camp Ridgedale
P.O. Box 10 (Bear Creek Road)
Vanleer, TN 37181
615-763-2200
**OTHER:** Our facilities are rented by specific groups who do their own programming. Camp Ridgedale offers a central lodge (near completion) which contains assembly space for 200, library, kitchen bath and shower facilities, two dormitory rooms for thirty persons. In addition there are overnight camping areas on 95 acres of woods and fields, bath house, laundry room, RV and tent sites with electric and water hook-ups, outdoor recreation (full-court basketball, softball fields, volley ball, soccer, hiking, etc.), swimming pool with change rooms.

### Cedine Bible Camp and Conference Center
Route 1, Box 2390
Spring City, TN 37381
615-365-9565
**SPECIAL ACTIVITIES:** May 17-19, 1991, Singles Retreat; July 5-7, 1991, Family retreat that invites single parents; October 4-6, 1991, Singles Retreat.

### Mountain Lake Ranch and Campground
Route 5, Box 181
Dandridge, TN 37725
615-397-3853
**OTHER:** We are open to singles groups who would like to plan a time to come. We can accommodate groups of up to 20 comfortably and twice that if they are willing to sleep in sleeping bags or mattresses on the floor. We provide hayrides, bonfires, barbecues, and are in close proximity to Gatlinburg and Pigeon Forge, offering all kinds or recreation. We are also next to Douglas Lake. We also have movies, videos, hiking. Our chalets are plush and comfortable, and we have other accommodations as well, plus a campground. We call it a "do it yourself" retreat as we do not provide food service, however, all accommodations have kitchen facilities.

# TEXAS

### Camp Copass Baptist Encampment
Route 2, Box 638
Denton, TX 76201
817-565-0050
**OTHER:** Available are 56 motel rooms with two double beds per room. Four hundred eight four dormitory type beds in co-ed dorms. Cafeteria food service with salad bar, ample conference room sand recreational facilities.

### Harambe Oaks Ranch
P.O. Box 645
Fischer, TX 78623
512-935-2557
**OTHER:** Anyone or group may come to Harambe. We have over 25 recreational activities and super facilities with great home-cooked food.

### The Pines Catholic Camp
Route 2, Box 373
Big Sandy, TX 75755
214-845-5834

# VIRGINIA

### Camp Bethel
P.O. Box 390
Wise, VA 24293
703-328-6876
**OTHER:** We are very interested in serving and making our facilities available to singles groups. Camp Bethel is a 165 acre wooded camp that includes a recreational lake, cabin bunkhouses, family campground with RV hook-ups, several wooded tent sites and showerhouse with laundry facilities, a gymnasium, basketball court, full-service kitchen and rock climbing.

### The Master's Inn Christian Conference Center
Route 2, Box 94-A (Hwy. 29)
Altavista, VA 24517
804-369-5053
**SPECIAL ACTIVITIES:** Retreats/conferences are scheduled throughout the year. Single adult conferences and ski conferences for various single parent families. Activities include: swimming, trail rides, beach and clay volleyball courts, tennis and basketball, archery, rifle range, ropes course, shuffleboard courts, hayrides and cookouts. All accommodations are deluxe. A free Quarterly Newsletter is available.

### Solo Con East
324-68th Street
Newport News, VA 23607
804-244-4649
**SPECIAL ACTIVITIES:** August 30-September 2, 1991. Labor Day Weekend Singles Retreat.

# WASHINGTON

### Camp Berachah
Christian Retreat Center
19830 S.E. 328th Place
Auburn, WA 98002
206-854-3765
**SPECIAL ACTIVITIES:** May 12, 1991 Mother's Day Banquet; March 27, 1991 Easter Program; March 31, 1990 Sunrise Services and Brunch; June 16 1991 Father's Day BBQ; 1992 - New Year's Singles Retreat with "Singles for Jesus"

### Crista Camps
12500 Camp Court, N.W.
Paulsbo, WA 98370
206-697-1212
**SPECIAL ACTIVITIES:** Single Parent Family Vacation Labor day (every year) at Island Lake Camp. This is a 2-day retreat with adult and youth workshops and activities focusing on needs of single parents.

### Noah's Ark Cruises and Tours
10900 N.E. 4th Street #1935
Bellevue, WA 98004
800-456-6269
**SPECIAL ACTIVITIES:** Singles Cruise.

# WISCONSIN

### Honey Rock/High Road
Wheaton College, Northwoods Campus
Three Lakes, WI 54562
715-479-7474 or 708-260-5124
**OTHER:** Challenging adult wilderness program for personal renewal and leadership development. Retreat Center for groups and individuals.

### Phantom Ranch Bible Camp
West 309, 910910 Hwy. I
Mukwonago, WI 53149
414-363-7291
**OTHER:** Phantom Ranch is a retreat facility.

### The Salvation Army
Wonderland Camp and Conference Center
P.O. Box 222
Camp Lake, WI 53109
414-889-4305
**OTHER:** We do have church groups using our conference facilities for singles' ministry. Our Facility can accommodate 500 in winterized accommodations from September through May. Activities include: cross-country skiing, tubing, ice skating. Olympic size pool open May through September (to be winterized by Fall 1991 or Spring 1992).

### Wesley Woods Conference Center
200 Stam Street
Williams Bay, WI 53191
414-245-6631
**OTHER:** We can help your group plan a retreat at our facility at a price that's affordable. Cribs, kitchens, meal service, A/V equipment available.

# Part 5

# Calendar of Events

Seminars, Retreats, Conferences, Leadership Training Events, White Water Rafting, and Other Events Scheduled in 1991 and 1992.

## Where To Find It:

# 1991-92 CALENDAR OF EVENTS

**Here's some of what is happening in 1991 and 1992 across North America. If you're looking for a single adult retreat, conference, leadership training seminar, white water rafting trip, or other events of interest, this is the place to begin.**

*NOTE: See "Retreat Centers" on page 73 for additional calendar items.*

## Divorce and Grief Recovery Workshops

***Spring - 1991***
*(call or write for exact dates)*
**Event:** Divorce Recovery Workshop (6 weeks)
**First Presbyterian Church of Salinas**
830 Padre Drive
Salinas, CA 93901
**Contact:** Peter Cantu
408-422-7811

***July 19-20, 1991***
**Event:** Divorce Recovery Workshop
**The Old Landmark Church,** 444 Alabama St., Vallejo, CA 94590
**Contact:** Booker Chandler
707-557-9038

***September 4, 1991***
**Event:** Divorce Recovery Workshop
**Victoria Community Church**
5320 Victoria Avenue
Riverside, CA 92506
**Contact:** Roy Ronveaux
714-788-9050

***Fall - 1991***
*(call or write for exact dates)*
**Event:** Divorce Recovery Workshop (6 weeks)
**First Presbyterian Church of Salinas,**
830 Padre Drive
Salinas, CA 93901
**Contact:** Peter Cantu
408-422-7811

***October 5, 1991***
**Event:** Grief Recovery Workshop
**Victoria Community Church**
5320 Victoria Avenue
Riverside, CA 92506
**Contact:** Roy Ronveaux
714-788-9050

***November 15,16, 1991***
**Event:** Divorce Recovery Workshop
**The Old Landmark Church**
444 Alabama Street
Vallejo, CA 94590
**Contact:** Booker Chandler
707-557-9038

***November, 1991***
*(call or write for exact dates)*
**Event:** Divorce Recovery Conference ("Looking In-Reaching Out II")
**Columbus Avenue Baptist Church**
1300 Columbus, P.O. Box 345,
Waco, TX 76703
**Contact:** Joe Carbonaro
817-752-1655

***March 20-21, 1992***
**Event:** Divorce Recovery Workshop
**The Old Landmark Church**
444 Alabama Street
Vallejo, CA 94590
**Contact:** Booker Chandler
707-557-9038

***March, 1992***
*(call or write for exact dates)*
**Event:** Divorce Recovery Workshop
**Victoria Community Church**
5320 Victoria Avenue
Riverside, CA 92506
**Contact:** Roy Ronveaux
714-788-9050

***March, 1992***
*(call or write for exact dates)*
**Event:** Grief Recovery Workshop
**Victoria Community Church**
5320 Victoria Avenue
Riverside, CA 92506
**Contact:** Roy Ronveaux
714-788-9050

***Spring, 1992***
*(call or write for exact dates)*
**Event:** Divorce Recovery Workshop (6 weeks)
**First Presbyterian Church of Salinas**
830 Padre Drive
Salinas, CA 93901
**Contact:** Peter Cantu
408-422-7811

***July 17-18, 1992***
**Event:** Divorce Recovery Workshop
**The Old Landmark Church**
444 Alabama Street
Vallejo, CA 94590
**Contact:** Booker Chandler
707-557-9038

# Get-Aways and Vacations

## For your single adults who would like to take a vacation with other Christian singles

***Spring - 1991***
*(call or write for exact dates)*
**Event:** Annual Camping Weekend
**St. Michael & All Angels Episcopal Church**
P.O. Box 12385
Dallas, TX 75225
**Contact:** Tom Blackmon
214-363-5471

***Spring - 1991***
*(call or write for exact dates)*
**Event:** White Water Rafting
**Ward Presbyterian Church**
17000 Farmington Road
Livonia, MI 48150
**Contact:** Andy Morgan
313-422-1854

***May, 1991***
*(call or write for exact dates)*
**Event:** Annual Trip to Holy Land USA
**East Taylorsville Baptist Church**
P.O. Box 906/First Avenue Drive, S.E.
Taylorsville, NC 28681
**Location:** Bedford, VA
**Contact:** John Alspaugh
704-632-7005

***May, 1991***
*(call or write for exact dates)*
**Event:** Memorial Day Weekend
**Eastside Baptist Church**
2450 Lower Roswell Road
Marietta, GA 30068
**Location:** Hilton Head
**Contact:** Gil Crowell
404-971-2323

***June 29-July 6, 1991***
**Event:** 4th of July Vacation Week - Program for singles, couples and families with small group studies
**Cedar Campus**
P.O. Box 425
Cedarville, MI 49719
**Location:** Cedar Campus, Cedarville, Michigan
**Contact:** 906-484-2294

***June, 1991***
*(call or write for exact dates)*
**Event:** Israel Tour
**New Hope Community Church**
11731 S.E. Stevens Road
Portland, OR 97266
**Location:** Israel
**Contact:** Richard Kraljev
503-659-5683

***June, 1991***
*(call or write for exact dates)*
**Event:** Group Trip to "Creation '91 Festival"
**Gloucester County Community Church,** P.O. Box 266
Pitman, NJ 08701
**Contact:** Robert Barber
609-582-0222

***June, 1991***
*(call or write for exact dates)*
**Event:** Backpacking Trip
**La Jolla Christian Chapel**
648 Center Street
La Jolla, CA 92037
**Location:** Yosemite
**Contact:** Stuart Fox
619-459-9569

***June, 1991***
*(call or write for exact dates)*
**Event:** Lake Powell Boat Trip
**Skyline Wesleyan Church**
1345 Skyline Drive
Lemon Grove, CA 92045
**Location:** Lake Powell
**Contact:** Larry White
619-460-5000

***Summer - 1991***
*(call or write for exact dates)*
**Event:** White Water Rafting
**Diocese of St. Petersburg**
2281 S.R. 580
Clearwater, FL 34523
**Contact:** John Moran
813-797-2375

***Summer - 1991***
*(call or write for exact dates)*
**Event:** Trip to Colorado Dude Ranch
**Ward Presbyterian Church**
17000 Farmington Road
Livonia, MI 48150
**Location:** Colorado
**Contact:** Andy Morgan
313-422-1854

***Summer - 1991***
*(call or write for exact dates)*
**Event:** Weekend Bicycle Tours
**Heartland Bicycle Tours**
1 Orchard Circle
Washington, IA 52353
**Contact:** 319-653-2277

***Summer - 1991***
*(call or write for exact dates)*
**Event:** Weekend Bicycle Tours (May-October); Beginner to Advanced cyclists
**Michigan Bicycle Touring**
3512 Red School Road
Kingsley, MI 49649
**Location:** Northern Michigan
**Contact:** 616-263-5885

***CONTINUED NEXT PAGE***

# Leadership Training Seminars and Conferences

## Opportunites to Better Equip You and Your Singles Ministry Leadership Team

***June 1, 1991***
**Event:** The National Association of Single Adult Leaders One-day Leadership Training Conference
**Quail Lakes Baptist Church**
1904 Quail Lakes Drive
Stockton, CA 95207
**Contact:** Patrick Allen
209-951-7380

***June 1, 1991***
**Event:** The National Association of Single Adult Leaders One-day Leadership Training Conference; Dennis Franck - Speaker
**Location:** Quail Lakes Baptist Church, 1904 Quail Lakes Drive, Stockton, CA 95207
**Contact:** Shellie Hakeem
209-951-7380

***October 20, 1991***
**Event:** Leadership Training
**The Peoples' Church**
374 Sheppard Avenue East
Toronto, Ontario, Canada
M2N 3B6
**Contact:** Glen Eagleson
416-222-3341

**CONTACT THE FOLLOWING FOR A COMPLETE AND CURRENT LIST OF LEADERSHIP TRAINING OPPORTUNITIES:**

- **The Singles Ministry Resources Leadership Training Group,** P. O. Box 60430, Colorado, Springs, CO 80960-0430
(719) 579-6471
*(Will begin sponsoring 40-60 one-day leadership training seminars annually in cities across North America—beginning Fall 1991.)*

- **The National Association of Single Adult Leaders** (NSL), 5910 West Lake Road, Twin Lake, MI 49457
(616) 828-4380
*(NSL has been sponsoring 30+ one-day leadership training seminars annually in cities across North America—since 1989.)*

## Get-Aways and Vacations . . . CONTINUED

***July 1-6, 1991***
**Event:** Singles' Canoe Trip
**Wilderness Outreach,**
P.O. Box 727
Grand Marais, MN 55604
**Contact:** 218-387-1620

***July 8-13, 1991***
**Event:** Singles' Canoe Trip
**Wilderness Outreach**
P.O. Box 727
Grand Marais, MN 55604
**Contact:** 218-387-1620

***July 15-27, 1991***
**Event:** Hawaii Vacation
**Fisherville Baptist Church**
P.O. Box 82
Fisherville, VA 22939
**Location:** Hawaii
**Contact:** Ann Higgins
703-332-7098

***August, 23-25***
Event: Singles' Summer Breakaway Cruise (3 night to Mexico on the Norwegian) with Gary and Gorgia Gonzales
Contact: 800-221-9479 or 800-339-9564

***August, 1991***
*(call or write for exact dates)*
**Event:** Wilderness Vacation
**Diakonos Singles**
595 East Colorado #331
Pasadena, CA 91101
**Location:** Yellowstone
**Contact:** Susan Highley-man,
818-792-8835

***August -Sept. 1991***
*(call or write for exact dates)*
**Event:** Singles' Canoe Trip
**Wilderness Outreach**
P.O. Box 727
Grand Marais, MN 55604
**Contact:** 218-387-1620

***Fall - 1991***
*(call or write for exact dates)*
**Event:** Weekend Bicycle Tours
**Heartland Bicycle Tours**
1 Orchard Circle
Washington, IA 52353
**Contact:** 319-653-2277

***October, 1991***
*(call or write for exact dates)*
**Event:** Singles' Cruise
**Second Baptist Church, Perth Amboy**
P.O. Box 1608, 101 Borad Street
Perth Amboy, NJ 08862
**Contact:** Frances L. Stanton,
201-826-5293

***October, 1991***
*(call or write for exact dates)*
**Event:** Wilderness Vacation
**Diakonos Singles**
595 East Colorado #331
Pasadena, CA 91101
**Location:** Bryce Canyon, Utah
**Contact:** Susan Highley-man,
818-792-8835

***Spring, 1992***
*(call or write for exact dates)*
**Event:** Rocky Mountain Ski Advance
**Faith Bible Chapel**
6210 Ward Road
Arvada, CO 80004
**Contact:** Daniel L. Fisher
303-424-2121

***Spring, 1992***
*(call or write for exact dates)*
**Event:** White Water Rafting
**Ward Presbyterian Church**
17000 Farmington Road
Livonia, MI 48150
**Contact:** Andy Morgan
313-422-1854

***Spring, 1992***
*(call or write for exact dates)*
**Event:** Annual Spring River Trip
**St. Michael & All Angels Episcopal Church,** P.O. Box 12385
Dallas, TX 75225
**Contact:** Tom Blackmon
214-363-5471

***May, 1992***
*(call or write for exact dates)*
**Event:** Yearly Trip to Holy Land USA
**East Taylorsville Baptist Church**
P.O. Box 906/246 1st Avenue, S.E.,Taylorsville, NC 28681
**Location:** Bedford, VA
**Contact:** John Alspaugh
704-632-7005

# Missions Involvement Opportunites

## Encourage your single adults to participate in short-term missions

*(See page 97-98 for additional information on short-term missions.)*

***May 24-31, 1991***
**Event:** Mexico/Ensenada Missions Outreach
**The Church of The Way**
14300 Sherman Way
Van Nuys, CA 91406
**Location:** Mexico; Ensenada, B.C.
**Contact:** John Tolle
818-373-8090

***May, 1991***
*(call or write for exact dates)*
**Event:** Vanguard in Concern (Evangelical outreach)
**Grace Church-Edina**
5300 France Avenue South
Edina, MN 55410
**Contact:** Dave Gibson
612-926-1884

***May, 1991***
*(call or write for exact dates)*
**Event:** Mission Trip
**First Baptist Church of Visalia**
1100 South Sowell
Visalia, CA 93277
**Location:** Ensenada, Mexico
**Contact:** Mike Popovich
209-732-4787

***June 1-10, 1991***
**Event:** Singles Mission Trip
**Village Baptist Church**
10600 North May Avenue
Oklahoma City, OK 73120
**Contact:** Jay Shepherd 405-751-1951

***June 7-15, 1991***
**Event:** Mexico Mission Trip
**Forest Park Baptist Church,** 725 Highview,
Joplin, MO 64801
**Location:** Mexico
**Contact:** John Scudder
417-623-4606

***June, 1991***
*(call or write for exact dates)*
**Event:** Single's Mission Trip
**Hoffmantown Baptist Church**
8888 Harper Drive, N.E.
Albuquerque, NM 87111
**Contact:** Paul A. Gossett
505-828-2600

***Summer - 1991***
*(call or write for exact dates)*
**Event:** Vacation with a Purpose (short-term missions)
**King of Glory Church**
6411 LBJ Freeway
Dallas, TX 75240
**Contact:** Scot Sorensen
214-661-9435

***Summer - 1991***
*(call or write for exact dates)*
**Event:** Short-Term Mission Projects
**Lake Avenue Congregational Church**
393 North Lake Avenue
Pasadena, CA 91101
**Location:** Worldwide
**Contact:** Steve Morgan
818-795-7221

***Summer - 1991***
*(call or write for exact dates)*
**Event:** Short Term Mission
**Providence Baptist Church**
9225 Leesville Road
Raleigh, NC 27613
**Location:** Brazil
**Contact:** David Williams
919-847-5410

***Summer - 1991***
*(call or write for exact dates)*
**Event:** Short-term Mission
**The Stone Church**
45 Davenport Road
Toronto, Ontario, Canada
M5R 1H2

**Location:** Cuba and Eastern Europe
**Contact:** Michael Krause
416-928-0101

***Summer - 1991***
*(call or write for exact dates)*
**Event:** Short-Term Mission
**Farmers Branch Church of Christ**
3035 Valley View Lane
Farmers Branch, TX 75234
**Location:** Honduras
**Contact:** Michael L. Pope
214-247-2109

***Summer - 1991***
*(call or write for exact dates)*
**Event:** One-Week Mission Trip
**Trinity Assembly of God**
2122 West Joppa Road
Lutherville, MD 21093
**Location:** Mexico
**Contact:** James A. Lex
301-821-6573

***Summer - 1991***
*(call or write for exact dates)*
**Event:** Mission Trip
**Evangelistic Temple**
5345 South Peoria
Tulsa, OK 74105
**Location:** Mexico
**Contact:** Harley E. Wideman, Jr.
918-749-9971

***Summer - 1991***
*(call or write for exact dates)*
**Event:** Team Asia - Short Term Mission
**Crossroads Neighborhood Church**
7555 Old Military Road, N.E.
Bremerton, WA 98310
**Location:** Thailand and Hong Kong
**Contact:** Scott Turner
206-692-1672

***July, 1991***
*(call or write for exact dates)*
**Event:** Short-term Mission Trip
**La Jolla Christian Chapel**
648 Center Street
La Jolla, CA 92037
**Location:** El Salvador
**Contact:** Stuart Fox
619-459-9569

***August 24-31,***
**Event:** Mission Trip
**Fair Oaks Presbyterian Church**
11427 Fair Oaks Boulevard
Fair Oaks, CA 95628
**Location:** San Quinton, Mexico
**Contact:** David Weidlich
916-967-4784

***August, 1991***
*(call or write for exact dates)*
**Event:** Two-Week Mission Trip
**Trinity Assembly of God**
2122 West Joppa Road
Lutherville, MD 21093
**Location:** East Germany
**Contact:** James A. Lex
301-821-6573

***August, 1991***
*(call or write for exact dates)*
**Event:** Mission Trip
**Grace Church, Edina**
5300 Frances Avenue South
Edina, MN 55410
**Location:** Lima, Peru (tentative)
**Contact:** Dave Gibson
612-926-1884

# 1992

***March, 1992***
*(call or write for exact dates)*
**Event:** Mexico Missions Trip
**Master Plan Ministries,** Box 542
Durango, CO 81302
**Contact:** Charles E. Helvoigt, II
303-385-7621

***June, 1992***
*(call or write for exact dates)*
**Event:** Singles' Mission Trip
**Hoffmantown Baptist Church**
8888 Harper Drive, N.E.
Albuquerque, NM 87111
**Contact:** Paul A. Gossett
505-828-2600

***Summer, 1992***
*(call or write for exact dates)*
**Event:** Short-Term Missions
**Providence Baptist Church**
9225 Leesville Road
Raleigh, NC 27613
**Location:** Israel or India
**Contact:** David Williams
919-847-5410

***Summer, 1992***
*(call or write for exact dates)*
**Event:** Team Asia - Short-Term Missions
**Crossroads Neighborhood Church,** 7555 Old Military Road, N.E.
Bremerton, WA 98310
**Location:** Thailand and Hong Kong
**Contact:** Scott Turner
206-692-1672

***Summer, 1992***
*(call or write for exact dates)*
**Event:** Short-Term Missions
**Lake Avenue Congregational Church**
393 North Lake Avenue
Pasadena, CA 91101
**Location:** Worldwide
**Contact:** Steve Morgan
818-795-7221

***Summer, 1992***
*(call or write for exact dates)*
**Event:** Short-term Missions Trip
**The Stone Church**
45 Davenport Road
Toronto, Ontario, Canada M5R 1H2
**Location:** Spain
**Contact:** Michael Krause
416-928-0101

***Summer, 1992***
*(call or write for exact dates)*
**Event:** Vacation with a Purpose Short-term Missions Trip
**King of Glory Church**
6411 LBJ Freeway
Dallas, TX 75240
**Contact:** Scot Sorensen
214-661-9435

**"According to the Bible, since my husband Ted died isn't his brother Ned supposed to marry me?"**

# Single Parent Family Retreats and Seminars

***May 10-12, 1991***
**Event:** Single Parent Families Retreat
**Hartland Christian Camp,** P.O. Box 25
Badger, CA 93603
**Location:** Hartland Christian Camp, Badger, California
**Contact:** 209-337-2349

***May 25-27, 1991***
**Event:** Single Parent Family Camp
**North Indiana Conference of the United Methodist Church**
P.O. Box 869
Marion, IN 46952
**Contact:** 317-664-5138

***May 31-June 2, 1991***
**Event:** Bible Conference for Singles and Single Parents (Childcare provided)
**Cannon Beach Conference Center**
P.O. Box 398
Cannon Beach, OR 97110
**Contact:** 503-436-1501

***July 5-7, 1991***
**Event:** Family Retreat that invites single parents
**Cedine Bible Camp & Conference Center**
Route #1, Box 2390
Spring City, TN 37381
**Location:** Cedine Bible Camp & Conference Center, Spring City, Tennessee
**Contact:** 615-365-9565

***July 19-21, 1991***
**Event:** Single Parent Retreat
**North Indiana Conference of the United Methodist Church**
P.O. Box 869
Marion, IN 46952
**Contact:** 317-664-5138

***July 19-21, 1991***
**Event:** Single Parent Family Weekend
**Elim Fellowship**
7245 College Street
Lima, NY 14485
**Location:** Lima, NY
**Contact:** Tony Martorana
716-582-2790

***August 9-11, 1991***
**Event:** Single Parent Family Weekend
**Elim Fellowship**
7245 College Street
Lima, NY 14485
**Location:** Thamesford, Ontario, Canada
**Contact:** Tony Martorana
716-582-2790

***September, 1991***
*(call or write for exact dates)*
**Event:** Single Parent Family Vacation Labor Day Retreat
**Crista Camps**
12500 Camp Court, N.W.
Poulsbo, WA 98370
**Location:** Island Lake Camp
**Contact:** 206-697-1212

List Your Upcoming Calendar Items FREE in SAM Journal

When you want to announce a seminar, conference or other event of interest to those involved in singles ministry, send it to *SAM Journal*. It will be listed FREE as space allows.

Send your listing (4-6 months ahead) to *SAM Journal*, P. O. Box 60430, Colorado Springs, CO 80960-0430

# Special Events, Single Adult Retreats, Conferences, and Seminars

**A catch-all list of events that you or your single adults may be interested in attending**

***May 3-4, 1991***
**Event:** Spring Conference
**Immanuel Baptist Church**
1000 Bishop (10th & Bishop)
Little Rock, AR 72202
**Contact:** Dianne Swaim
501-376-3071

***May 3-4, 1991***
**Event:** Metro '91
**Columbia Baptist Church**
103 West Columbia Street
Falls Church, VA 22046
**Location:** Washington, D.C.
**Contact:** James R. Perdew
703-534-5700

***May 17-19, 1991***
**Event:** Singles' Retreat
**Cedine Bible Camp & Conference Center**
Route #1, Box 2390
Spring City, TN 37381
**Location:** Cedine Bible Camp & Conference Center, Spring City, Tennessee
**Contact:** 615-365-9565

***May 24-26, 1991***
**Event:** Retreat, with Alan Basham as speaker.
**Kent Church of the Nazarene**
930 East James
Kent, WA 98031
**Location:** Miracle Ranch - $55
**Contact:** Gary L. Waller
206-852-5144

***May 24-26, 1991***
**Event:** Singles' Retreat (a separate camp is run in another part of the facility for children of singles)
**Thousand Pines, American Baptist Outdoor Center**
Box 3288, 359 Thousand Pines Road
Crestline, CA 92325
**Location:** Thousand Pines, American Baptist Outdoor Center, Crestline, California
**Contact:** 714-338-2705

***May 24-26, 1991***
**Event:** Single Adult Memorial Conference "Dare To Make A Difference." Ron Barker, Conference speaker; Keith Longbotham, Praise/Worship Leader.
**First Baptist Church**
205 West 8th Street
Plainview, TX 79072
**Contact:** Greg Griffin
806/296-6318

***May 24-17, 1991***
**Event:** Annual Memorial Day Weekend Single Adult Retreat
**Twin Pines Camp, Conference & Retreat Center**
3000 Twin Pine Road
Stroudsburg, PA 18260
**Location:** Twin Pines Camp, Conference & Retreat Center, Stroudsburg, Pennsylvania
**Contact:** 717-629-2411

***May 24-27, 1991***
**Event:** Singles' Conference
**Mount Hermon Christian Conference Center**
P.O. Box 413
Mount Hermon, CA 95041
**Location:** Ponderosa Lodge, Mount Hermon, California
**Contact:** 408-335-4466

***May 24-27, 1991***
**Event:** Spring Singles United Retreat
**Twin Pines Camp**
3000 Twin Pine Road
Stroudsbury, PA 18360
**Location:** Twin Pines Camp, cost $111 (includes housing, meals & program)
**Contact:** Pamela Rankin
717-629-2411

***May 30-June 2, 1991***
**Event:** Singles Retreat
**Overlake Christian Church**
9051 132nd Avenue, N.E.
Kirkland, WA 98034
**Contact:** Gary Winkleman
206-827-0303

***May 31-June 2, 1991***
**Event:** Singles Retreat
**Countryside Christian Center**
1850 McMullen Booth Road
Clearwater, FL 34619
**Contact:** Nick Panico
813-799-1618

***May 31-June 2, 1991***
**Event:** Bible Conference for Singles and Single Parents (Childcare provided)
**Cannon Beach Conference Center**
P.O. Box 398
Cannon Beach, OR 97110
**Contact:** 503-436-1501

***May, 1991***
*(call or write for exact dates)*
**Event:** Retreat
**Lake Avenue Congregational Church**
393 North Lake Avenue
Pasadena, CA 91101
**Location:** Southern California
**Contact:** Steve Morgan
818-795-7221

***May, 1991***
*(call or write for exact dates)*
**Event:** Retreat
**Meredith Drive Reformed Church**
5128 N.W. 46th Avenue
Des Moines, IA 50310
**Contact:** Virgil Dykstra 515-276-4901

***May, 1991***
*(call or write for exact dates)*
**Event:** Singles Weekend Conference
**Southeast Baptist Church**
1700 East 7000 South/P.O. Box 21399, Salt Lake City, UT 84121
**Contact:** Peter Cieslewski
801-943-2241

***May, 1991***
*(call or write for exact dates)*
**Event:** Weekend Retreat
**St. Luke's United Methodist Church**
700 Southway Boulevard East
Kokomo, IN 46902
**Contact:** Patricia Willhite
317-453-4867

***May, 1991***
*(call or write for exact dates)*
**Event:** Retreat
**The Stone Church**
45 Davenport Road
Toronto, Ontario, Canada
M5R 1H2
**Contact:** Michael Krause
416-928-0101

***May, 1991 (Every Memorial Day Weekend)***
*(call or write for exact dates)*
**Event:** Arizona District Singles Retreat
**West Rose Lane Assembly of God**
6145 North 36th Drive
Phoenix, AZ 48150
**Location:** District Campgrounds, Prescott, Arizona
**Contact:** Wesley G. Hodgkin
602-841-0610

***May, 1991***
*(call or write for exact dates)*
**Event:** Singles' Retreat
**Monadnock Bible Conference**
78 Dublin Road
Jaffrey Center, NH 03454
**Contact:** 603-532-8321 or 603-532-6267

***May, 1991 (tentative)***
*(call or write for exact dates)*
**Event:** Single Retreat
**Woodvale Pentecostal**
205 Greenbank Road
Nepean, Ottawa, Ontario, Canada K2H 8K9
**Location:** Ottawa Valley Pentecostal Camp, Pembroke, Ontario
**Contact:** Bob Lanoue
613-596-1950

***June 7-8, 1991***
**Event:** Becoming A Friend & Lover Conference
**Southeast Christian Church**
2840 Hikes Lane
Louisville, KY 40218
**Contact:** Ralph Dennison
502-451-0047

***June 10-14, 1991***
**Event:** Singles Seminar - "God, You and the Future"
**Trinity Lutheran Church**
800 Houston Avenue
Houston, TX 77007
**Contact:** Don Christian
713-224-0684

***June 21, 1991***
**Event:** Baptist Single Adult Convention
**First Baptist Church**
201 St. John Street
Monroe, LA 71210
**Location:** FBC, New Orleans, Louisiana
**Contact:** Steve Arledge
318-325-3126

***Summer - 1991***
*(call or write for exact dates)*
**Event:** Retreat
**Grace United Methodist Church**
1735 Morningside Avenue
Sioux City, IA 51106
**Contact:** Alaire Bornholtz
712-276-3452

***Summer - 1991***
*(call or write for exact dates)*
**Event:** Annual Summer Lake Days
**St. Michael & All Angels Episcopal Church,** P.O. Box 12385
Dallas, TX 75225
**Contact:** Tom Blackmon
214-363-5471

***Summer - 1991***
*(call or write for exact dates)*
**Event:** Retreat
**Columbus Avenue Baptist Church**
1300 Columbus/P.O. Box 345, Waco, TX 76703
**Location:** Glorieta, New Mexico and Colorado
**Contact:** Joe Carbonaro
817-752-1655

***July 4, 1991***
**Event:** Singles' Bar-B-Que
**The Old Landmark Church**
444 Alabama Street
Vallejo, CA 94590
**Contact:** Booker Chandler
707-557-9038

***July 5-7, 1991***
**Event:** "Life 101" - Singles' Retreat
**United Methodist Campground**
Lake Okoboji
Spirit Lake, IA 51360

***July 26-28, 1991***
**Event:** Singles Retreat, Tony Martorona, Speaker
**Fort Walton Beach Christian Center,** 1007 Gospel Road
Fort Walton Beach, FL 32548
**Location:** Fort Walton Beach, FL
**Contact:** Scott Hawkins
904-863-1323

***July 30-August 4, 1991***
**Event:** North American Baptist Trienial Singles Conference
6125 West Foster
Chicago, IL 60630
**Location:** Milwaukee, WI
**Contact:** Reverend Doug Harsch
312-763-5306

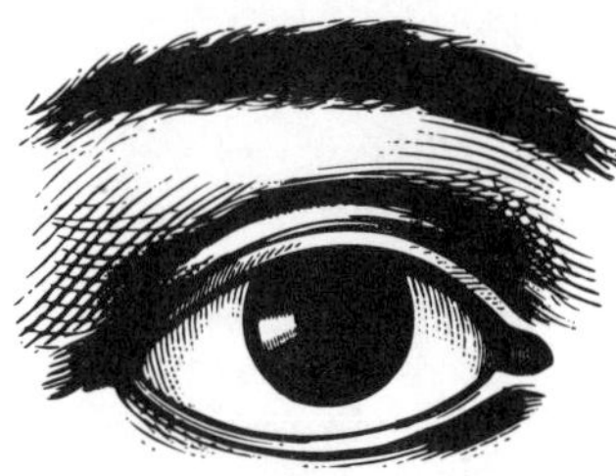

***July, 1991***
*(call or write for exact dates)*
**Event:** Summer Retreat
**Valley Community Baptist Church**
590 West Avon Road
Avon, CT 06001
**Contact:** John Busa
203-675-4714

***July, 1991***
*(call or write for exact dates)*
**Event:** Singles Retreat
**Chapel Rock Christian Church**
2220 North Girls School Road
Indianapolis, IN 46214
**Location:** FCA Camp in Marshall, Indiana
**Contact:** Paul E. Bledsoe
317-247-9739

***July, 1991***
*(call or write for exact dates)*
**Event:** Singles Retreat
**St. Luke's United Methodist Church**
700 Southway Boulevard East
Kokomo, IN 46902
**Contact:** Patricia Whillhite
317-453-4867

***August 1-4, 1991***
**Event:** Bible-Beach Conference
**First Baptist Church**
381 West Main Street
Hendersonville, TN 37075
**Location:** Panama City, Florida
**Contact:** Richard Gaia
615-824-6154

***August 3-10, 1991***
**Event:** Singles' Conference
**America's Keswick**
Keswick Grove
Whiting, NJ 98759
**Location:** America's Keswick, Whiting, New Jersey
**Contact:** 201-350-1187

***August 17-28, 1991***
**Event:** Retreat/Conference
**Second Baptist Church, Perth Amboy**
P.O. Box 1608/101 Broad Street
Perth Amboy, NJ 08862
**Location:** possibly Trinidad or Bahamas
**Contact:** Frances L. Stanton
201-826-5293

***August 22-September 2, 1991***
**Event:** Singles Labor Day Conference
**Village Baptist Church**
10600 North May Avenue
Oklahoma City, OK 73120
**Location:** New Mexico
**Contact:** Jay Shepherd
405-751-1951

***August 23-25, 1991***
**Event:** Singles Young Adult Retreat
**Victory Ranch (Regular Baptist Conference of Southern California)**
18080 Gilman Springs Road
Moreno Valley, CA 92360
**Location:** Victory Ranch, Moreno Valley, California
**Contact:** Gordon Nicholson, Administrator 714-654-7766

***August 30-***

***September 2,***
**Event:** Labor Day Weekend Singles' Retreat
Solo Con East, 324 - 68th St., Newport News, VA 236087
**Location:** Northern Virginia 4-H Center
**Contact:** 804-244-4649

***August 30-September 2, 1991***
**Event:** Singles' Weekend Camp
**South Dakota United Methodist Camps,** P.O. Box 460, Mitchell, SD 57301
**Contact:** 605-946-6552

***August 30-31, 1991***
**Event:** Singles' Conference and Bay Cruise
**The Old Landmark Church**
444 Alabama Street
Vallejo, CA 94590
**Contact:** Booker Chandler
707-557-9038

***August 30-September 2, 1991***
**Event:** Singles' Conference
**Mount Hermon Christian Conference Center**
P.O. Box 413
Mount Hermon, CA 95041
**Location:** Ponderosa Lodge, Mount Hermon, California
**Contact:** 408-335-4466

***August 30-September 2, 1991***
**Event:** Highland Conference/ Retreat Camp
**Hyde Park Baptist Church,** 3901 Speedway
Austin, TX 78751
**Contact:** John Walters
512-459-6587

***August 31-September 2, 1991***
**Event:** Singles' Retreat
**Thousand Pines, American Baptist Outdoor Center**
Box 3288, 359 Thousand Pines Road
Crestline, CA 92325
**Location:** Thousand Pines, American Baptist Outdoor Center, Crestline, California
**Contact:** 714-338-2705

***August 31-September 2, 1991***
**Event:** Acts 29-Labor Day Weekend
**South Fellowship**
3780 South Broadway
Englewood, CO 80014
**Contact:** Rob Cobb
303-761-8780

***August 31-September 2, 1991***
**Event:** Labor Day Retreat
**First Baptist Church**
Box 1080
Bartlesville, OK 74006
**Contact:** R.T. Shields
918-333-9607

***August 31-September 2, 1991***
**Event:** Singles Labor Day Weekend Campout
**Trinity Baptist Church**
1002 Cienegoitas Road
Santa Barbara, CA 93110
**Contact:** Mike Ballinger
805-687-7797

***August, 1991***
*(call or write for exact dates)*
**Event:** Camp Meeting
**New York Conference of Seventh Day Adventist**
P.O. Box 67
Syracuse, NY 13215
**Location:** Camp Cherokee
**Contact:** Carmen Gonzalez, 315-469-6921

***August, 1991***
*(call or write for exact dates)*
**Event:** Summer Explosion - Young Adults & Singles
**First Family Church**
8434 Greenleaf
Whittier, CA 90602
**Contact:** Douglas Healy
213-698-6737

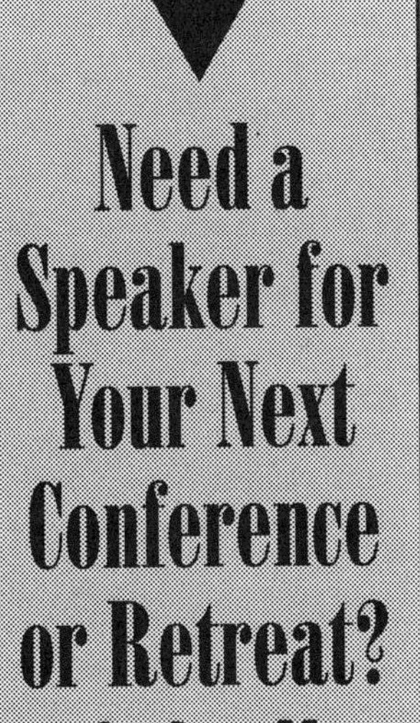


***August, 1991***
*(call or write for exact dates)*
**Event:** Singles Labor Day Conference
**New Faith Baptist Church**
4315 West Fuqua Road
Houston, TX 77045
**Contact:** Drew E. Marshall
713-433-6885

***September 6-7, 1991***
**Event:** Central Savannah River Area Single Adult Conference
**First Baptist Church**
3500 Walton Way
Augusta, GA 30909
**Contact:** Dr. J. Andrew Menger
404-733-2236

***September 13,14, 1991***
**Event:** "Becoming A Friend & Lover" Seminar, Dick Purnell - speaker
**Trinity Assembly of God,** 2122 West Joppa Rd
Lutherville, MD 21093
**Contact:** James A. Lex
301-821-6573

***September 13-15, 1991***
**Event:** Annual Fall Retreat for Single Adults
**Twin Pines Camp, Conference & Retreat Center,** 3000 Twin Pine Rd., Stroudsburg, PA 18360
**Location:** Twin Pines Camp, Stroudsburg, Pennsylvania
**Contact:** 717-629-2411

***September 13-15, 1991***
**Event:** Retreat, Harold Ivan Smith - Speaker
**Fair Oaks Presbyterian Church**
11427 Fair Oaks Boulevard
Fair Oaks, CA 95628
**Location:** Woodleaf
**Contact:** David Weidlich
916-967-4784

***September 14, 1991***
**Event:** Seminar To Remember
**First Baptist Church**
381 West Main Street
Hendersonville, TN 37075
**Contact:** Richard Gaia
615-824-6154

***September 19-22, 1991***
**Event:** Single Adult Extravaganza, Farris Gordon, Speaker; Keith Longbathem - Song Leader & Entertainer
**Fisherville Baptist Church,** P.O. Box 82
Fisherville, VA 22939
**Contact:** Ann Higgins
703-332-7098

***September 26-28, 1991***
**Event:** "Successful Single Living" Conference with Clyde Besson
**Trinity Baptist Church,** P.O. Box 3087
Lake Charles, LA 70602
**Contact:** John Kyle 318-439-8352

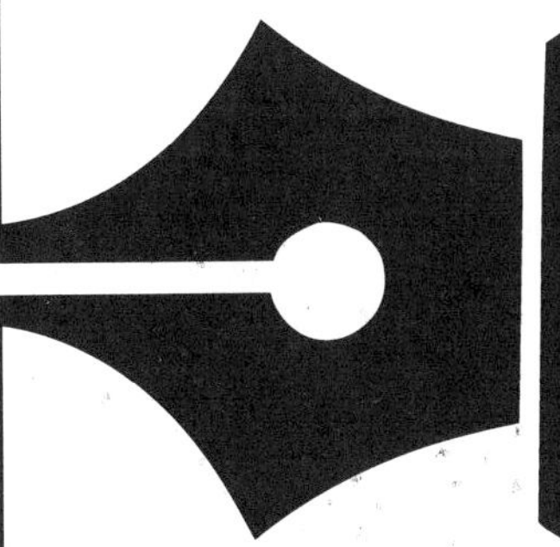

***September 27-29, 1991***
**Event:** 4th Annual Single Adult Conference
**Gull Lake Bible Conference**
1988 Midlake Drive
Hickory Corners, MI 49060
**Location:** Gull Lake Bible Conference, Hickory Corners, Michigan
**Contact:** 616-671-5155

***September, 1991***
*(call or write for exact dates)*
**Event:** Labor Day Singles' Retreat
**Sandia Baptist Church**
9429 Constitution, N.E.
Albuquerque, NM 87112
**Location:** West Coast, Glorieta, St. Louis or Ridge Crest
**Contact:** Elizabeth Riggins
505-299-7778

***September, 1991***
*(call or write for exact dates)*
**Event:** Singles' Labor Day Conference & Retreat
**Hermitage Hills Baptist Church**
3475 Lebanon Road
Hermitage, TN 37076
**Contact:** Gene Johnson
615-883-5034

***September, 1991***
*(call or write for exact dates)*
**Event:** Singles' Retreat
**Southeast Baptist Church**
1700 East 7000 South, P.O. Box 21399
Salt Lake City, UT 84121
**Location:** Glorieta, New Mexico
**Contact:** Peter Cieslewski
801-943-2241

***September, 1991***
*(call or write for exact dates)*
**Event:** Glorieta Single Adult Labor Day Conference
**Highland Baptist Church,** 4316 34th
Lubbock, TX 79410
**Contact:** Bob Batson
817-795-5910

***September, 1991***
*(call or write for exact dates)*
**Event:** Fall Retreat
**Grace Church, Edina**
5300 France Avenue South
Edina, MN 55410
**Contact:** Dave Gibson
612-926-1884

***September, 1991***
*(call or write for exact dates)*
**Event:** Singles Retreat
**Columbia-Mexico District Church,** 1910 Jackson ,
Columbia, MO 65202
**Location:** Blue Mountain
**Contact:** Marjorie Pickett
314-442-1353

***Fall - 1991***
*(call or write for exact dates)*
**Event:** Single Adult Conference
**First Baptist Church**
204 West Morgan Street
Brandon, FL 33510
**Contact:** Don Minton
813-689-1204

***Fall - 1991***
*(call or write for exact dates)*
**Event:** Mountain Retreat
**Rehoboth Baptist Church**
2997 Lawrenceville Highway
Tucker, GA 30084
**Contact:** John W. Rushing
404-939-3182

***Fall - 1991***
*(call or write for exact dates)*
**Event:** "God's Prescription for Mending" Seminar
**Christian Fellowship Church**
10237 Leesburg Pike
Vienna, VA 22182
**Contact:** Kelley Schroder
703-759-4210

***FALL - 1991***
*(call or write for exact dates)*
**Event:** Singles Retreat
**Countryside Christian Center**
1850 McMullen Booth Road
Clearwater, FL 34619
**Contact:** Nick Panico
813-799-1618

***Fall - 1991***
*(call or write for exact dates)*
**Event:** Singles' Conference
**Willoughby Hills Evangelical Friends Church**
2846 S.O.M. Center Road
Willoughby Hills, OH 44094
**Contact:** Craig Henry
216-944-1026

***Fall - 1991***
*(call or write for exact dates)*
**Event:** Single Adult Conference
**First Presbyterian Church**
1550 Pacific Avenue
Santa Rosa, CA 95404
**Location:** Westminster Woods, 6510 Bohemian Highway, Occidental, California
**Contact:** Gayle Turner
707-542-0205

***Fall - 1991***
*(call or write for exact dates)*
**Event:** Mountain Retreat
**Rehoboth Baptist Church**
2997 Lawrenceville Highway
Tucker, GA 30084
**Contact:** John W. Rushing
404-939-3182

***Fall - 1991***
*(call or write for exact dates)*
**Event:** Singles' Celebration
**Trinity Fellowship**
7910 South Bell
Amarillo, TX 79110
**Contact:** Jerry Billington
806-355-5652

***Fall - 1991***
*(call or write for exact dates)*
**Event:** Singles Crusade, Dick Purnell - Speaker
**The Neighborhood Church**
20600 John Drive
Castro Valley, CA 94546
**Contact:** Malcolm Cash
415-537-4690

***October 4-5, 1991***
**Event:** Singles' Workshop/ Seminar
**SOLO (sponsored by North Indiana Conference United Methodist Church)**
Epworth Forest Conference Center, North Webster, IN
**Contact:** Reverend Joe Smith, Box 5, Larwill, IN 46764, 219-834-2212

***October 4-6, 1991***
**Event:** Fall Retreat, Dick Purnell - Speaker
**Elmbrook Church**
777 South Barker Road
Waukesha, WI 53186
**Contact:** Lorin Staats
414-786-7051

***October 4-6, 1991***
**Event:** Singles' Retreat
**Cedine Bible Camp & Conference Center**
Route #1, Box 2390
Spring City, TN 37391
**Location:** Cedine Bible Camp & Conference Center, Spring City, Tennessee
**Contact:** 615-365-9565

***October 4-7, 1991***
**Event:** October Breakers, Ocean Retreat for Singles, Rick Hodge - Speaker
**Crossroads Neighborhood Church**
7555 Old Military Road, N.E.
Bremeton, WA 98310
**Contact:** Scott Turner
206-692-1672

***October 11-13, 1991***
**Event:** Tri-State Christian Singles' Retreat
**United Christian Youth Camp,**
1400 Paradise Valley Road,
Prescott, AZ 86303
**Contact:** 602-445-0391

***October 12-14, 1991***
**Event:** Singles Retreat
**Christian Fellowship Church**
10237 Leesburg Pike
Vienna, VA 22182
**Location:** Virginia Beach
**Contact:** Kelley Schroder
703-759-4210

***October 12-14, 1991***
**Event:** Fall Retreat
**The Peoples' Church**
374 Sheppard Avenue East
Toronto, Ontario, Canada
M2N 3B6
**Contact:** Glen Eagleson
416-222-3341

***October 12-13, 1991***
**Event:** LA District Church of the Nazarene Encampment
**L.A. District Church of the Nazarene**
P.O. Box 473
Baskin, LA 71219
**Location:** Pineville, Louisiana
**Contact:** Elizabeth Rigdon
318-248-2381

***October 12-23, 1991***
**Event:** Florida United Methodist Singles Retreat
**First United Methodist Church**
142 East Jackson Street
Orlando, FL 32804
**Contact:** Nancy Wood
407-849-6080

***October 12-23, 1991***
**Event:** Singles Retreat
**First Presbyterian Church of Salinas**
830 Padre Drive
Salinas, CA 93901
**Location:** Camp Koinonia, Watsonville, CA
**Contact:** Peter Cantu
408-422-7811

***October 16-18, 1991***
**Event:** Singles' Conference with Dr. Archibald Hart, Speaker
**Alpine Covenant Conference Center**
P.O. Box 155
Blue Jay, CA 92317
**Location:** Alpine Covenant Conference Center, Blue Jay, California
**Contact:** 714-337-6287

***October 18-20, 1991***
**Event:** Fall Retreat
**Park Street Church**
One Park Street
Boston, MA 02108
**Contact:** Doug Calhoun
617-523-3383

***October 25-27, 1991***
**Event:** Single Adult Conference
**Westminster Woods Presbyterian**
6510 Bohemian Highway
Occidental, CA 94565-9106
**Contact:** Bob Cordier
707-874-2426

***October 27, 28, 1991***
**Event:** Haunted Hayride, horseback riding
**High Places Ranch Camp**
P.O. Box 97
Mt. Morris, PA 15349
**Contact:** 412-324-2770 (or 324-2023) - Kingwood Pike, Morgantown, WV 26505

***October, 1991***
*(call or write for exact dates)*
**Event:** Retreat
**The Stone Church**
45 Davenport Road
Toronto, Ontario, Canada M5R 1H2
**Contact:** Michael Krause
416-928-0101

***October, 1991***
*(call or write for exact dates)*
**Event:** Singles' Celebration
**Prestonwood Baptist Church**
15720 Hillcrest
Dallas, TX 75248
**Contact:** Steve Cretin
214-387-4475

***October, 1991***
*(call or write for exact dates)*
**Event:** Retreat
**Lake Avenue Congregational Church**
393 North Lake Avenue
Pasadena, CA 91101
**Location:** Southern California
**Contact:** Steve Morgan
818-795-7221

***October, 1991***
*(call or write for exact dates)*
**Event:** Single's Celebration
**Hoffmantown Baptist Church**
8888 Harper Drive, N.E.
Albuquerque, NM 87111
**Contact:** Paul A. Gossett
505-828-2600

***October, 1991***
*(call or write for exact dates)*
**Event:** Retreat
**First Evangelical Free Church**
2223 North Mulford Road
Rockford, IL 61107
**Location:** Timber-Lee Christian Center
**Contact:** Wayne & Sharon Hilden 815-877-7046

***October, 1991***
*(call or write for exact dates)*
**Event:** Singles Retreat
**First Assembly of God**
2720 North Kesting Court
Appleton, WI 54914
**Contact:** Pastor Joe Ellis
414-738-3040

***October, 1991***
*(call or write for exact dates)*
**Event:** Singles Conference for Central California
**First Assembly of God**
3737 West Walnut
Visalia, CA 93277
**Contact:** Dan Holford
209-733-9504

***October, 1991***
*(call or write for exact dates)*
**Event:** October Singlefest
**Eastside Baptist Church**
1220 East Bryan Street/P.O. Box 1586
Douglas, GA 31533
**Contact:** Dr. John Dobbins, 912-384-7266

***October, 1991***
*(call or write for exact dates)*
**Event:** Singles Retreat
**First Baptist Church, Dade City**
417 West Church Avenue
Dade City, FL 33525
**Location:** Eustes, FL; sponsored by Lake Vale Baptist Assembly
**Contact:** Robin Quesenberry
904-567-3265

***November 8-10, 1991***
**Event:** Fall Retreat with Jary Corty
**The Valley Church**
10885 North Stelling Road
Cupertino, CA 95014
**Contact:** Richard Krikorian
408-739-4642

***November 15-16, 1991***
**Event:** Fall Singles' Conference (focusing on relationships)
**Trinity Baptist Church**
1002 Cienegoitas Road
Santa Barbara, CA 93110
**Contact:** Mike Ballinger
805-687-7797

***November 15-16, 1991***
**Event:** Singles' Fall Retreat
**Village Baptist Church**
10600 North May Avenue
Oklahoma City, OK 73120
**Contact:** Jay Shepherd
405-751-1951

***November 23-25, 1991***
**Event:** Singles' Conference
**America's Keswick**
Keswick Grove
Whiting, NJ 08759
**Location:** America's Keswick, Whiting, New Jersey
**Contact:** 210-350-1187

***November 28-29, 1991***
**Event:** Thanksgiving Celebration with Pete Carlson
**Gloucester County Community Church**
P.O. Box 266
Pitman, NJ 08071
**Contact:** Robert Barber
609-582-0222

***November 29-December, 1991***
**Event:** Singles Conference
**The Navigators, %Glen Eyrie**
P.O. Box 6000
Colorado Springs, CO 80934
**Location:** Glen Eyrie Christian Conference Center
**Contact:** 719-598-1212, ext. 460

***November 29-December, 1991***
**Event:** Singles' Retreat
**Hartland Christian Camp**
P.O. Box 25
Badger, CA 93603
**Location:** Hartland Christian Camp, Badger, California
**Contact:** 209-337-2349

***December 5, 1991***
**Event:** Singles' Christmas Banquet
**Village Baptist Church**
10600 North May Avenue
Oklahoma City, OK 73120
**Contact:** Jay Shepherd
405-751-1951

# 1992

***January 19-21, 1992***
**Event:** Single Life Celebration
**First Baptist Church**
P.O. Box 1000
Columbia, SC 29202
**Contact:** Clif Smith
803-256-4251

***January, 1992***
*(call or write for exact dates)*
**Event:** Weekend Retreat (offered by North Indiana Conference)
**St. Luke's United Methodist Church**
700 Southway Boulevard East
Kokomo, IN 46902
**Contact:** Patricia Willhite
317-453-4867

***March 6-7, 1992***
**Event:** Singles' Convention
**Overlake Christian Church**
9051 132nd Avenue, N.E.
Kirkland, WA 98034
**Contact:** Gary Winkleman
206-827-0303

***March 6-8, 1992***
**Event:** Celebrate Singleness Conference;
Harold Ivan Smith - Speaker
**Collier Street Church**
112 Collier Street
Barrie, Ontario, Canada L4M 1H3
**Contact:** Arthur Hiley
705-726-1511

***March 7, 1992***
**Event:** Tri-State Singles' Conference
**Garfield Park Church of God**
401 East Southern Avenue
Indianapolis, IN 46225
**Contact:** Sue Whitesel
317-786-0426

***March, 1992***
*(call or write for exact dates)*
**Event:** Oklahoma Single Adult Conference
**Northwest Baptist Church**
2200 North Drexel
Oklahoma City, OK 73107
**Contact:** Steve Fine
405-942-5557

***Spring, 1992***
*(call or write for exact dates)*
**Event:** Annual Advent & Lenten Retreat
**St. Michael & All Angels Episcopal Church**
P.O. Box 12385
Dallas, TX 75225
**Contact:** Tom Blackmon
214-363-5471

***Spring, 1992***
*(call or write for exact dates)*
**Event:** Annual Spring Camping Weekend
**St. Michael & All Angels Episcopal Church,** P.O. Box 12385
Dallas, TX 75225
**Contact:** Tom Blackmon 214-363-5471

***Spring, 1992***
*(call or write for exact dates)*
**Event:** Singles' Spring Retreat
**Hoffmantown Baptist Church**
8888 Harper Drive, N.E.
Albuquerque, NM 87111
**Contact:** Paul A. Gossett
505-828-2600

***Spring, 1992***
*(call or write for exact dates)*
**Event:** Westminster Woods Single Adults Conference
**First Presbyterian Church**
1550 Pacific Avenue
Santa Rosa, CA 95404
**Location:** 6510 Bohemian Highway, Occidental, California
**Contact:** Gayle Turner
707-542-0205

***April, 1992***
*(call or write for exact dates)*
**Event:** Singles' Retreat
**First Baptist Church of Dade City**
417 West Church Avenue
Dade City, FL 33525
**Location:** Lake Vale Baptist Assembly in Eustes, Florida
**Contact:** Robin Quesenberry
904-567-3265

***April 10-12, 1992***
**Event:** Tri-State Christian Singles' Retreat
**United Christian Youth Camp**
1400 Paradise Valley Road
Prescott, AZ 86303-4926
**Contact:** 602-445-0391

***May 4-5, 1992***
**Event:** Singles' Conference
**Farmer Memorial Baptist Church**
293 South Kingsway
Toronto, Ontario, Canada
**Contact:** Reverend Bill Webster
416-762-3061

***May 22-24, 1991***
**Event:** Retreat
**Kent Church of the Nazarene**
930 East James
Kent, WA 98031
**Location:** Miracle Ranch
**Contact:** Gary L. Waller
206-852-5144

***May, 1992***
*(call or write for exact dates)*
**Event:** Arizona District Singles' Memorial Weekend Retreat
**West Rose Lane Assembly of God**
6145 North 36th Drive
Phoenix, AZ 85019
**Location:** District Campgrounds, Prescott, Arizona
**Contact:** Wesley G. Hodgkin
602-841-0610

***May, 1992***
*(call or write for exact dates)*
**Event:** Weekend Retreat (offered by North Indiana Conference)
**St. Luke's United Methodist Church**
700 Southway Boulevard East,
Kokomo, IN 46902
**Contact:** Patricia Willhite,
317-453-4867

***May, 1992***
*(call or write for exact dates)*
**Event:** Retreat
**Lake Avenue Congregational Church**
393 North Lake Avenue
Pasadena, CA 91101
**Contact:** Steve Morgan
818-795-7221

***June, 1992***
*(call or write for exact dates)*
**Event:** Conference
**Lakeview Temple**
47 Beachway Drive
Indianapolis, IN 46224
**Contact:** Reverend Thomas W. Rakoczy
317-243-9396

***Summer, 1992***
*(call or write for exact dates)*
**Event:** Summer Lake Days
**St. Michael & All Angels Episcopal Church**
P.O. Box 12385
Dallas, TX 75225
**Contact:** Tom Blackmon
214-363-5471

***July 4, 1992***
**Event:** Singles' Bar-B-Que
**The Old Landmark Church**
444 Alabama Street
Vallejo, CA 94590
**Contact:** Booker Chandler
707-557-9038

***July, 1992***
*(call or write for exact dates)*
**Event:** Singles' Conference
**Farmer Memorial Baptist Church**
293 South Kingsway
Toronto, Ontario, Canada
**Contact:** Reverend Bill Webster
416-762-3061

***July, 1992***
*(call or write for exact dates)*
**Event:** Weekend Retreat (offered by North Indiana Conference)
**St. Luke's United Methodist Church**
700 Southway Boulevard East,
Kokomo, IN 46902
**Contact:** Patricia Willhite,
317-453-4867

***August 28-29, 1992***
**Event:** Singles' Conference and Bay Cruise
**The Old Landmark Church**
444 Alabama Street
Vallejo, CA 94590
**Contact:** Booker Chandler, 707-557-9038

***September, 1992***
*(call or write for exact dates)*
**Event:** Singles' Labor Day Conference & Retreat
**Hermitage Hills Baptist Church**
3475 Lebanon Road
Hermitage, TN 37076
**Contact:** Gene Johnson
615-883-5034

***September, 1992***
*(call or write for exact dates)*
**Event:** Acts 29 -Labor Day Weekend
**South Fellowship**
3780 South Broadway
Englewood, CO 80014
**Contact:** Rob Cobb
303-761-8780

***Fall, 1992***
*(call or write for exact dates)*
**Event:** Singles' Conference (tentative)
**Willoughby Hills Evangelical Friends Church**
2846 S.O.M. Center Road
Willoughby Hills, OH 44094
**Contact:** Craig Henry
216-944-1026

***Fall, 1992***
*(call or write for exact dates)*
**Event:** Mountain Retreat
**Rehoboth Baptist Church**
2997 Lawrenceville Highway
Tucker, GA 30084
**Contact:** John W. Rushing,
404-939-3182

***October 23-25, 1992***
**Event:** Single Adult Conference
**Westminster Woods Presbyterian Church**
6510 Bohemian Highway
Occidental, CA 94565-9106
**Contact:** Bob Cordier
707-874-2426

***October, 1992***
*(call or write for exact dates)*
**Event:** Singles' Celebration
**Hoffmantown Baptist Church**
8888 Harper Drive, N.E.
Albuquerque, NM 87111
**Contact:** Paul A. Gossett
505-828-2600

***October, 1992***
*(call or write for exact dates)*
**Event:** Singles' Conference
**Second Baptist Church, Perth Amboy**
P.O. Box 1608/101 Broad Street
Perth Amboy, NJ 08862
**Contact:** Frances L. Stanton
201-826-5293

***October, 1992***
*(call or write for exact dates)*
**Event:** Singles' Retreat
**First Presbyterian Church of Salinas**
830 Padre Drive
Salinas, CA 93901
**Location:** Camp Koinonia, Watsonville, California
**Contact:** Peter Cantu
408-422-7811

***October, 1992***
*(call or write for exact dates)*
**Event:** Singlefest
**Eastside Baptist Church**
1220 East Bryan Street/P.O. Box 1586, Douglas, GA 31533
**Contact:** Dr. John Dobbins
912-384-7266

***October, 1992***
*(call or write for exact dates)*
**Event:** Singles' Celebration
**Prestonwood Baptist Church**
15720 Hillcrest
Dallas, TX 75248
**Contact:** Steve Cretin
214-387-4475

Save Over $4 Each

To order additional copies of this *National Resource Directory* see page 248.

Get a copy for each member of your leadership team.

Save money by ordering five or more copies.

***October, 1992***
*(call or write for exact dates)*
**Event:** Retreat
**Lake Avenue Congregational Church**
393 North Lake Avenue
Pasadena, CA 91101
**Location:** Southern California
**Contact:** Steve Morgan
818-795-7221

***October, 1992***
*(call or write for exact dates)*
**Event:** Singles' Retreat
**First Baptist Church of Dade City**
417 West Church Avenue
Dade City, FL 33525
**Location:** Lake Vale Baptist Assembly in Eustes, Florida
**Contact:** Robin Quesenberry
904-567-3265

***October, 1992***
*(call or write for exact dates)*
**Event:** Retreat
**First Evangelical Free Church**
2223 North Mulford Road
Rockford, IL 61107
**Location:** Timber-Lee Christian Center
**Contact:** Wayne & Sharon Hilden 815-877-7046

***October, 1992***
*(call or write for exact dates)*
**Event:** Florida United Methodist Singles' Retreat
**First United Methodist Church**
142 East Jackson Street
Orlando, FL 32804
**Contact:** Nancy Wood
407-849-6080

***November 20-21, 1992***
**Event:** Singles' Conference and Bay Cruise
**The Old Landmark Church**
444 Alabama Street
Vallejo, CA 94590
**Contact:** Booker Chandler
707-557-9038

***November, 1992***
*(call or write for exact dates)*
**Event:** Retreat
**Lakeview Temple**
47 Beachway Drive
Indianapolis, IN 46224
**Contact:** Reverend Thomas W. Rakoczy 317-243-9396

"SINGLE ADULT MINISTRIES JOURNAL IS THE BEST RESOURCE OF ITS KIND. I READ IT COMPLETELY—USUALLY THE DAY IT ARRIVES—AND AM NEVER DISAPPOINTED. IT IS THE FIRST PUBLICATION I RECOMMEND TO ANYONE SERIOUS ABOUT A MINISTRY WITH SINGLES."

- DICK DUNN

ROSWELL UNITED METHODIST CHURCH, ROSWELL, GEORGIA

Call toll FREE today to get your subscription started.
**800-487-4-SAM or 719-488-2610**
Or write: *SAM Journal*, P. O. Box 62056,
Colorado Springs, Colorado 80962-2056.

A one-year subscription is $24 (10 issues); $29 in Canada; $33 for all other countries.
*U. S. funds only*. Payment by Visa, MasterCard, or "bill me" also available.

## *Part 6*

# Seminaries, Denominations and Missions Agencies

### Where To Find It:

# SEMINARY INFORMATION

**Would you like to do further study in the expanding field of single adult ministry? Here is a list of seminaries (along with some colleges) that provide such opportunities.**

## Bethany Bible College

26 Western St.
Sussex, New Brunswick, Canada
EOE-1PO/(506) 433-3668
**Contact:** Dr. Wm. Burbury, Vice President Academic Affairs
**Courses Offered:** Offers a number of courses in its Youth Ministries major: Leadership; Volunteer Ministry (How to acquire & train them); Counseling; Music; Broken Homes; Family Stress; Creative Ministries; Spiritual Walk; Young Adult Ministry & several others.

## Canadian Theological Seminary

4400 Fourth Ave.
Regina Saskatchewan, Canada
54T-0H8
(306) 545-1515 Ext. 247
**Contact:** Dr. James A. Davies, Associate Professor of Christian Education
**Courses Offered:** Church Ministries to Adults; Church Ministries to Singles; Family Life and Ministry; Church Ministries to Seniors.

## Central Baptist Theological Seminary

Seminary Heights
741 North 31st Street
Kansas City, KS 66102-3964
(800) 677-CBTS
**Contact:** John R. Landgraf, Ph.D., President and Professor of Theology and the Personality Sciences (913) 371-5313
**Courses offered:** Understanding and Ministering to Single Adults; Crisis Counseling; Introduction to Pastoral Care and Counseling; Human Sexuality in Christian Perspective; and others.
**Other:** Dr. Landgraf holds seminars/workshops and lectures on Singling and Singlehood (learning to live the single life).

## Dallas Seminary

3909 Swiss Avenue
Dallas, TX 75204
(214) 824-3094
**Contact:** Dr. Kenn Gangel, Department Chairman
**Courses offered:** Adult Ed. Ministry, Christian Home, Seminar on Family Problems.

## Fuller Theological Seminary

Pasadena, CA 91182
(800) 235-2222
**Contact:** Dr. Julie Gorman
**Courses offered:** Our Christian Formation and Discipleship Program includes courses applicable for ministry to single adults. Specific courses of interest would include: Adult Formation and Discipleship, Stages of Adult Development, and Ministry to Single Adults. (Issues concerning children of divorce are included in youth ministry courses.)

## Lincoln Christian College

100 Campus View Drive
Lincoln, IL 62656
(217) 732-3168
**Contact:** Dr. Gary Bussmann, Department Head—Christian Education
**Courses Offered:** One course, "Singles Ministry," in the context of Adult Education Specialization for a Christian Ed. Major.

## Methodist Theological School in Ohio

3081 Columbus Pike
Delaware, OH 43015
(614) 363-1146
**Contact:** Jay Edel, Director of Admissions, or Ed Trimmer, Associate Professor of Christian Education
**Courses Offered:** Offer a degree in Christian Education. The degree is designed so that one can specialize in any area they desire through supervised studies, individualized course and field education placements. They also address the areas of single adults, not through separate classes, but as part of courses in "Campus Ministry," "Family Ministry," "Older Adults," "Faith Development," etc.
**Other:** Several instructors are involved in writing and projects that relate to single adult ministry.

## New Orleans Baptist Theological Seminary

3939 Gentilly Boulevard
New Orleans, LA 70126
(504) 286-3617
**Contact:** Dr. Ferris Jordan, Professor of Adult Education
**Courses Offered:** 400-557 Ministry with Single Adults; 400-555 Family Life Education.
**Other:** Dr. Jordan has published a book regarding singles, *Living Values for Today's Singles*, and authored articles for *The Christian Single* (magazine). Additionally, the seminary also provides continuing educational opportunities related to starting and maintaining a single adult ministry in a church.

## North Park Theological

3225 W Foster Ave.
Chicago, IL 60625
(312) 583-2700
**Contact:** Dr. Francis Anderson, Professor of Christian Education
**Other:** No degree now, but plan to offer a degree in the Fall of 1991. Some current courses include segments or focus on Single Adult Ministries

## Steinbach Bible College

Box 1420 Steinbach
MB Canada R0A 2A0
(204) 326-6451
**Contact:** Gordon Daman, Public Relations Director
**Courses Offered:** Pastoral Care courses include Single Adult Ministry in curriculum.

## Trevecca Nazarene College

333 Murfeesboro Rd.
Nashville, TN. 37210

### Which Seminaries Are Having the Greatest Influence In the Field Of Single Adult Ministry?

Based on the results of a national survey of more than 600 singles ministry leaders, 16% said they have taken seminary or graduate course work specifically in single adult ministry. Those seminaries most attended by singles ministry leaders are:

1. Southwestern Baptist Seminary
2. Fuller Theological Seminary
3. Perkins School of Theology
   Southern Baptist Theological Seminary
   Talbot Theological Seminary
4. Bethel Theological Seminary
   New Orleans Baptist Theological Seminary

(615) 248-1308
**Contact:** Joe E. Bowers, Associate Professor of Christian Education
**Degree:** Special singles ministry emphasis offered by students' choice under Adult Ministries Classes and the Director of Christian Education degree.

### United Theological Seminary

1810 Harvard Boulevard
Dayton, OH 45406
(513) 278-5817
**Contact:** Debbie Holder, Christian Education Program Assistant.
**Courses Offered:** A person can take any of the following courses and specialize in single adult ministry: Christian Education of Adults; Beginning a Teaching Ministry; Life Stages: Educational Ministry to the Whole Congregation; Resources for Teaching; What is Christian Education?: Theoretical Foundations; Teaching the Bible; Administration of Christian Education.

### Wartburg Theological Seminary

333 Wartburg Place
Dubuque, IA 52001
(319) 589-0200
**Contact:** Dr. Norma Everist, Associate Professor of Educational Ministry
**Courses Offered:** Courses dealing with adult developmental stages and varieties of singleness are offered.

**EDITOR's NOTE:** In preparing this section of the directory, we mailed a questionnaire to every seminary in the United States and Canada. Those listed above are those who responded to this survey stating that they had courses/programs of interest to those seeking education in the field of single adult ministry. If you are aware of any other seminaries that offer courses in the field of single adult ministry, please contact us so that we can include them in future editions of this directory. Send this information to: SAM Resource Directory, P. O. Box 60430, Colorado Springs, CO 80960-0430. *Thanks for your help in making this the most complete Directory possible.*

# DENOMINATIONAL INFORMATION

**Here is a listing of those Denominational organizations and agencies who have a specific involvement in single adult ministry.**

### Antiochan Orthodox Archdiocese

Route 711 North
P.O. Box 638
Ligonier, PA 15658
**Contact:**
The Rt. Reverend George Gena
Department of Youth
(412) 238-3677
**Calendar/Events:**
Six Regional Conferences in which single adults participate — contact above for further information

### Assemblies of God

1445 Boonville Ave.
Springfield, MO 65807
**Contact:**
Bill Campbell, Adult Ministries Consultant, Sunday School Dept. (417) 862-2781
**Calendar/Events:**
Leadership Training Conference

### Baptist Convention Of Ontario & Quebec

217 St. George Street
Toronto, Ontario, Canada
M5R 2M2
**Contact:**
Rev. Dr. Bill Webster
Coordinator of Singles Ministry (416) 922-5163
**SAM Resources/Publications:**
"Journey"- Quarterly Newsletter featuring articles, information, events, etc.
**Calendar/Events:**
Singles Conference May 3-5 1991, McMaster University (Doug Fagerstrom - speaker); Single Adult Camp First week of July 1991, Baptist Camp; Kwasind Single Parent Family Camp last week of July 1991, Baptist Camp; Hermosa Singles Ministry Seminar November 1990-91, McMaster Divinity College

### Canadian Conference of Mennonite Brethren Churches

3-169 Riverton Avenue
Winnipeg, Manitoba, Canada
R2L 2E5
**Contact:**
David Wiebe, Executive Director (204) 669-6575
**Publications:**
"Idea Bank" - quarterly paper for working with singles

### Church of The Brethren General Offices

1451 Dundee Avenue
Elgin, IL 60120
**Contact:**
Chris Michael, Staff for Young Adult Ministry (708)742-5100

### Church of God/Anderson

2935 E. 6th Street
Anderson, IN 46012
(317) 644-7721
**Contact:**
William A. White

### Church of God

P.O. Box 2430
Cleveland, TN 37320
**Contact:**
T. David Sustar, Asst. International Director of Youth & Christian Education
(615) 478-7222
**Calendar/Events:**
National Singles Conference Nov. 9-11 1991, Perdido Beach, Alabama

### Church of God (Seventh Day Adventist)

P.O. Box 33677
Denver, CO 80233
**Contact:**
Calvin Burrell, President
(303) 452-7973

## Elim Fellowship

7245 College Street
Lima, NY 14485
**Contact:**
Rev. Joseph Jansen, Director, Mobilized to Serve
(716) 582-2790
**Calendar/Events:**
Mobilized To Serve North American Singles Conference, Nov. 16-18 '90 in Wyndham Franklin Plaza Hotel, Philadelphia, PA;
Mobilized to Serve 1991 Regional Singles Conferences: Greenbelt, MD Feb. 22-24 '91; Stamford, CT-Mar. 1-3 '91; Pittsburgh, PA Mar. 15-17 '91; S. Portland, ME-Apr.. 5-7 '91; Troy, MI-Apr. 19-21 '91; Lima, NY-May 17-19 '91
**Other:** Singles Leadership Days. Also: working on "Friends First: God's Plan to Relationships" a book on Christian dating from adult single perspective. (Author: Stacy Cline, Dean of Students at Elim Bible Institute, Lima, NY.)

## Evangelical Presbyterian Church

26049 Five Mile
Detroit, MI 48239
**Contact:**
Reverend L. Edward Davis, Stated Clerk
(313) 532-9555

## The Holy Apostolic Catholic (Assyrian) Church of The East

8908 Birch Avenue
Morton Grove, IL 60053
**Contact:**
The Most Rev. Mar Aprim Bishop, The Ordinary of the Diocese (Bishop)
(708) 966-0009

## Mennonite Church/ General Conference Mennonite Church

722 Main, Box 347
Newton, KS 67114-0347
**Contact:**
Ken Hawkley, Secretary for Adult/Young Adult Education
(316) 283-5100
**SAM Resources/Publications:**
"In Search" - quarterly newsletter focusing on topics of interest to young adults and students in transition. Goes to about 10,000 Mennonite students and 'scattered' young adults.
"Feedback" - quarterly congregational resource for young adults.

## Church of the Nazarene

6401 The Paseo
Kansas City, MO 64131
(816) 333-7000
**Contact:**
Linda Hardin, General Coordinator of Single Adult Ministries
**Calendar/Events:**
Several regional singles conferences plus single parenting conferences. (Write or call for complete details.)

## Pentecostal Assemblies of Canada

6745 Century Avenue
Mississauga, Ontario, Canada
L5N 6P7
**Contact:**
Rev. Rick Hiebert, Family Ministries Director
(416) 542-6460

## Pentecostal Free Will Baptist

P.O. Box 1568
Dunn, NC 28335
**Contact:**
Rev. J.T. Hammond, Christian Education Director
(919) 892-4161
**Calendar/Events:**
Single Adult Retreat - for all singles held in March of each year at the denominations youth camp facilities. The Retreat focus is fellowship, worship, and information relative to problems faced by singles.
Monthly meetings are held with singles; district chapters are being organized; special trips are planned during the year.

## Reformed Church In America

Office for Education and Faith Development
42 North Broadway
Tarrytown, NY 10591
**Contact:**
Jane Richardson, Associate for Young Adult Ministry
(914) 332-1311

## St. Gerard Parish

Young Adult Ministry
5550 W. Mall #3138
Lansing, MI 48917
**Contact:**
Anita Buessing, Young Adult Coordinator
(517) 323-2379
**SAM Resources/Publications:**
"VOICE" - Diocesan newsletter for Young Adults;
"Catholic Alumni Club of Lansing" - Newsletter;
"VIP" - Very Important Parties - Newsletter;
"CLASS" - Catholic Lansing Area Singles - Newsletter
**Calendar/Events:**
Leadership Development Program-Diocese; Young Adult Ministry (Gary Ashby - 517-342-2495 );
CHOICE Weekends - Paul Dagenais (303) 750-8155

## United Methodist

General Board of Discipleship
Box 840
Nashville, TN 37202
**Contact:**
Rev. Karen Greenwaldt
(615) 340-7132
**Calendar/Events:**
National Training Meeting for Leaders (United Methodist) of Single Adults

## Wesleyan Church

Box 50434
Indianapolis, IN 46250
**Contact:**
Larry Mitchell, Director of Young Adults International
(317) 576-8140
**SAM Resources/Publications:**
VUE Magazine - 3 times a year
Packet of training, curriculum, resources, etc. (5 per year)

**EDITOR's NOTE:** In preparing this section of the directory, we mailed a questionnaire to every denomination in the United States and Canada. Those listed above are those who responded to this survey. If you are aware of other denominations that offer specific ministries of interest to single adults, please contact us so that we can include them in future editions of this directory. Send this information to: SAM Resource Directory, P. O. Box 60430, Colorado Springs, CO 80960-0430. *Thanks for your help in making this the most complete Directory possible.*

**Looking For a Name For Your Singles Class or Group?**

Read through the Network (page 199) and let it be a catalyst for some creative name ides that can work for you.

# MISSIONS AGENCIES AND ORGANIZATIONS

**If you or your singles ministry would like to explore involvement in a short-term missions project, here is a list of some organizations and people who may be able to help.**

## A Growing Number of Single Adults Are Getting Involved in Short-term Missions

According to researcher Doug Millham, the short-term missions movement has had an exponential growth of more than one thousand percent over the past ten years. In fact, the growth of short-termers -- as compared to career missionaries -- has been phenomenal since 1967.

The growing single adult population has been one of the reasons short-term missions has seen such increased involvement.

Authors Engel and Jones, in their book, *Baby Boomers and The Future of World Missions*, describe how single adults are one of the most likely groups to get involved in short-term missions.

According to them, 43% of all Christian boomers are interested in volunteering for a short period (one month or less) with a Christian organization overseas. Specifically, those most willing to volunteer include:

- **Those 35 or younger:** 54% of those born since 1955 are interested and willing, compared to only 33% of those born prior to 1955;
- **Single adults:** More than 67% of the singles are open to this form of service, compared to only 36% for marrieds;
- **Those who have visited a Christian organization on site overseas:** Of the 22% who have done this, a remarkable 74% are interested in doing so again.

To explore short-term missions possibilities further, contact any of the following people.

### A.C.M.C.
**Ray Howard**
P.O. Box 24762
Denver, CO 80224

### Bridge Builders, Incorporated
**Chris Eaton**
9925 7th Way North #102
St. Petersburg, FL 33702

### Campus Crusade for Christ
**Beverly Jones and Milton Monnell**
Arrowhead Springs
San Bernardino, CA 92414

### Discover the World
**Doug and Jacquelyn Millham**
3255 East Orange Grove Boulevard
Pasadena, CA 91107

### English Language Institute/China
**Lois Broyles**
P.O. Box 265
San Dimas, CA 91773

### Gordon College
**Terry Bulicek and Sherrell Howe**
255 Grapevine
Wenham, MA 01984

### InterVarsity
**Scott Bessenecker**
P.O. Box 7895
Madison, WI 53707
or
**Linda Olson**
3181 South York Street
Englewood, CO 80110

### Life Ministries
**Kim Banton**
P.O. Box 200
San Dimas, CA 91773

### Mission to the World/SIMA
**Dan Camp**
P.O. Box 29765
Atlanta, GA 30359

### Missions Outreach International
**Jim Eschenbrenner**
P.O. Box 73
Bethany, MO 64424

### Northwestern College
**Becky King**
101 7th Street, N.W.
Orange City, IA 51041

### Overseas Crusades (STEP)
**Judy Shewey**
25 Corning Avenue
Milpitas, CA 95035

### SPRINT (WOF)
**Howard Lisech**
Box 585603
Orlando, FL 32585

### Sterling College
**Suzy Gaeddert**
Box 181
Sterling, KS 67579

### Student Missionary Project
**John Yoder**
Wheaton College
Wheaton, IL 60187

### Student Outreach
**David L. Hersberger**
Messiah College
Grantham, PA 17027

## Taylor World Outreach

**John Hein or Kathy Hassot**
Taylor University
Upland, IN 46989

## TEAM

**Barry Hancock**
P.O. Box 969
Wheaton, IL 60189-0969

## WEC

**Jill and Andrew Miles**
P.O. Box 1707
Fort Washington, PA 19034

## Wheaton College Christian Outreach

**Dennis Massaro**
Wheaton College
Wheaton, IL 60187

## World Concern

**Lisa Espinosa**
19303 Fremont Avenue North
Seattle, WA 98133

## World Relief

**Dr. Muriel Elmer**
450 East Gundersen
Carol Stream, IL 60188

## World Servants

**Ken Kendall**
8233 Gator Lane #6
West Palm Beach, FL 33411

## Wycliffe Translators

**Mark and Susan Chadwick**
720 West Victoria Apt. 2
Costa Mesa, CA 92627

## YUGO Ministries

**Leonard Janssen**
1622 Aurora Drive
El Centro, CA 92243

## Youth With A Mission

**Jim Rogers**
Box 1380
Lindale, TX 75771

**TO LEARN MORE ABOUT SHORT-TERM MISSIONS, ATTEND:**

**Miami '92**
**A Leadership Training Conference to Equip and Mobilize Single Adults for Short-Term Missions Teams**
(For complete details, write: P. O. Box 52-7900, Miami, FL 33152-7900 or call Donna at 305-884-8400.)

BRIDGE BUILDERS INC.

# Making SHORT-TERM MISSION a reality for your singles group!

*Bridge Builders can help you turn your dreams for meaningful short-term mission into reality. We offer all the assistance you need, including:*

- **Training** *for team members and leader(s).*
- **Logistics** *including travel, lodging, liaison with suitable host agencies or churches.*
- **On-field support** *including Bridge Builder personnel, familiar with local language and customs, traveling with your group.*
- **Post-trip follow-up** *with team members and leadership.*
- **Thorough assistance** *from start to finish!*

**Let us help you plan the right trip for your Single Adult Minstry!**

Bridge Builders, Inc.
9925 7th Way N., #102
St. Petersburg, FL 33702
(813) 576-4152
Attn: Chris Eaton

# WHEN GROUP LEADERS LOOK TO YOU, LOOK TO US.

NavPress Small Group Videos are specifically designed to give groups an experience they'll never forget—without pressuring the leader!

Each video package has everything a group needs for an exciting series of 60- to 90-minute discussion sessions, including:

- Powerful video segments, some including drama
- A viewer's discussion guide
- Leader's notes
- The popular book on which the video series is based

So when group leaders turn to you for a fresh, creative approach to discussion, turn to us.

**NavPress Small Group Videos**

- Special preview videos available for churches
- Regular book discounts apply
- Easy return policy

**1-800-366-7788**

"A HIGH PERCENTAGE OF CHURCH MEMBERS TODAY ARE SINGLE PEOPLE. TO EFFECTIVELY MINISTER TO THEM PASTORS MUST UNDERSTAND THEIR ISSUES AND CONCERNS. SAM JOURNAL PROVIDES THIS VALUABLE SOURCE OF INFORMATION."

- ANDRÉ BUSTANOBY

METROPOLITAN PSYCHOTHERAPY GROUP, WASHINGTON D.C.

Call toll FREE today to get your subscription started.
**800-487-4-SAM or 719-488-2610**
Or write: *SAM Journal*, P. O. Box 62056,
Colorado Springs, Colorado 80962-2056.

A one-year subscription is $24 (10 issues); $29 in Canada; $33 for all other countries.
*U. S. funds only*. Payment by Visa, MasterCard, or "bill me" also available.

*Part 7*

# Publications, Organizations, and Support Groups

People and Places to Contact For Information and Help

## Where To Find It:

# PROFESSIONAL PUBLICATIONS OF INTEREST

(Non-Religious)

**The following publications are:**

- **Designed primarily for counselors, social workers, clergy, educators, and other related professionals.**
- **Published by a professional or educational entity.(Generally speaking, they have no particular religious affiliation.)**

### STEPFAMILY BULLETIN
published by the Stepfamily Association of America, Inc.
900 Welch Rd., Suite 400
Palo Alto, CA 94304

### STEPFAMILIES AND BEYOND (STEPPARENT NEWS)
published by Listening Inc.
8716 Pine Ave.
Gary, IN 46403

### FAMILY RELATIONS JOURNAL
published by the National Council on Family Relations
1910 W. County Road B, Suite 147
St. Paul, MN 55113.

### SOLO PARENTING
published by the Cooperative Extension Education Department at the University of Delaware. Includes a wide variety of articles written specifically for the single parent.
The University of Delaware, Townsend Hall
Newark, DE 19717-1303
(302) 451-2538.

### DIVORCE CHATS
a publication dedicated to help remove divorce from the courts and treat it more as a human relations problem. Published by U.S. Divorce Reform, Inc.
Box 243, Kenwood, CA 95452.

### JOURNAL OF DIVORCE
published by Hayworth Press
12 West 32nd St., New York, NY 10010.
Covers clinical studies and research in family therapy, mediation studies and law.

### MARRIAGE AND DIVORCE TODAY
published by Atcom, Inc.
2315 Broadway, New York, NY 10024.
For marriage, divorce and family therapy professionals.

### MARRIAGE, DIVORCE
published by Gould Publishers
199-300 State St., Binghamton, NY 13901.
Comprehensive coverage of laws relating to marriage, divorce and adoption throughout the United States.

### STEP LIFE
the problems and joys of stepparenting and remarriage. Published by Wall Publishers, 901 Ivy Court, Eaton, OH 45320

### THE SINGLE PARENT
8807 Colesville Rd.,
Silver Springs, MD 20910
(800) 6388-8078.
Glossy magazine, 10 times per year.
Published by Parents Without Partners.

### UNMARRIED PARENTS TODAY
published by The National Committee for Adoption, 1346 Connecticut Ave. N.W., #326, Washington, DC 20036.

"This is the best resource available anywhere."

"SAM Journal is the best resource of its kind available anywhere. I read it completely—usually the day it arrives—and am never disappointed. It is the first publication I recommend to anyone serious about a ministry with single adults."

- DICK DUNN
Roswell United Methodist Church,
Roswell, Georgia

**Call toll FREE today to get your subscription started.**
**800-487-4-SAM or 719-488-2610**

Or write: *SAM Journal*, P. O. Box 62056, Colorado Springs, CO 80962-2056.

A one-year subscription is $24 (10 issues); $29 in Canada; $33 for all other countries. U. S. funds only.
Payment by Visa, MasterCard, or "bill me" also available.

# PUBLICATIONS FOR SINGLES AND SINGLE ADULT LEADERS

(Religious)

**The following publications are:**

- **Published by a Christian or religious organization or denomination.**
- **Intended for single adults, young adults, and/or pastors/leaders.**

### CATHOLIC SINGLES MAGAZINE
Box 1920
Evanston, IL 60204
(312) 731-8769
3 times yearly tabloid. Articles, personal ads.

### CHRISTIAN SINGLE
127 Ninth Ave., N., #140
Nashville, TN 37234
Monthly glossy magazine. Articles Published by the Southern Baptist Convention.

### FEEDBACK
Mennonite Student and Young Adult Services
c/o Rick Mojonnier, Editor
Box 370
Elkhart, IN 46515
Newsletter providing information and theological stimulation for student and young adult ministries, predominantly in Mennonite settings.

### JOURNEYS OF THE NEW APOSTLES
475 Riverside Dr., Room 710
New York, NY 10027
A newsletter about young adult ministry in 14 denominations and church-related agencies. Produced and published under the auspices of Young Adult Ministry Project, Dept. of Christian Life and Mission, National Council of Churches.

### MINISTRIES WITH YOUNG ADULTS
Division of Parish Services
2900 Queen Lane
Philadelphia, PA 19129
Monthly newsletter about young adult and singles activities in the Lutheran Church. Has resource listing.

### NATIONAL YOUNG ADULT REPORTER
Dept. of Education, U.S. Catholic Conference
1312 Massachusetts Ave.
Washington, DC 2005
A quarterly newsletter of young adult/singles activities in the Roman Catholic Church with a resource listing.

### S.A.M.I. (SINGLE ADULT MINISTRY INFORMATION)
Institute of Singles Dynamics
Box 11394
Kansas City, MO 64112
(816) 763-9401
National monthly newsletter for singles leaders. Resources reviewed. News about single adult groups/leaders. A calendar of current conferences listed nationwide.

### SINGLE ADULT MINISTRIES JOURNAL
P.O. Box 60430
Colorado Springs, CO 80960-60430
(719) 579-6471 (Editorial Office)
(800)487-4SAM (to subscribe)
Published 10 times a year.
Transdenominational publication dedicated to providing practical helps, ideas and encouragement for those involved in ministry to single adults.

### SINGLE IMPACT
Mobilized To Serve
7245 College St.
Lima, NY 14485
(716) 582-2790
Quarterly magazine for single adults, available on donation basis. Articles and news (primarily on Mobilized to Serve conferences). Transdenominational Christian Singles ministry.

### SINGLES NEWS, CHRISTIAN SINGLES INTERNATIONAL
Box 543, Harrison, OH 45030
Monthly publication.

### SINGLES SCENE
P.O. Box 310, Allardt, TN 38504
(615) 879-4625
Christian-oriented monthly magazine featuring articles on faith, Christian growth, self-help, health.

### TODAY'S SINGLES
1933 W. Wisconsin
Milwaukee, WI 53233
(414) 344-7300
Quarterly tabloid. Includes articles, events for Christian singles, reviews, etc. Available in bulk quantity. Donation.

### U.S. SINGLES TODAY
P. O. Box 927
Bedford, TX 76095
(817) 354-1103
Tabloid, display ads, some personals, singles events. Calls itself "A National Christian Singles Newspaper."

### YOUNG ADULT CONNECTION
The United Methodist Center, Y.A.C.
P.O. Box 840
Nashville, TN 37202
(615) 340-7000
News of what's happening, training sessions available, information on resources.

# PUBLICATIONS FOR SINGLE ADULTS

(Non-Religious)

**The following publications are:**
- **Primarily designed for single adults interested in meeting other singles through personal ads and in finding out about activities and events of interest in their city or state/region.**
- **Not generally religious in nature.**
- **An excellent place to advertise some of your singles ministry activities. (The readers of these publications are primarily single adults in search of love and friendship.)**

*(Editor's Note: Thanks to the Singles Press Association for compiling this list of publications. For more information on this Association, write Janet Jacobsen, 7432 E. Diamond, Scottsdale, AZ 85257.)*

## ARIZONA

### SINGLE SCENE
Box 10159, Scottsdale, AZ 85271 (602) 945-6746. Monthly newspaper. Articles, singles club directory, club calendar, poetry, personal ads. Per issue $1.00, yearly $8.50.

### ARIZONA SINGLES
PO Box 3424, Flagstaff, AZ 86003 (602) 779-0151. Monthly newspaper. Distributed free in northern & western Arizona. Articles. Yearly $12.00.

### THE TUCSON CONNECTION
Box 15114, Tucson, AZ 85708 (602) 749-9554. Monthly newspaper. Articles, personals. Free locally. Subscriptions $6.00.

## CALIFORNIA

### L.A. ALIVE
2029 Century Park, E., #1240, Los Angeles, CA 90067 (213) 556-0600. Bi-weekly tabloid. Articles, personals. Free locally, sample $1.00, yearly $12.50.

### NATIONAL SINGLES REGISTER
P.O. Box 567, Norwalk, CA 90650 (213) 864-2741. Bi-monthly newspaper. Articles, some singles events, personal ads. Per issue $1.00.

### BBW FRIENDSHIP EXPRESS
19611 Ventura Blvd., #200, Tarzana, CA 91356 (818) 881-9229. Monthly digest type. Friendship ads...from BBWs (Big Beautiful Women), men who love BBWs, and women who love BB Men. Single issue $2.00, yearly $15.00.

### LIFESTYLE
(Southern California edition), P.O. Box 5062. Van Nuys, CA 91413 (818) 980-4786. Monthly magazine. Articles, events, personal ads. Per issue $1.00, yearly $7.00.

### SINGLES MAGAZINE AND ENTERTAINMENT GUIDE
Box 5709, San Diego, CA 92105 (619) 296-6948. Bi-monthly newspaper. Articles, club directory, events, personal ads. Per issue $1.00, yearly $6.00.

### SINGLE LIFE MAGAZINE
18627 Brookhurst #293, Fountain Valley, CA 92708 (714) 549-5473. Personals, singles events.

### SINGLE FILE
1757 Mesa Verde Ave., #113, Ventura, CA 93003.

### TRELLIS SINGLES MAGAZINE
1260 Persian Drive, #6, Sunnyvale, CA 94089 (408) 747-1455. Bi-monthly newspaper. Personal ads and a schedule of events sponsored by magazine.

### LIFESTYLE
(northern California edition), 419 W. MacArthur Blvd., Oakland CA 94609 (415) 420-1381. Bi-monthly newspaper. Single issue $.75, yearly $7.00.

### SINGLES CHOICE
Box 58, Santa Barbara, CA 93102. Personals.

### AMICUS & DATIQUE, INC.
Box 1609, Pacifica, CA 94044. Quarterly newsletter and personalized relationship program. $45 and up.

### ENJOY LIFE
P.O. Box 2593, Santa Rosa, CA 95405 Bi-monthly publication. Subscriptions $8.

### SINGLES NEWS MAGAZINE
Box 61061, Sacramento, CA 95860 (916) 486-1414. Monthly newspaper. Articles, singles events, personal ads. Per issue, $.75, yearly $10.00.

## COLORADO

### THE SINGLE SOURCE
P.O. Box 460127, Aurora, CO 80015 (303) 692-5077. Monthly magazine. Articles, personal ads, calendar of events, singles organization/service. Per issue $1.00, yearly $10.00.

### THE SINGLES TRUMPET
Box 460303, Aurora, CO 80015 (303) 745-0818. Twice-monthly newspaper. Articles, poetry, personal ads. Yearly $25.00.

### GET-TWO-GETHER
Box 1413, Ft. Collins, CO 80522 (303) 211-4544. Bi-monthly magazine. Articles and personal ads. Per issue $1.00, 12 issues $9.99.

### SINGLESLINE
P.O. Box 16005, Colorado Springs, CO 80935 (719) 390-7503. Monthly newspaper. Articles, club directory, calendar, personal ads. Per issue $.75, yearly $7.00, sample $1.00.

## CONNECTICUT

### JEWISH SINGLES MAGAZINE
Box 728, Bloomfield CT 06002 (203) 243-1514. Magazine. Articles, personal ads for Jewish singles. Yearly $24.00.

## FLORIDA

### SINGLES SERENDIPITY
P.O. Box 5794, Jacksonville, FL 32247 (904) 399-5083. Bi-monthly magazine. Personal ads, local groups and activities, some articles. Per issue $1.95, yearly $11.00.

Fact:

According to the Vatican, more than three quarters of all annulments granted worldwide were to American Catholics.

*Washington Post, March 11, 1988*

### 1ST CLASS SINGLES LIFESTYLE
219 E. Commercial Blvd., Lauderdale, FL 33308.

### SOUTH FL SINGLES LIVING
300 S. Pine Island Rd. #247, Plantation, FL 33324 (305) 474-3999. Bi-monthly tabloid. Articles, personals, classified. Free locally.

### SINGLE LIVING MAGAZINE
4801 S.Univ. Dr. #226, Ft. Lauderdale, FL 33328.

### FLORIDA SINGLES AND E. COAST DATE BOOK
Box 1038, Jupiter, FL 33468. Bi-monthly magazine. Articles, personal ads.

### SINGLES NIGHT OUT
P.O. Box 235, Bradenton, FL 33505.

### SINGLES SERENDIPITY
P.O. Box 5794, Jacksonville, FL 32247 (904) 399-5083. Bi-monthly magazine. Personal ads, articles, listings of local groups and activities. Sample $2.50, subscription $11.

## GEORGIA

### ATLANTA SINGLES MAGAZINE
3423 Piedmont Rd. N.E. #320, Atlanta, GA 30305 (404) 239-0642. Monthly glossy magazine. Articles, activity & club guide, personal ads. Per issue $2.00, yearly $18.00.

## IDAHO

### SINGLES INDEX
2308 N. Cole Rd. Ste. G, Boise, ID 83715. Monthly magazine. Personal ads.

## ILLINOIS

### CHICAGO LIFE
Box 11311, Chicago, IL 60611. Irregularly published glossy magazine. Articles and activities. Yearly $26.00.

### NATIONAL DATING SCENE
Box 1307, Skokie, IL 60076 (312) 676-9860. Bi-monthly magazine. Articles and personal ads. Sample $1.50.

### SINGLES CHOICE
Box 4138, Arlington Heights, IL 60006 (312) 255-9940. Monthly magazine. Personals. Sample $1.00, subscription $24.00.

## KANSAS

### WICHITA SINGLES NEWSLETTER
Box 47482, Wichita, KS 67201. Monthly newspaper. Personal ads and articles. Sample $2.00, subscription $12.00.

## KENTUCKY

### TRI-STATE SINGLES CONNECTION
P.O. Box 17065, Covington, NY 41017 (406) 331-2374. Bi-monthly tabloid. Articles, personals.

### EXPRESSIONS OF LOVE
Box 1472, Ashland, KY 41105. Monthly publication. Subscriptions $30.00.

## LOUISIANA

### SINGLE ADULTS OF GREATER NEW ORLEANS
P.O. Box 8721, Metairie, LA 70011. Monthly newsletter. Membership $50.00.

## MAINE

### THE SINGLES NETWORK
P.O. Box 8751, Portland, ME 04104. Monthly newsletter. Membership $24.00.

## MARYLAND

### THE LITTLE BLACK BOOK
P.O. Box 352, Aberdeen, MD 21001. No other current info.

### CUPID
Box 2531, Gaithersburg, MD 20879. Monthly magazine. Articles, personals for mid-Atlantic singles (over 40). Sample $2.00, subscription $20.00.

## MASSACHUSETTS

### SINGLES ALMANAC
138 Brighton Suite 209, Boston, MA 02134 (617) 254-8810. Monthly magazine. Personal ads, events, articles. Per issue $2.00, yearly $12.00.

### INTRO SINGLES CLUB
Box 3006, Boston MA 02130. Bi-weekly newsletter. Personals. Subscription $10.00.

### SINGLES LIFELINE
Box 639, Randolph, MA 02368. No other current info.

### THE DATING PAGE
Box 310, Lynnfield, MA 01940. Twice monthly publication. Sample $5.00, subscription $25.00.

### SINGLES PERSONAL ADS
Box 850, Needham Heights, MA 02194. Monthly publication. Sample $1.00, subscription $4.00.

## MICHIGAN

### SINGLE FILE MAGAZINE
P.O. Box 6706, Station C, Grand Rapids, MI 49516 (616) 774-8100. Monthly glossy mini-magazine. Articles, events, club directory, personals. Per issue $2.00, yearly $16.00.

## MINNESOTA

### DI'S MEET PEOPLE
Box 247, Osseo MN 55369 (612) 593-0799. Monthly newspaper. Personals. Sample $1.50, subscription $11.95.

### THE GRAPEVINE
222 Riverwoods Lane, Burnsville, MN 55337. Directory of resources for singles in the Minneapolis and St. Paul metro areas. 100 plus listings. $5.00.

### SINGLES ALL TOGETHER
965 W. Larpenteur, St.Paul, MN 55113. Monthly newsletter.

## MISSOURI

### METRO SINGLES
Box 28203, Kansas City, MO 64118 (816) 436-8424. Bi-monthly newspaper. Personal ads, photos and feature articles. Per issue $2.00, yearly $12.00.

### REFLECTIONS - CONNECTIONS
P.O. Box 686, Liberty, MO 64608. Quarterly. Photo ads, personal ads, poetry, recipes, health and beauty tips. Per issue $3.00.

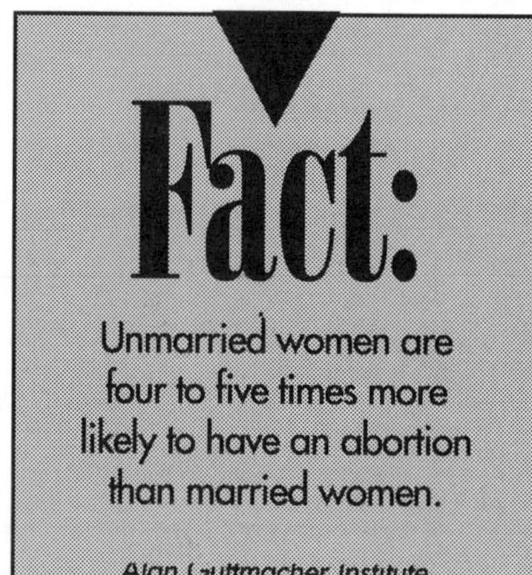


## NEBRASKA

### THE CONNECTOR
P.O. Box 24331, Omaha, NE 68124. Five times per year mini-magazine for Jewish singles. Personal "messages." Per issue $2.00, yearly $12.00.

### THE SINGLE LIFE
P.O. Box 83289, Lincoln, NE 68501 (402) 466-8521. Monthly newspaper. Articles, calendar of events, club directory, personal ads. Per issue $1.25, yearly $12.00.

## NEVADA

### LAS VEGAS SINGLE LIFESTYLE
3111 S. Valley View #A-220, Las Vegas, NV 89102 (701) 362-5800. Monthly tabloid. Articles, calendar, directory, personal ads. Free locally, yearly $14.95.

### TRUE MATCH
P.O. Box 18000-5, Las Vegas, NV 89114. Monthly magazine. Personal ads. Yearly $17.00.

### CUPID'S DESTINY
P.O. Box 5637, Reno, NV 89513. Quarterly magazine. Directory, personal ads, pictures. Per issue $1.00, yearly $24.00.

## NEW HAMPSHIRE

### DATELINE NEW HAMPSHIRE
P.O. Box 800, Greenland, NH 03840. Published 10 times per year. Subscription $12.00.

## NEW JERSEY

### SINGLES JOURNAL
103 Cobblestone Lane, Cherry Hill, NJ 08034 (609) 424-3080. Mini-tabloid. Personal ads. Per issue $1.75, yearly $15.00.

### HOMESTEAD HOTLINE
720 Morrow Avenue. Clayton, NJ 08312 (609) 881-0319. Quarterly tabloid. Personal ads. Per issue $1.00, yearly $15.00.

## NEW MEXICO

### CONNECTIONS
Box 37374, Albuquerque, NM 87176 (505) 345-4321. Monthly newspaper. Articles, singles groups, community events. Sample $1.50, subscription $15.

# NEW YORK

### CHOCOLATE SINGLES

Box 333, Jamaica, NY 11413. Monthly. Articles and personal ads for black singles. Subscription $25.00.

### SINGLES ALMANAC OF NEW YORK

80 E. 11th St., New York, NY 10003 (212) 673-3930. Bi-weekly tabloid. Personals, events. Per issue $.60, yearly $15.00.

### DATEBOOK

P.O. Box 473, Pleasantville, NY 10570 (914) 769-1365. Monthly mini-magazine. Personal ads, calendar of events, no articles. Free locally, yearly $18.00.

### LONG ISLAND SINGLES CLUB CALENDAR

1731 Prime St., West Babylon, NY 11704 (516) 669-6541. Monthly newsletter. Calendar of events, personal ads. Per issue $1.00, yearly $8.00.

# NORTH CAROLINA

### METORLINA SINGLES DATEBOOK

Box 11627, Charlotte, NC 28220 (704) 525-6200. Monthly magazine. Personal ads, singles events, club directory, some articles. Per issue $2.00, yearly $16.00.

# OHIO

### COLUMBUS SINGLE SCENE

P.O. Box 30856, Gahanna, OH 43230 (614) 476-8802. Monthly magazine. Articles, poetry, event calendar, personal ads. Per issue $1.00, yearly $10.00.

### CLEVELAND'S FINEST SINGLES

P.O. Box 79363, Cleveland, OH 44107, (216) 521-1111. Monthly tabloid. Articles, personal ads. Free locally, yearly $6.00.

### CAROL'S SINGLES ORGANIZATION

Box 998, Rootstown, OH 44272. Bi-monthly newspaper. Yearly $10.00.

# OREGON

### SINGLE SCENE

Box 5027, Salem, OR 97304 (503) 873-5637. Monthly newspaper. Singles Directory, activities, schedule, personal ads. Per issue $.50, yearly $6.00.

# PENNSYLVANIA

### LIFESTYLES PITTSBURGH

300 Mt. Lebanon Blvd. #210B, McMurray, PA 15234 (412) 941-5339. Bi-monthly glossy magazine. Articles, club directory, calendar of events, personal ads. Per issue $2.50, yearly $11.95.

# SOUTH DAKOTA

### SOLO RFD

Box 84428, Sioux Falls, SD 57118 (605) 335-0900. Monthly newspaper. Articles, poetry, club directory, personal ads. Per issue $1.00, yearly $15.00.

Many widows have limited financial resources. According to the U.S Census Bureau, in 1986 only 10% of all widows inherited benefits from their husbands. And while more than half of all men receive some kind of pension, only about 25% of women receive pension incomes of their own.

*Singlesline 4/89*

# TENNESSEE

### TENNESSEE SINGLE LIFE

P.O. Box 50711, Knoxville, TN 37950 (615) 524-4986. Monthly. Articles, directory, personals. Per issue $1.50, yearly $15.00.

# TEXAS

### U.S. SINGLES TODAY

P.O. Box 927, Bedford, TX 76095 (817) 540-2155. Frequency unclear. Tabloid. Display ads, some personals, singles events. Yearly, $36.00.

### SINGLE'S MONTHLY

P.O. Box 121999, Fort Worth, TX 76121. Monthly. Personals. Per issue $3.00, yearly $29.00.

### TOUCH OF CLASS

12603 Prima Vista, San Antonio, TX 78233 (512) 653-5357. Monthly magazine. Articles, directory of singles groups, personal ads. Per issue $1.00, yearly $10.00.

# WASHINGTON

### ACTIVE SINGLES LIFE

Box 80571, Seattle, WA 98108 (206) 282-0880. Twice-monthly newspaper. Articles, personal ads, some event listings. Per issue $1.00, yearly $20.00.

# WEST VIRGINIA

### SCAN (SINGLES CONNECT AND NETWORK)

P.O. Box 4561, Parkersburg, WV 26104 (304) 428-3283. Monthly magazine. Articles, personal ads. Per issue $2.50, yearly $24.00.

# WISCONSIN

### SINGLES LIFE

606 W. Wisconsin Ave., #703, Milwaukee, WI 53203 (414) 271-9700. Bi-monthly glossy magazine. Articles, events, personal ads. Per issue $1.95, yearly $9.99.

# ORGANIZATIONS AND SUPPORT GROUPS

## Consider the following organizations as a possible resource for your ministry with single adults.

### ALCOHOLICS ANONYMOUS
P.O. Box 459
Grand Central Station
New York, NY 10163
(212) 686-1100

### AL-ANON/ALATEEN FAMILY GROUP HEADQUARTERS
P.O. Box 182
Madison Square Station
New York, NY 10159
(800) 344-2666
(212) 302-7240

### ASSOCIATION FOR CHILDREN FOR ENFORCEMENT OF SUPPORT (ACES)
723 Phillips Ave., Suite 216, Toledo, OH 43612. Call: (419) 476-2511 or (800) 537-7072
For custodial parents who have problems collecting child support payments.

### ASSOCIATION OF COUPLES FOR MARRIAGE ENRICHMENT
P.O. Box 10596, Winston-Salem, NC 27108. Call: (919) 724-1526.
Network of couples seeking to enhance their own marriage and help strengthen the marriages of other couples through mutual support, retreats, and workshops.

### BIG BROTHERS/BIG SISTERS OF AMERICA
National Headquarters
230 North 13th St.
Philadelphia, PA 19107
(215) 567-7000

### CENTER FOR LOSS AND LIFE TRANSITION
3735 Broken Bow Road
Fort Collins, CO 80526
(303) 226-6050

### CHILD FIND OF AMERICA, INC.
P.O. Box 277, New Paltz, NY 12561. Call: 1-800-I-AM-LOST, or 1-800-A-WAY-OUT or (914) 255-1848.
Assistance for parents searching for missing children. Photo directory, registration and location, education programs, newsletter, and referrals.

### CHILD WELFARE LEAGUE OF AMERICA
67 Irving Place
New York, NY 10003
A national organization that offers information on child welfare issues and will refer families to appropriate agencies throughout the country.

### COMMITTEE FOR MOTHER AND CHILD RIGHTS, INC.
Rt. 1 Box 256A, Clearbrook, VA 22624. Call: (703) 722-3652.
Information and support for mothers with custody problems. Telephone support network.

### COMPASSIONATE FRIENDS
P.O. Box 3696
Oak Brook, IL 60522
(708) 990-0010
An organization for bereaved parents and siblings with more than 600 chapters nation-wide.

### COSA (CODEPENDENTS OF SEX ADDICTS)
P.O. Box 14537, Minneapolis, MN 55414. Call: (612) 537-6904.
12 step program for those who have relationships with people who have destructive sexual behavior.

### CULT AWARENESS NETWORK
2421 W. Pratt Blvd., Suite 1173, Chicago, IL 60645. Call: (312) 267-7777.
Education about mind-controlling cults. Help and support for friends and relatives of cult members. Help for former cult members.

### DEBTORS ANONYMOUS
314 W. 53rd St.
New York, NY 10019
(212) 969-0710

### DISPLACED HOMEMAKERS NETWORK
National Headquarters
1411 K St. N.W., Suite 930
Washington, D.C. 20005

### DIVORCE ANONYMOUS
Divorce Anonymous, 543 N. Fairfax Ave., Los Angeles, CA 90036. Call: (213) 651-2930.
Based on the 12 step program of Alcoholics Anonymous, this is a support group for those going through a divorce or separation.

### ELIM FELLOWSHIP
7245 College St.
Lima, NY 14485
(716) 582-2790
A charismatic ministry to all Christian denominations which conducts regional and North American singles conferences, as well as Singles Days, Single Parent Days, and leadership seminars throughout the United States and Canada. Produces *Single Impact* magazine and single ministry and single parent ministry kits.

### EMOTIONS ANONYMOUS
P.O. Box 4245
St.Paul, MN 55104
(612) 647-9712
A 12-step spiritual program (similar to AA) dealing specifically with the emotions such as anger, resentment, fears, phobias, loss/grief, low self-esteem and depression. Chapters world-wide.

### E.X.P.O.S.E. (EX-PARTNERS OF SERVICEMEN FOR EQUALITY)
P.O. Box 11191, Alexandria, VA 22312. Call: (703) 941-5844 or (703) 255-2917 hotline.
Works for changes in military divorce laws. Provides information of rights and legal assistance.

### FAMILY SERVICE ASSOCIATION OF AMERICA
44 E. 23rd St.
New York, NY 10010
Headquarters of a network of local family counseling agencies. If you are seeking counseling and cannot find a local listing, write for the name of an agency in your area.

### GAMBLERS ANONYMOUS
P.O. BOX 17173
Los Angeles, CA 90017
(213) 386-8789

## GRANDPARENTS' CHILDRENS' RIGHTS, INC.

5728 Bayconne Ave., Haslett, MI 48840 Call: (517) 339-8663. Information and assistance for grandparents who are being denied visitation rights with grandchildren.

## GRANDPARENTS RAISING GRANDCHILDREN

3851 Centraloma Dr., San Diego, CA 92107. Call: (619) 223-0344. Sharing of support and information for relatives who are raising a child, or who are concerned about a child's environment.

## IDAK CAREER MATCH

IDAK Group, Inc.
Banfield Plaza Building
7931 N.E. Halsey
Portland, OR 97213
(503) 257-0189
The first career matching system of its kind ever designed to help Christians find the right careers. IDAK Career Match uses state-of-the-art computer technology to help the person understand who they are, evaluate their occupational aptitudes and recommend best possible ministry and/or career matches.

## INCEST SURVIVORS ANONYMOUS

P.O. Box 5613
Long Beach, CA 90800

## INSTITUTE OF SINGLES DYNAMICS

Box 11394
Kansas City, MO 64112
(816) 763-9401
Conducts all-day workshops for singles leaders entitled, "How to Have Success With Singles." The workshops are presented by Don Davidson, editor of SAMI (Single Adult Ministry Information) newsletter and qualify for CEU credits. To host a workshop or to obtain a schedule in your area, contact Davidson at the address listed above.

## INTERCRISTO

19303 Fremont Ave. N.
Seattle, WA 98133
Contact: Karen Weschler
(206) 546-7330
Assists Christians in career decision making while offering job and service referrals for adults of all ages who want to work in Christian ministry.

## ITHEOS (They Help Each Other Spiritually)

717 Liberty Ave., 1301 Clark Bldg., Pittsburgh, PA 15222-3510. Call (412) 471-7779. Self-help groups for widows and widowers, focusing on recovery from grief. Chapters throughout the U.S. and Canada.

## JOINT CUSTODY ASSOCIATION

10606 Wilkins Ave., Los Angeles, CA 90024.Helps divorcing parents to work towards joint custody. Provides information regarding family law research and judicial decisions.

## MARKETPLACE

P.O. Box 7895
Madison, WI 53707-7895
Contact: Pete Hammond, Director
(608) 274-9001
A career oriented ministry of InterVarsity Christian Fellowship.

## MOTHERS WITHOUT CUSTODY

P.O. Box 56762, Houston, TX 77227-7418. Call: (713) 840-1622.
Network for support for women without custody of their children.

## NATIONAL ASSOCIATION for CHILDREN of ALCOHOLICS

31582 Coast Highway, Suite B
South Laguna, CA 92677
(714) 499-3889

## NATIONAL ASSOCIATION OF MILITARY WIDOWS

4023 25th Road, North Arlington, VA 22207. Call: (703) 527-4565.
Assists all military widows through changes in legislation and making referrals.

## (NSL) NATIONAL ASSOCIATION of SINGLE ADULT LEADERS

National Office
3777 Holton Road
Muskegon, MI 49445
(616) 744-4844 or 744-2546
A ministry dedicated to equip and encourage single adult leaders to more effectively reach single adults with the good news of Jesus Christ through His church. NSL sponsors several leadership training seminars annually, held throughout the U.S.

## NATIONAL ASSOCIATION of SINGLE PARENT EDUCATORS

Goddard College
Plainfield, VT 05667
(802) 454-8311
Contact: Douglas North

## NCSAS (NATIONAL CHILD SUPPORT ADVOCACY COALITION)

NCSAS, P.O.Box 4629, Alexandria, VA 22308. Call: (703) 799-5659.
Advocates for child support enforcement and collection.

## NATIONAL COUNCIL FOR CHILDREN'S RIGHTS

721 2nd St., NE, Washington, DC 20002. Call: (202) 547-NCCR. An organization of parents working towards reform of the legal system regarding child custody.

## NATIONAL CONGRESS FOR MEN

P.O. Box 202, Glenside, PA 19038-0202. Call: (215) 576-0177.
An organization working to reduce discrimination against men, especially in family court cases.

## THE NATIONAL FOUNDATION for SUDDEN INFANT DEATH, INC.

8200 Professional Place, Ste. 104
Landover, MD 20785
(800) 221-SIDS

## NATIONAL ORGANIZATION FOR MEN

381 Park Ave. S., New York, NY 10022. Call: (212) 686-MALE. Working for equal rights for men, uniform national divorce, custody, property, and visitation laws.

## NATIONAL SELF-HELP CLEARINGHOUSE

33 West 42nd St.
New York, NY 10036
(212) 642-2944

## NEW BEGINNINGS, INC.

13129 Clinfton Rd., Silver Spring, MD 20904. Call (301) 384-0111.
Discussion meetings, speakers, social events, workshops, newsletter for separated and divorced men and women.

## NORTH AMERICAN CONFERENCE OF SEPARATED AND DIVORCED CATHOLICS

NACSDC, 1100 S. Goodman St., Rochester, NY 14620. Call: (716) 271-1320.
Self-help groups, conferences, and training programs to examine the religious, educational, and psychological areas of divorce, separation, and remarriage. All faiths welcome.

## NO KIDDING!

Box 76982, Station "S", Vancouver, B.C., Canada V5R5S7. Call: (604) 538-7736.
Mutual support and social activities for married and single people who do not have children.

## PARENTS WITHOUT PARTNERS

National Headquarters
8807 Colesville Rd.
Silver Spring, MD 20910
Call: (301) 588-9354 or (800) 637-7974.
Educational organization for single parents.

## REMARRIEDS, INC.

Box 742
Santa Ana, CA 92702
Chapters in many states.

## S-ANON

P.O. Box 5117, Sherman Oaks, CA 91413. Call (818) 990-6910.
12 step program for those who have a friend or relative with a sexual addiction.

## SEXAHOLICS ANONYMOUS

P.O. Box 300, Simi Valley, CA 93062. Call (818) 704-9854.
Recovery program for those who want to end sexually destructive thinking and behavior. Work towards sexual sobriety.

## SEX ADDICTS ANONYMOUS

P.O. Box 3038, Minneapolis, MN 55403. Call: (612) 339-0217.
Fellowship of men and women who share support as they work to solve their common problems of compulsive sexual behavior.

## SEX AND LOVE ADDICTS ANONYMOUS

P.O. Box 119 New Town Branch, Boston, MA 02258.
12 step fellowship based on A.A. for those wanting to be free from obsessive/compulsive sexual behavior or emotional attachment.

## SINGLE MOTHERS BY CHOICE

P.O. Box 1642, Gracie Square Station, New York, NY 10028.
Call: (212) 988-0993
Support group for women having children while not in a permanent relationship with a man.

## SINGLE PARENT RESOURCE CENTER

1165 Broadway, New York, NY 10001. Call: (212) 213-0047.
Network of single parent groups. Information and referrals, seminars, consultation, and other resources for single parents.

## SINGLE PARENTS SOCIETY

527 Cinnaminson Ave., Palmyra, NJ 08065. Call: (609) 424-8872.
Discussion groups, social activities, educational programs to help the previously married single parent.

## THE SISTERHOOD OF BLACK SINGLE MOTHERS, INC.

1360 Fulton St., Rm. 413, Brooklyn, NY 11216. Call: (718) 638-0413.
Education and support for black single mothers, youth awareness project, newsletter.

## SOCIETY OF MILITARY WIDOWS

5535 Hempstead Way, Springfield VA 22151. Call: (703) 750-1342.
An organization to assist and support widows and widowers of members of all U.S. military services. Strives to promote public awareness. Newsletter.

## SPOUSE SURVIVORS

38 Sycamore Rd., Valley Stream, NY 11581. Call: (516) 791-7008.
This self-help group is for spouses of murder victims.

## STEPFAMILY ASSOCIATION OF AMERICA

900 Welch Rd., Suite 400
Palo Alto, CA 94304
Call: (301) 823-7570.
Chapters in many states and an annual national conference. Membership includes subscription to *Stepfamily Bulletin*.

## TALL CLUBS INTERNATIONAL

825 N. Hayden Rd., Suite C 108
Scottsdale, AZ 85257
Contact: John Young
(800) 521-2512
(602) 994-4502
Forty-seven chapters in the United States and Canada designed to promote social activities for single members who are at least 6'2" men or 5'10" women.

## TO LIVE AGAIN

P.O. Box 415,
Springfield, PA 19064.
Call (215) 353-7740.
An organization for widowed men and women experiencing the grief cycle. Monthly meetings, social events, conferences, newsletter.

## UNWED PARENTS ANONYMOUS

P.O. Box 44556, Phoenix, AZ 85064. Call: (602) 952-1463.
12 step program to help those affected by an out-of-wedlock pregnancy and parenting.

## W.E.S.O.M. (WE SAVED OUR MARRIAGE)

P.O. Box 46312, Chicago, IL 60646. Call: (312) 792-7034
Assists couples to deal with adultery and save their marriage.

## WIDOWED PERSON'S SERVICE

1909 'K' St., N.W.
Washington, D.C. 20049
Call: (202) 728-4370.
National organization has services for widowed person in over 150 communities around the United States. The organization sponsors outreach programs to assist the newly widowed, offering emotional support, a listening ear and referrals to appropriate community resources. The services are provided by volunteers who are widowed persons themselves.

## WOMEN ON THEIR OWN, INC. (W.O.T.O.)

P.O. Box 1026, Willingboro, NJ 08046. Call: (609) 871-1499.
A group for women who are single, divorced, separated, or widowed and who are raising children on their own.

**NOTE:** *For a more comprehensive listing of organizations, see the book, "The Self-Help Sourcebook." It provides information on over 600 organizations and support groups. (St. Clares-Riverside Medical Center, Denville, NJ 07834.)*

# Part 8

# Recommended Resources

## The Best Collection of Singles Ministry Resources Available Anywhere, Including Information on Books, Leader's Guides, Film, Audio, and Video

### Where To Find It:

# THE SINGLE ADULT MINISTRIES NATIONAL RESOURCE REVIEW BOARD

## Who evaluates and reviews all of the resources found on the following pages?

*Several years ago,* Single Adult Ministries Journal *established the National Single Adult Ministries Resource Review Board.*

*The challenge and responsibility of this national board is to rate and evaluate every product that has potential value to those involved in a ministry with single adults.*

*Each product is usually reviewed by at least three members of the board, providing a "Consumer Reports-like" evaluation and rating system. (Each product is given a composite score from 1 to 10, with 10 being the highest rating possible.) This method is a more reliable way of evaluating a product, since it reflects the opinions and perspectives of more than one singles ministry leader.*

*The following people are those currently serving on this national board. With more than 500 resources to review each year, their hard work and dependability is a vital contribution to singles ministry leaders across North America.*

**(For those interested in serving on this board, write *SAM Journal* and request a Review Board application.)**

**Albaum, Thomas**
Minister of Single Adults
First Presbyterian Church
Colorado Springs, CO

**Andress, Rubyanne**
Parish Assistant
St. Luke's United
Methodist Church
Jackson, MS

**Anthony, Michael**
Associate Pastor
Woodbridge Community Church
Irvine, CA

**Aumueller, Robert**
Singles Ministry Leader
Trinity Baptist Church
Manasquan, NJ

**Baker, David**
Singles Ministry Director
Crystal Cathedral
Irvine, CA

**Barber, Maryle J.**
Program Director
Central United
Methodist Church
Albuquerque, NM

**Basham, Alan**
Volunteer Leader/Counselor
University Presbyterian Church
Seattle, WA

**Bearden, Stephen R.**
Single Adult Pastor
Salem First Church
of the Nazarene
Salem, OR

**Bernstein, Scott W.**
Associate Singles Pastor
Bloomington Assembly of God
Bloomington, MN

**Bosch, Jim ten**
Associate Singles Pastor
Calvary Church of Santa Ana
Santa Ana, CA

**Bowen, Bob**
Volunteer Coordinator
Pompano Beach Church of God
Pompano Beach, FL

**Brown, Barbara E.**
Volunteer Leader/
Single Parents Ministry
Casos Adobes Baptist
Tucson, AZ

**Calhoun, Adele**
Womens Ministry Associate
Park Street Church
Boston, MA

**Calhoun, Douglas A.**
Minister to Young Adults
Park Street Church
Boston, MA

**Castaneda, Richard**
Associate Pastor of Singles
Full Faith Church of Love
Shawnee, KS

**Chandler, Rod**
Associate Pastor
Oakview Church
Centralia, WA

**Clark, M. Anne**
Volunteer Leader/
Board of Trustees
First United Methodist Church
Sarasota, FL

**Cumbie, Woody**
Adult Ministries
First Baptist Church
Fort Lauderdale, FL

**Curry, Judy**
Director of Singles
Bethel United MethodistChurch
Pond, MO

**D'Atri, Barbara**
Single Parent Ministry
Evangel Temple
Montgomery, AL

**Dennison, Ralph**
Associate Pastor of Singles
Southeast Christian Church
Lousiville, KY

**Dycus, Barbara**
Director of Single Parent
Family Program
Calvary Assembly of God
Winter Park, FL

**Dyke, James**
Minister of Single Adults
Grace Church
Edina, MN

**Eagleson, Glen**
Minister of Singles-
Young Adults
The Peoples Church
Willowdale, Ontario, Canada

**Eaton, Chris**
Executive Director
Single Purpose Ministries
St. Petersburg, FL

**Ellis, Stephen**
Volunteer Leader
Morris Hill Baptist Church
Chattanooga, TN

**Emery, Robert**
Minister of Single Adults
North Syracuse Baptist
North Syracuse, NY

**Etcheto, John**
Pastor to Single Adults
Reno Christian Fellowship
Reno, NV

**Fagerstrom, Doug**
Minister of Single Adults
Calvary Church
Grand Rapids, MI

**Fisher, Dennis**
Singles Ministry staff
WillowCreek
Community Church
South Barrington, IL

**Fisher, Terry**
Singles Ministry Leader
San Diego, CA

**Fleener, Bob**
Singles Pastor
Arcade Baptist Church
Sacramento, CA

**Fortner, Don**
Minister of Single Adults
Germantown Baptist Church
Germantown, TN

**Franck, Dennis**
Minister with Single Adults
Bethel Church
San Jose, CA

**Fulfer, Keith**
Associate Pastor
Glenwood Church
of Christ
Tyler, TX

**Fussell, Gloria J.**
Singles Associate
Evangel Temple
Montgomery, AL

**Gentry, Todd**
Minister with Singles
South MacArthur
Church of Christ
Irving, TX

**Gilbert, Dave**
Pastor to Singles/
Small Groups
Coast Hills
Community Church
Laguna Niguel, CA

**Gonzales, Georgia and Gary**
Singles Ministry Leaders
Upland, CA

**Griffin, Leland**
Volunteer Leader/Counselor
Northeast Christian Church
Grand Junction, CO

**Grzybowski, Jane**
Singles Ministry Staff
Ward Presbyterian Church
Livonia, MI

**Hagberg, Ron**
Director of Singles Ministries
Hennepin Avenue United
Methodist Church
Minneapolis, MN

**Hageman, Randy**
Associate Pastor with
Single Adults
First United Methodist Church
Lufkin, TX

**Halter, Joanne**
Director of Social Services
Atonement Lutheran
Milwaukee, WI

**Hardin, Linda**
General Coordinator of Single
Adult Ministries
International Church
of the Nazarene
Kansas City, MO

**Harding, Sandi**
Volunteer Leader
St. Stephens
Episcopal Church
Sewickley, PA

**Hare, Steve**
Pastor of Singles/
Small Groups
Highland Church of Christ
Abilene, TX

**Harper, Sherry**
Minister to Singles
Marin Covenant Church
San Rafael, CA

**Hemenway, Denise**
Volunteer Leader
Burton Church of God
Vancouver, WA

**Heppes, Lynn**
Volunteer Leader
Princeton Presbyterian Church
Princeton, NJ

**Herrick, Luralei**
Singles Ministry Director
First Assembly of God
McAlester, OK

**Hershey, Terry**
Speaker, Writer
Director of Christian Focus
Woodinville, WA

**Hollenbach, Mark**
Pastor of Singles/College
Central Christian Church
Mesa, AZ

**Holyfield, Billy**
Minister of Single Adults
Main Street Baptist
Hattiesburg, MS

**Howard, Willie**
Singles Director
Calvary Assembly of God
Winter Park, FL

**Hurst, Rich**
Singles Ministry Director
Crystal Cathedral
Garden Grove, CA

**Jackson, Karen**
Single Adult
Ministries Assistant
Second Presbyterian
Memphis, TN

**Jackson, Timm**
Minister with Single Adults
Second Presbyterian
Memphis, TN

**Johnson, David**
Minister with
Single Adults
Grace Chapel
Ipswich, MA

**Johnson, Kim**
Director of Singles Ministry
Community Church of Joy
Phoenix, AZ

**Keller, Jerry and Ruth**
Volunteer Leaders
Juniper Chapel
Redmond, OR

**Kennedy, Richard**
Single Adult/Discipleship Pastor
Big Valley Grace
Community Church
Modesto, CA

**Kent, Lawrence**
Pastor of Evangelism/ Singles
First Presbyterian Church
Flint, MI

**Kidd, Dwight**
Minister with Single Adults
Shades Mt. Baptist Church
Birmingham, AL

**Kirtland, Stephanie**
Young Adult Ministry Leader
Menlo Park Presbyterian
Menlo Park, CA

**Kline, Ann**
Singles Ministry Director
Frazer Memorial United
Methodist Church
Montgomery, AL

**Koppy, Kris**
Pastoral Care Minister
Lee Hwy. Church of God
Chattanooga, TN

**Kraljev, Richard**
Minister to Singles
New Hope Community Church
Portland, OR

**Krause, Michael**
Minister to Young Adults
The Stone Church
Toronto, Ontario Canada

**Krimbel, Stephanie**
Volunteer Leader
Kern Park Christian Church
Portland, OR

**Laughlin, Don**
Minister of Education/ Singles
First Baptist Church
Tyler, TX

**Lauterbach, Mark**
Senior Pastor
El Camino Baptist Church
Tuscon, AZ

**Lavik, Philip**
Pastor to Adults/Singles
Westminster Chapel
Bellevue, WA

**LeVan, Marlyn**
Counselor
Colorado Springs, CO

**Lehr, Brian**
Pastoral Intern
Living Stones Church
Red Deer, Alberta Canada

**Limiero, David**
Intern/Singles Ministry
Rocky Mountain Church
Longmont, CO

**Long, Stephen**
Associate Pastor
Bethel Evangelical
Baptist Church
Missisauga, Ontario Canada

**Lundblad, Daniel**
Counselor
Blue Water Counseling Center
Port Huron, MI

**Magon, Kathy**
Executive Producer,
singles radio program
Ward Presbyterian Church
Livonia, MI

**Mahan, Deborah**
Associate for Singles Ministry
First Presbyterian Church
Colorado Springs, CO

**McClay, Barry**
Volunteer Leader
Christ Community Church
Harrisburg, PA

**McCluskey, Gary**
Assistant Pastor
First Lutheran Church
Colorado Springs, CO

**McCoy, Timothy**
Minister of Singles
First Federated Church
Des Moines, IA

**McDonald, J. Mark**
Director of Young
Adult Ministries
Trietsch Memorial
United Methodist Church
Flower Mound, TX

**McInnes, Ronald**
Associate Director,
Seekers Singles Ministry
Jacksonville, FL

**Milam, Kenneth**
Associate Pastor
with Singles
Pioneer Drive Baptist Church
Abilene, TX

**Millenson, Carol**
Pastor to singles
Orlando Central Church
of the Nazarene
Orlando, FL

**Miller, Peter**
Minister to Singles
Memorial Drive United
Methodist Church
Houston, TX

**Morgan, Andy**
Minister with Single Adults
Ward Presbyterian Church
Livonia, MI

**Morphis, Doug**
Director of Community Life
First United Methodist Church
Wichita, KS

**Moses, Joyce**
Volunteer Leader
East Ridge Church of God
Chattanooga, TN

**Murrell, Deborah**
Minister of Education/Outreach
First Baptist Church
Winston-Salem, NC

**Oliver, Don and Linda**
Volunteer Leaders
Christian & Missionary Alliance
Church
Morgantown, WV

**Oyler, Bertie**
Singles Ministry
Coordinator
Trinity Lutheran Church
Sheboygan, WI

**Petersen, Paul**
Minister of Single Adults
Highland Park
Presbyterian Church
Dallas, TX

**Player, Gale**
Single Adult Leader
Foursquare Gospel Church
Rochester, NY

**Pratt, Gary L.**
Single's Pastor
First Assembly of God
Chickasha, OK

**Purnell, Dick**
Director, Single Life Resources
Cary, NC

**Randolph, Mary**
Director of Single Adult
Ministries
Asbury United Methodist
Tulsa, OK

**Reddy, Ellen**
Director of Singles Ministries
First United Methodist
Wichita, KS

**Reed, Bobbie**
Author, Singles Ministry Leader
Skyline Wesleyan Church
San Diego, CA

**Richwine, Jim**
Ministers of Singles
Coral Ridge
Presbyterian Church
Ft. Lauderdale, FL

**Ricotta, Bob**
Associate Singles Pastor
First Assembly of God
Clearwater, FL

**Rigdon, Elizabeth**
Volunteer Leader
Church of the Nazarene
Winnsboro, LA

**Rogers, Johnny**
Associate Pastor/
Director of Education
Zoar Baptist Church
Baton Rouge, LA

**Rogers, Linda**
Volunteer Leader
Aptos Foursquare Church
Aptos, CA

**Ronveaux, Roy**
Assistant Pastor with Singles
Victoria Community Church
Riverside, CA

**Rose, Bill**
Director,Touchstone
Singles Ministry
Lafayette, CA

**Santa-Maria, Maria**
Volunteer Leader/Counselor
South Jacksonville Presbyterian
Church
Jacksonville, FL

**Schiller, Barbara**
Assistant Director of
Singles Ministry
Central Presbyterian Church
St. Louis, MO

**Schroder, Kelley**
Minister with Single Adults
Christian Fellowship Church
Vienna, VA

**Scoles, Todd**
Director of College/Career
Ministries
Grace Brethren Church
of Columbus
Worthington, OH

**Senter, Robert**
Singles Ministry Leader
Living Word Church
Colorado Springs, CO

**Shaeffer, Dennis**
Singles Ministry Staff
First Baptist Church
Modesto, CA

**Shores, Chuck**
Pastor
Ojai Valley Wesleyan Church
Ojai, CA

**Simone, Michael**
Assistant Pastor/Singles
Virginia Beach
Community Chapel
Virginia Beach, VA

**Smith, H. Bret**
Minister of Single Adults
North Atlanta Church
of Christ
Atlanta, GA

**Smith, Harold Ivan**
Speaker, Author
St. Andrew's Episcopal
Kansas City, MO

**Smoke, Jim**
Director of the Center for
Divorce Recovery
Tempe, AZ

**Splinter, John**
Associate Pastor, Director of
Single Life Ministries
Central Presbyterian Church
Clayton, MO

**Staats, Lorin**
Associate Pastor/Singles
Elmbrook Church
Waukisha, WI

**Stifel, Fred**
Associate Pastor,
Singles/Visitation
Faith Presbyterian Church
Aurora, CO

**Suggs, Robert**
Director of Singles Ministries
Second Ponce De Leon
Baptist Church
Atlanta, GA

**Swanson, Terry**
Volunteer Leader
Calvary Chapel
Seattle, WA

**Talley, Jim**
Associate Minister to
Single Adults
First Baptist Church
Modesto , CA

**Taylor, Gary**
Pastor of Single Adults
Park Community Church
Chicago, IL

**Taylor, Tanya**
Volunteer Leader /Counselor
New Heritage Christian Center
Chicago, IL

**Thomas, Lyn**
Assistant Pastor, Education/
Singles and Young Adults
Arrow Highway
Wesleyan Church
Covina, CA

**Towns, Jim**
Volunteer Leader
Baptist Church
Nacogdoches, TX

**Van Loan, William**
Associate Pastor/
Single Adults
Arcadia Presbyterian Church
Arcadia, CA

**Vanden Bosch, Linda Brady**
Single Parent Ministries
Lodi, CA

**Vandewarker, Jim**
Pastor
Clarksville Wesleyan Church
Clarksville, MI

**Veale, Alan**
Pastor
Scottsdale Wesleyan Church
Scottsdale, AZ

**Vermillion, Tom**
Minister of Singles
Golf Course Road
Church of Christ
Midland, TX

**Victoriano, M. L.**
Volunteer Leader
United Methodist Church
Flagstaff, AZ

**Waller, Gary**
Associate Pastor of Adult
Ministries
Kent Church of the Nazarene
Kent, WA

**Westfall, John**
Associate Pastor of Adult
Ministries
University Presbyterian
Seattle, WA

**Wheeler, Dennis J.**
Associate Pastor of Adult
Ministries
First Church of Christ
Florence, KY

**White, William Larry**
Director of Singles/
Counseling
Skyline Wesleyan Church
Lemon Grove, CA

**Whitesel, Sue**
Director of Singles Ministry
Garfield Park Church of God
Indianapolis, IN

**Willhite, Patricia**
Singles Ministry Coordinator
St. Luke's United
Methodist Church
Kokomo, IN

**Winkleman, Gary**
Singles Minister
Overlake Christian Church
Kirkland, WA

**Wood, Nancy**
Diaconal Minister to Singles
First United Methodist Church
Orlando, FL

**Worley, Daryle**
Pastor of Singles
The Moody Church
Chicago, IL

**Young, Bob**
Director, Christian Singles
Tri City Baptist Temple
Gladstone, OR

**Yukers, Norman**
Director of Single Adults
Los Gatos Christian Church
Los Gatos, CA

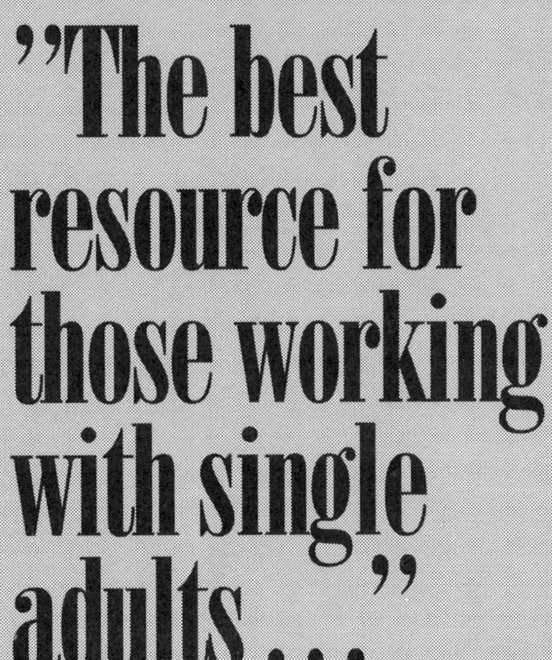


"I find practical ideas and insights in every issue of SAM Journal. It is the best resource available for pastors and leaders working with single adults . . . . Nothing else even comes close."

- PAUL PETERSEN
Highland Park Presbyterian Church,
Dallas, Texas

**Call toll FREE today to get your subscription started. 800-487-4-SAM or 719-488-2610.**

**Or write: SAM Journal, P. O. Box 62056, Colorado Springs, CO 80962-2056.**

A one-year subscription is $24 (10 issues); $29 in Canada; $33 for all other countries. U. S. funds only.
Payment by Visa, MasterCard, or "bill me" also available.

# Career and Work Related Issues

## Most Recommended Resource in This Section

(Based on evaluations and reviews made by *SAM Journal's* National Resource Review Board, using a 1-10 scale with 10 being the best possible score):

### 9.5 Your Work Matters To God

by D. Sherman and W. Hendricks (NavPress, 1987)

*(For more information on the above resource—plus other helpful products—find them listed in alphabetical order below.)*

### VIDEO/Called to the Marketplace

produced by 2100 Productions (InterVarsity Video, 1987) A two-tape, four-part series: Tape One, 26 min; Tape Two, 28 min. $59.95

***Not Yet Reviewed***

**NOTES:** Part I, "Being a Witness," focuses on how Christians can share their faith with co-workers by building relationships and being bold in their testimony. Part II, "Making the Right Choices," explores the moral and ethical dimensions of being a Christian in the marketplace. Part III, "Building the Kingdom," focuses on how God uses marketplace Christians to help build His kingdom. Part IV, "Following and Leading," focuses on how to follow and lead by serving others.

### Choosing Your Career, Finding Your Vocation: A Step by Step Guide for Adults and Counselors

by Roy Lewis (Paulist Press, 1989) 148 pp. $9.95

***Not Yet Reviewed***

**NOTES:** The author expands the present models, methods and practice of career counseling to include the spiritual dimension. He discusses the developmental stages that adults pass through, a theological understanding of work and vocation, assumptions about work and human potential, and the issues facing two-career families.

### On the Job: Survival or Satisfaction, How to Enjoy Your Work

by Jerry and Mary White (NavPress, 1988) 297 pp. $7.95

***Not Yet Reviewed***

**NOTES:** Because we spend as much as 40 percent of our waking hours working on a job, it is important for those hours to be fulfilling rather than frustrating. "On The Job" tackles the issues facing the Christian in the workplace, such as: how to handle adverse circumstances, the purpose of work in our lives, changing jobs, use of time, and ambition.

### Your Work Matters To God

by D. Sherman and W. Hendricks (NavPress, 1987) 286 pp. $14.95

***Overall Product Rating: 9.5***

**STRENGTHS:** Offers fresh new perspective on God's view of our jobs, our vocations... A must read for every young single adult (or anyone for that matter) trying to make career/life decisions...Comprehensive look at how believers have viewed work in the past and how it is viewed today...Written from within a Biblical framework...Helpful tool for leaders as they counsel single adults about living out their potential and making necessary life changes... Personable style holds your interest, very readable.

**WEAKNESSES:** Needs study guide, leaders guide, or questions for group interaction...It is a little long and at times technical, but overall a very helpful resource.

# Children of Divorce

## Most Recommended Resources in This Section

(Based on evaluations and reviews made by *SAM Journal's* National Resource Review Board, using a 1-10 scale with 10 being the best possible score):

### 8.3 Children and Divorce: What To Expect, How To Help

by Archibald Hart, Ph.D (Word Publishing, 1982)

### 8.3 Mom and Dad Don't Live Together Anymore

by Gary and Angela Hunt (Here's Life, 1989)

### 8.1 God Can Heal My Owies

by Barbara Dycus (self-published, 1986)

*(For more information on each of the above resources—plus many other helpful products—find them listed in alphabetical order below.)*

## How Does The National Review Board Function?

1. There are over 100 reviewers on this board, representing every major denomination and region of the country.
2. All reviewers are pastors, counselors or lay leaders involved in ministry with single adults.
3. Every product is reviewed and evaluated by *at least two - and in most cases, three - members* of this National Board. (When appropriate and possible, the product is actually used in a singles ministry prior to being evaluated.)
4. Each product is reviewed and evaluated on its own merit and not as it compares to other products or resources.
5. Reviewers' ratings for each product are tabulated and averaged by the staff of *Single Adult Ministries Journal* to determine each score. ***(Products are rated from 1 to 10, with 10 being the best rating possible.)***

## Adult Children of Divorce: Haunting Problems and Healthy Solutions

by Karen J. Sandvig (Word Publishing, 1990) 214 pp. $10.99

### Not Yet Reviewed

**NOTES:** Based on exhaustive research and real-life examples, the book grapples with the most prevalent feelings (loneliness, low self-esteem, fear of abandonment, need for consistency, tendency to extremes) and shows how to break the cycle and keep these feelings from contributing to dysfunctional relationships a generation later. More than just a catalog of ills, it prescribes positive, refreshing tips and exercises adults can apply to their wounds. Offers hope and wholeness for those who are still saddled with the trauma of their parent's divorce.

## Adult Children of Legal or Emotional Divorce

by Jim Conway (InterVarsity Press, 1990) 251 pp. $14.95

### *Not Yet Reviewed*

**NOTES:** Presents insights from author's own experience and shows adult children of divorce how to become healthy by helping them face their past; grieve their loss; shake off the victim mentality; forgive their parents and themselves; find spiritual direction; and receive support from others.

## Changing Families: A Guide for Kids and Grown-ups

by Fassler, Lash, and Ives (Waterfront Books, 1988) 180 pp. $14.95

### *Overall Product Rating: 6.6*

**STRENGTHS:** An on-target resource for helping meet the needs of children of divorce...The simplicity of this book is wonderful...The pictures and comments written by a child are especially appealing to children...Helps a child to openly discuss feelings...Written in a non-judgemental and supportive way that can help the child in a painful situation, one they have no control over.

**WEAKNESSES:** This book offers no Biblical basis for discussing separation, divorce or remarriage...It does not offer readers the hope of Christ nor the promise that God heals their hurts and understands their fears. With a Biblical base this would have been a powerful book...Lacks a study guide appropriate for lay leaders/facilitators.

## VIDEO/Children and Divorce

(Films Incorporated/Chicago, 1976) 37 min. $129.00

### *Not Yet Reviewed*

**NOTES:** The real victims of divorce are the children—bewildered at events they do not understand, harboring feelings of guilt that somehow they area at fault, suffering a sense of rejection. This study of the impact of divorce on children points at the necessity for parents to bury their own hostilities, to communicate without anger, and to provide the children with free access to both parents. (NBC News production.)

## Children and Divorce: What To Expect, How To Help

by Archibald Hart, Ph.D (Word Publishing, 1982) 156 pp. $8.99

### *Overall Product Rating: 8.3*

**STRENGTHS:** Very clearly written...An excellent discussion of the issues facing children of divorce and their parents... Because the author is a Christian psychologist (and the child of a single parent home) the treatment of the negative emotions experienced by a child going through divorce is especially helpful...Clear and concise... Good to see someone emphasize that a child needs lots of time to heal... Overall, a very solid book on the subject.

**WEAKNESSES:** Sometimes the material comes across in a clinical, detached manner ...I found it very useful for me personally but I probably would not use it as a text book with my single parents...Some of the solutions tend to be simplistic. For example, the author says "children must have a relationship with their father," but many times it is not that easy. What about the times when a parent is emotionally or psychologically unstable? There are many other factors to consider..

## Children Of Divorce

by Jim and Barbara Dycus (David C. Cook Publishing, 1987) 103 pp. $6.95

### *Overall Product Rating: 7.1*

**STRENGTHS:** The questions and answers were especially helpful. It gave good responses to many of the questions asked by divorced parents. This chapter alone makes the book worthwhile. I would like for each of my divorced parents to read this chapter... Very practical guidance. Specific enough that you can put it to use right away.

**WEAKNESSES:** Tries to cover too much material. I would rather they had tried to focus in on one particular area such as how the church needs to respond or counseling or help specifically for the parents. It's too much of a scattered, shotgun approach...The research is out of date...Too many quotes from other books...A bit simplistic at times.

## FILMSTRIP/Coping With Family Changes

(Sunburst Communications, 1982) 37 min. $175.00. (Also available in video.)

### *Not Yet Reviewed*

**Notes:** Three color filmstrips for teenagers of divorce. Shows how young people can help themselves and other family members cope with changing roles. Examples include single parent, stepparent and blended families. Three cassettes and teacher's guide included.

## Daughters Without Dads: Offering Understanding and Hope to Women Who Suffer From the Absence of A Loving Father

by Lois Mowday (Oliver Nelson, 1990) 224 pp. $13.95

***Not Yet Reviewed***

**NOTES:** Focuses on the emotional, physical, and spiritual consequences of the absent father syndrome. It offers guidelines for women about how to recognize the effects of an absent father and how to receive healing for inner pain. The author also address why Christians and the local church need to play a stronger role in providing help for this situation.

## VIDEO/Divorce and Other Monsters: Learning to Face Our Fears

A Barr Film (Franciscan Communications, 1989) 21.5 min. $34.95

***Not Yet Reviewed***

**NOTES:** Sandy reacts to her parents' divorce by talking to her parents, teacher, friend and directly to the viewer about her feelings of anger, fear, guilt and rejection.

## Divorce Recovery For Teenagers: How to Help Your Kids Recover, Heal, and Grow When Their Families Are Ripped Apart

by Stephen Murray and Randy Smith (Zondervan/YS, 1990) 155 pages. $12.95

***Not Yet Reviewed***

**NOTES:** Includes a complete divorce recovery workshop for teens along with several reproducible pages. Identifies stages of grief for kids; helps you help kids heal from the pain of divorce; helps kids improve their family relationships.

## Divorce Workbook, The

by Sally B. Ives, David Fassler, Michele Lash (Waterfront Books, 1985) 147 pp. $12.95

***Overall Product Rating: 6.5***

**STRENGTHS:** Good resource material to use with others in a workshop setting for kids of divorce (or by a parent or teacher-leader). A helpful catalyst to obtain response and discussion from children in counseling and or workshops...The simple children's drawings and statements appeal to children who are experiencing or have experienced divorce...Helps you better understand the feelings and experiences a child goes through when their parents divorce...Through the simplicity of this book, vocabulary that often is confusing to children becomes much more understandable...Written from the child's view...Facilitates drawing and coloring as an excellent therapy tool...Gives children permission to express emotions.
**WEAKNESSES:** Many good thoughts, but information is presented in such a way that may leave teachers/parents with the feeling, "OK, now what?" or "How should I do this with them?" No teacher's guide or instructions for leaders. Not cost-effective. With no rights to photocopy, few people will be able to buy multiple copies for children to color and use...Lacks spiritual/Biblical foundation which I find of paramount importance in dealing with kids of divorce.

## Divorced Kids: What You Need To Know To Help Kids Survive A Divorce

by Laurene Johnson and Georglyn Rosenfeld (Thomas Nelson, 1990) 218 pp. $8.95

***Not Yet Reviewed***

**NOTES:** Parents have the potential to help their kids not only survive but thrive, despite the pain of divorce. With the understanding of mothers who understand the difficult role of the divorced parent, Johnson and Rosenfeld provide answers to some of the tough questions moms and dads have: What is the best way to handle the situation when my ex comes to get the kids for the weekend? How do I establish discipline when my efforts are undermined every other weekend by my ex? What about dating and remarriage? What about grandparents? How about household chores?

## God Can Heal My Hurts

by Jim and Barbara Dycus (self-published, 1986) 91 pp. $6-students book; ($12-Teacher's Guide

***Overall Product Rating: 7.5***

**STRENGTHS:** Recognizes not only the needs of "divorce" children, but goes right to the heart with Biblical foundations...Provides curriculum for a very underdeveloped area of ministry in the church. The Bible stories (with the exception of a few) are well-chosen and provide a great source of understanding and comfort...The feelings addressed are right on target and the orientation at the beginning is very sensitive and helpful...We are just ready to launch a program for children of divorce and I'm sure we will be greatly enriched by some of these lessons.
**WEAKNESSES:** Low on creativity (i.e. the medium for teaching)...Basically a VBS version of working with children of divorce ...Appears targeted more to the charismatic/ Pentecostal persuasion (although good value can be gained by any church).

## God Can Heal My Owies

by Barbara Dycus (self-published, 1986) 62 pp. $6-students book; ($12-Teacher's Guide

***Overall Product Rating: 8.1***

**STRENGTHS:** An excellent resource for ministry to children of divorce...Effectively combines the basic principles of grief resolution with practical truth of God's love...Each lesson is designed to keep the children's attention through story/crafts helping them identify and resolve feelings resulting from their parent's divorce... Provides creative detailed group activities for each unit lesson. Even if one didn't imple-

## How Does The National Review Board Function?

1. There are over 100 reviewers on this board, representing every major denomination and region of the country.
2. All reviewers are pastors, counselors or lay leaders involved in ministry with single adults.
3. Every product is reviewed and evaluated by *at least two - and in most cases, three - members* of this National Board. (When appropriate and possible, the product is actually used in a singles ministry prior to being evaluated.)
4. Each product is reviewed and evaluated on its own merit and not as it compares to other products or resources.
5. Reviewers' ratings for each product are tabulated and averaged by the staff of *Single Adult Ministries Journal* to determine each score. ***(Products are rated from 1 to 10, with 10 being the best rating possible.)***

ment the entire course, most of the activities would be beneficial as an addendum to an already existing children's ministry...The section on "understanding children of divorce" in the teacher's manual is very useful.
**WEAKNESSES:** Some of the activities need a better explanation...Directions are sometimes incomplete and assumptions are made that all leaders have been in the church for a long time and understand and know songs to be sung. Many helpers may in fact be new Christians and need more complete direction...In many divorce recovery ministries, the majority of the families are unbelievers. This material seems to make the assumption that everyone involved is a Christian. Offering the Gospel is imperative but it must be done gently and sensitively... I disagree on their approach to handling anger and depression...Some of the coloring pages are too detailed for the age group.

## Helping Your Child Succeed After Divorce

by Florence Bienenfeld, Ph.D (Hunter House Inc., 1987) 206 pp. $9.95

***Overall Product Rating: 6.5***

**STRENGTHS:** Due to the thorough professional clinical research, it is valuable for diagnosing the needs and emotions of children of divorce. The section of children's drawings is particularly revealing and interesting...Very helpful in providing understanding of the struggles that children have as their parents fight over custody and visitation rights...An excellent resource for pastors or counselors who are dealing with persons in the midst of divorce or in the aftermath of divorce who are trying to decide the issues of custody and visitation...The pictures that the children have drawn say volumes and could be used with parents to show the pain that some children go through in the aftermath of divorce because of custody battles...Good diagnostic resource.
**WEAKNESSES:** The greatest weakness is its lack of spiritual perspective. Because of this, it will have limited value to church leaders who are developing a bible-centered ministry with children of divorce or single parents.

## Mike's Lonely Summer

by Carolyn Nystrom (Lion Publishing, 1986) 45 pp. $6.95

***Not Yet Reviewed***

**NOTES:** Looks at divorce through the eyes of 10-year-old Mike to help children find the answers to some of the questions that go through their mind when their parents divorce.

## Mom and Dad Don't Live Together Anymore

by Gary and Angela Hunt (Here's Life, 1989) 127 pp. $6.95.

***Overall Product Rating: 8.3***

**STRENGTHS:** Excellent resource tool for children/youth workers, SAM leaders and counselors...Contains many first hand comments from children and adults offering a realistic assessment of the divorce situation...Highlights various "booby-traps" to avoid...The "encouragements" for children and parents in the step-parenting chapter are excellent...Helps facilitate conversation between single parents and their children ...Would be useful for a group of teens with a facilitator or in a single parent support group.
**WEAKNESSES:** Sometimes does not do justice to the desperate nature of the divorced person's plight...The money issue often is much more grievous than the author acknowledges...Needed further discussion about the issues that arise when a parent dates...I would like to have seen more scriptural support given.

## FILM STRIP/My Mother and Father Are Getting Divorced

by Vanderslice/Davis (Sunburst Communications, 1984) 24 min. $119

***Overall Product Rating: 4.9***

**STRENGTHS:** If you had little or no background in this area it would sensitize you to children's feelings ...Looks at several different reasons for divorce...Represents a variety of emotional responses on the part of kids (especially from black families) and the way they deal with it...For a film strip, it is well done...Clearly states the objectives of the children's program...Labels the emotions and losses...Provides helpful and practical tools for help.
**WEAKNESSES:** Too elementary, too basic...A film strip is archaic in today's media generation and the dress of the kids is clearly outdated. I'm not sure I would use it...Quite expensive for the small amount of material.

## Our Family Got A Divorce

by Carolyn E. Phillips (Regal Press, 1979) 110 pp. $5.95

***Overall Product Rating: 7.5***

**STRENGTHS:** A sensitive story of a child struggling with his parents' divorce...One of the few narrative Christian children's books on this topic written from a child's perspective ...Written by a mom who has been there...Could be useful in helping other children explore and address the many emotions associated with divorce...A wonderful resource for leaders in single parent family ministries.
**WEAKNESSES:** The book needs to address more issues that do not have black-and-white answers. The truth is that some of the problems in divorce are unsolvable and it would have improved this book if that were made more apparent...Tended to focus more on solving external problems than on internal recovery...Tends to be written with a favorable bias towards the mother and a less than compassionate view of the absent father.

## Please Come Home: A Child's Book About Divorce

by Doris Sanford (Multnomah Press, 1985) 30 pp. $7.95

***Overall Product Rating: 6.9***

**STRENGTHS:** Divorce recovery from a child's view. Teddy (bear) talks directly to the problem...Is written simply with good art...The back two pages entitled "How to help a child with divorce," are really helpful as a discussion guide when talking to children about the subject...Sensitive handling of the subject...In a matter-of-fact manner, guides a child reader to understand the confusing emotions of divorce...Use of the teddy bear as a "constant" has a very stabilizing effect on a young reader.
**WEAKNESSES:** Slanted a bit towards the female being the "good gal" and the male being the "bad guy" ("Daddy wasn't going to live with them anymore;" "She was afraid Daddy might hit Mommy;" "She visited Daddy. It was fun at the park, but;" "Daddy has a girlfriend now;" "Mommy is so-o-o tired."... I'm not convinced that having the bear as the counselor is the best approach... Many subjects are covered very quickly. Sufficient discussion would need to accompany each page or two...Completely misses the opportunity to help a child see the love of God and His help in recovery. For this reason I'd hesitate to use it in our ministry.

## VIDEO/Single-Parent Families

(Sunburst, 1988) Includes Teacher's Guide, 37 min. $165

***Not Yet Reviewed***

**NOTES:** Examines several cases of single-parent families through the eyes of teenagers who are trying to cope with new responsibilities and changing roles in the family. Discusses the assignment of household chores and care for younger siblings as well as the impact of a parent's dating and socializing.

## What Children Need to Know When Parents Get Divorced

by William Coleman (Bethany House Publishers, 1983) 91 pp. $5.95

***Not Yet Reviewed***

**Notes:** A short, simple, understanding book to be read with a young child facing the agonizing trauma of divorce.

## VIDEO/Working with Students from the Broken Home

by Jim Burns (National Institute of Youth Ministry, 1989) 56 min. $49.00

***Not Yet Reviewed***

**NOTES:** The traditional family unit is rapidly deteriorating. Church leaders need handles and insights on how to work with kids from a disrupted family. Jim Burns helps pastors and youth workers understand the reactions of young people from a divorced background and offers thirteen practical ideas on how to have a more effective ministry to kids from broken homes.

# Counseling

## Most Recommended Resources in This Section

(Based on evaluations and reviews made by SAM Journal's National Resource Review Board, using a 1-10 scale with 10 being the best possible score):

### 9.3 Counseling For Family Violence and Abuse

by Dr. Grant Martin and Dr. Gary Collins (Word Publishing, 1987)

### 9.1 Christian Counseling: A Comprehensive Guide (Revised Edition)

by Dr. Gary Collins (Word Publishing, 1988)

### 9.0 Counseling Adult Children of Alcoholics

by Sandra D. Wilson, Ph.D. (Word Publishing, 1989)

### 8.7 Quick Scripture Reference For Counseling

by John G. Kruis (Baker Book House, 1987)

### 8.6 Help For The Post-Abortion Woman

by Terri and Paul Reisser (Zondervan, 1989)

### 8.5 Counseling and Homosexuality

by Earl D. Wilson (Word Publishing, 1988)

### 8.4 Counseling and Divorce

by David A. Thompson (Word Publishing, 1989)

### 8.0 Christian Peer Counseling: Love In Action

by Joan Sturkie and Gordon Bear (Word Pub., 1989)

### 8.0 Friendship Counseling

by Carol Lesser Baldwin (Zondervan, 1988)

*(For more information on each of the above resources—plus many other helpful products—find them listed in alphabetical order below.)*

## Christian Counseling: A Comprehensive Guide (Revised Edition)

by Dr. Gary Collins (Word, Inc. 1988) 711 pp. $18.99

***Overall Product Rating: 9.1***

**STRENGTHS:** Wide variety of subjects covered...Concise... Excellent reference book...Deals with various emotional issues well...The "case study" and "Biblical perspective" section of each chapter are especially helpful... Good balance between Biblical and psychological ...The section on counseling singles is very useful...A much needed, practical resource for those of us in singles ministry (both lay and clergy)...The extensive reference notes allow for further study on any given area... Provides a broad-based understanding of the issues we are called to address in the ministry.

**WEAKNESSES:** The print is a bit small for heavy reading...Not much "in-depth" study, but that is not the purpose of this book...I can't find anything to criticize about this excellent reference.

## Christian Peer Counseling: Love In Action

by Joan Sturkie and Gordon Bear (Word Pub., 1989) 201 pp. $12.99

***Overall Product Rating: 8.0***

**STRENGTHS:** A hands-on approach to this subject...Thorough coverage of how to begin a peer counseling ministry...Information and descriptions of present working ministries are a good resource ... Contains useful sample forms and specific program ideas... Compassionate style will motivate the reader...Provides good training for the peer counseling program and how to relate to hurting people...I found the possibilities of this concept as a ministry tool very exciting.

**WEAKNESSES:** Chapter One could have offered more direct incorporation of Biblical principles to help us see the ideal of Christian peer counseling...Could have given more information regarding recruiting/training of peer counselors—and how to handle those who should not be doing this...Gives the impression that anyone can be a counselor when some should not.

## How Does The National Review Board Function?

1. There are over 100 reviewers on this board, representing every major denomination and region of the country.
2. All reviewers are pastors, counselors or lay leaders involved in ministry with single adults.
3. Every product is reviewed and evaluated by *at least two - and in most cases, three - members* of this National Board. (When appropriate and possible, the product is actually used in a singles ministry prior to being evaluated.)
4. Each product is reviewed and evaluated on its own merit and not as it compares to other products or resources.
5. Reviewers' ratings for each product are tabulated and averaged by the staff of *Single Adult Ministries Journal* to determine each score. ***(Products are rated from 1 to 10, with 10 being the best rating possible.)***

## Counseling Adult Children of Alcoholics

by Sandra D. Wilson, Ph.D. (Word Publishing, 1989) 312 pp. $12.99

***Overall Product Rating: 9.0***

**STRENGTHS:** Presents a thorough, clear description of adult children of alcoholics and the alcoholic situation/pattern... Outlines well the types of counseling necessary for recovery ...The Christian leader will find a wealth of well-applied Scripture and theology to help "seekers" ...Author evidences excellent understanding ...A positive guide to help those who are victims of alcoholism.
**WEAKNESSES:** Needs a workbook to practice applying the insights gained before trying it out on clients...Study guide would be helpful.

## Counseling and Divorce

by David A. Thompson (Word Publishing, 1989) 199 pp. $12.99

***Overall Product Rating: 8.4***

**STRENGTHS:** Great book ...Author approaches pastors insightfully with this thorough, thoughtful, practical, theological and pastoral look at divorce... Provides healthy balance of anecdotal/ technical material...Realistic, Biblical in assessment of situations and people ...Gives grace to those who suffer divorce and to those who minister to them...Helps reader to recognize the many issues of divorce...Strong in counseling helps...Valuable material for divorce recovery ministries.
**WEAKNESSES:** Needed to explain and demonstrate the suggested counseling model for pastors more fully... Sometimes tended to identify issues without going deeper with solutions...Probably spent too much time in this book on remarriage (which could easily make another book).

## Counseling and Homosexuality

by Earl D. Wilson (Word Books, 1988) 225 pp. $12.95

***Overall Product Rating: 8.5***

**STRENGTHS:** Offers compassionate, non-judgemental approach... Helps counselor believe he can make a difference... Provides more than 100 practical ideas for counseling—ways to start the conversation, to summarize, to assess......Identifies important issues that Christians/counselors need to clarify for themselves ...A book every single adult leader should read...Helps us consider our theological position on homosexuality ...An exceptional book—best I've read on this subject.
**WEAKNESSES:** Would like to have seen more Biblical foundation relating to practical obedience for counselee...Little mention of the vast network of helpful ex-gay referral ministries nationwide.

## Counseling and Self-Esteem

by David Carlson (Word Publishing, 1988) 268 pp. $12.95

***Overall Product Rating: 7.6***

**STRENGTHS:** Offers practical guidelines for speaking to the issue of self-esteem and tools that can immediately be used by the counselor...Written for counselors, not for lay ministry...Provides clear cut relational process for facilitating the growth of healthy, self-esteem...Various case studies and practical application exercises are given with each major step.
**WEAKNESSES:** Needed to go more in depth on the issue of the self-esteem/identity of the "helper" counselor and how this relates to the counselee...Sometimes overly simple and does not assume enough ability and intelligence on the reader's part.

## Counseling For Anger

by Mark P. Cosgrove, Ph.D (Word Publishing, 1988) 176 pp. $12.99

***Overall Product Rating: 6.7***

**STRENGTHS:** Singles definitely struggle with this emotion. Could stimulate open discussion about anger and help overcome some unhealthy teaching/understanding in the Christian world...Provides several concise lists that would be helpful in counseling and teaching, each list dealing with a specific relational area of anger.
**WEAKNESSES:** Tends to be too theological and not practical enough ...Needs to be presented in a way that lay people would be interested in reading the book. The title leads one to believe it is mainly for counselors, but as a lay person I found it easy to read, understandable and a good resource.

## Counseling For Conflict Resolution

by Randolph Lowry and Richard Meyers (Word Publishing, 1991) $12.99

***Not Yet Reviewed***

**NOTES:** Sooner or later, conflict is inevitable in families, churches, organizations and ministries. But rather than adopting a fatalistic attitude, this book can help you manage the inevitable in such a way as to respect the relationships involved. This is a Biblical, practical guide for those Christians who must assist in the mediation of conflict between others.

## Counseling For Family Violence and Abuse

by Dr. Grant Martin and Gary Collins (Word Publishing, 1987) 280 pp. $12.99

***Overall Product Rating: 9.3***

**STRENGTHS:** The whole area of abuse and its effects on our lives is effectively addressed in this book...Outlines specific, clear steps to take to help someone in the recovery process who has experienced abuse in any form... Practical and clearly written. Excellent content.
**WEAKNESSES:** Ugly cover...Tends to be too academically-oriented. Not for the novice.

## Counseling For Problems of Self-Control

by Richard Walters (Word Publishing, 1987) 214 pp. $12.99

***Not Yet Reviewed***

**NOTES:** Defines self-control problems and the steps one needs to take to let go of compulsive behavior.

## Counseling For Unplanned Pregnancy and Infertility

by Everett Worthington (Word Publishing, 1987) 273 pp. $12.99

***Not Yet Reviewed***

**NOTES:** This book is written for counselors who are helping families with unplanned or unwanted pregnancies. Teen pregnancy, late-in-life pregnancy and unwed motherhood are viewed as crisis situations which can bring about life transitions. Infertility is also covered and the option of adoption is discussed.

## Counseling In Times Of Crisis

by Swihart and Richardson (Word Publishing, 1987) 210 pp. $12.99

***Not Yet Reviewed***

**NOTES:** Through years of experience in helping others cope with crises, the authors bring technical knowledge to this area of counseling. Crisis counseling is a unique ministry with specific goals and techniques that apply only in a crisis situation. The book examines the dynamics of various crises and uses a Biblical perspective to lay a foundation for counseling.

## Counseling Singles

by Keith Olson (Word Publishing, 1991) $12.99

***Not Yet Reviewed***

**NOTES:** Unlike any other group within the church and community, single adults simultaneously offer a vast reserve of unused talent while also requiring large amounts of sensitive counseling. As a result of this paradox, this book is designed to give the pastoral and professional counselor new and specific help for working with single adults. The author begins with the cultural, Biblical and historical perspectives, exploring the common myths and stereotypes about singleness. Then he presents specific counseling strategies for meeting needs. Finally, he provides support and guidelines which counselors can use in specific situations.

## Counseling the Depressed

by Archibald Hart (Word Publishing, 1987) 275 pp. $12.99

***Not Yet Reviewed***

**NOTES:** This book defines the various types of depression as well as the way depression relates to specific life problems. It advises the counselor in dealing with the wide range of depression problems, including suggestions for counseling the suicidal person.

## Friendship Counseling: A Biblical Guide to Helping Others

by Carol Lesser Baldwin (Zondervan, 1988) 309 pp. $12.50

***Overall Product Rating: 8.0***

**STRENGTHS:** Excellent suggestions for counseling and listening... Integration of confrontation and encouragement very helpful since most models emphasize one to the absence of the other...Good use of Scripture, not often seen in books like this...The study guide will help make anyone a better counselor/listener...Author gives scriptural backing or notations with each subject area. All of this would be beneficial to Bible study or group leader when preparing for a session...Some good role-play exercises are included to help in the teaching/ discussion...Well-written and understandable ...Excellent foundational tool for counseling... Provides good treatment of crisis counseling, great help.

**WEAKNESSES:** Illustrations were sometimes unrealistic, almost always showing a positive, successful response on part of person needing help...Theological models are sometimes too simplistic...Book not meant for light reading. It requires serious effort and much study...The book could mislead someone into believing that once having read the book, they are ready to save the world. The reader needs to be made more aware that counseling is not easy nor should everyone try it...Would like to have seen coverage on a greater variety of counseling problems.

## Heart of Pastoral Counseling, The: Healing Through Relationship

by Richard Dayringer (Zondervan, 1989) 173 pp. $8.95

***Not Yet Reviewed***

**NOTES:** The essence of pastoral counseling is in the relationship of the pastor with the parishioner. In 13 chapters, the author lays the foundation for utilizing the counseling relationship and explores such topics as observation, listening, communication, dealing with feelings, handling transference and termination.

## Help For The Post Abortion Woman

by Terri and Paul Reisser (Zondervan, 1989) 112 pp. $3.95

***Overall Product Rating: 8.6***

**STRENGTHS:** Presents compassionate help to women who struggle with P.A.S. symptoms as well as suggests avenues for treatment...Offers helpful "do's" and "don'ts" for counseling...Last chapter deals with how to begin much needed support groups ...This book helped me understand much better the P.A.S. woman, plus her emotional/physical pain...Is a great help for pastors, counselors and lay leaders...Helps us become more aware of the clues and symptoms of P.A.S. so we can help focus the healing light of Christ's love on this deep dark secret in so many women's lives...A must book for singles leaders.

**WEAKNESSES:** Would be good to have a workbook or journal for women to work through...Some quotes concerning God's forgiving power need to be given...No concrete scientific evidence is provided concerning P.A.S...Some will find it too simplistic (but its brevity makes it less intimidating).

## How Does The National Review Board Function?

**1.** There are over 100 reviewers on this board, representing every major denomination and region of the country.
**2.** All reviewers are pastors, counselors or lay leaders involved in ministry with single adults.
**3.** Every product is reviewed and evaluated by *at least two - and in most cases, three - members* of this National Board. (When appropriate and possible, the product is actually used in a singles ministry prior to being evaluated.)
**4.** Each product is reviewed and evaluated on its own merit and not as it compares to other products or resources.
**5.** Reviewers' ratings for each product are tabulated and averaged by the staff of *Single Adult Ministries Journal* to determine each score. ***(Products are rated from 1 to 10, with 10 being the best rating possible.)***

## Helping Victims of Sexual Abuse: A Sensitive, Biblical Guide for Counselors, Victims & Families

by Lynn Heitritter and Jeanette Vought (Bethany House Publishers, 1989) 272 pp. $8.95

***Overall Product Rating: 7.7***

**STRENGTHS:** Extremely informative, as abuse can be the root of many problems... Easy reading, not too technical...Includes excellent homework exercises...Offers expansive view of the issue...Practical resource, teachable ideas.

**WEAKNESSES:** Would like to have seen more Biblical correlations...Too fine print.

## Helping When It Hurts: A Practical Guide to Helping Relationships

by Robert L. Hunter (Augsburg Fortress, 1985) 80 pp. $4.95

***Not Yet Reviewed***

**NOTES:** The author provides practical illustrations of various types of counseling situations as well as suggested discussion questions and meditations.

## Hope For Hurting Relationships

by Myron Rush (Victor Books, 1989) 166 pp. $6.95

***Overall Product Rating: 6.5***

**STRENGTHS:** Book is laid out well...Helpful, personal illustrations...Most beneficial when working with separated or newly remarried people. The analysis of the causes of poor relationships is accurate and insightful as is the description of the different stages of deteriorating relationships...Well-organized and well-written, easy to understand.

**WEAKNESSES:** Most of the examples in the book are related to marriage relationships. By expanding the variety of examples to other binding relationships, this book could have had a much broader appeal...Author makes several therapeutic errors. He is not a counselor, yet sometimes tends to apply therapeutic techniques inappropriately.

## How to Help People Change

by Jay E. Adams (Zondervan, 1986) 203 pp. $7.95

***Overall Product Rating: 6.0***

**STRENGTHS:** Helps one understand the substantial change requiring the alteration of the heart and how the counselor works to bring about that change...A great guide in teaching one the steps of counseling...A simple, fundamental look at some of the basics required in helping people move toward change.

**WEAKNESSES:** I'm uncomfortable with his approach. He discredits the field of psychology except for those who buy his approach... Helping people change is not as simple as he implies ...Heavy and difficult to wade through, especially in the beginning.

## AUDIO CASSETTE/How to Reconcile A Marriage

by Dr. James Dobson with Jim Talley (Word Audio, 1987) 60 min. $9.95

***Overall Product Rating: 7.3***

**STRENGTHS:** Offers guidelines for talking about reconciliation between marriage partners whose marriage has dissolved. It would be an excellent tape to begin that process...The six requirements to pastors before performing a wedding are very useful.

**WEAKNESSES:** I realize there were time limitations on this tape but more facts on how the sessions on reconciliation are to be conducted would have been most helpful... Not for everyone who has experienced divorce, but could be valuable to those for whom it is intended.

## Innovative Approaches To Counseling

by Dr. Gary Collins (Word Publishing, 1986) 223 pp. $12.99

***Not Yet Reviewed***

**NOTES:** Working with people in the privacy and confidentiality of a counseling office is of crucial importance, but often there are other, less-traditional approaches to counseling that can be of equal or even greater effectiveness. This book describes some of these approaches.

## Pastoral Care Emergencies

by David K. Switzer (Paulist Press, 1989) 223 pp. $9.95

***Not Yet Reviewed***

**NOTES:** People in ministry interact with many people experiencing great emotional needs and spiritual hunger. Many in ministry hesitate to respond because they do not have advanced education in specialized pastoral care. This books provides a case for caring action as well as carefully developed information.

## Quick Scripture Reference For Counseling

by John G. Kruis (Baker Book House, 1987) 144 pp. $5.95

***Overall Product Rating: 8.7***

**STRENGTHS:** A handy, quick compilation by counseling topic...It is very important to back counseling with Scripture. This book allows you to do that.

**WEAKNESSES:** I would like to see a list of other Scripture references at the bottom of each topic.

## Short-Term Counseling

by David Dillion (Word Publishing, 1991) $12.99

***Not Yet Reviewed***

**NOTES:** Under ideal circumstances, pastors and Christian counselors can invest large amounts of time in diagnosing and treating a problem. But in today's fast-paced society, time frequently is limited and pro-fessional must intervene in emergencies. This book is a helpful resource for those situations. The author shows counselors how to guide patients through brief counseling opportunities while applying resources that have long-term impact.

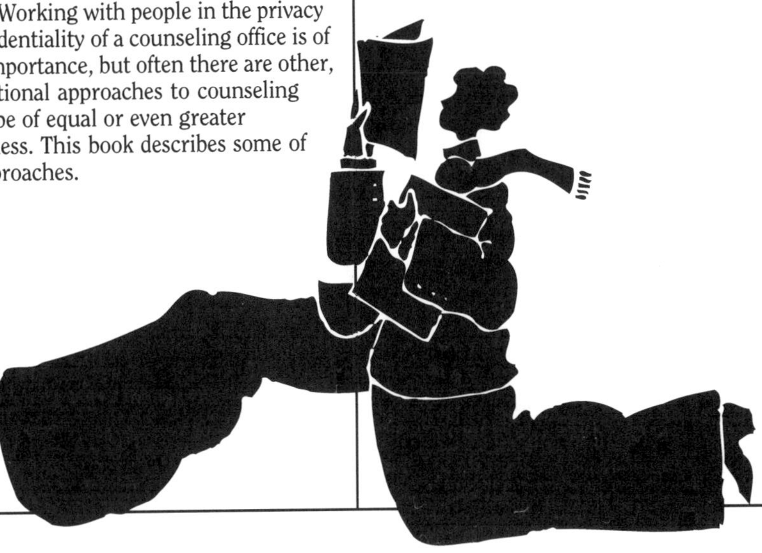

## Short-Term Pastoral Counseling

by Brian H. Childs (Abingdon Press, 1990) 135 pp. $10.95

***Not Yet Reviewed***

**NOTES:** Shows how certain problems such as poor job performance, minor depression, grief and some forms of obsession can be tackled by short-term pastoral counseling. Provides dialogue examples with sample questions that pastors can use to prepare for and conduct counseling sessions.

## Solving Marriage Problems

by Jay E. Adams (Zondervan, 1983) 122 pp. $4.95

***Overall Product Rating: 7.6***

**STRENGTHS:** Offers sound Biblical perspectives...Covers a wide range of marriage problems and suggested counseling for each in text-book fashion...Would be a helpful book in every pastor's and counselor's library...Useful information for pre-marital counseling.

**WEAKNESSES:** Idealistic and over-simplified because many issues are not as easy to resolve as the author sometimes implies. Issues can be deeply rooted and many faceted.

# Divorce & Remarriage

## Most Recommended Resources in This Section

(Based on evaluations and reviews made by *SAM Journal*'s National Resource Review Board, using a 1-10 scale with 10 being the best possible score):

### 9.6 But I Didn't Want a Divorce

by Andre Bustanoby (Zondervan, 1978)

### 9.5 No One Gets Divorced Alone: How Divorce Affects Moms, Dads, Kids and Grandparents

by H. S. Vigeveno & Anne Claire (Regal, 1987)

### 9.0 Starting Over Single: Life and Hope After the Death of a Marriage

by Mervin E. Thompson (Prince of Peace, 1985)

### 8.6 Courage to Begin Again: When Things Go Wrong, What Then?

by Ron Lee Davis and James Denney (Harvest House, 1988)

### 8.6 Hope For the Separated: Wounded Marriages Can Be Healed

by Gary Chapman (Moody Press, 1982)

### 8.6 I Wish Someone Understood My Divorce: A Practical Cope Book

by Harold Ivan Smith (Augsburg Fortress, 1986)

### 8.6 Reconcilable Differences: Mending Broken Relationships

by Jim Talley (Thomas Nelson, 1985)

### 8.6 Remarriage and God's Renewing Grace: A Positive Biblical Ethic For Divorced Christians

by Dwight H. Small (Baker Book House, 1986)

### 8.5 Beginning Again: Life After a Relationship Ends

by Terry Hershey and Lisa McAfee (Thomas Nelson, 1986)

### 8.3 Ministry of Divorce Recovery, The: A Workshop Development Manual

by Dr. Bill Flanagan (NSL Publications, 1987)
NOTE: This book is being revised and republished by Singles Ministry Resources/NavPress and will be available in early 1991 retitled, "Developing a Divorce Recovery Ministry."

*(For more information on each of the above resources—plus many other helpful products—find them listed in alphabetical order below.)*

## Ashes to Gold

by Patti Roberts with Sherry Andrews (Word Publishing, 1983) 171 pp. $4.99

***Not Yet Reviewed***

**NOTES:** Patti Roberts knows what it means to succeed. But she also knows what it means to fail in one of the most basic relationships—marriage. She and her husband projected an image of married bliss as they sang together on television. Yet, their marriage never grew strong in its own right for they did not take the time to nurture it. "Ashes To Gold" offers counsel, insights and spiritual inspiration concerning the meaning of commitment, loyalty and love in Christian marriage.

## How Does The National Review Board Function?

1. There are over 100 reviewers on this board, representing every major denomination and region of the country.
2. All reviewers are pastors, counselors or lay leaders involved in ministry with single adults.
3. Every product is reviewed and evaluated by *at least two - and in most cases, three - members* of this National Board. (When appropriate and possible, the product is actually used in a singles ministry prior to being evaluated.)
4. Each product is reviewed and evaluated on its own merit and not as it compares to other products or resources.
5. Reviewers' ratings for each product are tabulated and averaged by the staff of *Single Adult Ministries Journal* to determine each score. ***(Products are rated from 1 to 10, with 10 being the best rating possible.)***

## Beginning Again: Life After A Relationship Ends

by Terry Hershey and Lisa McAfee (Thomas Nelson, 1986) 165 pp. $7.95

***Overall Product Rating: 8.5***

**STRENGTHS:** The author does an excellent job of letting the single person know there is hope after a relationship ends...He not only deals with divorce recovery, but loneliness, sexuality, self-talk and several other issues that transcend divorce...He puts it into concise, organized sections...Includes "Affirmation Exercises" and study questions... This is an excellent resource for both the single adult as well as the single adult leader.

**WEAKNESSES:** Because the author covers several topics in the book, he doesn't elaborate much on any one area. Consequently, in at least some instances, he doesn't do justice to the concepts and this may frustrate some readers.

## Broken and Mended Again: Spouse Abuse

by Joy Loy (Harbour House, 1986) 160 pp.

***Not Yet Reviewed***

**NOTES:** How can a battered woman forgive? How can she start again? What does she do when the people in her church turn their back on her and ask her to step down as a Sunday school teacher? Is divorce, indeed, the unpardonable sin?

## But I Didn't Want a Divorce

by Andre Bustanoby (Zondervan, 1978) 174 pp. $6.95

***Overall Product Rating: 9.6***

**STRENGTHS:** Offers very clear, sound, common-sense information ...Easy to read...Well researched...If you were to only read one book on the subject, this one (Scripturally) covers nearly all the issues of divorce from separation to remarriage ...Written in a compassionate, non-judgemental style...Does not gloss over the sin of divorce but looks at the power of forgiveness and grace—and helps the individual move on in life...This was the first book I read on the subject after my divorce nearly eight years ago. It helped change my life—I've recommended it to many others since.

**WEAKNESSES:** I think the title is weak, and a table of information in the book (page 32) is hard to read... The author has a slight tendency to get too technical in places... Wish the title did not limit this book just to the divorce person. It is also an excellent book for married couples who think they could never get a divorce and for the family and friends of those going through divorce.

## By Death Or Divorce It Hurts to Lose

by Amy Ross Mumford (Accent Books, 1976) 160 pp. $4.95

***Overall Product Rating: 7.9***

**STRENGTHS:** The author writes with a "been there" authority... Clearly expresses the differences and similarities of both widowhood and divorce...The practical advise for how to change a life-style are excellent... Shows how Scripture can be a healing aid...I appreciated the authors candid view of herself as a committed Christian who failed in a marriage...Shows how she chose to be healed by God and grow closer to him in the process instead of becoming bitter and self-focused.

**WEAKNESSES:** The book starts off a little slow...I'm concerned that it may not be received as well by those struggling financially. Some of it may not be realistic for them...The book seemed to be inconsistent in places. For example, after an effective chapter suggesting ways to minimize being treated as a second-class citizen (page 95), the author advises the reader to accept that kind of treatment in his or her home church (page 129).

## Courage to Begin Again: When Things Go Wrong, What Then?

by Ron Lee Davis and James Denney (Harvest House, 1988) 186 pp. $5.95

***Overall Product Rating: 8.6***

**STRENGTHS:** Filled with great illustrations that offer hope..."Alone Again," the chapter on divorce, is excellent...Would be a great book to use for a small group to help people come back from set backs of any kind...Real experiences and realistic solutions...A very positive statement about God's grace... Theologically sound...Easy to read and understand.

**WEAKNESSES:** To make it more useful for a small group study, it needs some thought-provoking questions at the end of each chapter or in an appendix...Some may find it too anecdotal and not academic enough.

## Dance Of The Broken Heart

by John and Patti Thompson (Abingdon Press, 1986) 204 pp. $11.95

***Not Yet Reviewed***

**NOTES:** This is the story of how one couple's tragically-broken marriage was healed through a new covenant with God. She, the author of the best-seller, "Ashes to Gold," and he, the composer of Amy Grant's "El Shaddai" and other songs. They struggle with the compelling issues of our time: the meaning of marriage, the sanctity of the family and the potential for healing in a loving, blended family.

## Developing a Divorce Recovery Ministry: A How to Manual

by Dr. Bill Flanagan (Singles Ministry Resources/NavPress, 1991) $19.95

***Not Yet Reviewed***

**NOTES:** This book explores the rationale of divorce recovery ministry. And although it discusses some of the current theological arguments about divorce and remarriage in the church, its emphasis is practical. It gives sound step-by-step guidance for Christian pastors and lay leaders who are establishing a divorce recovery ministry in their own church, encouraging many to develop a ministry of hope and recovery with some of the church's most hurting members.

## Devotions For the Divorcing

by William Thompson (John Knox Press, 1985) 98 pp. $6.95

***Not Yet Reviewed***

**NOTES:** A glimmer of hope and inspiration for people in the midst of divorce. The meditations in this book cover depression, ecstasy, boredom, death, sexuality, church experiences, social settings, fears, family and job performance.

## Divorce: Legal and Personal Concerns

by Elizabeth Ogg (Public Affairs Pamphlet, 1987) 28 pp. $1.00

***Overall Product Rating: 5***

**STRENGTHS:** Some good statistical information...Highlights the many differences and injustices current U.S. divorce laws inflict on par-ticipants...Covers many divorce-related issues of interest to pastors and leaders.

**WEAKNESSES:** No theological basis...Gives the subtle suggestion that "it's OK to divorce" without any attempt to try to "work things out"...I would not give this to my single adults but would use it as an informational and statistical resource.

## Divorce: The Pain and the Healing (Personal Meditations When Marriage Ends)

by Judith Mattison (Augsburg, 1985) 95 pp. $6.50

***Not Yet Reviewed***

**NOTES:** This is a book of insights and devotions which address the healing process one must experience after divorce.

## Divorce and Remarriage: Four Christian Views

by Laney, Heth, Edgar and Richards (InterVarsity Press, 1990) 266 pp. $9.95

***Not Yet Reviewed***

**NOTES:** Not everyone who appeals to Scripture agrees about how we should understand what it says about divorce and remarriage. In this book, four authors present their distinct perspectives. Each essayist in this collection not only presents his own case but also critiques the position of the others. Case studies at the end of each essay help to make theory face reality.

## AUDIO CASSETTE/ Divorce and Remarriage in the Church

by Mark Lauterbach (self-produced) Three tapes x six talks x 30 min/talk $12.00

***Overall Product Rating: 7.5***

**STRENGTHS:** One of the best Biblical, cultural, historical and practical looks at the issue of divorce, remarriage and restoration that I have ever seen from a conservative, evangelical perspective. The speaker covers virtually every key passage on those issues, and refreshingly allows the Bible to speak louder than tradition...Each of the six talks can stand on their own and lend themselves well to discussion groups ...Matter-of-fact, not opinionated... The teaching on leadership in the church (when divorced or "fallen") was of great interest...This series clearly illustrates the forgiveness and grace of the Lord in action, upon repentance.

**WEAKNESSES:** The quality of the tapes need to be improved. The third tape is extremely short and the series ends very abruptly...Too much repetition...Without a printed guide or notes this series was hard to follow...Not a real dynamic presentation...These sermons need to be edited for broader appeal...At times the speaker walks a thin line between being authoritarian vs. the more positive authoritative.

## Divorce Decision, The

by Gary Richmond (Word Publishing, 1988) 214 pp. $9.95

***Not Yet Reviewed***

**NOTES:** This resource provides factual information and first-hand accounts from people who have experienced the trauma of divorce. For those considering divorce, this book challenges the couple to mend their own marital relationship, presenting the consequences of divorce in a frank and realistic manner.

## Divorce Handbook, The (Updated Edition)

by James T. Friedman (Random House, 1984) $7.95

***Not Yet Reviewed***

**NOTES:** A practical help for people who are divorced or considering divorce. Many suggestions for possible solutions to problems that are common to many divorced individuals.

## VIDEO/Divorce is Changing America

(Films Incorporated, Chicago, 1986) 50 min. $198.00

***Not Yet Reviewed***

**NOTES:** Divorce is creating a separate class of impoverished women, for modern American divorce laws presuppose full equality for both sexes in all areas, including the workplace, despite the fact that for many women such equal earning potential does not yet exist. In this NBC White Paper, Jane Pauley examines this sad situation. Divorce is also creating a society where it is socially acceptable for parents—particularly fathers—not to support their offspring. (An NBC News production.)

## Divorce Recovery: Piecing Together Your Broken Dreams

by Anita Brock (Worthy Publishing, 1988) 192 pp. $10.95

***Overall Product Rating: 7.5***

**STRENGTHS:** Offers a comprehensive, step-by-step guide to both understanding the emotions and stages of divorce, plus how to begin and conduct a divorce recovery workshop...The chapter on self-esteem is very good, the author's "S" formula will help the reader grow...The leader's guide is excellent... I already had much of this same information, but not in one handy book.

**WEAKNESSES:** Her information on the divorce recovery process is handled better in several other books on the market...There are not enough practical 1-2-3 suggestions...Too many case study examples given that may not accurately reflect the experiences of others.

## VIDEO/Divorce Recovery: Rebuilding the Castle That Has Come Down

by Bill Flanagan (Gospel Films, 1990) 3 video, 60 min. each, 30 min. per session. $149.95

***Not Yet Reviewed***

**NOTES:** Divorce is not about facts and figures, but about people who need support in their lives. This six-part video series focuses on people and their problems and feelings relating to divorce.

## Divorce Recovery Workshop

by Doug Morphis (Discipleship Resources, 1986) 27 and 74 pp. $3.45 ($6.95 for Leader's Guide)

***Overall Product Rating: 7.6***

**STRENGTHS:** Encourages participants to journal, to record their thoughts and feelings...Is presented in a non-intimidating way...Very logical and organized... Designed well for small group interaction, not just lecture.. .Could be especially useful for a first time divorce recovery program...Leader's Guide well outlined with step-by-step instruc-tions...Participants workbook has strong appeal to those who want to journal or

## How Does The National Review Board Function?

1. There are over 100 reviewers on this board, representing every major denomination and region of the country.
2. All reviewers are pastors, counselors or lay leaders involved in ministry with single adults.
3. Every product is reviewed and evaluated by *at least two - and in most cases, three - members* of this National Board. (When appropriate and possible, the product is actually used in a singles ministry prior to being evaluated.)
4. Each product is reviewed and evaluated on its own merit and not as it compares to other products or resources.
5. Reviewers' ratings for each product are tabulated and averaged by the staff of *Single Adult Ministries Journal* to determine each score. ***(Products are rated from 1 to 10, with 10 being the best rating possible.)***

write in a workbook.
**WEAKNESSES:** Too much material squeezed into each session. Need more time to explore identity, grief, survival...Due to a lack of psychological information or role playing guidelines, the enablers may find themselves over their heads...The danger is that, as written, this material might be presented in a superficial manner by an untrained or unqualified leader...Devoid of adequate encouraging spiritual reflection... Too few references to Scripture.

## VIDEO/Divorce Recovery Workshop

lead by Rev. Andy Morgan (Single Point Ministries, 1989) $100

***Not Yet Reviewed***

**NOTES:** This seven-part series is designed to help persons face and recover from divorce. It looks at: "Identity: Getting My 'Ex' in Focus;" "Forgiveness: Assuming Responsibility;" "Dating and Remarriage: Single Parenting;" and "Let Go and Live." Each session ends with questions that can be discussed in small groups.

## AUDIO CASSETTES/ Divorce Recovery Workshop

First Assembly of God, Rockford, Ill. (self-produced, 1988) $29

***Not Yet Reviewed***

**NOTES:** Six-cassette, seven-session series with accompanying leader's and participant's guides designed to assist separated and divorced people find answers, methods and hope to mental, emotional, financial, social, spiritual and relational problems.

## Divorced I Wouldn't Have Given a Nickel for Your Chances

by Suzanne Stewart (Zondervan, 1987) 224 pp. $7.95

***Overall Product Rating: 5.6***

**STRENGTHS:** Looks at a personal account of experiences encountered by a recently-divorced single parent ...The book helps the reader understand some of the roller coaster feelings and emotional ups and downs that affect many of those involved in our single adult ministries...Shows examples of God's provisions.
**WEAKNESSES:** Too much like a personal diary...The author is so specific that it seems to have limited application to people in my ministry. I couldn't hand it to them and expect them to identify with many of her experiences...The book seems to be written with a certain naivete to contemporary times. Seems more reflective of the 60s...Has little practical application...This book doesn't do much for me.

## Divorced Christian, The

by Charles Cerling (Baker Books, 1984) 194 pp. $9.95

***Overall Product Rating: 6.8***

**STRENGTHS:** This book will help the non-divorced become better acquainted with many of the issues and concerns facing Christians who experience divorce...Helpful reading when a friend of yours is going through divorce...Offers good discussion on many of the natural feelings and reactions of those experiencing divorce...I would recommend that all newly-divorced people read this and/or study it in a small group.
**WEAKNESSES:** Leaves out some important issues such as finances ...Lacks depth and freshness, often too superficial...Seldom offers Scriptural references to back up Biblical assumptions...Some illustrations are weak and inappropriate. Example: when author compares his loneliness from a two-day absent wife with the loneliness of those separated.

## Divorced Woman's Handbook

by Georgette McGrath (Globe Communications Corp., 1987) 64 pp. 75¢

***Overall Product Rating: 5.5***

**STRENGTHS:** Because the legalities involved in divorce are so confusing at times, this book's clarification of several terms was quite beneficial (such as joint legal custody vs. joint physical custody, when and who gets social security, getting credit etc.) ...Contains lots of useful information and general wisdom for divorcing women...The small size encourages women to keep it with them for reinforcement or easy use in discussion with others.
**WEAKNESSES:** Some inaccurate statements, such as on p. 55 where it is stated that most remarriages are successful. Statistics would discredit that remark. Other statistics/ statements were not footnoted or backed up in any way...The weakest sections are "dating again," and "getting serious." Much too superficial...Needed some material on the stages of grief and loss, also the subtle psychological factors at work in mate selection and marriage and remarriage ...The cover was pathetic. Artwork was cheaply done.

## Divorcing, Believing, Belonging

by James J. Young (Paulist Press 1984) 223 pp. $7.95

***Not Yet Reviewed***

**NOTES:** A series of essays or meditations which follow the divorcing person through the trauma of a broken marriage. This is a book about transforming painful experiences into life-giving experiences. Based on the author's ministry with Catholics.

## Divorcing Christian, The

by Lewis Rambo (Abingdon, 1983) 94 pp. $4.95

***Not Yet Reviewed***

**NOTES:** The author speaks about divorce by laying out his own experience as a divorced person and deals with specific theological problems presented to Christians who are divorced. He also discusses how and why the church needs to be a haven for hurting persons as well as a community of love and support.

## Finding Your Place After Divorce: How Women Can Find Healing

by Carole Sanderson Streeter (Zondervan, 1986) 144 pp. $6.95

***Overall Product Rating: 5.7***

**STRENGTHS:** A good book for women experiencing the struggles of divorce. Includes good exercises after each chapter to assist in the healing process...Challenges the church in its responsibility to minister to divorced persons...Offers good insight into decisions women have to make when suddenly alone...The author is very honest and open.

**WEAKNESSES:** Needs to go more in-depth. She whets the appetite, but doesn't always fulfill...The chapter about careers and working is inadequate and confusing...The book is directed too much to women from extreme theologically-conservative backgrounds.

## VIDEO/God's Blueprint: Divorce and Remarriage

Featuring Tony Evans (Moody Video, 1989) 50 minutes, $29.95

***Overall Product Rating: 5.3***

**STRENGTHS:** Strong exposition of classic Biblical passages on divorce and remarriage ...Puts in video format much of the "grounds for divorce" material presented in several books...Very evangelical presentation.

**WEAKNESSES:** The setting and delivery style tends to limit the potential audience to very churched, black evangelicals...It comes off quite hard-line fundamentalist which will limit its effectiveness...The tone of the message sometimes sounds too punitive... Grace as answer to divorce is only alluded to. ..This is not a video for divorce ministry, but an argument to discourage divorce before it happens...Although the speaker seemed theologically correct in most of what he said, he didn't seem to go far enough with a Biblical response to divorce once it happens ...This video would probably be inappropriate for persons without strong church/Bible background.

## VIDEO/God's Pattern Broken: Divorce and Remarriage ("The Family: God's Pattern for Living" series)

by Dr. John MacArthur (Moody Video, 1989) 50 min. $29.95

***Overall Product Rating: 5.1***

**STRENGTHS:** Gifted speaker...Sets forth a strong Biblical statement on divorce and remarriage...Uses a great deal of Scripture in his presentation.

**WEAKNESSES:** Weak ending...Needs more practical advise for those who are remarried. He simply states that they are to "live by God's will" but does not state what that is...There is a wider perspective in God's Word on this subject than was presented. The subject wasn't researched as much as it should have been. Divorce is not of God, but when someone does end a marriage, we shouldn't make them feel second class... Talked mostly about divorce, very little on remarriage or forgiveness...A presentation of one man's view/interpretation ...Not always accurate in my view.

## Growing in Remarriage: Working Through the Unique Problems of Remarriage

by Jim Smoke (Revell, 1990) 188 pp. $12.95

***Not Yet Reviewed***

**NOTES:** This eye-opening guide explores the wide range of questions, hopes and fears that comes with a new marriage. Among the wealth of sensitive, practical information the author presents here are seven keys for a successful second marriage, a chapter of questions and suggestions, the "Am I Ready for Remarriage?" test and a sample second-marriage ceremony.

## Growing Through Divorce (Expanded Edition)

by Jim Smoke (Harvest House, 1986) Includes Working Guide. 256 pp. $7.95

***Overall Product Rating: 8.1***

**STRENGTHS:** Excellent tool for divorce recovery workshops, especially with the Working Guide...Offers a healing orientation...Focuses on primary issues rather than extraneous ...Extensive coverage of the subject, including the "games" often played with children and ex-spouse...Emphasis placed on personal responsibility to get on with your life...One of the best resources for either doing a DR workshop or to use in counseling...I think this book could also be used for divorce prevention counseling...I recommend that every pastor and lay leader working with singles have a copy of this book.

**WEAKNESSES:** Although its not a significant factor, I felt the book could use some more Scriptural references ...The book tends to say "forget the past" when I think we need to sometimes honestly deal more with our mistakes and failures of the past before we can move on in healthy ways.

## Hate Divorce But Love the Divorced

by Tom Vermillion (The Single Life Institute, 1988) 12 pp. Free

***Overall Product Rating: 5.6***

**STRENGTHS:** Short, condensed presentation (from theologically conservative perspective) of a compassionate understanding for those persons caught in divorce... Easy-to-read pamphlet...May be helpful to those who feel ostracized as a result of divorce

## How Does The National Review Board Function?

1. There are over 100 reviewers on this board, representing every major denomination and region of the country.
2. All reviewers are pastors, counselors or lay leaders involved in ministry with single adults.
3. Every product is reviewed and evaluated by *at least two - and in most cases, three - members* of this National Board. (When appropriate and possible, the product is actually used in a singles ministry prior to being evaluated.)
4. Each product is reviewed and evaluated on its own merit and not as it compares to other products or resources.
5. Reviewers' ratings for each product are tabulated and averaged by the staff of *Single Adult Ministries Journal* to determine each score. ***(Products are rated from 1 to 10, with 10 being the best rating possible.)***

**WEAKNESSES:** Too general and shallow to be of much use to most singles...Due to its brevity, it does not adequately cover the theological issues of divorce.

## Home to Dwell In, A: One Woman's Journey Beyond Divorce

by Elise Chase (Ballantine, 1989) 172 pp. $3.50

***Not Yet Reviewed***

**NOTES:** The story of one woman's journey of recovery after her divorce. The book responds to the anger and pain of divorce with faith—faith in God, our abilities and ourselves. According to the author, this faith can guide one out of the depths of despair into a new, healthy and creative life.

## Hope For The Separated: Wounded Marriages Can Be Healed

by Gary Chapman (Moody Press, 1982) 119 pp. $6.95

***Overall Product Rating: 8.6***

**STRENGTHS:** Provides a basis of reasonable hope for reconciliation...Helpful, positive response to issues of separation. Leaves reader with the feeling that someone understands...Stresses responsibility.

**WEAKNESSES:** Out-of-date biography...The lack of a workbook and leader's guide limits its practical application.

## AUDIO CASSETTES/ How to Start a Beginning Again Ministry

by Terry Hershey (Christian Focus, Inc., 1989) $29.95

***Not Yet Reviewed***

**NOTES:** Single-cassette tape and accompanying 71-page guide designed to assist in the development of an effective ministry with anyone who has experienced a significant personal loss through a divorce, the death of a spouse or a friend, or the break up of an important relationship.

## AUDIO CASSETTE/How to Reconcile a Marriage

by Dr. James Dobson with Rev. Jim Talley (Word Audio, 1987) 60 min. $9.95

***Overall Product Rating: 7.3***

**STRENGTHS:** Offers guidelines for talking about reconciliation between marriage partners whose marriage has dissolved. It would be an excellent tape to begin that process...The six requirements to pastors before performing a wedding are very useful.

**WEAKNESSES:** I realize there were time limitations on this tape but more facts on how the sessions on reconciliation are to be conducted would have been most helpful... Not for everyone who has experienced divorce, but could be valuable to those for whom it is intended.

## VIDEO/How to Survive a Divorce

by Jim Smoke (Master Vision Inc., 1985) 180 min. $65

***Not Yet Reviewed***

**Notes:** Five part series on two tapes. The focus is on helping individuals turn their challenges and failures into positive learning, growing experiences. Topics include: Building a New Identity, Relating to your Former Spouse, Healing through Forgiveness.

## I Wish Someone Understood My Divorce: A Practical Cope Book

by Harold Ivan Smith (Augsburg Fortress, 1986) 157 pp. $8.95

***Overall Product Rating: 8.6***

**STRENGTHS:** A practical "how-to" cope book...The short chapters can easily be used for discussion group material...It reminds pastors not to overlook areas that are not part of their own personal experience ...Offers honest, frank discussion on the single life that many people think about but don't know how to verbalize.

**WEAKNESSES:** Several of my single-again leaders read it, and some felt it was too shallow and simplistic in places...Because the author doesn't give much emphasis on the possibilities of Biblical reconciliation, I wouldn't give this book to a separated person. But it's helpful for others.

## VIDEO/Intimate Relations

(Films Incorporated, Chicago, 1983) 50 min. $198

***Not Yet Reviewed***

**NOTES:** Explores the possible consequences of the breakdown of stable marital relationships in our society. Through the eyes of a small group of divorced women, the film looks at the changes that follow divorce. In interviews of couples and through observation, the film shows how long-term relationships increasingly depend on long-term rewards. Divorce may quite soon become the norm and stable long-term relationships the exception. (A BBC production.)

## Is There Life After Divorce in the Church?

by Richard L. Morgan (John Knox Press, 1975) 182 pp. $12.95

***Overall Product Rating: 4.0***

**STRENGTHS:** Good presentation of the difficulties, both theologically and practically, that divorce within the church brings to the minister and the believing community ...Hits head-on some of the really tough issues and questions relating to the divorced being cared for in and by the communities of faith.

**WEAKNESSES:** The author fails to address the sin issue Biblically. While decrying "cheap grace," he engages in it...I have a problem with his suggested service for "unmarry-ing"...Although there is an excellent section on forgiveness, the author does not do an adequate job of addressing the need to deal with the issues that may have led to the divorce. We need to learn from our mistakes, not just gloss them over.

## Living Beyond Divorce: The Possibilities of Remarriage

by Jim Smoke (Harvest House Publishing, 1984) 159 pp. $5.95

***Overall Product Rating: 7.9***

**STRENGTHS:** A helpful resource for small group discussion...Excellent for helping the individual who is struggling to reestablish healthy relationships following a divorce ...Good material to help the counselor/ pastor...Addresses practical issues the divorced person must face...Takes a lot of ideas and material that most of us already know and puts it into a very usable format...A challenge to the divorced person to live alone healthy and contented is an important aspect of this book...I appreciated the concept that divorce is not a stagnant state but that it is also life, and that it is possible to grow in divorce...The author has a very balanced approach to relationships for the divorced person.

**WEAKNESSES:** Biblically, it seems to be a soft sell approach. When I use this book in teaching or counseling, I will add more Scriptural application ...Doesn't deal deeply enough with issues that may have caused the divorce, such as dysfunctional personality problems, etc. These need to be addressed at some point before one can truly "Live Beyond Divorce"...I would have liked for this book to deal more with the doctrinal issues of remarriage, when it is okay, etc...A more expanded bibliography would have been nice.

## Living Through Your Separation or Divorce

by P. Mark Watts (C.S.S. Publishing) 23 pp. $2.25

***Overall Product Rating: 5.8***

**STRENGTHS:** This could be used as a handout in Sunday School or during counseling for people who are in the midst of divorce or separation...A nominal Christian could easily read and understand it...Provides a down-to-earth explanation of the feelings and thoughts of those going through a divorce or separation...Because it is only 23 pages long, it is something easy to read for those who are hurting.

**WEAKNESSES:** Most of this material is already available in better-written books... Nothing new or fresh...Spiritual comments seem limited to God's comfort without addressing His power and guidance.

## Marriage and Divorce

by John Stott (InterVarsity Press, 1987) 32 pp. $1.95

***Not Yet Reviewed***

**NOTES:** Explores God's ideal for marriage and what the Bible says about divorce and remarriage. For those struggling with their marriage and for those who counsel, this pamphlet brings a pastoral perspective.

## Marriage and Divorce: What the Bible Says

by James M. Efird (Abingdon Press, 1985) 93 pp. $6.95

***Overall Product Rating: 4.7***

**STRENGTHS:** Discusses a sometimes touchy subject with Scripture references that make for good study...A grace orientation toward divorce and remarriage with a brief overview of the Biblical texts...This could be a helpful book for those who would never read a more in-depth treatment on this subject.

**WEAKNESSES:** In my opinion, this is an example of the distortion of Scripture to fit a pre-determined con-clusion...Not an orthodox treatment of Scripture...Written in a very dry style...Exegesis is so brief and undocumented that I did not find it convincing...Such a controversial subject requires much more depth and discussion, even for the lay person.

## Marriage, Divorce, and Remarriage in the Bible

by Jay E. Adams (Zondervan, 1980) 99 pp. $6.95

***Overall Product Rating: 5.5***

**STRENGTHS:** Excellent content...Some of the Bible study on the definition of unequally yoked and divorce is useful (although one needs to be careful with some of this)... Systematically tackles the array of Biblical texts on divorce and remarriage. He has a way of unravelling the complicated into a single thread and then following it through the fabric of Scriptures. For example, difficult passages such as the "except clauses" in Matthew and the "causes to commit adultery" phrases are lucidly set forth with practical guidelines.

**WEAKNESSES:** The author seems peevish at times, taking pot shots at other perspectives on the topic of divorce and remarriage ...The danger in this book is substituting legalistic Bible study for serious examination of Scripture in light of a passage such as John 3:14-21.

## May I Divorce and Remarry: An Exegetical Commentary on 1 Corinthians 7

by Spiros Zodhiates (AMG Publishers, 1984) 343 pp. $8.95

***Not Yet Reviewed***

**NOTES:** As a Greek scholar, the author has delved into the deepest meaning of 1 Cor. 7 by examining each Greek word in the text. From this perspective, he provides his conclusions concerning the complex questions surrounding divorce and remarriage. The book also focuses on the issue that regardless of what situation we are in, our end goal should be a closer walk with Christ.

## Ministry of Divorce Recovery, The: A Workshop Development Manual

by Dr. Bill Flanagan (NSL Publications, 1987) 295 pp. $49.95

(NOTE: This book is being revised and republished by Singles Ministry Resources/ NavPress and will be available in early 1991 for $19.95. See "Developing a Divorce Recovery Ministry" listed earlier.)

***Overall Product Rating: 8.3***

**STRENGTHS:** A good, clear presentation of how to lead an effective divorce recovery ministry at a weekend retreat or during an 8-10 week period...Lay leaders would benefit by using this manual...Offers a concise review of Scripture as applied to divorce and remarriage ...An easy "add water and stir" resource to help people develop a divorce recovery program... Developed by a person who has had years of "hands on" experience.

**WEAKNESSES:** Needs to be published in paperback rather than three-ring binder. It's too expensive in its current format...Material could be more beneficial if sessions were designed to run over a longer period of time. It takes time to recover... Author quoted and referred too much to other previously-published books on the subject.

## Ministry to the Divorced: Guidance, Structure, and Organization that Promotes Healing in the Church

by Richards and Hagemeyer (Zondervan, 1986) 109 pp. $6.95.

***Overall Product Rating: 6.8***

**STRENGTHS:** Provides an organized, step-by-step process for leading a divorce recovery program... Provides forms, evaluations and discussion questions...Good use of illustrations about people going through the upheaval of divorce... Practical and comprehensive... Provides an excellent bibliography/ resource list... The second half of the book is a very helpful divorce recovery manual.

**WEAKNESSES:** Fails to adequately address what needs to happen after the healing begins. Unless we provide people with a purpose after their healing begins, we fail to make it a true "growth process"...It's a little confusing because it is almost two books in one. The first part is primarily anecdotal. The second part is nuts and bolts...The first part is too "surface."

## How Does The National Review Board Function?

1. There are over 100 reviewers on this board, representing every major denomination and region of the country.
2. All reviewers are pastors, counselors or lay leaders involved in ministry with single adults.
3. Every product is reviewed and evaluated by *at least two - and in most cases, three - members* of this National Board. (When appropriate and possible, the product is actually used in a singles ministry prior to being evaluated.)
4. Each product is reviewed and evaluated on its own merit and not as it compares to other products or resources.
5. Reviewers' ratings for each product are tabulated and averaged by the staff of *Single Adult Ministries Journal* to determine each score. ***(Products are rated from 1 to 10, with 10 being the best rating possible.)***

## No One Gets Divorced Alone: How Divorce Affects Moms, Dads, Kids and Grandparents

by H.S. Vigeveno & Anne Claire (Regal, 1987) 224 pp. $7.95

***Overall Product Rating: 9.5***

**STRENGTHS:** This book quickly outlines the reality of divorce. In an nonjudgemental manner the author looks at the effects of divorce and methods to lessen the pain, hurt and anger which accompany most divorces... The clarity and direct answers are clearly beneficial both to a person involved in divorce and those counseling them... Thoroughly covers every aspect of broken family relationships and the building of new ones...Reader can easily find any area related to broken families and find steps and principles to help them understand and resolve them.

**WEAKNESSES:** So clearly and concisely states the reality and covers so much ground that one not intimately acquainted with the pains, rejection, anger and hurt of a divorce may not accurately catch the significance of its accurate descriptions of the effects of divorce.

## Now That You Are Single Again: A Bible Study for the Separated and Divorced

by Gary Chapman (Here's Life Publishers, 1986) 94 pp. $3.95

***Overall Product Rating: 7.9***

**STRENGTHS:** An easy-to-use resource for self study or for small groups... Requires little or no preparation to use...The price of the book is appealing, especially for group use...Could be a valuable tool to use in divorce recovery groups...I plan to use this book in my ministry, especially with those in the first stages of healing...Offers personal "learning experience exercises" in each chapter.

**WEAKNESSES:** Definitely not an in-depth study for the divorced or separated. It is only "introductory material" and must be viewed as such...This book must be seen as useful only in the first phase of the recovery process...This is an "appetizer" for more thorough, helpful material...It tries to cover too much ground in too little time.

## Picking Up the Pieces: Successful Single Living For the Formerly Married

by Clyde Besson (Ballantine, 1984) 209 pp. $6.95

***Not Yet Reviewed***

**NOTES:** The author uses Biblical texts to explain the different kinds and levels of love as well as the ideal all-embracing human relationships toward which we should strive. He probes the reasons for marriage failure, thin offers new hope for finding the way out of despair.

## VIDEO/Power to Conquer Divorce, The

by Ray Mossholder (Marriage Plus Seminars, 1989) 45 min. $20.00

***Not Yet Reviewed***

**NOTES:** This is one segment in a video series entitled "Marriage Plus Seminar." According to Mr. Mossholder, over 400 divorces have been cancelled during the past year due to this video series, which is designed to cancel divorces and strengthen even the best of marriages.

## Preventing Divorce (Before You Get Married)

by McPhearson and Biehl (Multnomah, 1989) 124 pp. $9.95

***Overall Product Rating: 5.7***

**STRENGTHS:** Helpful to an engaged couple by helping them discuss areas of marriage that need to be explored before marriage... Good for couples who have difficulty communicating...The format and outline are helpful ...Encourages a response and is written in an inviting tone... Stimulating questions for engaged couples or those considering remarriage.

**WEAKNESSES:** Not a book at all, just a listing or questions...No scoring standard... Has little to do with preventing divorce...Too simplistic...Expects too little from its audience...Format is poor—should be in the format of a workbook... More space is needed for conflict resolution and how to settle differences...Needed some biblical suggestions for how to work on some of the trouble areas.

## Reconcilable Differences: Mending Broken Relationships

by Jim Talley (Thomas Nelson, 1985) 171 pp. $9.95

***Overall Product Rating: 8.6***

**STRENGTHS:** Addresses an issue that is a front-burner for most people going through a separation or divorce. (Is reconciliation a possibility?) ...Author provides readers with a clear, step-by-step process to follow for those who truly seek reconciliation.

**WEAKNESSES:** Author's engineering background shines through in his tendency toward charts, graphs and a "sliced, diced and cubed" view of life...Some areas of the book lacked scholarship...Sometimes sounds simplistic.

## Recovering From Divorce

by David A. Thompson (Bethany House Publishers) 94 pp. $6.95

***Overall Product Rating: 7.2***

**STRENGTHS:** Helpful in giving an inexperienced/unfamiliar pastor or counselor some structured suggestions for helping...Good, practical guide for working with people who are divorced in a counseling setting. The work pages positively guide people through a discovery process that allows them to deal with their feelings and problems.

**WEAKNESSES:** A simplistic approach...For the person who has little or no training/ experience, it does not give the necessary background information...Does not go far enough in suggesting positive interventions and alternatives for comforting and supporting strategies nor is it adequate in helping the counselor prepare for the sessions.

## Remarriage: A Healing Gift From God

by Larry Richards (Word Publishing, 1981) 165 pp. $9.99

***Not Yet Reviewed***

**NOTES:** The author makes a case for how remarriage can be God's gift of healing and a new beginning. Richards does not advocate divorce, but because men and women have fallen short of God's ideal for marriage, he writes that because of God's grace, there is an opportunity for forgiveness and a chance to begin again.

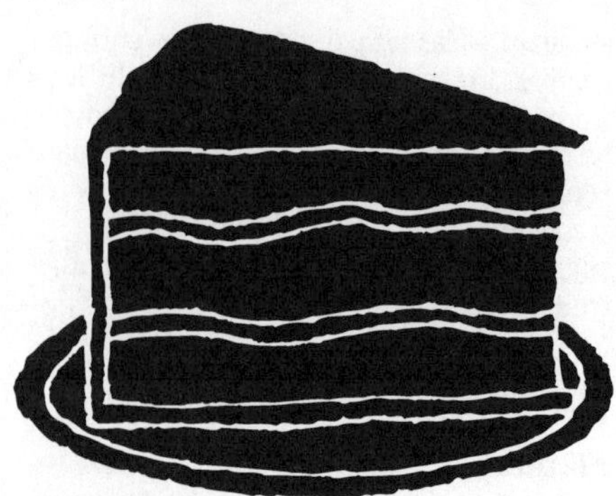

## Remarriage and God's Renewing Grace:
### A Positive Biblical Ethic For Divorced Christians

by Dwight H. Small (Baker Book House, 1986) 231 pp. $7.95

***Overall Product Rating: 8.6***

**STRENGTHS:** A positive, Biblically-oriented book which is faithful to Scripture...Offers an excellent re-emphasis of grace as a New Testament ethic...Helped make me more aware of the Scriptural authority I have when approaching divorce and remarriage...Gave me more Biblical perspective and guidance on this subject than anything I'd read previously.
**WEAKNESSES:** Sometimes the material is a little hard to get through. It must be read slowly...The author occasionally makes emotional remarks toward those who have differing theological persuasions. This sometimes distracts from the book.

## Second Chapter:
### New Beginnings After Divorce or Separation

by John P. Splinter (Baker Book House, 1987) 273 pp. $12.95

***Overall Product Rating: 8.1***

**STRENGTHS:** For those with a limited budget and library, it is an excellent one-book primer that covers the entire healing journey which singles experience in divorce recovery... Especially helpful for beginners in singles ministry...The book's "life-style profile" is an excellent tool for measuring a divorced person's progress, encouraging their growth...Includes an extensive bibliography for those wanting to dig deeper, plus helpful discussion questions.
**WEAKNESSES:** Needs more "life example" illustrations...Is sometimes too technical and cold...I was concerned that so little of the material in the book was attributed to specific sources. Obviously, the author spent a good deal of time researching, as shown by the further reading list. But many of the concepts were familiar and identifiable to specific authors. The failure to credit these authors seemed presumptuous...The Biblical perspectives chapter did not blend well...The preface states this book was a group effort, but the text does not credit or acknowledge the group involved... Poor cover design, not up to industry standards.

## Single Again: Remarrying For The Right Reasons

by Bud and Kathy Pearson (Regal Books, 1985) 133 pp. $6.95

***Not Yet Reviewed***

**NOTES:** The authors examine myths that many believe about being single, married or divorced and look at how important it is that one become a whole person prior to marriage. If remarriage is being considered, the book provides guidelines to help the couple assess their relationship, the prospects for a healthy marriage as well as an overview of the major issues that often surface in a second marriage.

## Single Again Man, The

by Jane K. Burgess (Lexington Books, 1988) 171 pp. $9.95

***Overall Product Rating: 5.5***

**STRENGTHS:** For those who have little awareness of the diversity and complexity of single again men—their issues and feelings—this might be a tool to expand understanding...Could be useful in helping the single again male to normalize his feelings and experiences by realizing others experience the same...Many case studies make real results of surveys. The frankness of many of the comments and the complexity of the responses help to tell it the way it is...A realistic appraisal of the single again phenomena.
**WEAKNESSES:** The book seems to be 150 pages of quotes from interviews, a descriptive study that feels like a thesis...Offers no Biblical perspective and no therapeutic solutions or aids...Tedious to read. I had to force myself to keep reading.

## Starting Over Single:
### Life and Hope After the Death Of A Marriage

by Mervin E. Thompson (Prince of Peace, 1985) 156 pp. $11.95

***Overall Product Rating: 9.0***

**STRENGTHS:** Hope for the divorced ...Explains how a divorce is like a death in the family and should be treated as such... Excellent explanation of Biblical principles concerning divorce...Good answers about God's forgiveness and grace (and the reminder to forgive ourselves)... Covers a full realm of problems and gives suggestions on how we should focus our thoughts...This book can help us help those who are going through a divorce.
**WEAKNESSES:** Author tends to meander some, but usually brings it back to his main point.

## VIDEO/Starting Over Single:
### A Help Seminar on Divorce

by various presenters/experts (Prince of Peace, 1987) a 5-part video series, $119.95

***Overall Product Rating: 7.9***

**STRENGTHS:** This video series opens the door for frank discussion about the nature of divorce and deals with the issues sensitively and in a sound way...The overall tone points to redemptive power, resurrection, renewal and re-creation rather than judgement and condemnation...Effectively addresses some addictive behaviors...Looks at many of the fears and feelings surrounding divorce.
**WEAKNESSES:** The sessions seem to have been prepared for television broadcasts rather than for a discussion group...Some of the material is too general...This video series had a hard time holding the attention of my people...Material is too vague and brief in some places... Each segment is—too long. Doesn't allow for discussion or interaction time.

## How Does The National Review Board Function?

1. There are over 100 reviewers on this board, representing every major denomination and region of the country.
2. All reviewers are pastors, counselors or lay leaders involved in ministry with single adults.
3. Every product is reviewed and evaluated by *at least two - and in most cases, three - members* of this National Board. (When appropriate and possible, the product is actually used in a singles ministry prior to being evaluated.)
4. Each product is reviewed and evaluated on its own merit and not as it compares to other products or resources.
5. Reviewers' ratings for each product are tabulated and averaged by the staff of *Single Adult Ministries Journal* to determine each score. ***(Products are rated from 1 to 10, with 10 being the best rating possible.)***

## AUDIO CASSETTES/ Successful Living After Divorce

by Laurene Johnson (self-produced, 1988) six x 20 min. $59.95

***Overall Product Rating: 5.0***

**STRENGTHS:** Offers one point of view of a family that has lived through divorce...Tapes are short enough to easily listen through in one sitting ...Good practical advice with suggestions on how to implement what she is talking about...Could be used as a starter for small group discussion or as a divorce recovery seminar in the smaller church... Insight for both children and adults.

**WEAKNESSES:** Does not bring Christianity in, talks about values but not Jesus... Sometimes I felt talked down to...Too much of the humanistic point of view...This resource has no application to a Christian seeking recovery from the difficult transition of divorce. There is a glaring omission to the need for Christian fellowship, Bible study or prayer. Secular self-help.

## VIDEO/Suddenly Single: What to Do When Divorce Strikes Home

by Clyde Besson (The Sampson Company, 1989) Four parts, 30 minutes each. Prices includes workbook. $99.95

***Not Yet Reviewed***

**NOTES:** This series deals with facing the facts; divorce, forgiveness and grace; leaving the past behind; and looking to the future.

## VIDEO/Surviving Broken Relationships

by Clayton Barbeau (Franciscan Communications, 1988) 21 min. $19.95

***Not Yet Reviewed***

**NOTES:** Explores the anger and pain that follow a broken relationship and helps the viewer to understand and work with the feelings experienced at the time.

## Surviving Divorce

by Jim Smoke (Harvest House Publishing, 1985) 46 pp. $2.25

***Overall Product Rating: 6.0***

**STRENGTHS:** A brief overview of the complex issue of divorce...Guidelines for helping get the divorced person headed in a positive direction...Reminds us that the divorce experience can be a useful teacher ...Concise and to the point...Practical suggestions in understandable language... Inexpensive enough to distribute to many people...Simple non-threatening questions that can be used as topic directed discussions.

**WEAKNESSES:** Too brief to get at the complex issues in a divorce ...Does not stress the importance of finding someone who will hold you accountable for the changes you want to make and/or the goals you set after a divorce...Very little emphasis on the role Christ plays in the healing process...Beyond the suggested venting of "war" stories, (a necessary part of the healing process), this booklet doesn't provide enough substantive material to "survive" divorce.

## Surviving Separation and Divorce

by Sharon Marshall (Baker Book House, 1988) 127 pp. $5.95

***Overall Product Rating: 7.9***

**STRENGTHS:** Singles pastors should keep a supply of this book on hand...Articulate in explaining the emotional/intellectual/ spiritual vacillations of the separated and divorced...The Epilogue concerning how to help and when responses are appropriate is worth the price of this book...The Epilogue with its specific suggestions should be shared with groups, marrieds and all pastors...Easy to read ...An excellent resource to put in the hands of those going through divorce.

**WEAKNESSES:** A little glib at points...The cover looks a little like curriculum, which is unfortunate for this book...Sometimes the writing gets too repetitive.

## Through The Whirlwind: A Proven Path to Recovery From the Devastation of Divorce

by Bob Burns (Thomas Nelson, 1989) 180 pp. $8.95

***Overall Product Rating: 7.8***

**STRENGTHS:** Uses good illustrations and case studies (believable "war stories")...Easy to follow... Encourages sharing of one's own personal experiences/struggles... The Biblical insights deal with all aspects of the divorce process in a most helpful way...An excellent section on how to deal with anger... Easy to understand illustrations... Unique insights on passive and active agents in the divorce process... Encourages use of small groups in the healing process.

**WEAKNESSES:** The doctrine of divorce given in appendix A was quite shallow from a Biblical perspective... Needs more practical helps. The descriptions and illustrations are fine, but what do I do about the various problems and immediate needs I need to address today...The Biblical examples of depressed men in the Bible (Elijah and Paul) seemed questionable to me in this context... There was not a lot of new, fresh material here for me.

## Untying The Knot: Help for Broken Families

by George E. Vandeman (Pacific Press, 1988) 48 pp. $5.00

***Overall Product Rating: 3***

**STRENGTHS:** Tries to be descriptive of the realities which divorced people face... Compassionate and affirms the working of God always on our behalf...Some of the personal testimonies are good.

**WEAKNESSES:** Needed a larger discussion of the theology of divorce and remarriage... No new ideas... Simplistic...Preachy...Poor docu-mentation...Another experiential book that we don't need.

## What About Divorce?

by Spiros Zodhiates (AMG Publishers, 1984) 303 pp. $7.95

***Overall Product Rating: 7.3***

**STRENGTHS:** Gives the history and truth of the Greeks wedding/marriage and divorce customs to help us better understand Biblical context...A helpful cultural, historical perspective that we seldom get... Provides a lot of textual analysis. It would be helpful for a scholarly study of divorce.

**WEAKNESSES:** Some of the book needs to be brought down to laymen's terms ...Heavy reading in places.

## When a Friend Gets a Divorce: What Can You Do?

by Sharon G. Marshall (Baker Book House, 1990) 128 pp. $6.95

***Overall Product Rating: 7.1***

**STRENGTHS:** Gives practical insight into the feelings of those going through a divorce...Reminds me that as the friend, I'm not the fixer, but am called to love them through it, including doing tangible things such as notes, calls, etc...A sound psychological approach for dealing with the process of divorce recovery ...The most helpful element in the book is the appendix with some guidelines for evaluating a person's need for professional help, with suggested sources to contact for assistance...Easy to read, short chapters with insight...Provides an excellent look at the downward spiral of emotions, feelings, hurts plus understanding about how a divorced person seeks to com-municate... Target for lay people who have a friend in the process of divorce...If the reader only uses half the insights in this book, their divorced friend will benefit greatly.

**WEAKNESSES:** Sometimes the author uses Scripture out of context ...Some chapters needed more research...This material is not designed so it could be easily used in a support group, which is unfortunate.

# Grief

## Most Recommended Resources in This Section

(Based on evaluations and reviews made by *SAM Journal*'s National Resource Review Board, using a 1-10 scale with 10 being the best possible score):

### 9.4 Comforter, The: A Journey Through Grief

by Doris Sanford (Multnomah, 1989)

### 9.1 December's Song: Handling the Realities of Grief

by Marilyn Willett Heavilin (Here's Life Publishers, 1988)

### 9.1 How Can I Help? Reaching Out to Someone Who is Grieving

by June Cerza Kolf (Baker House Books, 1989)

### 8.5 Helping People Through Grief

by Delores Kuenning (Bethany House Publishers, 1987)

### 8.5 Living Through the Loss of Someone You Love

By Sandra Aldrich (Gospel LIght/Regal, 1990)

*(For more information on each of the above resources—plus many other helpful products—find them listed in alphabetical order below.)*

## About Grief

(Channing L. Bete Co., Inc, 1984) 15 pp. 72¢

***Overall Product Rating: 7.3***

**STRENGTHS:** I really liked this simple little booklet...Good for early stages of grief when a more in-depth book could be overwhelming ...Covers the grief cycle, gives some resources and has a good section on what you can do for a grieving person...Excellent presentation...Helpful support group references...Easy to read and understand.

**WEAKNESSES:** Because it is such a small booklet, it tends to be superficial...Has good ideas but does not develop them very well...No Scripture references are given.

## Comforter, The: A Journey Through Grief

by Doris Sanford (Multnomah, 1989) 22 pp. booklet $4.95

***Overall Product Rating: 9.4***

**STRENGTHS:** A powerful little book that I've already ordered several copies of...There are many excellent books on the market dealing with grief. But most of them are too long and detailed for the person who needs it most. This booklet is short, honest, well written and easy to read, yet it packs in a great deal of hope and encouragement...This is the best book I have found for those in the beginning stages of grief... Describes key elements of the grief process as well as helpful suggestions for those comforting those who are grieving ...Beautiful, artistic design...A great tool for pastors and counselors to keep handy.

## How Does The National Review Board Function?

1. There are over 100 reviewers on this board, representing every major denomination and region of the country.
2. All reviewers are pastors, counselors or lay leaders involved in ministry with single adults.
3. Every product is reviewed and evaluated by *at least two - and in most cases, three - members* of this National Board. (When appropriate and possible, the product is actually used in a singles ministry prior to being evaluated.)
4. Each product is reviewed and evaluated on its own merit and not as it compares to other products or resources.
5. Reviewers' ratings for each product are tabulated and averaged by the staff of *Single Adult Ministries Journal* to determine each score. ***(Products are rated from 1 to 10, with 10 being the best rating possible.)***

**WEAKNESSES:** Because it is so short, it does not go into depth. Consequently, some people may find it too shallow...It needs a study guide to use in support groups.

## December's Song:
### Handling the Realities of Grief

by Marilyn Willett Heavilin (Here's Life Publishers, 1988) 138 pp. $6.95

***Overall Product Rating: 9.1***

**STRENGTHS:** Excellent. I've used this material several times in the past year... Although written by a lay person, this book is one of the most theologically-sound I have read in awhile...The author tackles hard issues courageously, fearlessly. She is realistic about the areas of pain, guilt and long-term recovery ...This book only gets better as you read along ...Includes a section on AIDS as well as for people who have experienced multiple loss...This is one book I will definitely pass along to the singles in my group who are experiencing grief...Also excellent for pastors/care givers.
**WEAKNESSES:** The chapter headings are sometimes artificial... The author referred too much to her previous book.

## Don't Take My Grief Away

by Doug Manning (Harper & Row, 1984) 128 pp. $8.95

***Not Yet Reviewed***

**NOTES:** Assists to understand what happens when someone dies, to accept it and to face the feelings of loss, separation and guilt that is experienced after the loss of a loved one.

## Early Widow:
### A Journal of the First Year

by Mary Jane Worden (InterVarsity Press, 1989) 189 pp. $14.95

***Overall Product Rating: 7.6***

**STRENGTHS:** Gives helpful insights into the grief process...It motivates and challenges people struggling with grief...Writing is poignant and powerful. I was deeply touched by the author's openness, honesty, strength and courage...This book got to me more deeply than most. It helped me recognize areas of my own grief process that still need work...Painful to read at times, yet helpful... Easy to read.
**WEAKNESSES:** This is not a very realistic book. The author seemed to have had an exceptionally supportive group of family and friends. Financially, she was not forced to go to work to care for her children, and she seemed to have an ideal marriage prior to her husband's tragic death. That's not the real world for most women who lose a mate (by death or divorce)...A beautiful, well-written story, but not transferable or very practical for most people (especially women) in her situation.

## God In The Dark:
### Through Grief and Beyond

by Luci Shaw (Zondervan, 1989) 266 pp. $16.95

***Not Yet Reviewed***

**NOTES:** A poet's record of her journey through grief and beyond. This is the author's journal account of her husband's terminal cancer for the months between the doctor's first diagnosis and the early months of her widowhood. With a poet's insight and honesty, the author probes the paradoxes of the faith with which we all struggle...when we are honest enough to admit it. A book for anyone who has lost a friend or relative and wonders, "Why does God darken his face when we need the comfort of his warmth and light?"

## Good Grief

by Granger E. Westberg (Fortress Press, 1979) 64 pp. $2.50

***Not Yet Reviewed***

**NOTES:** We all need a better understanding of the small griefs in life as well as those larger grief experiences which can overwhelm us. This book describes what happens to us whenever we lose someone or something important to us.

## Grief

by Haddon W. Robinson (Daybreak Books, 1974) 23 pp. $3.95

***Not Yet Reviewed***

**NOTES:** Collection of essays, poems, quotations and photographs on the subject of grief.

## Grief For a Season

by Mildred Tengbom (Bethany House Publishers, 1989) 155 pp. $5.95

***Overall Product Rating: 6.5***

**STRENGTHS:** Beautifully written, filled with wonderful poetry...Biblically well grounded... The author had a loving, deep relationship with her mother and you could feel her pain. It's a great book to give someone who has lost a parent or child...Offers good, practical advice for the grieving process... Realistic ...Very useful in counseling those who have experienced the loss of a loved one.
**WEAKNESSES:** Nothing specific pertaining to how the death of a parent affects the single adult...Probably not the best book for those who had a distant relationship with their parents...No leadership guide. More devotional than technical.

## Grief Process, The:
### Analysis and Counseling

by Yorick Spiegel (Abingdon Press, 1977) 348 pp. $5.95

***Not Yet Reviewed***

**NOTES:** Drawing from psychology, sociology and pastoral theology, the text contains comprehensive material on grief and empirical research, complete with case studies.

## VIDEO/Growing Through Grief:
### Personal Healing—The Five Tasks of Grief

by Dr. Howard Clinebell (EcuFilm, 1984) 180 min. $225.00

***Not Yet Reviewed***

**Notes:** Designed for people who want to help themselves and others find healing and growth from the painful experiences brought on by death or divorce.

How to use the Network:

**Have Lunch Together.**

Organize a luncheon with the other leaders in your city or region. Discuss common problems and concerns in singles ministry. Learn from one another. Network.

(See page 199)

## Guided Grief Imagery: A Resource for Grief Ministry and Death Education

by Thomas A. Droege (Paulist Press, 1987) 178 pp. $9.95

***Overall Product Rating: 6.9***

**STRENGTHS:** This book will help the reader become better acquainted with deep psychological and emotional aspects of death... Offers some suggested activities that might be useful to counselors...Since there is such little new material out on this subject, this book is refreshing to see...Offers a helpful overview of how death has been understood throughout Christian history... The studies of the images used in the Bible for understanding death is especially useful.

**WEAKNESSES:** Because of some of the "new age" terminology used, this book may be one of those that is praised by "liberals" and condemned by "conservatives"...The book is geared more to the Catholic audience than to the general evangelical audience...I would not trust much of this material in the hands of an inexperienced lay person who is trying to do some counseling. This book is primarily geared to the professional therapist.

## Helping People Through Grief

by Delores Kuenning (Bethany House Publishers, 1987) 272 pp. $6.95

***Overall Product Rating: 8.5***

**STRENGTHS:** Provides a good combination of personal experiences and practical suggestions for those experiencing a difficult situation and those who wish to be supportive ...Author clearly lists her own suggestions and then provides the readers with other pertinent resources and references at the end of each chapter... Presented in a very readable format and is organized well for quick references ...Each chapter shares real experiences of people experiencing a particular grief...A valuable resource for any library with practical suggestions and what to expect as we minister to those experiencing grief.

**WEAKNESSES:** While advise is given for family and friends, our reluctance to talk about suffering makes it difficult to prepare. A chapter or two addressed to the caregivers may have made this part of ministry easier to face.

## How Can I Help? Reaching Out to Someone Who is Grieving

by June Cerza Kolf (Baker House Books, 1989) 144 pp. $6.95

***Overall Product Rating: 9.1***

**STRENGTHS:** Many people avoid those in grief. This book helps us overcome our fears and prepares/equips us for ministry with the grieving...I lost my mate to death and I can say that this book is right on...Especially good suggestions for being supportive after the death and funeral...Excellent practical suggestions on how to respond to the bereaved...Written in short, concise chapters for easy reference...Easy to follow with explicit suggestions and instructions.

**WEAKNESSES:** This is not a book for the grieving person—it's strictly for the concerned person, the pastor, relative or friend...It's hard to give adequate depth to issues like "guilt" and "loneliness" in such short, concise chapters.

## It Hurts To Lose a Special Person

by Amy Ross Mumford (Accent Books, 1982) 24 pp. $4.95

***Overall Product Rating: 5.7***

**STRENGTHS:** Offers understanding and hope for people suffering grief, reminding them that they are not alone...Handy, attractive, easy to read booklet...Doesn't get bogged down in details...Helpful, appropriate Scriptural usage...Well done graphically ...Nice "pearls" and comforting thoughts.

**WEAKNESSES:** Quite expensive...Limits pain of loss to death only...Offers no direction to find help (other than Scriptural references)...Tends to oversimplify the recovery process.

## Jesus Wept: Trusting the Good Shepherd When You Lose a Loved One

by Leroy Brownlow (Brownlow Publishing Co., 1989) 47 pp. $7.95

***Overall Product Rating: 5.5***

**STRENGTHS:** Valuable Spiritual devotions for those who have lost a mate, child or close friend...Good poetry...The book comes in a gift box which makes it easy to give as a gift...Beautifully bound and illustrated... Highlights the Biblical truths of friends comforting one another and outlines the 23rd psalm dwelling on the love, protection and care of Jesus as Shepherd...A good job of explaining the necessity of death here on earth. I appreciated his ending the book with the knowledge that in "my Father's house there are many mansions".

**WEAKNESSES:** Because the book is short, it may not provide all the depth desired...This is book is clearly intended for believers only...Nothing new or particularly helpful about the grieving process ...Personal devotion material only... Good poems but nothing of depth.

## Living Through Grief

by Harold Bauman (Lion Publishing, 1989) 46 pp. $2.99

***Not Yet Reviewed***

**NOTES:** Explains the stages of grief and suggests practical steps for learning to live again.

## Living Through the Loss of Someone You Love

By Sandra Aldrich (Gospel LIght/Regal, 1990) 234 pp. $8.95

***Overall Product Rating: 8.5***

**STRENGTHS:** A personal case study that was easy to identify with...Raises many interesting, significant questions for thoughtful consideration. Section Two offers some very specific and realistic situations and suggestions ...Our singles ministries tend to focus primarily on the never married and divorced. This book is addressed to the widowed and done beautifully. We often

## How Does The National Review Board Function?

1. There are over 100 reviewers on this board, representing every major denomination and region of the country.
2. All reviewers are pastors, counselors or lay leaders involved in ministry with single adults.
3. Every product is reviewed and evaluated by *at least two - and in most cases, three - members* of this National Board. (When appropriate and possible, the product is actually used in a singles ministry prior to being evaluated.)
4. Each product is reviewed and evaluated on its own merit and not as it compares to other products or resources.
5. Reviewers' ratings for each product are tabulated and averaged by the staff of *Single Adult Ministries Journal* to determine each score. ***(Products are rated from 1 to 10, with 10 being the best rating possible.)***

include the widowed in our divorce seminar because we view the pain as similar (and in many ways it is). However, this book brings out areas where it is quite different...Good chapter about helping children work through their grief process.
**WEAKNESSES:** Would be a much stronger resource if there were a study guide or questions for discussion.

## Not By Accident:
### Comfort In Times of Loss
by Isabel Fleece (Moody Press, 1987) 28 pp. $1.95
***Overall Product Rating: 7.0***
**STRENGTHS:** Shows the importance of being ready to face death at any age and the comfort, peace and strength this mother received from God after the loss of her young son...Excellent insight into the feelings, ups and downs of someone grieving the death of a loved one...Very helpful for single adult pastors or lay leaders involved in counseling someone who has lost a family member...Many helpful Scripture references ...Could be an excellent evangelistic tool/gift for the unsaved grieving person.
**WEAKNESSES:** I wish the author would have shared about how her husband, church or friends helped her during the days of her son's funeral and afterward. This would have been helpful for the rest of us to see what she needed most during that time.

## On Being Alone
(AARP, 1987) 14 pp. Free
***Overall Product Rating: 6.5***
**STRENGTHS:** An excellent "one stop" information source...Section on grief was very well written...The details check list was useful, well put together...It's free and easy to read.
**WEAKNESSES:** General resources/ publications list needs to be updated...It would have been helpful to have included examples and contact people for some working programs to encourage/enable networking of support groups...Little spiritual input/guidance. A Bible study paralleling the topics presented in this booklet would be very helpful and could be developed to use with this product.

## Once in a Lifetime:
### Reflections upon the Death of a Father
by Harold Ivan Smith (Thomas Nelson, 1989) 156 pp. $10.95
***Not Yet Reviewed***
**NOTES:** "Once In A Lifetime" follows the grief process of the passing, the burying, the mourning and the remembering through the author's personal reflections along with the experiences of others who have lost a father in death. Memorable quotations, hymns, prayers and Scripture enhance the grief journey.

## Out of the Depths
by Robert V. Dodd (Abingdon Press, 1986) 22 pp. $1.95
***Not Yet Reviewed***
**NOTES:** Written to help the reader understand how grief affects everyone and how Jesus Christ can touch our lives in such a way that grief and tears give way to hope and joy.

## Tearful Celebration, A:
### Courage in Crisis
by James E. Means (Multnomah Press, 1985) 109 pp $6.95
***Overall Product Rating: 6.3***
**STRENGTHS:** A very personal grief story which may be of help to the pastor or leader dealing with terminal illness in a family... Realistic, readable and understandable ...Good treatment concerning the question of where is God when it hurts...Deals well with the fact that even Christians suffer trials in life...Shows how God can work in times of great distress... May be a helpful discussion starter for those who have lost a mate by death.
**WEAKNESSES:** Because of the subjective nature of this book, it fails to effectively communicate the objective statements about God... Does not deal with the subject as well as *A Grief Observed or Problems of Pain* by C. S. Lewis... It is theologically sound, but of several similar books in my library, this is not one of the first ones I would recommend.

## When Loved Ones Are Taken in Death
by Lehman Strauss (Daybreak Books, 1973) 32 pp. $3.50
***Not Yet Reviewed***
**NOTES:** Booklet of comfort for persons grieving the loss of a loved one.

# Homosexuality

## Most Recommended Resource in This Section
(Based on evaluations and reviews made by *SAM Journal*'s National Resource Review Board, using a 1-10 scale with 10 being the best possible score):

### 8.8 Overcoming Homosexuality:
### Helping Others in Crisis
by Ed Hurst with D. and N. Jackson (David C. Cook, 1987)

*(For more information on the above resource—plus other products—find them listed in alphabetical order below.)*

## Called Out Of The Gay Church
by Robert E. Middleton (Outpost, 1982) 9 pp. 50¢
***Overall Product Rating: 6.0***
**STRENGTHS:** It's hard to beat a true, personal story of how God works...Shows how God can have power over our bondage to sin...Helps us understand that a born-again believer can still struggle with homosexual feelings...Helpful information based on one man's story.
**WEAKNESSES:** May lead the reader to believe that it is possible to be free from this bondage in a few months rather than the two or more years that it usually takes...May not be a realistic portrayal for many who have

found it more difficult to be set free... Doesn't adequately explain what "freedom" means: Does it mean no more temptation or desire? The book is not clear...At times seems to use questionable theology.

## Factors In Freedom

by Ed Hurst (Outpost, 1986) 40 pp. $3.00

***Overall Product Rating: 7.0***

**STRENGTHS:** Portrays hope and release for the homosexual with the struggle of dominating sin as well as the need for Christian fellowship for strength to live a new life...Very realistic and practical for people who are involved in habitual homosexual life-styles and are trying to develop a "normal" Christian life-style...Suggests a reasonable path for change...Affirms Christ's victory over evil.

**WEAKNESSES:** Simplistic description of evil...Language is overly "churchy"...Too short, could easily be expanded.

## Homosexuality Information Packet

by Joanne Highley (L.I.F.E./Living In Freedom Eternally, pub. date unknown) Consists of a packet of six pamphlets, 87 pages total. $10

***Overall Product Rating: 7 .0***

**STRENGTHS:** This packet presents a comprehensive program for counseling and ministry with homosexuals...Well researched and presented material...Streamlines a lot of material into a workable format. Easy to understand. Does not get too technical or intimidating... Offers warnings about some of the common pitfalls that can be avoided in this ministry...A sincere desire to be Biblical. The material communicates love and compassion for the homosexual... Helpful to those of us with little background information in this area.

**WEAKNESSES:** It may not be a weakness, but rather a theological difference. There seems to be a good amount of focus on "demon spirits that need to be cast out" instead of a disobedient heart that needs repentance. This may make some theological persuasions view this material less useable ...Attributes a poor home life as the cause of homosexuality. No attentiveness given to physiological factors which may be the central determinative factor...Section on "Satanic attack on American society" is so laced with assumptions and generalities that it makes one question the quality of thought behind parts of the document.

## Homosexual Partnerships: Why Same-Sex Relationships Are Not A Christian Option

by John Stott (InterVarsity Press, 1987) 32 pp. $1.95

***Overall Product Rating: 5.8***

**STRENGTHS:** Stott is well-studied on the issue and gives careful, clear refutation of wrong ideas as well as a presentation of Scripture...Brief presentations of both sides of the argument...Refers to rational ideas previously published by homosexuals... Scholarly presentation.

**WEAKNESSES:** Because it presents both sides, the reader is left questioning as to where the author stands until the last few pages...Sometimes confusing...Comes to the conclusion that the homosexual "has suffered some deficit in the relationship with the parent of the same sex." This view is both naive and not well researched ...The primary source of hope is portrayed to be the Christian family and the promise that "one day it will be finished," which isn't much hope at all.

## Overcoming Homosexuality: Helping Others in Crisis

by Ed Hurst with D. and N. Jackson (David C. Cook, 1987) 119 pp. $9.95.

***Overall Product Rating: 8.8***

**STRENGTHS:** This book is written with understanding...Offers practical suggestions on how the counselor, pastor or leader can help and encourage people to overcome their homosexual sin...Helps open our eyes to the needs for ministry in this area...A very solid, helpful book... Provides a good bibliography for further reading...This is probably the best book I've read on the subject.

**WEAKNESSES**: The title is slightly misleading in that it implies that the book is primarily for individuals struggling with homosexuality. Instead, it is primarily for pastors, counselors and leaders, providing them insight and suggestions for a more effective ministry with others...I found no significant weaknesses in this book.

## How Does The National Review Board Function?

1. There are over 100 reviewers on this board, representing every major denomination and region of the country.
2. All reviewers are pastors, counselors or lay leaders involved in ministry with single adults.
3. Every product is reviewed and evaluated by *at least two - and in most cases, three - members* of this National Board. (When appropriate and possible, the product is actually used in a singles ministry prior to being evaluated.)
4. Each product is reviewed and evaluated on its own merit and not as it compares to other products or resources.
5. Reviewers' ratings for each product are tabulated and averaged by the staff of *Single Adult Ministries Journal* to determine each score. ***(Products are rated from 1 to 10, with 10 being the best rating possible.)***

# Leadership and Training Resources (plus Tools For Your Ministry)

## Most Recommended Resources in This Section

(Based on evaluations and reviews made by *SAM Journal's* National Resource Review Board, using a 1-10 scale with 10 being the best possible score):

### 9.4 Feeding and Leading
by Kenneth O. Gangel (Victor Books, 1989)

### 9.3 Leading With A Followers Heart: Practicing Biblical Obedience and Humility in the Workplace
by Eugene B. Habecker (Scripture Press Publications, 1990)

### 8.8 Increasing Your Leadership Confidence: Fine Tune Your Leadership Skills
by Bob Biehl (Questar Publishers, 1989)

### 8.7 Be a People Person
by John C. Maxwell (Victor Books, 1989)

### 8.5 Mastering Church Management
by Don Cousins, Leith Anderson, Arthur DeKruyter (Christianity Today, 1990)

### 8.5 No Foothold in the Swamp
by Charles Hollingsworth (Zondervan, 1988)

### 8.3 Heart and Soul of Effective Management, The
by James F. Hind (Victor Books, 1989)

### 8.2 Coping with Depression in the Ministry and Other Helping Professions
by Archibald D. Hart (Word Publishing, 1984)

*(For more information on each of the above resources—plus many other helpful products—find them listed in alphabetical order below.)*

## Antagonists In The Church
by Kenneth Haugk (Augsburg Fortress, 1988) 189 pp. $9.95

***Overall Product Rating: 7.5***

**STRENGTHS:** Does a good job of putting issues of conflict in the church in perspective ...Does a wonderful job of identifying and offering ways to deal with a variety of problems we all face at one time or another when providing leadership in the church... Helpful guidelines on how to identify problems, deal with disruptive people and circumstances, and respond effectively...Very helpful.

**WEAKNESSES:** Tries to back everything up with Bible verses which is cumbersome and not always necessary...Very boring style.

## Be a People Person
by John C. Maxwell (Victor Books, 1989) 156 pp. $12.95

***Overall Product Rating: 8.7***

**STRENGTHS:** Helpful information on the development of a leadership team and team relationship dynamics...Suggestions for how to keep a team and movement going forward...Uplifting...Gives great direction in how to build relationships with your leadership team.

**WEAKNESSES:** Needs more practical, specific how to illustrations and application ...Would be helpful to offer some guidelines about how to hire the right person in a ministry environment.

## VIDEO/Beyond the Church Walls
produced by 2100 Productions (InterVarsity Video, 1987) 18 min. $19.95

***Not Yet Reviewed***

**NOTES:** Provides a model for community services for every church based on the example of Pastor Arthur Kitonga of the Redeemed Gospel Church of Nairobi, Kenya.

## Broken Members, Mended Body: Building a Ministry With Love and Restoration
by Kathi Mills (Regal Press, 1988) 143 pp. $7.95

***Not Yet Reviewed***

**NOTES:** Being broken doesn't make people useless to God. Having been broken, they can become a blessing to others as they minister through understanding the deep needs of others. This book suggests an organizational structure through which to build a healing fellowship.

## Care and Feeding of Volunteers, The
by Douglas W. Johnson (Abingdon Press, 1978) 125 pp. $8.95

***Not Yet Reviewed***

**NOTES:** Discusses how to identify, recruit and train lay volunteers; how to enable and motivate them; how to assign appropriate tasks; how to help plan their work; and how to enable them to recruit and train other volunteers.

## Christian Caregiving — a Way of Life Leader's Guide
by Kenneth C. Haugk and William J. McKay (Augsburg, 1986) 141 pp. $9.95

***Not yet Reviewed***

**NOTES:** Leader's guide to the book on building community and training church members in distinctively Christian caring and relating skills.

## Contemplative Pastor, The
by Eugene Petersen (Word Publishing, 1988) 176 pp. $11.99

***Overall Product Rating: 7.9***

**STRENGTHS:** There is much wisdom for pastors in this book ...Many of the chapters begin with reference to one of the beatitudes and then contains very practical illustrations and experiences drawn from the authors

years of pastoring ...Stretches the pastor to rethink ways to do the duties and tasks before us...Easy to read...Keeps us focused on the right theological foundations of ministry and the right definition of the pastoral role. We need this kind of thinking and writing to keep us from degenerating into social directors, organizing one event after another.
**WEAKNESSES:** There is not much specific direction about how to redirect or refocus your life and ministry. We are left to ourselves and our own ingenuity to apply the principles and themes of the book...I don't agree with all of the author's presuppositions ...The main difficulty single adult pastors may have with this book is in translating the writings of a pastor who has settled into many years with one small congregation and writes from that perspective, into the more program-oriented and less durable tenures of ministry with singles.

## Coping with Depression in the Ministry and Other Helping Professions

by Archibald D. Hart (Word Publishing, 1984) 156 pp. $8.99
***Overall Product Rating: 8.2***
**STRENGTHS:** Comprehensive treatment of depression...Speaks to both its benefits and what happens when it becomes out of control... Most beneficial as it deals with the reality that we will all experience depression sometime during our lifetime...Offers hope to ministers. Recognizes that there are unique and often extraordinary pressures and demands on pastors that most of us aren't willing to admit...Could help someone on the road to burnout... Very helpful and insightful... Ideally suited for the pastor with a well-researched, clear understanding of our lifestyle. He "connected" with me...Well thought out theologically.
**WEAKNESSES:** Would like to have seen less emphasis on the descriptions of the various types of depression and more about why the pastoral profession is so prone to it...Needs more focus in the area of prevention ...A bit dry at times...Written more as a scholarly treatment than for general reading.

## VIDEO/Every Member Evangelism

produced by 2100 Productions (InterVarsity Video, 1987) 21 min. $19.95
***Not Yet Reviewed***
**NOTES:** Provides practical help for planning church outreach through the example of the Church of Santa Isabel in Bogota, Colombia, which is reaching out to a whole city through a strategic plan of witness.

## Feeding and Leading

by Kenneth O. Gangel (Victor Books, 1989) 329 pp. $14.95
***Overall Product Rating: 9.4***
**STRENGTHS:** This combines theology with the best of business/corporate mind set... Gives practical things that ministers/lay leaders can immediately use... Does an impressive job addressing various issues facing Christian leaders in a "user-friendly" style...Much more than a "how-to" book, it grapples with the underlying theological and philosophical "whys?"...A great trouble-shooting resource and reference tool...Good discussion of what true spiritual leadership means... Solid information on goals and planning... Although not uniquely useful for singles ministry, it offers excellent information for leaders...Valuable advice from a man well acquainted with leadership, management, etc.
**WEAKNESSES:** Occasionally too academic... The endnotes distracted me at times...A hierarchical rather than egalitarian view of male/female roles that artificially distinguished between "leadership roles" vs. "offices."

## Free To Dream

### Leadership Development Module

By Mark H. Senter, III (Scripture Press, 1984) 16 pp. $24.95
***Not Yet reviewed***
**NOTES:** This resource includes a film strip, audio cassette and a 16-page young adult Leader's guide. The dreams of young adults are crucial to the future of the local church, as well as the progress of the kingdom of God. This resource helps a church leader to assist the young adult in setting priorities and establishing goals.

## Healing The Wounded

by John White and Ken Blue (InterVarsity Press, 1985) 237 pp. $6.95
***Overall Product Rating: 5.5***
**STRENGTHS:** Challenges leaders to find their own strengths and weaknesses ...Sets a standard for love in action with leadership people... Provides some answers and guidelines to personal problems of healing in relationships.
**WEAKNESSES:** Needs good discussion questions at the end of each chapter...Does not address where we can find supportive mechanisms for restoration.

## Heart and Soul Of Effective Management, The

by James F. Hind (Victor Books, 1989) 132 pp. $7.95
***Overall Product Rating: 8.3***
**STRENGTHS:** Very helpful suggestions for pastors to implement in their own leadership style...Helpful in teaching singles how they can/should lead in their workplace... Extremely challenging...The author used good illustrations to make his point. I particularly enjoyed the emphasis on the importance of building up and caring for people...and the theme, "in the Kingdom of God, service to God is the measurement of true greatness."
**WEAKNESSES:** Not enough specific references to Scripture...Needs better follow through when identifying Jesus' model of leadership. When he gets to the "commandments of caring," he seems to lose his tie to the Jesus model and moves into human relationships. Not necessarily a bad approach, just different from he implied that he was going to do.

## How To Lead Small Groups

by Neal F. McBride (NavPress, 1990) 139 pp. $5.95
***Not Yet Reviewed***
**NOTES:** Covers leadership skills for all kinds of small groups—Bible study,

## How Does The National Review Board Function?

1. There are over 100 reviewers on this board, representing every major denomination and region of the country.
2. All reviewers are pastors, counselors or lay leaders involved in ministry with single adults.
3. Every product is reviewed and evaluated by *at least two - and in most cases, three - members* of this National Board. (When appropriate and possible, the product is actually used in a singles ministry prior to being evaluated.)
4. Each product is reviewed and evaluated on its own merit and not as it compares to other products or resources.
5. Reviewers' ratings for each product are tabulated and averaged by the staff of *Single Adult Ministries Journal* to determine each score. ***(Products are rated from 1 to 10, with 10 being the best rating possible.)***

fellowship, task and support groups. Provides step-by-step guidance and practical exercises to help grasp critical aspects of small group leadership and dynamics.

## Increasing Your Leadership Confidence: Fine Tune Your Leadership Skills

by Bob Biehl (Questar Publishers, 1989) 220 pp. $15.95

***Overall Product Rating: 8.8***

**STRENGTHS:** Good insights about human nature, helping you better understand people as you lead them...Quality book...The use of key questions throughout each chapter are especially effective—arresting and challenging, helpful in getting to the heart of the issue...The general format, combining philosophy, questions, brief commentary and review lends itself to easy and quick reference and use...Very user-friendly...Insightful and practical on issues that are not often addressed in Christian books on leadership... Helps you clarifying issues by leading you to ask pertinent questions. (Summary question sheets in back of book would be good to carry with you at all times)...The "leadership wisdom" gathered together in one place here is essential for those seeking to lead and manage a singles ministry (or any other ministry).

**WEAKNESSES:** No real theological base. Designed to be used in both church and non-religious settings... Not recommended to provide an initial understanding of spiritual leadership, but rather as a supplement to other books on Christian leadership...No attempt has been made to relate these leadership principles to the theological perspectives of those of us in church leadership positions, questions like: "Is this God's will?" "Have I prayed about this?"

## Leadership Inventory

by Bob Biehl (Masterplanning Group Intl., 1977) 14 pp. $5.00

***Overall Product Rating: 5.7***

**STRENGTHS:** Good resource for leaders... An excellent, easy-to-use tool to help a leadership team improve discussion and communication ...Helps us recognize a variety of leadership qualities.

**WEAKNESSES:** More suggestions on how to use this material are needed...Tends to be vague and too simplistic.

## Leadership Is Male: Truth Must Not be Based on Cultural Consensus But on the Revealed Mind of God

by J. David Pawson (Thomas Nelson, 1990) 127 pp. $11.95

***Overall Product Rating: 4.3***

**STRENGTHS:** Continues the ongoing dialogue of the woman's role in the church and attempts to be sensitive to the issues... Author tries to see both sides of the argument and remain fair to the controversy... Easy to understand...Offers several alternatives for exploration. The conclusion helps unscramble some of the more obvious tensions which is a good move on the authors behalf... Will challenge readers to know what personal beliefs they possesses.

**WEAKNESSES:** It doesn't take the reader long to see through the author's intentions or personal bias...By limiting God's alternative resources for revealing God's mind, culture is relegated to a separate and isolated island. Culture can also be a valuable alternative to revealing God's mind... Recognition of cultural differences which he feels is not an issue makes one wonder where he would stand on slavery in light of its acceptance in Scripture...Does not deal adequately with progressive revelation...The author's Old Testament theology is suspect ...Doesn't go deep enough...Faulty questions regarding spiritual gifts and their use by men and women...Doesn't honestly look at all sides of this tension.

## Leading with a Followers Heart: Practicing Biblical Obedience and Humility in the Workplace

by Eugene B. Habecker (Scripture Press Publications, 1990) 204 pp. $7.95

***Overall Product Rating: 9.3***

**STRENGTHS:** Applicable to a wide context of leadership (church, corporate, family). The author even presents the principles in terms which suggest multiple arenas... Material lends itself to leadership retreats. The questions at the end of each section are excellent.

**WEAKNESSES:** No separate work book is provided.

## Making of a Leader, The

by Dr. J. Robert Clinton (NavPress, 1988) 272 pp. $7.95

***Overall Product Rating: 4.5***

**STRENGTHS:** Looks at the importance of a philosophy of ministry and how to develop one...A systematic look at stages of leadership development and what to expect to happen at each stage...Helpful look at the process of becoming a leader. Very detailed.

**WEAKNESSES:** Too predictable. Each chapter's format is basically the same... Written in too much of an academic style...Nothing for the "wounded healers" in a singles ministry who often provide much of the leadership.

## Mastering Church Management

by Don Cousins, Leith Anderson, Arthur DeKruyter (Christianity Today, 1990) 166 pp. $12.95

***Overall Product Rating: 8.5***

**STRENGTHS:** Very strong in "how to" manage the church, and would be most helpful to pastors of small churches...Clear written with good examples...Good to have three different viewpoints... Well-presented wisdom gained by years of personal experience... Written in a usable form with skill and warmth...Although not directed towards singles ministry, it could be useful to the staff member working with singles.
**WEAKNESSES:** It would have been nice to have seen some specific singles ministry examples used.

## Maximum Ministry

by Robert E. Slocum (NavPress, 1990) 295 pp. $8.95

***Not Yet Reviewed***

**NOTES:** Outlines the essentials for preparing lay men and women for ministry. Includes a study guide for small group discussion and reflection.

## No Foothold In The Swamp

by Charles Hollingsworth (Zondervan, 1988) 154 pp. $10.95

***Overall Product Rating: 8.5***

**STRENGTHS:** An excellent book on pastoral burnout...Looks at how pastors who are high achievers are top candidates for burnout, how overwork and stress cause difficulty in marriage relationships and pastoral responsibilities ...The author explains how seeking a spiritual counselor was very important in saving his ministry ...Helps us see ourselves and the pressures that are inherent with the life of a minister...Gives us permission to call out for help before it's too late...The questions and suggestions at the back of the book are very helpful...Looks at both healthy and unhealthy ways ministers deal with burnout.
**WEAKNESSES:** Doesn't give much explanation as to why his particular coping mechanisms were used...His solution was not necessarily the best or only way to go. There could have been other approaches not discussed in the book...Solutions were not explicitly Biblically-based (though it was implied)...The price of this book may be limiting to some who most need this.

## Other Side of Leadership, The

by Eugene Habecker (Victor Books, 1987) 167 pp. $6.95

***Overall Product Rating: 7.6***

**STRENGTHS:** A very good book to use in leadership training to prepare lay leaders for the load of spiritual ministry...Transferable principles between ministry and the secular marketplace—Biblical life-style leadership... Excellent presentation on forgiveness and the hard issue of confrontation...Deals with the importance of follower-ship in leadership.
**WEAKNESSES:** Needs to be a study guide developed with overheads...A few illustrations as examples would be helpful...Needs a clear look at the "price" of leadership and the emotional drain one must face.

## Recruiting Volunteers in the Church

by Mark Senter III (Victor Books, 1990) 167 pp. $9.95

***Not Yet Reviewed***

**NOTES:** Provides information a church needs for recruiting, nurturing and keeping, as well as dismissing, if necessary, a strong staff of volunteers.

## Role of Women in Ministry Today, The

by H. Wayne House (Thomas Nelson, 1990) 192 pp. $9.95

***Not Yet Reviewed***

**NOTES:** Churches, denominations and Christian organizations have been split asunder over the issue of ordaining women for pulpit ministry. This books offers a fresh and challenging study on the specific Scriptures that shape modern views on the place of women in the church.

## Role Of Women In the Church, The

by Charles Caldwell Ryrie (Moody Press, 1970) 155 pp. $6.95

***Overall Product Rating: 4.3***

**STRENGTHS:** Presents a thorough, historical look at women of the Bible and in the church (albeit from a preconceived biased position)...A helpful exegesis on the passages about women in the Bible and about divorce...Provided information I can use in a Bible study with women about women.
**WEAKNESSES:** The basic conclusion that is arrived at could be found in any good commentary on the two Scriptural passages he uses as his primary source...I find little in this book of value in singles ministry... Quite dry. For a controversial topic, this book is boring...Leaves no room for varying opinions...Hard to understand at times...I cannot support his view of women. I feel he tried to slant his work toward his view even though he stated many times that he was merely reporting historical facts. A treatise on the letter, rather than the spirit, of the law.

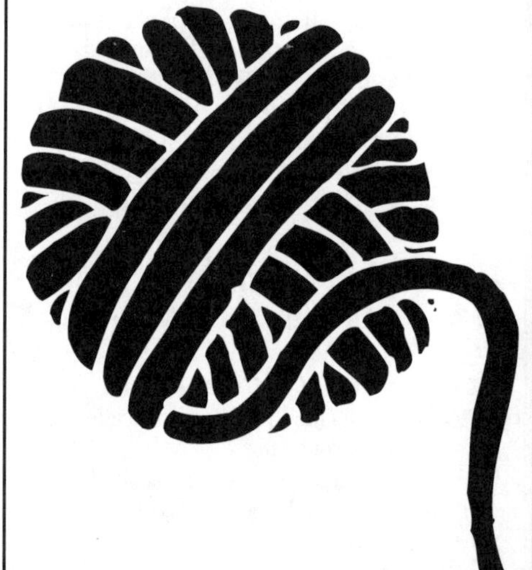

## How Does The National Review Board Function?

1. There are over 100 reviewers on this board, representing every major denomination and region of the country.
2. All reviewers are pastors, counselors or lay leaders involved in ministry with single adults.
3. Every product is reviewed and evaluated by *at least two - and in most cases, three - members* of this National Board. (When appropriate and possible, the product is actually used in a singles ministry prior to being evaluated.)
4. Each product is reviewed and evaluated on its own merit and not as it compares to other products or resources.
5. Reviewers' ratings for each product are tabulated and averaged by the staff of *Single Adult Ministries Journal* to determine each score. ***(Products are rated from 1 to 10, with 10 being the best rating possible.)***

## FILM STRIP/ Single Revolution

### Leadership Development Module

by Henry Jacobsen (Scripture Press, 1984) $24.95

***Not Yet Reviewed***

**NOTES:** This resource includes an 80-frame film strip, cassette tape and a 32-page Leader's guide. It is designed to use in four training sessions, each one hour in length. This will help equip the leader who is working with single adults in any age group.

## Solving Church Education's Ten Toughest Problems:

### An Experienced Educator Offers Sound Advice

by John R. Cionca (Scripture Press Publications, 1990) 187 pp. $7.95

***Not Yet Reviewed***

**NOTES:** Nearly every church struggles with at least one problem of the 10 most prevalent church education problems. This book gives information designed to relieve the problem and transform the church's educational program through using checklists and sample forms for getting the church ministry on target.

## Spiritual Leadership, Responsible Management

by Michael T. Dibbert (Zondervan, 1989) 207 pp. $5.07

***Not Yet Reviewed***

**NOTES:** The church needs spiritual leaders who manage well. This handbook brings together New Testament models for leadership and good management sense.

## Teach As He Taught:

### How To Apply Jesus' Teaching Methods

by Robert G. Delnay (Moody Press, 1987) 128 pp. $5.95

***Not Yet Reviewed***

**NOTES:** Describes the methods Jesus used to communicate to people, and how we can use those methods today. Robert Delnay focuses on teacher preparation and commitment, keeping students' attention, teaching techniques and lesson review.

## Team Spirit: A Management Book

by David Cormack (Pyranee/Zondervan, 1989) 216 pp. $9.95

***Overall Product Rating: 7.5***

**STRENGTHS:** Provides meaningful instructions and useful exercises to aid personal analysis and development as a leader...This book will help single adult leaders to effectively involve more people in the ministry.

**WEAKNESSES:** Tends to be introductory in nature...Sometimes the descriptions are very technical and somewhat difficult to grasp... There is such an abundance of material, lists, charts and graphs, that it almost overwhelms.

## Well-Managed Ministry, The

by Philip M. Van Auken (Scripture Press, 1989) 236 pp. $9.95

***Not Yet Reviewed***

**NOTES:** Certain managerial methods appropriate in today's business world are not compatible with the values of Christian organizations. This book develops effective and efficient management styles compatible to Christian values.

## Women In Ministry: Four Views

by Bonidell Clouse and Robert Clouse (InterVarsity Press, 1989) 250 pp. $9.95

***Overall Product Rating: 7.0***

**STRENGTHS:** While the book does not necessarily tackle an issue concerning single adults, it does address the perennial question of "What can women do in the ministry?" The book bravely provides a synopsis of four views on women with rebuttals for each...The last chapter is an appeal for unity and humility as regards this issue and is well taken...Clearly outlines all aspects of women involved in leadership roles in the organized church...Discusses various interpretations of Scripture and provides readers with a wealth of information in order to make an intelligent decision about where they stand in this debate...Prompts you to search deeper for scriptural bases for women in ministry...Puts some basic issues into perspective and into discussable chunks.

**WEAKNESSES:** After reading this, I have no clearer answer on this issue...Although this book gives four view points, it does not leave you satisfied with any of the answers...As someone primarily involved in a ministry with single parents, it has very little of relevance. We are busy doing the work of the church together, ministering to men and women after divorce or death of a spouse. This book is definitely geared to pastors who would be in the position to decide what roles women play in their particular church.

## You Can Teach Adults

by Henry Jacobsen (Victor Books, 1988) 64 pp. $4.95

***Not Yet Reviewed***

**NOTES:** Proven principles you can use to help your single adults link learning to living as they develop a mature understanding of the Word of God.

# Leadership Tools & Helps

## 99 Ways to Start a Study Group And Keep It Growing

by Lawrence O. Richards (Zondervan, 1987) 158 pp. $7.95

***Not Yet Reviewed***

**NOTES:** According to the author, this book offers a tested way to make the group experience successful and worthwhile. He suggests five principles needed to properly balance Bible study and fellowship in any group plus creative ideas for group involvement, ways to affirm each other with positive criticism, fresh ideas about studying Scripture and meaningful ways to worship as a group.

## Checklist for Planning A Special Event

by Ed Trenner (Masterplanning Group Int'l, 1983) 20 pp. $10

***Overall Product Rating: 8.1***

**STRENGTHS:** A 300-point checklist that can help cut your planning time...Outstanding resource and planning guide tool... Helps you see the big picture...Encourages you to ask the right questions when working with your various planning teams.

**WEAKNESSES:** The timetable help is weak—needed better guidelines for last minute details and specifics such as how to organize registration... Would be much more helpful if there were a timetable for each area... Assumes to much for the novice to use effectively...Might overwhelm someone new to planning and leading.

## Clip Art

(Youth Specialties, 1987) 131 pp. $11.95

***Overall Product Rating: 6.6***

**STRENGTHS:** Offers useful, easy-to-use art for newsletters, handouts, overheads, etc...Very good material for those working with teens.

**WEAKNESSES:** Is geared for youth and should be used by youth...Most of this would not be usable with single adults...Too juvenile.

## Creating Graphics That Communicate

by William M. Lessel (Moody Press, 1987) 133 pp. $6.95

***Overall Product Rating: 6.3***

**STRENGTHS:** Is concise but thorough, covering the basics...Uses lots of pictorial examples and de-scriptions...Easy to understand and aimed at readers with little or no experience in graphics...Text is written and illustrated in such a way as to make it possible for the reader to produce and excellent piece of art their first time.

**WEAKNESSES:** Cover design and the graphics pictures in the book have a very dated look compared to current trends in church singles artwork...Not very well composed ...Colors are garish.

## Emotional Balance Chart

by Bob Biehl (Masterplanning Group, 1983) 4 pp. $1.00

***Overall Product Rating: 3.0***

**STRENGTHS:** Provides some areas to help people consider where they living in balance...Offers some scriptural support... Gives minimal direction for reflection and attitude check.

**WEAKNESSES:** Tends to be unrealistic and simplistic in approach...Seems incomplete... Maybe beneficial on a one-shot basis but not as a ongoing tool.

## Six Skits For Singles: Short Scripts Ideal for Single Adult Retreats, Camps, Church Services or Youth Meetings

by Gail Blanton (Lillenas, 1980) 20 pp. $2.95

***Not Yet Reviewed***

**NOTES:** These six short, theatrical productions can be used in many ways, using the talents of your group members, and teaching/entertaining the remainder of your audience at the same time.

# Loneliness

## Most Recommended Resources in This Section

(Based on evaluations and reviews made by *SAM Journal's* National Resource Review Board, using a 1-10 scale with 10 being the best possible score):

### 9.1 How To Win Over Loneliness

by John Haggai (Harvest House Publishing, 1988)

### 8.3 How to Overcome Loneliness

by Elisabeth Elliot (NavPress, 1989)

### 8.1 Loneliness: It Can Be a Wilderness Or a Pathway to God

by Elisabeth Elliot (Oliver Nelson, 1988)

*(For more information on each of the above resources—plus many other helpful products—find them listed in alphabetical order below.)*

## About Loneliness

(Channing L. Betes Co., 1987) 15 pp. 72¢

***Overall Product Rating: 6.5***

**STRENGTHS:** Easy to read and understand. Persons when depressed and lonely do not want to read a complicated book and this would not discourage the reader...Strong outline of what loneliness is....Offers some good suggestions on growing through loneliness, and especially on the need to reach out to help others... Appreciated the part about accepting loneliness as a fact of life. It happens, don't try and run from it by doing things...Could be a good tool as a discussion starter.

**WEAKNESSES:** Several good ideas poorly developed.

## How to Overcome Loneliness

by Elisabeth Elliot (NavPress, 1989) 23 pp. $1.95

***Overall Product Rating: 8.3***

**STRENGTHS:** Directly addresses the difference between loneliness and "a-loneness"...Shares from the author's personal experiences...A thoughtful, well-written tool which tactfully addresses the subject...Small, inexpensive and interestingly written, this booklet would be easy to give to singles of all ages.

**WEAKNESSES:** For those persons less mature in their faith, they may view this booklet as somewhat pious, with an over-spiritualization of the emotional loneliness experience and the solution...Author doesn't effectively address the loneliness issues for younger singles (20s-30s).

## How to Win over Loneliness

by John Haggai (Harvest House Publishing, 1988) 167 pp. $5.95

***Overall Product Rating: 9.1***

**STRENGTHS:** Very enlightening, particularly in its description of different stages of loneliness...I particularly enjoyed the discussion of idealistic expectations of the lonely...A helpful plan to overcome loneliness no matter what stage of loneliness one is in...Very useful as a self-help book.

**WEAKNESSES:** For this material to benefit a larger group setting, much work would be

## How Does The National Review Board Function?

1. There are over 100 reviewers on this board, representing every major denomination and region of the country.
2. All reviewers are pastors, counselors or lay leaders involved in ministry with single adults.
3. Every product is reviewed and evaluated by *at least two - and in most cases, three - members* of this National Board. (When appropriate and possible, the product is actually used in a singles ministry prior to being evaluated.)
4. Each product is reviewed and evaluated on its own merit and not as it compares to other products or resources.
5. Reviewers' ratings for each product are tabulated and averaged by the staff of *Single Adult Ministries Journal* to determine each score. ***(Products are rated from 1 to 10, with 10 being the best rating possible.)***

required of the teacher/leader, which is unfortunate. This limits the number of people who would/could teach it.

## Loneliness

by Elizabeth Skoglund (InterVarsity Press, 1975) 36 pp. $1.00

***Not Yet reviewed***

**NOTES:** This pamphlet provides insights into the causes of loneliness and how it is related to low self-esteem. It then provides suggestions for alleviating loneliness by approaching it from its psychological and spiritual roots.

## Loneliness: It Can Be a Wilderness Or a Pathway to God

by Elisabeth Elliot (Oliver Nelson, 1988) 158 pp. $12.95

***Overall Product Rating: 8.1***

**STRENGTHS:** The author does an excellent job of showing how loneliness can be a time of growth—how it is our reaction to loneliness that determines our growth... Strong Scriptural support ...Based on the uncompromising truth of God's Word...Solid.

**WEAKNESSES:** At times the author is much too theological, sacrificing the relational aspects of this subject matter...Nothing very fresh or new ...Seems to be geared primarily to the older adult, which is unfortunate. Much of the material might be useful to younger people if it were written in a more contemporary manner... The author's openly "old-fashioned" references will create barriers to many who might otherwise benefit from this book...Although this is a new book, it seems dated.

## VIDEO/Surviving Loneliness

by Clayton Barbeau (Franciscan Communications, 1988) 24 min. $19.95

***Not Yet Reviewed***

**NOTES:** Examines loneliness as a part of everyone's life, especially in today's competitive society. Offers many concrete strategies to counteract loneliness.

## When You're Feeling Lonely

by Charles Durham (InterVarsity Press, 1984) 185 pp. $5.95

***Overall Product Rating: 6.0***

**STRENGTHS:** Realistic...The chapter on "Dangers of Loneliness" was exceptionally informing and challenging. It would be a good area to explore further with a person struggling with temptation.

**WEAKNESSES:** It needed a summary of some kind at the end of each chapter to help the reader digest the material.

## Why Be Lonely? A Guide To Meaningful Relationships

by Carter, Meier, Minirth (Baker Book House, 1982) 169 pp. $7.95

***Overall Product Rating: 7.6***

**STRENGTHS:** The book outlines practical steps for attaining emotional intimacy ...Maintains a balanced approach from medicine, psychiatry and theology...More than a "how to manual," it is a comprehensive understanding of behavior...Excellent description of loneliness...Strong emphasis on cognitive behavioral approach...Stays away from simplistic answers...Great illustrations ...Thorough discussion of the problem with solid answers and direction.

**WEAKNESSES:** Needs a study guide (although it may not be a good study book anyway)...At times a little preachy...Needs a bibliography...This book seems to be primarily an extension, rearrangement, and rewrite of the more recent Minirth Meier book, *Happiness Is A Choice*, which is a much better book than this.

# Pre-marriage and Remarriage Resources

## Most Recommended Resources in This Section

(Based on evaluations and reviews made by *SAM Journal*'s National Resource Review Board, using a 1-10 scale with 10 being the best possible score):

### 9.2 First Years of Forever

by Ed Wheat (with Gloria Perkins) (Zondervan, 1988)

### 8.5 Before You Say "I Do:" A Marriage Preparation Manual For Couples

by Wes Roberts and H. Norman Wright (Harvest House Publishing, 1978)

### 8.1 Handbook For Engaged Couples, A

by Alice and Robert Fryling (InterVarsity Press, 1977)

*(For more information on each of the above resources—plus many other helpful products—find them listed in alphabetical order below.)*

## About Preparing For Marriage

(Channing L. Bete Co., 1986) 15 pp. 72¢

***Overall Product Rating: 6.3***

**STRENGTHS:** Presentation is easy to outline and present...Easy to read and understand ...Could be given to couples to take home... Stresses the importance of pre-marital counseling plus things to discuss before marriage ...Gives some good general counsel on solving conflicts in a relationship.

**WEAKNESSES:** Absence of Scriptural references...Does not develop the good ideas. Too shallow.

## Before You Say "I Do:"
### A Marriage Preparation Manual For Couples

by Wes Roberts and H. Norman Wright (Harvest House Publishing, 1978) 76 pp. $5.95

***Overall Product Rating: 8.5***

**STRENGTHS:** Includes strong Scripture references...Activities involve the reader with exercises and open-ended questions...The list of books and other references at the end of each chapter allow the user to dig deeper... Can be an effective tool to help open lines of communication among couples...Great as homework in premarital counseling...Good discussion of money, in-laws, sex, etc.
**WEAKNESSES:** No table of contents ...The amount of Scripture referencing presumes users are reasonably mature Christians, which may limit its potential audience...Little writing with lots of questions...Requires considerable time to work through (which in many cases may be a strength rather than a weaknesses).

## VIDEO/Building A Christian Marriage

by Rev. Ron Brusius (Concordia Publishing House, 1987) $69.95

***Overall Product Rating: 6.2***

**STRENGTHS:** Excellent video quality, professionally produced... The case studies and Biblical examples used are an innovative approach to the material...Stimulates discussion better than many workbooks do... Addresses many vital issues facing people considering serious relationships or marriage... Although this material is lacking in several significant ways, I plan to incorporate some of it into my premarital counseling sessions.
**WEAKNESSES:** The acting on the video comes off overly melodramatic and trite... The situations portrayed by the actors tend to be stereotypical. Premarital problems are seldom as clear cut and well-defined...The material seems to be limited to a younger, less mature audience...The characters portrayed in the video are not overtly Christian in attitude or expression...I don't think single adults living in larger cities could relate to this material very well because the content is overly obvious and unsophisticated ...Too little Biblical instruction... Shallow ...If this is the best we can do toward helping our singles "build" a Christian marriage, then it is no wonder our divorce rates are so high.

## Counseling Before Marriage
### Resources for Christian Counseling

by Everett L. Worthington, Jr. (Word, Inc., 1990) 216 pp. $12.99

***Not Yet Reviewed***

**NOTES:** This book offers practical information on relationship development, psychology of marriage, preparation for marriage, forces that shape modern marriage, effects of widowhood and divorce, and the dynamics of remarriage.

## First Years of Forever

by Ed Wheat (with Gloria Perkins) (Zondervan, 1988) 191 pp. $8.95

***Overall Product Rating: 9.3***

**STRENGTHS:** I liked this book a lot. It presents an interesting blend of the practical and the ideal...Very refreshing to find an author who deals with sexuality so openly, yet with taste and sensitivity...A realistic look at what makes a marriage work...One of the best books I've read that addresses issues such as dating, pre-marriage and marriage in an up-to-date manner...An excellent book to use with both college students and single adults...A good resource for remarriage too... Many pre-marriage concerns/apprehensions are thoroughly covered...Great book!
**WEAKNESSES:** It lacks a workbook or study/discussion questions. That would have been a great benefit...The chapter on "Communicating" seemed to treat important concepts/issues too lightly.

## Getting Ready for a Great Marriage:
### For Those Who Want Their Love to Last

by R. Paul Stevens (NavPress, 1990) 109 pp. $5.95

***Not Yet Reviewed***

**NOTES:** In a day when divorce steadily stares down the best intentions and strongest commitments, it's important to plan for a marriage that will last "till death do you part." Focusing on the marriage covenant, a lifelong partnership that is in-dwelt by God, this book uses exercises and insights that will help you build foundations for a lasting marriage.

## How Does The National Review Board Function?

1. There are over 100 reviewers on this board, representing every major denomination and region of the country.
2. All reviewers are pastors, counselors or lay leaders involved in ministry with single adults.
3. Every product is reviewed and evaluated by *at least two - and in most cases, three - members* of this National Board. (When appropriate and possible, the product is actually used in a singles ministry prior to being evaluated.)
4. Each product is reviewed and evaluated on its own merit and not as it compares to other products or resources.
5. Reviewers' ratings for each product are tabulated and averaged by the staff of *Single Adult Ministries Journal* to determine each score. ***(Products are rated from 1 to 10, with 10 being the best rating possible.)***

## Getting Ready for Marriage

by David R. Mace (Abingdon Press, 1985) 113 pp. $6.95

***Not Yet Reviewed***

**NOTES:** Encourages partners to evaluate themselves, each other and their relationship before entering one of the most demanding of human relationships.

## Growing Into Love (Before You Marry)

by Joyce Huggett (InterVarsity Press, 1982) 128 pp. $5.95

***Overall Product Rating: 7.0***

**STRENGTHS:** An easy to use resource on dating...Covers such things as "learning to touch," "how far should we go?" etc... Potential differences in personality/temperament with a couple are faced squarely... Author is not afraid to say "perhaps you should break up"...The sexual relationship issues are handled well...Good questions for self-evaluation or discussion are included through-out...Could also be helpful in counseling

**WEAKNESSES:** Tends to quote other people too often ...Some of the book is outdated (i.e. AIDS, etc.)...Chapter 13 on "Love, Honor and Obey" is a well done statement on the conservative position of man's headship and woman's submission. But those of an egalitarian viewpoint will balk... Male/female roles are sometimes too stereotypical.

## Handbook For Engaged Couples, A

by Alice and Robert Fryling (InterVarsity Press, 1977) 71 pp. $4.95

***Overall Product Rating: 8.1***

**STRENGTHS:** An easy-to-follow look at some of the most important topics for engaged couples...Sections on problem solving will be very helpful for couples... Excellent discussion catalyst for engaged couples...Workbook format encourages work on communication...Honest and helpful examples from author ...Focuses on building a Scriptural foundation.

**WEAKNESSES:** Written in mid 70s, so resources/bibliography are not current... Primarily for the never-married single. No questions are included about divorce...Left out some important topics such as in-laws, self-esteem and parenting.

## Happily Ever After Is No Accident

by William Tapley (C.S.S. Publishing, 1987) Couple's Study Book 52 pp. $3.45; Leader's book 31 pp. $2.75

***Overall Product Rating: 4.0***

**STRENGTHS:** This product provides an orderly, structured approach to pre-marital counseling...Is reasonably thorough and involves the couple in discovering for themselves possible problem areas...Includes some thought provoking exercises in the workbook...Looks at some remarriage issues that may be helpful in leading the couple to assess things that they may not have considered.

**WEAKNESSES:** This material does not focus on the Christian aspects of a relationship so does not meet the needs of the singles ministry I work with...There are several areas where the wording indicated some confusion/ struggle concerning remarriage. Not clearly thought through...I feel the material is seriously undermined by the statement "results of questions are not the counselors business." This statement gives couples an out to dodge or ignore critical areas and not deal with the hard areas of disagreement in their relationship.

## How Can I Be Sure?

### A Pre-Marriage Inventory

by Bob Phillips (Harvest House Publishing, 1978) 153 pp. $4.95

***Overall Product Rating: 7.7***

**STRENGTHS:** Easy to use and understand... Comprehensive, thorough, yet not cumbersome... Especially with chapter 12 (on discerning true love) it helps bring application of scriptural principles and realities into the relationship...Practical questions, designed to show little prejudgment on any given issue... Helpful to include the wedding checklist...Covers a wide range of topics which pre-marital couples need to discuss... Provides pastors and leaders a checklist of most all problem areas...Includes tools to help the pastor to assist couples in discussing particularly sensitive or embarrassing issues.

**WEAKNESSES:** Bibliography is completely out of date...It gives the impression that once agreement on a particular question has been reached, a potential post-marital problem has been avoided, which is usually not true...Fails to include the perspective of real life, which on some issues is necessary to determine an honest response...The personal inventory sections were shallow compared to others I've seen on the market.

## How to Get Married and Stay That Way

by Cliff Albritton (Broadman Press, 1982) 144 pp. $5.95

***Overall Product Rating: 4.5***

**STRENGTHS:** Provides a positive outlook for singles...The personality profile comparison can result in a sensible evaluation of a prospective marriage partner...The checklist format for questions that need to be considered in mate selection is reasonable and helpful.

**WEAKNESSES:** The title may be misleading to some because this is not a marriage manual...The singular issue I found problematic is the close-ended statement on page 139 to the effect that to wait to accept Jesus is to reject Him, relying little on God's grace to complete the transformation.

## Journeying Toward Marriage

by Rev. William Anderson (Wm C. Brown, 1985) 165 pp. $6.75

***Overall Product Rating: 4.5***

**STRENGTHS:** The presentation in chapter five on love and communication is excellent. This chapter especially would be very helpful for pastors when counseling couples for marriage...The questions at the end of each section are quite helpful.

**WEAKNESSES:** The first part of the book is slow...Since it is Catholic in origin and theology, the ritual may be hard to accept for some Protestants.

## Making Marriage Work

### Developing Intimacy with the One You Love

by Truman Esau, MD with Beverly Burch (Victor Books, 1990) 180 pp. $12.95

***Overall Product Rating: 7.1***

**STRENGTHS:** Easy to understand... For the young single just entering into a first marriage, it would be a great book...Looks at the importance of bonding, sharing ones deepest thoughts and feelings. The book also helps us understand that the bonding that goes on in marriage owes a great deal to the kind of bonding received in childhood, how disruptions in this bonding process often lead to a history of abuse.

**WEAKNESSES:** Pretty basic. Most people probably desire something more thought provoking.

## VIDEO/Marital Counseling Series, The: Before and After You Say I Do

Features: H. Norman Write, Tim and Beverly LeHaye, Larry Burkett (Evangelical Films. 1986) 3-part series, 120 min. $295.00 (Includes 103 pp. Workbook and 70 pp. Leaders' Book.)

***Not Yet Reviewed***

**NOTES:** This three-part series helps the engaged couple examine their relationship in the areas of finances, spiritual needs, emotional and physical needs. An overview of marriage and marital expectations is given.

## Mystery of Marriage

by Mike Mason (Multnomah Press, 1985) 185 pp. $8.95

***Overall Product Rating: 7.3***

**STRENGTHS:** Sound portrayal of what marriage really is and what is involved in commitment...Beautifully written...The author writes as one who obviously loves marriage and loves his wife...Reminds us that a relationship is much more than merely living together...A helpful attempt to define that illusive, mysterious reality which must be present in every healthy, lasting marriage.

**WEAKNESSES:** Portions of this book will be difficult for a divorced person contemplating remarriage. His thoughts about divorce are quite black and white...Long on the poetic, short on the practical...Author seems eager to leave us with memorable word pictures which sometimes cloud his point and come off sounding effusive...Apparently the author has no children. The role of being both a parent and a spouse needs to be developed. He talks about being there or present with the spouse, but try to do that when little Johnny is trying to throw his potatoes across the room during dinner...Could have used some references for why living together is a life-style far different from marriage.

## Preparing For Christian Marriage

by Joan A. Hunt (Abingdon Press, 1987) 94 pp. $9.95

***Overall Product Rating: 6.5***

**STRENGTHS:** The work sheets and questionnaires are thorough, valuable, practical and interesting to answer...Not a theological handbook per se. Its strength is practical rather than theological...This workbook has excellent exercises for couples to use in exploring their relationship, attitudes, expectations and plans for the future. The chapter on communication is worth the price of the book.

**WEAKNESSES:** Limited Scriptural support. This is a significant problem and needs to be dealt with if you use it...I would not give this book to any couple to read. While many technical aspects are of high quality, this book teaches a philosophy of life, marriage and family that tends to be unbiblical and theologically unsound ...Does not get into controversial areas such as Eph. 5 or Tim. 2, which sooner or later we must deal with it.

## Preparing To Marry Again

by Dick Dunn (self-published, 1988) 142 pp. $15.00

***Overall Product Rating: 5.8***

**STRENGTHS:** Questions and activities at the end of each chapter are helpful...Provides a fairly thorough agenda for counseling those considering remarriage.

**WEAKNESSES:** The length is both an asset and a liability. An asset to the extent that it is pretty thorough, a liability in that most couples do not want more than 8-10 sessions... Insufficient questions and activities for a couple who are planning to marry. The questions and exercises should cause a couple to really deal with each subject area in detail. I don't think someone who worked through this would have sufficiently examined several vital topics.

## Preparing To Remarry

by Claire Berman (Public Affairs Pamphlets, 1987) 24 pp. $1.00

***Overall Product Rating: 5.1***

**STRENGTHS:** Provides helpful statistics that show how difficult remarriage can be, especially when children are involved... Offers practical advice and resources to help deal with difficult issues surrounding remarriage ...First part of book provides some excellent material that could be utilized in developing curriculum for a class on remarriage.

**WEAKNESSES:** God is not considered in this booklet...No Biblical perspective...Tends to promote the concept that living together without a marital contract is a viable option ...Not a book I would give to my singles but is one I would use as a resource for ideas and statistics.

## Promises of Marriage

by William H. Willimon (Discipleship Resources, 1987) 34 pp. $2.95

***Overall Product Rating: 6.7***

**STRENGTHS:** Good, sound theology...An excellent resource to provide a leader with theological and philosophical foundations for Christian marriage...Much of this material will find its way into my teaching, counseling and marriage ceremonies ...Provides a simple tool to give to couples in pre-marriage counseling.

**WEAKNESSES:** It is pretty heady stuff and would not be easy to hand to just anyone to read. Requires a thinking, reading, college graduate-level person.

## Should I Get Married?

by M. Blaine Smith (InterVarsity Press, 1990) 214 pp. $7.95

***Overall Product Rating: 7.6***

**STRENGTHS:** Easy to read, com-prehensive ...Dealt with most of the questions and issues Christians face in the dating/marriage world. Even dealt with some areas seldom addressed such as marriage to another race, computer-ized dating services and women taking the initiative...Very practical...Well-balanced, Scriptural approach to marriage and singleness, affirming both choices. For those desiring to marry, the author provides helpful advice on finding a mate, choosing the right kind of person and determining your readiness for lifelong commitment... Good material for the single adult, especially the never married...Sometimes books can be so heavenly minded they are no "earthly good." However, this book was practical and gave good, sound, solid advice.

**WEAKNESSES:** At times too general and brief. May try to cover too much in one book...The book does not specifically address the question of remarriage, although much of the material would still be helpful...No study guide was included with the book.

## How Does The National Review Board Function?

**1.** There are over 100 reviewers on this board, representing every major denomination and region of the country.
**2.** All reviewers are pastors, counselors or lay leaders involved in ministry with single adults.
**3.** Every product is reviewed and evaluated by *at least two - and in most cases, three - members* of this National Board. (When appropriate and possible, the product is actually used in a singles ministry prior to being evaluated.)
**4.** Each product is reviewed and evaluated on its own merit and not as it compares to other products or resources.
**5.** Reviewers' ratings for each product are tabulated and averaged by the staff of *Single Adult Ministries Journal* to determine each score.
***(Products are rated from 1 to 10, with 10 being the best rating possible.)***

## Two Friends In Love

by Ed and Carol Neuenschwander (Multnomah Press, 1986) 194 pp. $6.95

***Not Yet Reviewed***

**NOTES:** The authors share Biblical truth concerning interpersonal intimacy. With that foundation, they draw you into a realistic understanding of how to cultivate mature romantic love.

## When Victims Marry: Building a Stronger Marriage by Breaking Destructive Cycles

by Don and Jan Frank (Here's Life Publishers, 1990) 206 pp. $7.95

***Not Yet Reviewed***

**NOTES:** Explore the "foundations" of yourself and your mate (or future mate) to uncover any areas of dysfunction that may be hurting your relationship. Learn how to remove the debris and pour a new foundation that will increase the potential for success in even the most troubled marriage.

# Dating and Friendships-Relationships

## Most Recommended Resources in This Section

(Based on evaluations and reviews made by *SAM Journal*'s National Resource Review Board, using a 1-10 scale with 10 being the best possible score):

**9.5 Unfinished Business: Helping Adult Children Resolve Their Past**
by Charles Sell (Multnomah Press, 1989)

**9.2 Secret Of Loving, The: How a Lasting Intimate Relationship Can Be Yours**
by Josh McDowell (Here's Life Publishers 1985)

**9.2 201 Great Questions: (Conversation Starters For Times With Friends)**
by J. David Jones (NavPress, 1988)

**9.0 Caring Enough To Confront: How to Understand and Express Your Deepest Feelings toward Others**
by David Augsburger (Regal Press, 1981)

**8.7 One-Way Relationships: When you Love Them More than They Love You**
by Alfred Ells (Thomas Nelson, 1990)

**8.6 Love Is A Choice: Recovery For Codependent Relationships**
by Robert Hemfelt, Frank Minirth and Paul Meier (Thomas Nelson, 1989)

**8.5 Co-Dependent No More**
by Melody Beattie (Walker and Company, 1989)

**8.5 Language of Love, The: A Powerful Way to Maximize Insight, Intimacy, and Understanding**
by Gary Smalley and John Trent (Focus on the Family, 1988)

**8.5 Love and Its Counterfeits: It Looks Like Love, It Feels Like Love, But Is It Love?**
by Barbara Cook (Aglow Publications, 1989)

**8.5 You And Your Parents: Strategies for Building an Adult Relationship**
by Harold Ivan Smith (Augsburg Fortress, 1987)

**8.3 Restoring Broken Relationships**
by Don Baker (Harvest House, 1989)

**8.2 Can Christians Love Too Much: Breaking The Cycle of Codependency**
by Dr. Margaret J. Rink (Zondervan, 1989)

**8.0 Nothing To Hide: The Search for Authentic Relationships**
by William T. Rowley (Victor Books, 1989)

*(For more information on each of the above resources—plus many other helpful products—find them listed in alphabetical order below.)*

## Call It Love Or Call It Quits

by Tim Timmons and Charlie Hedges (Worthy, 1988) 179 pp. $12.95

***Total Overall Rating: 7.2***

**STRENGTHS:** A practical and sensible book on dating for single adults...Good reference or back-up source when teaching on relation-ships...Cleverly packaged diagnosis of relationships...Much of it is common sense, but it is made relevant and catchy so it doesn't just rehash on relation-ships...Could easily give it to a young adult to read—it's easy and quick.

**WEAKNESSES:** It's rather thin and "California-style" may not appeal to more serious intellectual sorts.

## Choices:
### Finding God's Way in Dating, Sex, Singleness and Marriage

by Stacy and Paula Rinehart (NavPress, 1983) 148 pp. $4.50

***Overall Product Rating: 5.8***

**STRENGTHS:** The study and application questions in this book make it an excellent resource for small groups, teachers and discussion leaders...The questions are thought-provoking and encourage digging into Scripture...The chapter on singleness—although short—is one of the best I've read on the subject ...Offers a strong Biblical perspec-tive...The book is comprehensive in scope, covering such things as the influence of culture on our attitudes, dating, sex and marriage...This book was more than I expected.

**WEAKNESSES:** The material is sometimes clinical in approach, making it a little hard to get into... The book cover was not very inviting ...The authors sometimes portray women in a subordinate role...Too many religious cliches such as "the world" and "godly"...I find the book naive especially when one out of two couples who come to me for counseling are already living together...An isolationist view of Christian-ity... Get's a bit preachy at times.

## VIDEO/Dating:
### Roots for Right Relationships

by Bob Stone (Personal Relationships, Inc.) Five-part series x 42 min. each $99.75

***Not Yet Reviewed***

**NOTES:** Includes the following sessions: "How to Know When It's Love," "Conse-quences of Messing Around," "Becoming Vulnerable," and much more.

## Dating and Waiting For Marriage

by Raymond Brock (Gospel Light, 1982) 128 pp. $4.50

***Total Overall Rating: 5.1***

**STRENGTHS:** A constructive hand book that does not put down single adults for waiting to get married.

**WEAKNESSES:** Overly simplistic in its presentation of the dilemmas of singleness ...Seems to be from another era...Poorly written and unattractively bound...The subject of sex was poorly addressed.

## Dating, Sex, and Friendship

by Joyce Huggett (InterVarsity Press, 1985) 204 pp. $7.95

***Overall Product Rating: 7.7***

**STRENGTHS:** The sections on sexuality and sex before marriage are frank, honest and well-presented... Challenges the reader to think through healthy limits in premarital intimacy ...Treatment of the topic of loneliness as a root cause of other problems presents an interesting new perspective.

**WEAKNESSES:** First part of book was basic and rather boring... Material may be too explicit for the less mature single...This book will not be as helpful for the older single adult or those who are divorced.

## God's Design For Christian Dating

by Greg Laurie (Harvest House Publishing, 1983) 94 pp. $2.25

***Overall Product Rating: 7.6***

**STRENGTHS:** A good guide to Christian dating...Author seems to be knowledgeable about the subject and is able to hold your attention...Helps the reader set and keep priorities in dating relationships.

**WEAKNESSES:** Needed more thorough development of some points.

## God Is A Matchmaker

by Derek Prince (Chosen Books, 1984) 221 pp. $7.95

***Overall Product Rating 6.8***

**STRENGTHS:** Practical, Scriptural, easy to read...Basically geared for singles themselves, but there are some clearly-presented patterns for character development that can be of use when counseling someone who has let the desire to marry overshadow personal development.

**WEAKNESSES:** Strong Pentecostal focus which could make some readers uncomfort-able ....May lead singles to expect the miracle of a "marriage made in Heaven"...Too black and white and formula-oriented for a world full of gray...The book seems to be geared to younger people still under the influence of parental guidance.

## Guidebook For Dating, Waiting, and Choosing A Mate

by H. Norman Wright and Marvin Inmon (Harvest House Publishing, 1978) 160 pp. $4.95

***Overall Product Rating: 5.7***

**STRENGTHS:** Challenges singles to examine the issues related to dating and marriage... Questions from the book could be helpful in teaching and counseling.

**WEAKNESSES:** Not much depth... Written primarily for the younger crowd...Needs a more comprehensive list of resources that people could refer to...The author's distinc-tions between sex and love are quite weak.

## How Does The National Review Board Function?

1. There are over 100 reviewers on this board, representing every major denomination and region of the country.
2. All reviewers are pastors, counselors or lay leaders involved in ministry with single adults.
3. Every product is reviewed and evaluated by *at least two - and in most cases, three - members* of this National Board. (When appropriate and possible, the product is actually used in a singles ministry prior to being evaluated.)
4. Each product is reviewed and evaluated on its own merit and not as it compares to other products or resources.
5. Reviewers' ratings for each product are tabulated and averaged by the staff of *Single Adult Ministries Journal* to determine each score. ***(Products are rated from 1 to 10, with 10 being the best rating possible.)***

# Give your singles a rich, rewarding single life

## with resources you can trust from Mobilized To Serve!

- **audio teaching tapes**
- **books**
- **Singles Days**
- **Regional/North American Conferences**
- **single parenting videos**

For a free information packet, contact:
Mobilized To Serve
Elim Fellowship
7245 College St.
Lima, NY 14485
(716) 582-2790

## Love Lines: A Light-Hearted Look at Love & Romance

by Vern McLellan (Harvest House, 1990) 185 pp. $3.95

***Overall Product Rating: 4.8***

**STRENGTHS:** If you've ever taught a lesson on love or marriage and wished you could break the tension with some comedy, this book is for you. The author includes sections on friendship, love, affection, dating, kissing, falling in love, courtship, engagement, weddings, honeymoons, marriage, singleness, divorce, alimony and senior love. Even the sections on divorce and alimony can break the emotional ice with humor ...The book has a few gems to possibly warrant its purchase as a resource.

**WEAKNESSES:** This is really a silly little book. Fluff. Groaners... Only possible purpose for buying this book would be for a speaker/teacher who's looking for clever quips, newsletter jokes or cartoons...As in any collection of this sort, some of the material is not that funny. Singles leaders ought to be aware that the chapter on "Spinsters and Bachelors" might be offensive to some single never-marrieds...Silly. Stereotype humor, ala Rodney Dangerfield. Could be offensive to women, mothers-in-law, etc.

## More Creative Dating

by Doug Fields and Todd Temple (Thomas Nelson, 1987) 160 pp. $5.95

***Overall Product Rating: 7.0***

**STRENGTHS:** Great content for persons who conduct single adult seminars...Has some fun and wild ideas. Some of the ideas could be used to show people how to have fun on a date and not be so serious and nervous...Provides suggestions to help one another feel special and to have permission to laugh at oneself. And laugh and laugh.

**WEAKNESSES:** Had difficulty at times believing this information was always legitimate or sincere...Is the energy expended for some of these creative dates really worth it?

## Next Time I Fall In Love

by Chap Clark (Zondervan, 1987) 144 pp. $5.95; Leader's Guide, $7.95

***Overall Product Rating: 4.7***

**STRENGTHS:** It is fine for its intended audience—teens...Would give leaders an easy outline for a discussion series on relationships and dating for teens. Provides some good discussion questions at the end of chapters...Defines different types of love... Offers practical dating tips on levels of intimacy.

**WEAKNESSES:** Written for audiences of 13-18, with 18 being the maximum age. Very teen-oriented... The back cover suggests it is for up to 25 years old—you've got to be kidding...The title is a little misleading, I think. It suggests that it might examine the ending of relationships and recovery more than it does. It's really a book about how to tell if you're really in love, or the difference between love and infatuation... Nothing of value for single adult ministries.

**Do You Feel Left Out?**

If you were left out of this National Directory, we have good news. There will be another Directory... and we want to make sure you are not left out again. Help us make this Directory complete. Let us know about your group.

**See page 249**

# Friendships-Relationships

## 201 Great Questions: (Conversation Starters For Times with Friends)

by J. David Jones (NavPress, 1988) 201 pp. $4.95

***Overall Product Rating: 9.2***

**STRENGTHS:** Creative new ideas for discussion starters ...This book takes seriously the importance of talking to one another ...Suggests ways for people to share, to be candid, creative and caring...Reminds us that people do not always want to be entertained but want to touch others lives and be touched...Offers a natural way of sharing our lives with others and learning more about them in the process...Great ice breakers ...A real time saver. As a minister, I don't have to worry about creating all my own questions...The questions are stimulating and concise...This book was a surprising discovery. The title sounded boring to me but the book was anything but boring...This book will make you laugh and think deeply at the same time.

**WEAKNESSES:** Too many serious questions. I would have liked to have had more light questions to use for openers and ice breakers.

## Addictive Personality, The: Roots, Rituals, and Recovery

by Craig Nakken (Hazelden Educational Materials, 1988) 125 pp. $6.95

***Overall Product Rating: 7.5***

**STRENGTHS:** An excellent book on compulsion and the addictive process. Good for therapists, church leaders in counseling roles, addicts and their friends and family... Helpful emphasis on building relationships rather than focusing on object or feeling... Easy to understand, well-researched, great illustrations ...Does not get bogged down in technical terms...It is evident the author understands this subject and has helped many people with a wide variety of addicts.

**WEAKNESSES:** Lacking in Biblical foundation, Scripture...Refers to a "higher

## How Does The National Review Board Function?

1. There are over 100 reviewers on this board, representing every major denomination and region of the country.
2. All reviewers are pastors, counselors or lay leaders involved in ministry with single adults.
3. Every product is reviewed and evaluated by *at least two - and in most cases, three - members* of this National Board. (When appropriate and possible, the product is actually used in a singles ministry prior to being evaluated.)
4. Each product is reviewed and evaluated on its own merit and not as it compares to other products or resources.
5. Reviewers' ratings for each product are tabulated and averaged by the staff of *Single Adult Ministries Journal* to determine each score. ***(Products are rated from 1 to 10, with 10 being the best rating possible.)***

power" without defining that power as the triune God...Could use more personal illustrations...A workbook or guide would have been useful.

## Always Daddy's Girl:
### Understanding Your Father's Impact on Who You Are

by H. Norman Wright (Regal Press,1989) 284 pp. $12.95

***Overall Product Rating: 7.6***

**STRENGTHS:** Helps a woman process her relationship with her father...A "hands-on" book providing many options on how to talk with your father, think through your relationship with him, forgive where it is needed and move on in life...Good at describing the affects of a traumatic relationship with a father... Author's style of writing makes you feel as if you are sitting across the table from him...Helps men better understand women.

**WEAKNESSES:** For a woman with serious sexual and emotional abuse it may not give due credit to her pain...Does not address sexual abuse directly and the ramifications to the adult woman...Needed to deal more with the results of a "good relationship" with a father...This book sheds light on where the root of the problem may lie, but it doesn't tell you where to go from there.

## Among Friends:
### You Can Help Make Your Church a Warmer Place

by James Hinkle and Tim Woodroof (NavPress, 1989) 230 pp. $7.95

***Not Yet Reviewed***

**NOTES:** Addresses the need for closer relationships in the church. The book provides practical guidelines, discussion material and insights for establishing a sense of community in the local church.

## Baby Hunger: Every Woman's Longing For A Baby

by Lois Leiderman Davitz (Winston Press, 1984) 136 pp. $8.95

***Not Yet Reviewed***

**NOTES:** According to the author, every woman knows about it and men are puzzled by it. This is one of the first books to discuss a nearly universal phenomenon, women's sudden and overwhelming urge to have a baby, most frequently between the ages of 27 and 30. Describes the physical and emotional symptoms of baby hunger, the effects on relationships with men, how this urge changes goals and values and how various women deal with this urge.

## Becoming a Better Friend:
### Secrets For Building and Maintaining Strong Friendships

by Melodie M. Davis (Bethany House Publishers, 1988) 141 pp. $5.95

***Not Yet Reviewed***

**NOTES:** Helps the reader to understand their own personality and be challenged to make life changes. The book also discusses what makes a person likable and how to work at improving relationships.

## Becoming A Friend and Lover

by Dick Purnell (Here's Life Publishers, 1986) 221 pp. $7.95

***Overall Product Rating: 7.3***

**STRENGTHS:** Easy to read...Offers a realistic, balanced approach to relationships ...Helpful use of Scripture gives added meaning to the qualities of love and friendship... Questions at the end of each chapter are good discussion starters... Encourages singles to develop personal, individual identities apart from depending on another for that identity...Discourages spending life "waiting for the right one"... Offers an excellent Biblical and psychological foundation for sexual intimacy... Practical approach for those struggling with relationships.

**WEAKNESSES:** Needs a study guide... Nothing particularly new.

## Building A Relationship That Lasts

by Dick Purnell with Jerry Jones (Here's Life Publishers, 1988) 140 pp. $7.95

***Overall Product Rating: 6.5***

**STRENGTHS:** Good basic outline that raises areas of concern in relationships. It would open a lot of doors for further discussion ...Clear and relevant...You sense the author has been there...Section on "How To Break Up" shows singles positive ways to deal with problems of confrontation. Leaders may also find this helpful when counseling singles who need help in taking steps toward closing unhealthy relationships.

**WEAKNESSES:** This book was originally entitled "Beating The Breakup Habit," which grabs some-one's attention much better. The existing title seems too general, too much like a host of other books, to catch my attention...Does not provide practical, specific steps on how one can work on several of the areas that are raised...The information is pretty basic. Other books treat this subject better...Seems geared only to younger singles.

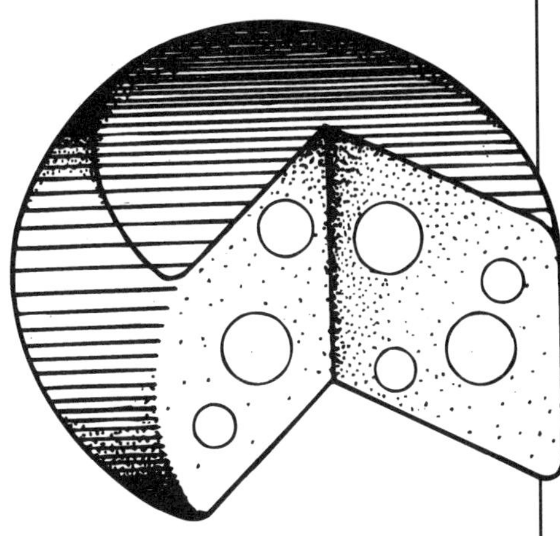

## Building Relationships With God and Others

by Jim Burns & Doug Webster (Harvest House Publishers, 1986) 64 pp. $4.95

***Not Yet Reviewed***

**NOTES:** Workbook based on Psalms 120-134 designed to be an encouragement and challenge to build a stronger relationship with God and others.

## Can Christians Love Too Much?
### Breaking The Cycle of Codependency

by Dr. Margaret J. Rink (Zondervan, 1989) 219 pp. $9.95

***Overall Product Rating: 8.2***

**STRENGTHS:** The product is very easy to use. That is something I look for in a product. It also has charts that make using the material helpful. This book refreshingly and succinctly defines and deals with codependency, the conflict of the Christian perspective, including the use of the 12 steps of recovery. Every Christian leader is getting in the way of Christ if he or she is unwilling or unable to identify and treat a co-dependent life-style. This book addresses this issue clearly and identifies the whys and what-nows of dysfunctional relationships many single adults experience. It is refreshing to see the topic of codependency among Christians addressed in such an honest and practical manner.

**WEAKNESSES:** Some of the material may be a little technical for the average reader. Information contained in the charts was somewhat hard to decipher and the charts themselves seemed to break up the continuity of the work. This is the same old story, nothing new but new labels. Personal questions to ponder at the end of each chapter would be helpful.

## Can Men and Women Be Just Friends?

by Andre Bustanoby (Pyranee/Zondervan, 1985) 144 pp. $7.95

***Not Yet Reviewed***

**NOTES:** The author looks at the sometimes perplexing matter of friendship: What is it? Who can be your friend? Does sexuality inevitably interfere with friendships between the sexes? Is friendship intimacy? He shows the difference between companionship, friendship and love in what they are and how they behave. Includes a helpful Couples Friendship Inventory.

## Caring And Commitment: Learning To Live the Love We Promise

by Lewis B. Smedes (Harper and Row, 1988) 153 pp. $7.95

***Overall Product Rating: 7.8***

**STRENGTHS:** Compassionately and clearly portrays Biblical commitment, what it takes to make it and to keep it. The author seems well aware of those places where we are most likely to break commitments along with practical suggestions for being stronger with our commitments... Wise insights into the dynamics of human relationships and our need for caring commitments...Covers a wide variety of commitments and relationships... Extensive.

**WEAKNESSES:** Focuses primarily on marital or family commitments, which is not apparent from the title. There is a section on friendships but most attention is given to marriage. It's unfortunate that the author did not make this book more practical for the single adult too...I don't think this was the author's intent, but I think some could read this book—especially the part about the role that grace plays when ending a commitment—and use it as an excuse to bail out of a commitment (such as a marriage).

## Caring Enough To Confront: How To Understand and Express Your Deepest Feelings Toward Others

by David Augsburger (Regal Press, 1981) 142 pp. $6.95

***Overall Product Rating: 9.0***

**STRENGTHS:** Helps people realize that confrontation can be a positive aspect of relationship building... Covers many of the "how to's and whys" in the confrontation communication process...Designed in such a way that it would be easy to adapt for group study...Offers personal application situations at the end of each chapter that would be great for discussion...Easy to follow...The author exposes our weaknesses and excuses we use to keep from being honest and real in our relationships ...Practical, realistic solutions and choices for healthier relationships.

**WEAKNESSES:** None noted.

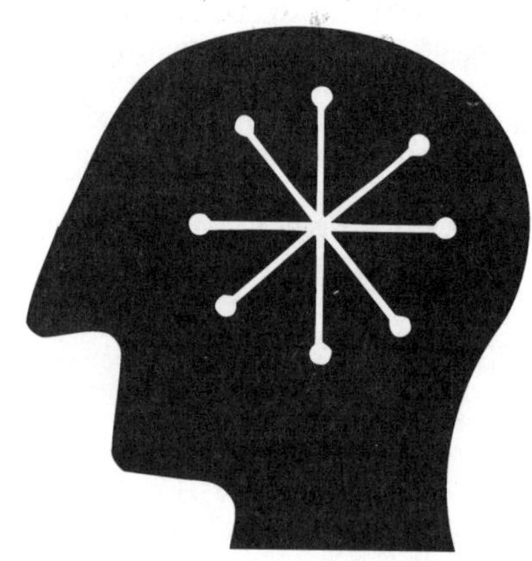

## Caring For Your Aging Parents: When Love is Not Enough

by Barbara Deane (NavPress, 1989) 276 pp. $9.95

***Overall Product Rating: 7.6***

**STRENGTHS:** This book has credibility because of the author's personal experiences and those of other caregivers referred to...In this day of do your own thing, she encourages Christian service, honor, support and respect for your aging parents while maintaining personal integrity...This is a topic that will become increasingly important as people live longer...The problems involved are especially difficult to handle since each case is different and there is no standard, pat answer. Because caring for an aging parent can even be more difficult for a single adult, this book is a most helpful resource for them.

**WEAKNESSES:** Although the book was easy to read once I got started, it wasn't an appealing book initially. The cover and title made me think that it would be a boring, hard-to-read book.

## Choices, Changes

by Joni Eareckson Tada (Zondervan, 1986) 286 pp. $14.95

***Overall Product Rating: 6.8***

**STRENGTHS:** Good insight into struggles of singleness...A refreshingly honest look at a well-known Christian leader's struggles and relationships in life...Encourages singles to deal with some of their own issues and not give up...A com-pelling, creative style of writing.

**WEAKNESSES:** Slow reading in the beginning, hard to get into...Needed more development on such issues as courtship and engagement, i.e. her doubts, fears and how she overcame them.

## Christian Men Who Hate Women: Healing Hurting Relationships

by Dr. Margaret J. Rinck (Zondervan, 1990) 205 pp. $8.95

***Not Yet Reviewed***

**NOTES:** The author examines how women-hating relationships begin, what happens in these relationships, how both parties contribute to the problem and the role of the church in such relationships. For men and women afflicted by misogyny, the book offers hope for reversing deeply established patterns of relating and coping in a cruel manner.

## How Does The National Review Board Function?

1. There are over 100 reviewers on this board, representing every major denomination and region of the country.
2. All reviewers are pastors, counselors or lay leaders involved in ministry with single adults.
3. Every product is reviewed and evaluated by *at least two - and in most cases, three - members* of this National Board. (When appropriate and possible, the product is actually used in a singles ministry prior to being evaluated.)
4. Each product is reviewed and evaluated on its own merit and not as it compares to other products or resources.
5. Reviewers' ratings for each product are tabulated and averaged by the staff of *Single Adult Ministries Journal* to determine each score. ***(Products are rated from 1 to 10, with 10 being the best rating possible.)***

## AUDIO CASSETTES/ Codependency

by Terry Hershey (Christian Focus, Inc.) 4 x 45 min. $25.95

***Not Yet Reviewed***

**NOTES:** Four-tape audio series on co-dependency. Tape 1 discusses "Coming Out of Hiding;" Tape 2, "Understanding Dysfunctional Families;" Tape 3, "Shame-Based Influences;" and Tape 4, "Acceptance: The Road to Health."

## Co-Dependent No More

by Melody Beattie (Walker and Company, 1989) 229 pp. $14.95

***Overall Product Rating: 8.5***

**STRENGTHS:** My single mothers' group is currently using this book. Of those in our group, four women had alcoholic fathers, six had alcoholic husbands, three were battered wives, two were victims of incest and the list goes on and on. This book has been tremendously helpful to all of us, and when supplemented with Biblical truths and Scripture, it is very powerful...The characteristics outlined in chapter four and the activity at the end was particularly insightful... Though a secularly-written book, it holds forth many truths that enhance Christian life... Good stuff on anger...The "drama triangle" (rescue, persecute, victimized) helps identify patterns of unhealthy interaction in relationships and gives some tools and motivation to break those patterns...Helps individuals understand the difference between rescuing (with mixed motivation) and helping people for the love of Jesus.

**WEAKNESSES:** The book, while not particularly anti-Bible, centers primarily on human experience. A non-Christian, especially a pantheist, could read this and probably not sense their vital need to have a relationship with Jesus Christ...The author is overly critical of the psychiatric and therapeutic world and their understanding of alcoholism and related diseases...I appreciate her focus on "a higher power" who is in control, all knowing, all loving, all powerful but would like to see this book have more spiritual depth.

## Connecting With a Friend: Eighteen Proven Counseling Skills To Help You Help Others

by Paul Welter (Tyndale, 1985) 223 pp. $6.95

***Not Yet Reviewed***

**NOTES:** The author draws on his years of experience as a counselor and a teacher as he describes effective means of connecting with a friend, helping guide them to wholeness and abundant life. The book offers advice on how to be more effective in asking questions, how to focus on the person rather than the topic, how to use you weaknesses to help others, how to resolve and mediate conflict, and how to use the Bible when counseling a friend.

## Creative Times With Friends

by Fields and Temple (Thomas Nelson, 1988) 154 pp. $6.95

***Overall Product Rating: 4.3***

**STRENGTHS:** Creative ideas that are fresh and fun...Could be used for ice breakers and reaching the hard to reach, etc....Tongue in cheek conversational material.

**WEAKNESSES:** It has relatively little to do with the friendship it purports to build...The sarcastic approach used can be quite offensive. Singles of any age have barriers they must face and this book makes fun of all of them. I don't see any new or enlightened ideas in this book.

## Dancing With Porcupines: Learning to Appreciate the Finer Points of Others

by Bob Phillips (Regal Books, 1989) 174 pp. $7.95

***Not Yet Reviewed***

**NOTES:** Family counselor Bob Phillips suggest that relating is a delicate art that requires a knowledge of differing social styles. With techniques for reducing tension and conflict, tips for improving communication, ideas for increasing your tolerance of others and practical suggestions for demonstrating love, the book offers help for getting along with the prickliest people in your life.

## AUDIO CASSETTES/ Delivering the Male

by Clayton C. Barbeau (St. Anthony Messenger Tapes) 255 min. $59.95

***Not Yet Reviewed***

**NOTES:** Six-tape audio series on getting "out of the tough-guy trap into a better marriage." Tape 1 examines "Man, Male, or Boy?;" Tape 2, "The Man-Woman Crisis;" Tape 3, "Corporate Castration;" Tape 4, "The Failure of Success;" Tape 5, "Separating the Men from the Boys;" and Tape 6, "Passion, Poetry, and Potency."

## Facing Codependence: What It Is, Where It Comes From, How It Sabotages Our Lives

by Pia Mellody, A.W. Miller, and J. Keith Miller (Harper and Row, 1989) $10.95

***Not Yet Reviewed***

**NOTES:** A new guide that traces the origins of codependence back to childhood, describing a wide range of emotional, spiritual, intellectual, physical and sexual abuses. Looks at how recovery from codependence may be possible by learning to re-parent oneself.

## VIDEO/Family Relationships (part of "The Family: God's Pattern For Living" series)

by Dr. John MacArthur (Moody Video, 1989) 50 min. $29.95

***Overall Product Rating: 6.8***

**STRENGTHS:** Useful for both small home group or a large class...Clearly states a Biblical pattern for relationships, especially family relationships ...Offers thorough historical under-standing...A gentle approach to Ephesians 5...Helpful material for singles to know whether or not they get married...A clear view of the fundamentalistic position that men have authority over women in function but equality in essence. Mutual submission is recommended but within the hierarchy of authority. Men are over women because woman sinned first.

**WEAKNESSES:** Gets lengthy and tiresome to watch. All lecture. Needs some humor and light hearted gestures, a bit too serious. Feels more like a sermon than an intro to study/ discussion time...Assumes any other interpretation or exegesis is wrong. Leaves no room for a different conviction regarding e.g. the meaning of submission, authority, "the curse," etc. John MacArthur preaches his convictions as if they were the only Gospel truth. He does have a grasp of some truth but certainly not the definitive last word.

## Friends and Friendship:
### The Secrets of Drawing Closer
by Jerry and Mary White (NavPress 1982) 191 pp. $7.95

***Not Yet Reviewed***

NOTES: God has placed within us a need for intimate companionship. When this need is unfulfilled, we are lonely. However, because of Christ's love we can deal with loneliness, according to the authors. This book suggests how to make friends, how to keep the ones you have, and when your're justified in backing off from making new friends.

## Friends and Lovers:
### How to Meet The People You Want to Meet
by Steve Bhaerman and Don McMillan (Writers Digest Books, 1986) 197 pp. $8.95

***Not Yet Reviewed***

**NOTES:** The ways in which to meet people that will be able to share common ground. The book discusses the idea of developing a personal agenda for your life and then building the friendships around your personal focus.

## Friendship:
### Skills For Having a Friend, Being a Friend
by Jim Conway (Zondervan, 1989) 207 pp. $8.95

***Overall Product Rating: 5.8***

**STRENGTHS:** Developing deep friendships is one of the most pressing needs among single adults. This book can be a useful tool in helping address this need...Is well designed for a small group study... Well organized... Offers good discussion questions and applications at the end of each chapter.

**WEAKNESSES:** I found nothing new in this book...Is sometimes plastic. In the beginning, the author says he wants to be the reader's friend, but how can one become friends by just reading a book?...Might be useful for someone who knows nothing about friendship or communications skills. But for me, it was redundant...Did not hold my attention... Does not read smoothly or energetically...Not enough Biblical examples of friendship used.

## Getting Along with People You Love:
### Building and Maintaining Healthy Relationships
by Marilyn Moravec (David C. Cook Publishing, 1989) 62 pp. $4.00

***Not Yet Reviewed***

**NOTES:** Discusses how to ease tension in your relationships, tell what loved ones really mean when they talk to you, accept and confront those you love, and let your commitment to Christ change how you relate to loved ones.

## VIDEO/Growing Closer
featuring Gordon and Gail MacDonald (InterVarsity Video, 1986) Three-tape, six-part series. Each tape is approx. 65 min. $59.95

***Not Yet Reviewed***

**NOTES:** Part I, "Building Commitment," shows how to deepen commitments to a specific person and to God. Part II, "Talking and Listening," identifies five levels of communication and shows how to deepen communication with others. Part III, "Affirming and Rebuking," helps audience members to grow in their ability to encourage positive qualities and lovingly confront negative qualities in friends and family members. Part IV, "Celebrating Our Sexuality," distinguishes the two kinds of sexual expression, "laying with" and "knowing," and encourages persons to pursue sexual fulfillment only within the scope of God's will. Part V, "Handling Excess Baggage," shows how to face past traumas that hurt present relationships with family and friends. Part VI, "Protecting One Another," shows how to discover and affirm the gifts, feeling and aspirations of friends.

**Fact:**

One out of every six women who have an abortion describes herself as an evangelical Christian.

*Alan Guttmacher Institute study*

## Hope for Hurting Relationships
by Myron Rush (Victor Books, 1989) 166 pp. $6.95

***Not Yet Reviewed***

**NOTES:** Explores why people seek relationships; why they deteriorate; how to handle conflict and build communications; and how relationships can be restored at any point in the four-stage cycle of deterioration.

## How To Find a Lasting Relationship
by Richard Gosse (R. and E. Publishers, Marin Publications, 1988) 230 pp. $9.95

***Overall Product Rating: 4.6***

**STRENGTHS: The** author offers some practical, relevant ideas and suggestions on relationship building ...Although I would not recommend this book to my singles, I could see using it some in my counseling...May provide some insight to singles pastors who are married.

**WEAKNESSES:** This book is totally secular, leaving no room for a theological perspective... I would never promote this book to my singles group...the book advocates some manipulative techniques...You have to wade through a lot of humanistic garbage to get to the worthwhile material in this book...In my opinion, this material makes light of many of our Christian values.

## How Does The National Review Board Function?

**1.** There are over 100 reviewers on this board, representing every major denomination and region of the country.
**2.** All reviewers are pastors, counselors or lay leaders involved in ministry with single adults.
**3.** Every product is reviewed and evaluated by *at least two - and in most cases, three - members* of this National Board. (When appropriate and possible, the product is actually used in a singles ministry prior to being evaluated.)
**4.** Each product is reviewed and evaluated on its own merit and not as it compares to other products or resources.
**5.** Reviewers' ratings for each product are tabulated and averaged by the staff of *Single Adult Ministries Journal* to determine each score. ***(Products are rated from 1 to 10, with 10 being the best rating possible.)***

## How to Have a Better Relationship with Anybody

by James Hilt (Moody Press, 1985) 116 pp. $5.95

***Overall Product Rating: 5.0***

**STRENGTHS:** Desires to be relevant in anticipating the wide web of human relationships. Sensitive to the need to weave Scripture into the fabric of interpersonal dynamics... Presented in a usable format, allowing the reader easy access to information concerning specific relationship problems...Covers a wide range of topics concerning developing and maintaining relationships.

**WEAKNESSES:** A simplistic approach to improving or healing damaged relationships ...Often fails to acknowledge any possible deeper issues ...Raises as many questions as it answers.

## AUDIO CASSETTE/ How To Meet People

by Jacobsen (Interpersonal Enterprise, date not known) 60 min. $10.00

***Overall Product Rating: 3.3***

**STRENGTHS:** Could stimulate some interesting discussion about various ways to meet people, especially for those individuals who are not "socially adept" or lack self-confidence ...A couple of the techniques for meeting people are interesting and unusual/creative...Might be of some benefit in teaching on fear of rejection.

**WEAKNESSES:** I wouldn't use this book in my singles ministry due to its total lack of spiritual content/sensitivity. Many of the illustrations are from the bar/nightclub scene... The suggestions really never advance beyond gimmicks or superficial tricks. Many of them require much more confidence to pull off effectively than most singles have ...Rather boring...Not worth the price.

## Invisible Partners, The: How the Male and Female in Each of Us Affects Our Relationships

by John A. Sanford (Paulist Press, 1980) 139 pp. $7.95

***Overall Product Rating: 4.6***

**STRENGTHS:** Explains in a readily understandable way the dynamic that we are

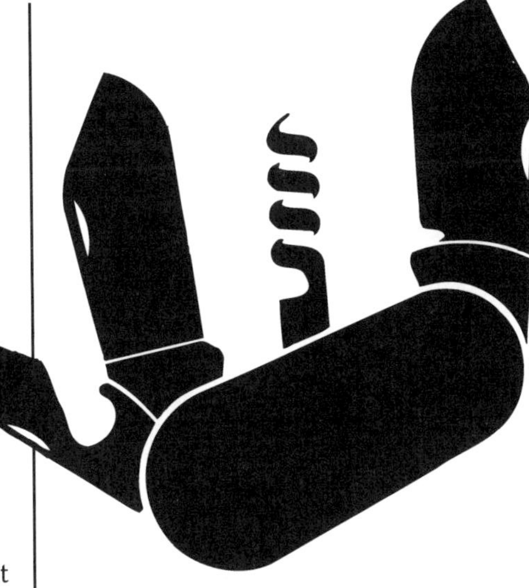

both masculine and feminine, and urges us to embrace both as part of our humanity. Cultures that don't attempt to balance both end up one-dimensional, e.g. modern America ...Stretches the mind to think in new areas. Helpful analysis of inner struggles...Well researched and footnoted, so the reader gets the benefit of the author's research.

**WEAKNESSES:** Too short and incomplete to adequately cover such an intense topic... The author takes an okay idea and carries it to an extreme. The opposite sex side is given almost a separate and independent personality. Every interaction is examined in terms of the primary person and that secondary person... Hard to teach...Must read slowly to digest what is being said...Would not be helpful unless someone has a direct interest in Jung.

## Language of Love, The A Powerful Way to Maximize Insight, Intimacy, and Understanding

by Gary Smalley and John Trent (Focus on the Family Publishing, 1988) 181 pp. $13.99

***Overall Product Rating: 8.5***

**STRENGTHS:** A practical method to help us communicate better... Beneficial for teaching our singles more effective communication skills in their relationships. Also a useful tool to help us improve our teaching/counseling skills...Provides a good number of examples that explain each step in the communication process...Useful to everyone not just singles...Biblically-based and well-supported by case studies...Provides hope for difficult relationships along with the specific parameters of how to construct word pictures in a healthy way...The authors practice throughout the book the message they are seeking to teach. They use emotional word pictures...Very readable, keeps your interest.

**WEAKNESSES:** Focuses primarily on married couples/families. Needs more specific examples/illustrations for single adults because the principles are not limited to married couples.

## Living in Harmony: Facing Conflict in Relationships

by Marilyn Moravec (David C. Cook Publishing, 1989) 58 pp. $4.00

***Not Yet Reviewed***

**NOTES:** Discover how to identify your own style of handling conflicts, tame your anger, state your needs clearly and fight fair, turning conflict into an opportunity for spiritual growth instead of revenge.

## Longing For Love

by Walter Trobisch (Crossway Books, 1979) 127 pp. $5.95

***Overall Product Rating: 4.5***

**STRENGTHS:** The author is very honest with his answers... Reassurance that each emotion we experience is normal and natural...He is an excellent model as a sensitive pastor/counselor.

**WEAKNESSES:** Basically geared to adolescents. Not very useful for singles.

## Love and Its Counterfeits: It looks like love, It Feels Like Love, But Is It Love?

by Barbara Cook (Aglow Publications, 1989) 197 pp. $8.95

***Overall Product Rating: 8.5***

**STRENGTHS:** A very worthwhile book to read...An eye opener for anyone struggling with love relation-ships...Easy to read, straight for—ward...Includes examples of relationships we've probably all been in or observed in our life...I've already given my copy away to a lady jolted by an irresponsible man who said he loved her but then skipped out.

**WEAKNESSES:** Lacked procedural help...Needed more specific, practical guidelines.

## Love Blocks: Breaking the Patterns That Undermine Relationships

by Mary Ellen Donovan and Dr. William P. Ryan (Viking, 1989) 412 pp. $18.95

***Not Yet Reviewed***

**NOTES:** We all want lasting relationships

that bring fulfillment and joy, but most of us have at least one relationship that brings disappointment and heartache instead. The authors look at such problems, "love blocks" as "I Don't Deserve Love," "I Don't Need Anyone—I'm Strong," and "I'll Never Get Another Chance." They offer a step-by-step guide to help readers overcome their love blocks and build more fulfilling relationships.

## Love Is a Choice
### Recovery For Codependent Relationships

by Robert Hemfelt, Frank Minirth and Paul Meier (Thomas Nelson, 1989) 284 pp. $14.95

***Overall Product Rating: 8.6***

**STRENGTHS:** A great basic book on codependency issues...Good use of illustrations ...Defines the problem, describes how it perpetuates itself and offers clear, Biblically-based solutions...Clear help for those counseling singles in addictive relationships ...Gives understandable, practical advice... Readable, organized...Has material which could be used in small group discussion...The best Christian book I've seen on this subject....A must for single adult leaders.
**WEAKNESSES:** More current research on topic would help... Needed discussion/reflection questions at end of each chapter... Should help facilitate self-examination better. People have to dig deep and ask hard questions for true recovery. The book could have more effectively helped facilitate this.

## Men Without Friends
### A Guide to Developing Lasting and Meaningful Friendships

by David W. Smith (Thomas Nelson, 1990) 227 pp. $9.95

***Not Yet Reviewed***

**NOTES:** The book identifies the components of friendship. What men share with other men is often a coworker or buddy relationship, not friendship. This book challenges one to build friendships that will stand the test of time.

## Misunderstood Man, The
### Why Men Suffer and What Can Be Done About It

by Walter Trobisch (InterVarsity Press, 1983) 103 pp. $3.95

***Not Yet Reviewed***

**NOTES:** Do men feel inferior to women? Is this why they put on a gruff voice or a silent exterior or act like a big chief? The author thinks so. He helps both men and women understand how men protect themselves with a variety of defenses. And he shows the way to become a redeemed man, a man free in his relationships to love, laugh, talk and be guided by God.

## Not Just Any Man: A Practical Guide to Finding Mr. Right

by Jennifer Logan (Word Books, 1989) 192 pp. $12.99

***Overall Product Rating: 4.4***

**STRENGTHS:** The book suggests that single women use a notebook to keep track of their positives and negatives, a good idea...Offers some good advice on how to build self-esteem...May be helpful for some pastors to better understand feelings and frustrations of single women.
**WEAKNESSES:** It should have been titled, "How to Manipulate a Man into Loving You"...If I were a man I would run fast from any woman who is using the author's suggested techniques...The author seems to believe that all single adults will be unhappy until they are married...On the inside back cover God's Will is mentioned—but it seems to be left out of the rest of the book...It's hard to tell this is a Christian book... Emphasis on church is to "find a mate" rather than ministry or community.

## Nothing To Hide:
### The Search for Authentic Relationships

by William T. Rowley (Victor Books, 1989) 192 pp. $7.95

***Overall Product Rating: 8.0***

**STRENGTHS:** Helps individuals peel away those things which keep us from acquiring that which we most desire—relationships... Reminds us of our individual beauty and uniqueness ...Doesn't gloss over difficulties in relationships...Author uses personal experiences, stories we can identify with... Questions at end of each chapter are valuable for review and to help apply personal evaluation/application.
**WEAKNESSES:** Sometimes was too general...Needed more in-depth treatment in some places.

## One-Way Relationships
### When You Love Them More Than They Love You

by Alfred Ells (Thomas Nelson, 1990) 211 pp. $9.95

***Overall Product Rating: 8.7***

**STRENGTHS:** This issue of codependency is an area that affects all of us in one way or another. The author does an excellent job of showing what it is, how it affects us and how to deal with it...From the very beginning it states the problem, shows the causes, shares God's answer...Written with clarity, directness, sensitivity and compassion for people who have been wounded in early life, and who have played that out in codependency... Affirms the place of choice and responsibility for each person... Provides a generally Christian approach to the topic.
**WEAKNESSES:** The book could have been a little more concise. At times it seems to lose your interest...The help that God offers seems to be just stated, but not discussed. Example: If a person's life or past is locked in shame

## How Does The National Review Board Function?

1. There are over 100 reviewers on this board, representing every major denomination and region of the country.
2. All reviewers are pastors, counselors or lay leaders involved in ministry with single adults.
3. Every product is reviewed and evaluated by *at least two - and in most cases, three - members* of this National Board. (When appropriate and possible, the product is actually used in a singles ministry prior to being evaluated.)
4. Each product is reviewed and evaluated on its own merit and not as it compares to other products or resources.
5. Reviewers' ratings for each product are tabulated and averaged by the staff of *Single Adult Ministries Journal* to determine each score. ***(Products are rated from 1 to 10, with 10 being the best rating possible.)***

over certain things, even though God loves and accepts us, the shamed person does not find that sufficient. While the author certainly encourages therapy and groups, a little more discussion of "how" a suffering person might be helped through relationship with God would have been useful.

### Parent Care

by Ruth M. Bathauer (Regal Books, 1990) 226 pp. $8.95

***Not Yet Reviewed***

**NOTES:** A practical guide for adult children who find themselves in the role of "caregiver." Offers ideas and suggestions for encouraging parents to remain active and involved; finding the best living situation for the parent; and dealing with care and finance issues.

### Please Don't Say You Need Me:
#### Biblical Answers for Codependency

by Jan Silvious (Zondervan, 1989) 159 pp. $7.95

***Overall Product Rating: 6.5***

**STRENGTHS:** A good overview of a complex topic...Identifies characteristics and traits of codependency... A good resource for building healthy relationships...Helpful appendices at the end of the book on relationship to Christ, value in Christ and attributes of God. Good practical examples.

**WEAKNESSES:** The repeated reference to prayer and Bible reading seem to indicate that they are the solution. As important as they are, it takes much more to overcome the dependency...Author offers little practical guidelines for overcoming our dependencies.

### Quality Friendship:
#### The Risks and Rewards

by Gary Inrig (Moody Press, 1981) 223 pp. $7.95

***Overall Product rating: 6.2***

**STRENGTHS:** This book gave me a much better understanding of 1 Samuel. Provides many Biblical references that could aid someone doing research on friendship or on this book of the Bible...Great insight...Help-ful material for all ages, married or single.

**WEAKNESSES:** Needs to be much more relevant concerning issues and situations of today if to be used effectively by Single


# Help Single Parents Succeed

$6.95

Single Christian parents face very unique challenges as they try to raise spiritually healthy, reasonably well-adjusted kids in today's world. Successful Single Parenting is an invaluable resource single parents and singles ministry leaders will turn to again and again. This complete handbook includes answers to the toughest questions:

- How to explain the absence of the other parent
- How to balance your kids' needs and your needs
- How to handle visitation rights and child support problems
- How to provide consistent discipline
- How to find the practical help you need and much more!

Available at Christian Bookstores everywhere.

"Personally, I know of no one better qualified to loosen the ties that bind the single parent than my friend and colleague in ministry, Gary Richmond. He not only has much to say, he has the wit and wisdom to say it well."
— CHUCK SWINDOLL, *Pastor, Author, Radio Bible Teacher*

"Successful Single Parenting is practical, powerful, and personal. This is a must read book!"
— REV. BOB GALLINA, *Minister to Single Adults, Bellevue Baptist Church, Memphis, Tennessee*

*Order by mail from*

HARVEST HOUSE PUBLISHERS
1075 Arrowsmith • Eugene, Oregon 97402
*or call toll free 1-800-547-8979 with Visa and MasterCard orders. Add $1.00 for phone and mail orders.*



## See the Index on Page 257

**When seeking information in the Reviews or Network section, use the handy index to help you find listings fast.**

Adult discussion leaders...The book seems to be choppy...I had a hard time finding this book interesting.

## Recovery from Codependency

by Dale & Juanita Ryan (InterVarsity Press, 1990) 62 pp. $3.95

***Not Yet Reviewed***

**NOTES:** According to the author, co-dependent behaviors are panic reactions to someone else's addictions or compulsions. This book helps the reader to let go of over-responsibility and to entrust the people we love to the care of God.

## Restoring Broken Relationships

by Don Baker (Harvest House, 1989) 176 pp. $5.95

***Overall Product Rating: 8.3***

**STRENGTHS:** Re-establishes the uncompromising necessity for Biblical forgiveness in the body of Christ. This book gives further instruction for practical repair and maintenance of broken relationships ...Challenges the church to look at itself in meeting the needs of people ...Easy-to-read and Biblically-based...Chapter five was most enlightening ...The last two chapters provide excellent guidelines for starting small groups.

**WEAKNESSES:** Author uses a few too many stories, few worth mentioning...Not nearly as strong as *Beyond Forgiveness*, the other book by this author...One would think that this is an in-depth look at how people can re-establish broken relationships. This is actually not done until the eleventh chapter. The first ten chapters look at the needs of people and how the church meets or doesn't meet these needs...Too simplistic at times, implying that if the relationship is broken, just ask for forgiveness and everything will work out okay.

## Roommate Connection, The: A Complete Guide to Successful Roommate Living

by Suzanne M. Hagopian (Reward Books, 1985) 192 pp. $7.95

***Not Yet Reviewed***

**NOTES:** A one-stop handbook with guidelines for making your roommate experience a happy one—from choosing a roommate, to getting the right apartment or house to share, to setting up an efficient household, to solving a myriad of common roommate conflicts.

## Seasons of Friendship: Naomi and Ruth as a Pattern

by Marjory Zoet Bankson (LuraMedia, Inc., 1987) 139 pp. $10.00

***Overall Product Rating: 6.3***

**STRENGTHS:** Helpful tool for understanding friendship in a transient world...Contains questions which engender reflection on one's own friendship history...This book might especially appeal to older adults interested in understanding the pattern of their friendships. It is affirming and comforting...Offers emphasis on the value of Christian friendships and changes (seasons) of relationships...Journal questions were good for personal growth. Could also be used for small group discussion...Good use of Biblical exegesis in relation to present day life...Well-organized. Well-written.

**WEAKNESSES:** The story of Ruth is interpreted through the eyes, sociology and psychology of 20th century relationships. I believe as exegesis the book is shaky. But as a tool for self-understanding, it can be beneficial. Its pattern on introducing summer, winter, spring and autumn into the Naomi/Ruth relationship is interesting but also somewhat artificial...Does not specifically address any singleness/friendship issues...Somewhat self-limiting in that it deals only with women. In our singles ministry, there is little interest in material directed to only one of the sexes because our groups prefer to meet in co-ed settings.

## Secret Of Loving, The: How a Lasting Intimate Relationship Can Be Yours

**by Josh McDowell (Here's Life Publishers 1985) Teacher's guide, 40 pp. $2.50; Student book, 207 pp. $8.95**

***Overall Product Rating: 9.2***

**STRENGTHS:** Designed with the leader's guide so that each session deals with a particular dynamic in loving. Addresses roadblocks and hindrances to each particular dynamic, then offers keys/tools for overcoming the walls and roadblocks we build. Focuses on why we're not loving (i.e. self-image) rather than why everyone else is a bad lover to us...Touches on major issues but also on seemly minor issue that can be very essential if not discussed during the relationship...Scriptural references are strongly supported ...Gives in clear detail what God wants for each one of us in our relationships with Him and with others... Everyone should read this book. I've given copies to several friends.

**WEAKNESSES:** The subject (loving) applies to everyone but it is written primarily from a married persons perspective, emphasizing marital issues and often using "married lingo"...Could have used some more examples/illustrations.

## How Does The National Review Board Function?

1. There are over 100 reviewers on this board, representing every major denomination and region of the country.
2. All reviewers are pastors, counselors or lay leaders involved in ministry with single adults.
3. Every product is reviewed and evaluated by *at least two - and in most cases, three - members* of this National Board. (When appropriate and possible, the product is actually used in a singles ministry prior to being evaluated.)
4. Each product is reviewed and evaluated on its own merit and not as it compares to other products or resources.
5. Reviewers' ratings for each product are tabulated and averaged by the staff of *Single Adult Ministries Journal* to determine each score. ***(Products are rated from 1 to 10, with 10 being the best rating possible.)***

## Trauma of Transparency: A Biblical Approach to Interpersonal Communications

by J. Grant Howard (Multnomah Press, 1979) 234 pp. $7.95

***Not Yet Reviewed***

**NOTES:** Divorce rates soar, families fragment, churches split as well as various groups within our society. Individuals increasingly feel alienated. We find it difficult to communicate in the critical areas of our lives. The author of this book offers evidence that the Bible speaks to both the problem and the solution.

## Two Sides of Love, The

by Gary Smalley and John Trent, Ph.D (Focus on the Family, 1990) 174 pp. $14.99

***Not Yet Reviewed***

**NOTES:** Explores the hard and soft sides of balanced love and offers practical counsel for getting and keeping relationships in a healthy, Christ-like balance.

## Understanding How Others Misunderstand You

by Ken Voges & Ron Braund (Moody Press, 1990) 264 pp. $14.95

***Not Yet Reviewed***

**NOTES:** Together with companion workbook, pinpoints the reader's behavioral style and secondary characteristics. Also helps reader to understand the behavioral traits of family, friends and co-workers in an effort to better relate to one another in Christian love.

## Understanding People: Deep Longings For Relationship

by Lawrence J. Crabb, Jr. (Zondervan, 1987) 223 pp. $12.95

***Not Yet Reviewed***

**NOTES:** Each of us wants someone to see us exactly as we are and still accept us. This book uses Biblical truth and practical theories of counseling to show why we must begin with repentance and submission to Biblical authority in order to bring healing and maturity.

## Understanding Women: A Book For Men

by Jan Silvious (Zondervan, 1989) 73 pp. $3.95

***Overall Product Rating: 5.1***

**STRENGTHS:** Practical insight into how men and women may misinterpret one another's messages because of their different orientations...The section on responding to the specific needs of a woman who has suffered sexual abuse provides good basic principles...Could help the pastor/leader when counseling a man working through difficulties in a female relationship... Understandable, non-technical language... Helps both men understand women and women understand themselves.

**WEAKNESSES:** Introduces ideas that are never developed...Most of this book should be common sense ...Covers some complex areas of communication and interaction with rather broad generalizations. For example, the author repeatedly states that men are goal-oriented and women are relationship-oriented. While this may often be true, how does our abuse of these traits affect our relationships with God and with each other? This is not addressed.

## Unfinished Business: Helping Adult Children Resolve Their Past

by Charles Sell (Multnomah Press, 1989) 280 pp. $8.95

***Overall Product Rating: 9.5***

**STRENGTHS:** An excellent book... Offers hope and practical suggestions on developing intimacy out of a difficult past...Here in a readable, accessible format lies help for adult children who have found it difficult to get close to others...The chapter on self-image and worth is Biblically-sound and encouraging... Empathic in tone yet helps one name problems, feelings and behavior patterns... Broken into a sequence of steps that target the problem and the solution... Factual but not so clinical as to discourage the average reader, not a lot of treatment jargon... Focused on the problem that results from living in a dysfunctional home, not just an alcoholic home. This gives the book a wider audience.

**WEAKNESSES:** We needed this book at least five years earlier...The cognitive approach and stress on cognitive resolve may not appeal to everyone. Though it is not the only style used in the book, it is the most frequent.

## Untwisting Twisted Relationships

by William and Candace Backus (Bethany House Publishers, 1988) 175 pp. $5.95

***Overall Product Rating: 6.7***

**STRENGTHS:** This is not a book geared specifically for single adults, but most singles pastors/leaders will recognize much of what is described in the book...Helpful for understanding the why of people's behavior... Helps you identify certain unhealthy group/individual personalities and how to help these individuals restore their lives...Gives both the pluses and minuses of personality traits...Guidelines for overcoming false belief systems that cause loneliness, jealousy, controlling behavior and people-pleasing...A crash course on friendship.

**WEAKNESSES:** The need for personal accountability was not emphasized. Nor was the responsibility of the Christian community to confront people in love when we see that they have a false belief system ...Approached subject in textbook style with too many case stories. Was boring and irrelevant at times ...For the person struggling with "unhealthy" relationships, it is doubtful that this book will enable them to change without counseling.

## Walls or Bridges:
### How to Build Relationships That Glorify God

by Jon Johnston (Baker Books, 1988) 250 pp. $7.95

***Overall Product Rating: 6.8***

**STRENGTHS:** Offers several specific ideas on how to encourage people to enhance their relationships with others...Pretty much covers the whole spectrum of ideas about friendship and healthy relationships ...Is filled with Scripture that is appropriately applied for the reader ...Could be used as a comprehensive study on the topic.

**WEAKNESSES:** The constant analogy to bridges and walls is a bit overdone...Much of this material (and the concepts) has been presented before...I would probably buy this book only because I am a pastor. But most of my singles would not purchase or read this book because it is a little bit hard to read. But I think they would attend a seminar or discussion on the topic.

## We Need Each Other:
### The Miracle of Relationships

by Keith & Gladys Hunt (Zondervan, 1985) 246 pp. $9.95

***Not Yet Reviewed***

**NOTES:** Relationships are what life is about and the truly independent person is a myth. The authors examine Biblical perspectives concerning what relationships need in order to grow and develop. How to handle conflict, finding time, dealing with change, improving marriage relationships and forming friendships are areas on which the book focuses.

## What a Question
### Opening Doors to Conversation and Windows of Discovery

by Daniel R. Murray (New Voyage Books, 1990) 221 pp. $7.95

***Not Yet Reviewed***

**NOTES:** After decades of mindless devotion to television, people are rediscovering the lost art of communication. This book is a springboard to meaningful conversations.

## When Someone You Love Is Someone You Hate

by Arterburn and Stoop (Word Publishing, 1988) 163 pp. $12.99

***Not Yet Reviewed***

**NOTES:** Love-Hate relationships may stem from many situations, such as an alcoholic parent or spouse, a broken home, a problem child. Questions that erupt from these stormy relationships involve the contradictory feelings that are experienced. The authors provide spiritual and emotional insights as to how one can make peace with these relationships.

## You And Your Parents:
### Strategies for Building an Adult Relationship

by Harold Ivan Smith (Augsburg Fortress, 1987) 154 pp. $8.95

***Overall Product Review: 8.5***

**STRENGTHS:** Provides honest insight into the fears and guilt that play such a significant role in most adults' relationships with their parents...Offers excellent insight into the struggle between honoring/loving parents and the breaking away to an independent, autonomous life as an adult...A good resource to give to those experiencing troubled relationships with parents...Very practical and easy to read...Must reading for those who work with young adults.

**WEAKNESSES:** Because the author attempts to cover so much material, some areas are shortchanged... Offers too many grocery list type solutions...Sometimes it gets repetitive.

# Sex & Intimacy

## Most Recommended Resources in This Section

(Based on evaluations and reviews made by *SAM Journal's* National Resource Review Board, using a 1-10 scale with 10 being the best possible score):

### 8.6 Free To Love Again: Coming to Terms with Sexual Regret
by Dick Purnell (Here's Life, 1989)

### 8.2 Intimacy: The Longing of Every Human Heart
by Terry Hershey (Harvest House, 1984)

### 8.1 Clear Headed Choices in a Sexually Confused World: (For adults in their 20s and 30s)
by Terry Hershey (Group Books, 1988)

### 8.1 Sex and the Single Christian
by Audrey Beslow (Abingdon Press, 1987)

*(For more information on each of the above resources—plus many other helpful products—find them listed in alphabetical order below.)*

## How Does The National Review Board Function?

1. There are over 100 reviewers on this board, representing every major denomination and region of the country.
2. All reviewers are pastors, counselors or lay leaders involved in ministry with single adults.
3. Every product is reviewed and evaluated by *at least two - and in most cases, three - members* of this National Board. (When appropriate and possible, the product is actually used in a singles ministry prior to being evaluated.)
4. Each product is reviewed and evaluated on its own merit and not as it compares to other products or resources.
5. Reviewers' ratings for each product are tabulated and averaged by the staff of *Single Adult Ministries Journal* to determine each score. ***(Products are rated from 1 to 10, with 10 being the best rating possible.)***

## Christians in a Sex Crazed Culture

by Bill Hybels (Victor Books, 1989) 155 pp. $11.95

***Overall Product Rating: 7.6***

**STRENGTHS:** Much research put into this effort, yet the book reads very smooth...Good handling to delicate situations...Very sensitive not to offend people...Excellent grasp of the overall scope of sex in America... While his book is realistic, it is a book of hope and does not rant and rave about all the problems... Very sound and thorough theology of sexuality provided...Good treatment of sexual aberrations...Well written section on forgiveness and overcoming sexual sin...Good section on sex and the single life...The chapters on homosexuality are relevant...Clear and creative in making his points.

**WEAKNESSES:** Superficial treatment of some subject matter...At times it reads like a sermon which would have been better to listen to in the context of his ministry... Shotguns at the broad topic of sexuality ...Tries to cover too much instead of focusing on specific areas...Would have liked discussion questions included at the end of each chapter.

## Clear Headed Choices in a Sexually Confused World:
### (For adults in their 20s and 30s)

by Terry Hershey (Group Books, 1988) 211 pp. $11.95

***Overall Product Rating: 8.1***

**STRENGTHS:** Better than most books today concerning singles and sex...Thorough and well-outlined ...Well-written in personal, interactive style...Offers insight into the life-style of a career single adult, how she faced the issues and found sound answers to her questions... Provides encouragement for single adults who struggle in this area...The book is divided into four sections which makes it easy to use in a retreat setting or for group discussion.

**WEAKNESSES:** Sometimes becomes a bit heavy...Author needed to better address the areas of Scripture that are clear. For example, when speaking about choices in chapter six, the author says that it would be difficult to develop a theology due to lack of Biblical clarity. But I believe the Scriptures are clearer on many points than he suggests...I feel the book may be too long and detailed to be read by many of those who need to read it most.

## Dance of Intimacy, The
### A Woman's Guide to Courageous Acts of Change In Key Relationships

by Harriet Goldhor Lerner (Harper & Row, 1989) 255 pp. $17.95

***Not Yet Reviewed***

**NOTES:** The author, a psychotherapist at the Menninger Clinic, looks at those relationships where intimacy is most challenged by too much distance, too much intensity or simply too much pain. She suggests changes we can make in one or two significant relationships that will affect our capacity for intimacy and selfhood over the long haul.

## Escape From Intimacy

by Anne Wilson Schaef (Harper & Row, 1989) 158 pp. $7.95

***Not Yet Reviewed***

**NOTES:** Examines the problem of relationship addictions to sex, love and romance.

## Free To Love Again:
### Coming to Terms with Sexual Regret

by Dick Purnell (Here's Life, 1989) 172 pp. $7.95

***Overall Product Rating: 8.6***

**STRENGTHS:** Deals frankly with the issue of past premarital sexual relationships and how to believe one can still have a pure, meaningful relationship in the future... Although this subject is seldom discussed, it is one that many single adults need to address...Offers steps to freedom... Gives practical advise, not just words...Provides direct application of Scriptural truth to the issues. I especially liked the "Quotes from God" section that offered relevant scriptural support...The author used many helpful real people illustrations ...I've already given this book away to some of my singles who need this book.

**WEAKNESSES:** There was no study guide...The only weakness I could find was that sometimes the author seemed to repeat himself from one chapter to the next.

## Gift Of Sex, The

by Clifford and Joyce Penner (Word Publishing, 1981) 352 pp. $11.99

***Overall Product Rating: 6.0***

**STRENGTHS:** Good theology about human sexuality...Excellent technical information/insights...Well written ...One of the most thorough treatments I've seen on the subject of marital sex.

**WEAKNESSES:** For the married couple, there are very few weaknesses with this book. Its just that it is written/designed for sexually active married partners, not single adults... Would be of great value in premarital or marital counseling ...Could maybe be better organized, using more charts.

## Givers, Takers, and Other Kinds of Lovers

by Josh McDowell and Paul Lewis (Tyndale House Publishers, 1981) 119 pp. $2.95

***Overall Product Rating: 7.1***

**STRENGTHS:** Helpful healthy dating section and also on setting clear goals for a future marriage...Easy and quick to read... Biblically based but not dogmatic...Attempts to help the reader understand the reasons why sex before marriage can be harmful in a non-preachy manner ...The perspectives on love and the various dimensions of sex were useful.

**WEAKNESSES:** Illustrations are definitely for college or young adult. (Book needs to more clearly specify its target audience)... Naive, too simplistic...Practical suggestions were too vague...Dealt with having or not having pre-marital sex, but lacked dealing with feelings, intimacy, closeness that can be ours without intercourse...Pretty much the "Just say no to sex" theme... While offering some good ideas for fun dates, it provided nothing on how to relate better one-on-one.

## Go Away Come Closer: A Book About Intimacy

by Terry Hershey (Word, Inc., 1990) 147 pp. $12.99

***Not Yet Reviewed***

**NOTES:** This book examines the risk taking involved in developing intimacy in our relationships. If we can sacrifice our illusions

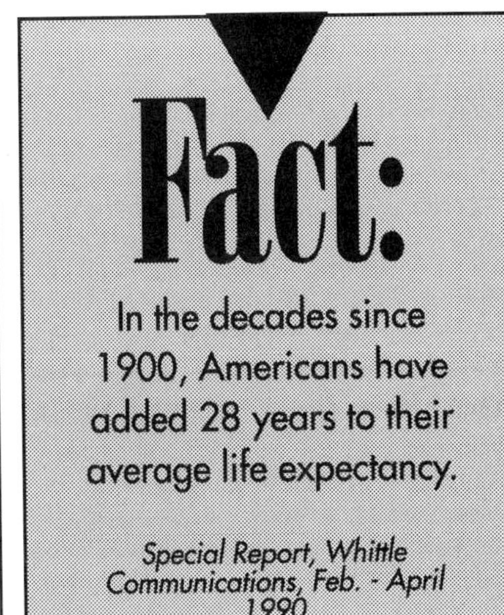

and some of our comfort, we can achieve touch, attention, warmth and affection within a wide range of life.

## VIDEO/How to Kiss

by Bill Plympton (Media, Inc., 1989) 7 min. $95.

***Not Yet Reviewed***

**NOTES:** A humorous discussion starter or crowd breaker. Animated, light-hearted tool to help with the often-taken-for-granted "art" of kissing.

## AUDIO CASSETTES/ Intimacy

by Clayton C. Barbeau (National Catholic Reporter Publishing Co., 1985) 160 min. $34.95

***Not Yet Reviewed***

**NOTES:** Four-tape audio series on intimacy. Tape 1 explores "Intimacy, Identity, and Awareness;" Tape 2, "You and I — Here and Now;" Tape 3, "Having Sex or Making Love;" and Tape 4, "Love: The Language of Life."

## Intimacy: The Longing of Every Human Heart

by Terry Hershey (Harvest House, 1984) 190 pp. $6.95

***Overall Product Rating: 8.2***

**STRENGTHS:** A very practical book... Author gets down to the nitty-gritty of what to do in a very honest way...Good chapters on "conflict" and "sexuality" ...Gives tangible expression to an elusive concept by first defining "intimacy" and then helping us understand what prevents us from achieving it and finishes by providing guidance in how we can work towards intimacy in all our relationships...One of the best resources I've read on understanding the dynamics of healthy relationships.

**WEAKNESSES:** The chapter on "ended" relationships is skimpy... Seems to be weak in providing guidelines and direction for interpersonal accountability...I would have liked to see less use of the author's personal illustration material...Lacks a study guide (which could help make this a much more useful resource within a singles ministry or for personal study).

## AUDIO CASSETTE/ Intimacy Without Guilt

by Dick Purnell (Life Lifters, 1989) 60 min. $10.00

***Overall Product Rating: 7.5***

**STRENGTHS:** Purnell was single until age 42 so he speaks from experience...In addition to looking at the theological basics for intimacy without guilt, he covers the emotional, psychological and physical as well...Offers a great deal of content for future discussion...Good use of humor.

**WEAKNESSES:** He speaks too fast on this tape, attempting to cover too much content in too little time...This tape would not be very effective with formerly married. Mostly directed to the never married.

## Intimate Deception: Escaping the Trap of Sexual Impurity

by P. Roger Hillerstrom (Multnomah, 1989) 156 pp. $7.95

***Overall Product Rating: 7.5***

**STRENGTHS:** Well-defined Scriptural reasons for sexual abstinence before marriage...Good discussion on impact AIDS (and other STD's) could have on one's life when sexually active outside of marriage... Also offers good section on abortion and unwed parenthood issues...Provides more rational guidelines than many other similar books... Has a sound Scriptural base...Clearly lays out God's intent when giving us the gift of sexuality.

**WEAKNESSES:** Too simplistic in its plan for rethinking sexuality as if it could be easily followed with no problems. Fails to acknowledge how terribly difficult this can be...Still does not adequately address issues concerning freedom of responsibility and the burden of freedom...Written with too many case studies... Could have had more strongly-stated statements to accompany Scripture ...Failed to hold interest in the second half of book.

## Let's Talk About Sex: A Straight Forward Guide for Today's Generation

by Larry Tomczak (Vine, 1987) 121 pp. $6.95

***Overall Product Rating: 3.1***

**STRENGTHS:** Some of the material could be used for group discussion ...Offers some sermon content on the subject.

**WEAKNESSES:** This book is predictable and shallow...Although I agree with many of his suggestions, I felt he could have approached the subject in a more "adult" manner... A simplistic re-hash of the same old stuff... There are much better books on the subject...The book is built on several inadequate assumptions. For example, the author assumes that sex equals intercourse. He misses the point that sex has to do with what it means to be human. It is not just a behavioral issue. The tragedy is that we assume by stopping or preventing or monitoring behavior we resolve the issue. Wrong. Sex is an identity issue and the behaviors are only symptoms of the underlying issues. Sex is not about what I do or don't do. It's about who I am, and about who I can become by God's grace.

## How Does The National Review Board Function?

1. There are over 100 reviewers on this board, representing every major denomination and region of the country.
2. All reviewers are pastors, counselors or lay leaders involved in ministry with single adults.
3. Every product is reviewed and evaluated by *at least two - and in most cases, three - members* of this National Board. (When appropriate and possible, the product is actually used in a singles ministry prior to being evaluated.)
4. Each product is reviewed and evaluated on its own merit and not as it compares to other products or resources.
5. Reviewers' ratings for each product are tabulated and averaged by the staff of *Single Adult Ministries Journal* to determine each score.

***(Products are rated from 1 to 10, with 10 being the best rating possible.)***

## VIDEO/Out in the Open:
### Plain Talk About Sex

produced by 2100 Productions (InterVarsity Video, 1989) 28 min. $29.95

***Not Yet Reviewed***

**NOTES:** Provides a unique opportunity for young adults to hear peers talk frankly about sexual struggles. They explore common problems in depth and speak of God's principles, forgiveness and healing.

## Positive Values of Chastity, The

by Eugene F. Diamond and Rosemary Diamond (Franciscan Herald Press, 1983) 95 pp. $7.50

***Not Yet Reviewed***

**NOTES:** In an era that some call the "Post-Christian" era, chastity may be an unfamiliar word to many. But as our society seems to sag from the consequences of unbridled sex, we must return to the virtue of chastity as an insulation against the baseness of self. In this book, chastity is treated against the backdrop of Christian love.

## Purity Makes the Heart Grow Stronger:
### Sexuality and the Single Christian

by Julia Duin (Vine Books, Servant Publications, 1988) 133 pp. $6.95

***Overall Product Rating: 6.8***

**STRENGTHS:** One of the most honest, "gutsy" books on the subject I've seen yet...The author writes with much clarity and realism ...This book can help many non-singles come to a better understanding of the struggles experienced by today's Christian single concerning sexual issues—and to also understand how many single adults perceive the church's response to their unique needs...In many ways, this book is a needed rebuke to the church as a whole.

**WEAKNESSES:** Some of the research data used by the author is woefully out of date (i.e. a 1958 study) ...There are too many broad, blanket generalizations in this book that may be true for the author but are simply not true for many other single adults...The author seems to view God as being some kind of cosmic yenta or matchmaker, relieving us from any personal responsibility for making dating/marital decisions...This is too much rah-rah for "us virgins." Where is the redemptive message in this book—or the grace—for the many singles out there who are not virgins? I'm not sure many of them would find this book realistic or helpful...It seems to be less about purity than about virginity. And there is a significant difference.

## Rebonding:
### Preventing and Restoring Damaged Relationships

by Donald M. Joy (Word Publishing 1986) 166 pp. $8.99

***Not Yet Reviewed***

**NOTES:** In this book the author examines the issues of broken bonds caused by premarital sex, how permissive society effects exclusive intimacy, Biblical definitions of virginity, fornication and adultery, the effects of adultery on marriage and why divorce isn't always the best answer. Dr. Joy calls for a society where principles of commitment and fidelity are the norm.

## Running The Red Lights

by Charles Mylander (Regal Press, 1986) 273 pp. $7.95

***Overall Product Rating: 5.7***

**STRENGTHS:** Covers some significant subjects concerning sex (including mental activity, forgiveness, overcoming sexual temptation) fairly and thoroughly...Provides good information for counseling and discussion...Comprehensive and Biblically-based...Presents practical, workable advice to people involved in sexual sin. I particularly appreciated Chapter Six, "What Do I Say to My Sinning Friend?" with a sample letter written to confront a friend... The compassion found in Chapter Nine, "How Can I Forgive Myself?," was also most helpful... Several good case histories.

**WEAKNESSES:** Speaks more about "the other guy who's at fault"...Not much new or fresh...Overly intense at times, and not easy reading... Written and organized in a somewhat confusing manner.

## Safe Sex

by Verne Becker (InterVarsity Press, 1989) 30 pp. 99¢

***Not Yet Reviewed***

**NOTES:** A short pamphlet which briefly examines critical questions related to health and moral issues of sexual involvement. It also looks at the role sex should play in the Christian life. Suggestions are given which could enable a person to make intelligent choices regarding sexual activity.

## VIDEO/Sex and the Search for Intimacy

by Tim Timmons (South Coast Community Church, 1989) 3 hrs. $39.95

***Not Yet Reviewed***

**NOTES:** Tim Timmons addresses the four steps in the search for intimacy with yourself, with God and other people that leads to true sexuality.

## Sex and the Single Christian (Beslow)

by Audrey Beslow (Abingdon Press, 1987) 176 pp. $6.95

***Overall Product Rating: 8.1***

**STRENGTHS:** Thorough presentation of the consequences of sex outside of marriage... Offers very practical, useful discussion questions ...Good insight on how relationships are damaged...Reaffirms that singleness is not just a time of waiting for a mate, but that it can be exciting, fulfilling—that God has designed us for His glory.

**WEAKNESSES:** Felt the author could have taken a stronger stand for celibacy outside of marriage... Would like to have seen more statistics/research rather than primarily author's opinion...Not very helpful for those seeking help in saying "no" in the middle of temptation... Seems to be written more for group discussion than personal reading, which is both good and bad.

## Sex And The Single Christian (Coleman)

by Barry Coleman, Editor (Regal Press, 1985) 135 pp. $6.95

***Overall Product Rating: 2.7***

**STRENGTHS:** Easy to read...Covers many questions regarding dating, sex and marriage... Formatted in such a way so you can turn to "your question" and read the answer as given by one of the authors.
**WEAKNESSES:** Not for the sophisticated reader...Canned and simplistic...Does little to make the reader feel understood...Title suggests it is addressed to all single Christians but the book demonstrates no understanding of the issues faced by the divorced Christian...Primarily finger-pointing "thou shalt nots" which would do more to turn off single adults than help them wrestle through personal issues...Not a recommendable book.

## Sex and Love When You're Single Again

by Thomas F. Jones (Thomas Nelson, 1990) 192 pp. $8.95

***Not Yet Reviewed***

**NOTES:** Many Christians in our society—the separated, the divorced, the widowed—are struggling with their sexuality in the single-again experience. This book discusses sexual frustrations and temptations yet maintains loyalty to Christian standards.

## Sexual Chaos:
### The Personal and Social Consequences of the Sexual Revolution

by John Vertefeuille (Crossway Books, 1988) 185 pp. $7.95

***Overall Product Rating: 4.4***

**STRENGTHS:** Open, frank discussion. Honest and quite explicit explanations of certain sexual issues and practices...Some interesting data on sexuality.
**WEAKNESSES:** Heavy reading. Too much background information given in first few chapters...Dry...A rehash of the old standard lines on sexuality...Rather narrow in its interpretation of Scripture...It feels harsh as if the author wants to repulse the reader with his explicit details.

## Sexual Christian, The

(Victor Books, 1989) 202 pp. $12.95

***Overall Product Rating: 6.5***

**STRENGTHS:** Challenges leaders to look at tradition and the world they face today in some non-traditonal ways...Provides some practical ideas for addressing sexuality...Is most helpful for young never-married singles.
**WEAKNESSES:** Somewhat intense. More a study than easy reading... Addressed more to youth workers than to single adult leaders... Handles the subject of homosexuality poorly, using little exegetical or textual support. Consequently, the information on homosexuality clearly seems to be the author's opinion only and it ignores several key issues.

## Sexual Freedom

by V. Mary Stewart (InterVarsity Press, 1979) 25 pp. 99¢

***Not Yet Reviewed***

**NOTES:** This pamphlet explores various sexual issues and describes the author's process of turning them over to God for correction and permanent change. Also gives some of the root causes of unhealthy sexual behavior.

## Sexual Sanity: Breaking Free From Uncontrolled Habits

by Earl D. Wilson (InterVarsity Press, 1984) 144 pp. $5.95

***Overall Product Rating: 7.9***

**STRENGTHS:** A great tool to use in one-on-one counseling...Good Biblical analysis of sexual sin and perver-sion...Doesn't deal just with surface, goes beyond actions to motivations... Covers many topics including masturbation, promiscuity, pornography, homosexuality and self-esteem... Looks at why people develop destructive habits and offers guidance on how to overcome them ...I plan to use this book in my counseling with singles.
**WEAKNESSES:** The author has a tendency to write over the heads of many people with his "educated style"...Poor book title—doesn't do justice to the content...Wish the book would have been better designed for use in group discussion.

## Sexual Temptation

by Randy C. Alcorn (InterVarsity, 1989) 32 pp. $1.95

***Overall Product Rating: 5.6***

**STRENGTHS:** Although the primary focus of this book seems to be for those in ministry leadership positions, I found that the Biblical presentation and the application on sexual temptation to be helpful for anyone...Could serve as a useful tool for introduction to sensitive, personal topics.
**WEAKNESSES:** Remedial and too "broad brush"...Attempts to deal with everything yet deals with very little new, helpful material.

## Sexual Understanding Before Marriage

by Herbert J. Miles (Zondervan, 1971) 222 pp. $6.95

***Overall Product Rating: 2.2***

**STRENGTHS:** Although this book is not written with single adults in mind, it may help leaders become more aware of the kind of sexuality education that some singles have received from their church, home and school background...Provides some very basic information about male and female sexuality.
**WEAKNESSES:** This book is written by one who is unable to affirm singleness, even listing the disadvantages of being single. It does not prepare young people for the option of singleness in adulthood. ...Clearly written for teens or those still supervised by parents...Much of this advice can be challenged on a number of grounds...The illustrative material and advice will not help much in a singles ministry...Many of the guidelines seem representative of the repressive, up-tight, stereotypical conservative Christianity of the 1950s. Not realistic or believ-able...A very dated book...The latter part of the book overly focused on the issue of sexual control rather than a more balanced Christian view of understanding the appropriate celebration of sexuality.

## Singles Ask:
### Answers to Questions About Relationships and Sexual Issues

by Harold Ivan Smith (Augsburg, 1988) 159 pp. $8.95

## How Does The National Review Board Function?

1. There are over 100 reviewers on this board, representing every major denomination and region of the country.
2. All reviewers are pastors, counselors or lay leaders involved in ministry with single adults.
3. Every product is reviewed and evaluated by *at least two - and in most cases, three - members* of this National Board. (When appropriate and possible, the product is actually used in a singles ministry prior to being evaluated.)
4. Each product is reviewed and evaluated on its own merit and not as it compares to other products or resources.
5. Reviewers' ratings for each product are tabulated and averaged by the staff of *Single Adult Ministries Journal* to determine each score. ***(Products are rated from 1 to 10, with 10 being the best rating possible.)***

***Overall Product Rating: 5.9***
**STRENGTHS:** A quick reference dealing with many real questions that singles ask...The author writes well and exhibits some street smarts that only a single person could articulate ...Covers many sexual issues that singles may be too embarrassed to talk about with their pastor...Offers different Biblical perspectives on such issues as masturbation and oral sex...Smith is at his best when he expresses strong, clear convictions.
**WEAKNESSES:** The answers are often not as straight forward as the questions...Just touches the surface on some very delicate issues... Too many pat answers...Felt that sometimes the author is given to cliches - like "mucho macho" that glibly describes a certain kind of male behavior that in fact is very complex.

## Snare, The:
### Avoiding Emotional and Sexual Entanglements
by Lois Mowday (NavPress, 1988) 231 pp. $12.95
***Overall Product Rating: 7.2***
**STRENGTHS:** A subject that needs to be addressed...Finally, a clear, precise look at our sexuality as human beings and how to incorporate that into our spiritual...Talks about real issues and real struggles...I was pleased at the strong Scriptural guidance but without judgmentalism or legalistic rules... Obvious the author has seriously dealt with this subject for herself and is at peace with the answers and God's guidance... I'm using this book in one of our women's small group studies and it has been great, a real help.
**WEAKNESSES:** Little hard research was done by the author on this topic. Seems to be primarily based on her personal experience/ opinion...Heavily influenced toward married women...Some professional singles out in the marketplace will find this material naive and unrealis-tic...Sometimes a bit preachy... Questionable theology concerning those unable to live a life of chastity ...Presented only from a feminine viewpoint. It desperately needs a man's point of view too.

Need a Speaker for Your Next Conference or Retreat?
See Page 55

## Song For Lovers, A
by S. Craig Glickman (InterVarsity Press, 1979) 188 pp. $8.95
***Overall Product Rating: 6.5***
**STRENGTHS:** A solid, Biblical presentation of romantic love...Would be useful to give to single adults who are approaching marriage... Could be used in marriage counseling to help the couple have a better understanding of sexual and romantic love.
**WEAKNESSES:** Long on exposition and short on application to everyday relational issues...Tends to promote an idealistic and unrealistic example of romantic love...It seems as though the author stretches some of the verses to make them fit his purposes.

## Struggling with Sex:
### A Serious Call to Marriage-Centered Sexual Life
by Arthur A. Rouner, Jr. (Augsburg Pub House, 1986) 112 pp. $6.50
***Overall Product Rating: 6.5***
**STRENGTHS:** This book offers a reason for giving our sex lives to God...Author has a very gentle approach...His focus on the purpose and value of sex is excellent....A frank discussion of sex which is not often found in Christian material (although I think it could still be more frank).
**WEAKNESSES:** In my opinion the title is weak. I don't know of too many people who would want to be seen reading this book...An inconsistency—the author stresses that premarital sexual expression must be withheld and then speaks of masturbation as a viable option. I do not oppose his position but only the inconsistent approach to this subject ...More statistical and factual evidence is needed. The author made statements as facts with no definite evidence to back them up, which I think happens far too often in the church, especially with such powerful issues as sex. To be an effective, credible witness today, we must have provable facts concerning this subject matter.

## Too Close Too Soon
by Jim Talley and Bobbie Reed (Thomas Nelson, 1989) 169 pp. $6.95 (Leader's Guide also available.)
***Overall Product Rating: 6.8***
**STRENGTHS:** The authors speak candidly concerning physical intimacy and its relationship to true love and friendship...I appreciate their attempt to offer understanding about male-female differences and the intensity of physical desires while still effectively advocating chastity...Warns singles concerning their inability to handle an intimate dating relationship on "your own"... Some excellent discussion questions and ideas for a two-part workshop.
**WEAKNESSES:** Too arbitrary with its time constraints and artificial standards for a dating relationship ...Too structured in perception of a problem and prognosis...Not for the average single adult because it is too simplistic and unrealistic in its approach.

## True Sexuality
by Ken Unger (Tyndale House Publishers, 1987) 240 pp. $6.95
***Overall Product Rating: 5.8***
**STRENGTHS:** Thoroughly covers the nature of our sexuality giving much attention to American culture and how we came to be where we are now, living for our own gratification...Gives churches a run for their money stating that we are a nation with a "surface conformity" to Christian values and principles but we have not truly known God! I appreciated his candor and his adherence to God's Word, pointing out that sin destroys and is often an attempt to fulfill our inner spiritual needs through outer physical pleasure...A good resource book for teaching Biblical sexuality...An excellent chapter for pre-marital counseling on how marriage is "the school of sacrifice"...Good stats.
**WEAKNESSES:** Profoundly narrow view and understanding of Christian feminism... Simplistic treatment of Freud and history... Explanation of sexual purity is weak... Constant use of undocumented sensationalism such as scare tactics on AIDs transmission in marriage...Does not deal with an older person's sexuality after divorce or the death of a spouse, treating "premarital sex" as only an issue young adults deal with...The writing style is to much like a research paper, failing to command attention after a few chapters.

# Single Adult Ministry

## Most Recommended Resources in This Section

(Based on evaluations and reviews made by *SAM Journal*'s National Resource Review Board, using a 1-10 scale with 10 being the best possible score):

### 8.8 Young Adult Ministry:
**Step-by-Step Help For Starting or Revitalizing Your Ministry With People Ages 18 to 35**
by Terry Hershey (Group Books, 1986)

### 8.2 Single On Sunday:
**A Manual For Successful Single Adult Ministries**
by Bobbie Reed (Concordia Publishing, 1979)

### 7.9 Successful Single Adult Ministry:
**It Can Happen in Your Church**
by Krista Swan Welsh (Standard, 1987)

### 7.7 Singles Ministry Handbook:
**A Practical Guide to Reaching Adult Singles in the Church**
Editor, Doug Fagerstrom (Victor Books, 1988)

*(For more information on each of the above resources—plus many other helpful products—find them listed in alphabetical order below.)*

## Challenge of Single Adult Ministry, The
by Douglas Johnson (Judson, 1982) 111 pp. $6.95

***Not Yet Reviewed***

**NOTES:** Not a "how-to" book, but help for those who minister in determining what might make a ministry with singles effective.

## Faces of Single Adult Ministries, The
Edited by Linda G. Hardin (Beacon Hill Press of Kansas City, 1990) 80 pp. $4.95

***Not Yet Reviewed***

**NOTES:** Chapters written from the editor's firsthand experience and by leaders of single adult ministries deal with the unique needs of various single adult groups, how the church can minister to them and how to begin single adult ministries.

## FILM STRIP/Free to Dream
by Mark H. Senter III (Scripture Press Ministries, 1984) $24.95

***Not Yet Reviewed***

**NOTES:** Film strip, audio cassette and leader's guide designed to discover and develop the dreams of young adults/singles which are crucial for the future of the Church.

## Half The Congregation: Singles
by R. T. Gribbon (Alban Institute, 1984) 30 pp. $7.50

***Overall Product Rating: 6.2***

**STRENGTHS:** An excellent research book which contains helpful ideas for reaching and keeping young adults...Contains an index of books helpful in the study...Concise.
**WEAKNESSES:** Not very up to date... Narrow definition of single adults (primarily only the young, never-married).

## How To Communicate With Single Adults
by Floyd A. Craig (Broadman Press, 1978) 46 pp. $13.95

***Overall Product Rating: 5.3***

**STRENGTHS:** The main benefit is that it gives a broad overview of steps to follow in planning/promoting an organization...Gives general background on characteristics of single adults in the United States... Includes several ideas for communication through newspapers, newsletters, etc....Offers information and visuals specifically related to reaching singles and visualizing singles ministry...Useful for both small and large singles ministries.
**WEAKNESSES:** Dated, giving background information that was relevant in the 70s...The book itself also does not apply some of its own recommendations. The content is cluttered and little white space is used to relieve the eye. Much of the content could be eliminated, and the basic message would still be understood. Illustrations do not support all elements of the content...Does not address some of the philosophical issues. For example: Can the meetings really produce what is promised in the ad? How far can attractive church publicity go before it becomes a projection of self-centered grandiosity or greatness which is essentially narcissistic and not characteristic of the self-giving, cross-bearing and servant life which is so central to the Gospel message?

## AUDIO CASSETTE/How To Start A Singles Ministry
by Dr. Britton Wood (Broadman, #4472-66) 60 min. $6.95

***Overall Product Rating: 7.6***

**STRENGTHS:** Continually stresses the importance of allowing the ministry to belong to the single adults themselves, allowing them to own it, lead it, etc....A well stated understanding of single adults and their needs...Encourages leaders to help singles recognize their potential as a part of the church...An excellent tape especially for those beginning a single adult ministry from scratch... Content could be useful when "making a case" with the church leadership

## How Does The National Review Board Function?

1. There are over 100 reviewers on this board, representing every major denomination and region of the country.
2. All reviewers are pastors, counselors or lay leaders involved in ministry with single adults.
3. Every product is reviewed and evaluated by *at least two - and in most cases, three - members* of this National Board. (When appropriate and possible, the product is actually used in a singles ministry prior to being evaluated.)
4. Each product is reviewed and evaluated on its own merit and not as it compares to other products or resources.
5. Reviewers' ratings for each product are tabulated and averaged by the staff of *Single Adult Ministries Journal* to determine each score. ***(Products are rated from 1 to 10, with 10 being the best rating possible.)***

about the need for a SAM.
**WEAKNESSES:** Is very basic and general so this would not be very helpful for anyone with much knowledge about, or experience with, singles ministry...Not as many specific "how to's" as some people might be looking for...The speaker tends to sound monotone on this tape.

## Idea Catalog for Single Adult Ministry, The

edited by Jerry Jones (Singles Ministry Resources/NavPress, 1991) $12.95

***Not Yet Reviewed***

**NOTES:** For nearly a decade singles ministers have turned to *Single Adult Ministries Journal* for help in their ministry with single adults. There they have found hundreds of helpful ideas. This book is the best of *SAM Journal*'s ideas, contributed by singles ministries from all across the country. Ideas gathered in this volume include help for building community, evangelism and outreach, advertising and promotion, special events, service and missions, plus much more.

## Launching and Sustaining a Successful Singles Ministry

by Dick Dunn (self-published, 1985) 106 pp. (Includes audio tape) $35.00

***Overall Product Rating: 4.9***

**STRENGTHS:** This product provides a thorough step-by-step guide for lay people who begin working with single adults... The Ice Breakers and Discussion Questions at the end of the book are very good...This resource does a good job of encouraging leaders to give ownership of the ministry to single adults...Simple for lay leaders to adapt...The tape is helpful.
**WEAKNESSES:** The price is much too high for what you get. It should be about half the price....Print quality is poor...Opinions seem to be biased and unresearched... "Ministry" is never defined. "Gospel" and "evangelism" seems primarily social and program-oriented...It seems the Number One goal is to produce "warm fuzzies" vs. developing or bringing singles to maturity in Christ.

## AUDIO CASSETTES/ Ministering To Single Adults

by Jim Talley (self-published, 1987) 4 x 60 min. $12.00

***Overall Product Rating: 6.8***

**STRENGTHS:** Covers four significant areas quite thoroughly (Starting a Singles Ministry, Interpersonal Relationships, Divorce and Remarriage, Dealing with Homosexuality) ...Good material at a reasonable price...Practical how-to's from an experienced single adult leader...A sensitive, logical and relevant presentation...Touches on several real-life needs and concerns of today's single adults...I was pleasantly surprised with the tape series.
**WEAKNESSES:** Some of the material is stated much too dogmatically and simplistically ...The concepts are excellent and often accurate, but I fear that many will stumble over the "rules" and miss the principles... Sometimes seems a bit condescending toward singles.

## Ministering to Young Adults

by Carol Gura (St. Marys Press, 1987) 233 pp. $28.95

***Not Yet Reviewed***

**NOTES:** This book provides practical ideas for gathering young adults to get a ministry started. It contains 30 specific programs that include step-by-step procedures and strategies. Learning activities, prayer services, models for Scriptural study groups and newsletter ideas are also provided. (Catholic in context.)

According to the U.S. Census Bureau, the likelihood of alimony being awarded divorced or separated women is twice as high if they are aged 40 or over than it is if they are under 30. Furthermore, alimony was significantly more likely for white women (than for blacks), and for college graduates.

*The Associated Press, 4/7/89*

## Ministry with Black Single Adults

by Sheron C. Patterson (Discipleship Resources, 1990) 59 pp. $1.92

***Not Yet Reviewed***

**NOTES:** According to the author, great need and opportunity currently exist for ministries with black single adults. Drawing on sociological statistics, Biblical insights and on her own experience as a leader of singles ministries, the author shows why the need for ministry is so great, and how to create singles ministries within the black church that deal with the real issues.

## Reach Out To Singles: A Challenge to Ministry

by Raymond K. Brown (Westminster Press, 1979) 191 pp. $8.95

***Not Yet Reviewed***

**NOTES:** A growing segment of our nation's adult population is single, yet singles comprise only a fraction of the church's membership. According to Dr. Brown, the problem with singles ministry is the church itself. Speaking to the problems, he offers some "how-to" options that any church can adapt to fit its own situation.

## VIDEO/Single

(Ecu-Film, 1980) 3 min. $9.00

***Not Yet Reviewed***

**Notes:** This film looks at being single and helps raise awareness for ministry needs. It's a good tool for use as a discussion starter or for planning meetings.

## Single Adult Ministry: The Authoritative Guide for Singles Ministry Leaders

Edited by Jerry Jones (Singles Ministry Resources/NavPress, 1991) $24.95

***Not Yet Reviewed***

**NOTES:** An exhaustive guide to ministering with today's single adults written by more than 50 of the field's nationally-known leaders. This book includes thorough explorations of the following: Building a Singles Ministry in the Local Church; Leadership for Your Single Adult Ministry; Programming for Your Singles Ministry; Divorce and Remarriage; Counseling Single Adults; Developing Single Parent Family Ministries; Reaching Unchurched Single Adults; Budgets and Promotion; and Contemporary Issues in Singles Ministry.

## Single Adult Ministry In Your Church

by Cliff Albritton, Tim Cleary, Ann Gardner, Horace Kerr (Convention Press, 1988) 128 pp. $3.25

***Overall Product Rating: 5.6***

**STRENGTHS:** Provides "thumbnail sketch" for those thinking about beginning a singles ministry...Offers some good information on the foundations of a singles ministry in the local church.

**WEAKNESSES:** Does not adequately address staff leadership issues, assuming that there is only lay leadership. This makes the leadership information unrealistic for many churches... References and resources given are exclusively denominational (Southern Baptist)...Too many diverse ideas from different authors without a sense of continuity and consensus...Not necessarily easy or enjoyable reading...Written too much like a text book.

## Single Adults: Resources and Recipients For Revival

by Dan R. Crawford, plus other contributing authors (Broadman Press, 1985) 182 pp. $5.95

***Overall Product Rating: 4.4***

**STRENGTHS:** If you like statistics, it was well researched (but is now already out of date)...Looks at a wide variety of life situations that singles find themselves in...A good "operators guide" for Singles ministry.

**WEAKNESSES:** As a leader who is single, I felt like I was reading about another group of people outside of this world and that I (and all other single adults) was only a category or number, not a real person...Very dry reading...Other contributing authors represent a narrow segment of Christianity (Southern Baptist). Some other perspectives would have rounded this out.

## Single Adults Want to Be the Church Too

by Britton Wood (Broadman Press, 1977) 186 pp. $9.95

***Not Yet Reviewed***

**NOTES:** One of the first books written on this subject, a pioneer. It can help churches become more aware of the needs of single adults and offers guidelines to help them develop an effective singles ministry. It is designed for both individual and group study/action.

## Single On Sunday: A Manual For Successful Single Adult Ministries

by Bobbie Reed (Concordia Publishing, 1979) 103 pp. $6.50

***Overall Product Rating: 8.2***

**STRENGTHS:** A very good "basic foundations" book for those interested in building a healthy singles ministry... Easy to use and under-stand...Offers a step-by-step process... This book does not lock ministries in a box because it helps leaders think about how to change the ministry as it grows...Provides some great ideas in the chapter on small groups...Gives practical guidelines for such areas as "Planning a Balanced Calendar," "Discussion Guide Sheets" and "Job Descriptions for the Leadership Team."

**WEAKNESSES:** The book tends to be dry and hard to get started with in the beginning ...It needs to be reedited and updated. Many of the references are out of date now.

## Singles Care One for Another

by Karen A. Greenwaldt (Discipleship Resources, 1989) 112 pp. $2.17

***Overall Product Rating: 6.0***

**STRENGTHS:** Focused and easy to read by a lay person. You don't have to wade through pages of material... Questions and guidelines given in the book can head singles into discovering how to address a particular need within the context of a singles ministry...A handy reference tool for those with little or no experience in ministry with single adults...Includes excellent, helpful sections on starting a singles ministry, complete with easy-to-use work sheets, surveys and further resources.

**WEAKNESSES:** Offers little new information...Seems aimed at a very general, elementary audience...Many deeper issues and needs that must be addressed in any healthy singles ministry are not even mentioned ...Although a good start, it appears that the author tried to cover too much ground in too little space. The result is a generic book with underdeveloped content...Was disappointed in the lack of theological foundations for what the author is proposing. Mostly a psychological approach.

## Singles Ministry Handbook: A Practical Guide to Reaching Adult Singles in the Church

Written by several authors, edited by Doug Fagerstrom (Victor Books, 1988) 304 pp. $17.95

***Overall Product Rating: 7.7***

**STRENGTHS:** A helpful collection of statistics...An excellent macro-view of the 'bones' of a ministry with single adults...A good introduction to various authors on a wide variety of subjects...The bibliography in back of the book is excellent ...I already had much of this same information, but not in one handy book.

**WEAKNESSES:** There are better authors to address some subjects covered...The book is almost too comprehensive to be as useful as

## How Does The National Review Board Function?

1. There are over 100 reviewers on this board, representing every major denomination and region of the country.
2. All reviewers are pastors, counselors or lay leaders involved in ministry with single adults.
3. Every product is reviewed and evaluated by *at least two - and in most cases, three - members* of this National Board. (When appropriate and possible, the product is actually used in a singles ministry prior to being evaluated.)
4. Each product is reviewed and evaluated on its own merit and not as it compares to other products or resources.
5. Reviewers' ratings for each product are tabulated and averaged by the staff of *Single Adult Ministries Journal* to determine each score. ***(Products are rated from 1 to 10, with 10 being the best rating possible.)***

it could be...This is just a handbook (vs. a step-by-step guide) and should be treated as such...Better footnotes on statistics and studies would have provided more credibility ...Most chapters are too short. Writers barely had chance to give the reader much helpful material.

## Successful Single Adult Ministry:
### It Can Happen In Your Church

by Krista Swan Welsh (Standard, 1987) 126 pp. $6.95

***Overall Product Rating: 7.9***

**STRENGTHS:** Easy to read and use, the kind of book I'll hand to new leaders in our single adult ministry ...Offers a general overview of single adults and program ministries designed for single adults plus it includes a few program "gems" that get a person brainstorming about the possibilities...As a full-time pastor of singes in a church with an established program, I found the "refresher course" (the statistics and need for singles ministry) to be an encouraging reminder of the validity of what I'm doing...Throughout, its value to me was a reminder of the basics, forgetting the stereotypes and getting on with the business of meeting needs in specific ways, determined by the life-situations of our people...Concise, articulate simplicity added to this book's overall effectiveness.
**WEAKNESSES:** Because of its brevity, this book serves only as an introduction to single adult ministry, and does not offer help for the challenges of maintaining an on-going ministry, especially regarding counseling and support group ministries and leadership recruitment.

## Vacations With a Purpose:
### Developing a Short-term Missions Ministry With Your Single Adults

by Chris Eaton and Kim Hurst (Singles Ministry Resources/NavPress, 1991) Leader's Manual, $16.95; Team Member's Manual, $5.95

***Not Yet Reviewed***

**NOTES:** Designed to assist American church leaders, singles ministers and overseas missions workers, this product gives solid, easy-to-follow guidelines for developing and implementing short-term missions teams. It also provides a philosophical foundation for short-term teams and gives examples of how churches and individual Christians have been changed and reinvigorated by a broader worldwide understanding of Christ's work on earth. This book provides anything you would need to know about recruiting and training your team, selecting a project plus short-term missions philosophy and logistics.

## Working with Single Adults in Sunday School

by Linda Lawson (Convention Press, 1978) 126 pp. $3.15

***Not Yet Reviewed***

**NOTES:** This book is designed to train workers in administration, teaching, learning, understanding single adults, outreach ministry, using space effectively and relating Sunday School to single adults within the context of a broad-based single adult ministry.

## VIDEO/Young Adult Ministry

Featuring Terry Hershey (International Lutheran Laymen's League, 1989) 72 min. $20.00

***Not Yet Reviewed***

**NOTES:** Four-session videotape designed to assist congregations in their ministry efforts toward young adults. Complete with leader's guide workbook and participant workbook.

## Young Adult Ministry:
### A Book of Readings

Editor, Ron Bagley (Don Bosco Multimedia, 1987) 131 pp. $12.95

***Overall Product Rating: 5.7***

**STRENGTHS:** The readings give a broad overview of the young adult, from high school to young married. The authors were experienced, which lends credibility to what they say. Gives a good idea of the concern within the Catholic church for young adults, single and married.
**WEAKNESSES:** This book is not a "how to." It does not provide much in programming or guidance. May be difficult reading for some non-Catholics.

## Young Adult Ministry
### Step-by-Step Help For Starting or Revitalizing Your Ministry With People Ages 18 to 35

by Terry Hershey (Group Books, 1986) 274 pp. $12.95

***Overall Product Rating: 8.8***

**STRENGTHS:** Provides excellent cultural/ Biblical analysis of the needs, philosophy of ministry... Offers many practical ideas for implementing a young adult ministry in your church...This book is worth the price and should be in every professional church staff person's library...I especially appreciated the group study materials section...This book provides some wonderful organizational concepts.
**WEAKNESSES:** It covers almost too much in one book, too diversified an age group (18 to 35)...There are several more excellent books on young adult ministry that were not mentioned in the resource section ...Book is geared to both marrieds and singles (although the primary focus is on singles), so the reader has to sometimes adapt it to singles.

# Single Parenting & Single Parent Families

## Most Recommended Resources in This Section

(Based on evaluations and reviews made by *SAM Journal*'s National Resource Review Board, using a 1-10 scale with 10 being the best possible score):

### 9.0 101 Ways To Be A Long Distance Super-Dad

by George Newman (Blossom Valley Press, 1981)

### 8.3 Second Chances: Men, Women, and Children a Decade After Divorce

by Judith Wallerstein (Ticknor and Fields, 1989)

### 8.0 Single Mothers Raising Sons

by Bobbie Reed (Thomas Nelson, 1988)

*(For more information on each of the above resources—plus many other helpful products—find them listed in alphabetical order below.)*

## 101 Ways To Be A Long Distance Super-Dad

by George Newman (Blossom Valley Press, 1981) 108 pp. $6.95

***Overall Product Rating: 9.0***

**STRENGTHS:** Extremely practical book for those non-custodial fathers who truly desire a relationship with their kids...Beneficial in providing creative communication ideas... I'm sending a copy of this book to a single parent father, who I know will find this material of real value...One of the greatest benefits of this book is its emphasis on learning to be a good parent and giving of oneself (which sometimes requires a great deal of involvement, especially when one lives many miles away)... Practical helps and projects for building a two-way relationship... Can also be used by non-custodial moms.

**WEAKNESSES:** The only drawback is that it has no Christian perspective (but I will still use it)...Would have appreciated a little more discussion on the whys and hows on the ideas plus better guidelines for age appropriateness.

## About Single Parenting

(Channing L. Bete Co., 1983) 15 pp. 72¢

***Overall Product Rating: 6.3***

**STRENGTHS:** Easy to understand... Would be a good booklet to give to those who have just recently become single parents...The "caring for yourself" and "sources of help" sections offered simple yet practical suggestions...The absence of condemning all single parent children to failure, doom and permanent injury.

**WEAKNESSES:** Very simplistic. Seems to almost be designed more for teenagers than adults...No Scriptural references.

## Advice To Single Parents

by Virginia Watts Smith (Focus On The Family, 1986) 15 pp. 35¢

***Overall Product Rating: 6.3***

**STRENGTHS:** Practical insight for single parents...Very good coverage of the various types of single parenting situations...The section for unmarried parents and their children was excellent...Concise and easy to read...Provides basic information for those working with single parents or for those who have just become single parents.

**WEAKNESSES:** This brief booklet covers so many different subjects that none of them are more than briefly introduced. Most people are going to be looking for much more than this booklet provides...The author drew very little from the authority of Scripture, relying primarily on the authority of his Ph.D.

## Being A Single Parent

by Andre Bustanoby (Zondervan, 1985) 280 pp. $8.95

***Overall Product Rating: 6.1***

**STRENGTHS:** An informational mini-encyclopedia on single parent-ing...A helpful resource for pastors and leaders to educate them regarding the many facets of single parenting...Offers facts, assistance and suggestions for helping single parents.

**WEAKNESSES:** This is a book *about* single parenting, not for single parents. It is far too technical for individuals struggling with the many demands of single parenting...Could be helpful as a book for parents needing encouragement or help...As a former single parent, this book would have overwhelmed me...Lacks emotion...Statistics are outdated.

## Complete Financial Guide For Single Parents, The

by Larry Burkett (Victor Books, 1991) $12.99

***Not Yet Reviewed***

**NOTES:** Single parents represent one of the most financially needy groups of people. With most of them being women—divorced or widowed—the struggle to make ends meet while juggling career and children often seems overwhelming. The author addresses the needs of this group through real-life illustrations, practical advice, and biblical truths. The book covers such areas as budgets, alimony, wills, and insurance.

## Do I Have a Daddy?

by Jeanne Lindsay (Morning Glory Press, 1982) 47 pp. $3.95

***Overall Product Rating: 6.0***

**STRENGTHS:** Valuable parent guide and information section, especially for the never-married parent... Focuses on the never-married mother and her young child who asks the questions children will ask... Well-researched by a credible author...Provides helpful, general information about single parent families...One of the few children's

## How Does The National Review Board Function?

1. There are over 100 reviewers on this board, representing every major denomination and region of the country.
2. All reviewers are pastors, counselors or lay leaders involved in ministry with single adults.
3. Every product is reviewed and evaluated by *at least two - and in most cases, three - members* of this National Board. (When appropriate and possible, the product is actually used in a singles ministry prior to being evaluated.)
4. Each product is reviewed and evaluated on its own merit and not as it compares to other products or resources.
5. Reviewers' ratings for each product are tabulated and averaged by the staff of *Single Adult Ministries Journal* to determine each score.

***(Products are rated from 1 to 10, with 10 being the best rating possible.)***

books for this targeted group.
**WEAKNESSES:** Disappointing that this book for emotionally hurt people offers no spiritual emphasis...Geared for the pre-schooler or young child thus narrowing its potential audience ...Did not encourage the parent to help the child express feelings.

## VIDEO/Family Matters, The:
### Parents Living Apart From Their Children

by Brenda Blackmon and Glenn Larson (EcuFilm, 1990) 30 min. $29.95

***Not Yet Reviewed***

**NOTES:** Interviews parents who are living apart from their children because of divorce. Offers suggestions for parents in this situation as well as discussion questions.

## VIDEO/Family Matters, The:
### Single Parents

by Brenda Blackmon and Glenn Larson (EcuFilm, 1990) 30 min. $29.95

***Not Yet Reviewed***

**NOTES:** Examines single parenthood through interviews with single parents. Suggests actions for single parents to consider and offers discussion questions.

## How To Single Parent

by Dr. Fitzhugh Dodson (Harper & Row, 1987) 197 pp.

***Overall Product Rating: 2.7***

**STRENGTHS:** Includes a lot of research from a secular, psychological viewpoint ...This is really a rehash of many books, videos, workshops, etc. of "how to" parent books. If you want "The Reader's Digest Book of Single Parenting" then this is probably the answer to your library needs. You can learn the buzz words of the field and sound like an expert.
**WEAKNESSES:** Few benefits. Its teachings are not Biblically based, sometimes even deceiving and false! The author tells us to set our own standards according to how we feel and what is "right" for us... Author's interpretation of what Jesus is telling us through Scripture is taken out of context and misconstrued to fit his own personal philosophy...A rewrite of much material that is already available in better forms...Suggests that only women are single parents and that men aren't...Nothing more than a "feel good" book that makes it a shallow effort at discussing life as a single parent ...Too secular and humanistic for my ministry. I didn't even agree with some of its psychological principles. There are many other better Biblically-based books for the single parent.

Women with incomes under $11,000 are over three times more likely to have an abortion than those with incomes above $25,000.

*Alan Guttmacher Institute*

## Just Me and the Kids:
### A Course for Single Parents

by Brandt and Jackson (David C. Cook Publishing, 1985) 82 pp. (Includes transparencies) $19.95

***Overall Product Rating: 7.8***

**STRENGTHS:** With a shortage of help for single parents, this material is of great benefit...The transparencies and work sheets provided in the book are most helpful...The topics covered are right on...The format and resources in this book make it appealing and convenient for those who want to begin a single parent ministry...Chapter five offers excellent guidelines for the parent on when a child needs professional help.
**WEAKNESSES:** A 13-week course can be too long for single parent. We used it, but cut it down to six...The main author is a single parent by choice. (She adopted two children). Consequently, the content is too simplistic for those who did not choose or want to be single parents.

## One Parent Families:
### Healing the Hurts

by Harold Ivan Smith (Beacon Hill, 1981) 104 pp. $2.95

***Not Yet Reviewed***

**Notes:** Helping heal the hurts in single parent homes should be a task addressed to the church and Christians who are interested in loving and ministering in this challenging area.

## Parents Divided, Parents Multiplied

by Margaret O. Hyde and E. Forsyth, M.D. (Westminster/John Knox, 1989) 115 pp. $13.95

***Not Yet Reviewed***

**NOTES:** As a result of many changes taking place in family life (blended families, one-parent families, etc.), children are often confused as to what behavior is expected or where their loyalties belong. Using true-to-life examples, these authors provide young people with a guide to various life-styles, including some of today's more unusual situations.

## Parenting Solo:
### How to Enjoy Life and Raise Good Kids

by Dr. Emil Authelet (Here's Life Publishers, 1989) 238 pp. $7.95

***Overall Product Rating: 7.9***

**STRENGTHS:** Very thorough and well-thought-out examination of the problems.... Thought-provoking study questions at end of chapters...We probably will use at least some of this book in our single parent support group... There is a lot of "meat" in this book...Very good in dealing with difficult job of single parenting and the single parent's needs and feelings. Also deals with children's needs and feelings....Raises a multitude of questions and issues that every single parent needs to address at some point...Would make a good resource for study/support group.
**WEAKNESSES:** May not get as much of an audience as it deserves just because it appears to be more conservative than it really is...The author's use of "lists" become tedious reading after a while...It needs a study guide...Tends to be more sociological than Biblical.

## Pregnant and Single:
### Help for the Tough Choices

by Carolyn Owens and Linda Roggow (Zondervan, 1990) 144 pp. $7.95

***Not Yet Reviewed***

**NOTES:** This book discusses pregnancy, adoption, single parenting and marriage so that the single pregnant woman can examine the alternatives and make an informed choice. The shock of realizing she is pregnant, readiness for motherhood, health of mother and baby, money matters and other problems are covered.

## Second Chances:
### Men, Women, and Children a Decade After Divorce

by Judith Wallerstein (Ticknor and Fields/ T.I.S. Enterprises, 1989) 352 pp. $19.95

***Overall Product Rating: 8.3***

**STRENGTHS:** Offers excellent information about the ongoing effects of divorce on children and the family...Provides previously unavailable research on how divorce impacts the lives involved... Fresh insight concerning the effects of divorce 10 years later...An excellent resource for anyone working with the divorced.

**WEAKNESSES:** The vast number of statistics can become overwhelming and distracting...The group surveyed for this book was too upper middle class. It would have been good to see more blue-collar people surveyed... The author is too reluctant to make recommendations based on her research...A helpful addition would have been an addendum in the back for professionals on how to effectively use the book.

## Single Again, This Time With Children
### A Christian Guide for Single Parents

by Alice Stolper Peppler (Augsburg Fortress, 1982) 136 pp. $6.95

***Not Yet Reviewed***

**NOTES:** This book provides an eye witness account of the difficulty of raising children alone. A wide range of topics is covered with Scriptural references used for support.

## Single Moms, Single Dads

by David R. Miller (Accent Books, 1990) 175 pp. $6.95

***Not Yet Reviewed***

**NOTES:** Reaches into everyday life of a single parent to offer practical, Biblical and common-sense insight and support for the single parent.

## Single Mothers Raising Sons

by Bobbie Reed (Thomas Nelson, 1988) 191 pp. $6.95

***Overall Product Rating: 8.0***

**STRENGTHS:** Addresses most major concerns a single mother would have in raising sons. Even mothers of daughters would benefit ...The chapter on male relationships is worth the price of the book alone. I share this chapter with many single moms in a custody battle with their former spouse...The discussion starters are excellent for helping single parents talk through their issues and concerns with others... Very good insights.

**WEAKNESSES:** Sometimes the book takes on a negative tone, going overboard in describing how difficult it is to raise children alone. I'd hate to see the book be more discouragement to already discouraged single moms...Sometimes the book carries a "tone" that if it were a two parent family, there would be no significant difficulties!

## Single Parent, The:
### A Christian Guide to Help You (Revised & Updated)

by Virginia Watts Smith (Revell, 1976) 192 pp. $6.95

***Not Yet Reviewed***

**NOTES: This** book covers the emotional levels of being a single parent. It deals with situations and circumstances of the never-married parent as will as the single-again parent.

## Single Parenting: A Wilderness Journey

by Robert G. Barnes, Jr. (Tyndale House Publishers, 1984) 199 pp. $5.95

***Not Yet Reviewed***

**NOTES:** Using Biblical insights and a common-sense approach, Robert Barnes writes on topics such as finances, communication, discipline, visitation, self-esteem, sex education, value building and remarriage for single parent families.

## Single Parent's Survival Guide

by Robert G. Barnes (Tyndale Publishers, 1987) 88 pp. $1.95

***Overall Product Rating: 6.7***

**STRENGTHS:** The small format of this booklet makes it convenient and handy to carry in pocket or purse...A brief, practical look at many of the biggest problems faced by single parents...The questions at the end of each chapter are good...Because of its size it is not too intimidating or time-consuming for the busy single parent...This would make an excellent item to give to new single parents.

**WEAKNESSES:** The eight chapter "plan" provided cannot be implemented successfully without further help in time management ...Has a tendency to make it sound easy: "Just follow these guidelines." There is no such thing as an "easy handbook" on how to be a single parent...Lacks specific tools or suggestions...Needs a little more emphasis on Christian principles.

## VIDEO/Successful Single Parenting

by Clyde Besson (Word, Inc., 1985) 180 min. $99.95

***Not Yet Reviewed***

**Notes:** This three video series looks at solutions to the problems and challenges of single parenting. Topics include: The Other Parent Still Counts, Understanding Your Child's Feelings, Helping Develop A Child's Identity and Discipline is Not A Dirty Word.

## Successful Single Parenting:
### Going It Alone

by Gary Richmond (Harvest House, 1990) 234 pp. $6.95

***Not Yet Reviewed***

**NOTES:** Trying to be a loving, nurturing parent while struggling with financial strain, work schedules, children's activities and the need for a social life is enough to drive the most energetic parent to the edge of frenzy. In this book, single parents pastor Gary Richmond gives advice and practical suggestions for meeting the challenges.

## How Does The National Review Board Function?

1. There are over 100 reviewers on this board, representing every major denomination and region of the country.
2. All reviewers are pastors, counselors or lay leaders involved in ministry with single adults.
3. Every product is reviewed and evaluated by *at least two - and in most cases, three - members* of this National Board. (When appropriate and possible, the product is actually used in a singles ministry prior to being evaluated.)
4. Each product is reviewed and evaluated on its own merit and not as it compares to other products or resources.
5. Reviewers' ratings for each product are tabulated and averaged by the staff of *Single Adult Ministries Journal* to determine each score. ***(Products are rated from 1 to 10, with 10 being the best rating possible.)***

# Singleness

## Most Recommended Resources in This Section

(Based on evaluations and reviews made by *SAM Journal*'s National Resource Review Board, using a 1-10 scale with 10 being the best possible score):

### 9.1 VIDEO/One is a Whole Number
by Dr. Harold Ivan Smith (Gospel Films, 1985)

### 9.0 STUDYWORKBOOK/ God's Call To The Single Adult
by Michael P. Cavanaughand Susan M. McCarthy (Oasis House, 1988)

### 8.7 Reflections For Women Alone
by Carole Sanderson Streeter (Victor Books, 1987)

### 8.5 Wide My World Narrow My Bed
by Luci Swindoll (Multnomah Press, 1982)

### 8.0 Great Leaps In A Single Bound
by Kaaren Witte (Bethany House Publishers, 1982)

*(For more information on each of the above resources—plus many other helpful products—find them listed in alphabetical order below.)*

## About Being a Single Christian
(Channing L. Bete Co., 1988) 15 pp. 72¢

***Not Yet Reviewed***

**NOTES:** This short pamphlet gives guidance for the single Christian in areas such as making wise choices and building healthy relationships.

## Bible Readings For Singles
by Ruth Stenerson (Augsburg Fortress, 1980) 112 pp. $4.50

***Not Yet Reviewed***

**NOTES:** The devotional writings in this book are intended for all those for whom the events of their lives have resulted in their living alone. Living alone can be a challenge and it can bring satisfaction. This book uses Scripture readings, prayers and insights to guide the single person as they accept the challenges.

## Complete As One
by Elizabeth Ann Horsford (Zondervan, 1987) 123 pp. $6.95

***Overall Product Rating: 5.2***

**STRENGTHS:** Good basic reading for the single person who is a new Christian...I appreciate the focus of the book, that fulfillment as a single is found through understanding and responding to God's direction in present circumstances. Emphasizes that being single is not a punishment or an oversight by God... Encourages singles to use their abilities, resources and experiences for God's glory now...Best suited for the newly single person (or one struggling with their singleness). The person who has been single for a longer period of time has learned and grown through these issues.

**WEAKNESSES:** Really doesn't offer that much...Never gets down to the nitty gritty...While the principles communicated are mostly sound, they are never addressed with much depth. Sometimes comes across more as a list of suggestions...There are several typing errors in the body of the book.

## Experiencing Singleness: A Process of Discovery
by Edward L. Boye (self-published, 1985) 138 pp. $6.00 ($7.50 for Leader's Guide)

***Overall Product Rating: 4.2***

**STRENGTHS:** This resource provides opportunities for significant sharing and group discussion...The author has attempted to develop some much-needed single adult ministries curriculum...The material touches on some key areas for singles.

**WEAKNESSES:** One of my singles read it and said, "'There's some good material here, but most of the group wouldn't use it because of its unattractive format plus the grammar and spelling errors." I agree... The material is theologically and Scripturally weak. The author seems to give as much weight to Gibran as to Christ...It seems more sociological than Biblical...Needs more focus on Christ's Lordship.

## Famous Singles of the Bible
by Brian L. Harbour (Broadman Press, 1980) 140 pp. $5.95

***Overall Product Rating: 6.7***

**STRENGTHS:** This book takes figures of the Bible and relates them to the struggles faced by present day singles...Offers ideas for dealing with the ups and downs of life as well as a note of inspiration and encouragement to the reader...Short, concise and easy to read...Could be used to stimulate discussion... Provides some good reference and statistics (although many are dated) ...Good source for devotionals/lesson studies.

**WEAKNESSES:** The greatest weakness is its male dominated language. The second greatest weakness is its stereotypical examples of promiscuous women and dedicated abstaining men. The third weakness is its lack of development of the Biblical characters before jumping to the contemporary issues. This causes the reader to feel disconnected...It does not so much focus on the Biblical figures as it does on helping people deal with modern life. This works out okay, but the title is misleading. The author uses the Biblical persons to reflect his ideas and thoughts. Again, this is okay, but not what I expected from the title... Author doesn't appear to have much personal knowledge. He's writing more from research than from personal experience.

By the mid-90s the stepfamily will be the most common family type in the U.S. And nearly 50 percent of these families will break up within the first five years.

*According to research at Northwestern University*

## Flying Solo

by Kaaren Witte (Abingdon Press, 1988) 175 pp. $9.95

***Overall Product Rating: 6.8***

**STRENGTHS:** Enjoyable reading. It hits on areas that singles are concerned with. I think many people would identify in part with her thoughts, struggles, temptations ...Author writes with personal touch and warmth...This personal insight into the author's life as a single adult is needed by married pastors/leaders to better understand the single adult experience...Somewhat autobiographical in nature.

**WEAKNESSES:** There is a considerable lack of chronological order when the author jumps in her story from 1973 to 1977...I felt too much time was spent on the issue of yearning for a mate. I kept hoping she would move on to alternative goals or expand personal anecdotes of herself or others she described... Needed to see more specific ways her experiences deepened her faith or enriched her professional life... You could possibly use this book as a resource but somebody with training would need to pick out sections to make it useful for small group study/discussion...Many of the deep questions were glossed over, failing to lead to real answers (which will frustrate some people).

## For Everything There is a Season

### A Book of Meditations for Single Adults

by Karen A. Greenwaldt (Discipleship Resources, 1988) 158 pp. $7.95

***Overall Product Rating: 6.6***

**STRENGTHS:** Some of the individual writers excerpted in this book are quite profound. I particularly appreciated all the writings of Glenda Taylor Emigh...Useful for a gift or a nurturing tool...The focus on Ecclesiastes 3 is great...Reflects a good cross section of life for singles ...Sincere in its desire to portray the various seasons of singleness.

**WEAKNESSES:** Writing is sometimes uneven...Suffers from too few authors... Much of the writing is so personal and self-centered that it becomes difficult to use as a meditation ...The chapter on celebration lacks celebration...Each section could use further explanation.

## God's Call To The Single Adult

by Michael Cavanaugh (Whitaker, 1986) 131 pp. $4.95 (See study workbook below.)

***Overall Product Rating: 6.0***

**STRENGTHS:** Very easy to read. Simple, free-flowing vocabulary ...Focuses on the need to be content as a single adult before walking down the marriage aisle...Provides excellent Biblical support...The overall tone reinforces that it really is okay to be single, a positive book...Helpful reading for all singles 18-35.

**WEAKNESSES:** Chapters seemed to be Sunday school sermons put to print. Not book quality...Comes across as preachy...No new content. It's the same old story written again...It appears that the author did no outside research when writing this book... The workbook (see below) is much better than this book.

## STUDY WORKBOOK/God's Call To The Single Adult

by Michael P. Cavanaughand Susan M. McCarthy (Oasis House, 1988) 88 pp. $3.95 (A Study to the book listed above.)

***Overall Product Rating: 9.0***

**STRENGTHS:** As a supplement to the book (see above), it maximizes personal application...Provides single adults with a tool to reflect on their singleness, write out their feelings... Helps single adults open up and discuss their feelings...Challenges singles to grow in their faith.

**WEAKNESSES:** A three-hole punch format would have been helpful, permitting additional pages for notes...Needs a few more "thinking" questions.

## VIDEO/God's Pattern For Successful Singlehood

Featuring Tony Evans (Moody Video, 1989) 50 minutes, $29.95

***Overall Product Rating: 7.9***

**STRENGTHS:** Provides in one source an excellent Scriptural view of singleness...as a black pastor, Tony Evans, a minority, addresses singleness which is often viewed as a minority issue in the church. It is effective ...This video pulled together nearly everything in a professional, well-done manner that I've heard over the years concerning a Biblical view of singleness ...This video really hit home with my mostly 30+ singles group... Theologically sound... This would make a good "teacher's aid" for those in singles ministry... An excellent "singles sermon." Hits home on several key issues.

**WEAKNESSES:** No outline or discussion questions were provided although they were referred to in the video...Uses very few examples of single men. Most examples of singleness given were female, which was unfortunate. We need male models too.

## Great Leaps In A Single Bound

by Kaaren Witte (Bethany House Publishers, 1982) 96 pp. $3.95

***Overall Product Rating: 8.0***

**STRENGTHS:** A useful tool to give to those who may be struggling with feelings of loneliness and discouragement because they are single...A book written with openness and honesty...It is a personal testimony of how God provides and cares for us in every detail of our lives...I like the bold print sayings that are scattered throughout the book. They are great "nuggets" to use in newsletters or for putting on cards ...The author made me laugh, cry and do some soul-searching about some of my attitudes towards single adults.

**WEAKNESSES:** The book appears to have been written just for single women. It also needs the male point of view...The material gets to be trite at times...Has a tendency to be repetitious.

## I Gave God Time

by Ann Kiemel Anderson (Tyndale House Publishers, 1982) 163 pp. $6.95

***Overall Product Rating: 7.8***

**STRENGTHS:** Authentic...The author sends the strong message: "Give God time to work in your life to prepare you for his best,

## How Does The National Review Board Function?

1. There are over 100 reviewers on this board, representing every major denomination and region of the country.
2. All reviewers are pastors, counselors or lay leaders involved in ministry with single adults.
3. Every product is reviewed and evaluated by *at least two - and in most cases, three - members* of this National Board. (When appropriate and possible, the product is actually used in a singles ministry prior to being evaluated.)
4. Each product is reviewed and evaluated on its own merit and not as it compares to other products or resources.
5. Reviewers' ratings for each product are tabulated and averaged by the staff of *Single Adult Ministries Journal* to determine each score. ***(Products are rated from 1 to 10, with 10 being the best rating possible.)***

whether that means marriage or not"...Gives those who expect a fairy tale, "happy ever after" life, a gentle, honest taste of reality—that even the best plans will have pain and adjustments...Encourages singles adults—regardless of the circumstances—to allow God to use them wherever they are.
**WEAKNESSES:** Sometimes the book almost seems too personal, as though you are a "peeping Tom"...The title does not appeal to men well...This book is not that helpful for leaders or pastors. It is primarily just for singles...The tone of the book sometimes reinforces the "only one man in the universe for me" fantasy.

## It's A One-derful Life:
### A Single's Celebration

by Mary Hollingsworth (Brownlow Pub Co., 1988) 63 pp. $7.95

***Not Yet Reviewed***

**NOTES:** Involved in a busy cycle of commitments and responsibilities, we seldom consider the importance of supporting and nurturing who we are ourselves. This book helps the single adult celebrate the joy of being the person they were created to be.

## Learn To Risk: Finding Joy As a Single Adult

by Bobbie Reed (Zondervan, 1990) 160 pp. $8.95

***Not Yet Reviewed***

**NOTES:** Anyone can be single, but it takes an adventurer to find joy as a single adult. By offering encouragement to the reader to be open, honest, caring and able to risk reaching out to others, the author invites the single adult to celebrate the abundant life God wishes for all of us.

## Making The Most of Single Life

by Bobbie Reed (Concordia Publishing House, 1980) 111 pp. $5.95

***Overall Product Rating: 7.1***

**STRENGTHS:** Provides a good overview of goal setting and possible blockages to achieving those goals... Helpful study questions in each chapter...It would be good to use in an issue-oriented small group... Each chapter deals with an issue that singles face and offers concise statements about how to deal with each area...A good book for leaders to give singles who are feeling depressed about being single...The "for further reading" section is excellent.
**WEAKNESSES:** Tends to give the impression that the single life is one long con-

tinuum of problems...There doesn't seem to be any logical progression in the book. Each chapter is independent of the other...The weakness is also one of its greatest strengths. Much of the material I have seen before in handouts or heard in other seminars so it is not new material. However, the material she uses is good...An index of issues would have been helpful...The discussion/challenge questions are sometimes a bit weak, pat.

## Men and Marriage

by George Gilder (Pelican, 1986) 215 pp. $17.95

***Not Yet Reviewed***

**NOTES:** The author examines the tenets of marriage and family life, arguing that both are essential for men. He argues that women can survive without being married much better than can men. Gilder also discusses the breakdown of the American family and the impact this breakdown has on our society, including single adults.

## Movers and Shapers

by Harold Ivan Smith (Revell Publishing, 1988) 192 pp. $6.95

***Not Yet Reviewed***

**NOTES:** The author introduces single men and women who did not allow their lack of marital status in a marriage-centered world to keep them from seeking first the kingdom of God. Each person presented provides a trustworthy role model.

## My Husband, My Maker

by Sharon Ries (Harvest House Publishing, 1989) 172 pp. $5.95

***Overall Product Rating: 4.0***

**STRENGTHS:** The story of what Christ can do in a person's life and how He is the answer to life's problems. I really liked the question that was raised at the end of the book: "God, do you date?" and the answer, "Of course you do, let's go!" The book was worth it just for that part...Very easy and interesting reading...A good testimony of how the Holy Spirit can change a life... Shows the real life problems of being unequally yoked in marriage.
**WEAKNESSES:** Attempted to make things sound too easy, too pat...A good book for individuals but not one that I would or could use in my ministry.

## My Life:
### Joy In Being

by James Towns (Convention Press, 1981) 48 pp. $4.15

***Overall Product Rating: 6.7***

**STRENGTHS:** The activities in each chapter are very helpful...Would be especially useful to a group of new Christians (including the chapter on "Perspective" which includes a concise, simple presentation of the spiritual gifts and the chapter on "Praise" which focuses well on praising the Lord regardless of your outward circumstances)...A self-contained study with a workbook, which can be used both individually and in a group setting...The research and resourcefulness of the material makes this an excellent tool for small churches as well as large metro churches...Very reasonably priced.
**WEAKNESSES:** The cover does not do the content justice. Very dated in appearance, unattractive and unappealing...Would be boring for some groups needing more meat... Issues discussed are too sketchy.

## On My Own:
### A Study Course for Young Singles

by Tom Eisenman (David C. Cook, 1986) pp 74, plus transparencies. $19.95

***Overall Product rating: 4.2***

**STRENGTHS:** The transparencies are well done...Provides a format for group discussion ...Good study/resource material for leaders... My group found unit three to be the best—it opened up great discussion on choosing a mate and why it is best to date and marry Christians.
**WEAKNESSES:** Doesn't cover the topics very well. A leader or teacher using this material would need to do more outside research ...Overall, the material comes across simplistic...My singles thought the material was "hokey"...The author never defines what he means by "young adults" or "young singles." Is he talking about college-age? The material needs to be more clearly targeted.

## VIDEO/One is a Whole Number

by Harold Ivan Smith (Gospel Films, 1985) Two tape, four-part series, 160 min. total. (Includes Study Guide) $129.95

***Overall Product Rating: 9.1***

**STRENGTHS:** Presents Biblical truths regarding singleness, marriage, divorce and sexuality...Offers a good Biblical standard for Christian living. While the approach is toward singles, the lessons are applicable to all...This format (using some comedy skits on the video) may be particularly appealing to younger singles (20s-30s)...Well put together tape series—entertaining and instructional at the same time...An excellent resource for any singles ministry...I enjoyed this video series a great deal. I highly recommend it.

**WEAKNESSES:** In a traditional Sunday school class, it's too hard to watch the video and then still have time for discussion. To effectively use this material you need a couple hours for each session.

## Positively Single

by Harold Ivan Smith (Victor Books, 1986) 168 pp. $6.95

***Not Yet Reviewed***

**NOTES:** An overview of many issues that Christian singles grapple with. Focuses on some areas that many other books do not, such as ministry, parents, and death.

## Reflections For Women Alone

by Carole Sanderson Streeter (Victor Books, 1987) 173 pp. $6.95

***Overall Product Rating: 8.7***

**STRENGTHS:** A most positive book offering a future and a hope for women alone...A fresh perspective ...The author honestly and bluntly addresses real life issues, such as sexuality, in a realistic, healthy, Biblical way...This book is long overdue. It requires and deserves more than one reading...The author is very open in sharing personal experiences, which reflects her understanding of real life situations which women alone encounter...This volume can replace several books in my professional library.

**WEAKNESSES:** This book is not easy to use in a group...Not a "quick read." One really must take time to process the content.... Almost too much material for one book.

## Season of Singleness, A

by Ray Larson (Gospel Light, 1984) 109 pp. $2.50

***Overall Product Rating: 7.6***

**STRENGTHS:** From the perspective of a pastor who was also single for several years as an adult...The personal illustrations of the author and his wife are the strong point of this book...Theologically sound and written with a strong, positive spiritual base...Clearly depicts a variety of negative emotions people have about singleness...Encourages living in the present, giving yourself to others and trusting God...Offers some good insight about reconciliation after a broken relationship... Refreshing. Reads like a conversation ...Makes for a good book to lend out to singles.

**WEAKNESSES:** Has very few "new" insights...Does not deal realistically with long-term singleness. The perspective is perhaps a bit too simple for complicated lives...The ongoing struggle is not clearly presented...Would be helpful to have a leader's guide and/or study workbook to use in teaching situations.

## VIDEO/Second Thoughts on Being Single

(Films Incorporated, Chicago, 1984) 52 min. $198.00

***Not Yet Reviewed***

**NOTES:** The fast-paced, carefree life pursued by millions of single young Americans no longer seems so glamorous or satisfying. Nearly 16 million young adults between 25 and 40 are single, but an increasing number wish they were not. Many single women believe that the sexual revolution has placed them at a disadvantage. They complain about rudeness, being stood up and the man who disappears at the first hint of a permanent relationship. (NBC News production.)

## Single Adults in America

by George Barna (Barna Research Group, 1987) 82 pp. $28.95

***Not Yet Reviewed***

**NOTES:** In a nationwide research study, the Barna Research Group looked at the single adult population. They asked such questions as "Do they attend church?" "What is important to them in a church?" "What are their top priorities in life?" and "How many of them have committed their life to Christ?" The book contains comparisons of Christians and non-Christians, males and females, the churched and the unchurched, singles and marrieds, age income groups, etc.

## Single Experience, The

by Keith and Andrea Wells Miller (Word Publishing, 1981) 262 pp. $8.95

***Not Yet Reviewed***

**NOTES:** Singleness is not just an unending series of painful and difficult experiences. It is an opportunity for self-examination and growth. The authors share the challenges common to singles: loneliness, search for a new identity, gaining emotional independence from parents, raising children alone, developing friendships, being financially responsible, and others.

## Singles: Looking Out For Number One (Small Group Study)

by Peter Menconi, Richard Peace, Lyman Coleman (Serendipity House, 1988) 63 pp. $3.95

***Overall Product Rating: 6.6***

**STRENGTHS:** True to the "serendipity" style of Lyman Coleman, this is a very practical study guide for small groups...Good questions for helping people get into the Scripture passages...Good tool for sparking group interest, trust and support... Subjects covered are especially good for those who struggle with their singleness...Helpful for singles who need/desire to grow spiritually.

**WEAKNESSES:** Sometimes the subjects are treated as more important than the Scriptures which address them. Scriptural application seems too surface at times...The

## How Does The National Review Board Function?

1. There are over 100 reviewers on this board, representing every major denomination and region of the country.
2. All reviewers are pastors, counselors or lay leaders involved in ministry with single adults.
3. Every product is reviewed and evaluated by *at least two - and in most cases, three - members* of this National Board. (When appropriate and possible, the product is actually used in a singles ministry prior to being evaluated.)
4. Each product is reviewed and evaluated on its own merit and not as it compares to other products or resources.
5. Reviewers' ratings for each product are tabulated and averaged by the staff of *Single Adult Ministries Journal* to determine each score. ***(Products are rated from 1 to 10, with 10 being the best rating possible.)***

format tends to make people give answers that they think they are supposed to give, rather than being challenged to be honest and real...The material seems to reflect an overly conservative, fundamental perspective/ bias on some subjects...The title and cover do not project a very positive image of singles.

## Single and Feeling Good

by Harold Ivan Smith (Abingdon Press, 1987) 160 pp. $9.95

***Overall Product Rating: 7.5***

**STRENGTHS:** Thought provoking. Single adults are challenged to take advantage of their single season and live life with purpose and enthusiasm ...Outlines many of the attitudes to be found regarding singleness in our culture, uncovering reasons as to why these attitudes exist... Encourages readers to see singleness as a possibility for doing good in God's kingdom, rather than as a liability.

**WEAKNESSES:** Since the chapters are short, the material tends to be choppy, not flowing well...No one topic is dealt with in any depth...In laying the groundwork for positive singleness, the author overemphasizes the wrong reasons for getting married, giving very little help to singles concerning the right reasons for getting married.

## Single and Whole:
### Singleness is a Gift

by Rhena Taylor (InterVarsity Press, 1985) 96 pp. $3.95

***Overall Product Rating: 7.2***

**STRENGTHS:** Presents positive reasons why God might call one to the single life, and may help educate married pastors to think this through ...Presents a sound theological position...Written by a single woman who has come to grips with the reality that "singleness" can be a special calling from God...As a single person in ministry, it helped reinforce God's call on my life, so for me, encouraging.

**WEAKNESSES:** Seems too narrowly focused. The author zeros in too specifically on single women in the mission field...I found the book rather dry to read...Though the author generally covers the positive points, much of the book is old material, old ideas.

## Single Person's Identity, A

by John Fischer and Lia O'Neil (Discovery Publishing, 1973) 17 pp. 50¢

***Overall Product Rating: 6.4***

**STRENGTHS:** Deals honestly with the "second class" status of being single...Takes single adults past self-pity to the greater work that God is doing. It lifts the head of the single person and gives them cause to celebrate today...An easy to understand approach in every day language ...Not a complicated approach to faith application and can be easily grasped.

**WEAKNESSES:** As are many sermons, it does not translate well to the written media. As a listener I probably would have gained a great deal from it. As a reader it is shallow and needs more thought development to really challenge me to action...It is written in the context of a church service and assumes that we are familiar with some things that we cannot possibly know (i.e. refers to morning sermon).

## Single Voices

edited by Bruce and Immo Jeanne Yoder (Herald Press, 1982) 126 pp. $6.95

***Overall Product Rating: 6.8***

**STRENGTHS:** A collection of insightful material presented in a sensitive, personal manner by mature single adults who are celebrating their single adult lives. I feel like I have just spent several hours unwrapping precious gifts of understanding from authors who have dared to be vulnerable with me by showing their deepest emotions. At no time did I want to put the book down...As a married pastor, I feel like I had just been filled with new understanding for the single adults I am called to shepherd. I have a new appreciation for the "single heart" and look forward to sharing this book with many in my ministry...Honest opinions from people living in the trenches of single adult life and ministry...Appeals to a broad audience because of the variety of authors and perspectives...Authors present some fresh encouraging ways to address and embrace one's sexual self, professional self, spiritual self, and how each of these fits into the body of Christ...I especially enjoyed the article, "Singles and Professionalism."

**WEAKNESSES:** Sometimes it seems outdated and narrow. Issues are still vital but the treatment of them is a bit dusty...For five months this book sat on my desk. Because of the title, I expected a boring discourse. Its unfortunate that the title could not have been more reflective of the quality material in the book... Because almost all of the authors are Mennonite, some of the chapters are a little too slanted with a Mennonite perspective in terms of ministry models, practices and theology.

## Singleness:
### Biblical Advice on Staying Single

by Charles Swindoll (Multnomah Press, 1981) 24 pp. $1.95

***Overall Product Rating: 6.7***

**STRENGTHS:** The prayer at the back of this booklet is an excellent tool for helping singles "recenter" their thinking, a reminder of "who I am"...Very easy to read...Due to its brevity, it is more likely to be read...It is compassionate...Offers a positive approach and several Biblical examples of the benefits of the single life...It helps the readers change their perspective from "seeking a mate" to "contentment in life," living each moment now.

**WEAKNESSES:** The book uses several stereotypes and makes some rather broad statements... Oversimplifies the single life... Presents somewhat of a utopian view of why it's so great to be single...Doesn't deal well with some of the real issues which face single adults.

## Singleness:
### An Opportunity for Growth and Fulfillment

by Gwen and Ed Weising (Radiant, 1982) 126 pp. $2.50

***Overall Product Rating: 6.0***

**STRENGTHS:** Helpful in its attitude of forgiveness and love towards the divorced... Provides practical steps to begin a singles program...Gives a quick overview of a healthy ministry with single adults...Concise and to the point.

**WEAKNESSES:** Author's denominational affiliation (Assemblies of God) takes a high role in interpretations and perspective, making it a less useful book for others.

## Singleness
### Find Fulfillment As a Single Woman, Explore Opportunities and Overcome Prejudice

by Dorothy Payne (Westminster Press, 1983) 112 pp. $7.95

***Not Yet Reviewed***

**NOTES: Single** women are able to enjoy life, using their positive energies for their own well-being and the good of others. The author explores the freedom, self-development, and self-determination of single women.

## Singles: The New Americans

by Jacqueline Simenauer and David Carroll (Signet Books, 1982) 419 pp. $3.95 paperback

***Not Yet Reviewed***

**NOTES:** A comprehensive, nation-wide study of single adults in America. The book answers such questions as: "Have you made any lasting contacts in a singles bar?" "What effect has being single had on your career?" "How do you feel about sex on the first date?" "How do your children react to your singles scene?" "What is the main reason you start or stop dating a particular person?" "What are the most valued qualities in someone of the opposite sex?" plus many more.

## Singles: Wants Vs. Shoulds

by W. Douglas Cole (Convention Press, 1980) 50 pp. $3.75

***Overall Product Rating: 6.5***

**STRENGTHS:** A "hands-on" book of stimulating questions for singles with Biblical application...For small group study...Designed primarily for a spiritually young singles group.
**WEAKNESSES:** Has little to offer the more mature singles group.

## Singles Alive

by Jim Towns (Pelican Publishing, 1984) 143 pp. $9.95

***Overall Product Rating: 5.6***

**STRENGTHS:** The encouragement for singles to be incorporated into the church as a whole is excellent...the overview of the book at the beginning is helpful and easy to follow...This is an effort to put together an encyclopedia of Biblical truths for the single adult. It contains some great spiritual truths on abundant living for single adults... Encourages singles to "keep the faith" even during the rough times... The "Declaration of Christian Singles" at the end of the book is one of the best summaries and practical approaches I've seen...Might be a useful study book for the most serious of Christian single adults.
**WEAKNESSES:** Much too presumptuous and simplistic...The material is presented as though everything is either all good or all bad...The book states that their are no magic answers or formulas—yet the book seems to be full of "magic answers and formulas" for abundant spiritual living...I never felt like I could catch the spirit or the heartbeat of the author...If I had not been asked to review this book, I would not have finished it...The material might be of value to the serious Christian single adult. But the majority of singles I come in contact with would be confused or overwhelmed by this material ...The cover looks unprofessional.

Need More Copies of This Directory?

Save nearly $4 each when you order five or more copies. Provide copies for each member of your staff. And raise money by selling extra copies at your next event.

See Page 248

## Singles Committed and Free

by Robert L. Spray, Jr. (Convention Press, 1988) 127 pp. $3.25

***Overall Product Rating: 5.5***

**STRENGTHS:** Economical to purchase... Brings together research from a number of areas to help singles understand themselves and others ...Good insights on the subject of commitment to God, to self and to others... Very organized—gives you everything you would need to lead a group through the materials each session from goals to central truth to materials needed...Excellent definition of L.O.V.E.—Living on the Vulnerable Edge...Author said some great things about relating to non-Christians... Emphasis on how freedom follows commitment is interesting thesis.
**WEAKNESSES:** Tries to cover too much material so does not deal with key issues in depth...To use this material in a study group, people would need to read the book in advance—which is not likely to happen in my singles ministry... Seems like an out of date book in terms of layout, pictures, etc. This detracted rather than enhanced communication...Too geared to Southern Baptist mind set and style...Study guide was pretty basic

## AUDIO CASSETTES/ Singles Plus Seminar

by Ray Mossholder (Marriage Plus, 1987) 6 tapes, 8 hrs. total. $38.50

***Overall Product Rating: 6.1***

**STRENGTHS:** Excellent for helping single adults appreciate their singleness as a gift from the Lord and in guidelines for how to handle their sexuality.
**WEAKNESSES:** These tapes would have a much wider audience if they were not so charismatic in theology and references/ style...I'm not sure very many singles would listen to this many tapes. Quite lengthy.

## How Does The National Review Board Function?

1. There are over 100 reviewers on this board, representing every major denomination and region of the country.
2. All reviewers are pastors, counselors or lay leaders involved in ministry with single adults.
3. Every product is reviewed and evaluated by *at least two - and in most cases, three - members* of this National Board. (When appropriate and possible, the product is actually used in a singles ministry prior to being evaluated.)
4. Each product is reviewed and evaluated on its own merit and not as it compares to other products or resources.
5. Reviewers' ratings for each product are tabulated and averaged by the staff of *Single Adult Ministries Journal* to determine each score. ***(Products are rated from 1 to 10, with 10 being the best rating possible.)***

## Singular Devotion, A

by Harold Ivan Smith (Revell, 1990) 336 pp. $8.95

***Not Yet Reviewed***

**NOTES:** A uniquely-designed collection of daily readings that profiles notable single men and women from the past or present. Each vignette is accompanied by a relevant Bible passage and a meditative thought or prayer. You will gain encouragement from the 366 examples of devoted men and women who obeyed God though times of adversity and prosperity.

## Singularly Significant

by Veronica Bandel (Evangelical Alliance-Britain, 1987) 17 pp. (Also includes audio cassette). $6

***Overall Product Rating: 5.5***

**STRENGTHS:** Includes some interesting questions to use in a small group setting... The tape is interesting to listen to because the people are from England and seem to have a more precise attitude toward singleness as an either/or state of living... Would be especially good for a small congregation since the emphasis is to have a discussion group of single and non-single people...Easy to use...Good poems and cartoons.

**WEAKNESSES:** Outdated. The British touch feels out of touch with singles (at least to me)...Very basic, nothing new...The study guide is much stronger than the cassette... Discussion of sexuality is weak, confusing.

## VIDEO/Successful Singles

by Jerry Brandt (self-produced, 1986) 13 x 60 min. $24.95 each

***Not Yet Reviewed***

Notes: A series of 13 tapes designed for use in both small and large study groups. Fifteen minute segments on topics such as: Sex and the Single, Improving your Self-Image, Jesus, the World's Most Successful Single, How to Love and be Loved, The New Single Woman, Successful Single Parenting, Healing the Wounds of Divorce, Killing Five Giants of Fear.

## Successfully Single

by Yvonne G. Baker (Accent Books, 1985) 187 pp. $6.95

***Overall Product Rating: 6.5***

**STRENGTHS:** At last someone has taken the time to compile practical suggestions, honest experiences, fears, frustrations of the day-to-day life of living as a single woman ...Provides an overview of areas single women need to become knowledgeable about...Good as a beginning book for newly

single people.

**WEAKNESSES:** Ignores whole areas of conflict that can occur in singleness...Treats several subjects in a superficial fashion.

## Suddenly Single

by Jim Smoke (Revell Publishing, 1988) $5.95

***Not Yet Reviewed***

**Notes:** Jim Smoke answers questions such as—Now that I'm alone, how can I start life over? Where do I belong? Who will comfort me, support and encourage me? How long do I wait before I start a new relationship? It gives examples to follow and mistakes to avoid.

## Tough Love For Singles

by Dr. James Dobson (Focus on the Family, 1986) 9 pp. 35¢

***Overall Product Rating: 7.8***

**STRENGTHS:** Offers 16 practical 'relationship suggestions" for single adults who would like to be married...Also provides affirma-tion and acceptance for those who have chosen to remain single...Much of the author's advice is so "common sense" that I wonder why somebody hasn't come up with it before... Provides several specific behaviors that singles need to avoid in their relationships.

**WEAKNESSES:** Over half of this booklet is an illustration to introduce the subject. Some of the "16 Tips" are only given a one-sentence explanation. Less introduction and more indepth explanation of the content would have been an improvement.

## When It Hurts To Be Single

by Randy Petersen and Anita Palmer (David C. Cook, 1988) 96 pp. $6.95

***Overall Product Rating: 7.4***

**STRENGTHS:** The authors convey an essential understanding of singleness and its problematic aspects... Offers thoughtful, professionally sound guidelines for those working with singles concerning the various challenges and concerns that may come up in a singles ministry...The "Questions and Answers" chapter is quite helpful...The tone of the book deals with single adults as whole people.

**WEAKNESSES:** The cover title and art work convey a negative picture (does not do justice to the insights and quality writing inside)... Some of the answers and suggestions given are much too simplistic. All problems cannot be solved just by obeying God more. The emotional and psychological aspects of some of these issues needed more thorough treatment.

## Wide My World Narrow My Bed:

### Living and Loving the Single Life

by Luci Swindoll (Multnomah Press, 1982) 175 pp. $7.95

***Overall Product Rating: 8.5***

**STRENGTHS:** Gives guidelines for living and making decisions...The author encourages you to live life to its fullest. The book is believable because she has been there and knows what she is talking about... Positive approach to singleness with practical ideas on how to enjoy being single...A good balance of humor and seriousness...Ms. Swindoll, thoroughly familiar with the battles each of us face as a single, shares her wit and wisdom of growing through those battles and discovering God's grace.

**WEAKNESSES:** Completely ignores serious treatment on the issue of singles and sexuality.

# Spiritual & Personal Growth

## Most Recommended Resources in This Section

(Based on evaluations and reviews made by *SAM Journal*'s National Resource Review Board, using a 1-10 scale with 10 being the best possible score):

### 9.6 Search for Significance

by Robert S. McGee (Rapha Publishing/ Word, 1990)

### 9.5 Turning Fear To Hope:

**Women Who Have Been Hurt For Love**

by Holly Wagner Green (Zondervan, 1989)

### 9.1 Hope For the Hurting (Booklet)

by Doug Sparks (NavPress, 1990)

### 9.0 Healing Life's Hurts

by Ron Lee Davis (Word, 1986)

### 8.8 Private Pain:

**Healing for Hidden Hurts**

by Rich Wilkerson (Harvest House, 1987)

### 8.6 Encourage Me:

**Caring Words For Heavy Hearts**

by Charles R. Swindoll (Multnomah Press, 1987)

### 8.5 Hidden Rift With God, The:

**Discover the Root Cause of Many of Our Common Emotional and Psychological Problems**

by William Backus (Bethany House Publishers, 1990)

### 8.5 Love, No Strings Attached:

**Talks From the Heart about Love and Approval**

by Rich Buhler (Thomas Nelson, 1990)

### 8.5 Missing Peace, The:

**Finding Emotional Balance**

by Les Carter (Minirth-Meier/Moody Press, 1987)

### 8.3 Love For All You're Worth:

**A Quest For Personal Value and Loveability**

by Joseph L. Aldrich (Multnomah Press, 1985)

### 8.2 Pain's Hidden Purpose:

**Finding Perspective in the Midst of Suffering**

by Don Baker (Multnomah Press, 1984)

### 8.2 Telling Yourself The Truth:

**Applying the Principles of Misbelief Therapy**

by William Backus and Marie Chapian (Bethany House Publishers, 1980)

### 8.2 You Don't Have to Quit

by Anne and Ray Ortlund (Thomas Nelson, 1986)

*(For more information on each of the above resources—plus many other helpful products—find them listed in alphabetical order below.)*

## About Believing In Yourself

(Channing L. Bete Co., 1988) 15 pp. 72¢

***Overall Product Rating: 6.5***

**STRENGTHS:** Many singles, especially after divorce, have problems with self-esteem. This would be good to have available for them. Also helpful to teenagers when parents are divorced...A good view of the psychological necessity to respect self-esteem as an area of growth in our Christian life...Booklet is very easy to read and understand...The three most helpful parts of this booklet for me were the focus on God's love for us, the importance of concentrating on positive thoughts and the need to reach out to others.

**WEAKNESSES:** Too general and simplistic.

## About Christian Values

(Channing L. Bete Co., 1987) 15 pp. 72¢

***Overall Product Rating: 5.6***

**STRENGTHS:** Good Biblical references. Presentation well-devised...Probably most helpful for younger kids and teenagers rather than adults...Simple and easy to read.

**WEAKNESSES:** Not sure singles leaders would get much use from this. Adults would probably be insulted if given this book due to its adolescent look and feel.

## About Forgiveness

(Channing L. Bete Co., 1987) 15 pp. 72¢

***Overall Product Rating: 6.7***

**STRENGTHS:** Easy to read and understand ...Would be useful for someone who has been the victim of divorce and needs help...I liked the way the process for forgiveness was presented, with steps about how to forgive others...Helpful when the author said to tell God how you feel, release your anger to Him,

## How Does The National Review Board Function?

1. There are over 100 reviewers on this board, representing every major denomination and region of the country.
2. All reviewers are pastors, counselors or lay leaders involved in ministry with single adults.
3. Every product is reviewed and evaluated by *at least two - and in most cases, three - members* of this National Board. (When appropriate and possible, the product is actually used in a singles ministry prior to being evaluated.)
4. Each product is reviewed and evaluated on its own merit and not as it compares to other products or resources.
5. Reviewers' ratings for each product are tabulated and averaged by the staff of *Single Adult Ministries Journal* to determine each score. ***(Products are rated from 1 to 10, with 10 being the best rating possible.)***

that it is okay to tell God you are angry. Gives one permission to release the pent up emotions in an honest way to the Lord...Good Biblical background. Psychologically sound. **WEAKNESSES:** Seems to be directed more towards teenagers than adults.

## Addiction and Grace

by Gerald G. May, M.D. (Harper and Row, 1988) 195 pp. $16.95

***Not Yet Reviewed***

**NOTES:** People can be addicted to many things today, from various substances to ideas, from junk food to pop psychology, from alcohol to security. This book provides insights that help guide the way through our modern idolatries to a place of freedom and grace.

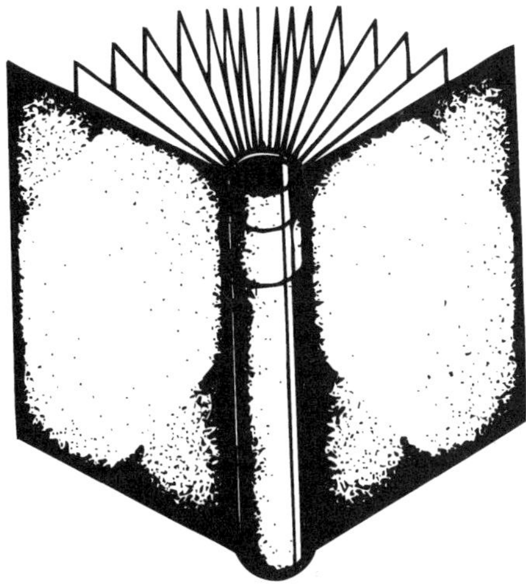

## Against The Odds

by Jill Briscoe and Judy Golz (Scripture Press, 1989) 142 pp. $6.95

***Overall Product Rating: 7.6***

**STRENGTHS:** Offers a more realistic and human look at certain Biblical characters that we sometimes idolize...An encouraging book...Simple and clear enough to easily be used with the unchurched or those with little Bible knowledge...Could work well in a support group for single mothers...The application section is great. Questions are thought provoking and challenging. **WEAKNESSES:** Lack of focus. Each chapter seems disconnected from the other chapters and the organizational structure is unclear. The Hagar/Ishmael story should have provided the unity which the book lacks... With two authors writing, it is sometimes difficult to distinguish who's writing what.

## Baby Boom Believers

by Mike Bellah (Tyndale House, 1988) 151 pp. $5.95

***Not Yet Reviewed***

**NOTES:** Looks at why baby boomers expect too much and what the Bible and its realistic view of the world has to say to an over-expecting generation.

## Beyond Forgiveness

by Don Baker (Multnomah Press, 1989) 102 pp. $8.95

***Overall Product Rating: 6.5***

**STRENGTHS:** Good theological treatment on the subject of church discipline, providing examples of how to treat and deal with a person in sin...Some of the Biblical approaches, thought processes and actions are applicable to singles ministry...Illustrates a success story of church discipline, something that seems to be rare. It contains a great example...It was refreshing to see the restoration process at work...Written primarily for church leaders. **WEAKNESSES:** In the author's primary example, the guilty party seemed to respond in an idealistic way, which in most cases, is probably not the way it would work out... Only addresses one story of someone who was repentant and had a submissive, obedient heart...a story-book ending. But not com-pletely realistic given all the issues that could have surfaced: What if church demanded he leave? What if wife divorced him? Too much 20-20 hindsight.

## Blessing, The

by Gary Smalley and John Treat (Thomas Nelson, 1986) 238 pp. $14.95

***Overall Product Rating: 7.5***

**STRENGTHS:** Offers a Biblical basis for self-esteem theology...Shows the importance of the spiritual and emotional legacy we receive from our parents and pass down to our children...A clear and simple evaluation of what many single adults sense in their lives —a lack of the blessing that affirms their worth...Offers suggestions and application for helping address and heal this inner pain and need...The book looks at the Biblical root cause of low self-esteem and helps us move on to bless others...I highly recommend this book to other single adult pastors/leaders. **WEAKNESSES:** It needs more study/ discussion questions for small groups...The dual authorship gets confusing at times...The book is not written specifically for singles so requires adaptation if used in a singles ministry.

## VIDEO/Blessings Out of Brokenness

(World Wide Pictures, 1990) 50 min. $5.95

***Not Yet Reviewed***

**Notes:** Four-part film series featuring Joni Eareckson Tada that offers hope and comfort to those who have personally experienced hurts. Topics include: Why the brokenness? Where are the blessings? Mending things. Healing and heaven.

## Broken and Mended Again

by Joy Loy (Harbour House, 1986) 159 pp. $7.95

***Not Yet Reviewed***

**NOTES:** The emotional story of a woman abused and battered by the man she loved, and how she struggled for the answers to the many questions she faced.

## Building a Positive Self-Image:

### A 31-Day Experiment

by Dick Purnell (Here's Life Publishers, 1990) 61 pp. $3.95

***Overall Product Rating: 6.1***

**STRENGTHS:** Author explains how to use the product well...Easy to read and do...Helps the individual increase their daily study of the Word, evaluate self and look beyond self to the Creator, seeing what God has said about us...The person willing to invest the time in this study will gain a better picture of how valuable he or she is in God's eyes. **WEAKNESSES:** After this 31-day experi-ment, the individual will have a more knowledgeable grasp of the Bible and their spiritual development may be strengthened, but I'm not sure it necessarily will help change one's self-image that much. It's a little simplistic in that regard...May be difficult for many to find another person to do this study with (as the author suggests).

## Coming Down the Mountain:

### How to Turn Your Retreat into Everyday Living

by Thomas Hart (Paulist Press, 1988) 101 pp. $3.95

***Not Yet Reviewed***

**NOTES:** You have just finished a retreat. You feel close to God and are eager to take your new energy and fresh Christian perspective out into the world and live the kind of life you deeply want to live. This book is written to help you do that. It is a follow-up to your retreat, designed to keep that experience alive and influential in your life. Not only does it look deepening your relationship with God but offers ideas for dealing with some of the troublesome areas of life such as loneliness, low self-esteem, difficult relationships, sexuality, grief and painful memories.

## Crises And Growth:
### Making the Most of Hard Times
by Anita L. Spencer (Paulist Press, 1989) 149 pp. $7.95

***Not Yet Reviewed***

**NOTES:** Takes you step-by-step through your crises, providing a map to positive growth that will turn necessary losses and hard times into new energy and a happier life-style.

## Disappointment With God:
### Three Questions No One Asks
by Philip Yancey (Zondervan, 1988) 260 pp. $14.95

***Not Yet Reviewed***

**NOTES:** Spiritual armor to deal with everything from personal losses to ongoing failures. Tackles some of the most critical questions of the Christian walk. It confronts the crises of faith that can shake the roots of any believer's spiritual life. And it brings to life the answers that help make a shattered faith whole again.

## Encourage Me:
### Caring Words For Heavy Hearts
by Charles R. Swindoll (Multnomah Press, 1987) 86 pp. $5.95

***Overall Product Rating: 8.6***

**STRENGTHS:** Meaningful encouragement for the discouraged...Concise, easy-to-read chapters which can be utilized several ways and in different kinds of groups...Good for devotional readings...Straight talk about the Christian's responsibility to encourage others...Insight, wisdom gained from experience.

**WEAKNESSES:** Much of this material is contained in Swindoll's other devotional books so there wasn't much new writing.

## VIDEO/Face to Face
by InterVarsity Christian Fellowship of the U.S.A. (InterVarsity Video, 1990) 30 min. $24.95

***Not Yet Reviewed***

**NOTES:** Discusses barriers that hinder racial reconciliation in the church, the community and organizations.

## For All Who Have Been Forsaken
by S. D. Gaede (Zondervan, 1989) 160 pp. $12.95

***Overall Product Rating: 6.5***

**STRENGTHS:** This is a thorough, simple study of the issues that create a sense of forsakenness. Especially helpful are the chapters on knowledge, independence and responsibility...End notes are helpful and informative...Good interaction of Scripture with the subject matter...Appeals strongly to the intellect...Several good illustrated stories are interspersed throughout the script. ..This author personalizes the subject of grief/loss and presents it in very readable form... Includes several good case studies.

**WEAKNESSES:** A bit too cognitive for most readers. Not the easiest to read. It fails to draw on the reader's imagination for participation...Each chapter could use clear applications, summary and affirmation exercises...It would have been more helpful to have the endnotes as footnotes because the author uses these to illustrate or defend his statements. Since they are related immediately to the text, it would have been more user-friendly to have them on the same page...The book could be better organized (by chapter definitions) and focus more fully on a single topic rather than the entire grief, loss, rejection, forsakenness arena.

## Freedom Factor, The:
### Overcoming the Barriers to Being Yourself
by R. Scott Walker (Harper & Row, 1989) 119 pp. $13.95

***Overall Product Rating: 7.5***

**STRENGTHS:** Author speaks openly and honestly about some of his struggles in life...Tackles some basic core issues that all of us face...Good use of illustration...Sound theologically and psychologically...Fresh approach...Easy to use as a study...Provides good insight into some of the situations encountered in single adult ministry...In an age of the Yuppie, the chapter on "The Tyranny of Possessions" is very helpful, eye-opening.

**WEAKNESSES:** Covers too many topics too briefly...May be a little too technical for lay people...Although there is an excellent chapter on being driven towards God, at times it seems the author relies more on psychological techniques than on Biblical counsel.

## Freeing Your Mind from Memories That Bind
by Fred and Florence Littauer (Here's Life Publishers, 1988) 302 pp. $8.95

***Overall Product Rating: 6.8***

**STRENGTHS:** Offers great insight for those who counsel people who have experienced abuse in their life and are holding onto related guilt feelings...Opens your eyes to the magnitude of the problem of abuse in the children of this country and the damaging effects this has on their relationships as adults...Will help me as a pastor to get to the root of people's problems rather than deal with just surface stuff, helping them identify the real source and work through it...Good insight into personality types...Good Bible study guide...Helpful restoration and prayer

## How Does The National Review Board Function?
1. There are over 100 reviewers on this board, representing every major denomination and region of the country.
2. All reviewers are pastors, counselors or lay leaders involved in ministry with single adults.
3. Every product is reviewed and evaluated by *at least two - and in most cases, three - members* of this National Board. (When appropriate and possible, the product is actually used in a singles ministry prior to being evaluated.)
4. Each product is reviewed and evaluated on its own merit and not as it compares to other products or resources.
5. Reviewers' ratings for each product are tabulated and averaged by the staff of *Single Adult Ministries Journal* to determine each score. ***(Products are rated from 1 to 10, with 10 being the best rating possible.)***

chapter...I loaned this book to a lady who was having marital problems because of experiences in her childhood and it was most helpful to her.
**WEAKNESSES:** I disagreed with the assumptions at the beginning of this book that all personalities are developed by abuse of some type in our childhood. I don't feel everyone is abused just because they are shy or outgoing, etc. Good experiences also develop our lives...Deals only with past sexual abuse overlooking the many other types of abuse...Repeatedly the authors state that one in four women were abused in childhood without ever giving the source. Needs more solid research and footnoting...At times, I felt the authors were being overly descriptive of sexual abuse cases simply for shock value... They appear to link all adult problems back to sexual abuse...If one had been sexually abused, they would need more than this book to help them along in their healing.

## From Rejection To Acceptance

by Barbara Taylor (Broadman Press, 1987) 190 pp. $9.95

***Overall Product Rating: 5.2***

**STRENGTHS:** Very well laid out...I appreciated her material on "tree of bondage" and the dilemma of "performance based acceptance".
**WEAKNESSES:** Overkill with personal opinions...A self-indulged fantasy of childhood rejection...Would not consider this book of real value in my singles ministry.

## VIDEO/Getting Your Act Together

hosted by Ivan Emke (Mennonite Board of Missions, 1989) A Four-part Series. Each part is 15 min. $60.00

***Not Yet Reviewed***

**NOTES:** Part I, "Preparing for God's Calling," emphasizes the need to recognize one's giftedness and to use those gifts in building God's kingdom. Part II, "Steps Toward Intimacy," emphasizes the need for experiencing intimacy first with God and then with others though a variety of caring relationships. Part III, "Cooperative Living for Singles" with Keith Graber Miller, offers four steps for young Christian singles to follow as they establish supportive community structures for themselves. Part II, "Living Unselfishly in a Selfish World" with Tom Sine, challenges young Christian singles to look for creative ways of being in mission in light of God's purposes for this world.

## VIDEO/God is Building a City

produced by 2100 Productions (InterVarsity Video, 1989) 14 min. $29.95

***Not Yet Reviewed***

**NOTES:** Reveals how the world is becoming less a world of independent countries and more a world of interconnected, international, multi-cultural cities. Helps develop world Christians.

## God is Not Fair: Coming to Terms with Life's Raw Deals

by Joel A. Freeman (Here's Life Publishers, 1987) 144 pp. $5.95

***Overall Product Rating: 6.0***

**STRENGTHS:** Excellent presentation of the relationship between man, suffering and God...Helpful discussion questions at the end of each chapter...Positive, realistic, applicable use of God's Word...A good book for people who feel they are getting a raw deal... Illustrations are personal and real...Could be a valuable tool for someone who is not necessarily "not into the Bible" because of the way the author entertwines Scripture with his main points.
**WEAKNESSES:** I am probably biased by having read *Disappointment With God* by Philip Yancey, as I find his treatment of this subject so far superior. This book is not satisfactory to me or to the situations I deal with...I do not hear arrogance (as this author suggests) from those who say God is not fair. I hear sadness and disappointment. People feel let down... No book, no matter how good, answers all our questions about why God sometimes seems to not be fair in this earthly life....No specific examples or illustrations that could be used in a singles ministry.

## God I've Got A Problem

by Ben Ferguson (Regal Press, 1987) 166 pp. $6.95

***Not Yet Reviewed***

**NOTES:** Christians are not immune from problems. We all experience loneliness, guilt, fear and much more. The author explores the principles God has given in His Word to help us handle the pressures and problems of everyday living.

## Gospel and the American Dream, The

by Bruce L. Shelley (Multnomah Press, 1989) 187 pp. $8.95

***Overall Product Rating: 7.1***

**STRENGTHS:** For those who live or work in American culture there's much in this book to chew on...Assists in one's understanding and analysis of this society and the development of workable and effective ministry... Helps define the cultural values in which the single under 35 has been indoctrinated and points to some of the issues that affect singles ministry as we bring our cultural thinking into the church. It points the singles ministry leader to possible teaching and program ideas to counter today's cultural influence...The major changes in American culture are helpfully described so that one is able to identify the morals and value conflicts at issue...Especially worthy of thought and discussion are the comments on Christian living responsibly in a pluralistic society and their attempts at political engagement. Also useful is the section on the uniqueness of the "Christian mind."
**WEAKNESSES:** The author is surveying society during a time (prior to the present) when Christianity had a firmer hold on personal and public life. He seems to see the present changes as evidence that Christianity is losing its grip or rightful place in society. Many of us lament the breakdowns in moral behavior and the great "self-absorption" of the present. But not all of us would see it as Christianity's call to keep society under control. We are to be salt, light, leaven, not a controlling power... Would be difficult to use as a tool for singles in any direct way although it might be useable in small group talk-it-overs etc. for thoughtful people...A bit conservative in parts but not so much so that it skews his observations.

## Healing for Damaged Emotions

by David Seamands (Victor Books, 1981) 144 pp. $5.95

***Not Yet Reviewed***

**Notes:** For those who are hurting emotionally. Seamands' sensitive insight into today's emotional stresses is especially helpful in spiritual growth and understanding. For professionals and lay people, with a leader's guide.

## Healing Life's Hurts

by Ron Lee Davis (Word, 1986) 186 pp. $8.99

***Overall Product Rating: 9.0***

**STRENGTHS:** Offers practical life applications and solutions to many of the hurts that we all experience (i.e. discouragement, conflict, mistreatment, illness, loss, loneliness, failure, inferiority, doubt and fear)... Does a great job of dealing with real people with real hurts in a real world... Provides leaders with excellent teaching material ...Shows that going through difficult life situations can be a definite part of our spiritual growth...Well-written... Reminds us that with God's help there can truly be light at end of every dark tunnel...Solid application from God's Word...A good picture of God's grace at work in our lives...I highly recommend this book. It is one of the best I've read in a long time.

**WEAKNESSES:** The final chapter is a letdown compared to the rest of the book.... Sometimes seems to ramble, but overall, it is a good, easy-to-read, fast-moving book.

## VIDEO/Heart of the Fighter, The

by Landon Saunders (Heartbeat, 1983) 360 min. $199.00

***Not Yet Reviewed***

**NOTES:** Six video tape, 12-part series designed to create and deepen "the heart of the fighter" in everyone by focusing on the courage to go forward into a meaningful, joyous life making creative use of disappointments and failures, whether of a person's own making or caused by roadblocks set up by others.

## Hidden Rift With God, The: Discover the Root Cause of Many of Our Common Emotional and Psychological Problems

by William Backus (Bethany House Publishers, 1990) 191 pp. $6.95

***Overall Product Rating: 8.5***

**STRENGTHS:** A great help to those who may hold inner bitterness, anger towards God due to loss...Will help single parents identify possible anger in their children and how to help them work through it...Allows every Christian to look within and discover God's mercy, love, even when we express bitterness or anger...A tool for counseling ...Helps people be honest in their "self-talk."

**WEAKNESSES:** Sometimes weak on the "how-to's."

## VIDEO/Holy Sweat

by Tim Hansel (Word, 1987) 120 min. $66.99

***Not Yet Reviewed***

**NOTES:** A three-session course which outlines 10 keys for becoming a peak performer in the kingdom of God by transforming Christianity from a cerebral commitment to a "hands and feet" commitment. Complete with the book on which the series is based and with a study guide.

## Hope For the Hurting

by Doug Sparks (NavPress, 1990) 24 pp. $1.95

***Overall Product Rating: 9.1***

**STRENGTHS:** This author does not write from an ivory tower. He honestly deals with the wide range of emotions that a person is confronted with when faced with a tragedy and how he tried to respond to them from a Biblical perspective...Obviously, this man's passion was to know God better through this crisis. He reminds us of where our source of strength and hope rest when facing life's dilemmas...Sound theological basis and Biblical support...Clear outline, well organized, practical personal illustrations ...Easy to understand...Good use of illustrations and Scripture...Excellent reflection questions.

**WEAKNESSES:** I wish he would have expanded on his own thoughts as well as his family's, telling us how he wrestled with God's Word when it was the last thing he wanted to hear or practice.

## How to Deal with Anger

by Larry Crabb (NavPress, 1989) 22 pp. $1.95

***Not Yet Reviewed***

**NOTES:** This booklet examines Biblical teaching on anger. It helps an individual to identify what is causing the anger. Lastly, it gives four specific ways to deal with anger.

## How to Find Your Church

by George Barna (World Wide Publications, 1989) 153 pp. $7.95

***Not Yet Reviewed***

**NOTES:** Nearly 90 million adult Americans have gone looking for a new church some time during their life. This book prepares readers, not just for another trip to the church supermarket, but for finding a church which will meet their needs and lead them into a rich experience of ministry.

## How Does The National Review Board Function?

1. There are over 100 reviewers on this board, representing every major denomination and region of the country.
2. All reviewers are pastors, counselors or lay leaders involved in ministry with single adults.
3. Every product is reviewed and evaluated by *at least two - and in most cases, three - members* of this National Board. (When appropriate and possible, the product is actually used in a singles ministry prior to being evaluated.)
4. Each product is reviewed and evaluated on its own merit and not as it compares to other products or resources.
5. Reviewers' ratings for each product are tabulated and averaged by the staff of *Single Adult Ministries Journal* to determine each score.
***(Products are rated from 1 to 10, with 10 being the best rating possible.)***

## How to Handle Adversity

by Charles Stanley (Thomas Nelson, 1989) 191 pp. $14.95

***Not Yet Reviewed***

**NOTES:** Biblical answers are offered for understanding why God lets us suffer and why God sometimes seems silent when we need Him the most. This book suggests how to glorify God and grow spiritually through pain.

## How to Know God's Will

by Charles Stanley (NavPress, 1989) 21 pp. $1.95

***Overall Product Rating: 6.1***

**STRENGTHS:** The question "How do I know God's will?" is so frequent that it's worthwhile to have a handy pamphlet such as this to give to your singles...Simple and clear, yet deep enough to cause singles to think through the process of listening to God's voice. A helpful summary and study guide adds to the booklet's usefulness...Fairly clear steps of the process involved for discerning God's will when faced with a decision.
**WEAKNESSES:** Nothing new...Simplistic ...There are more helpful books on the subject.

## I Know You're Hurting:
### God's Answer for Emotional Pain

by Lauren Stratford (Harvest House Publishing, 1989) 253 pp. $6.95

***Overall Product Rating: 6.1***

**STRENGTHS:** A very real, autobiographical book dealing openly and honestly with issues of pain...The book will make you cry and reflect...Author gives a strong testimony to the healing presence of Christ...I found myself drawn into the book as I read it...The exercises at the end are excellent...Although not specifically addressed for single adults, the book is geared for all who experience suffering as we live our lives in a sin-filled world...The author's greatest contribution in this book is her personal sharing of how she grew through the pain...I have read better written books on suffering, but she comes across as being sincerely interested in the reader's pain.
**WEAKNESSES:** The biggest problem is the lack of transition from pain to healing. She expressed the difficulties but did not really deal with the steps of the transition, which leads to an over-simplistic attitude that if only one believes then everything will work out okay...After reading *Pain's Hidden Purpose* I found this book lacking depth...Her examples were a bit mundane...Too many worn out expressions and old cliches were used...The author repeats herself at times.

## I'm Tired of Waiting

by Elisa Morgan (Victor Books, 1989) 154 pp. $6.95

***Overall Product Rating: 7.0***

**STRENGTHS:** Very practical Christian advice that speaks to those of us who have trouble being patient...Each chapter can stand by itself for a particular discussion or presentation...Well-written with good use of quotes from other sources, Biblical and other...Author encourages single adults to begin living rather than waiting for Mr. or Ms. Right...Deals with real issues, showing that waiting can be a time of growth... Describes the many reasons God has us wait...Outlines the glory God would receive if we would want for His best.
**WEAKNESSES:** At times I felt the book was written for a child...The chapter on prayer is weak. A serious subject is treated flippantly. The concept that we don't get what we want is okay but that doesn't mean God is withholding something or that "it's returned to sender"...Sometimes serious subjects are made trivial.

## In God's Waiting Room:
### Learning Through Suffering

by Lehman Straus (Moody Press, 1985) 103 pp. $5.95

***Overall Product Rating: 5.0***

**STRENGTHS:** Good use of Scriptural accounts to parallel situations which may arise in life, illustrating that God does indeed have all things in control, and sometimes it takes instances (such as a serious illness) for His love, caring and will to be made known... Good for those who are experiencing illness (or other tragedy/hardship) in their lives and/or families, who may be asking God "why?"...The author seems to have experienced what he is writing about.
**WEAKNESSES:** Seems to be more like a personal diary (low-key and slow-moving) than a book for the average adult...Written more for marrieds and the elderly than for the single adult... The writing style is not highly appealing to me...The suffering because of following Christ and the suffering for being a frail human being are quite different but seem to be blurred in this book.

## Inside Out

by Larry Crabb (NavPress, 1988) 223 pp. $12.95; Discussion Guide, $5.95

***Not Yet Reviewed***

**NOTES:** Are you becoming more like Christ or just acting that way? If you've got habits, weaknesses or personal problems you can't quite shake, don't act as it they didn't exist. This book helps you learn how to tell the difference between symptoms and root causes, and how to confront the things which have troubled you for years.

## Is It Real When It Doesn't Work?:
### When Formula Christianity Fails You

by Doug Murren and Barb Shurin (Thomas Nelson, 1990) 252 pp. $14.95

***Not Yet Reviewed***

**NOTES:** We think that if we have enough faith, or pray according to this formula, or spend enough time in confession of sin, or fast for so many days, or memorize this amount of Scripture, God will solve all our problems. What happens when He doesn't solve the problems? Is Christianity real when life isn't trouble free? This book says the answer is "Yes!"...helping you discover the basics of real faith.

**Advertise Your Upcoming Conferences and Retreats. FREE!**

Each issue of SAM Journal lists upcoming singles and leadership conferences free of charge (as room allows). Send the date and details of your next event 4 - 5 months in advance. Let SAM help you spread the word. Send to SAM Journal, P.O. Box 60430, Colorado Springs, CO 80960-0430

## Lies We Believe, The

by Dr. Chris Thurman (Thomas Nelson, 1989) 201 pp. $14.95

***Overall Product Rating: 7.5***

**STRENGTHS:** Deals with the harsh realities that life is neither fair nor easy, but we don't need to be victims of circumstances. We have control over our own actions and reactions ...Good emphasis on the work it takes to change and that truth stands the test of time, lies don't...Clear, practical advice...A needed message for people in churches... Useful study guide.

**WEAKNESSES:** The author rambles. You bog down in reading...Begins a process that it may take a counselor to sort out...Stresses cognitive restructuring therapy which has its limits...Some of the answers offered seemed simplistic.

## Lifestyles: Going in Style

by P. Menconi, R. Peace, L. Coleman (NavPress, 1988) 62 pp. $4.95

***Overall Product Rating: 8.0***

**STRENGTHS:** This booklet is one of a series which would prove very beneficial for small-group Bible studies for career-aged people, especially those in their 20s to early 40s...Subject material is relevant to issues of today...Of particular value are the Bible study Scriptures selected for each chapter, using a passage rather than jumping around from verse to verse...Leading discussion is normally difficult for most lay leaders. But this material provides very good ideas to promote interaction. Although its primary emphasis is group dynamics, the lessons also show a strong concern for getting participants to interact with the Bible...Application is relevant to today without violating the context of the Scriptures used in each lesson...Excellent format and reference notes.

**WEAKNESSES:** Book doesn't provide much information to the leaders, especially if you are a new leader..."Gospel study" section is too brief...Good material but does not deal specifically with single adult issues.

**Do You Like to Read?**

If you'd like to serve on SAM's National Resource Review, let us know.

*See Page 249*

## Lord, Heal My Hurts

by Kay Arthur (Multnomah Press, 1988) 280 pp. $8.95

***Overall Product Rating: 6.0***

**STRENGTHS:** Presents a well-organized, systematic guide to help someone through a period of hurt...Thorough list of suggested discussion questions at end of book, centering on each chapter...A very thorough Bible study...Good for personal use... Theologically sound.

**WEAKNESSES:** More useful for women than men...I felt worn down after reading through this book, even without doing all the exercises...The book seems best suited for individual study, but I think it would be a mistake to try to work through deep wounds and hurts without some group support. But if used with a group, the leader would need to be fairly skilled in helping to make this book real by going beyond what the author has included.

## Lord, If I Ever Needed You It's Now

by Creath Davis (Baker Book House, 1981) 137 pp. $5.95

***Overall Product Rating: 7.1***

**STRENGTHS:** Good useable Bible study book. Particularly easy to use in a lay-lead support group...Good resource for teaching or sermons...It endorses both God's willingness and ability to do the supernatural along with His sovereign right to work all things together for good...The questions at the end of the book can be used effectively to get people thinking, sharing and caring.

## Love, Acceptance and Forgiveness

by Jerry Cook with Stanley C. Baldwin (Regal Books, 1979) 128 pp. $6.95

***Not Yet Reviewed***

**NOTES:** Outlines how to apply Biblical principles to showing love, acceptance and forgiveness to non-Christians.

## Love For All You're Worth: A Quest For Personal Value and Loveability

by Joseph L. Aldrich (Multnomah Press, 1985) 140 pp. $6.95

***Overall Product Rating: 8.3***

**STRENGTHS:** The opening chapters on personal value and conscience are excellent. I particularly liked the tie-in to Peter on the issue of conscience...I found the author's stages of love to be an excellent summary... Accurate examination and evaluation of individual need to be loved, find self-worth and stay connected with God...Laid out very well with practical illustrations.

**WEAKNESSES:** Was not a very graphically appealing book...Some of the material is rehash.

## Love, No Strings Attached: Talks from the Heart About Love and Approval

by Rich Buhler (Thomas Nelson, 1990) 188 pp. $8.95

***Overall Product Rating: 8.5***

**STRENGTHS:** Well-written, easy to understand...Presents helpful methods of showing love and is able to show the pitfalls of confusing love with approval...Opens one's eyes to why people act the way the do. Once you understand the reasons behind their actions, it's easier to help them.

**WEAKNESSES:** Would like to have seen more Biblical support...Most of the examples deal with marriage, making it less applicable for the single adult (although still useable).

## How Does The National Review Board Function?

1. There are over 100 reviewers on this board, representing every major denomination and region of the country.
2. All reviewers are pastors, counselors or lay leaders involved in ministry with single adults.
3. Every product is reviewed and evaluated by *at least two - and in most cases, three - members* of this National Board. (When appropriate and possible, the product is actually used in a singles ministry prior to being evaluated.)
4. Each product is reviewed and evaluated on its own merit and not as it compares to other products or resources.
5. Reviewers' ratings for each product are tabulated and averaged by the staff of *Single Adult Ministries Journal* to determine each score. ***(Products are rated from 1 to 10, with 10 being the best rating possible.)***

## Loving Confrontation:
### How One Church Discovered the Biblical Principles of Speaking the Truth in Love

by Beverly Caruso (Bethany House Publishers, 1988) 159 pp. $5.95

***Not Yet Reviewed***

**NOTES:** With 25 years of pastoral experience, the author and her husband have learned Biblical and practical principles that transformed their individual lives, their marriage and their church. This book looks at how they discovered God at work in the area of speaking the truth in love.

## Measuring Up:
### Overcoming Rejection and Feelings of Inadequacy

by Dr. Kevin Leman (Revell, 1988) 256 pp. $14.95

***Overall Product Rating: 6.1***

**STRENGTHS:** A straight forward assessment of many of the issues single adults face, i.e. rejection, perfectionism, poor self-esteem, fear of failure, etc. Offers insights, exercises and advice on how people can grow and develop...The author is primarily cognitive in his approach to change. But he gives suggestions on how to undo habits that sabotage our lives and relationships...Advice on how to raise children so that they don't become defeated perfectionists...Valuable recommendations on how to overcome rejection and feelings of inadequacy.

**WEAKNESSES:** The cognitive approach is not the only vehicle for help, as the author implies...The areas that deal with how to overcome feelings of rejection and inadequacy sometimes seem to only be a gloss over. The book would have been much better if it dealt more with these issues and on a deeper level.

## Missing Peace, The:
### Finding Emotional Balance

by Les Carter (Minirth-Meier/Moody Press, 1987) 159 pp. $12.95

***Overall Product Rating: 8.5***

**STRENGTHS:** Good summary of Biblical origin of emotional struggles that show all mankind are prone to such struggles as pride, fear, loneliness, anger, inferiority...a reminder that inner peace is not automatic ...Deals with the emotional garbage individuals carry, how to find the underlying causes, and how to change...Provides solid Biblical foundation...Good integration of theology and psychology...Excellent chapter on communication skills that is useful for trained counselors as well as individuals... Easy to read, comprehend and apply...This may be the best book I've read on emotional peace and how it effects our life.

**WEAKNESSES:** Although it is easy to read for the most part, the author sometimes uses terminology and jargon that may be hard for some lay leaders to grasp...Some people will have trouble with the author's definition of sin.

## No Fear of Trying:
### Turn Your "I've Always Wanted To" Wishes into Realities

by Harold Ivan Smith (Thomas Nelson, 1988) 192 pp. $13.95

***Overall Product Rating: 8.0***

**STRENGTHS:** Easy reading...A motivational, emotional book rather than a factual, analytical one. But we all need a little encouragement and cheerleading! From that perspective, it is excellent...Especially rich source of illustrative/anecdotal real life material.

**WEAKNESSES:** Disappointed by the lack of Biblical/theological insight...Does not help the reader with any guided analysis or the setting of personal goals...Too much like current pop psychology books...This author has written on many other issues with much more credibility and effectiveness.

## One Anothering

by Simon Schrock (Harbour House, 1986) 144 pp. $7.95

***Not Yet Reviewed***

**NOTES:** A modern-day Mennonite writes a gentle reminder to Christians caught up in the competitive challenges of today's society. It's time for a return to a simple, practical life-style—getting along—helping each other! God created us as social beings. Christians' early survival was dependent on one another. That day has come again.

## VIDEO/Out of the Saltshaker and into the World:
### Evangelism as a Way of Life

by Rebecca Manley Pippert (InterVarsity Video, 1984) 160 min. $59.95

***Not Yet Reviewed***

**NOTES:** Four-part series encourages Christians to discover styles of personal evangelism suited to their own personalities and gifts. Part I looks at "Evangelism as a Way of Life;" Part II, "Getting the Story Straight;" Part III, "Learning to Love;" and Part IV, "Sharing the Message." Complete with discussion guide.

## Overcoming Anxiety

by Archibald D. Hart (Word, Inc., 1989) 224 pp. $14.99

***Not Yet Reviewed***

**NOTES:** Out-of-control anxiety can burden you with excessive fears, neurotic behaviors, sleeplessness, panic or physical illness. Excessive anxiety can be controlled and prevented. The author offers guidance to help you recognize if you have an anxiety problem, break the anxiety-depression cycle and work towards an anxiety resistant life-style.

## Pain and Pretending:
### You Can Be Set Free From the Hurts of the Past

by Rich Buhler (Thomas Nelson, 1988) 222 pp. $12.95

***Overall Product Rating: 8.0***

**STRENGTHS:** Helps people recognize the

root problem beneath the surface...Addresses severe cases of trauma in childhood (i.e. molestation, incest, abuse) but can be applied to anyone whose childhood affected them in a negative way...Integrates how this discovery and healing fits in with the Christian walk...Will help leaders help their people to be in touch with themselves...Helps people resolve their past...Challenges those of us who provide counseling not to be afraid to ask some of the hard questions.
**WEAKNESSES:** Not designed to be used as a leaders guide. More for individual use, one-on-one...Doesn't cover less traumatic experiences that affect us in the same way. For those who have not been a victim of molestation or abuse it may seem unusual to have a whole book written on the subject. If people do not know the number of the cases of these problems in the world they may think the book is over-exaggerated...There seemed to be an overabundance of case histories in the book. This is not necessarily bad, but I felt that fewer examples could have been given, allowing more time for "how to deal" with the various problems...Could have had more depth in its offering of solutions. I felt I was reading a pastor's diary and not getting enough of the "how to's."

## Pain's Hidden Purpose:
### Finding Perspective in the Midst of Suffering

by Don Baker (Multnomah Press, 1984) 104 pp. $5.95

***Overall Product Rating: 8.2***

**STRENGTHS:** A helpful resource for singles experiencing loss or painful life experiences ...Moves the reader from the self-centered position of wanting to know "why am I hurting" to who is the God I worship, i.e., His character...A wonderful realization/reminder that the battle was not between Satan and Job but between Satan and God...Several chapters are especially thought provoking: Chapter 11 on how Satan's goal was to discredit God, the meaning of curse; Chapter 13 explaining three reasons Job's friends' theology was wrong; Chapter 15 describing Job's sin of presumption; and Chapter 16 explaining how when God appears man changes...Easy to read and understand, written in today's language...A reminder that God is faithful even in the midst of our pain and trials.
**WEAKNESSES:** To benefit fully, one would need to have read the book of Job or to be quite familiar with it.

# AUDIO CASSETTES/

## Personal Renewal:
### Slowing Down in a Hurry Up World

by Terry Hershey (Christian Focus, Inc., 1988) 4 x 60 min. $25.95

***Not Yet Reviewed***

**NOTES:** Four-tape audio series on discovering what it means to find personal renewal in the midst of a busy world. Tape 1 outlines "Obstacles to Personal Renewal;" Tape 2, "Who Owns Me?"; Tape 3, "Sabbath: Learning How to Stop;" and Tape 4, "The Journey Toward Renewal."

## Power of Unconditional Love, The

by Ken Keyes, Jr. (Love Line Books, 1990) 214 pp. $7.95

***Overall Product Rating: 5.0***

**STRENGTHS:** Well-researched, adding credibility...The basic premise is that we are in control and responsible for our emotions ...Addresses relationships with marriage partners (but found application for any type of relationship). In fact, I learned something new and helpful regarding my relationship with my mom...Could help single adults move toward real commitment and discipline in their own personal lives... Emphasizes how it takes a lot of communication, caring and commitment to make any relationship work.
**WEAKNESSES:** After reading the book, I'm unsure whether he's New Age or Christian. He seems to mix theology and philosophy, never quite coming clean as to the source of the unconditional love...I find as questionable his solution on how to control or change our emotions...Seems to have an extremely lax attitude about divorce.

## Private Pain:
### Healing for Hidden Hurts

by Rich Wilkerson (Harvest House, 1987) 169 pp. $5.95

***Overall Product Rating: 8.8***

**STRENGTHS:** A wonderful restatement of the timeless basics of God's love, patience, commitment and willingness to not only restore broken people, but to allow the breaking process so that He can fill them with His power and glory...Combines stories from the Bible, church history and his own travels to paint a compassionate picture of "good" people as well as regular people who are suffering. The simple message of the book points people to Jesus, regardless of the cause, giving hope and courage to all who can't talk about their pain, shame or struggle...Easy to read with great illustrations to get points across...Excellent scriptural support...This book is superb reading for almost every person I can think of.

**Fact:**

The median income of unmarried men is less than that of married men but not much less. Here is the break-down among full-time workers, as of 1986:

Never-married......$17,300
Divorced men.........23,200
Widowed men........23,700
Married men..........28,400

*U.S. Census Bureau*

## How Does The National Review Board Function?

1. There are over 100 reviewers on this board, representing every major denomination and region of the country.
2. All reviewers are pastors, counselors or lay leaders involved in ministry with single adults.
3. Every product is reviewed and evaluated by *at least two - and in most cases, three - members* of this National Board. (When appropriate and possible, the product is actually used in a singles ministry prior to being evaluated.)
4. Each product is reviewed and evaluated on its own merit and not as it compares to other products or resources.
5. Reviewers' ratings for each product are tabulated and averaged by the staff of *Single Adult Ministries Journal* to determine each score. ***(Products are rated from 1 to 10, with 10 being the best rating possible.)***

**WEAKNESSES:** A more balanced perspective between pain and living life to the fullest would have been appreciated.

## Putting the Past Behind

by Les Carter (Moody Press, 1989) 191 pp. $8.95

***Overall Product Rating: 6.7***

**STRENGTHS:** While reading this book won't suddenly make a person whole again, it seems to be a valuable tool for reaching out and touching people where they hurt...A workshop or one-on-one counseling could be greatly enhanced by having this resource available...The author helps us utilize the strengths of our faith and our understanding of human psychology to move the person into forward movement...A practical book that gives hope...Well researched. Well written. Needed...Could be a good diagnostic tool for leadership...Combines psychological and scriptural principles.

**WEAKNESSES:** Sometimes the book seems theologically preachy...Maybe a little too deeply written for the lay person, more suited for professionals...An awkward format, making it difficult to follow...Too egocentric, concentrating on the satisfaction of unmet needs as the solution to all rather than on transformation of character.

## VIDEO/Quantum Connection:
### Is There a Link Between the New Physics and Faith?

produced by 2100 Productions (InterVarsity Video, 1989) 21 min. $29.95

***Not Yet Reviewed***

**NOTES:** Introduces non-scientist to the "New Physics," which is linked to the belief that everything is part of an impersonal divine oneness. Scholars and physicist challenge this claim and affirm the Biblical review of reality which gave rise to modern science.

## Real Christians Don't Dance

by John Fischer (Bethany House Publishers, 1988) 191 pp. $10.95

***Overall Product Rating: 8.1***

**STRENGTHS:** The best bennies of this book are that it will convict you if you're not right on track, and that it can help you find and work on your weaknesses...Brief chapters, easy to read...Unique insights, creative analogies.

**WEAKNESSES:** Would like to have seen some thought-provoking questions and a leader's guide...Not enough practical suggestions on how to repair or help self.

## Rebuilding Your Broken World

by Gordon MacDonald (Oliver Nelson, 1988) 235 pp. $12.95

***Not Yet Reviewed***

**NOTES:** Many men and women are dropping off the edge because of deep personal tragedy or even dramatic failure. Yet, the Bible offers a remarkable promise of rebuilding and renewal for which no one is exempt. This book offers the strength and compassion of Biblical hope to those who struggle with shattered ideals.

## Re-evaluating Your Commitments:
### How to Strengthen the Permanent and Reassess the Temporary

by Maxine Hancock (Bethany House Publishers, 1990) 155 pp. $6.95

***Not Yet Reviewed***

**NOTES:** In a hurried world that makes constant demands on one's time and resources, we need criteria to evaluate whether on not life is meaningful and worthwhile. This book helps show the reader how to discover those life-ordering commitments that are meant to put everything else into perspective.

## Regaining Control of Your Life

by Judson Edwards (Bethany House Publishers, 1989) 160 pp. $6.95

***Overall Product Rating: 8.0***

**STRENGTHS:** It discusses 10 of the many "joy killers" which prevents Christians from experiencing true joy and it could be used as part of a weekly Bible study by using the discussion questions at the end of each chapter...Can spark one's imagination and enable people to examine their own lives...Helps to evaluate one's self and to catch certain areas of life and ministry that need to be refocused...Reminds us Biblically that we are called to the abundant life and that Christianity should not rob us of our joy...Pastors/leaders will especially benefit because they are in the constant roving eye of the congregation and are always subjected to stress...This book provides insights on how to cope...Easy to read, well written...Good discussion questions...Very encouraging book to read...Openness of the author...Great quotes.

**WEAKNESSES:** Not written with singles specifically in mind...Several chapters could be expanded...Left one with a desire for more...Some chapters too broad and some too short...Reflections and discussion questions after every chapter could have been better prepared...Almost too simple...In one or two chapters more Biblical principles could have been applied to overcome the specific problem.

## Regaining Control:
### When Good Things Become Addictions

by Grant Martin (Scripture Press Publications, 1990) 192 pp. $7.95

***Not Yet Reviewed***

**NOTES:** A theological and understandable description of the addictive process. Areas of life that are not always considered addictions are discussed. Ways to work towards recovery are given.

## Rejection Syndrome, The

by Charles Solomon (Tyndale House Publishers, 1989) 141 pp. $5.95

***Overall Product Rating: 5.7***

**STRENGTHS:** Food for thought in areas of positional vs. experiential concepts concerning Christian life...Offers a model that uses a crises in one's life to begin the "exchanged life," which is living in Christ rather than in our own effort...Addresses a topic which many single adults experience, including many of our social and cultural issues yet did not excuse them as some illness.... Condemned sin and offered Christ...Thought provoking and convicting.

**WEAKNESSES:** Quite theoretical...Follows several tangents on humanism, psychology, theology, seminary training...Never fulfills the reader's expectations...Uses numerous religious cliches...Sees rejection being overcome by coming to Christ but gives too little attention to the diversity of circumstances Christ can use to eventually solidify our relationship with Him...There needs to be room for the reader to say more than "I experience rejection because I really don't know Jesus." Many other contributing factors may be below the surface, which this book does not cover...Flat and boring to read...The book began on a personal level but then attempted to take on the problems of the church, country and world. It tries to cover too much territory.

## Rest of Success, The:
### What the World Didn't Tell You About Having It All

by Denis Haack (InterVarsity Press, 1989) 173 pp. $7.95

***Overall Product Rating: 7.0***

**STRENGTHS:** Helps people understand that they are not to conform to this world (even in

the view of success) but are to transform their lives according to God's will (the author's view of success)...Is well-researched and provides good Biblical support for God's view of success...The study questions are great and really challenge you to apply the topic to your own life...Helpful reminder of how the world view has crept into Christian circles.
**WEAKNESSES:** Needs a study or leader's guide...The book didn't tie together as a whole in that it didn't flow from chapter to chapter. The theme stays consistent but the transitions are not good...The topic of Christian excellence was touched upon but not developed enough...The character studies are great but needed more direct, real-world application.

## Road Less Travelled, The

by Scott M. Peck, M.D. (Simon and Schuster, 1980)

***Not Yet Reviewed***

**Notes:** If life is a journey, the choice of roads we take is crucial. Peck invites us to travel towards spiritual growth and charts a new course for ways to deal with problems of everyday life.

## Search for Significance, The

by Robert S. McGee (Rapha Publishing/Word, 1990) Reading Book and Workbook, 479 pp. $12.99; Small Group Study Guide, Leader's Guide and Four-Part VIDEO kit, 25 min. each, $20.00

***Overall Product Rating: 9.6***

**STRENGTHS:** Provides step-by-step understanding of the meaning of the word "salvation"...Deals very well with self-esteem, a very important "singles" issue. It provides excellent measurement devices to enable an individual to see just how tied up they might be with shame, fear of punishment, etc.... Combines superb psychological and theological input creating a product which is excellent in almost any setting, for use by almost any individual or group...Does not compromise Biblical principles...A balanced approach to dealing with spiritual warfare... Provides application of truth on the basic issues of life: goals, motives and self-worth, and helps wean us from the worldly values such as status, beauty, wealth...Each chapter has a series of practical self-exams.
**WEAKNESSES:** It would have been helpful if this book would have exposed the dangers of radical extremes in a theological continuum (such as denying that Satan exists vs. seeing Satan behind every bush)...All in all, one of the best resources I've seen.

## VIDEO/Screen Test

by White Lion Video (Word, Inc., 1988) 25 min. $29.95

***Overall Product Rating: 5.1***

**STRENGTHS:** Shows truth of salvation in non-threatening manner...Easy to use... Humorous, unique method of presentation ...Fun to watch...Creative look at typical societies...Possible tool to keep group fresh and interactive.
**WEAKNESSES:** Better suited for younger audience (jr. high/high school/college) ...Priced too high...Message is oversimplified...Juvenile at times.

## Seeing Yourself Through God's Eyes:

### A Devotional Guide

by June Hunt (Zondervan, 1989) 95 pp. $6.95

***Overall Product Rating: 6.5***

**STRENGTHS:** For an individual struggling with self-worth and esteem, this book helps discover just how valuable God considers each one...Each devotional provides opportunity to personalize the information...A helpful resource to give to singles, especially those with low self-esteem...Encourages reader's to apply information to their current situation... Sincerely written...Uses Scripture frequently...Brief, concise, written to be easily used.
**WEAKNESSES:** Uses some quotations without credit to the source (p.69)...Not overly imaginative. Many other writers have covered this material with more depth and zip...As a devotional, it might be more helpful if it included a daily prayer...A bit too filled with cliches...Offers simplistic solutions. Seeing and valuing oneself as God does is often a daily and certainly (for most) more than a once in a lifetime experience.

## Self-Esteem: Gift from God

by Ruth McRoberts Ward (Baker Book House, 1984) 148 pp. $7.95

***Overall Product Rating: 6.3***

**STRENGTHS:** Biblically sound look at God's intention for people to have a good self-worth concept...Shows the impact that people have on each other's self-esteem. Reveals the potential we have in building up each other...Highlights a good tool in counseling—the Myers Briggs Personality Profile...If your singles have never been exposed to temperament information this is another book that brings out the importance of being knowledgeable about this key area of understanding. Friendships and relationships can be difficult but if we understand why people do what they do (temperaments) it can help illuminate a lot of misunderstanding.
**WEAKNESSES:** This book was a bit boring, did not hold my interest as it seemed to go on and on and on. I have read other books on the same subject and they increased my interest and were fun to read. The author is too laborious in her presentation... Emphasizes Myers Briggs too much in relationship to self-esteem...The author seems too focused on her own perceptions vs. sound research...The points made are generally too broad and don't acknowledge the many exceptions.

## How Does The National Review Board Function?

1. There are over 100 reviewers on this board, representing every major denomination and region of the country.
2. All reviewers are pastors, counselors or lay leaders involved in ministry with single adults.
3. Every product is reviewed and evaluated by *at least two - and in most cases, three - members* of this National Board. (When appropriate and possible, the product is actually used in a singles ministry prior to being evaluated.)
4. Each product is reviewed and evaluated on its own merit and not as it compares to other products or resources.
5. Reviewers' ratings for each product are tabulated and averaged by the staff of *Single Adult Ministries Journal* to determine each score.
***(Products are rated from 1 to 10, with 10 being the best rating possible.)***

## Sometimes It's Hard to Love God

by Dennis Guernsey (InterVarsity Press, 1989) 171 pp. $14.95

***Overall Product Rating: 8.0***

**STRENGTHS:** Appropriately blends Scripture and psychological insights to provide helpful guide for dealing with past hurts...Writes from personal experience, in an enjoyable, probing manner. The reader is continually encouraged to examine his/her own life...The perspective of the Kingdom of God in this book is sorely needed in our Christian culture which so often divorces spirituality (private) and public behavior... Challenges us in our secular life-style while calling ourselves Christian...Dealt with in a thorough manner...Could be especially helpful for divorced, separated and widowed ...Gives a fresh, indepth look at the Lord's prayer. Shows how our family relationships fit into the phrases of this prayer, helps us understand the effects family have on our spiritual walk and our self-imposed barriers with God.

**WEAKNESSES:** None noted.

## VIDEO/Stained Images

produced by 2100 Productions (InterVarsity Video, 1989) 25 min. $29.95

***Not Yet Reviewed***

**NOTES:** People talk honestly about their negative images and impressions of Christians and Christianity. A useful tool for helping your people get a better picture of how to communicate with the non-Christian and to understand how they perceive "us."

## Stressed-Out (Small Group Study)

by Peter Menconi, Richard Peace, Lyman Coleman (NavPress, 1988) 64 pp. $4.95

***Overall Product Rating: 6.2***

**STRENGTHS:** Attractively presented...Allows for differences of opinion in the study group...Simple format allows anyone from trained clergy/counselor to single adults themselves to lead the study...Very helpful to have the two tracks offered, one for more in-depth discussion/study...The subject (stress/burnout) is a subject of concern to active single adults, and is an area where many need to grasp some spiritual truths concerning their own life-styles.

**WEAKNESSES:** Wish there would have been more emphasis on how God helps us deal with stress...The dog illustration on the cover is a turn-off...Perhaps in an effort to create simplicity, a more detailed leader's guide was eliminated. Personally, I would liked to have this resource include more background material on the subject before leading a group.

## Strong-Willed Adult, The

by Dennis Gibson (Baker Book House, 1987) 188 pp. $7.95

***Overall Product Rating: 6.3***

**STRENGTHS:** Helps to identify those with a strong will and why they are the way they are...Gives practical and spiritual ways to overcome the strong will...Helps a person see how their strong will hurts their relationship with God...The author used Scriptural as well as psychological ways to deal with adults who have difficult personalities to deal with. I would recommend this book to those dealing with someone difficult to be around.

**WEAKNESSES:** The author seemed to take too long to define the strong-willed adult before getting to the "so what?"...It sometimes seemed to be attempting to turn the works of the flesh into a peculiar personality disorder. A better title might have been "Combating Our Pride."

## Success: Does the One with the Most Toys Win? (Small Group Study)

by Peter Menconi, Richard Peace, Lyman Coleman (NavPress, 1988) 64 pp. $4.95

***Overall Product Rating: 6.5***

**STRENGTHS:** Provides a study where all levels of spiritual maturity can be included ...Provides additional material to stimulate further thinking on the subject matter... Easy-to-use format, thought-provoking questions with an ability to get everyone who is involved in the Bible study to participate...Could be used by anyone... Questions focus specifically on the subject matter.

**WEAKNESSES:** It's not always clear where the each study is going. I would like to see the goals and objectives of each chapter clearly stated...Would like to have seen Scripture given more authority rather than the opinions of the participants. Opens the door for a possible pooling of ignorance... Needs to be tied together better as it relates to content and conclusions.

## VIDEO/Surviving Life Transitions

by Clayton Barbeau (Franciscan Communications, 1988) 26 min. $19.95

***Not Yet Reviewed***

**NOTES:** Guides the viewer through the process of change and offers stories and strategies for healthy personal growth.

## Telling Each Other the Truth

by William Backus (Bethany House Publishers, 1985) 189 pp. $6.95

***Overall Product Rating: 7.7***

**STRENGTHS:** An excellent resource for counseling with all singles...Includes very practical exercises for evaluating and improving truth-telling in our relationships ....Helps us see the subtle (and not so subtle) ways we are dishonest with others.

**WEAKNESSES:** Focuses too much on clinical and psychological examples and not enough on Biblical examples. If I were to use it in a small group, I might want to supplement the Biblical examples found in the text.

## Telling Yourself the Truth: Applying the Principles of Misbelief Therapy

by William Backus and Marie Chapian (Bethany House Publishers, 1980) 184 pp. $5.95

***Overall Product Rating: 8.2***

**STRENGTHS:** Applies the use of misbelief therapy to several disorders such as depression, fear, anxiety, etc...Well-illustrated with case studies...Biblically based, good use of Scripture...The chapters dealing with specific topics makes for quick reference. Examples and steps provided make it easy to apply...A reminder of the importance of communicating the truth of God's word to our people, and the hope God's word brings into our lives...Helps us as pastors and leaders to re-examine our own words: are we telling ourselves the truth or what others are trying to tell us?

**WEAKNESSES:** Once the concept of misbelief therapy is understood, the book can get repetitious. In some instances it takes an oversimplified approach. All problems are not the result of misbelief... Does not investigate the reasons why people don't tell themselves the truth...Needs more emphasis on how growth takes time. Learning to tell yourself the truth is not a quick fix, overnight process. It may take years to reshape the way we think about ourselves. Some insight on how to help people over the long haul would be helpful ...Examples tend to make one believe the process to changing self is quick and easy.

## Transitions:
### Savoring the Seasons of Life (Small Group Study)

by Peter Menconi, Richard Peace, Lyman Coleman (NavPress, 1988) 63 pp. $3.95

***Overall Product Rating: 8.0***

**STRENGTHS:** Solid, well-written Bible study...The dual track format allows tremendous flexibility...Discussion questions will stimulate rich discussion...This material (topic and treatment of Scripture) could be used with non-Christians in a small group setting. The potential results could be very positive...Price is great...We have used a number of the study books in this series and they have been well received by our people.
**WEAKNESSES:** Due to the wide span of age-specific topics in this study it is more difficult to use, for people to personally identify throughout. Especially difficult to use with younger singles. The lessons on mid-life and aging are not of high interest to them yet...Baby boomers are getting tired of some of these stereotypical classifications.

## True Believers Don't Ask Why

by John Fischer (Bethany House Publishers, 1989) 192 pp. $10.95

***Overall Product Rating: 8.1***

**STRENGTHS:** A good, thought-provoking book of essays about living out our faith in the real world...Very interesting reading... Chapters are short and inviting...Will be of great benefit to the reader.
**WEAKNESSES:** None noted

## Trusting God Even When Life Hurts

Jerry Bridges (NavPress, 1988) 215 pp. $12.95

***Not Yet Reviewed***

**NOTES:** Adversity is hard to endure and understand. Even when we know that God is in control it's difficult to trust Him. The author offers insights based on thorough Bible study of God's loving sovereignty.

## Turning Fear to Hope:
### Women Who Have Been Hurt For Love

by Holly Wagner Green (Zondervan, 1989) 223 pp. $8.95

***Overall Product Rating: 9.5***

**STRENGTHS:** All abused women should read this book. It reveals the truth of situations in Christian homes where men abuse women in the name of God...It's about time this subject was addressed in a confrontive way within the Christian community. Too many pastors, counselors, churches and Christians continue to be naive about the tremendous damage caused by abuse in the Christian home. Too many Christians who cry for help are not getting it. This book is a giant step forward, very enlightening theologically as well as providing practical solutions...Many singles are single because of abuse but without further help they may repeat the cycle in future relationships...Well researched.
**WEAKNESSES:** Perhaps a specific workbook addressed to the abused would be helpful as a companion with this book...Needs more information on how to minister to the abuser...The author sometimes appears to be slightly bitter towards men. I'm personally concerned about the men who are abusers. They also need help.

## Unlocking the Mystery of Your Emotions

by Archibald D. Hart, Ph.D. (Word, Inc., 1989) 161 pp. $8.99

***Not Yet Reviewed***

**NOTES:** Your emotions are a gift from God to enrich your life and alert you to threats. Feelings can be misunderstood and mis-handled. Many people either lose control of their emotions, creating pain and chaos, or overcontrol them, becoming stunted, distant and cold. This book looks at a healthier option, showing how with God's help you can learn to experience emotions without being controlled by them.

## Unlocking the Secrets of Being Loved, Accepted, and Secure

by Josh McDowell and Dale Bellis (Word Publishing, 1984) 117 pp. $7.99

***Overall Product Rating: 8.0***

**STRENGTHS:** The authors keep things simple and do not try to delve into heavy psychological problems. This book was not written for those with the heavy problems, but for those who struggle with basic self-image...Refreshing and encouraging...Easy to read and understand...Gives concrete believable examples and Biblical references. The author explains his points in detail without bogging the reader down with large vocabulary and wordy sentences.
**WEAKNESSES:** None stated.

## Up from the Ashes:
### How to Survive and Grow Through Personal Crisis

by Dr. Karl A. Slaikeu and Steve Lawhead (Zondervan, 1987) 236 pp. $7.95

***Not Yet Reviewed***

**NOTES:** A crisis does not have to end in total loss; it can mark the beginning of newer, more satisfying, and more productive ways of living. A crisis can be conquered. This book outlines four strategies for putting life together again after the worst is over.

## Waiting:
### Finding Hope When God Seems Silent

by Ben Patterson (InterVarsity Press, 1989) 170 pp. $12.95

***Overall Product Rating: 8.0***

**STRENGTHS:** This book deals with the truth of Job in an intellectually satisfying manner—yet throughout you sense the author's soft heart as he walks us through how to deal with life's uncertainties and unfairness....The very readable style and pleasant tone give this heavy topic a breath of fresh air....Helps lay the groundwork for a better understanding of how God works (very useful when we're counseling those in the process of "waiting upon God" for an answer

## How Does The National Review Board Function?

1. There are over 100 reviewers on this board, representing every major denomination and region of the country.
2. All reviewers are pastors, counselors or lay leaders involved in ministry with single adults.
3. Every product is reviewed and evaluated by *at least two - and in most cases, three - members* of this National Board. (When appropriate and possible, the product is actually used in a singles ministry prior to being evaluated.)
4. Each product is reviewed and evaluated on its own merit and not as it compares to other products or resources.
5. Reviewers' ratings for each product are tabulated and averaged by the staff of *Single Adult Ministries Journal* to determine each score. ***(Products are rated from 1 to 10, with 10 being the best rating possible.)***

or guidance).... I've already shared my copy with hurting people and it has helped bring healing... The little vignettes at the end of the chapters put flesh and blood on the printed words.
**WEAKNESSES:** At times, the author needed to be more concise...Wish book was available in paperback....Some chapters seemed too short to thoroughly cover the topics with depth.

## Waking from the American Dream

by Donald W. McCullough (InterVarsity Press) 156 pp. $7.95

***Overall Product Rating: 7.2***

**STRENGTHS:** Sheds light on the myth of the "Can-Do Faith," how it is an attempt to Christianize an illusion, which can only lead to illusion. Too often our view and presentation of the Gospel is a fairy tale approach when in reality we need to speak the truth in love. This book helps us do that...Single adults are very often people who have not yet experienced the "American Dream," so this book could help them see the way life really is...Provides realistic ideas for hope... Debunks "name it, claim it" theology.
**WEAKNESSES:** Sometimes the author gets bogged down and seems to lose sight of his objectives.

## Whatever Happened to Ordinary Christians

by Jim Smoke (Harvest House Publishing, 1987) 176 pp. $6.95

***Not Yet Reviewed***

**NOTES:** In this laser-swift, electronic age of instant everything, even Christians are influenced by the secular mentality and the unending drive to achieve material success and personal recognition. This pressure to be a Christian "superstar" could destroy the importance of living the simple, obedient Christian life. The author sends the strong message that God is seeking ordinary Christians to impact the world for Him.

## VIDEO/What Is God Like?

Directed by James F. Robinson (White Lion-Word, Inc., 1984) 30 min. $29.95

***Overall Product Rating: 6.1***

**STRENGTHS:** A great group discussion starter on who God is...Challenges people to evaluate their own belief systems and values...Good Biblical support with discussion guide...Interesting to hear the variety of opinions from common folk regarding "Is there a God and can He be known?"... Especially helpful for reminding that many in the world do not know much about God .
**WEAKNESSES:** The "unchurched" interviews were easier to relate to than the "Christian-ese" statements such as "the saved church people"...Does not provide solutions or answers to the questions it raises...Relies too heavily on the discussion guide to provide a benefit for the time to watch this material.

## When Life Is Unfair:
### Feeling God's Presence in Life's Dark Moments

by Larry Richards (Word, Inc., 1989) 155 pp. $10.99

***Not Yet Reviewed***

**NOTES:** The author blends the real life experiences of modern Christians and insights form Scriptures. He shows how tragedy can become a means of growth and grace. God's loving presence is with us in pain, offering hope and the prospect of peace.

## When Life Isn't Fair

by Dwight and Susan Wood Carlson (Harvest House Publishing, 1989) 235 pp. $6.95

***Overall Product Rating: 6.0***

**STRENGTHS:** Nice balance of personal experience and research...Helpful insight to why we suffer...Effectively relates to real life experiences.
**WEAKNESSES:** Gets too technical in some chapters. Many readers would get lost from one topic to the next...It would have been helpful to have Scripture references listed with text for easy reference, instead of in the notes...The questions and application exercises add to the value of this resource, but in this book they have been almost hidden in the appendix. They need to be placed at the end of the appropriate chapters.

**Fact:**

Roman Catholic women are more likely to have an abortion than either Protestant or Jewish women. Those with no religious affiliation are the most likely to receive an abortion of all groups in this survey.

*Alan Guttmacher Institute study*

## When the Night is too Long:
### Does God Know How Deep My Hurt Is? Then Why Doesn't He Do Something About It?

by Robert L. Wise (Thomas Nelson, 1990) 220 pp. $14.95

***Not Yet Reviewed***

**NOTES:** As a pastor, counselor, and friend trying to help others make sense out of questions, experiences and feelings, Robert Wise offers insights in the areas of pain and suffering. Wise extends the hope that even in the darkest of times, God is still working for good.

## Where is God When It Hurts

by Philip Yancey (Zondervan, 1977) 240 pp. $8.95

***Not Yet Reviewed***

**NOTES:** Many suffering people want to love God, but cannot see past their own tears. They feel hurt and betrayed. This book speaks to anyone in pain and also equips people who want to reach out to someone who is suffering.

## Who Am I and Who Cares?

by David Hocking (Multnomah Press, 1985) 165 pp. $3.95

***Overall Product Rating: 5.3***

**STRENGTHS:** Gives sound Biblical answers to questions about life and worth...Great Biblical direction to life situations...Offers hope...Includes most of the issues and stages of life...Comprehensive...Written without heavy technical jargon.
**WEAKNESSES:** The book has very small print making it extremely hard to read...I believe the message could have been given with fewer words pages...Trite. Makes self-esteem sound like an easy pursuit if only God is on your team.

## Winning by Losing:
### Eleven Biblical Paradoxes that Can Change Your Life

by Richard A. Fowler (Moody, 1986) 149 pp. $6.95

***Overall Product Rating: 6.1***

**STRENGTHS:** Helpful teaching against prevailing world philosophy...Very easy to read and understand...Study questions good

for group discussion and personal reflection ...Provides helpful word studies and background information for studying paradoxical teachings in the Bible...Since this is the Gospel that turns things up-side-down, it is a helpful resource for noting the world view of the Kingdom as contrasted to what's all around us.
**WEAKNESSES:** At a number of places, the examples and "preaching tone commentary" seem to be quite simplistic...The monolithic view on divorce and its effects will not be that helpful to divorcing singles. The larger, more complex aspects of the issue are avoided or not acknowledged...Some points are questionable theologically...Application is quite weak in places.

## Worry Free Living

by Frank Minirth, Paul Meier, Don Hawkins (Thomas Nelson, 1989) 223 pp. $15.95

***Overall Product Rating: 6.8***

**STRENGTHS:** Offers eight methods for fighting anxiety. These are practical and useful as well as often-overlooked matters of life-style...Stresses that anxiety is preventable, treatable and curable. If this book is followed, one could live a happier life...Lets readers know that their problem is not unique... Offers immediate help and steps for recovery ...Good material for group discussion... Provides technical info about physical results of anxieties. These are listed in a concise manner...Helpful for quick reference. The appendix is tremendous...The part on defense mechanisms and the treatment for anxiety will be helpful for years to come.
**WEAKNESSES:** Starts off too slow for most readers to continue and get to "the good stuff" later in the book...The first chapters were unnecessary. I would have quit reading if I hadn't promised to read for this review... The book is very wordy and repeats the same thoughts many times. I kept wanting to say "get on with it, I've got the idea"...Spent too much time explaining diseases such as bulimia instead of the anxiety the disease causes...Repetitive.

## You Don't Have to Quit

by Anne and Ray Ortlund (Thomas Nelson, 1986) 192 pp. $7.95

***Overall Product Rating: 8.2***

**STRENGTHS:** Helps us understand why people quit/give up with guidelines to help people overcome this problem...A good motivational book...Short, easy-to-read chapters with one point in each...Appreciated the abundant use of Scripture...Offers a myriad of ways to help people persevere in all of life's situations and circumstances, to win! Biblical principles applied to life.
**WEAKNESSES:** The use of A Zone, B Zone, etc. to prove points was a bit confusing. The material was sufficient without it...Parts of the book seemed dry.

## AUDIO CASSETTES/ You Gotta Keep Dancin': In The Midst of Life's Hurts, You Can Choose Joy! (Leader's Kit)

by Tim Hansel (LifeJourney/David C. Cook, 1988) Two cassettes, Leader's Guide and Book, $7.95

***Not Yet Reviewed***

**NOTES:** The message of this material is that no matter what your circumstances, you can choose to be joyful. This material can help your group members become more supportive and encouraging to one another.

## Your Hidden Half: Blending Your Private and Public Self

by Mark R. McMinn (Baker Book House, 1988) 227 pp. $8.95

***Overall Product Rating: 6.8***

**STRENGTHS:** A good job of building bridges between psychological theory and practical ministry. The author's diagrams are helpful especially for the visual learner... Good fresh ideas and concepts...The possibilities for this product are tremendous because it intrigued me as I began reading the book, especially the quotes from Dr. Jekyll and Mr. Hyde and some quotes from other resources as well. I believe that a great many people are interested in trying to blend their public and private selves as the author tries to do.
**WEAKNESSES:** Our private and public self is very complicated and a very intense issue. The author has tended to simplify this so much that the book loses its effectiveness. After reading this book, I am not sure where the author is really coming from...I'm a little disappointed because the subject matter in the introduction of this book really whet my appetite but the answers left me a little hungry for something deeper...The reader may need to be conversant with major psychological theories before reading this book...Better used as a college textbook than to be helpful in singles ministry...A workbook for group study would make this a more useful tool.

# StepFamilies

## Most Recommended Resources in This Section

(Based on evaluations and reviews made by *SAM Journal*'s National Resource Review Board, using a 1-10 scale with 10 being the best possible score):

### 8.2 Stepfamilies: A Growing Reality

by Claire Berman (Public Affairs Pamphlet, 1982)

### 7.9 Our Family Got A Stepparent

by Carolyn E. Phillips (Regal Press, 1981)

*(For more information on each of the above resources—plus many other helpful products—find them listed in alphabetical order below.)*

## Blended Family, The

by Tom and Adrienne Frydenger (Revell, 1985) 192 pp. $6.95

***Not Yet Reviewed***

**NOTES:** With sensitivity for the children's

## How Does The National Review Board Function?

1. There are over 100 reviewers on this board, representing every major denomination and region of the country.
2. All reviewers are pastors, counselors or lay leaders involved in ministry with single adults.
3. Every product is reviewed and evaluated by *at least two - and in most cases, three - members* of this National Board. (When appropriate and possible, the product is actually used in a singles ministry prior to being evaluated.)
4. Each product is reviewed and evaluated on its own merit and not as it compares to other products or resources.
5. Reviewers' ratings for each product are tabulated and averaged by the staff of *Single Adult Ministries Journal* to determine each score. ***(Products are rated from 1 to 10, with 10 being the best rating possible.)***

feelings and needs, this book offers insights and suggestions related to knitting a family together in a positive, healthy way.

## How To Blend A Family

by Carolyn Johnson (Pyranee-Zondervan, 1989) 223 pp. $8.95

***Overall Product Rating: 7.7***

**STRENGTHS:** Provides valuable, practical insights and suggestions...Shares personal stories and examples to emphasize suggestions ...Heart-felt story of blending a family...Powerful section in the book for those who have lost a spouse...Strong grief/anger process expressed in understandable terms...Personal experiences of writer give both real life to the book and practical suggestions...Topics are for the most part well-developed...Presents situations which many adults contemplating marriage/remarriage may not even think about, especially if children are involved...Shows thoughts and fears which children may pick up on during the formative years...Parents must put their children's welfare at the top of their priorities.

**WEAKNESSES:** Book was a little low-key and rather drawn out...Not sure the price of book is reasonable...Several statements were made and then are left dangling...Seems to run against the grain of most psychological thinking today. We need to know more about how she draws her conclusions...Better documentation needed...Very little theology or Bible used as rationale.

## Jigsaw Families:
### Solving the Puzzle of Remarriage

by Michelle Crese (Aglow Publications, 1989) 138 pp. $7.95

***Overall Product Rating: 7.6***

**STRENGTHS:** Will raise awareness about the challenges blended families face. It poses questions that a qualified discussion leader could use effectively as a springboard to discussion...An excellent book for group study with remarrieds, young adults, single parents, divorcees, those separated, etc. who now or later will be involved in a blended family...Provides thoughtful insights regarding little-realized difficulties remarrieds may experience, whether knowingly or unknowingly...Fast moving and touches on a wide variety of areas...Helpful discussion questions in the study guide.

**WEAKNESSES:** This book must not be viewed as the sole source for dealing with blended families. It's only a starter...Attempts to cover a lot of ground in a little space. May not be extensive enough for some.

## Our Family Got a Stepparent

by Carolyn E. Phillips (Regal Press, 1981) 79 pp. $5.95

***Overall Product Rating: 7.9***

**STRENGTHS:** Helpful in understanding stepparenting problems...Helps adults come to a better understanding of the emotional feelings of the child...Will help leaders recognize and identify symptoms of maladjustment in children...Provides specific suggestions on how parents/stepparents can make the adjustment easier for the children ...An excellent book to help understand stepparenting problems.

**WEAKNESSES:** The child in the story adjusts too easily to his stepparent situation. This might tend to make a child in a similar situation who is having adjustment problems feel different or bad about his/her own negative emotions. The reality is that few children adjust as easily as the boy in this story...The story is written about a middle class family with no financial struggles—not always realistic...This book was written several years ago.

## Stepfamilies:
### A Growing Reality

by Claire Berman (Public Affairs Pamphlet, 1982) 28 pp. $1.00

***Overall Product Rating: 8.2***

**STRENGTHS:** This is reliable, down-to-earth material that needs to be put into the hands of many single adults...The low cost makes it easy to distribute (quantity discounts are also available)...Offers great insight into the various problems that can develop when one marries someone with children...This pamphlet deals with many issues that are not being addressed in premarital counseling, but should be...Helps discourage fantasies and open eyes to real-world challenges for stepfamilies.

**WEAKNESSES:** Offers no reference to Scripture or Biblical principles...Leaves no room for how God can help overcome difficulties within blended families...The booklet is very short, so it doesn't go into much detail.

## VIDEO/Stepparents and Blended Families

(Sunburst, 1988) Includes Teacher's Guide, 37 min., $165

***Not Yet Reviewed***

**NOTES:** Points out the complexities of bringing children of different families into one household and shows it is possible to work though the inevitable rivalries and conflicts.

# The Resources That YOU Most Recommend . . .

The goal of this directory is to provide you with the best information on the most recommended resources available. That is why we put tremendous effort into rating and evaluating resources with the wonderful help of our National Single Adult Ministries Resource Review Board. But we also conduct a survey of singles ministry leaders for each directory to find out what resources they most recommend.

During 1990 we surveyed nearly 600 pastors and lay leaders from across the U. S. and Canada, asking, "What resources would you most recommend."

We believe the following survey results represent those resources that are currently most popular (or at least most visible) on the front lines of singles ministry.

## Resources I'd Most Recommend to Other Singles Ministry Leaders:

1. ***Singles Ministry Handbook***, edited by Douglas Fagerstrom (Victor Books)
2. ***Young Adult Ministry***, by Terry Hershey (Group Books)
3. ***Growing Through Divorce***, by Jim Smoke (Harvest House)
4. ***Single Adult Ministries Journal*** (SAM Resources)
5. VIDEO/***One Is A Whole Number***, by Harold Ivan Smith (Victory Films Gospel Films)
6. ***God's Call To The Single Adult***, by Michael Cavanaugh (Whitaker/Oasis House)
7. ***Single Adults Want To Be The Church Too***, by Britton Wood (Broadman)
8. ***National Single Adult Ministries Resource Directory*** (SAM Resources)
9. VIDEO/***Successful Single Parenting***, by Clyde Besson (Discovery Educational Service)
10. VIDEO/***Suddenly Single***, by Clyde Besson (Sampson Company)

## Resources I'd Most Like to See My Single Adults Use:

### BOOKS:

1. The Bible
2. ***Growing Through Divorce***, by Jim Smoke (Harvest House)
3. ***God's Call To The Single Adult***, by Michael Cavanaugh (Whitaker/Oasis House)
4. ***Too Close, Too Soon***, by Jim Talley and Bobbie Reed (Thomas Nelson)
5. ***Inside Out***, by Dr. Larry Crabb (NavPress)
6. ***Search for Significance***, by Robert S. McGee (Rapha)
7. ***Becoming A Friend and Lover***, by Dick Purnell (Here's Life)
8. ***The Road Less Travelled***, by Scott M. Peck (Simon and Schuster)
9. ***Intimacy***, by Terry Hershey (Harvest House)
10. ***Healing Damaged Emotions***, by David A. Seamands (Victor)
11. ***Ordering Your Private World***, by Gordon MacDonald (Thomas Nelson)
12. ***Celebration of Discipline***, by Richard Foster (Harper & Row)

### VIDEO:

1. ***One Is A Whole Number***, by Harold Ivan Smith (Gospel Films)
2. ***Successful Single Parenting***, by Clyde Besson (Discovery Educational Service)
3. ***Search for Significance***, by Robert S. McGee (Rapha)
4. ***Suddenly Single***, by Clyde Besson (Sampson Company)
5. ***Bonding/Rebonding***, by Donald Joy (Word)
6. ***Holy Sweat***, by Tim Hansel (Word)
7. ***Who Switched the Price Tags?*** by Tony Campolo (Word)

## Small Group Resources I'd Most Recommend to Other Singles Ministry Leaders:

1. Serendipity Materials, by Lyman Coleman (Serendipity/NavPress)
2. Lifestyle Small Group Studies (NavPress)
3. VIDEO/***Successful Single Parenting***, by Clyde Besson, (Discovery Educational Service)
4. VIDEO/***One Is A Whole Number***, by Harold Ivan Smith, (Victory Films/Gospel Films)
5. VIDEO AND STUDY BOOK/ ***The Search for Significance***, by Robert S. McGee (Rapha)
6. VIDEO/***Suddenly Single***, by Clyde Besson (Sampson Company)
7. ***The 2.7 Series*** (The Navigators)
8. ***Growing Through Divorce***, by Jim Smoke (Harvest House)
9. ***The Road Less Travelled***, by Scott M. Peck, M.D. (Simon and Schuster)

## How Does The National Review Board Function?

1. There are over 100 reviewers on this board, representing every major denomination and region of the country.
2. All reviewers are pastors, counselors or lay leaders involved in ministry with single adults.
3. Every product is reviewed and evaluated by *at least two - and in most cases, three - members* of this National Board. (When appropriate and possible, the product is actually used in a singles ministry prior to being evaluated.)
4. Each product is reviewed and evaluated on its own merit and not as it compares to other products or resources.
5. Reviewers' ratings for each product are tabulated and averaged by the staff of *Single Adult Ministries Journal* to determine each score. ***(Products are rated from 1 to 10, with 10 being the best rating possible.)***

# Part 9

# Network: Singles Ministries Listed by State

## The Largest, Most Comprehensive Listing of Singles Ministries in Existence

### Where To Find It:

# NETWORK: SINGLES MINISTRIES LISTED BY STATE

**On the following 46 pages you will find the most comprehensive listing of single adult ministries ever compiled. Use this like your telephone book to locate friends, ministry associates, peers, and those who may be able to assist you with a question or need about ministry with single adults. (If your ministry is not included in this issue of Network, please see page 249.)**

## ALEXANDER CITY

**Single Life Fellowship**
Lewis Archer
First United Methodist of Alexander City
101 Semmes Street
Alexander City, AL 30510
*United Methodist*
205/234-6323
**Years in existence:** 1
**Avg. attendance:** 20
**Primarily ages:** 26-30
**Main meeting time(s):** A week night (M-F)

## ANNISTON

**Faith Outreach Single Ministry**
Carolyn Funchess
Faith Outreach Ministry
3018 Moore Avenue
Anniston, AL 36201
*Interdenominational*
**Years in existence:** 2
**Avg. attendance:** 10
**Primarily ages:** 26-30
**Main meeting time(s):** Friday night

## BAY MINETTE

**Southside Baptist Singles in Fellowship**
Eugenia Harrelson
Southside Baptist
P.O. Box 418
Bay Minette, AL 36507
*Southern Baptist*
**Years in existence:** 1
**Avg. attendance:** 18
**Primarily ages:** 26-30, 46-50
**Main meeting time(s):** Sunday School Class and a week night (M-F)
**Singles classes:** Singles in Fellowship (28-50), College/ Career (18-30)

## BIRMINGHAM

**Birmingham Adult Christian Singles**
Wayne Mewbourne
2575 Columbiana Road
Birmingham, AL 35216
205/979-2273
**Years in existence:** 9
**Avg. attendance:** 95
**Primarily ages:** 36-50
**Main meeting time(s):** Sunday School Class

**Canterbury Seekers**
Virginia Weikel
Canterbury United Methodist Church
350 Overbrook Road
Birmingham, AL 35213
*United Methodist*
205/871-4695
**Years in existence:** 3
**Avg. attendance:** 100
**Primarily ages:** 26-35, 50+
**Main meeting time(s):** Sunday School Class **Singles classes:** Young Singles (23-35), Mid-Singles (30-45), Upper Singles (40+)

**Homewood Singles Ministry**
Rick Kanfhold
Homewood Church of Christ
265 West Oxmoor Road
Birmingham, AL 35209
*Church of Christ*
205/942-5683
**Years in existence:** 10
**Avg. attendance:** 200
**Primarily ages:** 26-40
**Main meeting time(s):** Sunday School Class, a week night (M-F)
**Singles classes:** College (Undergraduate) (17-24), Young Professional (24-40s), Older Professional (40+), Starting Over Singles (20s+)

**Independent Singles**
Mrs. Leigh Brown
Independent Presbyterian Church
3100 Highland Avenue
Birmingham, AL 35213
*Presbyterian Church, USA*
205/933-1830
**Years in existence:** 6
**Primarily ages:** 18-50+
**Main meeting time(s):** Sunday School Class **Singles classes:** Highlanders (22-35), Midtowners (35-50), Singles Now (50+)

**PCF Singles**
Marye L. Thrasher
Parkway Christian Fellowship
9753 Parkway East
Birmingham, AL 35215
*Interdenominational*
205/836-8845
**Years in existence:** 9
**Avg. attendance:** 60
**Primarily ages:** 26-50
**Main meeting time:** Sunday School Class
**Singles classes:** Singles I (21-32), Singles II (33-49), Singles III (50+)

**Shades Mountain Baptist Singles**
Jimmy Parrish
Shades Mountain Baptist Church
2017 Columbiana Road
Birmingham, AL 35216
*Southern Baptist*
205/822-1670
**Years in existence:** 12
**Avg. attendance:** 350
**Primarily ages:** 26-30
**Main meeting time(s):** Sunday School Class **Singles classes:** 1SA1 (21-30), 1SA2 (30-45), 1SA3 (45+), 2SA1A (21-30)

**First Christian Singles Ministry**
Dr. Drexel C. Rankin
First Christian Church
4954 Valleydale Road
Birmingham, AL 35242
*Christian Church (Disciples of Christ)*
205/991-5000

**STRONG (Singles, Thirty, Reaching Out, Nurturing, Growing)**
Millie J. Davis
East Lake United Methodist Church
7753 1st Avenue South
Birmingham, AL 35235
*United Methodist*
205/833-7958
**Years in existence:** 2
**Avg. attendance:** 10
**Primarily ages:** 31-40
**Main meeting time(s):** Sunday School Class

**Trinity United Methodist Single Adults**
Dale R. Cohen
Trinity United Methodist Church
P.O. Box 19069
Birmingham, AL 35219-9069
*United Methodist*
205/879-1737
**Years in existence:** 6
**Avg. attendance:** 65
**Primarily ages:** 26-30
**Main meeting time(s):** Sunday School Class **Singles classes:** Single Adult (All), Christian Single (26-30), Seekers (30-50), Faith (50+)

## GADSDEN

**Every Single Friday**
Jack Campbell
934 South 11th Street
Gadsden, AL 35901
205/547-7149
**Years in existence:** 10
**Avg. attendance:** 30
**Primarily ages:** 50+
**Main meeting time(s):** Friday night

## HUNTSVILLE

**SAM**
William O. Lipp
Trinity United Methodist Church
607 Airport Road
Huntsville, AL 35802
*United Methodist*
205/883-3215
**Years in existence:** 8
**Avg. attendance:** 45
**Primarily ages:** 26-30, 36-40+
**Main meeting time(s):** Sunday School Class
**Singles classes:** Winners (45+), New Life (24-33), New Directions (20-26), New Doorways (65+)

## MOBILE

**Dauphin Way Singles**
Scott White
Dauphin Way Baptist Church
3661 Dauphin Street
Mobile, AL 36608
*Southern Baptist*
205/342-3456
**Years in existence:** 20
**Avg. attendance:** 140
**Primarily ages:** 26-30
**Main meeting time:** Sunday School Class
**Singles classes:** Single Adults I (27-35), Single Adults II (36+)

## MONTGOMERY

**Aldersgate Christian Singles**
Steve Badskey
Aldersgate United Methodist Church
6610 Vaughn Road
Montgomery, AL 36116
*United Methodist*
205/272-6152
**Years in existence:** 1
**Avg. attendance:** 15
**Primarily ages:** 41-50+
**Main meeting time(s):** Sunday night

**First United Methodist Single Adult Ministry**
Miss Jane Parsons
First United Methodist Church
2416 West Cloverdale Park
Montgomery, AL 36106-1908
*Methodist*
205/834-8990
**Years in existence:**1
**Avg. attendance:** 50
**Primarily ages:** 26-35
**Main meeting time(s):** Sunday School Class
**Singles classes:** New Horizons (20-40)

**Frazer Memorial Single Adults**
Mrs. Ann L. Kline
Frazer Memorial
6000 Atlanta Highway
Montgomery, AL 36117
*United Methodist*
205/272-8672
**Years in existence:** 12
**Avg. attendance:** 450
**Primarily ages:** 26-30, 46-50
**Main meeting time(s):** Sunday School Class
**Singles classes:** Singles One (23-28), Single Life (28-38), PTS (38-58)

## OLD SPANISH FORT

**Old Spanish Fort Baptist Singles**
David Huggins
Old Spanish Fort Baptist
P.O. Box 547
Old Spanish Fort, AL 36527
*Baptist*
205/626-1379
**Years in existence:** 7
**Avg. attendance:** 35
**Primarily ages:** 31-45
**Main meeting time(s):** Sunday School Class, Friday night
**Singles classes:** Weekly (24+), Robinson (24+)

## PELL CITY

**Pell City Singles**
Ron DeThomas
Pell City Independent Church
P.O. Box 794
Pell City, AL 35125
*Independent*
205/338-2901
**Years in existence:** 2
**Avg. attendance:** 20
**Primarily ages:** 36-40
**Main meeting time(s):** A week night (M-F)
**Singles classes:** Young Adults (20-30)

## TUSCALOOSA

**First Baptist Single Adults**
Carol M. Woodruff
First Baptist Church
P.O. Box 031607
Tuscaloosa, AL 35403
*Baptist*
205/345-7554
**Years in existence:** 8
**Avg. attendance:** 70
**Primarily ages:** 26-30
**Main meeting time(s):** Sunday School Class **Singles classes:** Singles (18-30), Singles II (31-49), Singles III (50+)

## WIND COVE

**One In The Spirit Christian Adult Singles**
Martha Bryan
P.O. Box 652
Wind Cove, AK 99928
*One In The Spirit*
**Years in existence:** 3
**Avg. attendance:** 10
**Primarily ages:** 31-40
**Main meeting time(s):** Friday night
**Avg. attendance:** 30
**Primarily ages:** 18-45
**Main meeting time(s):** Sunday School Class, a week night (M-F)
**Singles classes:** Crossroads (18-25), Singles (25-45)

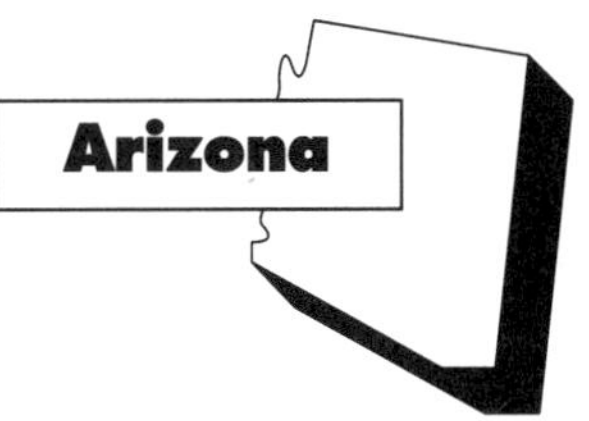


## GLENDALE

**Single With Joy**
Kim Johnson
Community Church of Joy
16635 N. 51st Avenue
Glendale, AZ 85306
602/938-1460
**Years in existence:** 4
**Avg. attendance:** 150
**Primarily ages:** 36-45
**Main meeting time(s):** Sunday School Class, Friday night
**Singles classes:** 50+ Singles (50+), Single With Joy (35-45)

## MESA

### Central Christian Singles
John Hendee
Central Christian
933 N. Lindsay Road
Mesa, AZ 85213
*Christian Church*
602/924-4946
**Years in existence:** 8
**Avg. attendance:** 70
**Primarily ages:** 31-40
**Main meeting time(s):** Sunday School Class, a week night (M-F)
**Singles classes:** Abijah (22-26), TNT (27-33), New Dawn (34-45)

### The Single Connections
Hope Mitchell
Grace United Methodist
2024 East University Drive
Mesa, AZ 85213
*Methodist*
602/964-8707
**Years in existence:** 5
**Avg. attendance:** 20
**Primarily ages:** 46-50+
**Main meeting time(s):** A week night (M-F)

## PHOENIX

### Christ Church Singles
Vernon Ermeling
Christ Church
3901 E. Indian School
Phoenix, AZ 85018
*Lutheran Church—Missouri Synod*
602/955-4830
**Years in existence:** 8
**Avg. attendance:** 30
**Primarily ages:** 18-45
**Main meeting time(s):** Sunday School Class, a week night (M-F)
**Singles classes:** Crossroads (18-25), Singles (25-45)

### New Life Singles
Bryan S. Latchaw
Bethany Bible Church
6060 N. 7th Avenue
Phoenix, AZ 85013
*Independent*
602/246-9788
**Years in existence:** 10
**Avg. attendance:** 80
**Primarily ages:** 26-35
**Main meeting time(s):** Sunday School Class

### Single Vision
Wesley G. Hodgkin
West Rose Lane Assemblies of God
6145 N. 36th Drive
Phoenix, AZ 85019
*Assemblies of God*
602/841-0610
**Years in existence:** 1
**Avg. attendance:** 10
**Primarily ages:** 26-30, 41-45
**Main meeting time(s):** Sunday School Class

### Valley Cathedral Singles
Randy Helm
The Valley Cathedral
6225 N. Central
Phoenix, AZ 80512
*Interdenominational*
602/266-6668
**Years in existence:** 10
**Avg. attendance:** 150
**Primarily ages:** 31-35
**Main meeting time(s):** Sunday School Class
**Singles classes:** Careers (25-39), Single Vision (40+), Successful Single Parents

## SCOTTSDALE

### Chaparral Christian Singles
David Totel
Chaparral Christian Church
6451 E. Shea Boulevard
Scottsdale, AZ 85254
*Non-denominational*
**Years in existence:** 3
**Avg. attendance:** 8
**Primarily ages:** 41-45
**Main meeting time(s):** A week night (M-F)

## SPRINGDALE

### First Baptist Singles Ministry
Wayne Cook
First Baptist Church of Springdale, AZ
1709 Johnson Road
Springdale, AZ 72764
*Baptist*
501/751-4523
**Years in existence:** 6
**Avg. attendance:** 120
**Primarily ages:** 31-40
**Main meeting time(s):** Sunday School Class, Saturday night
**Singles classes:** Singles I (19-23), Singles II (24-29), Singles III (30-43), Singles IV (44+)

## TEMPE

### Bethany Singles
Jeffrey R. King
Bethany Community Church
6240 South Price Road
Tempe, AZ 85283
Independent—Non-denominational
602/831-5005
**Years in existence:** 3
**Avg. attendance:** 60
**Primarily ages:** 31-35
**Main meeting time(s):** Sunday School Class
**Singles classes:** S.A.L.T. (Single Adults Learning Together) (30-45), Twenty-Something (23-30)

### Priority One
Ray Melser
Grace Community Church
3201 South Terrace
Tempe, AZ 85282
*Non-denominational*
602/894-2201
**Years in existence**: 5
**Avg. attendance**: 100
**Primarily ages:** 36-50
**Main meeting time**: Sunday School Class

## TUCSON

### Casas Adobes Singles Ministry
Larry Langley
Casas Adobes Baptist Church
2131 West Ina Road
Tucson, AZ 85741
*Southern Baptist*
602/297-7238
**Years in existence:** 10
**Avg. attendance:** 300
**Primarily ages:** 26-35
**Main meeting time(s):** Sunday School Class **Singles classes:** Single Adult I, Single Adult II, Single Adult III, Single Adult IV

### Single Pointe
Gale Trow
Emmanuel Baptist Church
1825 N. Alvernon
Tucson, AZ 85712
*Baptist*
602/323-9379
**Years in existence:** 10
**Avg. attendance:** 40
**Primarily ages:** 31-45
**Main meeting time(s):** Sunday School Class **Singles classes:** 2 (20s), 3 AS (30-34), 3B (35-40), 4 (40+)

## YUMA

### Singles Fellowship
Paula L. Killingsworth
First Assemblies of God
902 South 6th Avenue
Yuma, AZ 85364
*Assemblies of God*
602/782-9238
**Years in existence:** 1
**Avg. attendance:** 15
**Primarily ages:** 18-25
**Main meeting time(s):** Sunday night

## FORT SMITH

### Single Life
Grand Avenue Baptist
921 North 39th
Fort Smith, AR 72903
*Southern Baptist*
501/783-5161
**Years in existence**: 7
**Avg. attendance**: 90
**Primarily ages:** 26-30
**Main meeting time**: Sunday School Class
**Singles classes**: Dept. 18-32: 1 (18-22), 2 (23-25), 3 (26-29), 4 (30-32); Dept. 33-65: 1 (33-41), 2 (45-50), 3 (51-65)

## LITTLE ROCK

### Baring Cross Singles
Allan Greer
Baring Cross Baptist Church
13th & Franklin Streets
North Little Rock, AR 72114
*Southern Baptist*
501/375-2347
**Years in existence:** 6
**Avg. attendance:** 40
**Primarily ages:** 26-30
**Main meeting time(s):** Sunday School Class **Singles classes:** Wonder Years (18-21), Growing Pains (22-29), Thirty Something (30-39), Prime Time Live (40-55)

### First Baptist Singles Ministry
Theresa Anderson
First Baptist Church
62 Pleasant Valley Drive
Little Rock, AR 72212
*Southern Baptist*
501/227-0010
**Years in existence**: 12
**Avg. attendance:** 125
**Primarily ages:** 26-35
**Main meeting time**: Sunday School Class

### Grace Singles
Charles Boyd
Grace Community Church
2311 Biscayne #204
Little Rock, AR 72207
501/225-0843
**Years in existence:** 3
**Avg. attendance:** 35
**Primarily ages:** 26-35
**Main meeting time(s):** A week night (M-F)

### Immanuel Baptist Singles Ministry
Dianne Swaim
Immanuel Baptist
1000 Bishop (10th & Bishop)
Little Rock, AR 72202
*Southern Baptist*
501/376-3071
**Years in existence:** 12
**Avg. attendance:** 150
**Primarily ages:** 26-30, 41-45
**Main meeting time(s):** Sunday School Class
**Singles classes:** Career (22-31), Single Adult (32+)

### St. James United Methodist Singles
Rusty Johnson
St. James United Methodist Church
321 Pleasant Valley Drive
Little Rock, AR 72212
*United Methodist*
501/225-7372
**Years in existence**: 12
**Avg. attendance:** 100+
**Primarily ages:** 31-35
**Main meeting time**: Sunday School class
**Singles classes**: College & Careers (18-25), Cornerstone (25-35), Discovery (35-50), Fellowship (40-60)

## RUSSELVILLE

### West Side Singles
Mike Reeves
West Side Church of Christ
Box 1084
Russellville, AR 72801
501-968-1121
**Years in existence:** 3
**Avg. attendance:** 75
**Primarily ages:** 36-40
**Main meeting time(s):** A week night (M-F)

## SPRINGDALE

### Singles Alive
Wayne Cook
First Baptist Church
1709 Johnson Road
Springdale, AR 72764
*Southern Baptist*
501/751-4523
**Years in existence**: 8
**Avg. attendance:** 140
**Primarily ages**: 31-35
**Main meeting time:** Sunday School Class
**Singles classes**: Singles I (18-25), Singles II (26-32), Singles III (33-42), Singles IV (43+)

## ALAMEDA

### The Lighthouse Fellowship
Danny Turley
Westside Baptist Church
1531 Sixth Street
Alameda, CA 94501
*Conservative Baptist*
415/522-1696
**Years in existence:** 1
**Avg. attendance:** 2
**Primarily ages:** 18-25
**Main meeting time(s):** A week night (M-F)

## ALAMO

### Alamo Christian Singles
Bill Ambrose
Alamo Christian Assembly
2501 Danville Boulevard
Alamo, CA 94507
*Assemblies of God*
415/934-5449
**Years in existence:** 3
**Avg. attendance:** 15
**Primarily ages:** 26-30
**Main meeting time(s):** A week night (M-F)

## APTOS

### Twin Lakes Singles Network
Vince Turturice
Twin Lakes Baptist Church
2701 Cabrillo College Dr.
Aptos, CA 95003
*Conservative Baptist*
408/475-5284
**Years in existence**: 6
**Avg. attendance**: 100
**Primarily ages**: 18-30
**Main meeting time(s):** Sunday School Class, Wednesday night
**Singles classes:** New Life (45-60), Prime Time, Mom's Angels, In Step, Kid's Kloset

## ARCADIA

### Single Adult Fellowship
Rev. William Van Loan
Arcadia Presbyterian Church
121 Alice Street
Arcadia, CA 91006
*Presbyterian (American)*
818/445-7470
**Years in existence:** 12
**Avg. attendance:** 60
**Primarily ages:** 46-50+
**Main meeting time(s):** Sunday School Class, a week night (M-F)
**Singles classes:** Act I (30-40), Primetime (45+), 40s & 50s (40-50+)

## BAKERSFIELD

### Single Again
Don Bertrand
Calvary Bible Church
4850 Manor
Bakersfield, CA 93308
*Non-denominational*
805/327-5921
**Years in existence:** 8
**Avg. attendance:** 40
**Primarily ages:** 36-40
**Main meeting time(s):** A week night (M-F)

## BLYTHE

### Christian Singles
Ken Leonard
Streams In The Desert
361 N. Lovekin Boulevard
Blythe, CA 92225
*International Church of the Foursquare Gospel*
619/922-7210
**Years in existence:** 2
**Avg. attendance:** 8
**Primarily ages:** 31-35

## CASTRO VALLEY

### Single Purpose
Malcolm Cash
The Neighborhood Church
20600 John Drive
Castro Valley, CA 94546
*Christian & Missionary Alliance*
415/537-4690
**Years in existence:** 10
**Avg. attendance:** 40
**Primarily ages:** 50+
**Main meeting time(s):** Sunday School Class, a week night (M-F)

## CONCORD

### Ygnacio Valley Singles Fellowship
Sherry Boyle
Ygnacio Valley Presbyterian Church
2140 Minert Road
Concord, CA 94518
*Presbyterian*
415/682-8254
**Years in existence:** 4
**Avg. attendance:** 9
**Primarily ages:** 50+

## CORONA

### Crossroads Singles Network
Rick Stedman
Crossroads Christian Church
1775 S. Main Street/ P.O. Box 1775
Corona, CA 91718
*Independent*
714/737-4664

**Years in existence:** 10
**Avg. attendance:** 160
**Primarily ages:** 26-45
**Main meeting time(s):** Sunday School Class
**Singles classes:** 20 Something (20-30), Single Focus (25-70), Tuesday Night Fellowship (20-70)

## COSTA MESA

### Impact
Andy Stenhouse
New Port Mesa Christian Center
2599 New Port Blvd.
Costa Mesa, CA 92627
*Assemblies of God*
714/966-0454
**Years in existence:** 3
**Avg. attendance:** 150
**Primarily ages:** 26-30
**Main meeting time:** Sunday School Class **Singles classes:** Impact (21-35)

## CUPERTINO

### The Valley Church Career Group
Richard Krikorian
The Valley Church
10885 N. Stelling Road
Cupertino, CA 95014
*Bible Church Non-denominational*
408/739-4642
**Years in existence:** 10
**Avg. attendance:** 40
**Primarily ages:** 26-30
**Main meeting time(s):** Sunday School Class

## DEL MAR

### Vespers of St. Peters'
Mark Given
St. Peters' Episcopal Church
P.O. Box 336
Del Mar, CA 92014
*Episcopal*
619/755-1616
**Years in existence:** 2
**Avg. attendance:** 8
**Primarily ages:** 31-40
**Main meeting time(s):** A week night (M-F)

## DOWNEY

### First Baptist Singles
Denny Clementson
First Baptist Church
8348 Third Street
Downey, CA 90241
*American Baptist*
213/923-1261
**Years in existence:** 12
**Avg. attendance:** 120
**Primarily ages:** 26-30
**Main meeting time:** Sunday School Class **Singles classes:** College (18-22), Singles 1 (23-35), Singles Family (30-50), Koinonia (50+ single men)

### Serendipity Singles
Ken Campbell
Downey First Presbyterian Church
10544 Downey Avenue
Downey, CA 90241
*Presbyterian*
213/861-6752
**Years in existence:** 4
**Avg. attendance:** 12
**Primarily ages:** 31-40
**Main meeting time(s):** A week night (M-F)

### Singles Alive
Pastor Glenn Kravig
Calvary Chapel
12808 Woodruff Avenue
Downey, CA 90242
*Non-denominational*
213/803-5631
**Years in existence:** 11
**Avg. attendance:** 120
**Primarily ages:** 26-30
**Main meeting time:** A week night (M-F)
**Singles classes:** Picking Up the Pieces—divorce recovery; Growing Through Grief—support group; Fireside Fellowship—singles rap session; Positive Parenting—single parents; Men & Women Rap—facing personal issues

**Fact:**
*In the United States there are approximately 3,562 divorces every day, 148 every hour.*
*Pressing News, David C. Cook*

## ENCINITAS

### Presbyterian Singles United
James R. Bowen
Presbytery of San Diego
1901 Wandering Road
Encinitas, CA 92024
*Presbyterian*
619/544-7625
**Years in existence:** 8
**Avg. attendance:** 120
**Primarily ages:** 36-40

### San Dieguito Singles
Barb Hartman
San Dieguito United Methodist Church
170 Calle Magdalena
Encinitas, CA 92024
*United Methodist*
619/753-6582
**Years in existence:** 2
**Avg. attendance:** 25
**Primarily ages:** 36-50
**Main meeting time(s):** Sunday night

## ESCONDIDO

### Christian Singles Alive
Rev. Scott Last
Emmanuel Faith Community Church
639 E. Felicita
Escondido, CA 92025
*Non-denominational*
619/745-2541 X163
**Years in existence:** 9
**Avg. attendance:** 150
**Primarily ages:** 31-35
**Main meeting time(s):** Sunday School Class **Singles classes:** Spectrum (22-35), Single Purpose (30+)

### Neighborhood Church Singles
Dan Koeshall
The Neighborhood Church Singles
1001 Country Club Lane
Escondido, CA 92026
*Assemblies of God*
619/741-7881
**Years in existence:** 2
**Avg. attendance:** 20
**Primarily ages:** 18-25
**Main meeting time(s):** Sunday School Class

## FAIR OAKS

### Fair Oaks Presbyterian Singles
David Weidlich
Fair Oaks Presbyterian Church
11427 Fair Oaks Boulevard
Fair Oaks, CA 95628
*Presbyterian Church USA*
916/967-4784
**Years in existence:** 13
**Avg. attendance:** 150
**Primarily ages:** 36-50
**Main meeting time(s):** A week night (M-F)
**Singles classes:** Sunday Night Fellowship (30-55), Personal Growth (35-55), New Horizons (24-35), Senior Singles (65+)

## FREMONT

### Fremont Evangelical Free Singles
Fremont Evangelical Free Church
505 Driscoll Road
Fremont, CA 94539
*Evangelical Free*
415/651-2030
**Years in existence:** 10
**Avg. attendance:** 80
**Primarily ages:** 18-25
**Main meeting time:** Sunday School Class
**Singles classes:** Career Singles (8-26), SALT (26+)

### Singles Alive
Roger K. MCCarthy
First Assemblies of God
4760 Thorton Avenue
Fremont, CA 94536
*Assemblies of God*
415/793-8687
**Years in existence:** 7
**Avg. attendance:** 160
**Primarily ages:** 18-35
**Main meeting time(s):** A week night (M-F)
**Singles classes:** Single Parents Alive (all ages), Agape Class (all ages), New Life Singles (18-22)

## FRESNO

### The Peoples' Church Singles Ministry

Mick Wagenman
The Peoples' Church
7172 N.Cedar Avenue
Fresno, CA 93720-3368
*Independent*
209/298-8001
**Years in existence:** 14
**Avg. attendance:** 285
**Primarily ages:** 18-50
**Main meeting time(s):** Sunday School Class
**Singles classes:** College/Career (18-24), 20-Something (24-30), New Horizons (30+), Joint Heirs (40+)

## FULLERTON

### First Evangelical Free Singles

Jim Adkins
First Evangelical Free Church
2801 North Brea
Fullerton, CA 92635
*Evangelical Free*
714/529-5544
**Years in existence:** 17
**Avg. attendance**: 660
**Primarily ages:** 26-30
**Main meeting time(s)**: Sunday School Class **Singles classes:** 20/20 (23-27), Single Focus (27-40), Single Parent Fellowship

### Single Ministry

Doyle Duggins
Eastside Christian Church
2505 Yorba Linda Blvd.
Fullerton, CA 92631
*Non-denominational*
714/871-6844
**Years in existence:** 7
**Avg. attendance:** 100
**Primarily ages:** 26-35
**Main meeting time:** Sunday School Class **Singles classes:** S.I.F.T. (22-30), One in the Spirit (30-45)

## GARDEN GROVE

### Positive Christian Singles

David Baker and Rich Hurst
Crystal Cathedral Community Church
12141 Lewis Street
Garden Grove, CA 92640
*Reformed Church in America*
714/971-4061
**Years in existence:** 17
**Avg. attendance:** 150
**Primarily ages:** 31-45
**Main meeting time(s):** Sunday School Class, a week night (M-F)

## GILROY

### Gilroy Presbyterian Singles

Chuck Mallonee
Gilroy Presbyterian
6000 Miller Avenue
Gilroy, CA 95020
*Presbyterian Church (USA)*
408/842-3000
**Years in existence:** 3
**Avg. attendance:** 40
**Primarily ages:** 31-50
**Main meeting time(s):** Sunday School Class

## GLENDORA

### Glenkirk Singles Connection

Betty Naylor
Glenkirk Presbyterian Church
1700 E Palopinto Ave
Glendora, CA 91740
*Presbyterian*
818/914-4833
**Years in existence:** 11
**Avg. attendance:** 30
**Primarily ages:** 50+
**Main meeting time(s):** Sunday School Class

## HUNTINGTON BEACH

### Frontrunner

Paul Kaak
Calvary Baptist Church
8281 Garfield Avenue
Huntington Beach, CA 92646
*Conservative Baptist*
714/962-6860
**Years in existence:** 3
**Avg. attendance:** 25
**Primarily ages:** 18-25
**Main meeting time(s):** Friday night

## IRVINE

### South Coast Singles/Focus 20

Charlie Hedges
South Coast Community Church
5120 Bonita Canyon Drive
Irvine, CA 92715
**Years in existence:** 10
**Avg. attendance:** 250-300
**Primarily ages:** 36-50
**Main meeting time(s):** Sunday School Class, Friday night
**Singles classes:** South Coast Singles (35-55), Focus 20 (25-33)

## LA JOLLA

### La Jolla Christian Singles

Stuart Fox
La Jolla Christian Chapel
648 Center St.
La Jolla, CA 92037
619-459-9569
**Years in existence:** 2
**Avg. attendance:** 25
**Primarily ages:** 31-40
**Main meeting time(s):** Sunday School Class, Friday night
**Singles classes:** Cornerstone (30-35)

## LAFAYETTE

### Lafayette Orinda Presbyterian Singles

Rev. Terry Dawson
Lafayette Orinda Presbyterian
49 Knox Drive
Lafayette, CA 94549
*Presbyterian USA*
415/283-8722
**Years in existence**: 12
**Avg. attendance:** 500
**Main meeting time:** Sunday night
**Singles classes:** Castaways (20+), Shipmates (30s & 40s), Singleship (40+)

## LAGUNA NIGEL

### Single Focus

Dave Gilbert
Coast Hills Community Church
26041 Cape Drive #233
Laguna Nigel, CA 92677
*Independent*
714/582-6744
**Years in existence:** 3
**Avg. attendance:** 30
**Primarily ages:** 31-35
**Main meeting time(s):** Sunday School Class
**Singles classes:** Seven Thirtysomething (25-35), Streamers (35+)

## LEMON GROVE

### Skyline Singles Community

Larry White
Skyline Wesleyan
1345 Skyline Drive
Lemon Grove, CA 92045
*Wesleyan*
619/460-5000
**Years in existence:** 20
**Avg. attendance:** 140
**Primarily ages:** 36-45
**Main meeting time(s):** Sunday School Class
**Singles classes:** Single Adults (30-60), Thirty Something (30-45)

## LODI

### Temple Baptist Singles

David Lundy
Temple Baptist Church
801 S. Lower Sacramento Road
Lodi, CA 95242
*North American Baptist*
209/369-1948
**Years in existence:** 3
**Avg. attendance:** 5
**Primarily ages:** 26-45
**Main meeting time(s):** Sunday School Class

**Fact:**

In 1988, there were about 1.2 million divorced and widowed fathers raising their children, compared with 8.1 million single-parent mothers.

*U.S. Census Bureau*

## LOS ALTOS

### Christian Singles Fellowship
Brian D.N. Person
Union Presbyterian Church
858 University Avenue
Los Altos, CA 94024
*Presbyterian Church (USA)*
415/948-4361
**Years in existence:** 2
**Avg. attendance:** 12
**Primarily ages:** 31-35
**Main meeting time(s):** A week night (M-F)

### Single Focus
Chuck Grasse
First Baptist of Los Altos
625 Magdalena Avenue
Los Altos, CA 94024
*Baptist*
415/948-5698
**Years in existence:** 2
**Avg. attendance:** 20
**Primarily ages:** 31-35
**Main meeting time(s):** Sunday School Class

## LOS ANGELES

### Bel Air Adult Fellowship
Bob Henley
Bel Air Presbyterian Church
16221 Mulholland Drive
Los Angeles, CA 90049
*Presbyterian*
818/788-4200
**Years in existence:** 7
**Avg. attendance:** 125
**Primarily ages:**36-45
**Main meeting time(s):** A week night (M-F)
**Singles classes:** Koinonia (22-35), Bel Air Adult Fellowship (35-55), Bel Air Special Singles (56+)

### Single Adult Fellowship
Leland Chinn
First Chinese Baptist Church of Los Angeles
942 Yale Street
Los Angeles, CA 90012
*Southern Baptist*
**Years in existence:** 1
**Avg. attendance:** 20
**Primarily ages:** 31-40
**Main meeting time(s):** A week night (M-F)

## LOS GATOS

### Single Direction Ministries
Norman Yukers
Los Gatos Christian Church
16845 Hicks Road
Los Gatos, CA 95032
*Non-denominational*
408/268-6435
**Years in existence:** 10
**Avg. attendance:** 250
**Primarily ages:** 31-40
**Main meeting time(s):** Sunday School Class
**Singles classes:** Quest (24-32), Prime Time (33-45), Focus (46+)

## MENLO PARK

### Menlo Park Single Adult Ministries
Dan Chun
Menlo Park Presbyterian Church
950 Santa Cruz Avenue
Menlo Park, CA 94025
*Presbyterian Church, USA*
415/323-8631
**Years in existence:** 6
**Avg. attendance:** 350
**Primarily ages:** 26-35
**Main meeting time(s):** Sunday School Class, Sunday night
**Singles classes:** Twenty Something (21-25), Young Adults Fellowship (20s-30s), MSG (Mid Singles Group) (30-45), Singles Together (35+)

## MISSION VIEJO

### Saddleback "Successfull Singles"
Ross Shepherd
Saddleback Valley Community Church
24149 Alicia Parkway, Suite M
Mission Viejo, CA 92691
714/581-5683
**Years in existence:** 3
**Avg. attendance:** 300
**Primarily ages:** 26-35
**Main meeting time(s):** Sunday School Class, Sunday night, a week night (M-F), Saturday night
**Singles classes:** Successfully Single (25-35), Heart 'n' Soul (35-45), His Image (25-35), Open Forum (25-35)

## MODESTO

### Big Valley Singles Ministry
Jim Bouck
Big Valley Grace Community Church
4040 Tully Road
Modesto, CA 95356
*Non-denominatonal*
209/577-1604
**Years in existence:** 1
**Avg. attendance:** 75
**Primarily ages:** 36-40
**Main meeting time(s):** Sunday School Class, a week night (M-F)
**Singles classes:** Family Ties (35+), TNT (20s-30s)

### Singles Alive
Dr. Jim A. Talley
First Baptist Church
P.O. Box 4309
Modesto, CA 95352-4309
*Non-denominational*
209/521-0181
**Years in existence:** 16
**Avg. attendance:** 150+
**Primarily ages:** 31-40
**Main meeting time:** Sunday School Class **Singles classes:** Reconcilable Differences-divorced and separated; leadership training; single parenting classes

## MORAGA

### Singles Together
Mary Holder Naegeli
Moraga Valley Presbyterian Church
30 Idlewood Court
Moraga, CA 9456
*Presbyterian Church (USA)*
415/376-4800
**Years in existence:** 2
**Primarily ages:** 50+

## MORENO VALLEY

### The Edge
Martin Schlomer
Evangelical Free Church of Moreno Valley
23470 Olivewood Plaza #220
Moreno Valley, CA 92580
*Evangelical Free*
714/924-6832
**Years in existence:** 2
**Avg. attendance:** 15
**Primarily ages:** 18-25
**Main meeting time(s):** A week night (M-F)
**Singles classes:** College/Career (18-30)

## NAPA

### Positive Singles
David Scott
First Christian Church
2659 First Street
Napa, CA 94558
*Non-denominational*
415/895-4293
**Years in existence:** 2
**Avg. attendance:** 12
**Primarily ages:** 36-50
**Main meeting time(s):** Sunday School Class

## NEWPORT BEACH

### St. Andrews Singles
Dr. Bill Flanagan
St. Andrews Presbyterian
600 St. Andrews Road
Newport Beach, CA 92663
714/631-2885
**Years in existence:** 10
**Avg. attendance:** 150
**Primarily ages:** 41-45
**Main meeting time(s):** Sunday School Class, a week night (M-F), Friday night
**Singles classes:** Becomers (21-35), Illuminators (35-55), Ambassadors (55+), CLASP (Children, Love & Single Parents) (30-40s)

### Salt Company
Scott Rae
Mariners Church
1000 Bison Avenue
Newport Beach, CA 92660
*Non-denominational*
714/640-6010
**Years in existence:** 15
**Avg. attendance:** 150
**Primarily ages:** 31-35
**Main meeting time:** Sunday night
**Singles classes:** The Twenties Group (20s), graduated from college; Salt Company (30+)

## OCCIDENTAL

### Single Adult Conference
Bob Cordier
Westminster Woods Presbyterian
6510 Bohemian Highway

Occidental, CA 94565-9106
*Presbyterian Church (USA)*
707/874-2426
**Years in existence:** 10+
**Primarily ages:** 18-25, 31-50+

## OCEANSIDE

### Outriggers
William A. Wood
First Presbyterian Church
2001 El Camino Real
Oceanside, CA 92054
*Presbyterian Church (USA)*
619/757-3560
**Years in existence:** 8
**Avg. attendance:** 30
**Primarily ages:** 41-50+
**Main meeting time(s):** Sunday night
**Singles classes:** Outriggers (30-59), Spinnakers (20-39)

### Single's Again
Jeff Apsley
Tri City Church
302 N. Emerald Drive
Oceanside, CA 92083
*Baptist*
619/724-3957
**Years in existence:** 5
**Avg. attendance** 25
**Primarily ages:** 31-40
**Main meeting time(s):** Sunday School Class, Friday night
**Singles classes:** Focus (College) (19-30), Single Servants (20-30), Single Again (30+)

The segment of our society most unreached by the church is single men in their 20s.

*Lyle Schaller, church growth consultant*

## ORANGE

### Diocese of Orange— Young Adult Ministry
James F. Teixeira
Diocese of Orange
2811 E. Villa Real Drive
Orange, CA 92667-1999
*Roman Catholic*
714/974-7120 Ext. 214
**Years in existence:** 10
**Avg. attendance:** 200
**Primarily ages:** 18-30
**Singles classes:** Faith (18-30), Choice (18-30), Corpus Christi (18-35), Other Parish/Search Groups (18-30)

## PASADENA

### Diakonos
Susan Highleyman
595 E. Colorado #331
Pasadena, CA 91101
818/792-8835
**Years in existence:** 9
**Avg. attendance:** 60+
**Primarily ages:** 26-45

### Force of One Ministry
Jerry Homme
Pasadena Foursquare Church
174 N. Harkness Avenue
Pasadena, CA 91106
*Foursquare*
818/792-1803
**Years in existence:** 4
**Avg. attendance:** 55
**Primarily ages:** 31-35
**Main meeting time(s):** Friday night

### Lake Avenue Congregational Singles
Steve Morgan
Lake Avenue Congregational
393 N. Lake Avenue
Pasadena, CA 91101
*Congregational*
818/795-7221
**Years in existence:** 20
**Avg. attendance:** 350
**Primarily ages:** 26-30
**Main meeting time(s):** Sunday School Class **Singles classes:** Network (20-30s), Cornersone (40-50s), Single Again (40-50s)

## RANCHO CUCAMONGA

### Single With A Purpose
Richard A. May, III
Cucamonga Christian Fellowship
9592 7th Street
Rancho Cucamonga, CA 91730
*Non-denominational*
**Years in existence:** 5
**Avg. attendance:** 50
**Primarily ages:** 18-25
**Main meeting time(s):** A week night (M-F)
**Singles classes:** Single With A Purpose (24-29), Bub & Ted's Excellent Adventure (18-24), 30+ Singles (30-39)

## RIVERSIDE

### Club 10
Michael Valcarcel
Bethel Christian Center
2425 Van Buren Boulevard
Riverside, CA 92503
*Non-denominational*
714/359-1123 Ext 1240
**Years in existence:** 3
**Avg. attendance:** 74-100
**Primarily ages:** 26-35
**Main meeting time(s):** Sunday School Class, Friday night
**Singles classes:** Mission Won (18-22), Success Un-Ltd (22-30), The Connection (30+)

### Victoria Community Church Singles
Roy Ronveaux
Victoria Community Church
5320 Victoria Avenue
Riverside, CA 92506
*Christian Missionary Alliance*
714/788-9050
**Years in existence:** 13
**Avg. attendance:** 125
**Primarily ages:** 31-45
**Main meeting time(s):** Sunday School Class **Singles classes:** College & Career Network (18-23), Soul Purpose (23-35), SALT (30-40s), 50s Plus (50-65s)

## ROLLING HILLS

### Rolling Hills Singles Ministry
Pastor James J. Stewart
Rolling Hills Covenant Church
2222 North Palos Verde Drive North
Rolling Hills, CA 90274
*Covenant Church of America*
213/519-9406
**Years in existence:** 10
**Avg. attendance:** 100
**Primarily ages:** 41-45
**Main meeting time(s):** Sunday School Class, Friday night

## SACRAMENTO

### Arcade Singles
Bob Fleener
Arcade Baptist Church
3927 Marconi Avenue
Sacramento, CA 95821
*Conservative Baptist*
916/972-1617
**Years in existence:** 8
**Avg. attendance:** 400
**Primarily ages:** 26-40
**Main meeting time(s):** Sunday School Class, Friday night
**Singles classes:** Potter's Clay (22-30), Ekklesia (30-45)

### FOCUS
Ernie Woolner
First Covenant
9000 La Riveria Drive
Sacramento, CA 95826
*Evangelical Covenant Church*
916/363-9446
**Years in existence:** 6
**Avg. attendance:** 25
**Primarily ages:** 18-30
**Main meeting time(s):** Sunday School Class, a week night (M-F)
**Singles classes:** College (18-23), Roinonia (24-27), Focus (28-40)

### Single Life Ministries
Keith Standridge
Neighborhood Bible Church
6240 Verner Avenue
Sacramento, CA 95841
*Assemblies of God*
916/332-0863
**Years in existence:** 3
**Avg. attendance:** 35
**Primarily ages:** 18-40
**Main meeting time(s):** A week night (M-F)
**Singles classes:** S.A.I.L. (25+), College (18-25), Single Life (23-45)

**Singles Alive!**
Pastor Tim Clements
Captiol Christian Center
9470 Micron Avenue
Sacramento, CA 95827
*Assemblies of God*
916/363-5683
**Years in existence:** 22
**Avg. attendance:** 375+
**Primarily ages:** 18-50+
**Main meeting time:** Monday night

## SALINAS

**SASA**
Peter Cantu
First Presbyterian Church of Salinas
830 Padre Drive
Salinas, CA 93901
*Presbyterian*
408/422-7811
**Years in existence:** 2
**Avg. attendance:** 80
**Primarily ages:** 36-40
**Main meeting time(s):** Sunday School Class, a week night (M-F)
**Singles classes:** SASA 1 (23-34), SASA 2 (35-50)

## SAN BERNARDINO

**Singles Society**
Rob Cassata
Immanuel Baptist Church
2704 Del Rosa Ave
San Bernardino, CA 92404
*Southern Baptist*
714/886-7948
**Years in existence:** 9
**Avg. attendance:** 140
**Primarily ages:** 26-30
**Main meeting time(s):** Sunday School Class, Friday night
**Singles classes:** College/Young Career (18-23), Relational Career (24-30), Professional Career (31-39), Single Parents, Mature Life Managers (40+)

## SAN DIEGO

**Single-Phile**
Susan Gregg-Schroeder
San Diego First United Methodist
2111 Camino del Rio South
San Diego, CA 92108
*United Methodist*
619/297-4366
**Years in existence:** 13
**Avg. attendance:** 60
**Primarily ages:** 31-50
**Main meeting time(s):** A week night (M-F)

**College Avenue Singles**
College Avenue Baptist
4747 College Avenue
San Diego, CA 92115
*Baptist General Conference*
619/582-7222
**Years in existence:** 10
**Avg. attendance:** 170
**Primarily ages:** 26-30
**Main meeting time:** Sunday School Class **Singles classes:** Beyond College (20s), Single Celebration (30s & 40s), divorced, Victors (50s & 60s)

## SAN GABRIEL

**Joint Heirs Singles**
Tom H. McEnroe
San Gabriel Union Church
117 N. Pine Street
San Gabriel, CA 91775
*Non-denominational*
818/287-0434
**Years in existence:** 4
**Avg. attendance:** 25
**Primarily ages:** 41-50
**Main meeting time(s):** Sunday School Class **Singles classes:** Joint Heirs (40+), Twenty Something (22-35)

## SAN JOSE

**Single Life Ministries**
Dennis Franck
Bethel Church
1201 South Winchester Blvd.
San Jose, CA 95128
*Assemblies of God*
408/246-6790
**Years in existence:** 5
**Avg. attendance:** 80
**Primarily ages:** 26-50
**Main meeting time:** A week night (M-F)
**Singles classes:** Career Singles (20-30), Single Spirit (50+), Agape Singles (55+), Single Life Ministries (30+), Career Single Life Ministries (20-30)

**South Hills Community Church Singles**
Gary Rodriguez
South Hills Community Church
6601 Camden Avenue
San Jose, CA 95120
*Non-denominational*
408/268-1676
**Years in existence:** 5
**Avg. attendance:** 200
**Primarily ages:** 26-30
**Main meeting time(s):** Sunday School Class **Singles classes:** Singles (22-32), Singles Plus (35+)

## SAN MATEO

**Ovation Ministries**
Rev. George Pritchard
First Baptist Church
2801 Alameda
San Mateo, CA 94403
*American Baptist*
415/345-1965
**Years in existence:** 6
**Avg. attendance:** 55
**Primarily ages:** 26-30
**Main meeting time(s):** A week night (M-F), Sunday School class

## SAN RAFAEL

**Single's With Spirit**
Sherry Harper
Marin Covenant Church
195 North Redwood Drive
San Rafael, CA 94903
*Covenant*
415/479-1360
**Years in existence:** 10
**Avg. attendance:** 70
**Primarily ages:** 36-45
**Main meeting time:** Sunday School Class **Singles classes:** Divorce Recovery (all ages), Me & the Kids—single parents, Career Singles (20-35), Singles Creative (all ages), Caught in the Middle—children of divorce, Singles Bible Study (all ages), Singles Social (all ages)

## SAN RAMON

**Single Together (at Canyon Creek)**
Bob Scott
Canyon Creek Presbyterian Church
P.O. Box 597 (Meet at: Golden View Elementary School)
San Ramon, CA 94583
*Presbyterian Church in America*
415/833-7665
**Years in existence:** less than 1
**Avg. attendance:** 10
**Primarily ages:** 31-35
**Main meeting time(s):** A week night (M-F)

## SANTA ANA

**Calvary Church Singles**
Jim tenBosch
Calvary Church, Santa Ana
1010 North Tustin Avenue
Santa Ana, CA 92705
*Independent*
714/973-4800
**Years in existence:** 8
**Avg. attendance:** 400
**Primarily ages:** 26-35
**Main meeting time:** Sunday School Classes **Singles classes:** Bible & Breakfast (all ages), Career (25-35), 20+ (20-29), Sonshiners (30-35), single parents, Pathfinders (45+), Shared Life (35-50)

## SANTA BARBARA

**Singles Ministry at Trinity Baptist**
Mike Ballinger
Trinity Baptist Church
1002 Cieneguitas Road
Santa Barbara, CA 93110
*Baptist General Conference*
805-687-7797
**Years in existence:** 5
**Avg. attendance:** 50
**Primarily ages:** 26-40, 50+
**Main meeting time(s):** Sunday School Class, a week night (M-F)
**Singles classes:** Primetimers (35+), Singles in Action (30s), Roaring 20s (20s)

## SANTA CLARITA

**Roaring 20s & 30s**
Marianne Smith
Santa Clarita United Methodist Church
26640 Bouquet Canyon Road
Santa Clarita, CA 91350
*United Methodist*
805/297-3783
**Years in existence:** 1
**Avg. attendance:** 5
**Primarily ages:** 18-25
**Main meeting time(s):** Sunday School Class **Singles classes:** Roaring 20s & 30s (20-35), No Name Yet (30+)

## SANTA ROSA

**Seafarers**
Gayle Turner
First Presbyterian Church
1550 Pacific Avenue

Santa Rosa, CA 95404
*Presbyterian*
707/542-0205
**Years in existence:** 1
**Avg. attendance:** 7
**Primarily ages:** 36-50
**Main meeting time(s):** A week night (M-F)

## SIMI VALLEY

### FOCAS (Fellowship of Christian Adult Singles)

Dana Trotter
Simi Covenant Church
4680 Alamo Street
Simi Valley, CA 93063
*Evangelical Covenant*
805/526-8855
**Years in existence:** 1
**Avg. attendance:** 20
**Primarily ages:** 31-35, 41-45
**Main meeting time(s):** A week night (M-F)

## SOLANA BEACH

### Shipmates

Mary G. Graves
Solanda Beach Presbyterian Church
120 Stevens Avenue
Solana Beach, CA 92075
*Presbyterian Church (USA)*
619/755-9735
**Years in existence:** 8 to 10 years
**Avg. attendance:** 200+
**Primarily ages:** 41-50
**Main meeting time(s):** Sunday night

## SPRING VALLEY

### Faith Chapel Single Adults

Jim Berrier
Faith Chapel
9400 Campo Road
Spring Valley, CA 92077
*Assemblies of God*
619/461-7451
**Years in existence:** 10
**Avg. attendance:** 100
**Primarily ages:** 26-50+
**Main meeting time(s):** Sunday School Class
**Singles classes:** Cornerstone (25-39), Primetime (40-55), Discovery in Recovery (30-40)

## STOCKTON

### Fellowship of Christian Adult Singles

Patrick G. Allen
Quail Lakes Baptist Church
1904 Quail Lakes Drive
Stockton, CA 95207
*North American Baptist*
209/951-7380
**Years in existence:** 5
**Avg. attendance:** 100
**Primarily ages:** 31-45
**Main meeting time(s):** Sunday School Class
**Singles classes:** College/Career (18-23), FOLAS (23-50)

### Higher Ground Singles Ministry

Kevin Newton
Lakeview Assembly
2111 Quail Lakes Drive
Stockton, CA 95207
*Assemblies of God*
209/477-2645
**Years in existence:** -1
**Avg. attendance:** 40
**Primarily ages:** 26-30
**Main meeting time(s):** Friday night
**Singles classes:** Solo Walk (25-40), Relationship Class (21-29), Higher Ground (21-35)

## TWAIN HARTE

### Sierra Christian Singles

Pat and Sue Greenwell
Chapel in the Pines
Twain Harte, CA 95383
*Interdenominational*
209/928-1026
**Years in existence:** 1
**Avg. attendance:** 80
**Primarily ages:** 36-40
**Main meeting times:** Friday night

## UKIAH

### EFC College/Career

Dave Strem
Evangelical Free Church
750 Yosemite Drive
Ukiah, CA 95482
*Evangelical Free*
707/468-9251
**Years in existence:** 5
**Avg. attendance:** 20
**Primarily ages:** 18-25
**Main meeting time(s):** A week night (M-F)

## VACAVILLE

### Single Purpose Ministries of California

Ben Randall
Vaca Valley Christian Life Center
6391 Leisure Town Road
Vacaville, CA 95687
*Assemblies of God*
707/448-3124
**Years in existence:** 4
**Avg. attendance:** 100+
**Primarily ages:** 26-40
**Main meeting time(s):** A week night (M-F)
**Singles classes:** Prime-Time (30+), Heart Beat (20-30s), Just Me & The Kids (30s), Seekers (30s)

## VALLEJO

### Single Blessings

Booker Chandler
The Old Landmark Church
(Veteran's Building)
444 Alabama Street
Vallejo, CA 94590
*Pentecostal*
707/557-9038
**Years in existence:** 1 mo.
**Avg. attendance:** 2
**Primarily ages:** 36-40
**Main meeting time(s):** Friday night

## VAN NUYS

### Church on the Way Singles

John Tolle
The Church On The Way
14300 Sherman Way
Van Nuys, CA 91406
*Foursquare*
818/373-8090
**Avg. attendance:** 400-450
**Primarily ages:** 31-35, 41-45
**Singles classes:** Class Action (CA) (25-35), Eagles' Wings (EW) (35+)

## VENTURA

### First Baptist Singles

Suzanne Green
First Baptist Church Ventura
426 S. Mills Road
Ventura, CA 93003
*American Baptist*
805/642-3244
**Years in existence:** 10

**Avg. attendance:** 12
**Primarily ages:** 31-40
**Main meeting time(s):** Sunday School Class

### Ventura County Christian Singles
P.O. Box 1093
Ventura, CA 93002
**Years in existence:** 5
**Avg. attendance:** 50
**Primarily ages:** 31-50

## VISALIA

### Calvary Chapel Singles Ministry
K.R. Gildez
Calvary Chapel of Visalia
P.O. Box 3825
Visalia, CA 93278-3825
209/625-3622
**Years in existence:** 8-9 years
**Avg. attendance:** 30
**Primarily ages:** 26-40
**Main meeting time(s):** A week night (M-F)
**Singles classes:** College Cheer (18-23), Singles (25-48)

### First Assemblies Singles Ministry
Dan Holford
First Assemblies of God
3737 W. Walnut
Visalia, CA 93277
*Assemblies of God*
209/733-9504
**Years in existence:** 7
**Avg. attendance:** 30
**Primarily ages:** 41-45
**Main meeting time(s):** Sunday School Class, Friday night
**Singles classes:** Young Adult Ministry (22-33), Single Adults (35-50)

### First Baptist Singles Ministry
Mike Popovich
First Baptist Church of Visalia
1100 S. Sowell
Visalia, CA 93277
*American Baptist*
209/732-4787
**Years in existence:** 10
**Avg. attendance:** 45
**Primarily ages:** 26-35, 41-50+
**Main meeting time(s):** Sunday School Class, a week night (M-F)
**Singles classes:** Lifestyles (23-35), Encouragers (35-50), Agape (50+)

## WALNUT

### Christian Chapel Singles
Rob Leaf
Christian Chapel
1920 Brea Canyon Cutoff
Walnut, CA 91789
*Non-denominatonal*
714/598-1964
**Years in existence:** 4
**Avg. attendance:** 160
**Primarily ages:** 26-30
**Main meeting time(s):** Friday night

## WESTLAKE VILLAGE

### Calvary Singles
Scott Davis and Gordy Duncan
Calvary Community Church
31293 Via Colinas
Westlake Village, CA 91362
*Missionary Church*
805/496-2101
**Years in existence:** 9
**Avg. attendance:** 300
**Primarily ages:** 18-35
**Main meeting time(s):** Sunday night, a week night (M-F)
**Singles classes:** Carpenter's Guild (18-30), Oasis (25-35), TGIW (35+), Single Parents Network

## WHITTIER

### WABF Singles
Whittier Area Baptist Fellowship
8175 Villa Verde Drive
Whittier, CA 90605
*Baptist General Conference*
**Years in existence:** 2
**Avg. attendance:** 160
**Primarily ages:** 18-30
**Main meeting time:** Sunday School Class **Singles classes:** Club 20 (20-30), Unison (28-43), Single Focus (40+)

### Young Adults Ministry and Single Parents Ministry
Douglas Healy
First Family Church
8434 Greenleaf
Whittier, CA 90602
*Assemblies of God*
213/698-6737
**Years in existence:** 5
**Avg. attendance:** 60
**Primarily ages:** 26-35
**Main meeting time(s):** Sunday School Class **Singles classes:** New Dimensions YAM (22-35), New Seasons SAM (30-40s)

## ARVADA

### Singles Alive
Daniel L. Fisher
Faith Bible Chapel
6210 Ward Road
Arvada, CO 80004
*Non-denominational*
303/424-2121
**Years in existence:** 25
**Avg. attendance:** 125
**Primarily ages:** 26-40
**Main meeting time(s):** Sunday School Class

## AURORA

### Singles Alive
Nellie Smith
Aurora First Assemblies of God
11001 E. Alameda Avenue
Aurora, CO 80012
*Assemblies of God*
303/366-2603
**Years in existence:** 15
**Avg. attendance:** 55
**Primarily ages:** 26-30
**Main meeting time(s):** Sunday School Class

## BOULDER

### Single Light
Jim Brandenburgh
Boulder Valley Christian Church
5300 Baseline
Boulder, CO 80303
*Independent Christian*
303/494-7748
**Years in existence:** 2
**Avg. attendance:** 20
**Primarily ages:** 26-30
**Main meeting time(s):** Sunday School Class, a week night (M-F)
**Singles classes:** College (18-25), Singles (18-35), Single Parents (22-35)

## COLORADO SPRINGS

### First Methodist Singles
Steve Burnett
First United Methodist Church
420 N. Nevada
Colorado Springs, CO 80903
*United Methodist*
719/471-8522
**Years in existence:** 10+
**Avg. attendance:** 80
**Primarily ages:** 30-45
**Main meeting time(s):** Sunday night and Friday night
**Singles classes:** Sunday Night Live (25-40), Positive Single Image (45+), Buttons and Bows (65+), HUGS (Helping Us Grow As Singles-for ages 25-45).

### First Presbyterian Singles
Thomas Albaum/Deborah Mahan
First Presbyterian
219 E. Bijou Street
Colorado Springs, CO 80903
*Presbyterian Church (USA)*
719/471-3763 Ext. 125
**Years in existence:** 11
**Avg. attendance:** 400
**Primarily ages:** 26-50+
**Main meeting time(s):** Sunday School Class
**Singles classes:** Sojourners (20s-30s), Growing Edge (30s-40s), Going Concern (40s+)

### Mountain Singles Ministry
Tim Cox
Pulpit Rock Church
Colorado Springs, CO 80918
*Conservative Baptist*
719/598-6767
**Years in existence:** 3
**Avg. attendance:** 25
**Primarily ages:** 25-35
**Main meeting time(s):** Sunday School Class and Tuesday night Bible study
**Singles classes:** Mountain Singles

### Navigators—Singles' Conference
Del Lewis
Navigators
P.O. Box 6000
Colorado Springs, CO 80934
719/598-1212 Ext. 535
**Years in existence:** 10
**Primarily ages:** 18-30

### Lifeline
Dan Sarian
Fellowship Bible Church
421 S. Tejon
Colorado Springs, CO 80903
*Interdenominational*
719/633-5921
**Years in existence:** 3
**Avg. attendance:** 60
**Primarily ages:** 25-40
**Main meeting time(s):** Thursday Bible Study

### Singles Alive
Jonathan Batt
Radiant Church
4020 E. Maizeland Dr.
Colorado Springs, CO 80909
*Assemblies of God*
719/597-4402
**Years in existence:** 5+
**Avg. attendance:** 30
**Primarily ages:** 20-35
**Main meeting time(s):** Wednesday and Thursday night
**Singles classes:** Home Fellowship (all ages), Thursday Night Bible Study (all ages).

### Voyagers Singles Ministry
Beth Wilcox and Jeff Pluth
Village Seven Presbyterian Church
4050 S. Nonchalant Circle
Colorado Springs, CO 80917
*Presbyterian Church (PCA)*
719/574-6700
**Years in existence:** 6+
**Avg. attendance:** 70
**Primarily ages:** 25-45
**Main meeting time(s):** Sunday School Class
**Singles classes:** Voyagers, SPRING (Single Parents Resting in Grace)

## DENVER

### Calvary Temple SAM
Steve Gladen
Calvary Temple
200 S. University Boulevard
Denver, CO 80122
*Non-Denominational*
303/744-7213
**Years in existence:** 1
**Avg. attendance:** 100
**Primarily ages:** 26-40
**Main meeting time(s):** Sunday School Class
**Singles classes:** SAM (20-40), Biblical Backgrounds (40+)

## DURANGO

### Master Plan Ministries
Charles E. Helvoigt, II
Box 542
Durango, CO 81302
*Non-denominational*
303/385-7621
**Years in existence:** 3
**Avg. attendance:** 30
**Primarily ages:** 26-35

## ENGLEWOOD

### Career Fellowship
Rob Cobb
South Fellowship
3780 S. Broadway
Englewood, CO 80014
*Independent—Presbyterian*
303/761-8780
**Years in existence:** 15
**Avg. attendance:** 25
**Primarily ages:** 31-35
**Main meeting time(s):** Sunday night
**Singles classes:** Career Fellowship (30-45), Active 20-Something (22-29)

### Cherry Creek Singles
Brad Strait
Cherry Creek Presbyterian Church
10150 E. Belleview Avenue
Englewood, CO 80111
*Evangelical Presbyterian*
303/779-9909
**Years in existence:** 8
**Avg. attendance:** 160
**Primarily ages:** 26-30
**Main meeting time(s):** A week night (M-F)
**Singles classes:** Focus (20-39), Unison (40-60), Twenty Something (20-30), Divorce Recovery (all ages)

### Sole Mates
Louie Angone
Cherry Hills Community Church
3651 S. Colorado Boulevard
Englewood, CO 80110
*Evangelical Presbyterian*
303/781-0091
**Years in existence:** 4
**Avg. attendance:** 500
**Primarily ages:** 26-45
**Main meeting time(s):** Sunday School Class **Singles classes:** Prime Time (under 35), Top of The Rockies (35-50), Chosen (50+)

## LAKEWOOD

### Bear Valley Singles
Bill Donelson
Bear Valley Church
10001 W. Jewell Av
Lakewood, CO 80226
*So. Baptist/Con. Baptist*
303/935-3597
**Years in existence:** 13
**Avg. attendance:** 120
**Primarily ages:** 36-40
**Main meeting time:** Sunday School Class **Singles classes:** Singles Breakfast—divorced, single parents; Career Group (23-33); College Group (18-23)

## LITTLETON

### Arapahoe Road Baptist Singles
M. Wyss
Arapahoe Road Baptist Church
780 E. Arapahoe
Littleton, CO 80122
*Baptist*
303/794-3033
**Years in existence:** 6
**Avg. attendance:** 15
**Primarily ages:** 18-30
**Main meeting time(s):** Sunday School Class

### Single Again
Nancy Caproale
Ridgeview Hills Church
7140 South Colorado Boulevard
Littleton, CO 80122
*Christian Reform*
303/771-8663
**Years in existence:** 1
**Avg. attendance:** 12
**Primarily ages:** 31-35
**Main meeting time(s):** Sunday School Class
LOVELAND

### Champion Christian Singles
Mark Lucks
Resurrection Fellowship
6502 E. Crossroads Boulevard
Loveland, CO 80538
303/667-5479
**Years in existence:**6
**Avg. attendance:** 85
**Primarily ages:** 26-30
**Main meeting time:** Saturday night
**Singles classes:** A.C.T.S. (18-23), Single Women's Network (30-45), Single Men's Fellowship (25-35), Young Marrieds

## PARKER

### Faith Baptist Single Adult Ministry
Kyle Helmink
Faith Baptist Church
11150 Hilltop Road
Parker, CO 80134
*Baptist General Conference*
303/841-2273
**Years in existence:** 3
**Avg. attendance:** 8
**Primarily ages:** 41-45
**Main meeting time(s):** A week night (M-F)

## AVON

### Valley Community Singles/ Saturday Singles Club
John Busa
Valley Community Baptist Church
590 West Avon Road
Avon, CT 06001
*Northeast Baptist Conference*
203/675-4714 or
1-800-437-6278

**Fact:**
Women remain single longer in today's changing Japan than do American women. Today the average age of a new bride in Japan is 25.7; in the U.S., it's 23.6

*Newsweek, Jan. 22, 1990, page 50*

**Avg. attendance:** 12
**Primarily ages:** 36-40
**Main meeting time(s):** Sunday School Class, a week night (M-F)

## MERIDEN

### Calvary Baptist Single Adult Fellowship
Barbara D. Sarro
Calvary Baptist
262 Bee Street
Meriden, CT 06450
*Baptist General Conference*
203/238-1114
**Years in existence:** 2
**Avg. attendance:** 20
**Primarily ages:** 31-35
**Main meeting time(s):** A week night (M-F)
**Singles classes:** Singles (18-60), Divorce Recovery (25-50), Single Parents (20-40)

## MIDDLETOWN

### Single Purpose
Andrew Eiss
Fellowship Baptist Church
20 Brooks Road
Middletown, CT 06457
*Baptist*
203/346-1181
**Years in existence:** 2
**Avg. attendance:** 20
**Primarily ages:** 18-25
**Main meeting time(s):** Sunday School Class
**Singles classes:** Single Purpose (18-25), Lydia Class (35+)

## BRANDON

### First Baptist Singles
Don Minton
First Baptist Church
204 W. Morgan Street
Brandon, FL 33510
*Southern Baptist*
813/689-1204
**Years in existence:** 5-7
**Avg. attendance:** 90
**Primarily ages:** 31-35
**Main meeting time(s):** Sunday School Class
**Singles classes:** Adult 13 (46+), Adult 14 (32-45), Adult 15 (23-31), Adult 16 (18-22)

## CLEARWATER

### One In The Son
Bob Ricotta
First Assemblies of God
1739 S. Greenwood Avenue
Clearwater, FL 34616
*Assemblies of God*
813/585-5468
**Years in existence:** 8
**Avg. attendance:** 75
**Primarily ages:** 31-40
**Main meeting time(s):** Sunday School Class, a week night (M-F), Saturday night
**Singles classes:** Soulo I (18-25), Soulo II (25-35), Soulo III (35+)

### Single Life Fellowship
Nick Panico
Countryside Christian Center
1850 McMullen Booth Road
Clearwater, FL 34619
*Interdenominational*
813/799-1618
**Years in existence:** 6
**Avg. attendance:** 75-100
**Primarily ages:** 26-40
**Main meeting time(s):** Sunday School Class **Singles classes:** SLF I (25-40), SLF II (40-55), Single Parent (all ages)

### What's Up?
John Moran
Diocese of St. Petersburg
2281 S.R. 580
Clearwater, FL 34623
*Catholic*
813/797-2375
**Years in existence:** 2
**Avg. attendance:** 60
**Primarily ages:** 26-30
**Main meeting time(s):** A week night (M-F)
**Singles classes:** What's Up? Clearwater (18-35), What's Up? Tampa (18-35), What's Up? St. Petersburg (18-35)

## DADE CITY

### Singles Supporting and Serving
Robin Quesenberry
First Baptist Church of Dade City
417 W. Church Avenue
Dade City, FL 33525
*Southern Baptist*
904/567-3265
**Years in existence:** 4
**Avg. attendance:** 50
**Primarily ages:** 18-30
**Main meeting time(s):** Sunday School Class
**Singles classes:** Adult I (18-28), Adult II (25-55), Singles Supporting & Serving (23-55)

## FORT LAUDERDALE

### Alpha Judah
Rev. Sammy Lee Johnson
West Lauderdale Baptist
3601 Davie Blvd.
Ft. Lauderdale, FL 33312
*Southern Baptist/Charismatic*
305/791-8210
**Years in existence:** 4
**Avg. attendance:** 75
**Primarily ages:** 18-30
**Main meeting time:** Friday night

### Single Focus Ministries
Rev. James B. Richwine
Coral Ridge Presbyterian
5555 North Federal Highway
Ft. Lauderdale, FL 33308
*Presbyterian*
305/771-8840
**Years in existence:** 12
**Avg. attendance:** 100
**Primarily ages:** 26-50+
**Main meeting time:** Sunday School Class
**Singles classes:** College/Career (18-35), SEA (25-95), 39 and Holding (40-65), Discovery Groups—all age small groups

### The Singles Ministry
E.V. Clemeans
First Presbyterian Church
401 S.E. 15th Avenue
Ft. Lauderdale, FL 33301
*Presbyterian*
305/462-6200
**Years in existence:** 6
**Avg. attendance:** 55
**Primarily ages:** 41-50+
**Main meeting time(s):** Sunday School Class **Singles classes:** New Life Singles (35-50), First Class Singles (50+)

## FORT MYERS

### Ft. Myers Singles
David Persson
McGregor Baptist Church
3750 Colonial Blvd
Ft. Myers, FL 33912
813/936-1754
**Years in existence:** 12
**Avg. attendance:** 250
**Primarily ages:** 18-30, 50+
**Main meeting time(s):** Sunday School Class, a week night (M-F), Friday night
**Singles classes:** 18-31, 32+, 26-35, 36-45

## FORT WALTON BEACH

### FOCUS
Scott A. Hawkins
Fort Walton Beach Christian Center
1007 Gospel Road
Fort Walton Beach, FL 32548
*Non-denominational*
904/863-1323
**Years in existence:** 2
**Avg. attendance:** 25
**Primarily ages:** 18-30
**Main meeting time(s):** A week night (M-F)

### Single Heart
Samuel Davis
The Chapel
100 Jonquil Avenue
Ft. Walton Beach, FL 32548
*Interdenominational*
904/243-5814
**Years in existence:** 2
**Avg. attendance:** 35
**Primarily ages:** 26-30
**Main meeting time(s):** A week night (M-F)

## GULF BREEZE

### Gulf Breeze UMC Singles Ministry
Maryann J. Dotts
Gulf Breeze United Methodist Church
75 Fairpoint Dr
Gulf Breeze, FL 32561
*United Methodist*
904/932-3594

**Years in existence:** 3
**Avg. attendance:** 20
**Primarily ages:** 46-50
**Main meeting time(s):** A week night (M-F)
**Singles classes:** The Cross Roads Class (40-65), Foundations Class (23-60), Women's Bible Class (65-90)

## JACKSONVILLE

### ACTS (Active Community of Singles)
Bob Weigand
First Pentecostal Holiness Church
2550 Fouraker Road
Jacksonville, FL 32210
*Pentecostal Holiness*
904/783-3488
**Years in existence:** 1
**Avg. attendance:** 25
**Primarily ages:** 26-30
**Main meeting time(s):** A week night (M-F)

### First Baptist Singles
First Baptist Church
124 West Ashley Street
Jacksonville, FL 32202
*Baptist*
904/356-6077

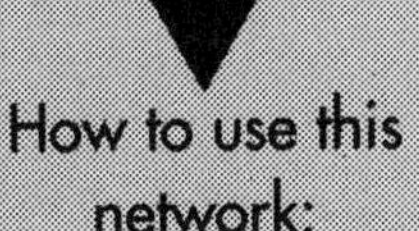

How to use this network:

**Have Lunch Together.**

Organize a luncheon with the other leaders in your city or region. Discuss common problems and concerns in singles ministry. Learn from one another. Network.

**Years in existence:** 16
**Avg. attendance:** 875
**Primarily ages:** 26-30
**Main meeting time:** Sunday School Class
**Singles classes:** College/Career (18-21), Career (22-28), Singles 1 (29-39), Singles 2 (40-49), Singles 3 (50-65), Single Professionals (27-45)

### The Seekers
Rod McIntyre/Ron McInnes
5545 Arlington Road, Office H
Jacksonville, FL 32211
*Non-denominational*
904/744-0144
**Years in existence:** 10
**Avg. attendance:** 125
**Primarily ages:** 31-40
**Main meeting time:** A week night (M-F)

### Lake Shore Singles
John R. Hamilton
Lake Shore United Methodist
2246 Blanding Boulevard
Jacksonville, FL 32210
*United Methodist*
904/388-1780
**Years in existence:** 4+
**Avg. attendance:** 10
**Primarily ages:** 26-35
**Main meeting time(s):** A week night (M-F)

### Trinity Singles
Michael Hamm
Trinity Baptist Church
800 Hammond Boulevard
Jacksonville, FL 32205
*Baptist*
904/786-5320
**Years in existence:** 6
**Avg. attendance:** 130
**Primarily ages:** 18-25
**Main meeting time(s):** Sunday School Class **Singles classes:** Singles I (18-22), Singles II (23-28), Singles III (29-38), Singles IV (39+)

## LAKE WORTH

### Emmanuel Single Adult Ministry
Michael Davis
Trinity Assemblies of God
7255 S. Military Trail
Lake Worth, FL 33463
*Assemblies of God*
407/965-4166
**Years in existence:** 3
**Avg. attendance:** 120
**Primarily ages:** 31-50
**Main meeting time(s):** Friday night
**Singles classes:** Single Parents, Young Adults (20-35), Adults (35+)

## LARGO

### First Baptist Singles
Phyllis Alderman
First Baptist Church of Indian Rocks
12156 Ulmerton Road
Largo, FL 34644
*Southern Baptist*
813/595-3421
**Years in existence:** 10
**Avg. attendance:** 150
**Primarily ages:** 31-35
**Main meeting time:** Sunday School Class

## LIVE OAK

### Suwannee Organization of Christian Singles (SOCS)
Michael W. Maloy
P.O. Box 1482
Live Oak, FL 32060-1482
904/362-2323
**Years in existence:** 3+
**Avg. attendance:** 15
**Primarily ages:** 46-50
**Main meeting time(s):** A week night (M-F)

## MARGATE

### Abundant Life Singles Ministry
Pastors Al & Micki Scavone
Abundant Life Christian Center
1490 Banks Road
Margate, FL 33063
*Interdenominational*
305/972-0660
**Years in existence:** 7
**Avg. attendance:** 150+
**Primarily ages:** 26-50
**Main meeting time:** Friday or Saturday night twice a month

## MERRITT ISLAND

### Single Heart Ministries
Reggie Joiner
First Baptist Church of Merritt Island
140 Magnolia Avenue
Merritt Island, FL 32952
*Southern Baptist*
407/453-2144 Ext. 212
**Years in existence:** 30
**Avg. attendance:** 140
**Primarily ages:** 26-30
**Main meeting time(s):** Sunday School Class, Friday night
**Singles classes:** Singles I (22-36), Singles II (37-53)

## MIAMI

### Single Side of Wayside
Wayside Baptist Church
7701 S.W. 98th Street
Miami, FL 33156
*Southern Baptist*
305/595-6550
**Years in existence:** 3
**Avg. attendance:** 55
**Primarily ages:** 26-35
**Main meeting time:** Sunday School Class
**Singles classes:** Singles I (25-35), Singles II (36+)

## ORANGE PARK

### Overcomers
William Lewis
Orange Park Assemblies of God
1324 Kingsley Avenue
Orange Park, FL 32073
*Assemblies of God*
904/264-5961
**Years in existence:** 4
**Avg. attendance:** 30
**Primarily ages:** 26-50+
**Main meeting time(s):** Friday night, Saturday night
**Singles classes:** College & Career (newly formed) (18-25), Overcomers (26-60)

## ORLANDO

### Single Christians United
Nancy Wood
First United Methodist Church
142 E. Jackson Street
Orlando,FL 32804
*United Methodist*
407/849-6080
**Years in existence:** 4
**Avg. attendance:** 150
**Primarily ages:** 26-45
**Singles classes:** Young Adult (25-35), Mid-Single (35-50), Adult (50+)

## PALM BEACH GARDENS

### PBCC Singles

Don Wilber
Palm Beach
Community Church
1211 Prosperity Farms Road,
Suite C-303
Palm Beach Gardens, FL 33410
*Non-denominational*
407/626-5683
**Years in existence:** 3
**Avg. attendance:** 150
**Primarily ages:** 18-45
**Main meeting time(s):** A week night (M-F)
**Singles classes:** College/Career (17-24), Various Bookstudy Groups (all ages), Professional Singles 1 (30-42), Professional Singles 2 (40+)

### Power & Light

Pastor Norman D. Benz
Maranatha Church of God
2575 Lone Pine Road
Palm Beach Gardens, FL 33410
*Church of God*
407/622-8330
**Years in existence:** 8
**Avg. attendance:** 130
**Primarily ages:** 26-35
**Main meeting time:** Friday night

### Trinity's Christian Friends Unlimited

Rosemary Corkwell
Trinity United Methodist Church
9625 N. Military Trail
Palm Beach Gardens, FL 33410
*United Methodist*
407/622-5278
**Years in existence:** 10
**Avg. attendance:** 40
**Primarily ages:** 50+
**Main meeting time(s):** A week night (M-F)
**Singles classes:** CFU (45+), TLCs (30-45), SOS (22-30)

## PANAMA CITY

### Panama City Singles

Michael McCollum
First Baptist Panama City
Box 1200
Panama City, FL 32402
*Southern Baptist*
904/785-6146
**Years in existence:** 10
**Avg. attendance:** 85
**Primarily ages:** 18-25
**Main meeting time(s):** Sunday School Class **Singles classes:** College (18-22), Career I & II (18-24/25+), Singles I & II (30-42/40+), Singles III (50+)

## PENSACOLA

### Focal Point

Rick Barnhart
East Hill Baptist Church
1301 E. Gadsden Street
Pensacola, FL 32501
*Southern Baptist*
904/433-0095
**Years in existence:** 1
**Avg. attendance:** 30
**Primarily ages:** 18-25
**Main meeting time(s):** Sunday School Class, Friday night
**Singles classes:** Singles 1 (18-30), Singles 2 (30-50)

### Singular Sensation

Pastor Mark LaBranche
First United Methodist
6 East Wright Street
Pensacola, FL 32501
*United Methodist*
904/432-1434
**Years in existence:** 4
**Avg. attendance:** 55
**Primarily ages:** 26-45
**Main meeting time(s):** Sunday School Class, Tuesday night

## POMPANO BEACH

### First Baptist Singles

New Life Singles
Jan Mohler
First Baptist Church of Pompano
138 N.E. First Street
Pompano Beach, FL 33060
*Southern Baptist*
305/943-3355
**Years in existence:** 13
**Avg. attendance:** 75
**Primarily ages:** 41-45
**Main meeting time(s):** Sunday School Class **Singles classes:** SA1 (23-30), SA2 (31-40), SA3 (41-50), SA4 (50+)

## ST. PETERSBURG

### Single Purpose Ministries

Chris Eaton
9455 Koger Blvd. N. #114
St. Petersburg, FL 33702
*Interdenominational*
813/578-0196
**Years in existence:** 10
**Avg. attendance:** 125
**Primarily ages:** 18-35
**Main meeting time(s):** A week night (M-F)

### Synergy & Circle of Friends

Carol Hutchinson
First United Methodist Church
P.O. Box 1138
St. Petersburg, FL 33731-1138
*United Methodist Church*
813/894-4661
**Years in existence:** 3
**Avg. attendance:** 30
**Primarily ages:** 26-35, 41-50
**Main meeting time(s):** Sunday School Class, a week night (M-F)
**Singles classes:** Circle of Friends (25-40), Synergy (35-55), Bible Study (35-55), Young At Heart (55+)

## STUART

### Redeemer Lutheran Singles

Thomas Keithley
Redeemer Lutheran Church
2450 S.E. Ocean Boulevard
Stuart, FL 34996
*Lutheran Church—Missouri Synod*
407/286-0911
**Years in existence:** 1
**Avg. attendance:** 20
**Primarily ages:** 26-50
**Main meeting time(s):** Sunday School Class

## TAMPA

### Bethel Temple Singles

Rod Taylor
Bethel Temple Assemblies of God
1510 W. Hillsborough Ave
Tampa, FL 33603
*Assemblies of God*
813/238-2348
**Years in existence:** 10
**Avg. attendance:** 50
**Primarily ages:** 18-25, 31-50+
**Main meeting time(s):** Sunday School Class

### Riverhills Singles

Darleen Allen
Riverhills Church of God
8718 North 46th Street
Tampa, FL 33617
*Church of God*
813/985-2388
**Years in existence:** 3
**Avg. attendance:** 35
**Primarily ages:** 31-35
**Main meeting time(s):** Sunday School Class, a week night (M-F)
**Singles classes:** Young Adult Singles (18-30), Single Support Group (24-45), College & Career (18-25), Single Connection (18-50)

### Singles Together

Molly Cox
University Church of God
10948 Central Avenue
Tampa, FL 33612
*Church of God*
813-933-3991
**Years in existence:** 10
**Avg. attendance:** 100
**Primarily ages:** 41-45
**Main meeting time(s):** Sunday School Class **Singles classes:**

Campus/Career (18-22), Young Adult (23-30), Middle Adult (30-40), Adults (41+)

## WEST PALM BEACH

### First Baptist Singles
Raymon Presson
First Baptist Church
1101 South Flagler Drive
West Palm Beach, FL 33401
*Southern Baptist*
407/650-7425
**Years in existence:** 17
**Avg. attendance:** 300
**Primarily ages:** 31-35
**Main meeting time(s):** Sunday School Class, Friday night
**Singles Classes:** 1 (18-24), 2 (25-30), 3 (31-38), 4 (39-45), 5 (46-55), 6 (55+)

## WINTER HAVEN

### Grace Singles
James N. Barnett
Grace Lutheran Church
327 Avenue C, S.E.
Winter Haven, FL 33880
*Lutheran*
813/293-8447
**Years in existence:** 2
**Avg. attendance:** 15
**Primarily ages:** 31-45
**Main meeting time(s):** Sunday School Class

## WINTER PARK

### Jireh Singles Ministry
Calvary Assembly of God
1199 Clay Street
Winter Park, FL 32789
*Pentecostal*
407/644-1199
**Years in existence:** 8
**Avg. attendance:** 300
**Primarily ages:** 26-45
**Main meeting time(s):** Sunday School Class, Friday night
**Singles classes:** 1 (25-35), 2 (36+), Divorce Recovery, Children of Divorce

### Singlelight Ministry
Kerry Webb
First Baptist Church
1021 North New York Avenue
Winter Park, FL 32789
*Baptist*
407/644-3061
**Years in existence:** 12
**Avg. attendance:** 165
**Primarily ages:** 18-35
**Main meeting time:** Sunday School Class
**Singles classes:** SC05 (college ages), Single Adult 04 (22-30), Single Adult 03 (31-41), Single Adult 02 (42-53), Single Adult 01 (54-65)

## ATHENS

### Prince Avenue Career Singles
David Johnson
Prince Avenue Baptist
595 Prince Avenue
Athens, GA 30603
*Southern Baptist*
404/353-1985
**Years in existence:** 12
**Avg. attendance:** 190
**Primarily ages:** 18-35
**Main meeting time:** Sunday School Class **Singles classes:** College (college ages), Career (18-28), Adult Singles (28+), Retreats/Special events

## ATLANTA

### First Baptist Single Adult Ministry
Richard Taylor
First Baptist Church
754 Peachtree Road
Atlanta, GA 30365
*Southern Baptist*
404/347-8222
**Years in existence:** 20
**Avg. attendance:** 600
**Primarily ages:** 31-35
**Main meeting time(s):** Sunday School Class **Singles classes:** SA1 (18-25), SA2 (26-30), SA3 (31-35), SA4, SA5

### North Atlanta Single Adults
H. Bret Smith
North Atlanta Church of Christ
5676 Roberts Drive
Atlanta, GA 30338
*Non-denominational*
404/399-5222
**Years in existence:** 8
**Avg. attendance:** 300
**Primarily ages:** 26-35
**Main meeting time(s):** Sunday School Class, a week night (M-F)
**Singles classes:** Singles In Christ (18-50), Single Support (18-50), Divorce Recovery (18-50)

### Peachtree Presbyterian Singles
Charles W. Roberts
Peachtree Presbyterian Church
3434 Roswell Road, N.W.
Atlanta, GA 30363
*Presbyterian*
404/842-5800
**Years in existence:** 12
**Avg. attendance:** 1,300
**Primarily ages:** 26-30
**Main meeting time(s):** Sunday School Class, a week night (M-F)
**Singles classes:** We have 12 Sunday School classes. Something for everyone!

### Singles Alive!
Jeff Bendert
Mt. Paran
2055 Mt. Paran Road, N.W.
Atlanta, GA 30327
*Church of God*
404/261-0720
**Years in existence:** 2
**Avg. attendance:** 80
**Primarily ages:** 26-30
**Main meeting time(s):** Sunday School Class **Singles classes:** Touch Stone (22-35), Complete In Him, Single Purpose (35-45), Single Adult Fellowship (45+)

### Singles at Second-Ponce
Rob Suggs
Second-Ponce De Leon Baptist Church
2715 Peachtree Road, N.E.
Atlanta, GA 30305
*Southern Baptist*
404/266-8111
**Years in existence:** 15
**Avg. attendance:** 70
**Primarily ages:** 26-30
**Main meeting time(s):** Sunday School Class
**Singles classes:** Singles I (20-32), Singles II (33+)

## AUGUSTA

### FBC: The Growth Place for Singles
Dr. J. Andrew Menger
First Baptist Church
3500 Walton Way
Augusta, GA 30909
*Baptist*
404-733-2236
**Years in existence:** 4
**Avg. attendance:** 102
**Primarily ages:** 26-40, 50+
**Main meeting time(s):** Sunday School Class
**Singles classes:** Singles I (18-33), Singles II (34-55), Singles III (56+)

### First Presbyterian Singles
Pastor Anthony J. Wheat
First Presbyterian Church
642 Telfair Street
Augusta, GA 30901
*Presbyterian*
404/823-2450
**Years in existence:** 12
**Avg. attendance:** 100
**Primarily ages:** 26-30
**Main meeting time:** Sunday School Class **Singles classes:** College Class, Seekers (20-29), Koinonia (30+)

## CONYERS

### SAM (Single Adult Ministry)
Chuck Williams
First Baptist Church, Conyers
958 Milstead Avenue
Conyers, GA 30207
*Southern Baptist*
404/483-8700
**Years in existence:** 5
**Avg. attendance:** 40
**Primarily ages:** 31-45
**Main meeting time(s):** Sunday School Class **Singles classes:** Single Adult A (under 35), Single Adult B (36+)

## DOUGLAS

### New Genesis Ministries
Dr. John Dobbins
Eastside Baptist Church
1220 E. Bryan Street
Douglas, GA 31533
*Southern Baptist*
912/384-6342
**Years in existence:** 2
**Avg. attendance:** 35

**Primarily ages:** 31-35
**Main meeting time(s):** Sunday School Class
**Singles classes:** New Genesis 1 (Mixed), New Genesis 2 (Mixed), New Genesis 3 (Mixed)

## DUNWOODY

**Dunwoody Baptist Single Adult Ministry**
Dunwoody Baptist Church
1445 Mount Vernon Road
Dunwoody, GA 30338
*Southern Baptist*
404/394-1277
**Years in existence:** 9
**Avg. attendance:** 130
**Primarily ages:** 26-30
**Main meeting time:** Sunday School Class **Singles classes:** Single Adult I Dept. 1 (22-26), Single Adult I Dept. 2 (27-30), Single Adult II Dept. 1 (31-47), Single Adult III Dept. 1 (48+)

## EAST POINT

**Southwest Christian Church S.A.M.**
Perry D. Rubin
Southwest Christian Church
4330 Washington Rd.
East Point, GA 30344
*Church of Christ/Christian Church*
404/766-1673
**Years in existence:** 7
**Avg. attendance:** 50
**Primarily ages:** 18-35
**Main meeting time(s):** Sunday School Class, a week night (M-F)
**Singles classes:** Singles 1 (23-35), Singles 2 (36-up), College Age (18-22), Single Parents (Mix)

## FAYETTEVILLE

**New Hope Single Adults**
Rick Nixon
New Hope Baptist Church
551 New Hope Road
Fayetteville, GA 30214
*Southern Baptist*
404/461-4337
**Years in existence:** 9
**Avg. attendance:** 400
**Primarily ages:** 18-25
**Main meeting time:** Sunday School Class **Singles classes:** College Dept. (active students), Singles I (18-28), Singles Again (28+), Divorcees & widows, Singles II (40+)

## JONESBORO

**Jonesboro First Baptist Singles**
Larry A. Lawrence
First Baptist of Jonesboro
147 Church St.
Jonesboro, GA 30236
*Southern Baptist*
404/478-6710
**Years in existence:** 7
**Avg. attendance:** 250
**Primarily ages:** 18-30
**Main meeting time:** Sunday School Class **Singles classes:** Single Adult-1 (18-25), Single Adult-2 (26-33), Single Adult-3 (34-45), Single Adult-4 (46+)

## LAWRENCEVILLE

**Lawrenceville Singles**
Sandra Smith-Franklin
First United Methodist
395 West Crogan Street
Lawrenceville, GA 30245
*United Methodist*
**Years in existence:** 6
**Avg. attendance:** 30
**Primarily ages:** 36-40
**Main meeting time(s):** Sunday School Class

## MARIETTA

**Eastside Singles**
Gil Crowell
Eastside Baptist Church
2450 Lower Roswell Road
Marietta, GA 30068
*Southern Baptist*
404/971-2323
**Years in existence:** 10
**Avg. attendance:** 200
**Primarily ages:** 26-35
**Main meeting time(s):** Sunday School Class

**Johnson Ferry Baptist Singles**
Ernie Faulkenberry
Johnson Ferry Baptist Church
955 Johnson Ferry Road
Marrietta, GA 30068
*Baptist*
404/973-6561
**Years in existence:** 2
**Avg. attendance:** 75
**Primarily ages:** 26-30
**Main meeting time(s):** Sunday School Class **Singles classes:** Seekers (22-35), One In Spirit (35+), College/Career (18-22)

**Roswell St. Baptist Singles Ministry**
William Rogers
Roswell Street Baptist Church
774 Roswell Street
Marietta, GA 30060
*Southern Baptist*
404/424-9836
**Years in existence:** 12
**Avg. attendance:** 385
**Primarily ages:** 18-30
**Main meeting time:** Sunday School Class
**Singles classes:** SCC1 (18-21), Single Adult 01 (20-25), Single Adult 02 (26-31), Single Adult 03 (32-41), Single Adult 04 (42-55), Single Adult 05 (56-70)

## MARTINEZ

**Carpenter Shop**
Jim Tripp
Carpenter Shop Bible Cathedral
3520 Washington Road
Martinez, GA 30907
404/863-7090
**Years in existence:** 2
**Avg. attendance:** 7
**Primarily ages:** 31-35
**Main meeting time(s):** Sunday School Class

## MONROE

**Young and the Restless**
Marcy Thobaben
1st United Methodist Church of Monroe
400 Broad St.
Monroe, GA 30655
*United Methodist*
404-267-6525
**Years in existence:** 2
**Avg. attendance:** 12
**Primarily ages:** 18-30
**Main meeting time(s):** Sunday School Class, a week night (M-F)

## SMYRNA

**Adventist Singles**
Gene Anderson
Adventist Singles Ministries
4467 King Springs Road
Smyrna, GA 30082
*Seventh-Day Adventist*
404/434-5111
**Years in existence:** 28
**Primarily ages:** 41-45

## STOCKBRIDGE

**Successfully Single**
Billy Miller
Metro Heights Baptist Church
2178 Highway 138
Stockbridge, GA 30281
*Southern Baptist*
404/474-6700
**Years in existence:** 1
**Avg. attendance:** 75
**Primarily ages:** 26-35
**Main meeting time(s):** Sunday School Class, a week night (M-F)
**Singles classes:** (18-29), (30-40), Rebuilders (20-60)

## STONE MOUNTAIN

**Christian Singles**
Webster Oglesby
Mount Carmel Christian Church
6015 Old Stone Mountain Road
Stone Mountain, GA 30087
*Christian*
404/279-8437
**Years in existence:** 5
**Primarily ages:** 26-30, 41-45
**Main meeting time(s):** Sunday School Class
**Singles classes:** Destiny (17-22), Pioneers (23-30), Encouragers (30+)

## TUCKER

**Rehoboth Singles**
John W. Rushing
Rehoboth Baptist Church
2997 Lawrenceville Highway
Tucker, GA 30084
*Southern Baptist*
404/939-3182
**Years in existence:** 10
**Avg. attendance:** 460
**Primarily ages:** 18-30
**Main meeting time(s):** Sunday School Class
**Singles classes:** College & Career (18-21), Career 1, 2 & 3 (22-24, 25-27 & 28-32), Singles 1 & 2 (33-38 & 39-48), Singles 3 & 4 (49-59 & 60+)

## BOISE

**Single Adults Learning Together (SALT Co.)**
Kris Rudell
Cole Community Church
8775 Ustick Road
Boise, ID 83704
208/375-3565
**Years in existence:** 8
**Avg. attendance:** 100
**Primarily ages:** 31-35
**Main meeting time(s):** Friday night

## MERIDIAN

**Valley Shepherd Singles**
Rick Waitley
Valley Shepherd Church
P.O. Box 267
Meridian, ID 83642
*Nazarene*
208/888-214
**Years in existence:** 8
**Avg. attendance:** 40
**Primarily ages:** 26-40
**Main meeting time(s):** Sunday School Class, a week night (M-F)

## NAMPA

**Solo Ministries**
Mary Cruz
First Church of the Nazarene
600 15th Avenue South
Nampa, ID 83686
*Interdenominational*
208/466-3549
**Years in existence:** 3
**Avg. attendance:** 40
**Primarily ages:** 26-30
**Main meeting time(s):** A week night (M-F)
**Singles classes:** Single Again (25+), Acts (20-40)

## CHICAGO

**Joy Ministry**
Nina Thompkins
New Heritage Christian Center
Send corresondence to: Robin Lay; 2001 S. Michigan
Chicago, IL 60616
*Non-denominational*
**Years in existence:** 2
**Avg. attendance:** 15
**Primarily ages:** 26-30
**Main meeting time(s):** Saturday night
**Singles classes:** Joy Ministry (18-35), Grace Ministry (35-40), Daughters of Hannah (33-40)

**Northwest Fellowship Singles**
Rev. Doug Harsch
Northwest Fellowship Baptist Church
6125 W. Foster Ave
Chicago, IL 60630
*North American Baptist*
312-763-5306
Years **in existence:** 1
**Avg. attendance:** 15
**Primarily ages:** 18-25
**Main meeting time(s):** A week night (M-F)

**Single Focus**
Daryl E. Worley, Jr.
The Moody Church
1609 N. La Salle Drive
Chicago, IL 60614
*Non-denominational*
312/943-0466
**Years in existence:** 20
**Avg. attendance:** 100
**Primarily ages:** 26-35
**Main meeting time(s):** Sunday School Class **Singles classes:** Single Focus (25-40), SALT (35-50), Business & Professional (45+)

## KENNER

**One In Christ**
John Ryan
Williams Blvd. Baptist Church
3000 Williams Blvd.
Kenner, IL 70065
*Southern Baptist*
504/443-2363
**Years in existence:** 5
**Avg. attendance:** 75
**Primarily ages:** 18-25
**Main meeting time(s):** Sunday School Class **Singles classes:** Young Adult I (18-25), Young Adult II-1 (26-30), Young Adult II-2 (31-35), Young Adult II-3 (36+)

## ROCKFORD

**J. C.'s Place**
Dean Niforatos
First Assembly of God Church
5950 Spring Creek Road
Rockford, IL 61111
*Assemblies of God*
815/877-8000
**Years in existence:** 14
**Avg. attendance:** 125
**Primarily ages:** 26-30
**Main meeting time:** Sunday School Class

**New Beginnings**
Wayne & Sharon Hilden
First Evangelical Free Church
2223 N. Mulford Road
Rockford, IL 61107
*Evangelical Free Church of America*
815/877-7046
**Years in existence:** 11
**Avg. attendance:** 55
**Primarily ages:** 31-35
**Main meeting time(s):** Sunday School Class

## SHAWNEE

**Positive Christian Singles**
Rev. Dwight Mix
First Baptist Church
11400 Johnson Drive
Shawnee, IL 66203
*American Baptist*
913/268-6500
Years **in existence:** 10
**Avg. attendance:** 30
**Primarily ages:** 46-50
**Main meeting time(s):** Sunday School Class **Singles classes:** New Beginnings (35-65), Career (25-35), College (18-25)

## SOUTH BARRINGTON

**FOCUS**
Marie Knee and Dick Schmidt
Willow Creek Community Church
67 East Algonquin Road
South Barrington, IL 60010
*Non-denominational*
708/382-6200
**Years in existence:** 4
**Avg. attendance:** 750, monthly events
**Primarily ages:** 30-45
**Main meeting time(s):** Weekly and monthly

## SPRINGFIELD

**First Singles**
Mary Sue Brenno
First United Methodist
501 E. Capitol
Springfield, IL 62701
*Methodist*
217/528-5683
**Years in existence:** 3
**Avg. attendance:** 50
**Primarily ages:** 31-40
**Main meeting time(s):** A week night (M-F)
**Singles classes:** Seekers (20-30), Challengers (30-45), Passages (45+)

**SALT (Single Adults Learning Together)**
Kip Knavel
West Side Christian
900 West Edwards
Springfield, IL 62704
*Christian*
217/528-0418
**Years in existence:** 10
**Avg. attendance:** 100
**Primarily ages:** 31-45
**Main meeting time(s):** Sunday School Class, Tuesday night
**Singles Classes:** Career Fellowship (18-28), Singles for Christ (28-60)

## BROWNSBURG

### Significant Singles
Rev. George Curry
Bethesda Baptist Church
7950 N. 650th East
Brownsburg, IN 46112
*General Association of Regular Baptist Churches*
317/852-3101
**Years in existence:** 8
**Avg. attendance:** 55
**Primarily ages:** 26-35
**Main meeting time(s):** Sunday School Class **Singles classes:** Singles I (under 28), Singles II (28-38), Singles III (38+)

### Phos Kosmos (Light of the World) Singles Ministry
Brian Williams
Cornerstone Christian Church
8930 N. SR 267
Brownsburg, IN 46112
*Independent Christian Church*
**Avg. attendance:** 10
**Primarily ages:** 18-25
**Main meeting time(s):** Sunday School Class

## CARMEL

### Indiana Singles Ministry
Sue Whitesel
Indiana Ministries
531 S. Guilford Street
Carmel, IN 46032
*Church of God—Anderson*
317/844-4224
**Years in existence:** 7
**Primarily ages:** 26-45

### Young Adult Fellowship (YAF)
Karl W. Haeussler
Carmel Lutheran Church
4850 East 131st Street
Carmel, IN 46032
*Lutheran Church—Missouri Synod*
317/844-8770
**Years in existence:** 3
**Avg. attendance:** 16
**Primarily ages:** 26-30
**Main meeting time(s):** A week night (M-F)
**Singles classes:** Thursday Night Class (21-35), Sunday Class (31-40)

## FORT WAYNE

### Sonlight Singles
Jeff Vaughn
Blackhawk Baptist Church
7400 E. State Boulevard
Fort Wayne, IN 46815
*General Association of Regular Baptist Churches*
219/493-7400
**Years in existence:** 10
**Avg. attendance:** 60
**Primarily ages:** 41-45
**Main meeting time(s):** Sunday School Class
**Singles classes:** College (18-22), Career (22-30), Sonlight Singles (30-60)

## GOSHEN

### Turning Point
Ritch Hochstetler
Clinton Frame Mennonite
63846 CR 35
Goshen, IN 46526
*Mennonite*
*219/642-3165*
**Years in existence:** 5
**Avg. attendance:** 30
**Primarily ages:** 26-30
**Main meeting time(s):** Sunday School Class

## GREENVILLE

### Faith Fellowship Singles Support Group
J.R. Mayhve
Faith Fellowship Center
600 W. Summer Road
Greenville, IN 37743
*Assemblies of God*
615/636-1369
**Years in existence:** 1
**Avg. attendance:** 5-8
**Primarily ages:** 46-50
**Main meeting time(s):** A week night (M-F)
**Singles classes:** Keen-Agers (50+), Other (Mixed)

## GREENWOOD

### Single for any Reason (SFAR)
Angie Baker
Greenwood Christian Church
512 S. Madison Avenue
Greenwood, IN 46142
*Independent New Testament*
317/881-9336
**Years in existence:** 1
**Avg. attendance:** 40
**Primarily ages:** 31-40
**Main meeting time(s):** A week night (M-F)

## INDIANAPOLIS

### Christian Singles of Indianapolis
John Simmons
4701 N.Keystone Av
Indianapolis, IN 46205
317-257-3339
**Years in existence:** 4
**Primarily ages:** 31-40

### CROSSROADS (Chapel Rock Outreach to Serve Singles)
Paul E. Bledsoe
Chapel Rock Christian Church
2220 N. Girls School Road
Indianapolis, IN 46214
*Christian Church (Independent)*
317/247-9739
**Years in existence:** 13
**Avg. attendance:** 100
**Primarily ages:** 31-40
**Main meeting time(s):** Sunday School Class **Singles classes:** Impact (18-22), Shalom (21-35), New Beginnings (30+)

### Jericho Road Ministries
Mark Wesner
East 91st Street Christian Church
6049 East 91st Street
Indianapolis, IN 46250
317-849-1261
**Years in existence:** 6
**Avg. attendance:** 250
**Primarily ages:** 31-35
**Main meeting time(s):** Sunday School Class

### Single Life Ministries
Rev. Thomas W. Rakoczy
Lakeview Temple
47 Beachway Drive
Indianapolis, IN 46224
*Assemblies of God*
317/243-9396
**Years in existence:** 13
**Avg. attendance:** 70
**Primarily ages:** 31-50+
**Main meeting time(s):** A week night (M-F)

**Advertise Your Upcoming Conferences and Retreats. FREE!**
Each issue of SAM Journal lists upcoming singles and leadership conferences free of charge (as room allows). Send the date and details of your next event 4 - 5 months in advance. Let SAM help you spread the word. Send to SAM Journal, P.O. Box 60430, Colorado Springs, CO 80960-0430

**Single Side**
Sue Whitesel
Garfield Park Church of God
401 E. Southern Avenue
Indianapolis, IN 46225
*Church of God*
317/786-0426
**Years in existence:** 2
**Avg. attendance:** 30
**Primarily ages:** 31-45
**Main meeting time(s):** A week night (M-F)

## KOKOMO

**Solitaire**
Patricia Willhite
St. Luke's United Methodist
700 Southway Boulevard E
Kokomo, IN 46902
*United Methodist*
317/453-4867
**Years in existence:** 9
**Avg. attendance:** 18
**Primarily ages:** 50+
**Main meeting time(s):** Sunday School Class

## SEYMOUR

**Immanuel Single Adults Ministry (SAM)**
David McClean
Immanuel Lutheran Church
605 S. Walnut Street
Seymour, IN 47274
*Lutheran*
812/522-3118
**Years in existence:** 4
**Avg. attendance:** 30
**Primarily ages:** 26-45
**Main meeting time(s):** A week night (M-F), Friday night

## SOUTH BEND

**Little Flower Young Adult Ministry**
Julie Lytle
Little Flower Catholic Church
54191 North Ironwood
South Bend, IN 46635
*Catholic*
219/272-7070
**Years in existence:** 3
**Avg. attendance:** 50
**Primarily ages:** 26-30
**Main meeting time:** A week night (M-F)

## CEDAR FALLS

**IT (Individuals Together)**
Ella Hansen
Nazareth Lutheran Church
University & Main Street
Cedar Falls, IA 50613
*Evangelical Lutheran Church of America*
319/266-7589
**Years in existence:** 6
**Avg. attendance:** 76
**Primarily ages:** 36-45
**Main meeting time(s):** Sunday School Class, a week night (M-F), Saturday night
**Singles classes:** Sunday School Class (30-70), DSG (30-50), W/W (50-70)

## CEDAR RAPIDS

**Christian Adult Singles Activities (CASA)**
Jill Jennewein
St. Paul's United Methodist Church
Cedar Rapids, IA 52403
*Methodist*
319/363-2058
**Years in existence:** 1
**Avg. attendance:** 110
**Primarily ages:** 31-40
**Main meeting time(s):** Sunday night
**Singles classes:** Uno (30-45), Yes (19-30), New (30-45), Mature (45+)

**DWAS**
Jim McDaniel
New Covenant Bible Church
1800 46th Street, N.E.
Cedar Rapids, IA 52403
319/395-0021
**Years in existence:** 1
**Avg. attendance:** 15
**Primarily ages:** 36-40
**Main meeting time(s):** Saturday night

**First Assemblies Single Adults**
Richard L. Summerhays
First Assemblies of God
3233 Blairsferry Rd., N.E.
Cedar Rapids, IA 52402
*Assemblies of God*
319/393-1216
**Years in existence:** 4
**Avg. attendance:** 20
**Primarily ages:** 31-35
**Main meeting time(s):** Sunday School Class, a week night (M-F)

**FOCAS (Fellowship of Christian Adult Singles)**
Rich Batten
New Covenant Bible Church
1800 46th Street N.E. (meeting location only)
Cedar Rapids, IA 52405
319/395-0021
**Years in existence:** 3
**Avg. attendance:** 35
**Primarily ages:** 18-30
**Main meeting time(s):** Sunday night

## DAVENPORT

**St. John's Single Adult Ministry (SAM)**
Dottie Hoy
St. John's United Methodist Church
109 E. 14th Street
Davenport, IA 52807
*United Methodist*
319/324-5278
**Years in existence:** 2
**Avg. attendance:** 116
**Primarily ages:** 46-50
**Main meeting time(s):** Sunday night
**Singles classes:** Crossroads Sunday School Class (all ages), Younger Singles (18-35)

## DES MOINES

**Faith Aflame Singles; Steadfast Singles**
Rob Jones
Des Moines Baptist Church
950 35th Street
Des Moines, IA 50312
*Independent Baptist*
515/279-6440
**Years in existence:** 4
**Avg. attendance:** 100
**Primarily ages:** 18-25
**Main meeting time(s):** Sunday School Class **Singles classes:** Faith Aflame Singles (18-26), Steadfast Singles (27-40)

**First Federated Singles Ministry**
First Federated Church
4801 Franklin Avenue
Des Moines, IA 50310
*Non-denominational*
515/255-2122
**Years in existence:** 4
**Avg. attendance:** 200
**Primarily ages:** 18-30
**Main meeting time:** Sunday School Class
**Singles classes:** New Horizons (18-25), Career Class (25-35), Sojourners (35+)

**YACS (Young Adult Christian Singles)**
Virgil Dykstra
Meredith Drive Reformed Church
5128 N.W. 46th Avenue
Des Moines, IA 50310
*Reformed Church in America*
515/276-4901
**Avg. attendance:** 35
**Primarily ages:** 26-30
**Main meeting time(s):** Sunday School Class, a week night (M-F)

## SIOUX CITY

**Singles With Christ**
Alaire Bornholtz
Grace United Methodist Church
1735 Morningside Avenue
Sioux City, IA 51106
*United Methodist*
712/276-3452
**Years in existence:** 1
**Primarily ages:** 36-40

## EMPORIA

**Single Adult Fellowship of Emporia**
Dr. John Williams
12th Avenue Baptist Church
2023 W. 12th Avenue, P.O. Box 2023
Emporia, KS 66801-2023
*Southern Baptist Conference*
316/342-8830
**Years in existence:** 5

**Avg. attendance:** 35
**Primarily ages:** 26-50
**Main meeting time(s):** Sunday School Class, Sunday night

## NEWTON

### Student/Young Adult Services (SYAS)

Ken Hawkley
Box 347
Newton, KS 67114
*General Conference Mennonite & Mennonite Conference*
316/283-5100
**Years in existence:** 20
**Primarily ages:** 18-25

## PRAIRIE VILLAGE

### Nall Avenue Single Adults

Joyce Haynie
Nall Avenue Church of the Nazarene
6301 Nall Avenue
Prairie Village, KS 66206
*Nazarene*
913/384-3040
**Years in existence:** 1
**Avg. attendance:** 15
**Primarily ages:** 18-25
**Main meeting time(s):** Sunday School Class

**Fact:**
In Romania, during Nicolae Ceaucescu's rule, adult women who did not have children, even if they could not, were forced to pay a "celibacy tax" of up to 10 percent of their monthly salaries.

*Newsweek, Jan. 22, 1990, page 35*

### Village Church Singles Ministry

Pat Jackard
Village Presbyterian Church
P.O. Box 8050
Prairie Village, KS 66208
*Presbyterian*
913/262-4200
**Years in existence:** 10
**Avg. attendance:** 700
**Main meeting time(s):** A week night (M-F)
**Singles classes:** Young Adult Singles (20-30)

## SHAWNEE

### Single Vision

Richard Castaneda
Full Faith Church of Love
6824 Lackman Road
Shawnee, KS 66217
*Non-denominational*
913/631-1100
**Avg. attendance:** 80
**Primarily ages:** 26-35
**Main meeting time(s):** Sunday School Class
**Singles classes:** College Ministry (TNT) (18-24), Young Singles (22 to 30 Something), Adult Singles (30+)

## TOPEKA

### Northland Christian Singles

Dan Muzzy
Northland Christian Church
3102 N. Topeka
Topeka, KS 66617
*Non-denominational*
913/286-1204
**Years in existence:** 5-7
**Avg. attendance:** 15
**Primarily ages:** 31-50+
**Main meeting time(s):** Sunday School Class, Friday night
**Singles classes:** TNT (20s-30s), Solo's (40s+)

## WICHITA

### First Nazarene Singles

Vernon Haller
First Church of Nazarene
1400 E. Kellogg
Wichita, KS 67211
*Nazarene*
316/264-2851
**Years in existence:** 10
**Avg. attendance:** 100-120
**Primarily ages:** 18-50
**Main meeting time(s):** Sunday School Class **Singles classes:** Alpha (18-24), Light (25-45), Salt (40-65)

### Positive Christian Singles

Doug Peake
Central Community Church
6100 W. Maple
Wichita, KS 67209
*Church of God*
316-943-1800
**Years in existence:** 15
**Avg. attendance:** 150
**Primarily ages:** 36-45
**Main meeting time(s):** A week night (M-F)

### Singles at First

First United Methodist
330 N. Broadway
Wichita, KS 67206
*United Methodist*
316/267-6244
**Years in existence:** 10
**Avg. attendance:** 400
**Primarily ages:** 41-45
**Main meeting time(s):** Sunday School Class, a week night (M-F)
**Singles classes:** Cornerstone (30-45), SAM (55+), Koinonia (45+)

### Single Direction

George Granberry
Eastminster Presbyterian Church
1958 N. Webb Road
Wichita, KS 67206
*Presbyterian (USA)*
316/634-0337
**Years in existence:** 10
**Avg. attendance:** 70
**Primarily ages:** 26-35
**Main meeting time(s):** A week night (M-F)
**Singles classes:** Young Adults (18-25), Single Direction (25-35), Christian Singles (30-45), Singles Fellowship (45+)

### Westlink Singles

H. Henry Williams
Westlink Christian Church
8810 W. 10th
Wichita, KS 67212
*Non-denominational*
316/722-8020
**Years in existence:** 5
**Avg. attendance:** 30
**Primarily ages:** 26-30
**Main meeting time(s):** Sunday School Class **Singles classes:** Single Focus (22-35), Single Adults Class (35-50), SAS (Monthly) (60+), First Friday (Monthly) (30-50)

## ELIZABETHTOWN

### LAFFS

Brenda Durham
Memorial United Methodist
P.O. Box 97
Elizabethtown, KY 42701
*United Methodist*
502/769-3331
**Years in existence:** 5
**Avg. attendance:** 6
**Primarily ages:** 31-35
**Main meeting time(s):** Sunday School Class

## FLORENCE

### Singleheart

Barry Tucker
First Church of Christ
8453 U.S. 42
Florence, KY 41042
*Non-denominational*
606/525-8227
**Years in existence:** 4
**Avg. attendance:** 40
**Primarily ages:** 18-45
**Main meeting time(s):** Friday night, Saturday night
**Singles classes:** Metanoia (30+), New Directions (21-30)

## LEXINGTON

### Odyssey

Mark A. Brewer
Broadway Christian Church
187 N. Broadway
Lexington, KY 40508
*Christian Non-denominational*
606/278-6721 or 252-5638
**Years in existence:** 2
**Avg. attendance:** 40
**Primarily ages:** 36-40
**Main meeting time(s):** Sunday night

**Singleminded**
Bret R. Robbe
Immanuel Baptist Church
3100 Tates Creek Road
Lexington, KY 40502
*Southern Baptist*
606/266-3174
**Years in existence:** 3
**Avg. attendance:** 130
**Primarily ages:** 31-45
**Main meeting time:** Sunday School Class **Singles classes:** SA2 (20-27), SA3 (28-35), SA4 (36+)

**Trinity Hill Singles**
Marcia Weeks
Trinity Hill United Methodist
3600 Tates Creek Road
Lexington, KY 40517
*United Methodist*
606/272-3456
**Years in existence:** 10
**Avg. attendance:** 15
**Primarily ages:** 31-40
**Main meeting time(s):** A week night (M-F)
**Singles classes:** Tuesday Night Fellowship (22-50+), Sunday School (22-50+)

**Young Adult Ministries of SCC**
Monte J. Wilkinson
Southland Christian Church
P.O. Box 23338
Lexington, KY 40523
*Christian Church/Church of Christ*
606/223-3071
**Years in existence:** 5+
**Avg. attendance:** 125
**Primarily ages:** 26-30
**Main meeting time(s):** A week night (M-F)
**Singles classes:** Sunday School Classes (18-35), Wednesday Night Bible Study (18-35), Impact Prayer Groups (18-35)

## LOUISVILLE

**Injoy!**
Wayne Hunsucker
Ormsby Heights Baptist Church
2120 Lower Hunters Trace
Louisville, KY 40165
*Southern Baptist*
502/447-6867
**Years in existence:** 2
**Avg. attendance:** 35
**Primarily ages:** 26-30
**Main meeting time(s):** Sunday School Class **Singles classes:** Singles I (18-24), Singles II (25-34), Rebuilders

**Southeast Christian Church**
Ralph Dennison
Southeast Christian Church
2840 Hikes Lane
Louisville, KY 40218
*Independent Christian*
502/451-0047
**Years in existence:** 7
**Avg. attendance:** 325
**Primarily ages:** 31-35
**Main meeting time(s):** Sunday School Class **Singles classes:** B.Y.K.O.T.A. (41+), OASIS (49+), Young Adults (22-32), Venture (30-41)

## BASKIN

**LA District Singles**
Elizabeth H. Rigdon
LA District of the Nazarene
P.O. Box 473
Baskin, LA 71219
*Church of the Nazarene*
318/248-2381
**Primarily ages:** 36-40

## BOSSIER CITY

**Airline Drive Singles Ministry**
Gary Hatcher
Church of Christ
2125 Airline Drive
Bossier City, LA 71111
*Christian*
318/746-2645
**Years in existence:** 1
**Avg. attendance:** 12
**Primarily ages:** 26-35
**Main meeting time(s):** Sunday School Class


**Nice singles with Christian values wish to meet others!**

SINGLES SCENE, a monthly tabloid publication, is the nation's **number one** meeting place for Christian singles. **Since 1981 we have had hundreds of success stories reporting marriages** and lasting friendships begun through our pages. **Could we help you make more friends and possibly find that special someone?** You'll get a 25-word personal ad **FREE** with your one-year subscription. OR you can get **two FREE ads** with a two-year subscription. Print your ad in the space below or on a separate sheet of paper. Send it with your payment to: *Single Scene*, P. O. Box 310, Allardt, TN 38504.

**ORDER FORM**

☐ **YES I'd like to subscribe to *Singles Scene* and run my personal ad. I have printed my ad below or on a separate sheet of paper and I have checked the services I want below. Please rush !!!**

________ 1-year subscription and one FREE 25- word ad ($20.00)

________ 2-year subscription and a FREE 25-50 word ad to run two months in *Singles Scene* ($36.00)

_____a 25-50 word ad to run one month ($10.00) (to run 6 months - $50.00) (checking copy sent)

______TOTAL ☐ I enclose my check or money order

Charge my ☐Visa ☐ MasterCard
Card #____________Expires ______
Signature ____________Phone________

NAME________________

ADDRESS________________

CITY__________STATE_____ZIP________

Clip or duplicate and mail to:
*SINGLES SCENE*, Dept. SRD, P.O. Box 310, Allardt, TN 38504

## LAFAYETTE

### Aspires
Rev. Charles R. Langford
Asbury United Methodist Church
101 Live Oak Boulevard
Lafayette, LA 70503
*United Methodist*
318/984-4211
**Years in existence:** 9
**Avg. attendance:** 95
**Primarily ages:** 31-50
**Main meeting time(s):** Sunday School Class
**Singles classes:** Phoenix (30-50), New Class (unnamed) (30-60)

## LAKE CHARLES

### Trinity Baptist Singles
John Kyle
Trinity Baptist Church
P.O. Box 3087
Lake Charles, LA 70602
*Southern Baptist*
318/439-8352
**Years in existence:** 1
**Avg. attendance:** 63
**Primarily ages:** 18-40
**Main meeting time(s):** Sunday School Class
**Singles classes:** Singles 1 (22-29), Singles 2 (30+)

## MONROE

### Christian Singles
Steve Arledge
First Baptist Church
201 St. John Street
Monroe, LA 71210
*Southern Baptist*
318/325-3126
**Years in existence:** 10
**Avg. attendance:** 25
**Primarily ages:** 31-40
**Main meeting time(s):** Sunday School Class
**Singles classes:** Single Adult 1 (up to 30), Single Adult 2 (31-45), Single Adult (45+)

### First Presbyterian Singles
Lina Robinson
First Presbyterian Church
1201 Stubbs Avenue
Monroe, LA 71201
*Presbyterian Church (USA)*
318/323-9402
**Years in existence:** 1
**Avg. attendance:** 10
**Primarily ages:** 41-45, 50+
**Main meeting time(s):** Sunday School Class
**Singles classes:** Singly Yours (36-60)

## NEW IBERIA

### Singles at First
Donald McLeod
First United Methodist
119 Jefferson
New Iberia, LA 70560
*Methodist*
318/685-2324
**Years in existence:** -1
**Avg. attendance:** 24
**Main meeting time(s):** Friday night

## NEW ORLEANS

### Berean Singles
Jim Smithies
Berean Bible Church
3712 Herschel St.
New Orleans, LA 70114
*Berean*
504-362-3254
**Years in existence:** 1
**Avg. attendance:** 25
**Primarily ages:** 26-30
**Main meeting time(s):** Sunday School Class
**Singles classes:** Sunday School class (20-35), Single Parent Support Group (25-45)

## RUSTON

### Pathfinders
Dewey Myles
Trinity United Methodist
1000 W. Woodward
Ruston, LA 71270
318-251-0750
**Years in existence:** 1.5
**Avg. attendance:** 30
**Primarily ages:** 41-45
**Main meeting time(s):** Sunday School Class

## SHREVEPORT

### Brookwood Baptist Singles
Lana Elrod
Brookwood Baptist Church
8900 Kingston Road
Shreveport, LA 71118
*Baptist*
318/686-2898
**Years in existence:** 2
**Avg. attendance:** 35
**Primarily ages:** 18-25
**Main meeting time(s):** Sunday School Class
**Singles classes:** College/Career (18-22), Singles 1 (30+), Single 2 (21-30)

## ABERDEEN

### Bible Church Singles Fellowship
Daphney Gwynn
Aberdeen Bible Church
529 Edmund Street
Aberdeen, MD 21001
*Non-denominational*
301/272-3278
**Years in existence:** 6
**Avg. attendance:** 20
**Primarily ages:** 26-30
**Main meeting time(s):** Friday night
**Singles classes:** (17-20), Single Adults (21-30), Single Parents (Open), Widows/Widowers (Open)

## CAPITOL HEIGHTS

### SMILE (Singles Ministering In Love Edified)
Laura L. Dean
Cornerstone Peaceful Bible Baptist
6076 Central Avenue
Capitol Heights, MD 20743
*Baptist*
301/209-0030
**Years in existence:** 3
**Avg. attendance:** 105
**Primarily ages:** 26-30
**Main meeting time:** Friday night

## ELLICOTT CITY

### First Lutheran Singles Support Ministry
Audrey D. Forbes
First Lutheran Evangelical Church
3604 Chatham Road
Ellicott City, MD 21043
*Lutheran*
301/465-2977
**Years in existence:** 2
**Avg. attendance:** 12
**Primarily ages:** 41-45
**Main meeting time(s):** A week night (M-F)

## GAITHERSBURG

### IMPACT!
Mark Rowe
Church of the Redeemer
504 E. Diamond Avenue #F
Gaithersburg, MD 20877
*Non-denominational*
301/926-0967
**Years in existence:** 1
**Avg. attendance:** 35
**Primarily ages:** 26-30
**Main meeting time(s):** Friday night

## JOPPATOWNE

### Ministry to Single Adults
Dan Weaver
Joppatowne Christian Church
P.O. Box 216
Joppatowne, MD 21085
*Christian Church*
301/679-9366
**Years in existence:** 2
**Avg. attendance:** 15
**Primarily ages:** 18-25
**Main meeting time(s):** Sunday night
**Singles classes:** College Age Sunday School (18-22), CAYAC (18-25), Serendipity Class (22-30)

## LUTHERVILLE

### Mainstream
James A. Lex
Trinity Assemblies of God
2122 W. Joppa Road
Lutherville, MD 21093
*Assemblies of God*
301/821-6573
**Years in existence:** 2
**Avg. attendance:** 70
**Primarily ages:** 26-40
**Main meeting time(s):** A week night (M-F)
**Singles classes:** Young Adults (20-30), Single Adults (30s-40s)

## ROCKVILLE

### Montrose Singles
Reiff Lesher
Montrose Baptist Church
5100 Randolph Road
Rockville, MD 20852

*Southern Baptist*
301/770-5335
**Years in existence:** 12
**Avg. attendance:** 75
**Primarily ages:** 26-30
**Main meeting time(s):** Sunday School Class
**Singles classes:** Single Young Adults (25-35), Singles Enjoy (45+)

## SIMPSONVILLE

### Delmarva-D.C. Single Adult Ministry (State Office)
William A. Reid
Church of God
P.O. Box 98
Simpsonville, MD 21150
*Church of God—Cleveland, TN*
301/531-5351
**Years in existence:** 1
**Primarily ages:** 18-30
**Main meeting time(s):** Sunday School Class

## WESTMINSTER

### Open Door Single Adults
Dale Kidd
Church of the Open Door
550 Baltimore Boulevard
Westminster, MD 21157
*Independent*
301/848-8840
**Years in existence:** 6
**Avg. attendance:** 50
**Primarily ages:** 26-40
**Main meeting time(s):** Sunday School Class **Singles classes:** New Horizons (18-22), Single Focus (23-32), Abundant Life (33+)

## BOSTON

### Young Adult Ministry
Doug Calhoun
Park Street Church
One Park Street
Boston, MA 02108
*Conservative Congregation Christian Conference*
617/523-3383
**Years in existence:** 22
**Avg. attendance:** 145
**Primarily ages:** 26-30
**Main meeting time(s):** A week night (M-F)

## HINGHAM

### Unison
Suzanne Tanner and James Weston
South Shore Baptist Church
578 Main Street
Hingham, MA 02043
*Conservative Baptist*
617/749-2592
**Years in existence:** 3
**Avg. attendance:** 125
**Primarily ages:** 26-36
**Main meeting time:** A week night (M-F)

## LEXINGTON

### Grace Chapel Singles
Pastor David A. Johnson
Grace Chapel
59 Worthen Road
Lexington, MA 02173
*Interdenominational*
617/862-6499
**Years in existence:** 7
**Avg. attendance:** 200
**Primarily ages:** 31-35
**Main meeting time:** Friday night
**Singles classes:** Basic—college/career; Alive (27-38), Single Adult Fellowship (30-45), Carpenters—single parents

## MAYNARD

### One In Christ Fellowship
Carol Cousins
2 Riverbank Road
Maynard, MA 01754
**Years in existence:** 5
**Avg. attendance:** 10
**Primarily ages:** 31-35
**Main meeting time(s):** Saturday night

## MILFORD

### Reach Out
Pastor Carl Kuhn
Milford Bible Baptist Church
P.O. Box 597
Milford, MA 01757
*Baptist*
508/883-3490
**Years in existence:** 3
**Avg. attendance:** 10
**Primarily ages:** 26-30
**Main meeting time(s):** Saturday night

## WORCESTER

### Singles-Diocese of Worcester
Karen Daige
Office of Youth Ministry
781 Grove Street
Worcester, MA 01605
*Roman Catholic*
508/852-7877
**Years in existence:** 2
**Primarily ages:** 18-35
**Singles classes:** We serve 128 parishes in the Worcester Diocese to enable and advocate for Young Adult Ministry

## ALLEN PARK

### Downriver Presbyterian Singles
Wendy S. Bailey
Allen Park Presbyterian Church
7101 Park Avenue
Allen Park, MI 48101
*Presbyterian Church (USA)*
313/383-0100
**Years in existence:** 1
**Avg. attendance:** 20
**Primarily ages:** 36-50
**Main meeting time(s):** Sunday night
**Singles classes:** Sunday Night Singles (25-55), Divorce Recovery (25-55)

## ANN ARBOR

### New Directions
David Krehbiel
First Presbyterian Church
1432 Washtenaw
Ann Arbor, MI 48104
*Presbyterian*
313/662-4466
**Years in existence:** 10
**Avg. attendance:** 75
**Primarily ages:** 36-40
**Main meeting time:** Sunday School Class **Singles classes:** Wayfarers (18-30), New Directions (30+)

## FERNDALE

### YESS (Young Adult Education for Single's Session )
Brenda Waller
P.O. Box 20715
Ferndale, MI 48220
**Years in existence:** 5
**Avg. attendance:** 50
**Primarily ages:** 18-30

## FLINT

### Caring Christian Singles
Dr. Lawrence W. Kent
First Presbyterian Church of Flint Michigan
746 S. Saginaw
Flint, MI 48502
*Presbyterian*
313/234-8673
**Years in existence:** 6
**Avg. attendance:** 120
**Primarily ages:** 41-45
**Main meeting time(s):** A week night (M-F)

### Singleness of Purpose Ministries
Keith McAr
Faith Fellowship Ministries
P.O. Box 303
Flint, MI 48501
*Non-denominational*
313/743-2484
**Years in existence:** 3
**Avg. attendance:** 40
**Primarily ages:** 26-40

## GRAND RAPIDS

### Calvary Single Adults
Doug Fagerstrom
Calvary Church
777 E. Beltline Ave. N.E.
Grand Rapids, MI 49506
*Non-Denominational*
616/956-9377
**Years in existence:** 8
**Avg. attendance:** 350-400
**Primarily ages:** 31-35
**Main meeting time(s):** Sunday School Class, Saturday night
**Singles classes:** Pier 127 (18+),

Roaring 20s (23+), S.A.M. (26+), Focus (39+)

## GRANDVILLE

**Single Focus**
Kent Walters
Grace Bible Church
3715 Wilson
Grandville, MI 49418
*Non-denominational*
616/538-9350
**Years in existence:** 4
**Avg. attendance:** 17
**Primarily ages:** 31-35
**Main meeting time(s):** Sunday School Class

## HOLLAND

**Sole Concern**
Elizabeth Veldink
Christ Memorial Church
595 Graafschap Road
Holland, MI 49423
*Reformed Church of America*
616/396-2305
**Years in existence:** 3
**Avg. attendance:** 30
**Primarily ages:** 26-35
**Main meeting time(s):** A week night (M-F)
**Singles classes:** Sole Concern (Thursday) (25-40), Singles Forum (25-40), Single Again Support Group (30-40), Single Parent Support Group (30-40)

*During the 1980s, the number of families headed by married couples rose by 3 million—but the number headed by single parents increased by 3.3 million.*

*U.S. Census Bureau*

## HUDSONVILLE

**Single Adult Ministry**
Mark S. Tans
Classis Georgetown
P.O. Box 124
Hudsonville, MI 49426-0124
*Christian Reformed*
616/669-2600
**Years in existence:** 1
**Primarily ages:** 18-35

## LANSING

**Central Singles**
Del Shinabarger
Central Free Methodist
828 North Washington
Lansing, MI 48906
*Free Methodist*
517/485-2232
**Years in existence:** 5
**Avg. attendance:** 75
**Primarily ages:** 18-25, 36-45
**Main meeting time(s):** Sunday School Class **Singles classes:** Singles #1 (18-30), Singles #2 (30-45)

**S.A.M**
Mark W. Harbison
East Lansing Trinity Church
841 Timberlane
E. Lansing, MI 48823
517/351-8200
**Years in existence:** 7
**Avg. attendance:** 80
**Primarily ages:** 26-40
**Main meeting time(s):** Sunday School Class **Singles classes:** S.A.M. (25-40), Single Parents (25-40)

**Single View**
Val Chappell
South Baptist Church
1518 S. Washington Avenue
Lansing, MI 48910
*Independent*
517/482-0753
**Years in existence:** 10
**Avg. attendance:** 80
**Primarily ages:** 18-25, 41-45
**Main meeting time(s):** Sunday School Class **Singles classes:** Koinonia (18-30), Focus (35+)

## LIVONIA

**SPM (Single Point Ministry)**
Andy Morgan
Ward Presbyterian Church
17000 Farmington Road
Livonia, MI 48150
*Evangelical Presbyterian Church*
313/422-1854
**Years in existence:** 15
**Avg. attendance:** 550
**Primarily ages:** 31-50+
**Main meeting time(s):** Sunday School Class, Friday night
**Singles classes:** Upward Bound (18-22), Single Spirit (22-35), Single Point (30+)

## PORT HURON

**Singles Christian Fellowship**
Max Amstutz
Colonial Woods Missionary
3240 Pine Grove Avenue
Port Huron, MI 48060
*Missionary Church*
313/984-5571
**Years in existence:** 8
**Avg. attendance:** 70
**Primarily ages:** 36-40
**Main meeting time(s):** Sunday School Class

## ANOKA

**Whole-In-One**
Mike Johnson
Elim Baptist Church
503 Polk Street
Anoka, MN 55303
*Baptist General Conference*
612/421-8124
**Years in existence:** 5
**Avg. attendance:** 30+
**Primarily ages:** 36-50
**Main meeting time(s):** A week night (M-F)
**Singles classes:** Whole-In-One (36-60s), Young Elim Singles (YES) (23-35), Ice Collegiate Encounter (ICE) (18-22)

## BLOOMINGTON

**Life Styles**
Scott Bernstein
Bloomington Assemblies of God
8600 Bloomington Avenue South
Bloomington, MN 55425
*Assemblies of God*
612/854-1100
**Years in existence:** 11
**Avg. attendance:** 80
**Primarily ages:** 26-30
**Main meeting time(s):** Sunday School Class, a week night (M-F)

## BURNSVILLE

**Prince of Peace Singles**
Dee Bailey
Prince of Peace Lutheran Church
200 East Nicollet Blvd.
Burnsville, MN 55337
*Evangelical Luthern Church of America*
612/435-8102
**Years in existence:** 12
**Avg. attendance:** 100+
**Main meeting time:** A week night (M-F)
**Singles classes:** Singles Organized South (all ages), Starting Over Single—divorce recovery, Positive Christian Singles (all ages), Singles Bible Study (all ages)

## EDEN PRAIRIE

**Wooddale Singles Ministry**
Wooddale Church
6630 Shady Oak Road
Eden Prairie, MN 55344
*Baptist General Conference*
612/944-6300
**Years in existence:** 10
**Avg. attendance:** 200+
**Primarily ages:** 26-30
**Singles classes:** College Class (18-22), Career Singles (18-22), Singles Life Fellowship (22-35), Single Adults (35+), One-by-One (30s), Uplifters (40-60s), formerly married, The Wright Ones—divorced

## EDINA

**Grace Single Adults**
Jim Dyke
Grace Church of Edina
5300 France Avenue S.
Edina, MN 55410
*Independent*
612/926-1884
**Years in existence:** 8
**Avg. attendance:** 200

**Primarily ages:** 26-35
**Main meeting time(s):** Sunday School Class **Singles classes:** Single Spirit (40s-50s), Single Focus (20s-30s), Single Fellowship (30s), Single Heart (20s)

## HASTINGS

**Jubilee Singles**
Bill Ruhr
Jubilee Christian Church
11125 W. Pt. Douglas Road
Hastings, MN 55033
*Non-denominational*
612/437-9770
**Years in existence:** 5
**Avg. attendance:** 20
**Primarily ages:** 26-30
**Main meeting time(s):** Saturday night

## MINNEAPOLIS

**New Directions**
Ron Hagberg
Hennepin Avenue United Methodist
Lyndale & Goveland Avenues
Minneapolis, MN 55403
*United Methodist*
612/871-5303
**Years in existence:** 6
**Avg. attendance:** 50
**Primarily ages:** 41-45
**Main meeting time(s):** Sunday School Class **Singles classes:** Alpha Group (25-35), Alternatives (35-45)

## ROCHESTER

**First Baptist Singles**
Rev. Jeff McNicol
First Baptist Church
415 - 16th Street S.W.
Rochester, MN 55902
*Non-denominational*
507/288-8880
**Years in existence:** 14
**Avg. attendance:** 80
**Primarily ages:** 18-40
**Main meeting time:** Sunday School Class **Singles classes:** Singles I (post college age-35), Singles II (30+)

## ST. PAUL

**St. John's Young Adults**
Vicki Osendorf
St. John's
380 E. Little Canada Road
St. Paul, MN 55117
*Catholic*
612/484-0048
**Years in existence:** 1
**Avg. attendance:** 25
**Primarily ages:** 26-30
**Main meeting time(s):** Sunday night

**St. Paul Area Singles**
Leland Jackson
Bethel Lutheran Church
670 W. Wheelock Parkway
St. Paul, MN 55117
*Lutheran Church—Missouri Synod*
612/488-6681
**Years in existence:** 6
**Avg. attendance:** 22
**Primarily ages:** 26-35
**Main meeting time(s):** A week night (M-F)

## JACKSON

**One by One**
Rubyanne Andress
St. Luke's United Methodist Church
621 Duling Street
Jackson, MS 39216
*United Methodist*
601/362-6381
**Years in existence:** 4
**Avg. attendance:** 25
**Primarily ages:** 31-40, 50+
**Main meeting time(s):** Sunday School Class
**Singles classes:** Career (22-35), Pathfinders (35-40+), Seekers (50-60+)

## QUITMAN

**Bethany Christian Singles**
Gwen Hayes
Bethany
123 Long Boulevard
Quitman, MS 39355
*Pentecostal Holiness*
**Years in existence:** 3
**Avg. attendance:**14
**Primarily ages:** 36-40, 46-50+
**Main meeting time(s):** Sunday School Class

## BOLIVAR

**Every Single Person (ESP)**
Maeanne Browning
First Baptist Church
316 North Main
Bolivar, MO 65613
*Southern Baptist*
417/326-2431
**Years in existence:** 3
**Avg. attendance:** 15
**Primarily ages:** 31-40, 50+
**Main meeting time(s):** Sunday School Class

## CHESTERFIELD

**Perspectives**
Mary L. Wigton
Green Trails United Methodist
14237 Ladue Road
Chesterfield, MO 63017
*United Methodist*
314/469-6740
**Years in existence:** 1
**Avg. attendance:** 15
**Main meeting time(s):** Sunday School Class

## COLUMBIA

**Columbia-Mexico District Singles**
Marjorie Pickett
Columbia-Mexico District Church
1970 Jackson
Columbia, MO 65202
*United Methodist*
**Years in existence:** 2
**Avg. attendance:** 18
**Primarily ages:** 41-45
**Main meeting time(s):** Sunday School Class

**Travelers**
Randall F. Kilgore
First Baptist—Columbia
112 East Broadway
Columbia, MO 65201
*Southern Baptist/American Baptist*
314/442-1149
**Years in existence:** 3+
**Avg. attendance:** 18
**Primarily ages:** 31-35
**Main meeting time(s):** Sunday School Class

## FLORISSANT

**First Christian Singles**
Steve Wingfield
First Christian Church of Florissant
2890 Patterson Road
Florissant, MO 63031
*Nondenominational*
314/837-2269
**Years in existence:** 4
**Avg. attendance:** 45
**Primarily ages:** 18-30, 41-45
**Singles classes:** LAF (18-35), ASC (30-55)

## JOPLIN

**Forest Park Baptist Singles**
John Scudder
Forest Park Baptist Church
725 Highview
Joplin, MO 64801
*Southern Baptist*
417/623-4606
**Years in existence:** 3
**Avg. attendance:** 55
**Primarily ages:** 31-45
**Main meeting time(s):** Sunday School Class
**Singles classes:** Singles I (18-22), Singles II (23-35), Singles III (36+)

## KANSAS CITY

### Country Club Christian Singles Ministry
Carla Aday
Country Club Christian Church
6101 Ward Parkway
Kansas City, MO 64112
*Christian Church (Disciples of Christ)*
816/333-4917
**Years in existence:** 7
**Avg. attendance:** 60
**Primarily ages:** 50+
**Main meeting time(s):** Sunday School Class **Singles classes:** Genesis (20s), Christian Lifestyles (30s), One-ders (40-50s), 50+ Singles (65-80)

### Holmeswood Baptist Single Adults
Nancy Brown
Holmeswood Baptist Church
9700 Holmes Road
Kansas City, MO 64131
*Southern Baptist Convention*
816/942-1729
**Avg. attendance:** 75
**Primarily ages:** 31-35
**Main meeting time(s):** Sunday night
**Singles classes:** AS-1 (18-26), AS-2 (27+)

### New Life Singles
Barbara Youree
Colonial Presbyterian
9500 Wornall Road
Kansas City, MO 64114
*Presbyterian*
**Years in existence:** 15+
**Avg. attendance:** 20
**Primarily ages:** 50+
**Main meeting time(s):** Sunday School Class **Singles classes:** Colonial Singles Fellowship (40s), Thirty-Something (30s)

### Northland Cathedral Singles
Pastor Lowell Harrup
Northland Cathedral
600 N.E. 46th Street
Kansas City, MO 64116
*Assemblies of God*
816/455-2555
**Years in existence:** 5
**Avg. attendance:** 100
**Primarily ages:** 36-50
**Main meeting time(s):** Sunday School Class, Tuesday night
**Singles classes:** Young Adults (21-35), single & married, Confident Singles (all ages), Singles Experience (all ages), Tuesday Night Singles (all ages)

### Red Bridge Baptist Single Adults
Victor Borden
Red Bridge Baptist
4901 Red Bridge Road
Kansas City, MO 64137
*Baptist*
816-761-1194
**Years in existence:** 8
**Avg. attendance:** 40
**Primarily ages:** 18-30
**Main meeting time(s):** Saturday night

### Single Adult Fellowship
Bob Hodges
Broadway Baptist
3931 Washington Street
Kansas City, MO 64111
*Interdenominational*
816/561-3274
**Years in existence:** 8
**Avg. attendance:** 270
**Primarily ages:** 41-45
**Main meeting time(s):** Sunday night, Sunday morning

**Do You Feel Left Out?**
If you were left out of this National Directory, we have good news. There will be another Directory... and we want to make sure you are not left out again. Help us make this Directory complete. Let us know about your group.
*See page 249*

### Single Adult Ministry
Ken Greene
Catholic Diocese of Kansas City/ St. Joseph
P.O. Box 419037
Kansas City, MO 64141-6037
*Catholic*
816/756-1850
**Years in existence:** 1
**Primarily ages:** 26-30

### Solo Con
Linda Hardin
Church of the Nazarene
6401 The Paseo
Kansas City, MO 64131
*Nazarene*
816/333-7000 Ext. 257
**Years in existence:** 7
**Primarily ages:** 31-40

## LEE'S SUMMIT

### First Baptist Singles
Steve Treece
First Baptist —Lee's Summit
2 North Douglas
Lee's Summit, MO 64063
*Southern Baptist*
816/525-0700
**Years in existence:** 4
**Avg. attendance:** 10
**Primarily ages:** 18-25
**Main meeting time(s):** Sunday School Class

### Lee's Summit Singles
Dan Chorny
Lee's Summit United Methodist Church
P.O. Box 362
Lee's Summit, MO 64063
*Methodist*
816/524-4966
**Years in existence:** 3
**Avg. attendance:** 35
**Primarily ages:** 26-50+
**Main meeting time(s):** Sunday School Class, a week night (M-F)
**Singles classes:** Sunday Singles (25-50), Summit Singles (50+), Singles Meeting Singles (20-50)

## LIBERTY

### Pleasant Valley Baptist Single Adults
Jim Danielson
Pleasant Valley Baptist Church
6816 Church Road
Liberty, MO 64068
*Southern Baptist*
816/781-5959
**Years in existence:** 10
**Avg. attendance:** 100
**Primarily ages:** 18-40
**Main meeting time(s):** Sunday School Class
**Singles classes:** College Bible Study (18-22), Singles 1 (18-25), Singles 2 (26-37), Singles 3 (37+)

## POND

### Bethel Singles
Judy Curry
Bethel United Methodist Church
17500 Manchester
Pond, MO 63038
*United Methodist*
314/275-7772
**Years in existence:** 2
**Avg. attendance:** 15
**Primarily ages:** 50+
**Main meeting time(s):** A week night (M-F)

## SPRINGFIELD

### Evangel Single Adult Ministry
Gary York
Evangel Temple Christian Church
2020 E. Battlefield
Springfield, MO 65804
417-883-0676
**Years in existence:** 5
**Avg. attendance:** 12
**Primarily ages:** 31-45
**Main meeting time(s):** A week night (M-F)
**Singles classes:** Singles Overcomming Life's Obs (25+)

### Rolling Hills Singles
Dane Brandwein
Rollings Hills Baptist Church
3304 S. Cox
Springfield, MO 65807
*Baptist (Spirit Filled)*
417/887-7760
**Years in existence:** 2
**Avg. attendance:** 130
**Primarily ages:** 18-25, 31-45
**Main meeting time(s):** Sunday School Class, Friday night

### Singles at Second
Vic Almen
Second Baptist Church
1201 S. Oak Grove
Springfield, MO 65804
*Southern Baptist*
417/841-4111

**Years in existence:** 8
**Avg. attendance:** 180
**Primarily ages:** 18-25
**Main meeting time(s):** Sunday School Class, Friday night
**Singles classes:** Singles I (18-34), Singles II (35-54), Singles III (55+), College (18-23)

### Sojourner Ministries, Inc.
Scott Shemeth
P.O. Box 9101
Springfield, MO 65801-9101
*417/863-9160*
**Years in existence:** 3

### Young Adult Singles
Roger Tiller and Jerry Bear
High Street Baptist
900 North Eastgate Road
Springfield, MO 65802
*Baptist*
417/862-5502
**Avg. attendance:** 140
**Primarily ages:** 18-25
**Main meeting time:** Sunday School Class

## ST. LOUIS

### First Baptist Church Singles
Rev. Wesley V. Owens
First Baptist Church of Ferguson
333 North Florissant Road
St. Louis, MO 63135
*Southern Baptist*
314/521-1515
**Years in existence:** 7
**Avg. attendance:** 200
**Primarily ages:** 18-50
**Main meeting time(s):** Sunday School Classes **Singles Classes:** Single Adult 1E (18-24), Single Adult 2E (25-30), Single Adult 3E (31-40), Single Adult 4E (41-60), Single Adult 1L (18-40), Single Adult 2L (41-65), University Form (college age)

### Focus-St. Louis
Thomas Merkel
Archdiocese of St. Louis
4140 Lindell Boulevard
St. Louis, MO 63108
*Roman Catholic*
314/371-4980
**Years in existence:** 2
**Primarily ages:** 18-35

### Single Life Ministries
John P. Splinter/Barb Schiller
Central Presbyterian Church
7700 Davis Drive
St. Louis, MO 63105
*Presbyterian*
314/727-2777
**Years in existence:** 6
**Avg. attendance:** 120
**Primarily ages:** 36-40
**Main meeting time(s):** Sunday School Class, Monday and Wednesday nights
**Singles classes:** Sunday School Class (30+), Just Me & The Kids—single parents, Second Chapter—divorce recovery, FOCUS (30+), Relationships Anonymous (30+), Prime Time (20-35), XYZ (50+), Cursillo (30-60).

## BELLEVIEW

### Adult Career Singles
Barbara Mehrens
Calvary Christian Church
Cornhusker at Cedar Island Road
Bellevue, NE 68005
*Nondenominational*
402/293-1700
**Years in existence:** 1
**Avg. attendance:** 12
**Primarily ages:** 18-35
**Main meeting time(s):** Sunday School Class

## KEARNEY

### SAM Council
Nona Morrison
First United Methodist Church
4500 Linden Drive
Kearney, NE 68847
*United Methodist*
308/237-3158
**Years in existence:** 2
**Avg. attendance:** 15
**Primarily ages:** 36-50+
**Main meeting time(s):** Sunday night
**Singles classes:** Cast (35-55), Spice (55+)

## LINCOLN

### St. Mark's Singles Ministry
Sue Nilson
St. Mark's United Methodist Church
740 N. 70th
Lincoln, NE 68505
*United Methodist*
402/489-8888
**Years in existence:** 5
**Avg. attendance:** 100
**Primarily ages:** 31-50
**Main meeting time(s):** Sunday School Class, a week night (M-F)
**Singles classes:** Heart & Soul (20-30s), Single Adults (30-50), Network (45-60), Pacesetters (50+)

## RENO

### Single Life Fellowship
John R. Etcheto
Reno Christian Fellowship
1700 W. Zolezzi Lane
Reno, NV 89511
702/853-4234
**Years in existence:** 6
**Avg. attendance:** 60
**Primarily ages:** 31-45
**Main meeting time(s):** Sunday School Class, a week night (M-F)

## ALLENWOOD

### Young Adults
Bob Aumueller
Trinity Baptist Church
P.O. Box 523, Allenwood/ Lakewood Roads
Allenwood, NJ 08720
*Conservative Baptist (American)*
201/544-3106
**Years in existence:** 7
**Avg. attendance:** 22
**Primarily ages:** 18-25
**Main meeting time(s):** A week night (M-F)

### Younger Singles
Douglas & Tisha Dial
Shore Christian Center Church
4041 Squantrum Road
Allenwood, NJ 08720
908/229-0415
**Years in existence:** 1
**Avg. attendance:** 15
**Primarily ages:** 18-25
**Main meeting time(s):** Saturday night

## ALTANTIC HIGH-LANDS

### King's Highway Singles
William R. Walters
King's Highway Faith Fellowship
44 Memorial Parkway
Atlantic Highlands, NJ 07716
908/291-2915
**Years in existence:** 1
**Avg. attendance:** 4-12
**Main meeting time(s):** A week night (M-F)

## CHERRY HILLS

### Singles Class
Hank Lancaster
Cherry Hill Baptist
Browning Road (behind Woodcrest Shopping Center)
Cherry Hill, NJ 08003
*Baptist*
604/854-7000
**Years in existence:** 3
**Avg. attendance:** 20
**Primarily ages:** 26-35
**Main meeting time(s):** Sunday School Class

## ESSEX FELLS

### Tuesday Night Live
Stephen Maret
Calvary Evangelical Free Church
450 Fells Road
Essex Fells, NJ 07021
*Evangelical Free*
201/226-5272
**Years in existence:** 9
**Avg. attendance:** 100
**Primarily ages:** 18-35

**Main meeting time(s):** A week night (M-F)
**Singles classes:** Solid Rock Group (18-23), Tuesday Night Live (24+)

## MEDFORD

### Alliance Singles

Bob Ricoord
Fellowship Alliance Chapel
199 Church Road
Medford, NJ 08055
*Christian & Missionary Alliance*
609/953-7333
**Years in existence** 4
**Avg. attendance:** 2 groups/18 each
**Primarily ages:** 26-40
**Main meeting time(s):** Sunday night, Friday night
**Singles classes:** Alliance Singles Fellowship (18-35), Alliance College Fellowship (18-23), Barnabas Fellowship (25-45), Single Mothers Fellowship (25-45)

## PERTH AMBOY

### PLUS (Power Filled Living for Unifying Singles)

Frances L. Stanton
Second Baptist Church, Perth Amboy
101 Broad Street/P.O. Box 1608
Perth Amboy, NJ 08862
*Baptist (Full Gospel)*
201/826-5293
**Years in existence:** 6
**Avg. attendance:** 25
**Primarily ages:** 26-30
**Main meeting time(s):** Friday night

## PITMAN

### The Alternative for Single Adults

Robert Barber
Gloucester County Community Church
P.O. Box 266
Pitman, NJ 08071
*Interdenominational*
609/582-0222
**Years in existence:** 1
**Avg. attendance:** 70
**Primarily ages:** 18-45
**Main meeting time(s):** A week night (M-F)
**Singles classes:** The Alternative—Volleyball/Bible Study (18-45), Sounds of Praise (Singles Choir) (20-35), Single Parents Fellowship (30-45), Home Bible Studies (2) (varies)

## WILLINGBORO

### FRIENDS, INC.

Pat McLain
18 Hamilton Lane
Willingboro, NJ 08046-1705
**Avg. attendance:** 20
**Primarily ages:** 26-40
**Main meeting time(s):** A week night (M-F)

## WYCKOFF

### The New Christian Singles Ministry

Douglas A. Landau
Christian Reformed Church
530 Sicomac Avenue
Wyckoff, NJ 07481
*Christian Reformed Church in America*
201/848-0639
**Years in existence:** 5
**Avg. attendance:** 85
**Primarily ages:** 36-45
**Main meeting time(s):** Sunday night, Saturday night

## ALAMOGORDO

### Grace United Methodist Singles

Theresa Tally
Grace United Methodist Church
1206 Greenwood Lane
Alamogordo, NM 88310
*Methodist*
505/437-7640
**Years in existence:** 5
**Avg. attendance:** 20
**Primarily ages:** 18-25
**Main meeting time(s):** Sunday School Class

## ALBUQUERQUE

### Bethany Singles

Mark Vanderput
Heights Cumberland Presbyterian
8600 Academy N.E.
Albuquerque, NM 87111
*Presbyterian*
505/822-8722
**Avg. attendance:** 55
**Primarily ages:** 46-50
**Main meeting time(s):** Sunday night
**Singles classes:** Bethany Singles (30+), Single Life Fellowship (22-30), University Singles Fellowship (18-24)

### Sandia Baptist

Elizabeth Riggins
Sandia Baptist Church
9429 Constitution N.E.
Albuquerque, NM 87112
*Southern Baptist*
**Years in existence:** 10
**Avg. attendance:** 60
**Primarily ages:** 26-30
**Main meeting time(s):** Sunday School Class
**Singles classes:** Singles I (18-30), Singles II (30-45), Singles III (46+), College (18-22)

### Single Hearted

Paul A. Gossett
Hoffmantown Baptist Church
8888 Harper Dr. NE
Albuquerque, NM 87111
*Baptist*
505/828-2600
**Years in existence:** 6
**Avg. attendance:** 125-150
**Primarily ages:** 18-35
**Main meeting time(s):** Sunday School Class **Singles classes:** LSA3 (21-34), LSA2 (34-44), LSA1 (45+)

## CLOVIS

### Single Adult Ministry

Phyllis Macmillan
Central Baptist Church
800 Hinckle
Clovis, NM 88101
*Southern Baptist*
**Primarily ages:** 46-50+
**Main meeting time(s):** Sunday School Class
**Singles classes:** Single Adult I (22-29), Single Adult II (30-45), Single Adult III (46+)

## FARMINGTON

### Single Servants

Jay Wendeborn
Chapel of the Valley
2016 E. 16th
Farmington, NM 87401
*Non-denominational*
505/327-0941
**Years in existence:** 4
**Avg. attendance:** 25
**Primarily ages:** 26-40
**Main meeting time(s):** Friday night

## BROCKPORT

### CCAOS (College/Career and/or Single)

Dave Livermore
Grace Baptist Church
5220 Lake Road South
Brockport, NY 14420
*Regular Baptist Fellowshp*
716/637-2470
**Years in existence:** 1
**Avg. attendance:** 10
**Primarily ages:** 18-25
**Main meeting time(s):** Sunday School Class, Sunday night

## BRONX

### Glad Tidings Singles

Marlene Henderson
Glad Tidings Church
3 Van Cortland Avenue East
Bronx, NY 10467
*Assemblies of God*
212/367-4040
**Years in existence:** 5
**Avg. attendance:** 150
**Primarily ages:** 18-30
**Main meeting time(s):** Sunday School Class
**Singles classes:** Singles (19-35)

## BUFFALO

### One by One Singles

Charles Douglas
New Covenant Tabernacle
345 McConkly Drive

Buffalo, NY 14223
*Assemblies of God*
**Years in existence:** 8
**Avg. attendance:** 40
**Primarily ages:** 18-35
**Main meeting time(s):** Friday night

## CIRCLEVILLE

### Circleville Singles Ministry
May R. Lennon
Circleville Presbyterian Church, Box 141
Circleville, NY 10916
*Presbyterian (USA)*
914/361-2381
**Years in existence:** 2
**Primarily ages:** 46-50
**Main meeting times:** A week night (M-F)

## CLIFTON SPRINGS

### Singles Connection
Lynn Spence
Clifton Springs United Methodist
Main Street at Crane St.
Clifton Springs, NY 14432
*Methodist*
315/462-2274
**Years in existence:** 1
**Avg. attendance:** 30
**Primarily ages:** 36-50+
**Main meeting time(s):** Friday night
**Singles classes:** We are all equal (30+)

## FISHKILL

### Steppin' Stone Cafe: Christian Singles Over Thirty
Jim Chercio
Fishkill Nazarene Church
201 Main Street
Fishkill, NY 12534
*Nazarene*
914/896-8203
**Years in existence:** 4
**Avg. attendance:** 50
**Primarily ages:** 18-50+
**Main meeting time(s):** Friday night, Saturday night

## GENEVA

### Geneva Interfaith Young Adults
Julie Russell
First United Methodist Church
738 Castle Street
Geneva, NY 14456
*United Methodist*
315/787-2221
**Years in existence:** 1
**Avg. attendance:** 12
**Primarily ages:** 26-40
**Main meeting time(s):** A week night (M-F)

## JOHNSON CITY

### Lifebuilders/ Careerbuilders
Brian Eichelberger
First Baptist Church
12 Baldwin Street
Johnson City, NY 13790
*Baptist*
607/797-1635
**Years in existence:** 6
**Avg. attendance:** 30
**Primarily ages:** 18-40
**Main meeting time(s):** Sunday School Class
**Singles classes:** Lifebuilders (18-26), Careerbuilders (27-36)

## KATOMAH

### Singles In Spirit
Ann Delorier
12 North Street (meet at Bedford Community Church)
Katomah, NY 10536
*Interdenominational*
**Years in existence:** 5
**Primarily ages:** 46-50
**Singles classes:** 30-50, 30-60, 50-60

## LIMA

### CHIPS (Christ's Helpers In Parental Strife)
Tony Martorana
Elim Fellowship
7245 College Street
Lima, NY 14485
716/582-2790
**Avg. attendance:** 250
**Primarily ages:** 36-40

## NEW YORK CITY

### FOCUS (Fellowship of Christians United In Service)
Rev. David Miles
Fifth Avenue Presbyterian Church
7 West 55th Street
New York, NY 10019
*Presbyterian*
212/247-0490
**Years in existence:** 6
**Avg. attendance:** 80+
**Primarily ages:** 26-45
**Main meeting time:** Sunday night monthly

### SPLASH (Single People Loving and Serving Him)
Elizabeth D. Rios
Primitive Christian Church
207-09 East Broadway
New York, NY 10002
*Pentecostal*
212/439-2005
**Years in existence:** 1
**Avg. attendance:** 40
**Primarily ages:** 18-25
**Main meeting time(s):** Friday night

## SYRACUSE

### 121 Singles Ministries
Doug Brushell
Believers' Chapel
7912 Thompson Road
North Syracuse, NY 13212
315-699-4140
**Years in existence:** 3
**Avg. attendance:** 90
**Primarily ages:** 26-30
**Main meeting time(s):** Friday night
**Singles classes:** Young Adults (19-23), Singles (23+)

### Agape Network
Rev. Robert G. Emery
North Syracuse Baptist Church
420 S. Main Street
Syracuse, NY 13212
*Baptist*
315/458-0271
**Years in existence:** 6
**Avg. attendance:** 125
**Primarily ages:** 26-30
**Main meeting time(s):** Sunday School Class **Singles classes:** Antioch (18-24), Galations (22-24), Phillipians (30-43), Ephesians (40+)

## ROCHESTER

### Calvary Singles
John H. Myers
Calvary Evangelical Free Church
5500 25th Avenue, N.W.
Rochester, NY 55901
*Evangelical Free Church of America*
507/282-4612
**Years in existence:** 5
**Avg. attendance:** 40
**Primarily ages:** 26-30
**Main meeting time(s):** A week night (M-F)

### Foursquare Single Adult Ministry (SAM)
Gale L. Player
Rochester Foursquare Gospel Church
312 Fisher Road
Rochester, NY 14624
*International Church of the Foursquare Gospel*
716/247-7226
**Years in existence:** 4
**Avg. attendance:** 15
**Primarily ages:** 41-50+

### Single Harvest
Rev. N. Jean Cupp
Bethel Full Gospel
321 East Avenue
Rochester, NY 14604
*Assemblies of God*
716/232-1136
**Years in existence:** 10
**Avg. attendance:** 300
**Primarily ages:** 36-45
**Main meeting time(s):** Sunday School Class, Saturday night

### Victory Class/College & Career
Gary Sauer
First Bible Baptist Church
1039 N. Greece Road
Rochester, NY 14626
*Independent*
716/225-3493
**Years in existence:** 8
**Avg. attendance:** 40
**Primarily ages:** 18-25
**Main meeting time(s):** Sunday School Class

## SCHROON LAKE

### Fellowship Singles
Jim Williams
Word of Life Fellowship
Pine Lake Box 529
Schroon Lake, NY 12870
*Baptist Doctrine*
518/7111 X228
**Years in existence:** 13
**Primarily ages:** 18-30
**Main meeting time(s):** Sunday School Class, a week night (M-F)

**Harvest Singles Ministries**
Ronald Svejkovsky
Grace Assemblies of God
4220 Fay Road
Syracuse, NY 13219
*Assemblies of God*
315/488-8013
**Years in existence:** 7
**Avg. attendance:** 15
**Primarily ages:** 26-30
**Main meeting time(s):** Sunday School Class **Singles classes:** Single Parents (30-50), Special Singles (Handicapped) (30-45), Young Adults (18-35)

**N.Y. Conference Singles of SDA**
Carmen Gonzalez
N.Y. Conference of Seventh Day Adventist
P.O. Box 67
Syracuse, NY 13215
*Seventh Day Adventist*
315/469-6921
**Years in existence:** 1
**Avg. attendance:** 18
**Primarily ages:** 36-45
**Main meeting time(s):** Saturday night

## WHITE PLAINS

**Westchester Christian Singles Fellowship**
Stephen P. Sacco
Ridgeway Alliance Church
465 Ridgeway
White Plains, NY 10605
914/633-9272
**Years in existence:** 16
**Avg. attendance:** 30
**Primarily ages:** 36-40
**Main meeting time(s):** Friday night

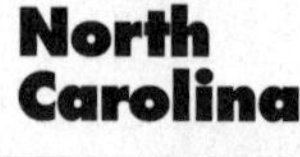

## CHARLOTTE

**Calvary Singles**
Paul Rhonds
Calvary Church
5801 Pineville Matthews Rd
Charlotte, NC 28226
*Interdenominational*
704/543-1200
**Years in existence:** 12
**Avg. attendance:** 120
**Primarily ages:**26-35
**Main meeting time:** Sunday School Classes **Singles classes:** Singles 1 (18-25), Singles 2 (25-up), Singles Again

**Myers Park Young Adult Singles**
Ron L. Hall
Myers Park United Methodist Church
1020 Providence Road
Charlotte, NC 28207
*United Methodist*
704/376-8584
**Years in existence:** 5
**Avg. attendance:** 150
**Primarily ages:** 26-35
**Main meeting time(s):** Sunday School Class, a week night (M-F)
**Singles classes:** Young Adults (26-35)

## CONOVER

**Trinity United Singles**
J. Eric Davis
Trinity United Church of Christ
217 - 2nd Avenue N.E.
Conover, NC 28613
*United Church of Christ*
704/464-1666
**Years in existence:** 3
**Avg. attendance:** 65
**Primarily ages:** 36-40
**Main meeting time:** Friday night

## GREENSBORO

**Westover Singles/Careers**
Jerry Aldridge
Westover Presbyterian Church
908 Westover Terrace
Greensboro, NC 27408
*Unaffiliated*
919/273-0807
**Years in existence:** 12
**Avg. attendance:** 25
**Primarily ages:** 26-35
**Main meeting time:** Sunday School Class **Singles classes:** Singles/College (18-21), Singles/ Career (22-39), Singles III—single again

## HIGH POINT

**Wesleyan Church Singles Ministries**
Greg Remole
First Wesleyan Church
1915 N. Centennial
High Point, NC 27265
*The Wesleyan Church*
919/884-1111
**Years in existence:** 5
**Avg. attendance:** 44
**Primarily ages:** 18-30
**Main meeting time(s):** Sunday School Class
**Singles classes:** ACTS (College & Career) (18-25), SOUL (Singles Offering Unconditional Love (23-38), SOS (Starting Over Single) (35-49)

## PINEVILLE

**Lifespring Single Adults**
Dianne Maynard
Lifespring Church of God
13733 Highway 521 South
Pineville, NC 28134
*Church of God*
704/542-9951
**Avg. attendance:** 15
**Primarily ages:** 26-30
**Main meeting time:** Friday night
**Singles classes:** Singles I (18-30), Singles II (31-45), Singles III (45+)

Parade Magazine reports that only five U.S. states have more men than women: Alaska, Hawaii, Nevada, North Dakota and Wyoming.

## RALEIGH

**Airborn**
Rev. Ron G. Body
Raleigh Christian Community Church
7000 Destiny Drive
Raleigh, NC 27604
919-266-7000
**Years in existence:** 3
**Avg. attendance:** 75
**Primarily ages:** 26-40
**Main meeting time(s):** Sunday night

**SALT/Single Vision**
David Williams
Providence Baptist Church
9225 Leesville Road
Raleigh, NC 27613
*Southern Baptist*
919/847-5410
**Years in existence:** 5
**Avg. attendance:** 50
**Primarily ages:** 26-30
**Main meeting time(s):** Friday night
**Singles classes:** SALT (20-33), Single Vision (34+)

**Forest Hills Baptist Church**
Bo Prosser
Forest Hills Baptist Church
3110 Clark Avenue
Raleigh, NC 27607
*Baptist*
919/828-6161
**Years in existence:** 10
**Avg. attendance:** 90
**Primarily ages:** 26-35
**Main meeting time(s):** Sunday School Class **Singles classes:** 18-26, 26-31, 31-44, 44+

**Single Adult Ministry**
Paul L. Geldart
Hayes Barton Baptist Church
1800 Glenwood Avenue
Raleigh, NC 27609
*Southern Baptist*
919/833-4617
**Years in existence:** 1
**Avg. attendance:** 4
**Primarily ages:** 31-35
**Main meeting time(s):** Sunday School Class **Singles classes:** Singles Sunday School (18-65)

**SOLO Inc. (Singles Offering Life To Christ)**
Chuck Milian
P.O. Box 17501
Raleigh, NC 27619
919/782-1838

**Years in existence:** 3
**Avg. attendance:** 500
**Primarily ages:** 26-35
**Main meeting time(s):** A week night (M-F)
**Singles classes:** Charlotte/ Durham/Chapel Hill (all ages), Fayetteville/Winston/Salem (all ages), Wilmington (all ages), Montgomery (all ages)

## TAYLORSVILLE

### START (Singles That Are Reaching Together)

John Alspaugh
East Taylorsville Baptist Church
246 1st Ave. Drive, S.E.
P.O. Box 906
Taylorsville, NC 28681
*Southern Baptist*
704/632-7005
**Years in existence:** 3
**Avg. attendance:** 25
**Primarily ages:** 18-25
**Main meeting time(s):** Sunday School Class **Singles classes:** College & Career (18-25), New Beginnings (26+)

## BEDFORD

### SALT Ministries

Bedford Church of the Nazarene
365 Center Road
Bedford, OH 44146
*Nazarene*
216/232-7440
**Years in existence:** 6
**Avg. attendance:** 30
**Primarily ages:** 26-35
**Main meeting time:** Sunday School Class
**Singles classes:** College/Career (18-23), Young Professionals (24-39), Middle Singles (40+)

## CINCINNATI

### Hyde Park Community Singles Ministry

Steve Gill
Hyde Park Community United Methodist
1345 Grace Avenue
Cincinnati, OH 45208
*United Methodist*
513/871-1345
**Years in existence:**17
**Avg. attendance:** 300
**Primarily ages:** 31-35
**Main meeting time:** Sunday night
**Singles classes:** New Beginnings—Widowed, Singles Together (20-35), never-married, Friday Night Social—middle-aged dance, Polygons—middle-aged singles, Prime Time Singles—older singles

### SALT (Single Adults Learning Together)

Jeff Lewellyn
White Oak Christian Church
3675 Blue Rock Road
Cincinnati, OH 45247
*Independent*
513/385-0425
**Years in existence:** 5
**Avg. attendance:** 25
**Primarily ages:** 31-40
**Main meeting time(s):** Sunday School Class

### Sharonville United Methodist Singles

Sharonville United Methodist Church
3751 Creek Road
Cincinnati, OH 45241
*United Methodist*
513/563-0117
**Years in existence:** 5
**Avg. attendance:** 12
**Primarily ages:** 31-50
**Main meeting time(s):** Sunday School Class, a week night (M-F)

## COLUMBUS

### Lane Avenue Baptist Singles

Victor Fanberg
Lane Avenue Baptist Church
1610 West Lane Avenue
Columbus, OH 43221
*Southern Baptist*
614/488-6260
**Years in existence:** 12
**Avg. attendance:** 13
**Primarily ages:** 18-40
**Main meeting time(s):** Sunday School Class
**Singles classes:** College (18-25), Singles (22-40)

### Nazarene Student Fellowship

Steve Myers
First Church of the Nazarene
142 King Avenue
Columbus, OH 43201
*Nazarene*
614/294-4717
**Years in existence:** 1
**Avg. attendance:** 12
**Primarily ages:** 18-25
**Main meeting time(s):** Sunday School Class

### The S.T.E.P.S. Brigade

Diane T. Jackson
Rhema Christian Center
2116 Agler Rd
Columbus, OH 43224
614/228-3907
**Years in existence:** 3
**Avg. attendance:** 6
**Primarily ages:** 31-35
**Main meeting time(s):** A week night (M-F)
**Singles classes:** Never married Single Adults (25-35), Single Parents (22-50)

## DAYTON

### Single Life Ministries

Frank Drago
Bethel Temple
327 S. Smithville Road
Dayton, OH 45703
*Assemblies of God*
513/253-4161
**Years in existence:** 4
**Avg. attendance:** 75-130
**Primarily ages:** 26-30
**Main meeting time(s):** Sunday School Class, a week night (M-F)

## DEFIANCE

### SAM: Single Adult Ministry

Donald Luhring
St. John Lutheran Church
655 Wayne Avenue
Defiance, OH 43512
*Lutheran Church—Missouri Synod*
419/782-5766
**Years in existence:** 5
**Avg. attendance:** 15
**Primarily ages:** 36-40
**Main meeting time(s):** Saturday night
**Singles classes:** Second Chapter, Widows/Widowers (Older), Single Topics (36-40), Single Volleyball

## ELYRIA

### Singles In Harmony

Alan L. Schafer
Church of The Open Door
43275 Telegraph Road
Elyria, OH 44035
*Non-denominational/ Fundamental*
216/775-8789
**Years in existence:** 8+
**Avg. attendance:** 50
**Primarily ages:** 36-40
**Main meeting time(s):** Sunday School Class

## STOW

### Holy Family Young Adults

Cindee Case
Holy Family Parish Community Church
3450 Sycamore
Stow, OH 44224
*Roman Catholic*
216/688-6411
**Years in existence:** 1
**Primarily ages:** 18-35
**Main meeting time(s):** A week night (M-F)

**Fact:** Within 10 years of the wedding, 38 percent of those who had lived together before marriage had split up, compared with 27 percent of those who simply married.

*University of Wisconsin study*

## TIPP CITY

### SAM at GUM
Deborah Campbell
Ginghamsburg United Methodist Church
7695 S. County Road 25A
Tipp City, OH 45371
*United Methodist*
513/667-1069
**Years in existence:** 3
**Avg. attendance:** 40
**Primarily ages:** 26-30
**Main meeting time(s):** Friday night
**Singles classes:** Young Singles (18-24), Young Adults (21-40), More Mature Singles (35+), Single Parents

## WADSWORTH

### First Christian Singles Ministry
Peggy Rowe
First Christian Church
116 Boyer Street
Wadsworth, OH 44281
*Disciple of Christ*
216/336-6697
**Years in existence:** 5
**Avg. attendance:** 30
**Primarily ages:** 36-40
**Main meeting time(s):** Sunday School Class
**Singles classes:**Rebuilding (35-40), Living Single Successfully (40+)

## WILLOUGHBY HILLS

### Single, Divorced & Widowed Group
Patricia Berthelot
Holy Family
3450 Sycamore Dr.
Stow, OH 44224
216/688-4147
**Years in existence:** 1
**Avg. attendance:** 35
**Primarily ages:** 36-45, 50+
**Main meeting time(s):** Friday night

### Single Friends Ministries
Craig Henry
Willoughby Hills Evangelical Friends Church
2846 S.O.M. Center Road
Willoughby Hills, OH 44094
*Evangelical Friends Church*
216/944-1026
**Years in existence:** 8
**Avg. attendance:** 80
**Primarily ages:** 26-45
**Main meeting time(s):** Sunday School Class
**Singles classes:** Single Direction (18-23), Singles Sunday A.M. (24+)

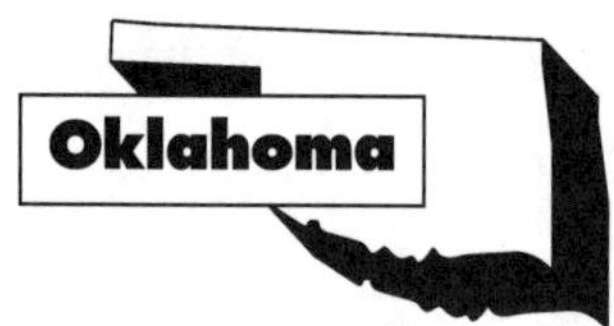


## BARTLESVILLE

### First Baptist Church
R.T. Shields
First Baptist Church
Box 1080
Bartlesville, OK 74006
*Baptist*
918/336-6172
**Years in existence:** 8
**Avg. attendance:** 110
**Primarily ages:** 46-50
**Main meeting time(s):** Sunday School Class, Friday night
**Singles classes:** Career (18-26), Singles I (26-35), Singles II (36-50), Singles III (51+)

## BETHANY

### Bethany First Nazarene Singles Ministry
Rick Eastman
Bethany First Church of the Nazarene
6789 N.W. 39th Expressway
Bethany, OK 73008
*Nazarene*
405/789-2056
**Years in existence:** 15
**Avg. attendance:** 150
**Primarily ages:** 26-35
**Main meeting time(s):** Sunday School Class, a week night (M-F)
**Singles classes:** College/Career Singles (18-25), W.H.A.M. (20s-30s), Becomers (30s-40s), Living Water (40s-50s)

### Singles In Touch
Alan Damron
Council Road Baptist Church
2900 N. Council Road
Bethany, OK 73008
*Southern Baptist*
405/789-3175
**Years in existence:** 6
**Avg. attendance:** 125
**Primarily ages:** 36-45
**Main meeting time(s):** Sunday School Class
**Singles classes:** SA I (18-22), SA II (23-29), SA III (30-36), SA IV (37-44)

## CHICKASHA

### SAM (Single Adult Ministry)
Gary L. Pratt
First Assemblies of God Church
3340 South 16th Street
Chickasha, OK 73018
*Assemblies of God*
405/224-1599
**Years in existence:** 6
**Avg. attendance:** 125
**Primarily ages:** 31-35
**Main meeting time(s):** A week night (M-F)

## ENID

### Emmanuel Single Adult Ministry
Pastor Steve Mortensen
Emmanuel Baptist Church
2505 W. OK Garriott Road
Enid, OK 73703
*Southern Baptist*
405/237-0602
**Years in existence:** 12
**Avg. attendance:** 80
**Primarily ages:** 50+
**Main meeting time(s):** Sunday School Class, Thursday night
**Singles classes:** Single Women's Class, Single Adult 1 (22-27), Single Adult 2 (28-36), Single Adult 3 (37-45), Single Adult 4 (46+)

## MOORE

### Single Adult Ministry of First
Larry Ellis
First Baptist Church
201 S. Howard
Moore, OK 73160
*Southern Baptist*
405/794-5541
**Years in existence:** 3
**Avg. attendance:** 175
**Primarily ages:** 18-25
**Main meeting time(s):** Sunday School Class **Singles classes:** College (18-24), Young Single Adults (18-28), Single Adults 1 (29-38), Single Adults 2 (39+)

## OKLAHOMA CITY

### Single Tracks
Steve Fine
Northwest Baptist Church
2200 N. Drexel
Oklahoma City, OK 73107
*Southern Baptist*
405/942-5557
**Years in existence:** 21
**Avg. attendance:** 143
**Primarily ages:** 26-35
**Main meeting time(s):** Sunday School Class
**Singles classes:** SA1 (18-22), SA2 (23-26), SA3 (27-30), SA5 (27-34), SA (35-39), SA7 (40-48), SA9 (60+), Ladies Only

### Village Baptist Singles
Jay Shepherd
Village Baptist Church
10600 N. May Avenue
Oklahoma City, OK 73120
*Southern Baptist*
405/751-1951
**Years in existence:** 25
**Avg. attendance:** 140
**Primarily ages:** 18-30
**Main meeting time(s):** Sunday School Class **Singles classes:** SA5 (67+), SA4 (55-66), SA3 (45-54), SA2 (30-44)

## STILLWATER

### Nehemiah Singles Fellowship
Bill Russell
Hillcrest Baptist Church
902 North Washington
Stillwater, OK 74075
*Southern Baptist*
405/372-7330
**Years in existence:** 2
**Avg. attendance:** 18
**Primarily ages:** 26-45
**Main meeting time(s):** Sunday School Class

## TULSA

### Asbury's SAM
Mary Randolph
Asbury United Methodist
5838 South Sheridan Road
Tulsa, OK 74145
*United Methodist*
918/492-1771
**Years in existence:** 12
**Avg. attendance:** 400
**Primarily ages:** 26-50
**Main meeting time(s):** Sunday

School Class
**Singles classes:** CIA (Christians In Action) (20-35), ATS (All-Together Singles) (32-45), NBC (New Beginnings Class) (40+), Encore, College/Career Student Ministries.

**E.T. Singles Ministry**
Harley E. Wideman, Jr.
Evangelistic Temple
5345 South Peoria
Tulsa, OK 74105
*Pentecostal Holiness*
918/749-9971
**Years in existence:** 3
**Avg. attendance:** 20
**Primarily ages:** 26-30
**Main meeting time(s):** Sunday School Class, Friday night

**First Methodist Singles**
Dr. Mel Whittington
First United Methodist Church
1115 South Boulder
Tulsa, OK 74119
*United Methodist*
918/587-9481
**Years in existence:** 32 years
**Avg. attendance:** 200
**Primarily ages:** 18-50+
**Main meeting time(s):** Sunday School Class **Singles classes:** Ambassadors (20-29), Upper Room (20s & 30s), Women's Bible Class—women who come to church alone, Saints & Sinners (40+)

**Grace Fellowship Singles Ministry**
John Olin
Grace Fellowship Church
P.O. Box 55236
Tulsa, OK 74155-1236
918/252-1611
**Years in existence:** 12
**Avg. attendance:** 75
**Primarily ages:** 18-30
**Main meeting time(s):** Sunday School Class

**Single Spirit**
Ann Huddleston
First Baptist Church
403 S. Cincinnati
Tulsa, OK 74103
*Baptist*
918/587-1571
**Years in existence:** 20
**Avg. attendance:** 150
**Primarily ages:** 18-30, 50+
**Main meeting time(s):** Sunday School Class, Sunday night
**Singles classes:** Singles 1 (18-30), Singles 2&3 (28-40/38+), Singles 4 (50+), Singles 5 (25-45)

**Young Adult Ministry**
Bill Turner
Memorial Bible Church
415 S. Memorial
Tulsa, OK 74112
*Non-denominational*
918/835-2051
**Years in existence:** 1
**Avg. attendance:** 10
**Primarily ages:** 18-25
**Main meeting time(s):** Sunday School Class

## ALBANY

**SOLO (Serving Our Lord Only)**
Tim Brown
First Assemblies of God
2817 Santiam Highway
Albany, OR 97321
*Assemblies of God*
508/926-2291
**Years in existence:** 4
**Avg. attendance:** 40
**Primarily ages:** 36-40
**Main meeting time(s):** Sunday School Class
**Singles classes:** SOLO (25-45), 20/20 Vision (45+)

## BEAVERTON

**Positively Single Fellowship**
Lance D. Kamstra/Dick Rohrer
Beaverton Christian Church
13600 S.W. Allen
Beaverton, OR 97007
*Non-denominational*
503/238-9700
**Years in existence:** 2
**Avg. attendance:** 80-90
**Primarily ages:** 36-40
**Main meeting time(s):** A week night (M-F)
**Singles classes:** College and Career (19-25), Singles (25-60)

## BEND

**New Life**
Frank Patka
First Baptist Church
60 N.W. Oregon Road
Bend, OR 97701
*Conservative Baptist (CBA)*
503/382-3862
**Years in existence:** 5
**Avg. attendance:** 15
**Primarily ages:** 26-30
**Main meeting time(s):** A week night (M-F)

## BORING

**SAM Congregation**
Bob Billstein
Good Shepherd Community Church
28986 S.E. Haley Road
Boring, OR 97009
*Non-denominational*
503/663-5050
**Years in existence:** 1
**Avg. attendance:** 40-50
**Primarily ages:** 26-30, 36-45
**Main meeting time(s):** Sunday School Class, Friday night

## CORVALLIS

**Chi Alpha Christian Fellowship**
M.J. Johnson
Kings Circle Assemblies of God
2110 N.W. Circle Boulevard
Corvallis, OR 97330
*Assemblies of God*
503/757-9080
**Years in existence:** 20
**Avg. attendance:** 15
**Primarily ages:** 18-25
**Main meeting time(s):** Friday night

## EUGENE

**Single Adults Ministry**
Glen Eickmeyer
First Baptist Church
868 High Street
Eugene, OR 97401
*Conservative Baptist*
503/345-0341
**Years in existence:** 16
**Avg. attendance:** 50
**Primarily ages:** 31-45
**Main meeting time(s):** Sunday School Class
**Singles classes:** Transition (22-35), Single Parents (28-40), New Beginnings (40+)

## HOOD RIVER

**Fellowship of Christian Adult Singles (FOCAS)**
Steven P. Ballweber
Hood River Assemblies of God
1110 May Street
Hood River, OR 97031
*Assemblies of God*
503/386-3656
**Years in existence:** 3
**Avg. attendance:** 15
**Primarily ages:** 18-35, 50+
**Main meeting time(s):** A week night (M-F)

## McMINVILLE

**Splash**
Jim Peterson
Bethel Baptist Church
325 Baker Creek Road
McMinnville, OR 97128
*Conservative Baptist*
503/434-5541
**Years in existence:** 2
**Avg. attendance:** 40
**Primarily ages:** 36-45
**Main meeting time(s):** Sunday School Class, a week night (M-F)

## PORTLAND

**Hinson Singles Network**
Hinson Memorial Baptist Church
P.O. Box 14186
1315 S.E. 20th
Portland, OR 97214
*Conservative Baptist*
503/232-1156
**Years in existence:** 12
**Avg. attendance:** 140
**Primarily ages:** 31-35
**Main meeting time:** Sunday School Class

**New Beginnings for Singles**
Chip Nichols
Portland Christian Center
5700 S.W. Dosch Road
Portland, OR 97201
*Assemblies of God*
503/245-7735
**Years in existence:** 2
**Avg. attendance:** 60
**Primarily ages:** 18-30, 41-45, 50+
**Main meeting time(s):** Sunday

School Class, a week night (M-F)
**Singles classes:** Becomers (18-25), Destiny (21-35), Agamos (21-60)

### New Hope Positive Singles
Richard Kraljev
New Hope Community Church
11731 S.E. Stevens Road
Portland, OR 97266
*Non-denominational*
503/659-5683
**Years in existence:** 15
**Avg. attendance:** 300
**Primarily ages:** 36-40
**Main meeting time(s):** A week night (M-F)
**Singles classes:** Focus (18-23), Pacesetters (23-30), Achievers (30+)

### Singles Celebration
John Sturm
Greater Portland Bible Church
1820 S.W. Vermont
Portland, OR 97219
*Non-denominational*
503/452-9375
**Years in existence:** 5
**Avg. attendance:** 120
**Primarily ages:** 26-35
**Main meeting time:** Sunday School Class
**Singles classes:** Single Parent Adventure, Singles Celebration

## SALEM

### Christian Singles Alive!
Steve Bearden
Salem First Nazarene
1550 Market Street N.E.
Salem, OR 97303
*Nazarene*
503/581-3680
**Years in existence:** 5
**Avg. attendance:** 275
**Primarily ages:** 31-50
**Main meeting time(s):** Sunday School Class **Singles classes:** New Horizions (35+), Salt (25-40), Light (25-40), More Light (25-40)

## ALLISON PARK

### The Single Circle
Gary Weston
Memorial Park Church
8800 Peebles Road
Allison Park, PA 15101
*Presbyterian Church in America*
412/364-9492
**Years in existence:** 10
**Avg. attendance:** 75
**Primarily ages:** 41-50+
**Main meeting time(s):** A week night (M-F)

## BETHEL PARK

### FOCAS on Jesus
Jef Marshall
South Hills Assemblies of God
2725 Bethel Church Road
Bethel Park, PA 15102
*Assemblies of God*
412/854-4040
**Years in existence:** 2
**Avg. attendance:** 30
**Primarily ages:** 26-35
**Main meeting time(s):** A week night (M-F)

## BRISTOL

### LAMB Young Adult Ministry
Daryll Adsit
Calvary Baptist Church
250 Green Lane, P.O. Box 704
Bristol, PA 19007
*Independent*
215/788-8418
**Years in existence:** 6
**Avg. attendance:** 30
**Primarily ages:** 26-30
**Main meeting time(s):** A week night (M-F)

## BROOMHALL

### Frontline Singles Ministry
Warren Boettcher
Covenant Fellowship of Philadelphia
450 Parkway Dr. #200
Broomhall, PA 19008
*Non-denominational*
215/359-1180
**Years in existence:** 4
**Avg. attendance:** 145
**Primarily ages:** 18-30
**Main meeting time(s):** A week night (M-F)

## CAMP HILL

### Crossfire Interchurch Singles Ministry, Inc.
Rev. James E. Schamback
2645 Lisburn Rd. Suite B
Camp Hill, PA 17001
*Interdenominational*
717/975-2776
**Years in existence:** 12
**Avg. attendance:** 200
**Primarily ages:** 26-35
**Main meeting time:** Tuesday night

## DRESHER

### SALT (Single Adults Linked Together)
Stan Hagberg
Chelten Baptist Church
1601 Limekiln Pike
Dresher, PA 19025
*Conservative Baptist*
215/646-5557
**Years in existence:** 12
**Avg. attendance:** 50
**Primarily ages:**18-25
**Main meeting time:** A week night (M-F)
**Singles classes:** SALT 1 (college age to 24), SALT 2 (25-39), SALT 3 (40+)

## ERIE

### Singles Alive Ministry (SAM)
Mary C. Stewart
Eastminster Presbyterian
2320 E. Lake Road
Erie, PA 16511
*Presbyterian (USA)*
814/455-7819
**Years in existence:** 5
**Avg. attendance:** 20
**Primarily ages:** 46-50
**Main meeting time(s):** Friday night

## HERSHEY

### Common Bond
Jim Erb
Evangelical Free Church
P.O. Box 648
Hershey, PA 17033
*Evangelical Free Church*
717/533-4848
**Years in existence:** 9
**Avg. attendance:** 50
**Primarily ages:** 18-25
**Main meeting time(s):** Sunday School Class, a week night (M-F)

## HOUSTON

### SOLO (Singles Outreach through Love and Obedience)
David J. Falvo
Central Assemblies of God
155 McGovern Road
Houston, PA 15342
*Assemblies of God*
412/746-4900
**Years in existence:** 3
**Avg. attendance:** 50
**Primarily ages:** 36-40
**Main meeting time(s):** Friday night

## McMURRAY

### C-3s (Center's Christian Core)
Don Steele
Center Presbyterian Church
255 Center Church Road
McMurray, PA 15317
*Presbyterian*
412/941-9050
**Years in existence:** 3
**Avg. attendance:** 12
**Primarily ages:** 26-35
**Main meeting time(s):** Saturday night
**Singles classes:** Single Adults (living at home) (26-36), College Students (18-22)

## MECHANICSBURG

### SALT (Single Adults Living Triumphantly)
David Hedeen
Immanuel Alliance Church
800 S. Market Street
Mechanicsburg, PA 17055
*Christian & Missionary Alliance*
717/766-4633

**Years in existence:** 4
**Avg. attendance:** 30
**Primarily ages:** 26-35
**Main meeting time(s):** A week night (M-F)
**Singles classes:** SALT (20-35), SALT II (35+)

## PENNSBURG

**Lighthouse Singles**
David Martino
Lighthouse Tabernacle
P.O. Box 88
Pennsburg, PA 18073
*Assemblies of God*
215/679-4482
**Years in existence:** 3
**Avg. attendance:** 10
**Primarily ages:** 18-25
**Main meeting time(s):** Sunday School Class

## PHILADELPHIA

**Tenth Presbyterian Singles**
Rev. Glenn N. McDowell
Tenth Presbyterian Church
1700 Spruce Street
Philadelphia, PA 19103
*Presbyterian*
215/735-7688
**Avg. attendance:** 150
**Primarily ages:** 26-45
**Main meeting time(s):** Sunday School Class

## SEWICKLEY

**Uni Son Ministries**
Woody Volland
St. Stephen's Episcopal Church
P.O. Box 401
Sewickley, PA 15143
*Episcopal*
412/741-1790
**Years in existence:** 7
**Avg. attendance:** 75
**Primarily ages:** 31-45
**Main meeting time(s):** A week night (M-F)
**Singles classes:** Fresh Start (25-40), Aftershock (25-45)

## STROUDSBURG

**Singles Unite Retreat**
Pamela Rankin
Twin Pines Camp
3000 Twin Pine Road
Stroudsburg, PA 18360
*Evangelical Congregational Church*
717/629-2411
**Years in existence:** 6
**Avg. attendance:** 30-40
**Primarily ages:** 26-30

## TITUSVILLE

**Never Alone Singles Group**
L. Kay Cribbs
First Presbyterian
Franklin & Walnut Street
Titusville, PA 16354
*Presbyterian*
814/827-3664
**Years in existence:** 5+
**Avg. attendance:** 30
**Primarily ages:** 41-50
**Main meeting time(s):** Saturday night

## WASHINGTON CROSSING

**Single Purpose**
Pastor David Burke
1895 Wrightstown Rd
Washington Crossing, PA 18977
*United Methodist*
215/493-5080
**Years in existence:** 1
**Main meeting time(s):** Friday night

## WAYNE

**Church of the Savior Network**
Church of the Savior
651 N. Wayne Avenue
Wayne, PA 19087
*Evangelical, Independent*
**Years in existence:** 11
**Avg. attendance:** 200
**Primarily ages:** 31-40
**Main meeting time(s):** Sunday School Class **Singles classes:** Focus (32-60), Vision (25-35)

## WEST CHESTER

**Young Adults Group**
Chris Foster
First Presbyterian Church
Miner & Darlington Streets
West Chester, PA 19382
*Presbyterian*
215-696-0554
**Years in existence:** 1
**Avg. attendance:** 10
**Primarily ages:** 26-30
**Singles classes:** Young Adults (18-35)

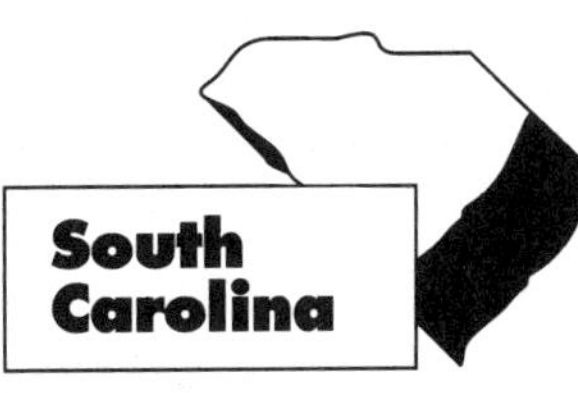


## AIKEN

**Single Adult Ministry of Millbrook**
Stephen Burnette
Millbrook Baptist Church
176 E. Pine Log Road
Aiken, SC 29803
*Southern Baptist*
803/648-4220
**Years in existence:** 3
**Avg. attendance:** 51
**Primarily ages:** 26-45, 50+
**Main meeting time(s):** Sunday School Class
**Singles classes:** College-Career (19-21), Burnette Class (24-34), Elliott Class (35-46), Smith Class (50+)

## CHARLESTON

**Grape Vine**
Alice M. Robinson
Grace United Methodist Church
1601 Sam Rittenberg Boulevard
Charleston, SC 29407
*United Methodist*
803/766-1621
**Years in existence:** 3
**Avg. attendance:** 12
**Primarily ages:** 31-35
**Main meeting time(s):** Sunday School Class
**Singles classes:** Disciples Class (25-45), Methodist Singles (Singles from 10 area U.M. Churches)

## COLUMBIA

**First Baptist Singles**
Clif Smith
First Baptist
P.O. Box 1000
Columbia, SC 29202
*Southern Baptist*
803/256-4251
**Years in existence:** 15
**Avg. attendance:** 125
**Primarily ages:** 31-35
**Main meeting time(s):** Sunday School Class
**Singles classes:** Single Adult 1 (23-27), Single Adult 2 (28-35), Single Adult 4 (36+), Single Adult 5 (all ages)

## SIMPSONVILLE

**Focus Ministries**
Larry L. Kiser
Southside Baptist Church
111 Woodruff Road
Simpsonville, SC 29681
*Independent Baptist*
803/234-7575
**Years in existence:** 12
**Avg. attendance:** 175
**Main meeting time(s):** Sunday School Class
**Singles classes:** Roaring Twenties (19-25), Central Focus (26-45)

## SPARTANBURG

**The Single Adventure**
Becky Smith-Greer
First Baptist of Spartanburg
201 East Main Street
Spartanburg, SC 29301
*Southern Baptist*
803/583-7245
**Years in existence:** 16
**Avg. attendance:** 140
**Primarily ages:** 26-30, 41-45
**Main meeting time(s):** Sunday School Class
**Singles classes:** Department I (under 32), Department 2 (33-42), Department 3 (43+)

## CHATTANOOGA

**Lee Highway Singles**
Kris A. Koppy
Lee Highway Church of God
7120 Lee Highway
Chattanooga, TN 37421
*Church of God*
615/894-6982
**Years in existence:** 4
**Avg. attendance:** 25
**Primarily ages:** 26-35
**Main meeting time(s):** A week night (M-F)

**Positive Christian Singles**
First Centenary United Methodist
P.O. Box 208
Chattanooga, TN 37401
*United Methodist*
615/756-2021
**Years in existence:** 11
**Avg. attendance:** 85
**Primarily ages:** 46-50
**Main meeting time:** A week night (M-F)
**Singles classes:** In-Sync (24-30), Odyssey (30-45), Trinity (30-45), singles & married couples, Pacesetters (40-60)

**Singles-Plus Ministry**
Grace P. Byrd
Chattanooga Christian Fellowship
P.O. Box 8308
Chattanooga, TN 37411-0308
615/899-6187 (Pastor)
**Years in existence:** 1
**Avg. attendance:** 20
**Primarily ages:** 41-45
**Main meeting time(s):** Sunday School Class

## CORDOVA

**Bellevue Singles Ministry**
Bob Gallina
Bellevue Baptist Church
2000 Appling Road
Cordova, TN 38018
*Southern Baptist*
901/385-5780
**Years in existence:** 25
**Avg. attendance:** 400
**Primarily ages:** 26-35
**Main meeting time(s):** Sunday School Class **Singles classes:** Singles I (26-29), Singles II (30-39), Singles III (40-49), Singles IV (50-59)

## FRANKLIN

**Sojourners**
Mike Smith
Christ Community Church
136 Third Avenue South
Franklin, TN 37064
*Presbyterian Church in America*
615/794-6904
**Years in existence:** 3
**Avg. attendance:** 80
**Primarily ages:** 26-30
**Main meeting time(s):** Sunday School Class

## GERMANTOWN

**Germantown Singles**
Don Fortner
Germantown Baptist Church
2216 Germantown Rd. S
Germantown, TN 38138
*Baptist*
901/754-1723
**Years in existence:** 6
**Avg. attendance:** 120
**Primarily ages:** 18-30
**Main meeting time(s):** Sunday School Class **Singles classes:** SA1 (18-27), SA2 (28-35), SA3 (36-45), SA4 (46+)

## HENDERSONVILLE

**First Baptist Singles**
Richard Gaia
First Baptist Church
381 W. Main Street
Hendersonville, TN 37075
*Southern Baptist*
615/824-6154
**Years in existence:** 7
**Avg. attendance:** 85
**Primarily ages:** 18-25, 31-35
**Main meeting time(s):** Sunday School Class **Singles classes:** Young Singles (21-30), 25-35, 36-45, 46+

## HERMITAGE

**Singles Alive**
Gene Johnson
Hermitage Hills Baptist Church
3475 Lebanon Rd
Hermitage, TN 37076
*Baptist*
615/883-5034
**Years in existence:** 8
**Avg. attendance:** 80-100
**Primarily ages:** 26-30, 36-40
**Main meeting time(s):** Sunday School Class
**Singles classes:** College (18-24), Singles (24+), Single Again (all ages)

## KNOXVILLE

**Calvary Baptist Singles**
Tony Connors
Calvary Baptist Church
3200 Kingston Pike
Knoxville, TN 37919
*Southern Baptist*
615/523-9419
**Years in existence:** 11
**Avg. attendance:** 170
**Primarily ages:** 18-30
**Main meeting time:** Sunday School Class **Singles classes:** Single Adult I (22-29), Single Adult II (30-42), Single Adult III (42+)

**Cedar Springs Singles**
Roy Zinn
Cedar Springs Presbyterian
9132 Kingston Pike
Knoxville, TN 37923
*Presbyterian Church in America (PCA)*
615/693-9331
**Years in existence:** 9
**Avg. attendance:** 100
**Primarily ages:** 26-35
**Main meeting time(s):** Sunday School Class **Singles classes:** Career (21-25), Singles I (24-37), Priority One (30-45), College (18-23)

**Central Singles**
Robert Bowman
Central Baptist Church Bearden
6300 Deane Hill Drive
Knoxville, TN 37919
*Baptist*
615/588-0586
**Years in existence:** 14
**Avg. attendance:** 250
**Primarily ages:** 31-50
**Main meeting time(s):** Sunday School Class
**Singles classes:** Eleven classes all integrated— 2 classes (21-27), 3 classes (28-35), 3 classes (35-57), 3 classes (58+)

## MEMPHIS

**Positive Christian Singles**
Nick Clark
Christ United Methodist
4488 Poplar
Memphis, TN 38117
*United Methodist*
901/683-3521
**Years in existence:** 10
**Avg. attendance:** 175
**Primarily ages:** 31-50
**Main meeting time(s):** Sunday School Class **Singles classes:** Young and Single (26-35), Social Singles (30-55), Super Singles (50+), Singles at 11:00 (26-30)

**Raleigh Singles Ministry**
Brenda J. Hunter
The Raleigh Church
P.O. Box 281085
Memphis, TN 38168
*Church of God in Christ*
901/377-1195
**Years in existence:** 1
**Avg. attendance:** 20
**Primarily ages:** 18-25, 31-45

### Singles at Raleigh
David Reinhard
Raleigh Assemblies of God
3683 Austin Pezy Highway
Memphis, TN 38128
*Assemblies of God*
901/386-5055
**Avg. attendance:** 25
**Primarily ages:** 41-45
**Main meeting time(s):** Sunday School Class

### Singles At Second
Timm Jackson
Second Presbyterian Church
4055 Poplar Avenue
Memphis, TN 38111-7699
*Evangelical Presbyterian*
901/454-0034
**Years in existence:** 7
**Avg. attendance:** 200
**Primarily ages:** 36-40
**Main meeting time(s):** Sunday School Class

## NASHVILLE

### Belmont Singles
Jim Bevis
Belmont Church
68 Music Square East
Nashville, TN 37203
*Non-denominational*
615/256-2123
**Years in existence:** 5
**Avg. attendance:** 150
**Primarily ages:** 26-40
**Main meeting time(s):** Sunday School Class, Sunday night, a week night (M-F)

### First Baptist Downtown Single Adults
Dan Jones
First Baptist Church Downtown
108 7th Avenue S.
Nashville, TN 37203
*Southern Baptist*
615/664-6000
**Years in existence:** 20
**Avg. attendance:** 200
**Primarily ages:** 26-30
**Main meeting time(s):** Sunday School Class **Singles classes:** Single Adult 1A (18-25), Single Adult 1B (26-31), Single Adult 2A (32-46), Single Adult 2B (47-65)

### Woodmont Baptist Singles
Harry M. Rowland, Jr.
Woodmont Baptist Church
2100 Woodmont Boulevard
Nashville, TN 37215
*Southern Baptist*
615/287-5303
**Years in existence:** 15
**Avg. attendance:** 200
**Primarily ages:** 26-35, 41-45
**Main meeting time(s):** Sunday School Class
**Singles classes:** Under 30 (4 classes), 30-40 (3 classes), over 40 (3 classes)

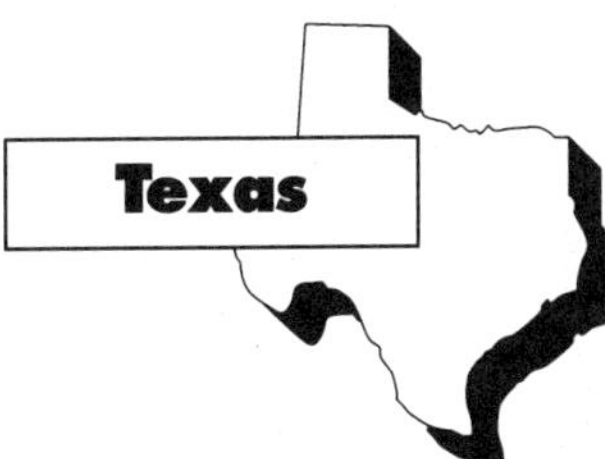


## ABILENE

### Pioneer Drive Singles
Randy White
Pioneer Drive Baptist Church
701 South Pioneer Drive
Abilene, TX 79605
*Southern Baptist*
915/692-6776
**Years in existence:** 12
**Avg. attendance:** 160
**Primarily ages:** 26-35
**Main meeting time:** Sunday School Class **Singles classes:** Single Adult 1 (22-25), Single Adult 2 (26-28), Single Adult 3 (29-33), Single Adult 4 (34-38), Single Adult 5 (39-43), Single Adult 6 (44-49), Single Adult 7 (50-56), Single Adult 8 (57+), Single Adult 9 (all ages)

### SALT
Marvin Rumbaugh
First Church of the Nazarene
1389 Vine Street
Abilene, TX 79602
*Nazarene*
915/677-0805
**Years in existence:** 1
**Avg. attendance:** 20
**Primarily ages:** 31-45

## AMARILLO

### Paramount Terrace Singles Ministry
Bob Schroeder
Paramount Terrace Christian Church
4000 Mays
Amarillo, TX 79109
*Non-denominational*
806/353-6615
**Years in existence:** 7
**Avg. attendance:** 170
**Primarily ages:** 41-45
**Main meeting time(s):** Sunday School Class, a week night (M-F)
**Singles classes:** Singles, Too (35+), Balcony People (35+), YES (Young Enthusiastic Singles) (20-35)

### SOAR (Singles Outreach and Restoration)
Jerry Billington
Trinity Fellowship
7910 S. Bell
Amarillo, TX 79110
*Inter-denominational*
806/355-5652
**Years in existence:** 5
**Avg. attendance:** 160
**Primarily ages:** 18-40
**Main meeting time(s):** Sunday School Class
**Singles classes:** College (19-23), Young Adult (23-33), Cornerstone (33+)

## ARLINGTON

### Single Adult Ministry of First Baptist
Martin K. Scirrat
First Baptist Church
300 S. Center
Arlington, TX 76010
*Southern Baptist*
817/277-6353
**Years in existence:** 10
**Avg. attendance:** 200
**Primarily ages:** 18-30
**Main meeting time(s):** Sunday School Class
**Singles classes:** YSA2 (20-25), YSA3 (26-29), YSA4 (30-36), MSA (37+)

## AUSTIN

### First Methodist Singles
David Gilliam
First United Methodist Church
P.O. Box 1666
Austin, TX 78767
*United Methodist*
512/478-5684
**Years in existence:** 8
**Avg. attendance:** 90
**Primarily ages:** 18-25, 50+
**Main meeting time(s):** Sunday School Class
**Singles classes:** Crossroads (22-26), New Visions (29-40), Becomers (41-60)

### GANGG (Greater Austin Non-Married Guys & Gals)
Jeannie Whitehurst
Northwest Hills United Methodist Church
7017 Hart Lane
Austin, TX 78731
*United Methodist*
512/345-1743
**Years in existence:** 2
**Avg. attendance:** 45
**Primarily ages:** 31-45
**Main meeting time(s):** Sunday School Class
**Singles classes:** Kiononia Sunday School Class (25-35), New class (one month old) (40-60), BYOB (Bring Your Own Bible) (23-45), Single Parent Support Group (30-40s)

### Hyde Park Baptist Singles
John Walters
Hyde Park Baptist Church
3901 Speedway
Austin, TX 78751
*Baptist*
512/459-6587
**Years in existence:** 14
**Avg. attendance:** 250
**Primarily ages:** 26-30
**Main meeting time(s):** Sunday School Class
**Singles classes:** Career 1 (18-24), Career 2 (25-27), Career 3 (28-31), Singles 1 (32-37)

### Texas District Lutheran Singles
Lori L. Bachmann
Texas District Lutheran Church—Missouri Synod
7900 E. Highway 290
Austin, TX 78724
*Lutheran Church—Missouri Synod*
512/926-4272
**Years in existence:** 6+
**Primarily ages:** 31-35

## BEAUMONT

### Singles of Calvary
Carlton Berry
Calvary Baptist Church
3650 Dowlen Road
Beaumont, TX 77706
*Southern Baptist*
409/898-7074
**Years in existence:** 4
**Avg. attendance:** 130
**Primarily ages:** 18-30
**Main meeting time(s):** Sunday School Class, Friday night
**Singles classes:** University (18-22), Singles 2 (18-40), Singles 1 (41-65), Rebuilders (20-50s)

## BELTON

### First Baptist Career/ Singles
Kandy Kirkley
First Baptist, Belton
506 N. Main
Belton, TX 76513
*Baptist*
817/939-0705
**Years in existence:** 6
**Avg. attendance:** 40
**Primarily ages:** 26-30, 41-45
**Main meeting time(s):** Sunday School Class
**Singles classes:** Career (20-35), Single A7 (35-60)

## BURLESON

### SOS (Serving Our Singles)
Cory Smithee
Stepping Stone
P.O. Box 144
Burleson, TX 76028
*Non-denominational*
817/295-7671
**Years in existence:** 6
**Avg. attendance:** 40
**Primarily ages:** 18-25
**Main meeting time(s):** Friday night
**Singles classes:** SOS (18-35), HIS (35-50)

## COPPELL

### Single Threads
Cheryl Meyers
First United Methodist of Coppell
Heartz at Bethel School Roads
Coppell, TX 75019
*United Methodist*
214/239-7446
**Years in existence:** 4
**Avg. attendance:** 10
**Primarily ages:** 36-40
**Main meeting time(s):** Sunday School Class
**Singles classes:** Singles Sunday School (26-70)

## CORPUS CHRISTI

### Calallen Baptist Singles Department
Don Neal
Calallen Baptist Church
13505 Leopard
Corpus Christi, TX 78410
*Southern Baptist*
512/387-5727
**Years in existence:** 4
**Avg. attendance:** 12
**Primarily ages:** 36-40
**Main meeting time(s):** Sunday School Class
**Singles classes:** Single I (18), Single II (25+)

### First Baptist Singles
Bruce Peterson
First Baptist Church
3115 Ocean Drive
Corpus Christi, TX 78404
*Southern Baptist*
512/888-8228
**Years in existence:** 10
**Avg. attendance:** 80
**Primarily ages:** 36-40
**Main meeting time(s):** Sunday School Class, Sunday night
**Singles classes:** College (18-24), New Horizons (25-29), Disciples (30-37), Seekers (38-44), Saints Alive (43-73)

## DALLAS

### Highland Park Single Adult Ministry
Eric Folkerth
Highland Park United Methodist Church
3300 Mockingbird Lane
Dallas, TX 75205
*United Methodist*
214/521-3111
**Years in existence:** 17
**Primarily ages:** 26-40
**Main meeting time(s):** Sunday School Class
**Singles classes:** Agape (40s+), Becomers (20s-30s), Crossroads (20s-30s), Dialogue (55+)

### King of Glory Singles
Scot Sorensen
King of Glory
6411 LBJ Freeway
Dallas, TX 75240
*Evangelical Lutheran Church of America*
214/661-9435
**Years in existence:** 8
**Avg. attendance:** 30
**Primarily ages:** 26-35
**Main meeting time(s):** Sunday School Class

### Lakeside Singles
John C. Horn
Lakeside Baptist Church
9150 Garland Road
Dallas, TX 75218
*Southern Baptist*
214/324-1425
**Years in existence:** 15
**Avg. attendance:** 90
**Primarily ages:** 26-35
**Main meeting time(s):** Sunday School Class **Singles classes:** College & Career/Class 1B (18-23/24+), Class 1C (29-34), Class 2A (35-47), Class 2B & 2C (48-60/60+)

### Lovers Lane United Methodist Singles
R. Ben Marshall
Lovers Lane United Methodist
9200 Inwood Road
Dallas, TX 75220
*United Methodist*
214/691-4721
**Years in existence:** 15
**Avg. attendance:** 400
**Primarily ages:** 31-50
**Main meeting time(s):** Sunday School Class **Singles classes:** Disciples (22-27), 30 Something (30-40), Celebrations (40-50), Single Friends (40-50)

### Metroplex Chapel Single Adults
Ron and Nancy Myers
Judy Everett
Metroplex Chapel
P.O. Box 612047
Dallas/Ft. Worth, TX 75261
*Nazarene*
817/267-8000
**Years in existence:** 7
**Avg. attendance:** 65
**Primarily ages:** 26-30
**Main meeting time:** Sunday night
**Singles classes:** College/Career (18-25), Primarily Singles (all ages)

### Northway Singles
Marilyn Dickson
Northway Christian Church
7202 W.N.W. Highway
Dallas, TX 75225
*Disciples of Christ*
214/361-6641
**Years in existence:** 8
**Avg. attendance:** 30
**Main meeting time(s):** Sunday School Class **Singles classes:** Singles I (25-40), Seekers (35-60)

### Northwest Bible Singles
Dwayne Adams
Northwest Bible Church
8505 Douglas Avenue
Dallas, TX 75225
*Independent Bible*
214/368-6436
**Years in existence:** 7
**Avg. attendance:** 300
**Primarily ages:** 26-30
**Main meeting time(s):** Sunday

School Class, Sunday night, **Singles classes:** Morning Career Class (25-35), Young Singles Class (21-30), Evening Career Class (21-35), Singles and Singles Again (30+)

**Reinhardt Bible Singles**
Rev. G. Jerry Martin
Reinhardt Bible Church
10123 Garland Rd.
Dallas, TX 75218
*Non-denominational*
214/327-9351
**Years in existence:** 9
**Avg. attendance:** 110
**Primarily ages:** 26-35
**Main meeting time:** Sunday School Class **Singles classes:** Roaring 20s (23-29), Reinhardt Singles (29-39)

**St. Michael Singles Ministry**
Tom Blackmon
St. Michael & All Angels Episcopal Church
P.O. Box 12385
Dallas, TX 75225
*Episcopal Church*
214/363-5471
**Years in existence:** 6
**Avg. attendance:** 40
**Primarily ages:** 31-45
**Main meeting time(s):** Sunday School Class, Sunday night, a week night (M-F)
**Singles classes:** Younger Singles (23-33), Singles+ (33-50), Divorce Support (30-60), Single Parents (30-45)

**Highland Park Singles Ministry**
Paul M. Petersen
Highland Park Presbyterian
3821 University Blvd.
Dallas, TX 75205
*Presbyterian Church (USA)*
214/526-7457
**Years in existence:** 20
**Avg. attendance:** 1,000
**Primarily ages:** 26-35
**Main meeting time(s):** Sunday School Class **Singles classes:** Bridges (21-35), Cornerstone (20s-30s), Connections (40s-50s), Singleterians (40+)

**The Singles of Prestonwood**
Steve Cretin
Prestonwood Baptist Church
15720 Hillcrest
Dallas, TX 75248
*Baptist*
214/387-4475
**Years in existence:** 11
**Avg. attendance:** 650
**Primarily ages:** 26-30
**Main meeting time(s):** Sunday School Class **Singles classes:** Singles I (11 classes) (18-32), Singles II (7 classes) (33+)

## DENTON

**Grace Temple Baptist SAM**
Ron Lewis
Grace Temple Baptist Church
1106 West Oak
Denton, TX 76201
*Southern Baptist*
817/387-6137
**Years in existence:** 4
**Avg. attendance:** 75
**Primarily ages:** 18-25
**Main meeting time:** Sunday School Class **Singles Classes:** Class 1 (18-23), never-married, Class 2 (24-28), Class 3 (29-33), Class 4 (34-45), single parents & older singles

## FARMERS BRANCH

**BEST (Bible Enriched Singles Team)**
Michael L. Pope
Farmers Branch Chuch of Christ
3035 Valley View Lane
Farmers Branch, TX 75234
*Church of Christ*
214/247-2109
**Years in existence:** 3
**Avg. attendance:** 25
**Primarily ages:** 26-30
**Main meeting time(s):** Friday night

## FLOWER MOUND

**Ecumenical Singles' Group**
Robert S. Hanson
Trinity Presbyterian Church
2100 Kirkpatrick
Flower Mound, TX 75028
*Presbyterian Church (USA)*
214/539-0514
**Years in existence:** 2
**Avg. attendance:** 20
**Main meeting time(s):** A week night (M-F)

## FORT WORTH

**Birchman Singles Ministry**
John Crawford
Birchman Baptist Church
9100 North Normandale
Fort Worth, TX 76116
*Southern Baptist*
817/244-6590
**Years in existence:** 18
**Avg. attendance:** 150
**Primarily ages:** 18-35
**Main meeting time:** Sunday School Class
**Singles classes:** College/Career (18-23), Young Professionals (23-29), Singles I (30-38), Singles II (39+)

**Richland Hills Singles**
Don Phillips
Richland Hills Church of Christ
6300 N.E. Loop 820
Fort Worth, TX 76180
*Church of Christ*
817/281-0773
**Years in existence:**12
**Avg. attendance:** 300
**Main meeting time(s):** Sunday School Class, Sunday night,
**Singles classes:** Family Unit 1 (18-24), Unit 2 (25-30), Unit 3 (30-40), Unit 4 (35-40), Unit 5 (40-50), Unit 6 (50+)

**Single Light**
Jack Norville & Mike Jackson
Bethel Temple
6801 Meadowbrook Drive
Fort Worth, TX 76112
*Assemblies of God*
817/457-1111
**Years in existence:** 14
**Avg. attendance:** 60
**Primarily ages:** 50+
**Main meeting time:** Sunday School Class (in a restaurant A.M.)

**Single Spirit**
Bob Neely
North Richland Hills Baptist
4001 Vance Road
Ft. Worth, TX 76180
*Southern Baptist*
817/284-9206
**Years in existence:** 9
**Avg. attendance:** 104
**Primarily ages:** 18-35
**Main meeting time(s):** Sunday School Class **Singles classes:** Single Adult 1 (18-29), Single Adult 2 (18-39), Single Adult 3 (30-45), Single Adult 4 (40-54)

**Southcliff Singles**
Rick Patrick
Southcliff Baptist Church
4100 S.W. Loop 820
Fort Worth, TX 76109
*Southern Baptist*
817/924-2241
**Years in existence:** 17
**Avg. attendance:** 130
**Primarily ages:** 18-30
**Main meeting time:** Sunday School Class **Singles classes:** Single Adult 2 (20-32, 6 classes), Single Adult 3 (30-59, 2 classes recovery), Retreats/Special events

**Travis Avenue Single Adults**
Tommy Gowan
Travis Avenue Baptist Church
3041 Travis Avenue
Fort Worth, TX 76110
*Southern Baptist*
817/924-4266
**Years in existence:** 37
**Avg. attendance:** 400
**Primarily ages:** 26-40
**Main meeting time:** Sunday School Class **Singles classes:** Single Adult 1 (21-30), Single Adult 2 (21-30), Single Adult 3 (31-40), Single Adult 4 (41-55), Single Adult 5 (56+)

## HOUSTON

**Brookhollow Baptist Single Adults**
Terri Alexander
Brookhollow Baptist Church
5314 Bingle
Houston, TX 77050
*Baptist*
713/374-2119
**Years in existence:** 1
**Avg. attendance:** 15
**Primarily ages:** 26-30
**Main meeting time(s):** A week night (M-F)

**Lone Stars**
John Kaster
Gloria Dei Lutheran Church
18220 Upper Bay Road
Houston, TX 77058
*Lutheran*
713/333-4545
**Years in existence:** 10
**Avg. attendance:** 40
**Primarily ages:** 26-35
**Main meeting time(s):** A week night (M-F)

**Memorial Drive Singles**
Peter Miller
Memorial Drive Church
12955 Memorial Drive
Houston, TX 77079
*United Methodist*
713/468-8356
**Avg. attendance:** 180
**Primarily ages:** 31-35
**Main meeting time(s):** Sunday School Class **Singles classes:** Sunrizons (28-35), Young Singles (23-28), Pathfinders (35-50), New Horizons (45-60)

**New Faith Singles Ministry**
Drew E. Marshall
New Faith Baptist Church
4315 W. Fuqua Road
Houston, TX 77045
*Baptist*
713/433-6885
**Avg. attendance:** 70
**Primarily ages:** 36-45
**Main meeting time(s):** Friday night
**Singles classes:** Singles (18-27), Singles (28-35), Singles (36+)

**St. John Singles**
Rev. Randall Trego and Rev. Beth Green
St. John The Divine Episcopal Church
2450 River Oaks Blvd.
Houston, TX 77019
*Episcopal*
713/622-3600
**Years in existence:** 4
**Avg. attendance:** 50
**Primarily ages:** 18-35
**Main meeting time:** A week night (M-F)
**Singles classes:** Collegiate Fellowship (19-25), Roaring Twenties (20s), Baby Boomers (30s)

**Singles for Christ**
Tina M. Jones
St. John Missionary Baptist
2222 Gray Avenue
Houston, TX 77003
*Baptist*
713/659-7703
**Years in existence:** 7
**Avg. attendance:** 15
**Primarily ages:** 36-45
**Main meeting time(s):** A week night (M-F)

**Singles in the City**
Alan D. Allen
Church in the City
1035 E. 11th Street
Houston, TX 77009
713-869-9070
**Primarily ages:** 18-35
**Singles classes:** Crossroads (19-25), SITC (Singles in the City) (26+)

**South Union Singles Ministry**
Maurice S. Davis
South Union Church of Christ
3569 Lydia Street
Houston, TX 77021
*Church of Christ*
713/747-5440
**Years in existence:** 1
**Avg. attendance:** 15
**Primarily ages:** 26-30
**Main meeting time(s):** Sunday night

**Spring Branch Community Singles**
Brian Myers
Spring Branch Community Church
9560 Long Point Road
Houston, TX 77055
*Independent Bible*
713-465-3473

Need More Copies of This Directory?
Save nearly $4 each when you order five or more copies. Provide copies for each member of your staff. And raise money by selling extra copies at your next event.
*See page 248*

**Years in existence:** 20
**Avg. attendance:** 70
**Primarily ages:** 26-30
**Main meeting time(s):** Sunday School Class

**Trinity Lutheran Single Adult Ministry**
Don Christian
Trinity Lutheran Church
800 Houston Avenue
Houston, TX 77007
*Lutheran Church—Missouri Synod*
713/224-0684
**Years in existence:** 3
**Avg. attendance:** 30
**Primarily ages:** 31-35
**Main meeting time(s):** Sunday School Class
**Singles classes:** Single Parent Fellowship (28-40), Sunday Singles Class (20-45)

## IRVING

**Single Adult Ministry**
Larry Frederick
First Baptist Church, Irving
403 S. Main Street
Irving, TX 75060
*Southern Baptist Convention*
214/253-1171
**Years in existence:** 8
**Avg. attendance:** 40
**Primarily ages:** 31-40
**Main meeting time(s):** Sunday School Class **Singles classes:** Single Adult 1 (20-30), Single Adult 2 (30-45), Single Adult 3 (45-60)

**Single Together Ministries**
Todd Gentry
South MacArthur Church of Christ
1402 S. MacArthur Boulevard
Irving, TX 75060
214/986-8989
**Years in existence:** 5
**Avg. attendance:** 209
**Primarily ages:** 26-40
**Main meeting time(s):** Sunday School Class
**Singles classes:** S0 Unwed Mothers (16-22), S1 Transitions (18-23), S2 Young Professionals (22-35), S4 Singles (31-45)

## KATY

**New Lites**
Richard Bauman
St. Peter's United Methodist Church
20775 Kingsland Boulevard
Katy, TX 77450
*United Methodist*
713/492-8031
**Years in existence:** 2
**Avg. attendance:** 10
**Primarily ages:** 31-50
**Main meeting time(s):** Sunday School Class
**Singles classes:** New Lites (30+)

## LEWISVILLE

**Lakeland Baptist Single Adults**
Keith Utley
Lakeland Baptist Church
397 S. Stemmons
Lewisville,TX 75067
*Southern Baptist*
214/436-4561
**Years in existence:** 8
**Avg. attendance:** 65
**Primarily ages:** 18-25
**Main meeting time(s):** Sunday School Class **Singles classes:** SAI Co-ed (18-22), SA 2 (23-29), 30 Something (30-39), SA III (40+)

## LUBBOCK

**First United Methodist Singles**
Rev. Kay Reed
First United Methodist
1411 Broadway
Lubbock, TX 79401
*United Methodist*
806/763-4607
**Years in existence:** 14
**Avg. attendance:** 85
**Primarily ages:** 36-45
**Main meeting time:** A week night (M-F)

**Highland Baptist Singles**
Bob Batson
Highland Baptist Church
4316 - 34th
Lubbock, TX 79410
*Southern Baptist*
817/795-5910
**Years in existence:** 5
**Avg. attendance:** 25
**Primarily ages:** 31-35
**Main meeting time(s):** Sunday

School Class
**Singles classes:** Singles I (18-30), Singles II (31-45), Singles III (46+)

### Trinity Singles
David Savage
Trinity Church
7002 Canton Avenue
Lubbock, TX 79413
*Independent*
806/792-3363
**Years in existence:** 10
**Avg. attendance:** 120
**Primarily ages:** 31-45
**Main meeting time:** Sunday School Class
**Singles classes:** Young Adults (to mid 20s), Careers (up to mid 30s), Conquerors (mid 30s to mid 40s), Cornerstone (mid 40s+)

### University Singles
Betty Dotts
St. John's United Methodist Church
1501 University
Lubbock, TX 79401
*Methodist*
806/762-0123
**Years in existence:** 10
**Avg. attendance:** 18
**Primarily ages:** 26-35
**Main meeting time(s):** Sunday School Class
**Singles classes:** University (18-22), Covenant Singles (22-35)

## LUFKIN

### First United Methodist SAM
Randy Hageman
First United Methodist Church
805 E. Denman Avenue
Lufkin, TX 75901
*United Methodist*
409/639-3141
**Years in existence:** 6
**Avg. attendance:** 30
**Primarily ages:** 36-50
**Main meeting time(s):** A week night (M-F)
**Singles classes:** Discovery (30-55), Revelation (20-35), TNT (Tuesday Nights Together) (30+)

## MIDLAND

### Kelview Heights Baptist Singles
Jerry Berry
Kelview Heights Baptist
402 W. Scharbauer
Midland, TX 79705
*Independent*
915/682-3842
**Years in existence:** 8
**Avg. attendance:** 85
**Primarily ages:** 31-35
**Main meeting time(s):** Sunday School Class
**Singles classes:** College & Career (18-24), Singles (25+)

## ODESSA

### Temple Baptist Singles
Gail Teegarden
Temple Baptist Church
1000 North Texas
Odessa, TX 79760
*Baptist*
915/337-3641
**Years in existence:** 10
**Avg. attendance:** 120
**Primarily ages:** 31-40
**Main meeting time:** Sunday School Class

## PASADENA

### Single Adult Ministry
Ron Jenkins
First Baptist Church
1604 S. Tatar
Pasadena, TX 77502
*Southern Baptist Convention*
713/475-1231
**Years in existence:** 12
**Avg. attendance:** 180
**Primarily ages:** 31-35, 50+
**Main meeting time(s):** Sunday School Class **Singles classes:** SA 1 (19-27), SA 2 (28-38), SA 3 (2 classes) (38-48), SA 4 (2 classes) (48+)

## PLAINVIEW

### Single Heart Ministries
Greg Griffin
First Baptist Church
205 W. 8th Street
Plainview, TX 79072
*Southern Baptist*
806/296-6318
**Years in existence:** 4
**Avg. attendance:** 60
**Primarily ages:** 26-30


"Singling, or creative singleness, is a process by which singles in a couple–oriented world can achieve emotional and financial self-reliance as well as a sense of self-worth and accomplishment. . . . The message of this work is positive and reassuring and reaffirms the joy of becoming an independent, complete human being."–*Booklist (American Library Association )*

SINGLING–
A New Way to Live the Single Life
*by John R. Landgraf*

Viewed as an objective to be reached rather than a condition to be endured, the singles experience is seen as a complete, fulfilling lifestyle. John Landgraf discusses how to become single (even if married!), how to become whole without a primary relationship, and how to stay whole within one. Many fears are explored and debunked, such as the fear of becoming too self-absorbed, the fear of the unknown, and the fear of being alone. Paper $10.95

"A significant part of my counseling practice includes persons who are single, having never married, or are rebuilding their lives after a failed marriage. Landgraf's book provides an honest discussion of such issues as loneliness, sex, and money, as well as other troubling concerns that face the single adult." –***Charles L. Rassieur, Licensed Consulting Psychologist and Licensed Marriage and Family Therapist, New Brighton, Minnosota***

**JOHN R. LANDGRAF, Ph.D.,** is President and Professor of Theology and the Personality Sciences, Central Baptist Theological Seminary, Kansas City. His professional memberships include the American Psychological Association for Counseling and Development, and the American Association of Pastoral Counselors.

At your bookstore or call toll free
**1-800-227-2872**

WESTMINSTER/JOHN KNOX PRESS
100 Witherspoon Street, Louisville, KY 40202-1396

**Main meeting time(s):** Sunday School Class
**Singles classes:** (18-25), (26-28), (29-35), (36-42)

## PLANO

### Custer Road United Methodist
Vicki Smith
Custer Road United Methodist
6601 Custer Road
Plano, TX 75023
*Methodist*
214/618-3450
**Years in existence:** 4
**Avg. attendance:** 45
**Primarily ages:** 26-40
**Main meeting time(s):** Sunday School Class **Singles classes:** Rainbow Singles (30-50), S.A.L.T. Singles S.S. (24-35), Thursday Night Live! (30-50), Divorce Recovery (20-60)

## RICHMOND

### Pathway to Freedom (for Divorced & Widowed)
Joe E. Jones
First Baptist Church
239 Stuart
Richmond, TX 77531
*Southern Baptist*
409/265-4848 or
409/233-5641
**Years in existence:** 7
**Avg. attendance:** 30
**Primarily ages:** 46-50
**Main meeting time(s):** Sunday School Class

## SUGAR LAND

### Sugar Creek Singles
Mark R. Harris
Sugar Creek Baptist Church
13213 Southwest Freeway
Sugar Land, TX 77478
*Southern Baptist*
713/242-2858
**Years in existence:** 7
**Avg. attendance:** 100
**Primarily ages:** 41-45
**Main meeting time(s):** Sunday School Class

## TEXARKANA

### Texarkana Single Adults
Ed Kohl
First Baptist Church Texarkana
3015 Moores' Lane
Texarkana, TX 75503
*Southern Baptist*
214/831-6000
**Years in existence:** 10
**Avg. attendance:** 90
**Primarily ages:** 26-45
**Main meeting time(s):** Sunday School Class
**Singles classes:** Single Adults I (A&B) (20-27), Single Adults II (A&B) (28-34), Single Adults III (35-44), Single Adults IV (45+)

## TEXAS CITY

### Single Purpose
Steve Hardwick
First Baptist Church
1710 4th Avenue North
Texas City, TX 77590
*Baptist*
409/945-2309
**Years in existence:** 2
**Avg. attendance:** 90
**Primarily ages:** 31-35
**Main meeting time(s):** Sunday School Class
**Singles classes:** College & Career (18-25), Single Adult I (26-39), Single Adult II (40-55), Single Adult III (55+)

## TYLER

### Glenwood Singles
Keith Fulfer
Glenwood Church of Christ
807 W. Glenwood
Tyler, TX 70701
*Church of Christ*
214/592-3858
**Years in existence:** 1
**Avg. attendance:** 10
**Primarily ages:** 26-30
**Main meeting time(s):** Sunday School Class

### Green Acres Singles
Ken Brumley
Green Acres Baptist
1612 Leo Lynn
Tyler, TX 75701
*Southern Baptist*
214/593-9424
**Years in existence:** 10
**Avg. attendance:** 250
**Primarily ages:** 26-30
**Main meeting time:** Sunday School Class
**Singles classes:** 1 (20-25), 2 (26-30), 3 (31-36), 4 (37-43), 5 (44-51), 6 (50-60), 7 (60+)

### Marvin Single Adult Ministry
Dr. Lyle Dabney
Marvin United Methodist Church
300 West Erwin
Tyler, TX 75702
*United Methodist*
214/592-7396
**Years in existence:** 5
**Avg. attendance:** 60
**Primarily ages:** 26-45
**Main meeting time:** Sunday School Class **Singles Classes:** Single Young Adults (late teens to early 20s), Covenant (mid 20s to late 30s), Genesis (late 30s to late 40s), Sonrise (late 40s to mid 60s)

## WACO

### Columbus Avenue Single Adult Ministry
Joe Carbonaro
Columbus Avenue Baptist Church
1300 Columbus
P.O. Box 345
Waco, TX 76703
*Southern Baptist*
817/752-1655
**Avg. attendance:** 60
**Primarily ages:** 26-45
**Main meeting time(s):** Sunday School Class
**Singles classes:** Single Adult 1 (18-25), Single Adult 2 (26-30), Single Adult 3 (31-38), Single Adult 4 (39-50)

## WICHITA FALLS

### Singles On Christ's Side (SOCS)
Wade Reynolds
Loop II Church of Christ
1420 Loop II
Wichita Falls, TX 76305
*Non-denominational*
817/855-3183
**Years in existence:** 6
**Avg. attendance:** 25
**Primarily ages:** 31-40
**Main meeting time(s):** Sunday School Class

## SALT LAKE CITY

### Southeast Singles
Peter Cieslewski
Southeast Baptist Church
1700 E. 7000 South, P.O. Box 21399
Salt Lake City, UT 84121
*Southern Baptist*
801/943-2241
**Years in existence:** 3
**Avg. attendance:** 25
**Primarily ages:** 18-40, 50+
**Main meeting time(s):** Sunday School Class **Singles classes:** Adult Singles I (18-25), Adult Singles II (25-50), Adult Singles III (50+)

## FALLS CHURCH WEST

### Columbia Singles
James R. Perdew
Columbia Baptist Church
103 W. Columbia St.
Falls Church, VA 22046
*Baptist*
703/534-5700
**Years in existence:** 10
**Avg. attendance:** 210
**Primarily ages:** 26-35
**Main meeting time(s):** Sunday School Class
**Singles classes:** Singles Adult I (24-35), Singles Adult II (36-45), Singles Adult III (46+)

## FISHERVILLE

### Fisherville Baptist Singles Ministry
Ann Higgins
Fisherville Baptist
P.O. Box 82
Fisherville, VA 22939
*Southern Baptist*
703/332-7098
**Years in existence:** 5
**Avg. attendance:** 30
**Primarily ages:** 46-50, 50+
**Main meeting time(s):** Sunday School Class
**Singles classes:** The Seekers (40+), The Kingdom Heirs (25-39), Saints Alive (18-24)

## LURAY

### Dimensions
Mike Nochols
Mt. Carmel Regular Baptist
P.O. Box 31
Luray, VA 22835
*Independent Baptist*
703/743-5645
**Years in existence:** 2
**Avg. attendance:** 5
**Primarily ages:** 18-25
**Main meeting time(s):** Sunday School Class

## MANASSAS

### Manassas Baptist Singles
Mark G. Cooke
Manassas Baptist
8800 Sudley Road
Manassas, VA 22110
*Southern Baptist*
703/361-2146
**Years in existence:** 11
**Avg. attendance:** 35
**Primarily ages:** 31-35, 50+
**Main meeting time(s):** Sunday School Class
**Singles classes:** Singles I (18-35), Singles III (30-49), Singles V (45+)

## RICHMOND

### Grove Avenue Baptist Singles
Rusty Coram
Grove Avenue Baptist Church
8701 Ridge Road
Richmond, VA 23229
*Southern Baptist*
804/740-8888
**Years in existence:** 8
**Avg. attendance:** 105
**Primarily ages:** 26-35
**Main meeting time:** Sunday School Class

## ROANOKE

### Cave Spring Singles
Jeffery S. Alphin
Cave Spring Baptist Church
4873 Brambleton Ave, SW
Roanoke, VA 24018
*Southern Baptist*
703/989-6136
**Years in existence:** 1
**Avg. attendance:** 50
**Primarily ages:** 26-30
**Main meeting time(s):** Sunday School Class **Singles classes:** Lamplighters (18-24), A.C.T.S. (25-35), New Beginnings (35-55)

## SPRINGFIELD

### Singles at Messiah
Lucy B. Marsden
Messiah United Methodist Church
6215 Rolling Road
Springfield, VA 22153
*United Methodist*
703/569-9862
**Years in existence:** 6
**Avg. attendance:** 50+
**Primarily ages:** 36-45
**Main meeting time(s):** Sunday School Class **Singles classes:** Singles at Messiah (35-55), Young Adults (20-35)

## VIENNA

### Single Diversity
Kelley Schroder
Christian Fellowship Church
10237 Leesburg Pike
Vienna, VA 22182
*Interdenominational*
703/759-4210
**Years in existence:** 10
**Avg. attendance:** 135
**Primarily ages:** 26-50
**Main meeting time(s):** Sunday School Class, a week night (M-F)
**Singles classes:** Single Vision/ New Horizons (20-34), Singles of the Son (35+)

## VIRGINIA BEACH

### London Bridge Baptist Single Adults
Chuck Callis
London Bridge Baptist
2460 Potters Road
Virginia Beach, VA 23454
*Southern Baptist*
804/486-7900
**Years in existence:** 3
**Avg. attendance:** 100
**Primarily ages:** 18-25
**Singles classes:** Singles I (18-24), Singles II (25-30), Single III (31+)

## BREMERTON

### Crossroads College/Career & Single Adults Ministry
Scott Turner
Crossroads Neighborhood Church
7555 Old Military Road, N.E.
Bremerton, WA 98310
*Christian & Missionary Alliance*
206/692-1672
**Years in existence:** 5
**Avg. attendance:** 50
**Primarily ages:** 18-30, 36-45
**Main meeting time(s):** A week night (M-F)
**Singles classes:** College/Career Fellowship (18-29), Single Adults Fellowship (30-50)

## EVERETT

### New Beginnings
Doreen J. Fox
Our Saviors' Lutheran Church
P.O. Box 2927
Everett, WA 98203
*Lutheran*
206/252-0413
**Years in existence:** 7
**Avg. attendance:** 20
**Primarily ages:** 41-50+
**Main meeting time(s):** Sunday night
**Singles classes:** Workshops (All singles)

## KENT

### Kent Positive Singles
Gary L. Waller
Kent Church of the Nazarene
930 East James
Kent, WA 98031
*Nazarene*
206/852-5144
**Years in existence:** 8
**Avg. attendance:** 85
**Primarily ages:** 31-35
**Main meeting time(s):** A week night (M-F)
**Singles classes:** Young Adult (20-30), Growing Tree (30-50)

## KIRKLAND

### Assemblies of God Singles
Ed Weising
Assemblies of God
P.O. Box 699
Kirkland, WA 98083
*Assemblies of God*
206/827-3013
**Years in existence:** 12

### Northwest Christian Singles
Ed Weising
Assemblies of God
P.O. Box 699
Kirkland, WA 98083
*Assemblies of God*
206/827-3013
**Years in existence:** 5

### SWAT (Singles With A Task)
Gary Winkleman
Overlake Christian Church
9051 132nd Avenue N.E.
Kirkland, WA 98034
*Non-denominational*
206/827-0303
**Years in existence:** 15
**Avg. attendance:** 400-500
**Primarily ages:** 31-45
**Main meeting time(s):** Sunday School Class, a week night (M-F)
**Singles classes:** Agamos (40+), Acts (30-40), Life (18-26)

## LONGVIEW

**Koinonia Christian Singles**
Rev. Michael A. Dekraa
Emmanuel Lutheran Church
2218 E. Kessler Blvd
Longview, WA 98632
*Lutheran*
206-423-3250
**Avg. attendance:** 35
**Primarily ages:** 31-50+
**Main meeting time(s):** Sunday School Class, a week night (M-F)

## RICHLAND

**Central United Singles Ministry**
Jo Kimmel
Central United Protestant
1124 Stevens
Richland, WA 99352
*Methodist, Presbyterian, American Baptist*
509/943-1143
**Years in existence:** 10
**Avg. attendance:** 50
**Primarily ages:** 41-50+
**Main meeting time(s):** A week night (M-F)
**Singles classes:** Monday Discussion (40+), Quest (20-30s), Single on Sunday (20s+), Remarried Couples Support (40+)

## SEATTLE

**University Presbyterian Singles**
John Westfall
University Presbyterian Church
4540 15th Avenue N.E.
Seattle, WA 98105
*Presbyterian*
206/524-7300
**Years in existence:** 9
**Avg. attendance:** 500
**Primarily ages:** 26-40, 50+
**Main meeting time(s):** Sunday School Class
**Singles classes:** Post-College Fellowship (21-27), Cornerstone Fellowship (25-35), Streamers (31-45), Genesis Fellowship (50+)

## TACOMA

**Single Focus**
Greg Chantler
Central Baptist Church
5000 - 67th Avenue W.
Tacoma, WA 98467
*Baptist*
206/565-6500
**Years in existence:** 2
**Avg. attendance:** 75
**Primarily ages:** 26-30
**Main meeting time(s):** A week night (M-F)
**Singles classes:** College Age (18-23), Single Focus (24-49), Single Focus IV (50+)

**A Single Purpose**
Pastor Chuck Hushek
The Peoples Church
1819 East 72nd Street
Tacoma, WA 98404
*Independent*
206/475-6454
**Years in existence:** 5
**Avg. attendance:** 120
**Primarily ages:** 18-45
**Main meeting time:** Sunday School Class **Singles classes:** Young Adults (18-29), SALT (30-55), Prime Timers (55+), SPAN (Single Parents Assistance Network); Big Brother/Sister (Kids ages 5-12)

## VANCOUVER

**Christ Centered Singles**
Denise M. Hemenway
Burton Church of God
3611 N.E. 132nd Avenue
Vancouver, WA 98662
*Pentecostal*
206/892-3650
**Years in existence:** 2
**Avg. attendance:** 25
**Primarily ages:** 36-40, 46-50
**Main meeting time(s):** Sunday School Class, a week night (M-F), Friday night

**Crossroads Singles**
Rob Oberto
Crossroads Community Church
7708 N.E. 78th Street
Vancouver, WA 98662
*Interdenominational*
206/256-9711
**Years in existence:** 4
**Avg. attendance:** 150
**Main meeting time:** Sunday School Class

## YAKIMA

**ACTS (Active Christians In Training and Service)**
Reagan Couch
Yakima Foursquare Church
3414 Tieton Drive
Yakima, WA 98902
*Foursquare*
509/575-1490
**Years in existence:** 6
**Avg. attendance:** 40
**Primarily ages:** 26-40
**Main meeting time(s):** Friday night
**Singles classes:** ACTS - Under 30 (under 30), ACTS - Over 30 (30-45)

## MORGANTOWN

**Single Adults Living The Truth (SALT)**
Don Oliver
Christian & Missionary Alliance
308 Elmhurst St.
Morgantown, WV 26505
*Christian & Missionary Alliance*
304-284-2237
**Years in existence:** 4
**Avg. attendance:** 25
**Primarily ages:** 36-40
**Main meeting time(s):** Sunday School Class

## PARKERSBURG

**Single Path Ministries**
Paul Morton
North Parkersburg Baptist Church
3109 Emerson Avenue
Parkersburg, WV 26102
*American Baptist*
304/428-3293
**Years in existence:** 17
**Avg. attendance:** 60
**Primarily ages:** 31-40, 46-50
**Main meeting time(s):** A week night (M-F)

**Singles classes:** Dynamics (all ages), Path Finders (24-35), Pace Setters (35-50), Motivators (50+)

## APPLETON

**Singles Alive**
Pastor Joe Ellis
First Assemblies of God, Appleton
2720 N. Kesting Ct.
Appleton, WI 54911
*Assemblies of God*
414-738-3040
**Years in existence:** 4
**Avg. attendance:** 60
**Primarily ages:** 18-25, 36-40
**Main meeting time(s):** A week night (M-F)
**Singles classes:** Potters Clay (18-28), Singles Alive (23-60)

## CHEPPEWA FALLS

**STEAM (Singles Together Enjoying A Ministry)**
Cheryl Vogler
Christ Lutheran Church
467 E. Colome
Chippewa Falls, WI 54729
*Lutheran*
715/723-8273
**Years in existence:** 5
**Avg. attendance:** 20
**Primarily ages:** 41-45
**Main meeting time(s):** Friday night

## MADISON

**Animations**
Warren Keapproth
Madison Gospel Tabernacle
4909 E. Buckeye Road
Madison, WI 53716
*Non-denominational*
608/221-1528
**Years in existence:** 2
**Avg. attendance:** 70

**Primarily ages:** 31-35
**Main meeting time(s):** A week night (M-F), Friday night

## MILWAUKEE

**Garfield Singles**
David W. Loftis
Garfield Baptist Church
4400 N. Mayfair Road
Milwaukee. WI 53225
*General Association of Regular Baptist Churches*
414/464-9190
**Years in existence:** 7
**Avg. attendance:** 45
**Primarily ages:** 26-35
**Main meeting time(s):** Sunday School Class

## MONROE

**Single Path**
Gale Craig
Monroe United Methodist Church
2227 - 4th Street
Monroe, WI 53566
*United Methodist*
608/325-6700
**Years in existence:** 6
**Avg. attendance:** 100
**Primarily ages:** 18-45
**Main meeting time:** A week night (M-F)

## WAUKESHA

**Elmbrook Church Single Adult Ministry**
Lorin Staats
Elmbrook Church
777 S. Barker Road
Waukesha, WI 53186
*Non-denominational*
414/786-7051
**Years in existence:** 15
**Avg. attendance:** 110
**Primarily ages:** 31-35
**Main meeting time(s):** A week night (M-F), Friday night
**Singles classes:** Single Parents (30-40), Waukesha Group (25-40), Thirty-Plus (35-45), Northside (35-45)

## WHEATLAND

**First Christian Singles**
Andrew J. Gudahl
First Christian Church
95 19th Street
Wheatland, WY 82201
*Non-denominational*
307/322-3132
**Years in existence:** 2
**Avg. attendance:** 15
**Primarily ages:** 26-30
**Main meeting time(s):** A week night (M-F)

# INTERNATIONAL SINGLES MINISTRIES

# CANADA

## CALGARY

**Full Gospel Singles Ministry (FGSM)**
Lucy Lutz
The Full Gospel Church of Calgary, Alberta
917 14th Avenue S.W.
Calgary, Alberta
Canada AB T2R 0N8
*Apostolic Church of Pentecost*
403/244-2948
**Years in existence:** 10
**Avg. attendance:** 50
**Primarily ages:** 31-35
**Main meeting time(s):** A week night (M-F)

## EDMONTON

**Contact Ministries**
Walter Hnatko
P.O. Box 11601
Edmonton, Alberta
Canada T5J 3K7
*Non-denominational*
403/426-1797
**Years in existence:** 7
**Primarily ages:** 26-45
**Singles classes:** Singles (24-45)

**Evangle Pentecostal Assembly**
Pastor Dale Reesor
Evangle Pentecostal Assembly
7907 86 Ave.
Edmonton, Alberta
Canada T6C 1J2
*Pentecostal Assemblies of Canada*
403/468-4714
**Years in existence:** 4
**Primarily ages:** 26-30
**Main meeting time(s):** Friday night

**Gospel Centre Singles**
Lissa Wray
Gospel Centre
9445 - 153rd Street
Edmonton, Alberta
Canada T5R 1R2
*Pentecostal Assemblies of Canada*
403/484-0085
**Years in existence:** 1
**Avg. attendance:** 12
**Primarily ages:** 26-40
**Main meeting time(s):** A week night (M-F)

**Singles' Church**
Blair Donnelly
Peoples' Church
11205 - 101st
Edmonton, Alberta
Canada T5G 2A4
*Pentecostal Assemblies of Canada*
403/474-8091

**Years in existence:** 15
**Avg. attendance:** 90
**Primarily ages:** 26-30
**Main meeting time(s):** A week night (M-F)
**Singles classes:** Single Parents (27-50)

## ABBOTS FIELD

### CAM (Career Adult Ministries)

Howard Phillips
Central Heights Church
1661 McCallum Road
Abbots Field, British Columbia
Canada V2S 3M4
*Mennonite Brethren*
604/852-1001
**Years in existence:** 4
**Avg. attendance:** C/C, 90; CAM, 25
**Primarily ages:** 18-25
**Main meeting time(s):** Sunday School Class, a week night (M-F)
**Singles classes:** College & Careers (18-25), CAM (25-35)

## BURNABY

### Single Adult Living Today (SALT)

Brian Carlson
Willingdon Church
4812 Willingdon Avenue
Burnaby, British Columbia
Canada V5G 3H6
*Mennonite Bretheren*
604/435-5544
**Years in existence:** 14
**Avg. attendance:** 125
**Primarily ages:** 26-50
**Main meeting time(s):** A week night (M-F), and Saturday night
**Singles classes:** Positive Christian Singles 40+, Connections 34-44, Young Adults 25-35, Parentime (all ages)

## LANGLEY

### Christian Life Assembly Single Adults

Brian Pierson
Christian Life Assembly
Box 3123, 21277 - 56th Avenue
Langley, British Columbia
Canada V3A 4R5
*Pentecostal Assemblies of Canada*
604/530-7344
**Years in existence:** 4
**Avg. attendance:** 60
**Primarily ages:** 41-45
**Main meeting time(s):** A week night (M-F)
**Singles classes:** Sunday School (30-55), Single Moms (25-35), Home Groups (30-55)

## VANCOUVER

### Cornerstone

Karen Reed
Broadway Tabernacle
2677 E. Broadway
Vancouver, BC
Canada V5M 1Y6
*Pentecostal Assemblies of Canada*
604/253-4167
**Years in existence:** 5
**Avg. attendance:** 275
**Primarily ages:** 26-30
**Main meeting time(s):** Sunday School Class, Friday night
**Singles classes:** College & Career (18-25), Cornerstone (25-40)

## MONCTON

### Single Visions

William Annis
Sound of Pentecost
Box 1202
Moncton, New Brunswick
Canada E1C 8P9
*Pentecostal*
**Avg. attendance:** 20
**Primarily ages:** 31-35

## BARRIE

### Collier Christian Singles

Arthur Hiley
Collier Street Church
112 Collier Street
Barrie, Ontario
Canada L4M 1H3
*United Church of Canada*
705/726-1511
**Years in existence:** 12
**Avg. attendance:** 30
**Primarily ages:** 36-50
**Main meeting time(s):** Sunday night

## KIRKLAND LAKE

### Adults Without A Partner

Raymond Martel
Living Faith Assembly
Highway 66 (Box 96)
Kirkland Lake, Ontario
Canada P2N 3M6
*Pentecostal*
705/567-7407
**Years in existence:** 1
**Avg. attendance:** 8
**Primarily ages:** 31-35

## LONDON

### SALT Ministries

Lorraine St. John
Glad Tidings Assembly
556 Wonderland Road N.
London, Ontario
Canada N6H 3E3
*Pentecostal Assemblies of Canada*
519/473-2804
**Years in existence:** 2
**Avg. attendance:** 35
**Primarily ages:** 31-45
**Main meeting time(s):** Saturday night

## NEPEAN

### Fellowship of Christian Adult Singles (FOCAS)

Bob Lanoue
Woodvale Pentecostal
205 Greenbank Road
Nepean (Ottawa), Ontario
Canada K2H 8K9
*Pentecostal Assemblies of Canada*
613/596-1950 (Bob)
**Years in existence:** 5
**Avg. attendance:** 25
**Primarily ages:** 41-50
**Main meeting time(s):** Saturday night

## TORONTO

### Farmer Memorial Baptist Singles

Rev. Dr. Bill Webster
Farmer Memorial Baptist Church
293 South Kingsway
Toronto, Ontario
Canada
*Baptist*
416/762-3061
**Years in existence:** 4
**Avg. attendance:** 20
**Primarily ages:** 31-45
**Main meeting time(s):** A week night (M-F)

### Peoples Singles' Ministry

Glen A. Eagleson
The Peoples' Church
374 Sheppard Avenue E.
Toronto, Ontario
Canada M2N 3B6
*The Peoples' Church*
416/222-3341
**Years in existence:** 10
**Avg. attendance:** 140
**Primarily ages:** 26-45
**Main meeting time(s):** Sunday School Class, a week night (M-F)
**Singles classes:** P.S.M. (35-50), Young Adults (25-35)

### Stone Church College & Careers

Michael Krause
The Stone Church
45 Davenport Road
Toronto, Ontario
Canada M5R 1H2
*Pentecostal Assemblies of Canada*
416/928-0101
**Years in existence:** 10
**Avg. attendance:** 120
**Primarily ages:** 26-30
**Main meeting time(s):** A week night (M-F)

## MONTREAL

### Groupe Personnes Seules

Florence Dutaud
Le Centre Evangelique
1455 Papineau
Montreal, Quebec
Canada H2K 4H5
*Pentecostal (French)*
514/522-8781
**Years in existence:** 3
**Avg. attendance:** 50
**Primarily ages:** 50+

# ISRAEL

### Living Stones

Reuven Ross
King of Kings Assembly
P.O. Box 427
Jerusalem, Israel
*Interdenominational*
02/232016
**Years in existence:** 2
**Avg. attendance:** 45
**Primarily ages:** 26-30
**Main meeting time(s):** A week night (M-F)

**For additional order forms... or other information, please write:**

**Singles Ministry Resources**
P.O. Box 62056
Colorado Springs,
CO 80962-2056

Or call:
Customer Service
(719) 488-2610

To order product or to subscribe to *SAM Journal*, call toll-free
(800) 487-4-SAM

When ordering by phone, have your VISA or MasterCard available.

**We want to hear from you!**

Make Sure You Are Included In The Next

# NATIONAL SINGLE ADULT MINISTRIES RESOURCE DIRECTORY

❑ **Yes, I want to be included.**

Please send me your application form when you begin compiling the next Directory. *(Note: If you are a subscriber to* SAM Journal, *you will automatically receive all the necessary information.)*

**Send to:**

Name____________________________________

Address__________________________________

City____________________State______Zip______

Church___________________________________

R.D./91-92

**I'm interested in the following:**

*(Please check all that apply.)*

❑ I want to make sure our singles ministry is listed in the next Directory.

❑ I may want to be listed as a speaker/singer in the next Directory.

❑ I may want to advertise in the next Directory. Please send me your advertising rates.

❑ I would be interested in serving on SAM's National Resource Review Board. (Must be a pastor or lay leader in singles ministry.)

❑ Please send me information on how I can subscribe to *Single Adult Ministries Journal.*

❑ Other:__________________________________

**Send to:** *SAM Resources,* P.O. Box 62056, Colorado Springs, CO 80962-2056

# ORDER FIVE OR MORE COPIES OF THIS DIRECTORY...

## *And Save Over $4 Each!*

When you order five or more copies of the *National Single Adult Ministries Resource Directory*, you pay only $8.75 each, plus postage and handling. (That's a savings of $4.20 per Directory over the $12.95 cover price!)
**Help us put this valuable Resource Directory into the hands of your leadership team...the people who can most benefit from this helpful information.**

**Ways to use additional copies of this Directory:**

❑ Make them available to all your key ministry leaders and staff

❑ Sell them to other pastors and leaders at your singles conferences and leadership training events. Use the profit for a special project or fund in your singles ministry. *(For even larger quantitiy discounts of 10, 20, 50 or more copies, call 800-487-4-SAM.)*

❑ Make them available to key pastors in your community to help them become more aware of single adult ministries nationwide.

❑ Give one to your mom.

❑ **Yes,** please send me ___ copies of the National Resource Directory at the special reduced rate of only $8.75 each, plus postage and handling. This is a savings of more than $4 per Directory from the cover price of $12.95. (Offer good only with a minimum order of 5.)

**Payment:** ❑ Bill me (A 5% billing charge will be added to total.)
❑ Check (Make payable in U.S. funds to SAM Resources)
❑ Credit Card ___VISA ___ MasterCard
Card #___________________________Exp. Date_________

**Postage and handling rates:** Add $4 for orders up to $25; $6 for orders up to $50; $8 for orders up to $75; $9 for orders up to $100; all orders over $100, 10% of total. *Please double shipping charges for rush orders or orders outside of U.S.*

Name___________________________________ Church__________

Address_______________________________________________

City_____________________________State________ Zip__________

R.D./91-92

**Send to:** *SAM Resources*, P.O. Box 62056, Colorado Springs, CO 80962-2056

**For additional order forms... or other information, please write:**

**Singles Ministry Resources**
P.O. Box 62056
Colorado Springs, CO 80962-2056

Or call:
Customer Service
(719) 488-2610

To order product or to subscribe to *SAM Journal*, call toll-free
(800) 487-4-SAM

When ordering by phone, have your VISA or MasterCard available.

**We want to hear from you!**

**For additional order forms... or other information, please write:**

**Singles Ministry Resources**
P.O. Box 62056
Colorado Springs, CO 80962-2056

Or call:
Customer Service
(719) 488-2610

To order product or to subscribe to *SAM Journal*, call toll-free (800) 487-4-SAM

When ordering by phone, have your VISA or MasterCard available.

**We want to hear from you!**

**Make Sure You Are Included In The Next**

# NATIONAL SINGLE ADULT MINISTRIES RESOURCE DIRECTORY

❑ **Yes, I want to be included.**

Please send me your application form when you begin compiling the next Directory. *(Note: If you are a subscriber to* SAM Journal, *you will automatically receive all the necessary information.)*

**Send to:**

Name________________________________

Address______________________________

City____________________State________Zip_______

Church_______________________________

R.D./91-92

**I'm interested in the following:**

*(Please check all that apply.)*

❑ I want to make sure our singles ministry is listed in the next Directory.

❑ I may want to be listed as a speaker/singer in the next Directory.

❑ I may want to advertise in the next Directory. Please send me your advertising rates.

❑ I would be interested in serving on SAM's National Resource Review Board. (Must be a pastor or lay leader in singles ministry.)

❑ Please send me information on how I can subscribe to *Single Adult Ministries Journal.*

❑ Other:______________________________

**Send to:** *SAM Resources,* P.O. Box 62056, Colorado Springs, CO 80962-2056

# HOW CAN WE IMPROVE THIS NATIONAL RESOURCE DIRECTORY?

This is the second-ever resource directory of its kind for those involved in ministry with single adults. (As with anything, this product can always be improved.)

We want to make this Directory as effective and helpful a resource for you as possible. So *talk* to us. Your feed-back, ideas and suggestions are very helpful to us.

**What would you like to see more of in future Directories?**

**What would you like to see less of?**

**What did we forget that you would like to see included next time?**

**How can we make this directory more helpful and useful in your ministry with single adults?**

**Other comments:**

**Send to:** *SAM Resources*, P.O. Box 62056, Colorado Springs, CO 80962-2056

R.D./91-92

## For additional order forms... or other information, please write:

**Singles Ministry Resources**
P.O. Box 62056
Colorado Springs,
CO 80962-2056

Or call:
Customer Service
(719) 488-2610

To order product or to subscribe to *SAM Journal*, call toll-free
(800) 487-4-SAM

When ordering by phone, have your VISA or MasterCard available.

## We want to hear from you!

**For additional order forms... or other information, please write:**

**Singles Ministry Resources**
P.O. Box 62056
Colorado Springs, CO 80962-2056

Or call:
Customer Service
(719) 488-2610

To order product or to subscribe to *SAM Journal*, call toll-free (800) 487-4-SAM

When ordering by phone, have your VISA or MasterCard available.

**We want to hear from you!**

# ORDER FIVE OR MORE COPIES OF THIS DIRECTORY...

## *And Save Over $4 Each!*

When you order five or more copies of the *National Single Adult Ministries Resource Directory*, you pay only $8.75 each, plus postage and handling. (That's a savings of $4.20 per Directory over the $12.95 cover price!)
**Help us put this valuable Resource Directory into the hands of your leadership team...the people who can most benefit from this helpful information.**

**Ways to use additional copies of this Directory:**

❑ Make them available to all your key ministry leaders and staff

❑ Sell them to other pastors and leaders at your singles conferences and leadership training events. Use the profit for a special project or fund in your singles ministry. *(For even larger quantitiy discounts of 10, 20, 50 or more copies, call 800-487-4-SAM.)*

❑ Make them available to key pastors in your community to help them become more aware of single adult ministries nationwide.

❑ Give one to your mom.

❑ **Yes,** please send me ___ copies of the National Resource Directory at the special reduced rate of only $8.75 each, plus postage and handling. This is a savings of more than $4 per Directory from the cover price of $12.95. (Offer good only with a minimum order of 5.)

**Payment:** ❑ Bill me (A 5% billing charge will be added to total.)
❑ Check (Make payable in U.S. funds to SAM Resources)
❑ Credit Card __VISA __ MasterCard
Card #________________________Exp. Date__________

**Postage and handling rates:** Add $4 for orders up to $25; $6 for orders up to $50; $8 for orders up to $75; $9 for orders up to $100; all orders over $100, 10% of total. *Please double shipping charges for rush orders or orders outside of U.S.*

Name________________________ Church__________

Address________________________

City________________ State________ Zip__________

R.D./91-92

**Send to:** *SAM Resources*, P.O. Box 62056, Colorado Springs, CO 80962-2056

# HOW CAN WE IMPROVE THIS NATIONAL RESOURCE DIRECTORY?

This is the second-ever resource directory of its kind for those involved in ministry with single adults. (As with anything, this product can always be improved.)

We want to make this Directory as effective and helpful a resource for you as possible. So *talk* to us. Your feed-back, ideas and suggestions are very helpful to us.

**What would you like to see more of in future Directories?**

**What would you like to see less of?**

**What did we forget that you would like to see included next time?**

**How can we make this directory more helpful and useful in your ministry with single adults?**

**Other comments:**

**Send to:** *SAM Resources*, P.O. Box 62056, Colorado Springs, CO 80962-2056

R.D./91-92

**For additional order forms... or other information, please write:**

**Singles Ministry Resources**
P.O. Box 62056
Colorado Springs, CO 80962-2056

Or call:
Customer Service
(719) 488-2610

To order product or to subscribe to *SAM Journal*, call toll-free
(800) 487-4-SAM

When ordering by phone, have your VISA or MasterCard available.

**We want to hear from you!**

# ORDER FORM

# Resources For Your Ministry With Single Adults

Cut along the dotted line and mail this page to: SAM Resources, P.O. Box 62056, Colorado Springs, CO 80962-2056. Or place your order by phone. Call toll-free (800) 487-4-SAM or (719) 488-2610.

## NEWSLETTER

❑ ***Single Adult Ministries Journal***. Ideas, resources and guidance for leaders . . . the most recommended publication for those involved in ministry with single adults. Ten issues per year. **One-year subscription, $24.** *(Add $5 in Canada and $9 for all other countries.)* **Two-year subscription (SAVE $10) $38.** *(Add $10 in Canada and $18 for all other countries.)*

## RESOURCE DIRECTORY

❑ **National Single Adult Ministries Resource Directory**, *"The complete 'Yellow Pages' to ministry with single adults."* Every kind of useful information—from A to Z—is in this directory to help you save time, be more effective, and become 'networked' with the best singles ministry people and resources. **$12.95**

## BOOKS

❑ **Single Adult Ministry: 60 Leaders Tell How You Can Build and Nurture a Healthy Ministry**. Edited by Jerry Jones. *"The authoritative guide for singles ministry leaders."* How do you build a singles ministry that's effective? How do you keep it from slipping into a rut? How do you deal with the obstacles and opportunities that are unique to working with single adults? This book has the answers to these questions and many more. A collection of the best articles from the first eight years of *Single Adult Ministries Journal*, this excellent resource features insights and suggestions from 60 of the most knowledgeable leaders in singles ministry. **$24.95**

❑ **Developing a Divorce Recovery Ministry: A How-to Manual**, by Dr. Bill Flanagan. As one of the pioneers of 'the small group model' of divorce recovery ministry, in this book Dr. Flanagan shows you how to design the program, gather a leadership team, create a caring community and reach out to the growing number of divorced persons in your community. Everything you need to get started is in this book. **$19.95**

❑ **Divorce Recovery For Teenagers: How to Help Your Kids Recover, Heal, and Grow When Their Families are Ripped Apart**, by Stephen Murray and Randy Smith. The concept of divorce recovery for adults is generally accepted in the church. But what about the kids of divorce? While they suffer as much as (if not more than) their parents, too often they are left to fend for themselves as they are buffeted by life-wrenching events they cannot control. This resource offers a step-by-step workshop that you can use to begin an adolescent divorce recovery ministry right now. **$12.95**

**Continued on other side**

# ORDER FORM

❑ **The Idea Catalog for Single Adult Ministry**, edited by Jerry Jones. Here are hundreds of ideas to spark your imagination and help you and your leadership team build your singles ministry. These ideas have been contributed by singles ministry leaders from across North America. They are ideas that have been successfully used in singles ministries for special events, socials, retreats, single parent ministry, leadership training, publicity/promotion, fund-raising, evangelism, and more. **$12.95**

❑ **Vacations With a Purpose: A Planning Handbook for Your Short-term Missions Team**, by Kim Hurst and Chris Eaton. The authors of this book are hands-on pioneers in preparing single and young adults for short-term team missions trips. This helpful guide will be a must-have for anyone seeking to challenge and involve their people in world missions. The two books in this series (one for leaders and one for team members) provides everything you will need to know about philosophy, putting the team together, advance preparation, maximizing the benefits of the trip, selecting a project, raising the necessary funds, as well as all the logistical questions and issues that need to be addressed. **Leader's Manual, $16.95; Team Member's Handbook, $5.95.**

❑ **Singles Ministry Handbook: A Practical Guide to Reaching Adult Singles in the Church**, edited by Douglas Fagerstrom. Over 60 million single adults live in the United States and most of them don't attend church. This book includes help for reaching and ministering to this neglected and diverse segment of our society, with guidance and help from more than 30 singles ministry experts. **$18.95**

❑ **Young Adult Ministry: Step-by-step Help for Starting or Revitalizing Your Ministry With People Ages 18 to 35**, by Terry Hershey. One of the most-recommended books for leaders in singles ministry. This excellent resource will help address such questions as: How do I minister to this diverse age group? How do I revive a struggling young adult ministry? How can I reach unchurched single and young adults? How can I address their needs? What type of programming works? and How can I motivate my congregation to take a more supportive role in this ministry? **$12.95**

## PLEASE SEND ME THE FOLLOWING RESOURCES

Send this page to: SAM Resources, P.O. Box 62056, Colorado Springs, CO 80962-2056.
Or place your order by phone. Call toll-free (800) 487-4-SAM or (719) 488-2610.

Your Name ______________________ R.D./91-92

Church or Organization ______________________ Day Phone ( ) ______

Street ______________ City ______ State ______ Zip ______

| Quantity | Product Description | Unit Price | Amount |
|---|---|---|---|
| | | | |
| | | | |
| | | | |
| | | | |

**Check method of payment below:**

❑ Check (Make payable in U.S. funds to SAM Resources)
❑ Credit Card ____VISA ____MasterCard
Card # ______________ Exp. Date ______
Exact name on card: ______________

Add postage and handling charges. *(See rates below)* ______
Colorado residents add 6.5% sales tax ______
**TOTAL:** ______

**Postage and handling rates:** Add $2 for orders up to $10; Add $4 for orders up to $25; $6 for orders up to $50; $8 for orders up to $75; $9 for orders up to $100; all orders over $100, 10% of total. *Please double shipping charges for rush orders or orders outside of U.S.*

# ORDER FORM

# Resources For Your Ministry With Single Adults

Cut along the dotted line and mail this page to: SAM Resources, P.O. Box 62056, Colorado Springs, CO 80962-2056. Or place your order by phone. Call toll-free (800) 487-4-SAM or (719) 488-2610.

## NEWSLETTER

❑ ***Single Adult Ministries Journal***. Ideas, resources and guidance for leaders . . . the most recommended publication for those involved in ministry with single adults. Ten issues per year. **One-year subscription, $24.** *(Add $5 in Canada and $9 for all other countries.)* **Two-year subscription (SAVE $10) $38.** *(Add $10 in Canada and $18 for all other countries.)*

## RESOURCE DIRECTORY

❑ **National Single Adult Ministries Resource Directory**, *"The complete 'Yellow Pages' to ministry with single adults."* Every kind of useful information—from A to Z—is in this directory to help you save time, be more effective, and become 'networked' with the best singles ministry people and resources. **$12.95**

## BOOKS

❑ **Single Adult Ministry: 60 Leaders Tell How You Can Build and Nurture a Healthy Ministry**. Edited by Jerry Jones. *"The authoritative guide for singles ministry leaders."* How do you build a singles ministry that's effective? How do you keep it from slipping into a rut? How do you deal with the obstacles and opportunities that are unique to working with single adults? This book has the answers to these questions and many more. A collection of the best articles from the first eight years of *Single Adult Ministries Journal*, this excellent resource features insights and suggestions from 60 of the most knowledgeable leaders in singles ministry. **$24.95**

❑ **Developing a Divorce Recovery Ministry: A How-to Manual**, by Dr. Bill Flanagan. As one of the pioneers of 'the small group model' of divorce recovery ministry, in this book Dr. Flanagan shows you how to design the program, gather a leadership team, create a caring community and reach out to the growing number of divorced persons in your community. Everything you need to get started is in this book. **$19.95**

❑ **Divorce Recovery For Teenagers: How to Help Your Kids Recover, Heal, and Grow When Their Families are Ripped Apart**, by Stephen Murray and Randy Smith. The concept of divorce recovery for adults is generally accepted in the church. But what about the kids of divorce? While they suffer as much as (if not more than) their parents, too often they are left to fend for themselves as they are buffeted by life-wrenching events they cannot control. This resource offers a step-by-step workshop that you can use to begin an adolescent divorce recovery ministry right now. **$12.95**

**Continued on other side**

# ORDER FORM

❑ **The Idea Catalog for Single Adult Ministry**, edited by Jerry Jones. Here are hundreds of ideas to spark your imagination and help you and your leadership team build your singles ministry. These ideas have been contributed by singles ministry leaders from across North America. They are ideas that have been successfully used in singles ministries for special events, socials, retreats, single parent ministry, leadership training, publicity/promotion, fund-raising, evangelism, and more. **$12.95**

❑ **Vacations With a Purpose: A Planning Handbook for Your Short-term Missions Team**, by Kim Hurst and Chris Eaton. The authors of this book are hands-on pioneers in preparing single and young adults for short-term team missions trips. This helpful guide will be a must-have for anyone seeking to challenge and involve their people in world missions. The two books in this series (one for leaders and one for team members) provides everything you will need to know about philosophy, putting the team together, advance preparation, maximizing the benefits of the trip, selecting a project, raising the necessary funds, as well as all the logistical questions and issues that need to be addressed. **Leader's Manual, $16.95; Team Member's Handbook, $5.95.**

❑ **Singles Ministry Handbook: A Practical Guide to Reaching Adult Singles in the Church**, edited by Douglas Fagerstrom. Over 60 million single adults live in the United States and most of them don't attend church. This book includes help for reaching and ministering to this neglected and diverse segment of our society, with guidance and help from more than 30 singles ministry experts. **$18.95**

❑ **Young Adult Ministry: Step-by-step Help for Starting or Revitalizing Your Ministry With People Ages 18 to 35**, by Terry Hershey. One of the most-recommended books for leaders in singles ministry. This excellent resource will help address such questions as: How do I minister to this diverse age group? How do I revive a struggling young adult ministry? How can I reach unchurched single and young adults? How can I address their needs? What type of programming works? and How can I motivate my congregation to take a more supportive role in this ministry? **$12.95**

## PLEASE SEND ME THE FOLLOWING RESOURCES

Send this page to: SAM Resources, P.O. Box 62056, Colorado Springs, CO 80962-2056.
Or place your order by phone. Call toll-free (800) 487-4-SAM or (719) 488-2610.

Your Name ______________________________ R.D./91-92

Church or Organization ______________________ Day Phone ( ) __________

Street ______________ City __________ State ______ Zip ______

| Quantity | Product Description | Unit Price | Amount |
|---|---|---|---|
| | | | |
| | | | |
| | | | |
| | | | |
| | | Add postage and handling charges. (See rates below.) | |
| | | Colorado residents add 6.5% sales tax | |
| | | **TOTAL:** | |

**Check method of payment below:**

❑ Check (Make payable in U.S. funds to SAM Resources)
❑ Credit Card ____VISA ____MasterCard
Card # ______________ Exp. Date ________
Exact name on card: ______________

**Postage and handling rates:** Add $2 for orders up to $10; Add $4 for orders up to $25; $6 for orders up to $50; $8 for orders up to $75; $9 for orders up to $100; all orders over $100, 10% of total. *Please double shipping charges for rush orders or orders outside of U.S.*

# Index

## Here's another way to help you find helpful information fast.

*(Note that only the two largest sections—Recommended Resources and Network—have been included in this index.)*

### Where To Find It:

# NETWORK INDEX

**Use this index to quickly find a singles ministry leader or church by name. *(To search by state or city, refer to the Network section beginning on page 199.)***

## B

# F

# I

# K

# N

# Q



# R

# RESOURCES INDEX

**Use this index to search for a book or video by title, author, or publisher. *(To find a resource by topic, refer to the Recommended Resources section beginning on page 111.)***

# C



***CONTINUED NEXT PAGE***

# Audio and Video Index

**Here's the place to come for a quick search of audio, video and filmstrips listed in the Resource section of this Directory.**

## AUDIO CASSETTES



## VIDEO



## FILMSTRIPS

## S

***CONTINUED NEXT PAGE***

**Did You Get Left Out Of This Directory?**

*Help us make this publication complete.*
*If you—or anyone else you might know—*
*should be included in the next Directory,*
*please see page 249.*

# ORDER FORM

# Resources For Your Ministry With Single Adults

Cut along the dotted line and mail this page to: SAM Resources, P.O. Box 62056, Colorado Springs, CO 80962-2056. Or place your order by phone. Call toll-free (800) 487-4-SAM or (719) 488-2610.

## NEWSLETTER

❑ ***Single Adult Ministries Journal.*** Ideas, resources and guidance for leaders . . . the most recommended publication for those involved in ministry with single adults. Ten issues per year. **One-year subscription, $24.** *(Add $5 in Canada and $9 for all other countries.)* **Two-year subscription (SAVE $10) $38.** *(Add $10 in Canada and $18 for all other countries.)*

## RESOURCE DIRECTORY

❑ **National Single Adult Ministries Resource Directory,** *"The complete 'Yellow Pages' to ministry with single adults."* Every kind of useful information—from A to Z—is in this directory to help you save time, be more effective, and become 'networked' with the best singles ministry people and resources. **$12.95**

## BOOKS

❑ **Single Adult Ministry: 60 Leaders Tell How You Can Build and Nurture a Healthy Ministry.** Edited by Jerry Jones. *"The authoritative guide for singles ministry leaders."* How do you build a singles ministry that's effective? How do you keep it from slipping into a rut? How do you deal with the obstacles and opportunities that are unique to working with single adults? This book has the answers to these questions and many more. A collection of the best articles from the first eight years of *Single Adult Ministries Journal,* this excellent resource features insights and suggestions from 60 of the most knowledgeable leaders in singles ministry. **$24.95**

❑ **Developing a Divorce Recovery Ministry: A How-to Manual,** by Dr. Bill Flanagan. As one of the pioneers of 'the small group model' of divorce recovery ministry, in this book Dr. Flanagan shows you how to design the program, gather a leadership team, create a caring community and reach out to the growing number of divorced persons in your community. Everything you need to get started is in this book. **$19.95**

❑ **Divorce Recovery For Teenagers: How to Help Your Kids Recover, Heal, and Grow When Their Families are Ripped Apart,** by Stephen Murray and Randy Smith. The concept of divorce recovery for adults is generally accepted in the church. But what about the kids of divorce? While they suffer as much as (if not more than) their parents, too often they are left to fend for themselves as they are buffeted by life-wrenching events they cannot control. This resource offers a step-by-step workshop that you can use to begin an adolescent divorce recovery ministry right now. **$12.95**

**Continued on other side**

# ORDER FORM

❑ **The Idea Catalog for Single Adult Ministry**, edited by Jerry Jones. Here are hundreds of ideas to spark your imagination and help you and your leadership team build your singles ministry. These ideas have been contributed by singles ministry leaders from across North America. They are ideas that have been successfully used in singles ministries for special events, socials, retreats, single parent ministry, leadership training, publicity/promotion, fund-raising, evangelism, and more. **$12.95**

❑ **Vacations With a Purpose: A Planning Handbook for Your Short-term Missions Team**, by Kim Hurst and Chris Eaton. The authors of this book are hands-on pioneers in preparing single and young adults for short-term team missions trips. This helpful guide will be a must-have for anyone seeking to challenge and involve their people in world missions. The two books in this series (one for leaders and one for team members) provides everything you will need to know about philosophy, putting the team together, advance preparation, maximizing the benefits of the trip, selecting a project, raising the necessary funds, as well as all the logistical questions and issues that need to be addressed. **Leader's Manual, $16.95; Team Member's Handbook, $5.95.**

❑ **Singles Ministry Handbook: A Practical Guide to Reaching Adult Singles in the Church**, edited by Douglas Fagerstrom. Over 60 million single adults live in the United States and most of them don't attend church. This book includes help for reaching and ministering to this neglected and diverse segment of our society, with guidance and help from more than 30 singles ministry experts. **$18.95**

❑ **Young Adult Ministry: Step-by-step Help for Starting or Revitalizing Your Ministry With People Ages 18 to 35**, by Terry Hershey. One of the most-recommended books for leaders in singles ministry. This excellent resource will help address such questions as: How do I minister to this diverse age group? How do I revive a struggling young adult ministry? How can I reach unchurched single and young adults? How can I address their needs? What type of programming works? and How can I motivate my congregation to take a more supportive role in this ministry? **$12.95**

## PLEASE SEND ME THE FOLLOWING RESOURCES

Send this page to: SAM Resources, P.O. Box 62056, Colorado Springs, CO 80962-2056.
Or place your order by phone. Call toll-free (800) 487-4-SAM or (719) 488-2610.

Your Name ______________________________ R.D./91-92

Church or Organization ______________________ Day Phone ( ) ______________

Street ______________ City ______________ State ________ Zip ________

| Quantity | Product Description | Unit Price | Amount |
|---|---|---|---|
| | | | |
| | | | |
| | | | |
| | | | |

**Check method of payment below:**

❑ Check (Make payable in U.S. funds to SAM Resources)
❑ Credit Card ____ VISA ____ MasterCard
Card # ______________________ Exp. Date __________
Exact name on card: ______________________

Add postage and handling charges. *(See rates below)* ________

Colorado residents add 6.5% sales tax ________

**TOTAL:** ________

**Postage and handling rates:** Add $2 for orders up to $10; Add $4 for orders up to $25; $6 for orders up to $50; $8 for orders up to $75; $9 for orders up to $100; all orders over $100, 10% of total. *Please double shipping charges for rush orders or orders outside of U.S.*